50 YEARS OF
TEXT GAMES

"A **fascinating** peek into the history and evolution of interactive storytelling."

—Serenity Caldwell

"**If *Zork* means more to you than *Fortnite* ever will**, if you know exactly which items to take with you in *Hitchhiker's Guide to the Galaxy,* or if you have ever typed the words SOUTH and HELP into a white-on-black text box, then you may be interested in this book..."

—Nintendo Life

"**An exceptional survey of the form**: I learned new things even about games I know well, and had a delightful introduction to some I'd never heard of. ...both thoroughly researched and full of joy."

—Emily Short (Galatea)

"**Essential... excellent**."

—BoingBoing

"**Mandatory reading**. This is the really good kind of nonfiction writing where it's well-researched, consise, and so good at getting to the heart of why something is important or what's surprising about it. If you're interested in games writing or design **you really must read this**."

—Bruno Dias

"A **favorite**... takes a wider view to try to understand why this game at that moment was particularly significant or representative."

—Tim Carmody

"An **awesome** exploration of the long history of the genre."

—Nick Walton (AI Dungeon)

"Every article in this series has been **a gift**."

—Rose Behar

"My favorite thing in 2021. **If you haven't read it, you should**."

—Christopher Gates

"**Would recommend** it to anyone curious about gaming history in general, and text in specific."

—Mike Laidlaw

"A staggering history of text games... It's **an incredible accomplishment** and a wellspring of historical knowledge."

—Cat Manning

"**One of the best reads on the internet** about games right now. Highly recommended!"

—Gil Hova

"Aaron's **exhaustively researched** *50 Years of Text Games* is one of the best newsletters I've ever read, and now he's turning it into a book... Instabacked."

—Andy Baio

"**Fascinating**. Some stuff I knew, some stuff I didn't know. But just great."

—John August

"Absolutely essential... a **stunning**, peerless introduction to IF specifically and game-oriented e-lit more generally."

—Colin Post

"A highlight of 2021 for me—**I learned so much**."

—@Spookysoft_Hi

"**One of the coolest things I've had the pleasure of reading this past year**."

—Matthew Trost

"A fascinating read... really opened my eyes to **games history I never knew about**."

—@Science_Maybe

50 YEARS OF
TEXT GAMES

FROM OREGON TRAIL TO AI DUNGEON

Aaron A. Reed

First edition
Changeful Tales Press
Oakland, California

Hardcover ISBN: 979-8-9859661-3-8
Paperback ISBN: 979-8-9859661-4-5
E-book ISBN: 979-8-9859661-2-1
Print on Demand Hardcover: 979-8-9859661-0-7
Print on Demand Softcover: 979-8-9859661-1-4

Name: Reed, Aaron A.
Title: 50 Years of Text Games: From Oregon Trail to AI Dungeon / Aaron A. Reed
Description: First Edition. Oakland: Changeful Tales Press, 2023
Identifiers: ISBN 9798985966107 (print-on-demand hardcover) / ISBN 9798985966114 (print-on-demand softcover) / ISBN 9798985966138 (hardcover) / ISBN 9798985966145 (paperback) / ISBN 9798985966121 (e-book)
Subjects: LCSH: Computer Games—History.
Library of Congress Control Number: 2022949771

First Edition March 2023
10 9 8 7 6 5 4 3 2

Copyedited by Emily Morganti.
Ebook production by Electric Book Works (electricbookworks.com).
Typeset in Baskerville URW, Aktiv Grotesk, Bebas Neue, Calibri, & Nexus Typewriter.
Covers use Color Basic by Typodermic and Ac437 IBM BIOS by VileR (CC BY-SA 4.0).

Changeful Tales Press
Oakland, California

aaronareed.net

For Willie, Don, Roberta, Steve, Brian, Ron, Graham, Andrew, Adam, Emily,
Nick, Victor, Carl, Peter, Dan, Jacq, Yoon, Tarn, several Sams,
and everyone else who built me a world of words

And for Dad

CONTENTS

ACKNOWLEDGME

CROWDFUNDING COLLECTOR

12-Bit Team Retrogaming · Aaron Cincinatus · Aaron I Sanders · Aaron J. Massey · Aaron Jamieson · Aaron Polans · Aaron Selby · Aaron Seymour · Aaron Smischney · Aaron Spurloc Aaron Walsh · Aaron Williams · Abby Braunsdorf · Abigail D. · Abraham Liebrecht Aucamp · Adam Bradley S · Adam Conover · Adam Eccleshall · Adam Hill · Adam Kempa · Adam Sale Adam Small · Adam Thornton and One Of The Bruces · Adrian Ford · Aelfrin · Agarose Gel · AJ Flenard · AJ Low · Alain 'FuFxs' Baxter · Alan Gratz · Alan Shutko · Alan Yu · Albert Bassi Albino Zeb · Alex Folch · Alex Genco · Alex Korntner · Alex Martinez · Alex Peachey · Alex Wiltshire · Alexander J. King · Alexander King · Alexander Morse-Hambrock · Alexander Re Alexandr Mac · Alexey Timakov · Alfredo Escudero Diaz · Alice Bowman · Alicia Neptune · Alistair Forbes · Allan Christophersen · Allen T. Garvin · allen tingley · Alper Tasci · Altaïr Peliss · altsoph · Alyce Caswell · Ambrosia J Webb · Amir Rahmati · Ån · Anastasia Salter · Andrea "Vyrelion" Back · Andreas Kotsakis · Andreia "shana" Gaita · Andres Rojas · Andrew Alan M Andrew Arthur · Andrew Badr · Andrew Bogue · Andrew Childs · Andrew Corvin · Andrew Ferguson · Andrew Garvin · Andrew Hatchell · Andrew Judd · Andrew K. Milton · Andrew Kraus Andrew LaCortiglia · Andrew Lee Dolan · Andrew Marks · Andrew Petro · Andrew Tomko · Andrew Vestal · Andrew W. Smith · Andrew Wainwright · Andrew Wood · Andy Baio · Andy Beatt Andy Culler · Andy Grossberg · Andy Libecki · Angela Mazur · anjakefala · Antha Ann Adkins · Anthony Micari · Anthony Phillips ("Benji Dahood") · Apollo Thomas · Arnd B. · Arrith · Arr Reed · Art d'Os · Arthur Avitia III · Arthur Bollis · Ashley Cooper · Athyro Metagames · ATS · Atul Varma · Auribouros · Austin Grant · Austin Wilson · Axel Hassen Taiari · B Davis-Shannon · Baldur Brückner · Barney/Nagasaki/ Naedea/Deadmoon/Vaerys/Jonx · Barrett Anderson · Barrington "nemodos" Lloyd-Lovett · Barry Walker · Bart Krieger · Bay Chang · bbz · Beat Suter · Becki Lee · Ben Black · Ben Combee · Ben Cressey · Ben Dodson · Ben Esacove · Ben Monroe · Ben Nichols · Ben Rathert · Ben Unsworth · B "535" Blank · Benedict Steele · Benesumi · Bernard M. Wright · Big Tyler · Bill Kratzer · Bill Loguidice · Bill MacKenty · Bill Sheakoski · Billy Peery · Björn Ehlert · Blair Leggett · Blair Norri BleakBob · BlurryPixle · Bo Williams · Bob Fleck · Bob Freed, blotter-size graph paper cartographer · Bogusław Szawara · Books Above the Bend · Boris Demaria · bpcmusic · Brad Bidnic Brad David Grierson · Brad Justus · Braden E. Bishop · Brandon Boyer · Brandon S Higa · Brendan Hennessy · Brendan Martin · Brennon Church · Brett B. · Brett Watson · Brett Witty · hefele · Brian Conway · Brian Covault · Brian J. Parker · Brian K. Perry · Brian Lavelle · Brian M. Workman · Brian Medendorp · Brian Ott · Brian P. Evans @evansdawg · Brian Pilnick · Bri R. Boisvert · Brian R. Maggi · Brian Simpson · Brian Stolz · Brian Young · Brigi Fodor · Brook Miles · Brownzelman · Bruce and Christe McMenomy · Bruce G. Felkins · Bruno Setola · Bry Owen · Bryan Walker · Bryan "Cybershaman(X)" Logie · Bryant Moscon · BShep · Bucky Thuerwachter · Budgieboyo · Bukkaroo · C. S. Kessler · C1506 · C64 "Suspended" Rob Commander Marcus · Cabel Sasser · Caffo · Caitlin Fisher, Immersive Storytelling Lab, Toronto · Cal Henderson · Calvin and Drew Thornton · Cameo Wood · Cameron Bowes · Camer Friend · Cameron Hunt · Camille Dickinson · Captain Keith "Chewie" Surowiec · Carl Muckenhoupt · Carla L. · Carlo Luciano Bianco · Carly Soule · Carolyn VanEseltine · Cary Hazelwood · Casey Andrew Tuckerson · Cat & George Drayer · Cat N. · Cedric "3vyl" Robichaud · Celeste Birzgalis · Cena Ringwald · Chad Dylan Long · Chad Freeburg · Chad "Hello Sail Briggs · ChainsawHunter · Channing King · Charibdys · Charity A. Petrov · Charles · Charles "TRS-80" Hunsinger · Charley Dupré (Charlex Duralex) · Charlie Cameron · Chas. D. Bade Cheryl Howard · Chill Mill · chip · Chip Long · Chloé Balmat · Chris Ainsworth · Chris Angelini · Chris Belanger · Chris Boehme · Chris Bracy · Chris Chapman · Chris Eng · Chris Foster · Ch Godlewski · Chris Grapes · Chris Harvey · Chris J. Young · Chris Larson[Eaten by a grue.] · Chris Maxwell, founder of Pod&Hive · Chris Mikesell · Chris Otto (Papergreat.com) · Chris Pau Chris Scruton and Alexander Goodland · Chris Tonkinson · Chris Wilkes · Chris "Superfreak1000" Anderson · Christian · Christian · Christian Davis · Christian Iñiguez · Christian J. Estra · Christian Neuhaus · Christian Sykes · Christine Simoes Tilden · Christophe PÉRICARD · Christophe Rhodes · Christopher Chestnut · Christopher Harris - PlayPlayLearn · Christoph Helmke · Christopher Hill · Christopher Reagoso · Christopher Sacchi · Christopher Schance · Christopher Sousa · Christopher Strege · Christopher "Bos" Bosdal · Chrysostom Nicopoulos · Chuck Michael · Clara Fernández-Vara · Clarice Meadows · Clay Gardner · clifford longino · Clint and Connie · Clive Naish · Coby Randquist · Cody Konior · Colin Djukic · Co Liotta (Lifeline) · Colin Paterson · Colin Post · Collin Gifford Brooke · Collin Pieper · Connor Milligan · Connor Moran · Cory Bryant · Cory Ringdahl, "Zork VR" Designer · Cousin Artaud · C Pantaloons · cqr · Craig Anderson · Craig DeGraff · Curtis Frye · CWM1414 · D. Kevin Stilwell Jr. · D. Wilson · Daag · Damiancito Rodko · Dan Alexander · Dan Hallock · Dan Renkin · D Sanderson · Danger and Joanna Geist · Daniel (bitmeise) Pinske · Daniel C. Hodges · Daniel G. Stephens · Daniel Gelon · Daniel Gonçalves · Daniel Kennett · Daniel Landau · Dan Monson · Daniel Pancotto · Daniel Poggenpohl · Daniel Ravipinto · Daniel Sharpe · Danny Whitehead · Dario Scarpa · Dark Lord Leon · Dark Star · Darkwolf · Darren Monahan · Darr Whiting · Daulton James Whitehead III · Dave Holets · Dave LeCompte · Dave Otaguro · Dave Rogers, There can be only one! · David A Dillow · David B. Garson · David Buksbaum killed a Kobold. · David Clarke · David Dovel · David Engles · David Gauntt · David Guiot · David HM Spector · David Horgan · David James (DJ) · David Klco · David L. · David McCully · Dav Millar · David Moon, Chastain Jr. High's Zork Team, 1983 · David Ortega · David P Anderson · David Phelps · David Platt · David Stark (Zarkonnen) · David Stephenson · David Tai · Dav vun Kannon · David W Franklin · david wolfpaw · David Youd · Davis "Blaktyde" Cole · Deacon Wardlow · Dean Nones · Deanna Light Amar · Dee Cooke · Deirdre and Robyn McLeo Delilah Robinson · Dennis Keith Earl II · Dennis Stanke · Dennys Antunish · Derek Alexander · Derek Felton · Derek Golden · Derek J. Balling · Destina Connor · detrohutt · Devendra · Dev Patterson (MI, USA) · Devin R.E.M. Windfield · Devlin Rourke · Doctor Andy · Donald Byron Johnson · Donald K Mc · Doug Jones · Doug McIntyre · Doug Valenta & John Zajac · Doug Childs · Douglas R. White · Douglas "Adoru" Alves · Dr Claw - Santa Cruz BBS - 1980s · Dr Glen Spoors · Dr Melissa J. Rogerson · Dr Nic Velissaris · Dr. April Grow · Dr. Daniel A. Ray · M Emily C. Friedman · Dr. Scott Patterson · Drew Czosek · Drew Powers · Duncan Bowsman · Duncan Harvey · Dustin Campbell · Dustin Norman · Duston Williams · Dutchess Von Bee Dylan Baker · Dylan "A Mind Forever Voyaging" Distasio · DYoung · E. A. C. Moreno-Davis · Éamonn O'Moore BL · Eaton · Ed Geist · ed. blair · EDOUARD LOMBARD · Eduardo Pelos Edward Blanch · Edward Breathe · Edwin Durning · Elena Bartlett · Eli Shupe · Eli Zupke · Elizabeth Daggert · Elizabeth Norton · Ella Korhonen · Emanuel Bettelheim · Emily Kawasal Emily Short · Emma Krantz · Empish · Ender Montgomery · Eric Alba · Eric Cassady · Eric Chon · Eric de Broche des Combes · Eric Floehr · Eric Ho · Eric J Leslie · Eric Keller · Eric Laird · E Liga · Eric Litman · Eric McAfee · Eric Neustadter (e) · Eric Nichols · Eric Sanders - Apple][+ Gamer Since 1983 · Eric Swain · Eric Vitiello · Erica McCowan · Erik Andersen · Erik Jay Webe Erik Knechtel · Erik Lind · Erik Malinowski · Erik Marple · Erik Max Francis · Erik Moeller · Erin Valenciano · ERKetchum · Ernst Krogtoft · Ernst Paunzen · Ernst „Zitatwaffe" Jammerman Ethan Koester · Evelyn Rossing · Evgenia Kleidona · Evie · Fabrizio Pedrazzini · Falcon Street · Fatima Fayez · Federico Rocha · Fejérvári Boldizsár, Luca, Berengár, Kilián, and Sóthy Vir (V-LAB/K) · Felix Ruzzoli · Fenric Cayne · FF · Finn Orion · Fiona Hartmann · Fletcher Adamowicz · Fletcher G.W. Christensen · For my loving wife, Julia Kathleen Ramsey · Forrest Emerson · Forrest Greenwood · Francis Wallace · Frank Moskal · Frank Tinschert, Germany · Frankie B · G. Hartman · Gabriel Bit-Babik · Gabriel L. Helman · Gabriel Luthier · Garrett Olive Garry Lancaster · Gary Driggs · Gary J. Anderson · Gaspar Rey Alvarez · Gavin Craig · Gavin Dalton · Geir Norheim · Geoff Giordano · Geoff Shearer · Geoffrey A. Rosen · Geoffrey Gold (AdventureSnack.com) · Geoffrey Long · Geoffrey Riutta · Geoffrey Roth · Georg Wille · Gerald Shroyer · Gerry McFatridge · Gilles Gobron · Gino Roncaglia, Roma Tre University · Giorg Maria Di Nunzio · Giovanni Riccardi · Giuseppe Brindisi · Glen West · Glenn Greene · Glenn "Justicar" White · Gold Machine · Gollybea · gonk gonk gonk · Graeme Devine · Grayson Shipl · Greg Aronowitz · Greg Savage · Greg Smith · Greg, aka Ace · Gregorio Giacchetti · Gregory Wild-Smith · Grey Williams · Gui Ambros · guregu · Gwendelyn Foster · Gábor Téglás · HAROL (Batman) Batson Jr · Harrison Page · Harrison "mossflwer" · Havilah McGinnis · Hazardous · Heath D. Alberts · Heather Albano · Hector Nun · Helrayzer · Henning Naarlien-Tolpinru Henning Schmiedehausen · Henry Burrows · Hilary Mason · Hiok · hollowaytape · Hot Coffee · Hrvoje Harvey Vrsalovic · Hugo Stieglitz · Humberto R. Baptista · Hungry Cat Game Hussain class · Ian Blizzard · Ian Gowen · Ian Michael Waddell · Ian W. Parker · Igor "kibertoad" Savin · Iman Rastegari · IndustrialRobot · ios.hex · Isaiah Whisner · Ismail · Iván de Neyr Franco · J Earl · J French · J Krzyzanowski · J. Marshall Pittman · J. Ramirez · J. Sison · J. Slutter · Jack B. Everitt · Jack Posont · Jack Schlesinger · Jacob Childress · Jacob Tende

cqueline & Sam Ashwell · Jake Gonnella · James Buchanan · James Burt · James Chivers · James Klingler and family · James Pontolillo · James Rodgers · James Ryan · James Terr
mie Law · Jamie Vann · Jan F. Daldrup · Jan "Shakchal" Chaloupka · Jared Cherup · Jason 'XenoPhage' Frisvold · Jason Breti · Jason C. Penney · Jason Cavaliere · Jason Dyke · Jason
er · Jason Grinblat · Jason Joyce · Jason Kapalka · Jason Kerchner · Jason Lamb · Jason Mehmel · Jason Newberry · Jason Ruvinsky · Jason Sanchez · Jason Santilli · Jason Scott ·
son Varcoe · Jason "jasonnomore" Li · Jason "Opie" Babo · Javier Pedreira «Wicho» · Jay C. Parangalan · Jay Phillips · JB Klug · JediGameFreak · Jeff Boschee · Jeff Charleston · Jeff
lley · Jeff Hungerford · Jeff Lunt, a.k.a. normalocity · Jeff Ryder · Jeff Somers · Jeff W Hardin · Jeff Zahnen · Jeffery Wright the Sightless Scholar · Jeffrey A. Ow · Jem Manley-Buser ·
nnifer S. McCandless · Jenny Wilkes · Jeremy Kleier · Jeremy Kuhne · Jeremy P. Wright · Jess Haskins · Jess Poore · Jess Ruefli · Jesse Burneko · Jesse C. Polhemus · Jessica Smith ·
zacain · Jim Bailey · Jim Horvath · Jim Java · Jim Spring · Jim Whitehead · Jimmy Dib · Joan "Wohali" Touzet · Joe Gimblett · Joe Goldston · Joe Halliwell · Joe McReynolds · Joe Pereira ·
e Valdez · Joe W. Aultman · Joel Marshall · Joel Panther · Joey Nirschl · Johan Franzén · Johan "Burre" Burell · John A Guzik, Jr. · John Amerisun · John Desmarais · John Doty · John
scoll · John Ewalt · John Faulkenbury · John G. McDaid · John Hammersley · John Hooloovoo Bosico · John Jacobsen · John Kelly · John Koschwanez · John Leen · John Mettraux ·
John Muellerleile @jrecursive · John Ohno · John Paul Ashenfelter · John Philip Law · John Stallings · John Steinmann · John Winner · John Wood ·
John-tan Pham · Jon Kopetz · Jon Moore · Jon Newlands · Jon Satrom · Jon Veen · Jonah Shafran · Jonas Jacobsson · Jonathan Blackwell ·
Jonathan Carpenter · Jonathan Chan · Jonathan Huston · Jonathan Kimrey · Jonathan Sato · Jonathan Wilson · Jordan Magnuson · Jordan White ·
Jordin Kee (Path of Adventure) · Jordy van Opstal · Jorn Lavoll · Jose P. Zagal · Jose Paredes · Joseph A. Stanko · Joseph Boyd · Joseph "Zafyr Goa-
Lum Dragon" Marcus · Josh Hepola · Josh LaMar · Josh Lawrence · josh_g · Joshua Burdick · Joshua D. Johnson · Joshua Lake · Joshua LaMont ·
Joshua Marcus · Joshua Yuan · Josiah Lebowitz · Jouko Strömmer · João G.M. Araújo · JSG · jsj01 · Juande Santander-Vela · Juggleware Games ·
Jukka Raskinen · Julia Blackwood · Julian Fleetwood · Julie Mundt · Julien T. · Julien Zamor (smwhr) · Justin A. Bortnick · Justin Drew · Justin Peck ·
Justin Reiter · Justin "MzRie" Tokarski · Justin "Neodolphino" Orenich · K Bex · K. Goldstrohm Jr. · K.G. Orphanides · Kaerubot · Kai Hagenburg · Kai
Nikulainen · KailelleXD · Kake · Kaleb Mic · Kaltin Kirby · Karen and Barry Wallis · Karl Erickson · Karl J. Smith · Karl Mayer · Karl Parakenings · Karl
ade · Kasey McKenna · Kassandra Walker · Kat A. · Kat Crispin · Kate Strong Stadt · Kate 'lurking grue' Peterson Koch · Katherine Morayati · Katherine Prevost · Katherine "KZD" Jarrard ·
tie Lamonica Joh · Kaveru Lam · Kayaba · Kayla Brown · Keeks and Aive · Keiran Harcombe · Keith Armonaitis · Keith R. Hayden · Keith Rose · Keith W. Sheehan · Kel Cecil · Kelly Roberge
elly Ziemski · Kelsey R. Marquart · Ken Finlayson · Kenna W · Kenton at The Archaeogaming Museum · Kenzie Du · Kernelcoremode · Kes Sampanthar · Keunwoo Lee · Kevin & Amanda
rtin · Kevin and Divi Greene · Kevin Bachus · Kevin Bales · Kevin Cafferty · Kevin Harman · Kevin Keller · Kevin Lo · Kevin Loken · Kevin Sargent · Kevin Snow · Kevin Wong · Keyfire (PJ
I) · Kian Ryan · Kian S. Bergstrom · kibwashere · Killroy - Now more than ever · Kippy Tidwell · Kirk Lund · kit Geraghty · KJ, Alien in the Village · Knox Family · Konrad 'kuororath'
biński · Kori Joyce · Kory Dondzila · Kostadis Roussos · KPOW · Krispijn James Larrison · Kristian Grossman-Madsen · Kristian Rodriguez · Kristina Born · Kristoffer Björkman · Kurt
hann Klemm · Kurtiss Keefner · Kyle Dean · Kyle K Boyd · Kyle Scheele · Kyle Schumacher · Kyle Thorson · Kyne · Kyra Romanello · Kyungdahm Yun (tomyun) · L. Ross Raszewski · Lace
Iliamson · Ladyoflight, aka: Chelsea · Lan D Ho · Lance Bohy · Lance Hurst · Lance Jordan · Lane Becker · Larry Anderson · Lars-Ove Karlsson · Latitude, Inc. · Lauren A. Merriman ·
uren MacDonald · Lee Hammerton · Leif "Eightywithout" Groome · Lena Maximilian Siess · Lennart Niemelä · Lenny - yes, that one · Leo Horovitz (Lehooo) · Leonard Souza · Leslie B · Li
ung Wang · Light Bates · Lightning Dave Bolton · Lily Kennison · Linus and Clementine Griggs · Linus Gustavsson · Lisa Wolf · Liza Daly · Lord Kronious Haecheon · Lorenzo "N3rdcore"
ntoni · Lowell David Denning · Loïc Celestin Hon-Yu · Luca Ruella · Lucas Endres · Lucas Wagner · Lucila Mariel Neira · Lucy Lin · Luke Beeman · Luke Boyett · Luke Dicken · Luke Hsu
ke M Reilly · Luke Ryan & Chaotic Good · Luke van den Barselaar · Lyla Snowlocke · Léa Talbot · m0v3 · Maciej Piwoda · MacLaren North · MaddenJester · Magdalena Cielecka · Magnus
rdin · Maik Schmidt · Mainframe5 = LadyKeli + PadrePablo · Maja B. Kubel Højmose and Christian Kubel Højmose · Malanius Privierre · Marc Beltmann · Marcin Blacha · Marcin Segit ·
rcin Wichary · Marco Alpert · Marcos Juarez · Marcy Lerner · Marie Mitoufle · Mariko Ayotte · Marina Müller · Mario Schlosser @mariots · Marisa Parham @amplify285 · Mark A-J.
ught · Mark A.R. Thompson · Mark Allen Buckner · Mark B. Parsell · Mark Best · Mark Chapple Baumann · Mark Davis · Mark McKibben · Mark Nieman · Mark Pilgrim · Mark Rickerby ·
rk S. · Mark Sample · Mark Slutsky · Mark Stephan · Mark Sztainbok · Mark W. Greaves · Mark Wentzell · Marri Lynn Knadle · Married to Stinkyhead · Marshall McGowan · Marti Shirley,
Instructor · Martin Ender · Martin Grider · Marty · Mason Armstrong · Matt Brandwein · Matt Brier · Matt Griffin · Matt H · Matt Howard · Matt Leitzen · Matt Porter · Matt Schneider · Matt
ne, Mayor of Falken's Maze · Matt Sylvia · Matt Taylor · Matt Waxler · Matt Webb · Matt "East Of A White House" Andrysiak · Mattaui · Matteo Settenvini · Matthew Gingerich · Matthew
re · Matthew LeHew · Matthew Noe · Matthew Peterson · Matthew R.F. Baloušek · Matthew Sharun · Matthew Stibbe · Matthew Turk · Matthew Yancer · Matthias De Aliaga · Mattias
uzelius · Mattroid · Maurizio Pistelli · Max Schilling · Max Smith · Maxi Organ · Maximilian Weigand · maxpev · MC Augstkalns · Megan Condis · Meghan Couture · Mel O'Neill · Melinda
mphreys · Mica · Micah Silverman · Michael & David DeGusta · Michael Amundson · Michael Bailey · Michael Bikovitsky · Michael C. Bernier · Michael DeCristofaro · Michael Everson ·
chael Geoffrey Scharnberg · Michael Guerin · Michael H. Chopade · Michael H.W. Driesen · Michael Hanscom · Michael Hobbs · Michael Keith · Michael Lane · Michael M. Kroeker ·
chael Mauzy · Michael McCollum @gnustoboz · Michael Miley · Michael Phillips · Michael Piotrowski · Michael Poley · Michael Robertson · Michael S. Siegel · Michael Schwartz · Michael
ughn Green · Michel Lichand · Michel Meeuwesen · Michi Behrens · Midnite Watchman · Mike Blanckaert · Mike Burgess · Mike Cummins · Mike Gregory · Mike Laidlaw · Mike McFarland
like Mika · Mike Miller · Mike Piontek · Mike Smith · Mike Westley · Mike, Janet, and Johnston Moore · MikeDemo · Mikko Parviainen · misartventure · Mishra 'Nemo' Hamelin · mitcharf
tri Van · Mo Nassar · Molley the Mage · monolar · Morgan Smith · Motoharu Ito · Myles O'Neill · N.S. · Nate Lucier · Nathan Cheever · Nathan Janos · Nathan Ladd · Nathan Mumm
chTimeRadio.com · Nathan Wray · Nathaniel Mathias Ford · Nay Saysourinho · Neal R. · Neffi Pamin · Neil Estacio · Nelson Tiago Remoaldo de Oliveira · Nic Gard · Nicholas Newell ·
cholas Sinlock · Nick Brooker · Nick Burtner · Nick Gibbins · Nick Lines · Nick Mc · Nick Osborn · Nick Plante RIP ThE FiNaL ZoNe · Nick Scheiblauer · Nick Tierce · Nick Vargish · Nick
ornick" Albright · Nicolas Ezeyza-Alvear · Nicole Zeltzer · Nigel Sood · NightsoN Blaze · Nikolas Sinkola · Ninebit · Ninotchka · Niraj Sanghvi · Noah Dunn · Noah "Old Lingolf House"
een · Noble Fisk · Noel Warford · Nostalgia_Chaser · Nuutti-Iivari Merihukka · OgreTech, Inc. · Old Olaf Fowles · Olegus t.Gl. · Oliver Corpuz · Oliver Knagge · Olivier S. Baillif · Omer Raviv ·
an Nordhus Karlsson · Oscar González Cabo · Oscar Nearly · Owen Wiggins · Pa · Pablo M. Martínez Merino · Pablo Merino Sáez · Paisley Green · Pam Drouin · Parker Davis · Partha
thore · Pat Breen · Patricia Doll · Patricia Landers · Patricia Ramsey · Patrick Clapp · Patrick Colombo · Patrick Fowler · Patrick Grenier · Patrick Rafferty · Paul A. Martin · Paul Heindl ·
ul Horbal · Paul J Hodgeson · Paul Jimenez · Paul Lindblad · Paul Marzagalli · Paul Player 1 · Paul Popernack · Paul S. Urbanski · Paul Saunders · Paul Southerington · Paul "Emperor XLII"
nsen · Pedro Fernández López · Pedro Martins · Pedro, Lisa, Jonathan and Katarina · Pete Shaw · Peter Alau · Peter C. Earle · Peter Landers · Peter Liebert (aka Dragonlord) · Peter Lux ·
ter McCowie · Peter Mietlowski · Peter Mount · Peter Neufeld · Peter van Hardenberg · Peter Wilkinson · pettersson · Phantom Watson · Phil James · Phil Palmieri · Philip W Rogers Jr ·
oenix Toews · Picaro · Piepie · Pierino Gattei · pigfinite · Pippa Brooks · PJ Thum · plaid1swb · Pliny the Gamer / Kinjiru · Plum Creek Retro · Pomegranate_VI · Poppy Haralson · Preston
exander Reece Beall · Priya J. · Q.M. · R. · R37R0 · [[Rabbit,Rabbit]] · Rachael David Farrar · Rachel Helps · Rachel Joy Victor · RadioactiveCrow · Rafael Mondragón · Rafael Oliveira · Ralf
hn · Raliedir · Ralph J Ciotti · Ramon Macias · Randall Neff · Randy Peck · Raph D'Amico · Ray Cornwall · Rebecca Rouse · Reginald T. Gardner · Reid Miles · Reinik · RemoR · Ren Gaudet ·
tro Ojisan · RetroStation Hungary (Lawry) · Reuben Tekoeti-Mead from Aotearoa · Rex and Rebecca Reed · Rex van Der Spuy · rexlexfex · Ri'en Karrot · Ricardo "Manny" Belano · Rich
ugherty · Rich Fletcher · RIchard 'Lord Papflower' Cosgrove · Richard Charles St.Clair · Richard Dunlap · Richard F. Nelson · Richard Francis Homann · Richard G. Hallas · Richard Gillin ·
chard Hunton · Richard Johnson · Richard L Dufresne · Richard R. Phillips · Richard Smyth · Richard "Flexman" Hawley · Richie Franklin · Rick Ohnemus · Rick Radzville · Rick Rambo ·
ck Reynolds · Rick Rezinas · Riddlemaster · Ridge "Deadite" Briel · Ridzuan Ashim @ridz84 · Rob Birnie · Rob MacAndrew · Rob Michalchuk · Rob Myall · Rob Prouse · Rob Wynne & Larissa
rch · Robb Ballard · Robbie Honerkamp · Robert (R2) Radune · Robert B. Linton, OG Text Gamer · Robert Bailey · Robert Drescher · Robert H Wilde · Robert J. Hardy · Robert Kubin ·
bert Poss · Robert Ross · Robert VanFleet · Robert Zubek · Robert Ödman · Robert "Jefepato" Dall · Robin Horton · Robin Ray and Dan Hon · RobMSantos · Rocco Buffalino · Rodger
nson · Rodney Lelah · Roel Herberghs · Roland Gaida · Romain Savioz · Ron 'Coyote' Lussier · Ron Boerger · Ron Hale-Evans · Ron Roff · Ronald H. Miller · Ronald "Pluribus" McCormick ·
ss Freshwater · Ross Heflin · Roy Hollis & Family · Roy J Leatherberry IV · Royal McGraw · Rui Caneira · Russell J. Ward · Ruth Lin · Ryan Adams · Ryan Andrew Dibble · Ryan Campbell ·

Ryan Coombes · Ryan Dahlgren · Ryan De La Torre · Ryan Mannion · Ryan Myers · Ryan North · Ryan Patterson - "LinkIron" · Ryan van Barneveld · Ryan Whitcomb · Ryan Wyatt · Ry
"Rybread" Stevens · Ræv42 · S Busby · Sabrina Gannon · Salamander · Sam Breese · Sam Kleb · Sam LC · Sammy G. · Sandra Ringgaard Coyle · Sara Clemens · Sara R. Johnson · Sa
"Witt's End" Keesler · Sarah Grimsley · Sarah Mei · Sarinee Achavanuntakul · Scarlet & Chel Foster · Scott Adams · Scott Anderson · Scott Barrett · Scott Blomquist · Scott Butler · Sc
Elson · Scott Klein · Scott M. Behren · Scott McMillin · Scott Mohler · Scott Mohnkern · Scott Pezza · Scott Richards aka Major Sirius · Scott Seago · Scott Thede · Scott Tyack · Sc
Williamson · Scott Youngdahl · SDF II · Seafoe Araven · Sean Barnes · Sean Duncan · Sean Flannigan · Sean Gugler · Sean Kelly · Sean Krauss · Sean Murphy · Sean O'Neill · Sean Siche
Seb Chan · Sebastian and Valerie · Seiromem · Serena "Intendant S" Nelson · Seth E. Ober's memories of his childhood · SGOT Denver · Shahar "AJRION" Matsa · Shane Brennan · Sha
G. · Shannon Appelcline · Shannon Crock · Shawn Clary · Shawn Flowers · Shawn L. Reed · Shawna Kelly · Shelley L. Doty - Explorer · Sheridan Delaine Youngblood Reid · Sherol Che
Shervyn · Shy Ruparel · Siddharth M · SIlverBeard · Simon Campbell · Simon Hudson @sliktrik · Simon J Canham · Simon Louis · Simon Wistow · Sir Mark of House Estonia · skipclark
Skye Nathaniel Schiefer · Snacksnicky · SneakyGit · Snicker Furfoot · Sony Valdez · Sophia Chen · sozin · Spelkollektivet · SpielmannSpiel · spookylabs.co · Spun Counterg · Stacy E. Re
· Stanislav Hrda · Stanley Winters ·
Starye · Stef van Hooijdonk · Stefan
Meier · Stefano "Mando" Zocchi · Stella
Wisdom · Stephan Belin · Stephan Hüper
· Stephan Junker · Stephen and
Christine Smith · Stephen Baker ·
Stephen Ball · Stephen Boucher ·
Stephen D. Rynerson · Stephen G. Shaw ·
Stephen G. Ware · Stephen Granade · Stephen P. Anderson · Stevan Hird · Steve Alcorn · Steve Eisner · Steve J. Hodges · Steve Margolis · Steve Meretzky · Steven and Elizabeth Wei
Steven B. Davis · Steven Berg · Steven Bodnar · Steven Dast · Steven Feurer · Steven Marsh · Stian Rødven-Eide · Still mapping the maze. XYZZY! - Dan Cooley · Stoffe · Strider Jone
Stuart Adair · Stuart Feldhamer · Stuart McInally · Stuart Rice · @stv · summervillain · Sunny Chow They Guy · Susan Heinick · Susannah Mansky · Sylvain Petit · Syncoplay Retro Gamin
T.R. Fullhart · Tabitha Nichols · Tamzen Cannoy · Tanio Klyce · taraliu · Tarn Adams · Tarus L Latacki Jr · Taylor Stratton · Ted Reed · Tejas Shirodkar · Terence Chua · Teresa Marcus · Te
Wilson · Tess Kinniburgh · Thadeus Smith · Thanh Coong · Thank you Ernie aka the Brogmoid! Love, David & Eric · ThaRealMcCoy77 · The Ancient Alchemist · The Casuists · The Gre
Quux · The Nicholson Family · The Pittman Family · The Rebelskys · thegleek · TheGreatMadOne · Thelgor · Thierry Clavel · Thierry "tym" MÉCHAIN · thisisbeth · Thomas E. Marsha
Thomas Fitzsimons · Thomas Insel · Thomas Kullmann · Thomas M. Smith · Thomas Mark Sørensen · Thomas Stassin · Thomas Øhrbom · Thraka - Thanks Dad for that copy of Hitchhike
Tim · Tim Appleton · Tim Berry · Tim Burnett · Tim Gilberts · Tim Kirby · Tim O'Brien · TimeSyphon · Timmy & Linda Durnan · Timothy Bazalgette · Timothy L. Crabtree · Timothy Star
Tobias Hodges · Tobias Kruse · Tobias Paul · Todd Guill · Todd O. Dampier · Todd Paoletti · Todd W Ramsey · Tom Foster · Tom Hickerson · Tom Houston-Harley · Tom Mohan · Tom Seag
Tom "Mad Dog" Batchik · Tomas Pettersson · Tommy Chu · Tommy Nyquist · Tomás AF · Toni Westbrook · Tony A. Rowe · Tony Goggin · Tony Joe Chriscoe · Tony Kapolka · Tony Piscu
Tony "tonhe" Mattke · Torbjörn Andersson · Toshiya Nakamura · Trajecient · Transmissible Games, The Netherlands · Travis Fouche · Travis Moy · Trenton Wynter Brown · Trevor Bramb
Trevor Johnson · Trevor Smith · Tristan Louis, TNL.net · Tristan Ostrowski · Troy Gilbert · Troy Sabean · Truchainz · Trynity Mirell · Tucker McKinnon · Tyler Kieft · Tyler Sigman · Ty
Datwyler · ubuntor · Vasco Dunker · Vasilis Papaioannou · Vasyl Tsvirkunov · VCF Midwest · Vendetta Psychon · Victor Gijsbers · Vin de Silva · Vincent Latour · Vincent Szopa · Vince
Verhoeven · Vittorio Rosati · Vivi Gibbens/Sarnai Himaa · Vivienne Dunstan · Vojtěch Balák · VoodooLilium · Vsevolod Zubarev · W. Dean Thrasher · W. Scott Neal Reilly · Wade Woodsc
Walt Stoneburner · Ward Childress · Warren H Tutwiler · WarWizard Games · Wayne Sung · Wei Li · Wendell Duellman · Wendy, Lisa, Murphy & Lily · Wilhelm Fitzpatrick · Will Day · W
Ellwood · Will Hopkins · Willem B. · William Bull · William Combs · William D. Smith · William G Wu · William Hampton · William Neilson · William P. Newhall, Jr. · William Wentwor
Sheilds · Wizard Maximilian · WJ McCormick · Wtchet · Wyatt Draggoo · Wyatt Lee Chastain · Wyatt Walker · Xander Purcell · Xavier 'FenriX' Bodénand · Xavier Couët · Xevi · Xris Parsell
K. Lee · YAKOUSEI · Yann R. Fernandez · Yee Cang Ling · Yellis · Yifat Shaik · yomidian · YunYan Chi · Zac Bir · Zach Ehrlich · Zach Kamsler · Zachary Tellman · Zachary "Professor" Edgert
· Zack R. · Zain Jarrar · Zak McClendon · Zanthax · Zdeněk Pavlátka · Zeke Fiddler · ZorkFox: THIS SPACE INTENTIONALLY LEFT BLANK

ACKNOWLEDGME

CROWDFUNDING PATRONS

Alan Hinchcliffe
(in memoriam—miss you, pal)

Adam Summerville
Adrian Hon
BLAST RETRO GAMING BOOKS
Botta Family
Chad Barb
Chelsea Stearns
Chris Charla
David Rheingold
Garnulf the Grey
Gwenda Obels
Hans Petter Jansson
Herní historie, z.s.
Jake Rodkin

James 'Matty' Farrow
John Urquhart Ferguson
Matt Hargett
Nathan "instigator" Green
Patrick Coleman
Peter Engrav
Petrov Neutrino
Ridzuan Ashim @ridz84
Sean B Swick
Serhii Mozhaiskyi / Ukrainian Interactive Fiction Community
Stacey Mason
starmaru
Stephen Lafleur
Steven Velozo
Thomas Biskup
Tommy Honton

THIS BOOK would not have been possible without the generosity of many folks who answered questions, assisted my research efforts, offered feedback or corrections, helped with translations, or otherwise lent support. Thanks to Tarn Adams, Jacqueline Ashwell, Richard Bartle, Stephanie Boluk, Justin Bortnick, Jason Castonguay of ACB Radio, Lynn Cherny, Nyeogmi Choi, Raph D'Amico, Depresiv, Tamara Duplantis, Ruber Eaglenest, the Electronic Literature Organization, Clara Fernández-Vara, Hannah Flynn, Jeremy Freese, Jacob Garbe, Tim Gilberts, Stanislav Hrda, Isaac Karth, Hugo Labrande, Jennifer Loredo at the US Army Heritage and Education Center, Pablo Martinez, Steve Meretzky, Matt Mihály, Nicola Newton, Andrew Plotkin, Jenni Polodna, John Pritchett, Jason Scott, Isabella Shaw, Emily Short, Rebecca Slitt, Gillian Smith, Vojtěch "sCZther" Straka, Nic Velissaris, and Noah Wardrip-Fruin.

Also worthy of special thanks is the Internet Archive, without which hundreds of online and early print sources cited in this volume might have been lost forever; the physical archives of the Computer History Museum in Mountain View, California; MobyGames for their work cataloging vintage game credits and reviews; and every academic institution that open-sources its research rather than locking it behind a paywall. (In this spirit, the chapters in this book first appeared as free posts on Substack, and will remain accessible that way indefinitely.)

I am inspired by and indebted to Jason Dyer, Jimmy Maher, and David Welbourn for their ongoing work documenting text games and their history with a passion and attention to detail I can only aspire to. Their work has proved invaluable time and time again, and each have their own projects well-deserving of your support.

Maps and flowcharts were created by the author except where noted, using the tools GitMind and Dungeon Scrawl (by Keir a.k.a ProbableTrain).

My copyeditor, Emily Morganti, and decade game listings research assistant, Duncan Bowsman, both provided invaluable assistance; their attention to detail helped make this book the best it could be, though any remaining mistakes are certainly my own.

As this project evolved, it gathered an invaluable online community of fans and fellow researchers. Initial work was supported by paid subscribers to the "50 Years of Text Games" Substack, who believed in the free blog series enough to financially support it even without exclusive content; their continued votes of confidence helped keep me going. Thanks also to my crowdfunders who helped bring the print and e-book version of this project to life, and to the participants in the "50 Years" Discord who caught typos, offered feedback, and provided much-needed cheerleading and advice.

AI Artificial Intelligence; in the context of text games, common AI domains include natural language understanding, characters who make plans or try to achieve goals, and generating grammatically correct or narratively interesting sentences.

ANSI graphics A way of rendering simple images on computers using colored text characters, popular in the early to mid-90s especially on BBSes; the name refers to the American National Standards Institute, though not a particular standard.

ARPANET A precursor to the modern internet developed in the 1960s and 70s by the US military's Advanced Research Projects Agency.

ASCII One of various standards for encoding text on computers defined by the American Standard Code for Information Interchange; often used to distinguish text-based from graphical game interfaces.

BASIC A programming language targeted at beginning computer users, developed in the 1960s and popular through the late 80s.

BBS Bulletin Board System, a computer connected to one or more telephone lines that allowed users with accounts to dial in via modem to access files, chat with other users, and play games (see **1991**).

C, C++ Mainstream programming languages used for many professional applications and forming the basis of many graphical game engines.

CD-ROM A media format based on compact discs, capable of holding about 650 MB of data; replaced floppy disks with far less storage capacity in the 1990s and helped bring video and multimedia to computer gaming.

changelog A file that holds a record of changes made to a program in each of its previous releases.

chatbot A program designed to converse via text with a human interactor.

choice-based In reference to interactive fiction games, those that provide a list of actions the player can take at each turn (contrast with the open-ended prompt in a parser-based game, or clickable links in hypertext fiction).

command line A computer interface based on typing textual commands at a prompt.

compass navigation In text adventures, the convention of using cardinal directions like *north* and *east* to move between areas.

compile The process of converting human-readable source code into executable machine code that runs on a particular kind of computer system.

core loop Game design term for the central cycle of player activity in a particular game; the core loop of Monopoly is rolling dice to move around a board and pay rent or buy properties.

corpus, corpora In the context of text games with AI, a data set used by a program for analysis or training, such as a corpus of public-domain novels used to train a program to recognize well-constructed sentences.

cutscene A noninteractive segment of a game, often used for exposition or major plot events in which the player isn't allowed to intervene.

CYOA Short for Choose Your Own Adventure, the popular 1980s gamebook series (see **1979**); often used generically to refer to any choice-based interactive story.

D&D *Dungeons & Dragons*, a tabletop roleplaying game first published in the 1970s and influential on many early computer games (see **1975–7**); one player (the "dungeon master") creates a fictional story or setting for the other players, each controlling a specific character, to explore.

dial-up An online service requiring a modem and telephone landline to connect.

domain-specific language (DSL) A programming language designed to author one specific kind of program, like Inform for text adventures; contrast with a general-purpose language like C++.

DOS Disk Operating System, one of several pregraphical command-line operating systems for early computers, of which Microsoft's MS-DOS was the most popular.

dumb terminal A keyboard and display with little or no local computing power, allowing a user to run a program on a distant computer. *See also* mainframe.

dungeon master *See* D&D.

emulator A program that allows software for one computer platform to be run on another; often used in games preservation to run old programs on modern machines.

flag A variable tracking a single piece of state in a program, often boolean (either set or unset); a game character might have an alive/dead flag, for example.

Flash A software platform from Macromedia (later Adobe) for creating graphical animations and user interfaces, commonly used in the 2000s to create more visually sophisticated games and apps for the web, before support for advanced styling and JavaScript features became commonplace.

floppy disk Early computer storage medium, used from the late 1970s through early 90s; common sizes included 5.25″ disks (often holding 360 KB of data) and 3.5″ disks (1.44 MB).

freemium, free-to-play A monetization strategy that became popular in the 2010s, especially for mobile games, where rather than purchasing a game outright, players are encouraged to pay for upgrades to free (but often annoyingly constrained) gameplay.

gamebook An interactive story that is

GLOSSARY

(or could be) realized as a printed book.

gamemaster A system-neutral term for "dungeon master." *See also* D&D.

GDC The Game Developers Conference, held annually in the San Francisco Bay Area since 1988; one of the digital game industry's major trade shows.

Glulx A 32-bit virtual machine format designed by Andrew Plotkin in 1999 that extends Infocom's 16-bit Z-machine, allowing for text adventure games significantly larger in size and scope than those made during the 80s.

handle An alias used online, often consistently across multiple systems.

Hello World A simple example program often used as the first code encountered in a tutorial, generally printing *Hello World* to the screen or some equally simple task.

high-level In the context of programming, code that centers big-picture structures and concerns rather than underlying execution, letting authors focus on the specifics of a problem at the expense of slower execution or less control over minutia. *See also* low-level.

hypertext A textual work consisting of passages connected via clickable words, allowing multiple possible pathways through a reading.

IDE Integrated Development Environment, a tool for editing code, often with advanced features to assist and streamline common programming tasks and workflows.

IF *See* interactive fiction.

IF Comp The Interactive Fiction Competition, an annual online event since 1995, invites authors to submit an interactive story that can be enjoyed in two hours or less; players rank entries on a ten-point scale.

Infocom A 1980s game company known for releasing high-quality, imaginative parser interactive fiction games (see **1983–5**).

Inform A popular language for creating parser interactive fiction, first released in **1993**; Inform 6 became a standard from the mid-90s on, and Inform 7, with a new natural language syntax, was released a decade later (see **2008**).

interactive fiction In this book, any text-based interactive story (though the term has been used in various ways by various people, often to mean parser-based text adventures specifically).

iOS Apple's mobile operating system, which drove devices like the iPhone and iPad from the 2000s on.

IT Information Technology, often used as a shorthand for staff in charge of maintaining computer systems at a company.

Java An object-oriented programming language popular from the late 90s on, often used in the 2000s to embed complex programs on websites.

JavaScript A programming language (largely unrelated to Java) designed originally to support lightweight scripting on websites; became the dominant platform for nearly all web-based apps and games.

low-level In the context of programming, code that is conceptually closer to the functioning of specific hardware, offering the author more control at the expense of less portability, readability, and fewer helpful abstractions. *See also* high-level.

mainframe A powerful, expensive central computer designed for many users to connect to and share, often via a teletype or dumb terminal; common before the 1980s when computers were too expensive for individual users to own. *See also* timeshare.

mechanic In a game, a rule or set of rules that enable a particular kind of action from the player; combat games might have a dodging mechanic.

microcomputer, micro A personal computer; useful term in the late 70s and early 80s contrasting with mainframes or smaller (but still massive) minicomputers.

MMO, MMORPG A massively multiplayer online game (or specifically role-playing game) that lets hundreds or thousands of players coexist within the same virtual world.

modem Hardware allowing one computer to remotely connect to another over a standard telephone landline.

MUD Multi-User Dungeon, a game genre named after progenitor *MUD* (see **1980**); multiplayer text-based virtual world, often with a fantasy setting.

newsgroups *See* Usenet.

NPC Non-Player Character: any character in an interactive story who is part of the game world but not controlled by a human player. *See also* PC.

parser A text input system designed to read a command and parse it into a form the program can understand; often used as shorthand for parser-based interactive fiction.

pathfinding Code that helps a computer-controlled game character to move from one point to another in a simulated world, or more generally, to find a route between two nodes on a graph.

PC Personal Computer; usually used to differentiate DOS- or Windows-compatible machines from Apple or other architectures, as in "PC gaming."

PC Player Character; any character in an interactive story controlled by a human. *See also* NPC.

port To rewrite or modify a program so it can run on a different kind of computer.

procgen, procedural generation A class of techniques used to build large amounts of random content (often environments, items, or characters for a game world) based on rules created by a coder or designer.

punch card, punch tape Early methods of storing binary data by punching and reading holes in paper media; mostly replaced by magnetic media by the late 1970s.

puzzle In text games, a challenge or obstacle blocking narrative progress, often used for pacing; waned in popularity during the 1990s.

PvP Player versus Player; multiplayer games that allow human players to pit their characters against each other to win points, treasure, clout etc.

QA Quality Assurance, the process of testing gameplay and reporting bugs, or the team in charge of this process.

readme A file included with a download that often explains its contents, gives instructions, and provides the author's contact details.

repo, repository A digital storehouse for a program's code, often part of a version control system that archives each prior revision.

roguelike A style of game named after *Rogue* [1980] characterized by exploring dangerous randomly generated environments, a top-down view that uses text characters as surrogate graphics, and frequent deaths and restarts as a core part of its gameplay.

roleplaying game A kind of tabletop or digital game centered on the narrative or numeric improvement over time of a strong central character or cast.

room A discrete location in a text game, which could be anything from an actual indoor room to a huge outdoor space.

RPG *See* roleplaying game.

SPAG The Society for the Promotion (originally Preservation) of Adventure Games, online newsletter promoting interactive fiction founded in 1994.

storylet A piece of content in an interactive story with rules for when it can appear; often contains attached choices and consequences.

string In programming, a piece of textual data (likely named based on its implementation as a sequence of single characters).

sysop System Operator, administrator of a networked computer system or BBS.

tabletop roleplaying game, a nondigital roleplaying game played with dice, a rulebook, a gamemaster, and a group of players.

TADS The Text Adventure Development System, a C-like language for interactive fiction authoring popular in the 1990s and 2000s.

teletype, teleprinter A typewriter that can send and receive text from a connected computer, local or remote; the primary interface for most computer users in the 1970s.

text adventure A game style characterized by a command-line parser and second-person explorations of a simulated world (see **1976**).

text game A digital game that uses primarily written or spoken language, rather than multimedia, to tell its story.

time-share A method of allocating mainframe computer time allowing many users share a single system, taking advantage of the fact that much of an interactive section is idle time as the system waits for the user to respond.

transcript A record of one playthrough of a text game.

UI User Interface, the part of a program the user directly sees and interacts with.

Usenet A distributed online discussion network organized by topic popular in the 90s and early 2000s; groups like rec.arts.int-fiction hosted important early text game design conversations.

virtual machine A computer platform designed to be easily emulated in software; useful for running the same code on many different kinds of computers.

visual novel A style of interactive story popularized in Japan in the 1990s and 2000s, characterized by conversation-heavy stories illustrated by full-screen character portraits.

walkthrough A step-by-step guide to playing through a game; for text games, often in the form of a list of commands.

Win Short for Windows, dominant operating system on PCs from the early 90s on.

Z-machine A virtual machine developed by Infocom in the early 80s to run games compiled into **Z-code**, a custom format; this let them easily port their games to many computer systems (see **1978**). The format was later repurposed by fans and used well into the 2000s. *See also* Inform.

ZIL The Zork Implementation Language, a Lisp-like programming language used by Infocom to create their games.

INTRODUCT

ION

THE EARLIEST VERSION OF *THE OREGON TRAIL*—the text-only original, made long before the green-tinged Apple remake played by 80s kids in their school computer labs—debuted in a Minnesota classroom on December 3, 1971. In the fifty years since, text games—fiction you can play—have evolved from rough-hewn prototypes to mainstream successes to commercial pariahs to underdog heroes. They've been resurrected as indie punk games, award-winning art games, viral sensations, and groundbreaking pioneers of interactive storytelling techniques. Their popularity has waxed and waned, but they've never been dead, and they've never gone away. Often overlooked, frequently dismissed, these games are a vibrant part of gaming history worth remembering, playing, and continuing to make.

In this book we'll take a journey through fifty text games, one for each year of the medium's first half century. We'll take a close look at how each game works, what it says, who made it, and how it fits into the rapidly changing historical and technological context of its time. These aren't necessarily the most famous fifty games from these years, nor the best-loved, the most influential, or the most important (whatever that might mean). The constraint of picking one and only one game for each year instead suggests a grand tour, a journey that can't possibly include everything but aims to stop at many interesting sites along the way.

On our tour we'll meet games famous and obscure, amateur and commercial, some with millions of words of content and others so small their source code can fit on a single printed page. Our fifty titles hail from a surprising breadth of genres and intertwine with a vast array of technologies, from teletypes to iPhones to virtual machines to virtual reality, from cassette tapes to spoken words to paper tape to Kindles. Collectively, their story cuts a fascinating cross section through the history of computing, from the dawn of stored programs up through the cutting edge of today's AI.

Why do these games matter? Unlike mainstream computer games, they're often made by sole creators with something to say, and the freedom to explore and experiment with new ways of saying it. They have pioneered new genres and mechanics years before the same ideas make it into graphical games. They have explored countless ways stories can be dynamic, debuted influential creators who found success in the wider game or publishing industries, and served as a constant source of inspiration as creators redefine what games made of words can do, mean, and be, over and over again.

WHAT IS A TEXT GAME? In brief, it's a game you want to share excerpts from, not screenshots. The broader game industry is primarily visual, trafficking in colorful screen grabs and trailers full of motion. But a screenshot of a text game is missing the point. There are few screenshots in this book, but many excerpts.

A text game tells its story with words, thus connecting more to written than filmic traditions. Some might have illustrations, as do some books, but these are not required to play (as they are in graphical adventures like *Mystery House* [On-Line Systems 1980] or *Disco Elysium* [ZA/UM 2019]), and neither are they foundational to the experience of play (unlike, say, the art in visual novels). Text games are interactive, which differentiates them from animated concrete poetry or digital word art. They use words as words, not as placeholder graphics as in roguelikes (which we'll mostly skip over but for a few exceptions that also meaningfully engage with language). Finally, the kinds of text games we talk about here are mostly digital (excluding tabletop storytelling games like *Dungeons & Dragons*) and exclusively narrative (excluding pure wordplay or other kinds of linguistic fun not concerned with story).

While there are many traditions of text games in languages other than English, this book mostly limits its scope to the English-speaking world, with a few exceptions.

see *P.R.E.S.T.A.V.B.A.* **1988**; and *El Museo de las Consciencias / Lieux Communs* **2007**

TEXT GAME STYLES can vary considerably, but the games discussed in this book can be roughly clustered by technology, structure, or audience into about a dozen nonexclusive categories.

» Resource Management. Games primarily concerned with managing a set of numeric qualities. Modern idle and clicker games fall into this category, as do many early computer games.

The Oregon Trail **1971**; *ROCKET* **1972**; *Universal Paperclips* **2017**

» Parser. A simulated world explored by typing imperative commands that are then "parsed" into valid actions. Also called text adventures or interactive fiction, parser games were massively popular in the 1980s and continue to be made today.

Adventure **1976**; *Zork* **1977**; *Pirate Adventure* **1978**; *The Hobbit* **1982**; *Suspended* **1983**; *The Hitchhiker's Guide to the Galaxy* **1984**; *A Mind Forever Voyaging* **1985**; *Plundered Hearts* **1987**; *P.R.E.S.T.A.V.B.A.* **1988**; *Silverwolf* **1992**; *Curses* **1993**; *So Far* **1996**; *Photopia* **1998**; *Galatea* **2000**; *The Fire Tower* **2004**; *El Museo de las Consciencias* and *Lieux Communs* **2007**; *Violet* **2008**

» MUD (Multi-User Dungeon). Parser games hooked up to a persistent, multiplayer world.

MUD **1980**; *LambdaMOO* **1990**; *Achaea* **1997**

» Hypertext. A tree of story nodes often explorable in nonlinear order, generally navigated by clicking linked words.

Uncle Roger **1986**; *Patchwork Girl* **1995**; *Howling Dogs* **2012**

» Choice-Based. Story nodes connected by explicit decision points, usually moving forward through a possibly-branching plot.

The Cave of Time **1979**; *Digital: A Love Story* **2010**; *80 Days* **2014**; *Lifeline* **2015**; *Choices: The Freshman* **2016**; *Weyrwood* **2018**

» Storylet-Driven. An unordered set of story nodes presented to the player in an order based on randomness, simulation qualities, or player stats.

King of Dragon Pass **1999**; *The Kingdom of Loathing* **2003**; *Fallen London* **2009**; *80 Days* **2014**

» **Procedural Story**. Interactive narratives shaped by complex procedures as well as player choices, usually offering multiple and sometimes emergent outcomes.

The Hobbit **1982**; *The Playground* **1994**; *King of Dragon Pass* **1999**; *Dwarf Fortress* **2006**; *Versu: A Family Supper* **2013**; *AI Dungeon* **2019**; *Scents & Semiosis* **2020**

» **Roguelike**. A challenging world with procedurally generated elements, often explored from a top-down perspective. Roguelikes often use text as stand-in graphics rather than primarily as words and sentences.

Hunt the Wumpus **1973**; *Super Star Trek* **1974**; *dnd* **1975**; *Shades of Doom* **2005**; *Dwarf Fortress* **2006**

» **ARG** (Alternate Reality Game). A live multiplayer game usually running for a limited time, often extending through multiple media and communication channels including text (though many are not primarily text-based).

The Beast **2001**

» **BBS**. Multiplayer games for a bulletin board system, usually designed to be played by one player at a time rather than simultaneously.

Trade Wars 2002 **1991**

» **Play-by-Mail**. Multiplayer games where players send in orders by mail or email, with a central computer batch processing turns at a slow cadence (often once a week) and sending personalized results as a turn report.

Monster Island **1989**

» **Experimental**. Text games that don't fit into any of the above styles.

His Majesty's Ship "Impetuous" **1981**; *Screen* **2002**; *Nested* **2011**

WHILE YOU CAN READ THIS BOOK STRAIGHT THROUGH, each entry is also cross-linked to other games connected through threads of inspiration, technology, or tradition. References to other games featured in this volume are indicated by a stylized year reference **2022**, often in a sidebar. Years are printed on the bottom outside corners of pages, making it easy to navigate through decades as well as by page numbers. Mentions of games not covered in this book are cited with [Author/Publisher and Year].

Spoilers are sometimes inevitable in a detailed discussion of a game. Especially egregious ones are indicated with a vertical black bar.

> Sidebars alongside underlined body text provide additional commentary or cross-references.

Game excerpts are shown in a bordered gray box; if the excerpt is from a different game than the main topic of a chapter, the border is omitted. Player input is indicated by:

> `TEXT LIKE THIS`

In games where the player selects from a list of inputs rather than typing directly,

» *Each presented option is*
» *shown individually, and*
» *the one selected is reversed.*

> *Spoilers for how excerpts are styled in this book.*

> In games where the player interacts with text directly, <u>interactable text</u> is shown underlined in the <u>excerpt</u> (if that text was <u>styled distinctly</u> in the original), and the player's choice is repeated at the bottom with a cursor icon:
>
> ▸ interactable text
>
> ---
>
> A horizontal line indicates a page clear; otherwise text scrolled in the original presentation.

If the original version is not the one being excerpted, this will be indicated.

Care has been taken to keep the content of excerpts as close as possible to the game's original release, including idiosyncrasies of spelling, line breaks, and indentation. One exception is that, in most cases, paragraphs have been rewrapped to look more natural given the book's column width. When game transcripts have been shortened for clarity, brackets [...] indicate ellipses not in the original. Game names match the title screen or opening text of the original release (hence *Adventure*, not *Colossal Cave Adventure* or *ADVENT*), except in the case of an online game later better known by a different name. Author names are their preferred name at death or publication time.

Early text games ran on systems that COULD NOT DISPLAY LOWERCASE CHARACTERS. This convention has been preserved in relevant excerpts. Until the mid-1990s, computer text was generally displayed with a fixed-width font; this has not been preserved except for games where this was a key part of their layout or aesthetic. In all other cases excerpts have been styled with a consistent modern font rather than attempting to emulate period text styles, not all of which are especially friendly to unpracticed eyes today.

10 Source code excerpts are presented in a fixed-width font.

Citations are numbered alphabetically at the end of each chapter. "Direct quotations only are attributed" using citation number[5] or in a sidebar for chapters without endnotes. Bibliography links to online content are given a date prepended with either *a* and date of access, or *s* and date of a snapshot from the Wayback Machine at the Internet Archive (https://archive.org).

The book is divided into five parts by decade, each beginning with a brief summary of the larger trends in text games of that period beyond the specific ten games covered. The chapter "Before the 70s" also covers the years leading up to the start of this history. A brief sampling of other noteworthy text games from each decade with capsule summaries can be found at the end of these intros.

Robert Pinsky. 1995. "The Muse in the Machine: Or, The Poetics of Zork." *New York Times*, Mar 19, 1995, sec. Books.

"WHAT HAS POETRY TO DO WITH COMPUTER SOFTWARE?" asked Robert Pinsky in 1995, precisely the middle of this history. Pinsky, a future US poet laureate, had a decade earlier authored the surreal text adventure *Mindwheel* [Brøderbund Software 1984]. Still enamored of the possibilities of "the muse in the machine," he wrote a piece for the *New York Times* defending interactive text, a uniquely contested art form that, like poetry, "suspicious guardians of the past may hug … protectively" while "preening advocates of the future may scorn … as outmoded."

> What has this activity amounted to so far? Less than enthusiasts claim, more than the scornful might assume—an interesting infancy.… On the peculiar terrain of literature-for-the-monitor, where the most innocent science fiction adventure may overlap with the most fashionable of nonreferential language theory, the future and the past are conducting their perennial transaction.

Text and language have endured far longer than most technologies for storing information and sharing stories. The next fifty years of interactive prose, and the next after that, will build on the craft and wisdom of the pioneers in these pages, whose stories we would do well not to forget.

Index to Games by Creation Tool

An enormous variety of programming languages and authoring tools were used to create the games in this book; here's an index to games by creation tool.

ASP: The Beast 2001 (server)

BASIC: Oregon Trail 1971; ROCKET (1972 version); Hunt the Wumpus 1973; Super Star Trek 1974; Pirate Adventure 1978; His Majesty's Ship "Impetuous" 1981; Uncle Roger 1986 (commercial version); P.R.E.S.T.A.V.B.A. 1988

BCPL: MUD 1980 (version 3)

C/C++: LambdaMOO 1990 (server); Achaea 1997; King of Dragon Pass 1999; Screen 2002; Dwarf Fortress 2006; Choices: The Freshman 2016

ChoiceScript: Weyrwood 2018

Flash: The Beast 2001 (multimedia)

FOCAL: ROCKET 1972 (original version)

Fortran: Adventure 1976

Hap: The Playground 1994 (character logic)

Hourglass: Achaea 1997 (original server)

Inform: Curses 1993; So Far 1996; Photopia 1998; Galatea 2000; The Fire Tower 2004; Lieux communs and El museo de las consciencias 2007

Inform 7: Violet 2008; Scents & Semiosis 2020

JavaScript: The Beast 2001 (websites); Fallen London 2009 (frontend); Nested 2011; Universal Paperclips 2018; AI Dungeon 2019 (frontend)

Lisp: The Playground 1994 (engine)

Lua: Achaea 1997 (scripting)

MACRO-10: MUD 1980 (versions 1 & 2)

MDL: Zork 1977

MOO: LambdaMOO 1990 (world)

MUDDL: MUD 1980 (world)

NodeJS: Fallen London 2009 (backend, 2019 redesign)

Objective C: Lifeline 2015 (app)

Pascal: Trade Wars 2002 1991

PAW: Silverwolf 1992

Perl: The Kingdom of Loathing 2003 (backend)

PHP: The Kingdom of Loathing 2003 (backend)

Praxis: A Family Supper 2013 (content)

Python: AI Dungeon 2019 (backend)

QuickBasic: Monster Island 1989

Rapture: Achaea 1997 (2001 server)

Ren'Py: Digital: A Love Story 2010

StoryNexus: Fallen London 2009 (content)

Storyspace: Patchwork Girl 1995

TUTOR: dnd 1975

Twine: Howling Dogs 2012; Lifeline 2015 (story)

Unix shell scripts: Uncle Roger 1986

Versu: A Family Supper 2013 (engine)

Visual Basic: Shades of Doom 2005

Vortex: Achaea 1997 (1998 server)

Z80 Assembler: The Hobbit 1982

ZIL: Suspended 1983; The Hitchhiker's Guide to the Galaxy 1984; A Mind Forever Voyaging 1985; Plundered Hearts 1987

BEFORE THE

70s

GRAPHICS CAME FIRST, despite the popular tale of primitive text games that pretty pictures displaced. While the story holds true for some of the first generation of home computers, digital games had been around for a long time by then. The earliest, from Bertie the Brain's *Tac-Tac-Toe* [1950] to *Tennis for Two* [1958] to *Spacewar!* [1962], were all visual. It was language and text—storing it, assembling it, understanding it—that, at first, was hard.

The earliest digital games used mothballed World War II radar displays, oscilloscopes, or grids of blinking lights for their graphics. In 1947, two New Jersey physicists submitted a patent for a Cathode-Ray Tube Amusement Device, which let the player shape arcs of curved light on a screen. The beams signified the paths of virtual artillery shells, and plastic airplane decals attached to the screen showed the position of targets. If the player could align their beam with a target, they scored. Though it never moved beyond the prototype phase, even this early game had flashy graphics. On a hit, a clever engineering trick forced a resistor overload, causing the display to briefly lose focus and the bright dot of the missile to blur into a fuzzy circle—a tiny expanding explosion.

People were playing with cathode ray tubes on the other side of the Atlantic too. A technology developed in England—the Williams-Kilburn tube, after its two inventors—could both store and display persistent binary data using a grid of visible dots. By reading the location of the brightened phosphors (which represented ones) and looping back a signal to keep them lit, the tube could "store" the very data it was displaying. The technology opened up a relatively inexpensive way to give a computer random-access memory, using the electrical signal to determine whether the phosphor dot at a given position was bright or dim. The visible grid of bits could give human operators an invaluable window into a running program, but it also gave them a canvas. In 1947, Williams and Kilburn configured their prototype to display the blocky words "C.R.T. STORE," perhaps the first bitmapped text ever drawn to a screen.

The two engineers developed a computer that could use their memory tube: the Manchester Baby, the first stored program computer. In a later incarnation, the Ferranti Mark 1, it also became one of the world's first computers to be commercially sold. One of the earliest software games without dedicated hardware was devised for the Ferranti, first running successfully in 1952. It played a game of draughts (checkers), using the grid of phosphor dots on one of its small round

Reconstruction of early digital text on a prototype Williams-Kilburn tube in 1947, configured with a 32 x 32 grid of phosphor dots. These were called "picture elements" by the tube's inventors. In later years, this would evolve into the shorthand word "pixel."

Also called a teleprinter or teletype, these devices had been in use for much of the twentieth century for sending telegrams and news wires, and were rapidly repurposed as computer interfaces. Effectively, a teletype is just a typewriter that can also send and receive keystrokes as electrical signals.

Noah Wardrip-Fruin has dubbed this previously unnamed game *M.U.C. Draughts*, after the system's informal name: the Manchester University Computer.[29]

The / . at the end of the last line above may have signified an exclamation mark, since the teleprinter hooked up to the Ferranti Mark 1 had no such dedicated symbol.

Williams-Kilburn screens to draw the board and pieces. But the program could also output text to an attached teletypewriter, making it likely the earliest digital game to print full sentences. On startup, the machine would print:

```
PLEASE READ THE INSTRUCTION CARD.
```

This was necessary because playing moves meant inputting a series of 5-bit numbers via a long row of switches—the computer could print English text more easily than it could receive it. After the user learned from the card that they needed to press a particular button on the console to proceed, the printer continued:

```
SHALL WE TOSS FOR THE FIRST MOVE? WILL YOU SPIN A COIN?
TAILS
HAVE I WON?
```

Once the player answered, the game could begin. While moves were primarily shown visually on the CRT grid, the program would use the teletype to offer occasional feedback, which could get testy if the human took too long to move or entered incorrect data:

```
YOU MUST PLAY AT ONCE OR RESIGN.
```

```
KINDLY READ THE INSTRUCTIONS AND START THE MOVE AGAIN.
```

```
I REFUSE TO WASTE ANY MORE TIME. GO AND PLAY WITH A HUMAN
BEING/.
```

The text, and the rather clever draughts-playing program itself, were written by an unlikely programmer named Christopher Strachey. A brilliant mathematician, he had suffered a nervous breakdown halfway through his undergraduate coursework, later attributed to a struggle to reconcile his sexuality with the rigidly heteronormative world of the 1940s. Though he returned to finish his degree, he did not test well enough to continue on to graduate work and settled instead into a quiet life as a schoolteacher. But one of his college chums had been computing pioneer Alan Turing, and years later, idly curious, Strachey was able to get access to the Manchester computer through his old acquaintance.

Strachey threw himself into the extraordinary challenge of programming early computers with an almost obsessive passion. A famous anecdote tells that he asked Turing for ideas: what should he write for his first program? Without cracking a smile, Turing suggested he write some code to make the computer simulate itself. Not knowing the task would be extraordinarily difficult, Strachey nevertheless came back some weeks later with a program not only far longer than any yet written for the machine, but one that ran correctly and played "God Save the King" through the system's alert speaker

1952

when it finished—incidentally, one of the earliest pieces of computer music. Turing, refusing to be drawn out, responded only by muttering, "Good show."

After teaching the Manchester University Computer to play draughts, Strachey next programmed it to print out procedurally generated love letters. His code filled in template sentences with random words from a list of flowery adjectives, entered one tedious character at a time into the machine. Strachey pinned the printed love notes anonymously to the department's notice board, to the consternation of colleagues:

```
HONEY DEAR
   MY SYMPATHETIC AFFECTION BEAUTIFULLY ATTRACTS YOUR
AFFECTIONATE ENTHUSIASM. YOU ARE MY LOVING ADORATION: MY
BREATHLESS ADORATION. MY FELLOW FEELING BREATHLESSLY HOPES
FOR YOUR DEAR EAGERNESS. MY LOVESICK ADORATION CHERISHES
YOUR AVID ARDOUR.
                        YOURS WISTFULLY
                           M. U. C.
```

Strachey would go on to a long career as a computer scientist, pioneering many ideas in programming language design and time-sharing architecture. He was one of the very first software developers, and one of the earliest authors of prose meant for computers to perform—the godfather to all text games in the decades to come.

In the **1950s**, **programming computers to play games** or write love letters was somewhat akin to blasphemy. Computers cost millions of dollars and were used almost exclusively for important matters like codebreaking or calculating ballistic trajectories. And indeed, some of the earliest complex computer games were wargames created by the US military as training exercises. One of these was a game called *HUTSPIEL* (1955) in which two players used a bank of dials and switches to interact with a real-time simulation—a complex model of a hypothetical battle in Europe between NATO and Soviet forces. The models that drove the game came from an unlikely source: a historian, Dr. Dorothy Kneeland Clark, whose career had centered around statistical analyses of real-world military conflicts, generalizing the messy data into reusable heuristics and equations. When a computer wargame project needed a numerical model on which to base its combat simulation, Dr. Clark was brought aboard to computerize her equations. Largely forgotten by gaming history, her work formed the foundation of one of the first complex computer games, and one of the earliest not based on an existing tabletop game like draughts.

Another thread of complex early computer games was evolving in the world of business management. (This might seem incongruous until you remember that management executives were some of the first customers of early computers.) In 1957, the American Management Association (AMA) ran an exclusive retreat for "participants in executive decision-making programs"[31] where attendees were placed in teams to play, essentially,

HUTSPIEL ran on a custom analog computer (using continuous voltages to represent values, rather than ones and zeros) called the Goodyear Electronic Differential Analyzer.

STATEMENT OF ASSETS

YEAR 0 QUARTER 0

		TOTAL	NET CHANGE
CASH		$ 4,425,000	$25,000
INVENTORY	150,000 units @ $4.50	$ 675,000	$ 0
PLANT INVESTMENT	1,010,000 units @ $5.00	$ 5,050,000	$50,000
TOTAL ASSETS		$10,150,000	$75,000

ANNUAL STATEMENTS

YEAR 0

	COMPANY 1	COMPANY 2	COMPANY 3	COMPANY 4	COMPANY 5
CASH	$ 4,425,000	$ 4,425,000	$ 4,425,000	$ 4,425,000	$ 4,425,000
INVENTORY	$ 675,000	$ 675,000	$ 675,000	$ 675,000	$ 675,000
PLANT INVESTMENT	$ 5,050,000	$ 5,050,000	$ 5,050,000	$ 5,050,000	$ 5,050,000
TOTAL ASSETS	$10,150,000	$10,150,000	$10,150,000	$10,150,000	$10,150,000

INCOME STATEMENT

SALES INCOME	900,000 units @ $5.00		$4,500,000
COST OF GOODS SOLD & OPERATING EXPENSES			
COST OF GOODS SOLD		$4,050,000	
MARKETING & RESEARCH AND DEVELOPMENT		$ 300,000	
OTHER (MARKET RESEARCH)		$ 0	$4,350,000
			$ 150,000
OTHER INCOME (PLANT DISPOSAL)			$ 0
INCOME BEFORE TAXES			$ 150,000
TAXES			$ 75,000
NET INCOME			$ 75,000

MARKET INFORMATION

	COMPANY 1	COMPANY 2	COMPANY 3	COMPANY 4	COMPANY 5
PRICE	$ 5.00	$ 5.00	$ 5.00	$ 5.00	$ 5.00
SHARE OF MARKET	20.00%	%	%	%	%
TOTAL MARKET	4,500,000				
POTENTIAL SALES	900,000				

MARKET RESEARCH REPORT

TOTAL INDUSTRY MARKETING EXPENDITURE	$
TOTAL INDUSTRY RESEARCH & DEVELOPMENT EXPENDITURE	$
POTENTIAL SHARE OF MARKET — MAXIMUM MARKETING	%
POTENTIAL SHARE OF MARKET — MAXIMUM PRICE	%

OPERATING AND DECISION INFORMATION
(for next period)

	1	2	3	4	DECISIONS LAST PERIOD (5)	6	7	8	9
UNIT COST OF PRODUCTION	$ 4.65	$ 4.61	$ 4.57	$ 4.54	$ 4.50	$ 4.49	$ 4.48	$ 4.46	$ 4.45
UNITS OF PRODUCTION	720,000	765,000	810,000	855,000	900,000	918,000	936,000	954,000	972,000

— DECISION ALTERNATIVES —

	1	2	3	4	DECISIONS LAST PERIOD (5)	6	7	8	9
COST OF PRODUCTION	$ 3,348,000	$3,526,700	$3,701,700	$3,881,700	$4,050,000	$4,121,800	$4,193,300	$4,254,800	$4,325,400
MARKETING		$ 170,000	$ 180,000	$ 190,000	$ 200,000	$ 210,000	$ 220,000	$ 230,000	
RESEARCH & DEVELOPMENT		$ 85,000	$ 90,000	$ 95,000	$ 100,000	$ 105,000	$ 110,000	$ 115,000	
ADDITIONAL PLANT INVESTMENT	$ 0	$ 10,000	$ 20,000	$ 30,000	$ 40,000	$ 50,000	$ 60,000	$ 70,000	$ 80,000

MARKET RESEARCH INFORMATION

S = COMPETITORS' SHARE OF MARKET
M = TOTAL INDUSTRY MARKETING EXPENDITURE
R = TOTAL INDUSTRY RES. & DEVELOP. EXPENDITURES
A = POTENTIAL MARKET SHARE — MAX. MARKETING
P = POTENTIAL MARKET SHARE — MAX. PRICE

	1	2	3	4	5	6	7	8	9
	NONE	S $ 5,000	M $ 10,000	R $ 10,000	S&M $ 15,000	S&R $ 15,000	M&R $ 20,000	S,M&R $ 25,000	
				NONE	A $ 22,500	P $ 22,500	A&P $ 45,000		
PRICE	$ 4.80	$ 4.85	$ 4.90	$ 4.95	$ 5.00	$ 5.05	$ 5.10	$ 5.15	$ 5.20
PLANT DISPOSAL (in units)				NONE	5,000	10,000			

IBM 650 REPORT — TOTAL FUNDS AVAILABLE → $4,425,000 — COMPANY 1 PERIOD 1 GAME 1

1957

business wargames. Each team controlled a virtual firm manufacturing a product in a competitive market, setting a retail price and dividing expenditures between five possible categories including a marketing budget and production capacity. An IBM 650 would run each team's decisions against a simple economic model and churn out quarterly reports. This was AMA's *Top Management Decision Simulation*, and while it was a relatively simple demonstration for a very niche audience, it caught the attention of many businesses and business colleges eager to ride the wave of the future.

A much more complex business game, *The Carnegie Tech Management Game* (first played in 1959), was created by a group of faculty members in the institution's Graduate School of Industrial Administration. The game was designed to be played by a full class of second-year graduate students, divided into teams of five to ten that each managed a simulated company making detergent (selected, ironically, as a stable product mostly untouched by technological progress). Over the course of two semesters, teams would compete to make their company's detergent products the leader in a virtual market, with the computer crunching hundreds of variables representing everything from tax rates to warehouse storage costs, production expenses, losses from union strikes, how consumers in various regions felt about three simulated detergent characteristics (washing power, sudsing power, and gentleness), and more. Players could make over three hundred unique decisions, and the program could generate reports with thousands of individual points of data.

But the early business management sims were very different from later generations of computer games, because most of the time spent playing them happened offline, away from the machine. Computer time in the 50s was still incredibly precious, with programs processed in stages that involved human labor and mechanical action at each step. After a program had been written and encoded on a stack of punch cards, it would be loaded into a computer's memory via a dedicated appliance the size of a refrigerator. A second stack of cards with data for the program to operate on would be loaded next. The program would execute, and the computer would output the results via another specialized appliance—a card printer, teletype, or magnetic tape storage system—that might then in turn be connected to a bulky printer to render output in a human-readable format. This system of "batch processing" programs meant dozens could be queued up for technicians to run in sequence, but it rarely allowed users to intervene in the middle of a run. Usually the earliest you could see the output of a program you wanted to run was the following day.

In Carnegie Tech's management game, turns were batch processed at the end of each week and represented one month's worth of business decisions. In the interim, most of the game was played in person. Each week's turn began with the delivery of a series of "information reports," printouts detailing the status of your team's company. During the week, teams were encouraged to schedule meetings, strategize over product directions and marketing strategies, sort out issues with production lines or backlogs, and even report to a board of directors made up of faculty. Consensus would be reached through whatever org structures each team devised. By noon on Friday, teams were expected to submit a stack of "decision records" detailing changes to their corporate strategy over the next month; there were twelve different kinds of these forms, from "Production and Raw Material Ordering Decisions" to "Product Comparison Test Orders." A clerk would convert the form submissions into a stack of data punch cards for each team and hand them to an operator to run through the program over the weekend, with the next set of information reports delivered the following Monday.

The early wargames (and business wargames) were an important step toward the text games of later decades, but they lacked two defining qualities those descendants would have. First, they weren't technically interactive (an adjective that today applies to nearly all computer programs) because they couldn't be played in real time. Strachey's draughts program had allowed a user to sit in front of it and play out a full game, but this had only been

Batch process games had mostly died out by the 1970s as interactive computer terminals became widespread, but a curious thread of their descendants survived in the form of play-by-mail games—see **1989**.

possible in a research lab. In the real world, a computer's time had to be allocated far more carefully to justify its expense. Computer access would need to become more readily available before interactive programs, and games in particular, could flourish. Second, computers and their users needed a language that each could speak with equal fluency, lest specialists remain the only ones who could use them. The most obvious choice for such a language was one the users already spoke. The quest to enable real-time, back-and-forth natural language dialogue between humans and machines would occupy the bulk of the 1960s, and many of the decades since.

A BETTER LANGUAGE WAS OF LIMITED USE while the chances to speak it were rare. Stuck in dedicated air-conditioned rooms guarded by trained technicians, each computer installation could only support a handful of users. The first time-sharing systems would go a good way toward solving this problem by the early 60s.

Time-sharing turned a weakness of early human-computer interaction into a strength. The reason most mainframes couldn't afford to be interactive was the long delay imposed by a human reading the results of an input, thinking about their next command, and typing it in—all wasted computer cycles. But if a single computer could split its time between multiple people, each connected to a remote terminal with their own sandboxed sessions, one computer might serve dozens or even hundreds of simultaneous users. Christopher Strachey filed the first patent for a time-sharing system in 1959, and by 1961 a system called CTTS (the Compatible Time-Sharing System) was running at MIT.

Time-sharing was a force multiplier on the democratizing trends in computing. Not only was hardware getting smaller, cheaper, and faster, but each machine could now be used by more people—none of whom needed physical access to the actual computer, eliminating a security risk. All that users needed was a cheap "dumb terminal," often just a teletype that could send and receive text when connected to a phone line. And that terminal might just as easily be across campus as around the world. Time-sharing began a chain of technical innovations that would lead to the modern internet.

One of the first games to take advantage of time-sharing was the brainchild not of a hacker, but of a school teacher named Mabel Addis. At fifty-two years old, with hair beginning to go gray, she would design probably the earliest text game by the definition we use here. It was called *The Sumerian Game*.

Many teletypes featured two ink ribbons, often colored black and red, to differentiate words typed by the computer and the human when looking at the scrollback—then, a literal scroll of printer paper.

1961

```
    IMAGINE THAT YOU HAVE JUST BEEN MADE RULER OF LAGASH,
A CITY-STATE OF SUMER, IN THE YEAR 3500 B.C. TWICE YEARLY
YOUR ROYAL STEWARD, URBABA, WILL REPORT TO YOU THE ECONOMIC
CONDITION OF THE KINGDOM. GUIDED BY THESE REPORTS, YOU WILL
DECIDE THE USE OF YOUR GRAIN AND OTHER RESOURCES, TRYING TO
KEEP YOUR POPULATION STABLE AND WELL FED. BETWEEN REPORTS,
YOUR COURT ADVISOR WILL COME TO YOU WITH NEWS OF YOUR
KINGDOM.
```

```
     THE STEWARD WILL USE THE TYPEWRITER TO REPORT AND ASK
FOR YOUR DECISIONS. WHEN THE "PROCEED" LIGHT COMES ON, TYPE
YOUR ANSWER IN FIGURE AND PRESS "RETURN". (IF YOU MAKE A
MISTAKE, PRESS "CANCEL" INSTEAD AND TRY AGAIN). GOOD LUCK!
```

The first inklings of *The Sumerian Game* came in the summer of 1962, when a cooperative of rural New York schools arranged a workshop with IBM. The goal was to brainstorm how computers could help students not just at the college level, but in primary schools too. At the workshop, IBM's Bruse Moncreiff spitballed an idea for a simulation of supply and demand that could teach students basic economic theory. The meetings would lead to a grant from the US Office of Education, eager to catch up with Soviet classrooms in science and technology, for a series of pilot projects. Mabel Addis, an elementary school teacher with a degree in ancient history, pitched a project inspired by Moncreiff's idea: an economics simulation set in ancient Sumer. Working with IBM programmer William McKay, she created a scenario designed for a teletype hooked up to an off-site IBM 7090 time-sharing mainframe. The ambitious program would take sixth-grade students through a succession of increasingly difficult scenarios playing as three generations of Mesopotamian rulers trying to keep their people fed.

The PLATO program also arose from these same concerns; see *dnd* **1975**.

```
ECONOMIC REPORT OF THE RULER'S STEWARD FOR THE SPRING
SEASON IN THE YEAR 1 OF LUDUGA I.

POPULATION AT PREVIOUS REPORT                    500
CHANGE IN POPULATION                            -155
TOTAL POPULATION NOW                             345

THE QUANTITY OF FOOD THE PEOPLE RECEIVED LAST SEASON WAS
FAR TOO LITTLE.
HARVEST LAST SEASON                            13000
HARVEST THIS SEASON                            14393

PREVIOUS INVENTORY                              1301
CHANGE IN INVENTORY                             -640
PRESENT INVENTORY                                661

TOTAL RESOURCES, HARVEST + INVENTORY           15054
YOU MUST NOW DECIDE HOW TO USE YOUR RESOURCES.
HOW MANY BUSHELS OF GRAIN DO YOU WISH TO FEED YOUR PEOPLE?
3500
HOW MANY BUSHELS OF GRAIN DO YOU WANT PLANTED FOR THE NEXT
CROP?
10000
THIS MEANS THAT 893 BUSHELS MUST BE PLACED IN STORAGE. IS
THIS ALL RIGHT? DO YOU WISH TO 1-LET YOUR DECISIONS STAND
OR 2-REVISE THEM?
1
RESULTING INVENTORY                             3993
THE STEWARD WILL EXECUTE THE ROYAL COMMANDS AND RETURN IN 6
MONTHS.
```

Addis and McKay began work on the game in 1963 and tested it with a group of students in 1964; a later grant provided funds for a major revision, which was played in 1966. The transcripts quoted here are from the 1966 version.

Addis faced a difficult challenge: how to turn a dry simulation into a story. Numbers were interesting to business grad students (presumably), but capturing the attention of twelve-year-olds would take more care. Addis devised a slideshow with recorded audio that would play before the student sat down at the computer, introducing the world of Sumer and the player's role in the game. But the program itself would also need to be compelling. Addis would have to devise a narrative to frame the numbers as well as a character to tell it, the mildly obsequious steward to the king:

```
I LEAN HEAVILY UPON YOUR WISDOM, LUDUGA, BUT I AM ALSO HERE
TO HELP YOU. TELL ME, IF YOUR POPULATION IS INCREASING,
WOULD YOU EXPECT THE QUANTITY OF GRAIN FED TO YOUR PEOPLE
TO 1-INCREASE 2-DECREASE?
1
OF COURSE IT SHOULD INCREASE. FORGIVE ME IF MY QUESTIONS
SEEM SIMPLE. IT IS MY DUTY TO URGE YOU TO SEE THE
RELATIONSHIP AMONG THE ITEMS IN YOUR STEWARD'S REPORTS.
```

Like other early computer games, the heart of the program was a simple simulation—in this case, of crops and population. But this simulation was married to a story. Addis supplemented the dry progression of rising and falling numbers with anecdotes and events—disasters like floods or fires—that gave the losses a human cost, and gave students an emotional reason to learn how to manage them:

```
NE-SAG'S FAMILY BECAME ILL WITH A FEVER WHILE CUTTING
REEDS IN THE MARSH LANDS. I AM SORRY TO REPORT THAT HE AND
FOUR GROWN SONS HAVE DIED. FORTUNATELY THE DISEASE DID NOT
SPREAD, BUT ANY LOSS OF FARMERS IS NOT TO BE TAKEN LIGHTLY.
```

The Sumerian Game would pass through many hands and sundry reinventions, eventually morphing into a game known as *Hammurabi* that became part of an early canon of personal computer games ported to each new system and rewritten for each new language. While the original's source code is believed lost, the surviving transcripts show nearly all the qualities we identify in modern text games: a narrative and a simulation, natural language prose, and real-time interaction.

But there was still one piece missing. While *The Sumerian Game* spoke eloquently with the words Addis wrote for it, players could only respond with numbers. Teaching computers to understand English input would be the hardest challenge yet.

WHEN COULD YOU FIRST type words into a computer and get words back in return? Like many firsts, it's difficult to pinpoint with certainty. In their earliest decades, computers evolved so quickly that many innovations were made and lost and made again before spreading far enough to be standardized. Programming pioneer Grace Hopper recalled that "back in the early days [of the 1950s] there was a gadget called a Unityper" that

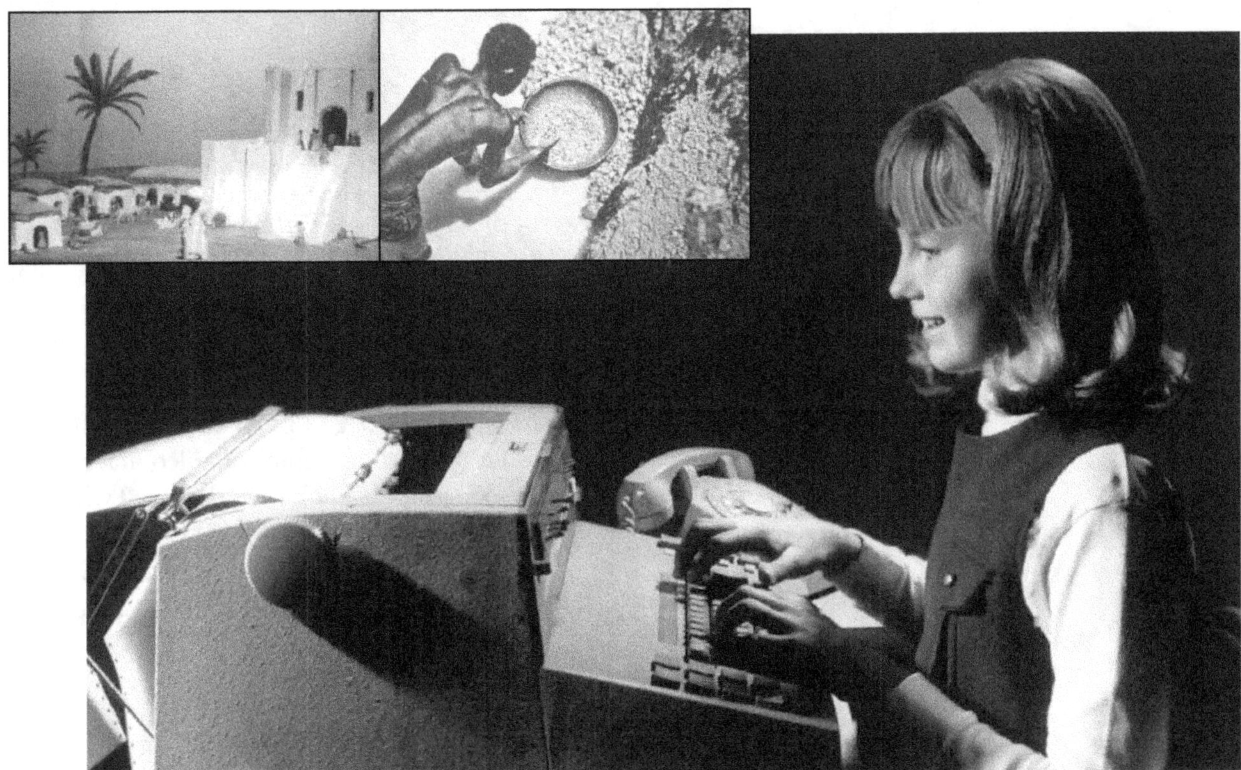

Photo from an IBM press release of a student playing *The Sumerian Game* via an IBM 1052 Model 3 terminal. The phone used to connect to the mainframe is visible in the background. Inset: two slides from the game's introductory presentation.

would let you type programs directly onto magnetic tape: "Of course, it disappeared and we had to reinvent that wheel some years later."[15]

Computers had been hooked up to typewriters from the very beginning. Even the punch card output of the ENIAC, progenitor of the twentieth-century computer revolution, could be fed into a tabulator to render its results into more human-readable forms. But sending data back into the computer via keyboard was trickier. "In the early years of programming languages, the most frequent phrase we heard was that the only way to program a computer was in octal," Hopper remembered,[15] referring to the base-8 numeric system some machines used for data and program statements. Christopher Strachey's code had been entered with a system that assigned a different typewriter key to each possible 5-bit word the machine could store. This meant input looked, to anyone but the well initiated, like gibberish:

```
/I//OZ//:/AZO&ED
B&IA:/EROL:SOWSD
/TSIATU/OPACOQAT
/TU/NPKCH/E:J/SB
```

As computer capabilities expanded, these codes became somewhat less arcane. By the 1950s most programmers were using some form of assembly language, which could at least be read by humans and had visible divisions between operators and operands. But assembly was still largely inscrutable to outsiders. Hopper would spearhead one of the earliest projects advancing the notion that computers might be configured to understand something far

Sample code from IBM 704 assembler. The first line uses the instruction CLA ("clear and add to accumulator").

```
CLA 1,4
STA LDQ
CLA 2,4
STA FMP
SXD SAVE,1
CLA 3,4
PAX 0,1
PXD
```

closer to human language. In December 1953, she and her team delivered a report that

> proposed to management that … data processing programs should be
> written in English statements, and we would be delighted to supply [the
> compiler]. I was promptly told that I could not do that. And this time the
> reason was that computers couldn't understand English words. [*Laughter.*]
> Well, I allowed as to how I never expected any computer anywhere
> to understand anything; that all I intended to do was to compare bit
> patterns. But it was not until January of 1955 that we were able to write a
> formal proposal for writing a data processing compiler.[15]

Hopper's proposal would result in the language FLOW-MATIC, which could turn a restricted subset of English statements into compiled machine code. It was one of the first times a computer could be programmed with English sentences.

```
(1) COMPARE PRODUCT-NO (A) WITH PRODUCT-NO (B); IF GREATER GO
       TO OPERATION 10; IF EQUAL GO TO OPERATION 5; OTHERWISE
       GO TO OPERATION 2 .
(2) TRANSFER A TO D .
(3) WRITE-ITEM D .
(4) JUMP TO OPERATION 8 .
(5) TRANSFER A TO C .
(6) MOVE UNIT-PRICE (B) TO UNIT-PRICE (C) .
(7) WRITE-ITEM C .
```

FLOW-MATIC inspired Cobol, which would remain in use through the rest of the century and beyond. Along with Fortran (developed in a parallel line of work at IBM), it signaled a decisive end to the days of coding in octal and demonstrated the potential for humans and computers to speak the same language.

BY THE EARLY 1960s, the front lines of research had moved to enabling untrained users, not just skilled programmers, to have natural language interactions with a computer. At Massachusetts research firm Bolt Beranek and Newman (BBN), which would soon develop much of the foundational technology behind the internet, an interactive program was running that could generate the following strange transcript:

As with all transcripts in this book, the user's input is in REVERSE CAPS.

```
Start when ready.
CURVES?
One.
LOOSE ENDS?
Two.
OBLIQUES?
Zero.
C.
You don't have enough information yet to get the right
answer. How do you know it isn't J, for example?
J.
You don't have enough information yet. How do you know it
isn't C, for example?
```

1963

```
HORIZONTALS?
Zero.
That was a wasted question. It did not eliminate any
possibilities.
```

Baffling without context, the transcript was from *The Alphabet Game*, created by Judith Harris at BBN. The player is trying to guess which letter the computer is thinking of by asking questions about its shape. The curious game was a test case for a general-purpose program called *The Socratic System*, developed by colleague Wallace Feurzeig. After reading a 1959 conference paper describing a hypothetical computer program that could be interrogated with English questions—a tool for didactic learning—Feurzeig felt sure he could actually design such a program. He imagined medical students able to practice diagnosing patients in a risk-free virtual environment. Following Harris's proof of concept, Feurzeig enlisted medical doctor Preston K. Munter and BBN coder Myra Breen to build a med student scenario for *The Socratic System*. In what would become a common theme for programs with natural language interfaces, its transcripts suggested far more intelligence than was actually present:

```
PHYSICAL EXAM?
Fine. What in particular would you like to know?
CHEST EXAM?
It is common practice in the medical profession to begin an
examination by checking the patient's general appearance.
GENERAL APPEARANCE?
Acutely prostrated, lying in bed on his right side. Looks
acutely ill, sweaty, apprehensive, but alert. Paroxysmal
cough, bringing up a little rusty streaked sputum.
Breathing with difficulty.
EENT EXAM?
Check all of the vital signs first!
TEMPERATURE?
103.
BLOOD PRESSURE?
150/84.
PULSE?
100 a minute. Occasional extra systole.
RESPIRATORY RATE?
20 a minute and shallow.
RESPIRATORY EXCURSION?
Apparently equal. Questionable pain on right side on
inspiration.
```

The Socratic System was a database of human-authored questions and their answers, without much real intelligence. Its key benefit was that the questions might be asked in any order, as lines of thought occurred to a user. The program gained an illusion of liveliness through its ability to know which questions had already been asked and adjust responses accordingly—chastising a student who performs tests in the wrong order, for instance, or

Harris, a footnote in this history, was the star of her own. After being dismissed from a Harvard psychology PhD by an all-male review board, who wrote "we are in considerable doubt that you will develop into our professional stereotype of what an experimental psychologist should be," she became an independent researcher. Decades after her time at BBN, she would upend conventional wisdom around child psychology with her bestselling book *The Nurture Assumption: Why Children Turn Out the Way They Do*, which made the cover of *Newsweek* in 1998.

leaps to diagnostic conclusions without sufficient evidence. The program could also be coded to take the lead at times, prodding the student into a particular line of thought via scripted questions:

```
Before proceeding with the reexamination it might
be instructive to pause and consider the diagnostic
implications of the information at hand. Perhaps you think
it too early to arrive at any definitive conclusion. On the
other hand, you may be prepared to make the diagnosis now.
Are you?
NO.
Fine. Nevertheless, we've got a fair amount of information
- at least enough to raise some, perhaps several,
diagnostic possibilities. Have you any in mind?
YES.
Name one.
PNEUMOCOCCAL PNEUMONIA.
Good. The general signs of a pneumonic process are present.
Of course, you haven't isolated the bug. Do you think
the belly pain and flank pain reinforce the case for
pneumococcal pneumonia?
NO.
Right. Though the white count is consistent, isn't it?
YES.
```

Despite its intelligent veneer, *The Socratic System*'s responses are all canned, and it has no complex simulation going on under the surface: it can't reason about a patient's condition, make inferences, or indeed recognize any inputs other than the those printed on the vocabulary list given to players in advance. But its transcripts proved incredibly alluring. Dozens like them were appearing in the computer literature and spreading like wildfire. To novices, and even to many experts, they made the state of the art seem to be advancing in scarcely credible leaps and bounds.

Perhaps the most famously alluring computer conversationalist was a program originally designed as a takedown of those misleading transcripts. Joseph Weizenbaum's *ELIZA*, created in 1966, was in part meant to puncture the myth that contemporary computer programs could actually approach a real human's capacity for language and reasoning. "Machines are made to behave in wondrous ways," he wrote of the transcripts breathlessly shared,

> often sufficient to dazzle even the most experienced observer. But once a particular program is unmasked, once its inner workings are explained in language sufficiently plain to induce understanding, its magic crumbles away; it stands revealed as a mere collection of procedures.[30]

The sentiment was not new. Christopher Strachey had said almost exactly the same thing more than a decade earlier, writing about his draughts-playing and romance-writing programs:

> The whole behaviour of the machine, though perfectly determinate and simple if you know the rules, appears to the uninitiated as complex and

unpredictable.… [These kinds of programs] are, of course, the most spectacular examples and ones which are easily understood by laymen. As a consequence they get much more publicity—and generally very inaccurate publicity at that—than perhaps they deserve.[27]

Both Strachey's and Weizenbaum's words would prove prophetic. *ELIZA*, explained in detail in a paper Weizenbaum wrote to introduce it, was a general-purpose program for conversing with a user at a keyboard, driven by recognizing keywords in their input. Certain words could trigger stock responses, or use some basic linguistic transformation of the input to make it appear the program had understood what had been said. For example, an input like "You are not very aggressive" might be transformed into the response "What makes you think I am not very aggressive?" The most famous *ELIZA* script was called *Doctor*, and it emulated—or, perhaps, parodied—a conversation between a therapist and their patient:

```
HOW DO YOU DO. PLEASE STATE YOUR PROBLEM.
I SPEND TOO MUCH TIME WITH COMPUTERS.
WHY DO YOU MENTION COMPUTERS?
YOU ARE ONE.
DOES IT PLEASE YOU TO BELIEVE I AM ONE?
YES.
YOU SEEM TO BE QUITE POSITIVE.
I SUPPOSE I AM.
HOW LONG HAVE YOU BEEN?
31 YEARS.
I'M NOT SURE I UNDERSTAND YOU FULLY.
JOIN THE CLUB.
PLEASE GO ON.
```

"A large part of whatever elegance may be credited to *ELIZA* lies in the fact that *ELIZA* maintains the illusion of understanding with so little machinery," Weizenbaum wrote, careful to never use a pronoun like "she." He even included the entire *Doctor* script in his paper, noting that it demonstrated "if nothing else, how easy it is to create and maintain the illusion of understanding, hence perhaps of judgment deserving of credibility. A certain danger lurks there."[30]

Indeed. Weizenbaum's project backfired: it became exactly the kind of "wondrous" and "dazzling" example he had hoped to deflate. Sample transcripts from his program were shared far and wide, often wildly out of context. After a 1967 *Playboy* article on the growing reach of computers into everyday life quoted an *ELIZA* conversation, Weizenbaum's lab was flooded with reactions from readers assuming the digital therapist already had human patients. It

Another early conversation program, created in 1959 at the University of Toronto, tried to enable a free-form chat about the weather between an unscripted human and an IBM 650. Like much later programs, *The Conversation Machine*[12] would scan user input for keywords, assigning each a topic and a strength. A word like *drizzle*, for instance, would become (3, 1): the first number indicating a strength of opinion out of ten, and the second meaning topic #1, precipitation. *Downpour* would translate to (9, 1).

Other keywords signifying negation, or references to particular times like *yesterday* or *December*, could also be recognized. Put together with a knowledge base of recent and historical weather patterns, semiplausible conversations were made possible, though with a fragility typical to keyword-based systems. The user might state "When Christmas comes we will have some colder weather," and the machine could respond "COLD? YES, IT'S USUALLY PRETTY FROSTY DURING DECEMBER." But it might also respond to "Can you tell me what the weather is like?" with "I LIKE SUNNY WEATHER."

became one of the most famous programs of the decade and, eventually, the century. In the 1970s Weizenbaum would write an entire book trying to undo the perceived damage he had caused, an attempt to discredit what he saw as the dangerous lure of anthropomorphizing computers, and of trusting in artificial intelligence when you don't understand what complexities—or simplifications—are behind it.

ELIZA SHOWED HOW THE DREAM OF CONVERSING with a computer could be an incredibly compelling illusion, and that the trick could be pulled off by a relatively simple program. Not long after Weizenbaum debuted his experiment, a PhD candidate in mathematics named Terry Winograd would attempt to put some substance behind the smoke.

His improvements came on two main fronts. First, neither *ELIZA* nor *The Socratic System* had included a simulation behind their conversational models, instead using simple lookups and transformations to maintain a dialogue. Winograd wanted to build a program that could converse about something it actually understood. Second, for the user to freely converse about a running simulation, the program needed to recognize more than just keywords. It needed to understand something about linguistics and grammar—sentence structure, clauses, modifiers, articles. Winograd would need to teach the computer to understand English, not merely memorize a vocab list.

```
PICK UP A BIG RED BLOCK.
OK.
GRASP THE PYRAMID.
I DON'T UNDERSTAND WHICH PYRAMID YOU MEAN.
FIND A BLOCK WHICH IS TALLER THAN THE ONE YOU ARE HOLDING
AND PUT IT INTO THE BOX.
BY "IT", I ASSUME YOU MEAN THE BLOCK WHICH IS TALLER THAN
THE ONE I AM HOLDING.
OK.
WHAT DOES THE BOX CONTAIN?
THE BLUE PYRAMID AND THE BLUE BLOCK.
WHAT IS THE PYRAMID SUPPORTED BY?
THE BOX.
HOW MANY BLOCKS ARE NOT IN THE BOX?
FOUR OF THEM.
IS AT LEAST ONE OF THEM NARROWER THAN THE ONE WHICH I TOLD
YOU TO PICK UP?
YES, THE RED CUBE.
```

To limit the scope of his problem, Winograd simulated only a limited subset of the world: a toy universe of colored blocks on a table. The program he wrote to interact with it was called *SHRDLU*. Even in the tiny block world, the scope of the challenge was immense, encompassing not only a huge swath of linguistics but also commonsense concepts of space, geometry, gravity, and even memory and causality:

```
HAD YOU TOUCHED ANY PYRAMID BEFORE YOU PUT THE GREEN ONE ON
THE LITTLE CUBE?
```

SHRDLU's name came from the arrangement of letter keys on a Linotype, the machine used to typeset books and newspapers (just a few years away themselves from being replaced by computers). Linotype letters were arranged in descending order of their frequency in English: the first twelve were ETAOIN SHRDLU.

1971

```
(CLAUSE MAJOR QUESTION NGQ SUBJQ PASV AGENT)

    (NG  QUEST DET NUMDET NPL INDEF)              (how many blocks)
        (DET QDET NPL INDEF)                                   how
        ()                                                    many
        (NOUN NPL)                                          blocks

    (VG NAUX VPL PASV (PRES))                     (are supported)
        (VB AUX BE PRES VPL)                                   are
        (VB MVB EN TRANS)                               supported

    (PREPG AGENT)       (by the cube which I wanted you to pick up)
        (PREP)                                                  by

        (NG OBJ PREPOBJ DET DEF NS)
                        (the cube which I wanted you to pick up)
            (DET DEF NPL NS)                                   the
            (NOUN NS)                                         cube

        (CLAUSE RSQ WHRS NGREL DOWNREL TRANS)
                            (which I wanted you to pick up)
            (RELWD)                                         which

            (NG SUBJ PRONG NFS)                               (I)
                (PRON NFS)                                      I

            (VG NAGR (PAST))                             (wanted)
                (VB MVB PAST TRANS TOOBJ SUBTOBJ)        wanted

            (CLAUSE RSNG SUBTO OBJ OBJ1 PRT
                    TRANS UPREL OBJ1UPREL)       (you to pick up)

                (NG SUBJ PRONG NPL)                        (you)
                    (PRON NPL)                               you

                (VG TO NAGR)                          (to pick)
                    ()                                         to
                    (VB MVB INF TRANS VPRT)                 pick

                (PRT)                                         up
```

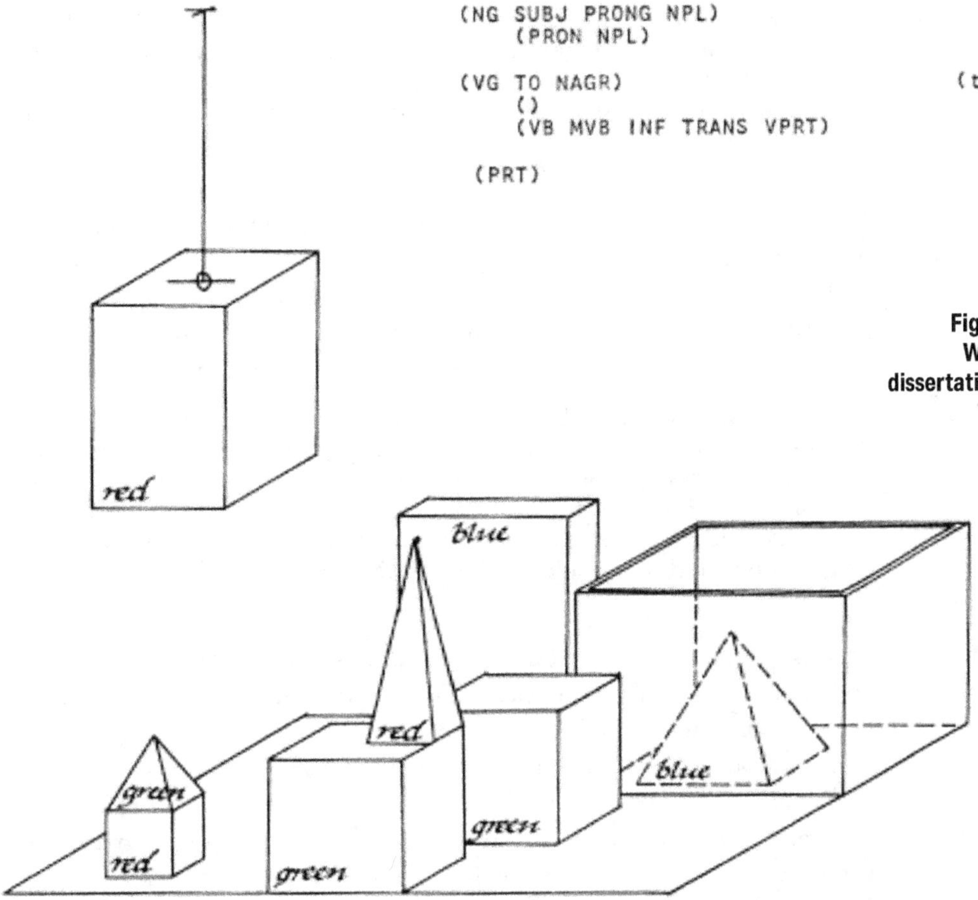

**Figures from Terry
Winograd's 1971
dissertation on *SHRDLU*.**

```
YES, THE GREEN ONE.
WHEN DID YOU PICK IT UP?
WHILE I WAS STACKING UP THE RED CUBE, A LARGE RED BLOCK AND
A LARGE GREEN CUBE.
WHY?
TO GET RID OF IT.
WHY DID YOU DO THAT?
TO CLEAN OFF THE RED CUBE.
WHY DID YOU CLEAR OFF THAT CUBE?
TO PUT IT ON A LARGE GREEN CUBE.
WHY DID YOU DO THAT?
TO STACK UP THE RED CUBE, A LARGE RED BLOCK AND A LARGE
GREEN CUBE.
WHY DID YOU DO THAT?
BECAUSE YOU ASKED ME TO.
```

Winograd worked in a dialect of Lisp, one of the earliest high-level programming languages designed to operate more on abstractions than basic symbols. The intoxicating power of the language and the increasing sophistication of computers put a fire in Winograd—the ideas he was swimming in seemed on the cusp of changing the world. "Let us envision a new way of using computers," his 1971 dissertation begins,

> so they can take instructions in a way suited to their jobs. We will talk to them just as we talk to a research assistant, librarian, or secretary, and they will carry out our commands and provide us with the information we ask for. If our instructions aren't clear enough, they will ask for more information before they do what we want, and this dialog will all be in English.[34]

In the end Winograd wrote nearly thirty thousand lines of Lisp, but his program was never finished. He got it to parse many kinds of questions and commands, but the transcripts often shared of *SHRDLU* are façades. The program could in no way carry out an unscripted conversation with a naïve user, even about its simple block world. It couldn't even come close.

> I mean, you know, the famous dialogue with *SHRDLU* where you could pick up a block, and so on, I very carefully worked through, line by line. If you sat down in front of it, and asked it a question that wasn't in the dialogue, there was some probability it would answer it…. But there was no attempt to get it to the point where you could actually hand it to somebody and they could use it to move blocks around.[35]

IN A WAY, *SHRDLU* WAS AS MUCH AN ILLUSION AS *ELIZA*, though with far more code required to pull off the trick. The two programs make an interesting contrast, showing how little it takes to create a beguiling semblance of conversation, yet how much to lend the illusion some substance. A medium is often defined by its limitations, and as time went on, a defining feature of text games would become this tension between illusion and understanding, show and simulation. Should creators of interactive stories spend their time on the technical innovations of a program's code, or on the artful mirage of its surface text? As the 1970s dawned, the question was still unresolved. Fifty years later, text game authors are still exploring new ways to answer it.

References

1 Clark, Dorothy K., Archie N. Colby, Paul Iribe, Nicholas M. Smith, and Lloyd D. Yates. 1958. "HUTSPIEL: A Theater War Game." ORO-SP-53. Johns Hopkins University: Operations Research Office. archive.org/details/hutspiel-a-theater-war-game | a Feb 22, 2022

2 Cohen, D.S. 2019. "Cathode-Ray Tube Amusement Device: The World's First Video Game?" *Lifewire* (blog). Mar 14, 2019. www.lifewire.com/cathode-ray-tube-amusement-device-729579 | a Feb 22, 2022

3 Cohen, Kalman J., Richard M. Cyert et al. 1960. "The Carnegie Tech Management Game." *Journal of Business* 33 (4): 303–21.

4 Cohen, Kalman J., and Eric Rhenman. 1961. "The Role of Management Games in Education and Research." *Management Science* 7 (2).

5 Copeland, B. Jack. 2012. *Turing: Pioneer of the Information Age*. Oxford University Press.

6 Copeland, B. Jack, Jonathan Bowen, Mark Sprevak, and Robin Wilson. 2017. *The Turing Guide*. Oxford University Press.

7 Copeland, Jack, and Jason Long. 2016. "Restoring the First Recording of Computer Music." *Sound and Vision Blog* (British Library). Sep 13, 2016. blogs.bl.uk/sound-and-vision/2016/09/restoring-the-first-recording-of-computer-music.html | a Feb 22, 2022

8 Feurzeig, Wallace. 1964a. "The PDP-1 Computer as a Teaching Aid in Problem-Solving." In *DECUS Proceedings 1963*. Maynard, Masschusetts: Digital Equipment Computer Users Society.

9 Feurzeig, Wallace. 1964b. "Conversational Teaching Machine." *Datamation*, June 1964.

10 Feurzeig, Wallace, Preston Munter, John Swets, and Myra Breen. 1964. "Computer-Aided Teaching in Medical Diagnosis." *Journal of Medical Education* 39 (8).

11 Gaboury, Jacob. 2013. "A Queer History of Computing: Part Three." *Rhizome* (blog). Apr 9, 2013. rhizome.org/editorial/2013/apr/09/queer-history-computing-part-three/ | a Feb 22, 2022

12 Green, L.E.S., E.C. Berkeley, and C.C. Gotlieb. 1959. "Conversation With a Computer." *Computers and Automation*, Oct 1959.

13 Harrison Jr, Joseph O., and Mary Frances Barrett. 1964. "Computer-Aided Information Systems for Gaming." RAC-TP-133. McLean, Virginia: Research Analysis Corporation. apps.dtic.mil/dtic/tr/fulltext/u2/623091.pdf | s Nov 12, 2020

14 Havemann, Ernest. 1967. "Computers: Their Scope Today." *Playboy*, Oct 1967.

15 Hopper, Grace. 1978. "Keynote Address." Presented at the ACM SIGPLAN History of Programming Languages Conference, Jun 1978.

16 Lee, J.A.N. 1995. "Christopher Strachey." In *International Biographical Dictionary of Computer Pioneers*. Chicago: Fitzroy Dearborn.

17 Link, David. 2006. "There Must Be an Angel: On the Beginnings of the Arithmetics of Rays." *Variantology* 2.

18 Link, David. 2012. "Programming ENTER: Christopher Strachey's Draughts Program." *Computer Resurrection*, Winter 2012.

19 Mackenzie, Charles E. 1980. *Coded-Character Sets: History and Development*. Reading, MA: Addison-Wesley.

20 Napper, Brian. 1998. "Programming on the Ferranti Mark 1." Computer 50. 1998. www.computer50.org/mark1/program.html | s Mar 14, 2011

21 Reed, Aaron A. 2022. "HUTSPIEL and Dr. Dorothy K. Clark." *50 Years of Text Games* (blog). Jan 26, 2022. if50.substack.com/p/hutspiel-and-dr-dorothy-k-clark | a Feb 22, 2022

22 Ricciardi, Franc M., Clifford J. Craft, Donald G. Malcolm, Richard Bellman, Charles Clark, Joel M. Kibbee, and Richard H. Rawdon. 1957. *Top Management Decision Simulation: The AMA Approach*. Ed. Elizabeth Marting. New York: American Management Association, Inc.

23 Roberts, Siobhan. 2017. "Christopher Strachey's Nineteen-Fifties Love Machine." *New Yorker*, Feb 14, 2017. www.newyorker.com/tech/elements/christopher-stracheys-nineteen-fifties-love-machine | a Feb 22, 2022

24 Shrager, Jeff. 2021. "Joseph Weizenbaum's Original ELIZA." ELIZAGEN (website). May 23, 2021. sites.google.com/view/elizagen-org/the-original-eliza | a Feb 22, 2022

25 Smith, Alexander. 2014. "The Priesthood at Play: Computer Games in the 1950s." *They Create Worlds* (blog). Jan 23, 2014. videogamehistorian.wordpress.com/2014/01/22/

the-priesthood-at-play-computer-games-in-the-1950s/ | a Feb 22, 2022

26 Sperry Rand Corporation. 1958. *UNIVAC FLOW-MATIC Programming System* (Manual).

27 Strachey, Christopher. 1954. "The 'Thinking' Machine." *Encounter* 3 (4).

28 Wardrip-Fruin, Noah. 2005. "Christopher Strachey: The First Digital Artist?" *Grand Text Auto* (blog). Aug 1, 2005. grandtextauto.org/2005/08/01/christopher-strachey-first-digital-artist/ | s Jan 27, 2010

29 Wardrip-Fruin, Noah. 2021. "Who Invented Video Games?" *The Conversation*. Nov 29, 2021. theconversation.com/who-invented-video-games-169792 | a Feb 22, 2022

30 Weizenbaum, Joseph. 1966. "ELIZA—a Computer Program for the Study of Natural Language Communication between Man and Machine." *Communications of the ACM* 9 (1).

31 Wiemer, Serjoscha. 2011. "Computer History and the Movement of Business Simulations." In *Proceedings of DiGRA 2011 Conference: Think Design Play*. Utrecht.

32 Willært, Kate. 2019. "The Sumerian Game: The Most Important Video Game You've Never Heard Of." *A Critical Hit!* (blog). Sep 9, 2019. www.acriticalhit.com/sumerian-game-most-important-video-game-youve-never-heard/ | a Feb 22, 2022

33 Wing, Richard L., Mabel Addis, Walter Goodman, Jimmer Leonard, and William McKay. 1967. "The Production and Evaluation of Three Computer-Based Economics Games For the Sixth Grade." Project No. 2841, Grant No. OE-5-10-203. Westchester County, New York: The Board of Cooperative Educational Services. archive.org/details/ERIC_ED014227 | a Feb 22, 2022

34 Winograd, Terry. 1971. "Procedures as a Representation for Data in a Computer Program for Understanding Natural Language." Dissertation, Cambridge: MIT. archive.org/details/bitsavers_mitaiaimAI_20368805 | a Feb 22, 2022

35 Winograd, Terry. 1991. An Interview With Terry Allen Winograd. Interview by Arthur L. Norberg. conservancy.umn.edu/bitstream/handle/11299/107717/oh237taw.pdf | a Feb 22, 2022

THE

19

1971	**The Oregon Trail**
1972	**ROCKET**
1973	**Hunt the Wumpus**
1974	**Super Star Trek**
1975	**dnd**
1976	**Adventure**
1977	**Zork**
1978	**Pirate Adventure**
1979	**The Cave of Time**

70s

AT THE DAWN OF THE 1970s, computers were bulky, expensive, and mostly locked away in office buildings and universities. By the end of the decade you could buy one from the corner electronics store, small and light enough to carry out yourself—often for less than a thousand dollars—and about half a million customers would have preceded you. While mainframes had increasingly given way to minicomputers like the PDP-8, which were closer in cost and size to a car than a home, by the end of the 70s momentum had conclusively shifted to microcomputers like the Apple II, the TRS-80, or the Commodore PET. The personal computer revolution had arrived, and it would exponentially accelerate in the decade to come.

An irony of the transition to micros was that it forced game design ambition to take a serious step backward. The earliest home systems had crushingly small storage and memory footprints compared to their mainframe ancestors. Take the IBM System/370 mainframe line launched in 1970, for instance: a typical model offered up to 512 kilobytes of memory and ran at around ten million cycles per second. The first-generation TRS-80 that launched in 1977, while orders of magnitude cheaper, was far slower, and had only 4K of memory to store a running program and

see **1976**, **1977**, and **1978**

see **1948–1970**

see **1975** and **1976**

see **1986**, **1995**, **2012**

see **1979**

DEC had branded their
PDP minicomputer
a *Programmed Data
Processor* to avoid the word
computer.

see **1990**, **1993**, **2008**,
2012, and **2018**

1970s

all its data. Mainframe games like *Adventure* were thus vastly more capable
and expansive than the home computer games that followed them. The
mainframe text game *Acheton* [Jon Thackray et al. 1978] grew to over four hundred
rooms, and the original PDP-10 *Zork* eventually used up a full megabyte of
data—comparable to the amount of text in four hundred pages of this book.
Contemporary PC games like *Pirate Adventure*, by contrast, had to fit in the
equivalent of a single page spread. It would take microcomputer text games
quite a while to improve on the ambitions of their mainframe predecessors.

While digital text games had existed in various forms before the 70s, it
wasn't until then that they came into their own as a medium with trends,
traditions, and tropes. Many of that medium's most recognizable forms were
born in the 70s. The release of *Dungeons & Dragons* in 1974 spawned at least
three digital game genres as early hackers tried various ways of digitizing the
immersive tabletop game with its numerical systems for simulating fantasy
adventures: roguelikes and computer roleplaying games, which trended
more toward graphics and action, and prose-based text adventures focused
on puzzles and immersion. All would become foundational and remain
active in one form or another for at least the next fifty years. Experiments
with hypertext in the 60s and 70s were mostly centered around nonlinear
information retrieval, not interactive fiction, but they laid technical
and conceptual groundwork for storytellers in later decades to explore.
And gamebooks, after many earlier experiments, would break into the
mainstream with the massively popular Choose Your Own Adventure book
series; easy to implement on a computer, the digital gamebook would be a
popular low-tech way of telling an interactive story in years to come.

While the 70s brought many hardware innovations, perhaps the most
significant advance for text games was in software with the widespread
adoption of the programming language BASIC. Invented at Dartmouth in
1964, BASIC displaced earlier teaching languages like FOCAL or Fortran
over the next decade, its simplicity and clarity of syntax inviting younger
and less technical computer users to build their own programs instead of
just using those written by others. At a time when computers were still often
distrusted by the general public—seen as tools of big government and big
business—the notion that anyone could (or everyone should) learn to code
was radical, even revolutionary. The first issue of the People's Computer
Center newsletter in 1972 included a cartoon (reprinted in this book's
coverage of **1973**) showing protesters of all ages and skin tones demanding
to be part of the computer revolution. One holds a sign reading, "No more
Fortran! BASIC is the people's language!" BASIC let nearly anyone write
code and make games, foreshadowing future tools that would open the doors
to digital storytelling even wider, and it remained a popular game-creation
tool through the 1980s.

Communities of computer users numbered in the single digits before
the 70s, but that changed as magazines, newsletters, computer shows, and
local user groups created national and international networks of coders
and game makers. *Creative Computing* magazine, founded in 1974, shared
BASIC program listings users could type into their minis or micros, along

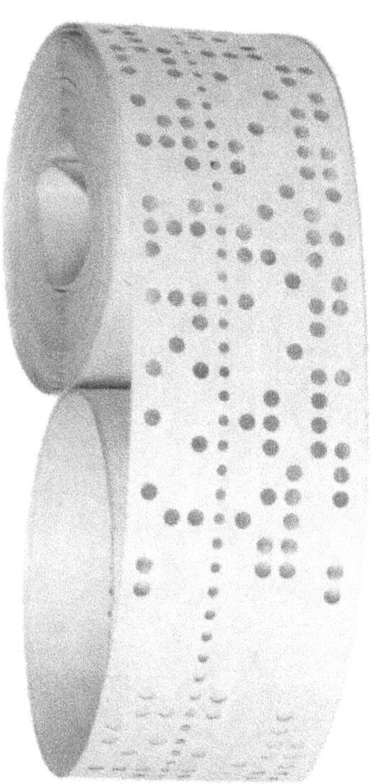

with interesting projects from their members that brought computers into the domains of art, education, and music; the first West Coast Computer Faire in 1977 brought ten thousand enthusiasts together in San Francisco. Years before the idea that software could be copyrighted was legally entrenched, "folk games" like *ROCKET* **1972**, *Star Trek* **1974**, and *Hunt the Wumpus* **1973** often passed from author to author, each one improving, tweaking, and sharing their code and text. Early enthusiasts spent the decade exploring the possibilities of computer games, not yet yoked to the constraints a commercial game industry would bring in the years to come.

Computer technology in the 1970s was often transitional, with existing analog infrastructure bootstrapping the emerging digital world. The punch cards of the earliest computers had evolved into punch tape, inch-wide paper reels that encoded bits as tiny round holes. Punch tape was easy and cheap to duplicate, write to, or read from, with support built in to many models of teletype. Some of the earliest computer game sales were for mail-order rolls of punch tape holding BASIC code at the rate of about three lines per foot. Later in the decade, audio cassettes became a common interface to home computers: users could often grab off-the-shelf tape players and blank cassettes to store data as screeching audio and play it back into their machines. Many early PCs likewise used stock television sets as monitors, replacing the printouts earlier systems had relied on in the absence of cheap CRTs (or the video RAM required to drive them). Tellingly, the most common way to mass distribute a program in the 1970s was still to print its source code in a magazine or book. By the 80s, software was distributed on disks.

While even the original *Oregon Trail* was played via connection to a distant computer, that link was to a single mainframe over a phone line, offering no way to interact with other connected users. That would change through the 1970s with the emergence of the ARPANET, ancestor of the modern internet. Bringing pairs, dozens, or even hundreds of far-flung players together into the same virtual space would enable radically new kinds of games in the decades to come, a development foreshadowed by *dnd*. But even in the 70s, the ARPANET's collapsing of distance was profoundly influential. *Adventure* only grew into its addictive final form through an indirect collaboration between authors on opposite coasts, while *Zork* evolved in response to a growing community of fans watching its development in real time and offering feedback and suggestions.

It's not too far a stretch to claim that text games could only emerge because of the communities the internet would enable. Each early computer

Repurposed analog tech for early computers: a rebranded television serves as monitor for the TI-99/4, a cassette tape holds software for the Apple II, and a roll of paper tape encodes a program in 8-bit rows of punched holes (plus smaller sprocket holes to advance the tape).

see **1971**

see **1975**; developed for the non-ARPANET network PLATO

see **1976** and **1977**

was a pocket of isolation; ideas and innovations were hard to spread. But like any art form, text games required conversation to develop. As networks of fans emerged, they could begin to explore and define what computer games in general, and interactive prose in particular, might become.

More Text Games from the 1970s

Given the difficulties of dating early computer programs and the multiyear periods of development and evolution many went through, some dates listed, especially early in the decade, are only approximate.

1970 **KING** *(James A. Storer, BASIC)*; also known as *Pollution Game*. Early land and resource management sim inspired by Doug Dyment's *King of Sumeria*, itself a recreation of *The Sumerian Game* 1964. **Nuclear Destruction** *(Rick Loomis, play-by-mail)*. The first computer-moderated play-by-mail game.

1971 **Baseball** *(Don Daglow, PDP-10)*. Strategic all-text baseball simulator that describes
The Oregon Trail play on the field in dynamic English sentences, like a commentator. **Hammurabi** *(David H. Ahl, BASIC)*. Influential port of *King of Sumeria* to BASIC.

1972 **ANIMAL** *(Nathan Teichholtz, BASIC)*. Guessing game the player could extend with new
ROCKET questions and answers. **Empire** *(Peter Langston, HP 2000)*. Early 4X wargame with dozens of commands; later extended by Ben Norton and others; original version believed lost. **PARRY** *(Kenneth Colby, Lisp)*. Chatbot by a psychiatrist that tried to emulate a paranoid schizophrenic. **Trek73** *(William Char et al., HP 2000)*. Distinct from the Mike Mayfield *Trek* lineage 1974; featured an all-text interface and dialogue from TV show characters.

1973 **Caves1** *(Dave Kaufman, PDP-8)*. Cave exploration program that may have influenced
Hunt the Wumpus *Hunt the Wumpus* 1973. **Ecala** *(Don Daglow, PDP-10)*. Improved *ELIZA* chatbot. **FURS** *(Dan Bachor, BASIC)*. Simulates a French fur trading expedition with strategies around buying/selling and supplies. **Lemonade Stand** *(Bob Jamison, MECC)*. Simple business game later popularized in various Apple ports.

1974 **Star Trader** *(Dave Kaufman, HP 2000F)*. Space trading game influential on *Trade Wars*
Super Star Trek 1991. **Wander** *(Peter Langston, BASIC)*. Early program for making text exploration games with rooms and portable objects; *Castle*, written for this system, may predate *Adventure* 1976 but original version is believed lost.

1975 **The Dungeon** *(Rusty Rutherford, PLATO)*; aka *pedit5*. D&D adaptation that inspired
dnd *dnd* 1975. **Dungeon** *(Don Daglow, PDP-10)*. D&D adaptation where multiple players at one keyboard could control members of an adventuring party. **DUNGEON** *(John Daleske et al., PLATO)*. D&D adaptation with first-person view. **The Great Guano Gap** *(Bill Roper et al., PLATO)*. One of the earliest known hypertext fictions for a public network; simulated navigating the PLATO account of a fictional character who'd become trapped in the machine.

1976 **Buffalo Castle** *(Rick Loomis, Flying Buffalo)*. Choice-based gamebook that introduced
Adventure readers to the *Tunnels & Trolls* roleplaying game. **Dukedom** *(Vince Talbot, PL/1)*. More extensive descendant of *Hammurabi* involving land purchases, taxes, wars, and plagues. **Moria** *(Kevet Duncombe and Jim Battin, PLATO)*. Inspired by earlier PLATO dungeon games; had dynamically generated dungeon levels, multiplayer with up to ten players, and a large persistent game world. **Starweb** *(Rick Loomis, Flying Buffalo)*. Space-based play-by-mail game that remained popular for more than twenty years. **Sugarcane Island** *(Edward Packard, WH Allen)*. First published version of
1970s the book series that would become Choose Your Own Adventure 1979.

Aldebaran III *(Peter Langston, BASIC)*. *Wander* game based on Keith Laumer's stories of space diplomat Jame Retief. **Atom20** *(Ray Brander, Apple II)*. Post-apocalyptic clone of *The Oregon Trail 1971*. **Oubliette** *(Jim Schwaiger et al., PLATO)*. Another multi-player dungeon game; may have influenced *Wizardry*. **Trek80** *(Processor Technology, Sol 20)*. *Trek* clone with the twist that you could place an AM radio near your computer to get sound effects.

1977
Zork

Acheton *(Jon Thackray et al., IBM 360/165)*. Vast mainframe adventure written at Cambridge; lots of mazes. **Adventureland** *(Scott Adams, Adventure International)*. One of the earliest text adventures written for a personal computer. **Beneath Apple Manor** *(Don Worth, The Software Factory)*. Early roguelike dungeon crawler, one of the first games to use procedural generation. **DECWAR** *(Bob Hysick et al., PDP-10)*. Multiplayer evolution of *Super Star Trek 1974*, later rebranded as *MegaWars* on CompuServe. **Empyrean Challenge** *(Vern Holford, Superior Simulations)*. Sci-fi play-by-mail game with incredible complexity, supporting 150 players; turn results could be hundreds of pages long. **Mystery Mansion** *(Bill Wolpert, HP-1000)*, aka *Mansion*. Murder mystery set in a monster-filled manor house. **Scepter** *(Alan E. Klietz, CDC Cyber 6600)* aka *Scepter of Goth* and *Milieu*. One of the earliest MUDs and the first to go commercial. **Stuga** *(Kimmo Eriksson et al., PDP-10)*. Goofy Swedish text adventure, perhaps the earliest in a language other than English; authors were between ten and fourteen years old when they wrote it.

1978
Pirate Adventure

Brand X *(Peter Killworth and Jonathan Mestel, IBM 370)* aka *Philosopher's Quest*. Difficult parsed-based puzzle game. **The Count** *(Scott Adams, Adventure International)*. Well-reviewed game from Adventure International set in Dracula's castle. **Dog Star Adventure** *(Lance Micklus, TRS-80)*. *Star Wars* inspired; one of the first parser games with type-in source code published in a magazine. **Eamon** *(Donald Brown, Apple II)*. Text-based roleplaying game series and game creation tool that let players transfer their character between games. **Empire of the Over-Mind** *(Gary Bedrosian, Apple II)*. Early text game to navigate via landmark rather than compass directions and use emergent solutions; came with a long narrative poem containing vital hints. **Goblins** *(Hal Antonson and Linda Stix, Apple II)*. One of the earliest computer games with a credited female programmer. **Haunt** *(John E. Laird, PDP-10)*. Haunted mansion game influential on several early designers. **Local Call for Death** *(Robert Lafore, Adventure International)*. Conversational detective story from the Interactive Fiction label *1981*.

1979
The Cave of Time

THE OREGON TRAIL

Don Rawitsch, Bill Heinemann, and
Paul Dillenberger

Style **Resource Management**
Debuted **Dec 3, 1971**
(Jordan Junior High School)
Launch Platform **HP 2100**
Language **BASIC**

> " THIS PROGRAM SIMULATES A TRIP OVER THE OREGON TRAIL FROM INDEPENDENCE, MISSOURI TO OREGON CITY, OREGON IN 1847. YOUR FAMILY OF FIVE WILL COVER THE 2000 MILE OREGON TRAIL IN 5-6 MONTHS --- IF YOU MAKE IT ALIVE.

IN THE MIDST OF THE COLD BUT SNOWLESS Minnesota December of 1971, a twenty-one-year-old student teacher named Don Rawitsch wheeled a bulky teletypewriter into his eighth-grade history class. Students gathered around curiously as he plugged in power and phone cables, switched on the humming machine, and dialed the number on a rotary phone that would connect him to a $100,000 minicomputer fifty miles away. The students, Mr. Rawitsch said, were going to play a game.

Rawitsch had been asked three weeks earlier by his supervising instructor to cover the class's unit on the western expansion period of US history. Eager to engage with his students, Rawitsch had already tried showing up to classes dressed as historical figures like Meriwether Lewis, and he quickly hit

1971

MAJOR RELEASES

» **Original**, Dec 1971.

» **1974 version**, CDC Cyber 70, MECC. Retyped by Rawitsch from printout of original code; adjusted some details of events and probabilities based on settlers' journals.

» **OREGON**, Mar 1975. Made available to Minnesota schools on time-share network.

» **1977 version**, CDC Cyber-73. Added difficulty setting for timed hunting and multiple words. Source printed in *Creative Computing* May/Jun 1978 issue (as *Oregon Trail*).

» **OREGON (Apple II)**, John Cook, 1978. Adds simple graphics.

» **Oregon** (in *Expeditions*), MECC, Atari/C64/TRS-80, 1983. Commercial port.

» **The Oregon Trail**, R. Philip Bouchard, MECC, 1985. Redesigned with full-color illustrations, geographic landmarks, characters to interact with; first to become nationally popular.

» **Oregon Trail Deluxe**, DOS/Macintosh, 1992.

» **Oregon Trail II**, CD-ROM, 1995. Major revisions.

» **The Oregon Trail 5th Edition**, The Learning Company, Win/Mac, 2001.

» **Mobile version**, Gameloft, iOS, 2008.

» **Facebook version**, The Learning Company, 2011.

on the further idea of a board game about traveling west in a covered wagon. He shared an apartment with two other student teachers, Bill Heinemann and Paul Dillenberger, who had each taken Carleton College's single five-week computer course the previous year. As they gathered around the board game to workshop it with Rawitsch, they started wondering if it might work better as a computer program instead. Heinemann recalled:

> I was fascinated by the power of the computer to not only calculate, but also to interact with written language. I had been thinking about writing a program to interact with a human through language, but the content of such a program remained a mystery to me.[10]

Maybe a simulated journey was just the ticket. The computer could handle all the math of tracking miles and supplies for students, and it could generate faster and more complex randomness than the roll of a die. Computers in the classroom had to date mostly been used for math, not history, but the three roommates warmed to the challenge of turning the board game concept into a program. In the two weeks remaining before Rawitsch's unit was meant to start, the three somehow managed to piece together the core of what would become the best-known educational game ever written.

```
MONDAY MARCH 29 1847


TOTAL MILEAGE IS 0
FOOD   BULLETS   CLOTHING   SUPPLIES   CASH
 100    2500        50         50        200


DO YOU WANT TO (1) HUNT or (2) CONTINUE?2


DO YOU WANT TO EAT
(1) POORLY (2) MODERATELY OR (3) WELL?2


RIDERS AHEAD. THEY LOOK HOSTILE.
TACTICS:
(1) RUN         (2) ATTACK
(3) CONTINUE    (4) CIRCLE WAGONS
IF YOU RUN YOU'LL GAIN TIME BUT WEAR DOWN YOUR OXEN.
IF YOU CIRCLE YOU'LL LOSE TIME.
?
```

Written in BASIC, the six hundred–line program let players purchase supplies in five categories (oxen, food, ammunition, clothing, and medicine) before starting a simulated journey across the country, tracked in miles traversed and two-week turns. Each move, the player chooses whether to continue or hunt, with the option to purchase additional supplies from a fort on every second turn. Due to obstacles encountered along the way, the supply numbers go down as the mileage goes up, complicating the player's goal of traversing 2,040 miles—the significant distance of the historic route from Independence, Missouri, to Oregon City, Oregon—before supplies run out.

The students who clustered around the teletype in Rawitsch's classroom would have had a vastly different experience from gamers today, or even players of text games in later decades. In 1971 there were fewer than a thousand computers in the world with monitors, and most were locked away at research labs and universities. Users would instead connect to a distant, expensive system via time-share, typing command-line instructions on a machine that looked much like a typewriter, except that it would type back to you—at a crawling ten characters per second, accompanied by a sound only slightly removed from machine gun fire. With only a single terminal available, Rawitsch had to cycle his students through in groups, one sitting at the keyboard while the others clustered around making suggestions or tracking resources on scratch paper.

Previous attempts had been made through grants and special programs to get computers into schools, and even to make educational games, but the machines' intimidating sounds and obtuse interfaces meant they were often underused. Rawitsch and his collaborators hoped to entice students to play through friendly and jargon-free output, but also via clever uses of the limited affordances of their platform. The HP-2100 mainframe on the other end of their teletype ran a version of BASIC that would record not only characters typed into a line of input, but the time it had taken to type them. This became the core of a timed hunting minigame within their program:

```
DO YOU WANT TO (1) STOP AT THE NEXT FORT, (2) HUNT,
OR (3) CONTINUE?2
TYPE BANG:BANG
RIGHT BETWEEN THE EYES---YOU GOT A BIG ONE!!!!
```

The time it took a student to type BANG and press return was used to judge the accuracy of their shot, and thus how much food was gathered and ammo lost. If the response took too long or the word was mistyped, the shot might miss, leaving the virtual settlers hungry.

The authors also took advantage of the fact that their teletype had an internal bell, used as in a traditional typewriter to mark the end of a line while typing, but also activated by the computer at the other end of the connection to signal errors or alerts. In the game, certain noteworthy events like scoring a perfect shot while hunting would ring this bell. The line of BASIC that outputs the message above reads:

```
1755  PRINT "RI"'7"GHT BETWEE"'7"N THE EYE"'7"S---YOU GOT
         A"'7" BIG ONE!!"'7"!!"
```

The 7 is the ASCII code to ring the bell, and as the 7s are spaced about ten characters apart, this meant the bell would ring once per second as this line was printed—an aural reward perhaps reminiscent of midway games and doubtless accompanied by a thrilling whoop of victory from the students gathered around the machine.

As players continued their journey in two-week increments, they encountered random events, usually mishaps that reduced their stock of resources. The original version of the game included some twenty of these

see *The Sumerian Game*
1964

Excerpts are from the 1975 version of the game, the earliest known to have survived. Code archaeology by Jimmy Maher suggests this version had only minor differences from the original.[7]

incidents, summarized in single lines like WAGON GETS SWAMPED FORDING RIVER--LOSE FOOD AND CLOTHES or YOUR SON GETS LOST---SPEND HALF THE DAY LOOKING FOR HIM. If vital supplies like food ever ran out, or situational supplies like clothing or medicine were depleted when a random event tested them, the game ended in failure with one of a small handful of cheerful messages like YOU RAN OUT OF FOOD AND STARVED TO DEATH. It would be more than a decade before a version of the game included the message "You have died of dysentery," destined to become one of *Oregon Trail*'s lasting touchstones.

A key to the game's success—even in its original version, which was shorter and simpler than later iterations—was its use of sensible randomness. Almost every event in the game involves some random variation in its outcome, but rarely so much as to seem unfair or unpredictable. For example, a random event testing your preparedness against cold weather in a mountain pass is instantiated by this source code:

```
2935   PRINT "COLD WEATHER---BRRRRRRR!---YOU ";
2940   IF C>22+4*RND(0) THEN 2955
2945   PRINT "DON'T ";
2950   C1=1
2955   PRINT "HAVE ENOUGH CLOTHING TO KEEP YOU WARM"
2960   IF C1=0 THEN 3100
2965   GOTO 4700
```

The variable C in line 2940 stores the dollar amount the player has spent on cold-weather gear, so this code means "If the player has at least (22 + a random number between 0 and 4) clothing, that's sufficient to stay warm." A player might figure out through trial and error that while twenty dollars spent on clothes is never enough and thirty dollars seems always sufficient, there's some uncertainty from game to game about where exactly in the middle is safe—a difference it's easy to imagine correlating to the unpredictable strength of a winter storm. Years later, *Zork* co-creator Dave Lebling would say of adventure games: "Obviously, no small computer program can encompass the entire universe. What it can do, however, is simulate enough of the universe to appear more intelligent than it really is."[5] *Oregon Trail* often leans on the illusion of deeper complexity to be surprising and entertaining, and the measured use of randomness helps maintain this effect.

Another example can be seen in the sketch at a narrative arc enabled by this code, which determines the likelihood each turn of being attacked:

```
2100   IF RND(0)*10>((M/100-4)^2+72)/((M/100-4)^2+12)-1 THEN
          2500
```

The details are gnarly, but the equation pivots on the M variable, representing the number of miles traversed. Offsetting it and dividing it by differently scaled amounts creates a probability distribution curve across the player's journey, making attacks more likely as the player moves away from settled Missouri, and then less likely again as they approach their final destination. This mathematical trick establishes a deepening and then easing sense of

see **1977**

danger, without printing any text to this effect explicitly. A similar trick increases the chance of cold-weather hazards during the middle of the journey when the homesteaders would logically be crossing the Rocky Mountains, even though the game never mentions this geography in its prose. *Oregon Trail* lacks explicit markers of progress other than the increasing mileage number—the concept of "rooms" from later adventure games didn't yet exist—but still gives players a sense of forward progress and geographical consistency.

Oregon Trail is not just a technological artifact—it's also a cultural one. Like most media about the western expansion from its time, the game tells only half a story. Native Americans exist explicitly in the original game only as a single random event—HELPFUL INDIANS SHOW YOU WHERE TO FIND MORE FOOD—but might also be the presumed attackers whose numbers increase, according to the logic of that single line of code, as the player moves farther away from lands settled by whites. Rawitsch has said the vague word RIDERS in those events was deliberately chosen to not solely implicate Native Americans, noting that settlers were historically more likely to be attacked by white bandits than natives. But later, more visual adaptations of the game generally interpreted this word, in their illustrations and animations, to mean hostile native peoples—arguably, just as millions of young players had done given the lack of explicit language to the contrary.

In a lengthy critique of the game's graphical remake, teacher Bill Bigelow noted the danger in teaching history through a game that was silent about the historical Oregon Trail's role in enabling and strengthening white America's project of expansion and extermination:

> The consequences of the Oregon Trail for the Plains Indians, the Indians of the Northwest and for the earth were devastating…. [Pioneers] cut down all the cottonwood trees found along the rich bottomlands of plains rivers … [and] killed tremendous numbers of buffalo that Plains Indians depended upon for survival…. The game fails to alert students that white hostility was one feature of the westward migration. The omission is significant because the sanitized, nonviolent *Oregon Trail* fails to equip students to reflect on the origins of conflicts between whites and Indians.
>
> …Once we arrive, the game awards us points and tells us how our life in Oregon turned out. And yet it fails to raise vital questions about our right to be there in the first place, and what happened to the people who were there first.[1]

```
YOU FINALLY ARRIVED AT OREGON CITY
AFTER 2040 LONG MILES---HOORAY!!!!!
PRESIDENT JAMES K. POLK SENDS YOU HIS
     HEARTIEST CONGRATULATIONS


     AND WISHES YOU A PROSPEROUS LIFE AHEAD


              AT YOUR NEW HOME
```

Bobbie Conner, a former director of the only Native American museum along the historical Oregon Trail, has further noted: "Most of what is written

1971

about the Oregon Trail is about the triumph of the United States." In the game, students are "learning about the settling of the West"—what Conner calls its *unsettling*—"but not the way the US government steamrolled lots of people to accomplish its goals.… So many people were dying for so many reasons. That gets lost when you learn a shallow version of history."[4]

The scope of stories the game could include were naturally limited by the capabilities of early computers. But those limitations had more than mere technical implications. In later decades, game scholars would advance theories of procedural rhetoric: the notion that an algorithm can encode an opinion, and make playable a theory about how the world works.[2] Games would come to be seen as having the power to bring ideas to life in a more experiential and immediate way than any prior medium. In the twenty-first century, we're still coming to terms with the way they can also concretize dangerous misconceptions—or omissions—when they claim their small simulations encode truths about the complexities of the world outside their code.

But the reason we're still talking and thinking about this game today is its remarkable longevity and popularity. Something about it clicked, right from that first version in Rawitsch's class, so engaging that some of his students would come in before school or stay late to keep playing. When spring term ended and Rawitsch graduated from college, he dutifully deleted the game off the mainframe before closing his student account, and it might have been lost forever had he not kept a printout of its source code. Years later, while working for the Minnesota Educational Computing Consortium (MECC), a new nonprofit dedicated to supporting the use of computers in Minnesota schools, he retyped and began improving it, sharing it in 1975 on a new mainframe system available to teachers across the state. Thousands of students began to play.

Over the next decade, the program would become one of the most popular educational games, first in Minnesota, and then across the United States. After several interstitial upgrades were made, a 1985 Apple II version (completely rewritten by R. Philip Bouchard with more events and simple graphics) would be played by millions, firmly cementing the game into a generation's cultural memory. Dozens of versions and editions have appeared since, collectively selling over sixty-five million copies.

While some of *Oregon Trail*'s popularity can doubtless be attributed to the many entertaining ways to die along the way, the game's creators also keenly grasped the storytelling potential of inviting the player into a simulated world. If your journey fails, you're asked a series of questions, a sort of consolation prize for failing:

```
DO TO YOUR UNFORTUNATE SITUATION, THERE ARE A FEW
FORMALITIES WE MUST GO THROUGH
WOULD YOU LIKE A MINISTER?Y

WOULD YOU LIKE A FANCY FUNERAL?N

WOULD YOU LIKE US TO INFORM YOUR NEXT OF KIN?N
```

```
YOUR AUNT NELLIE IN ST. LOUIS IS ANXIOUS TO HEAR

WE THANK YOU FOR THIS INFORMATION AND WE ARE SORRY YOU
DIDN'T MAKE IT TO THE GREAT TERRITORY OF OREGON
BETTER LUCK NEXT TIME


                        SINCERELY

        THE OREGON CITY CHAMBER OF COMMERCE
```

Though the game does nothing with the answers, the mere fact of being asked makes you feel like a part of the story being told. It was a trick that would continue to work across half a century of computer games and counting; a good reminder that no game is too old to learn from.

References

1   Bigelow, Bill. 1997. "On the Road to Cultural Bias: A Critique of 'The Oregon Trail' CD-ROM." *Language Arts* 74 (2).

2   Bogost, Ian. 2007. *Persuasive Games: The Expressive Power of Videogames*. MIT Press.

3   Bouchard, R. Philip. 2017. "I Designed The Oregon Trail, You Have Died of Dysentery." *Format*. Jul 24, 2017. www.format.com/magazine/features/design/you-have-died-of-dysentery-oregon-trail-design | a Mar 5, 2022

4   Landry, Alysa. 2017. "'It's a White Thing': 'The Oregon Trail' Game Doesn't Tell Complete History." *Indian Country Today*. Jun 8, 2017. indiancountrytoday.com/archive/it-s-a-white-thing-the-oregon-trail-game-doesn-t-tell-complete-history-xQAG3I7o0EKeeEGw7sCkbQ | s Oct 21, 2020

5   Lebling, P. David, Marc S. Blank, and Timothy A. Anderson. 1979. "Zork: A Computerized Fantasy Simulation Game." *IEEE Computer* 12 (4): 51–59.

6   Lussenhop, Jessica. 2011. "Oregon Trail: How Three Minnesotans Forged Its Path." City Pages, Jan 19, 2011. www.citypages.com/news/oregon-trail-how-three-minnesotans-forged-its-path-6745749 | s Mar 29, 2016

7   Maher, Jimmy. 2011. "On the Trail of the Oregon Trail, Parts 1-5." *The Digital Antiquarian* (blog). Mar 27, 2011. www.filfre.net/2011/03/on-the-trail-of-the-oregon-trail-part-1 | a Mar 5, 2022

8   Rawitsch, Dan. 1978. "Oregon Trail." *Creative Computing* June 1978, 4(3): 132-139.

9   Whitaker, Robert. 2021. "He Created The Oregon Trail." *Slate*. Nov 17, 2021. slate.com/news-and-politics/2021/11/oregon-trail-game-history-inventor-don-rawitsch.html | a Mar 5, 2022

10 Wong, Kevin. 2017. "The Forgotten History of 'The Oregon Trail,' As Told By Its Creators." *Vice*. Feb 15, 2017. www.vice.com/en/article/qkx8vw/the-forgotten-history-of-the-oregon-trail-as-told-by-its-creators | a Mar 5, 2022

ROCKET

Jim Storer

Also Known As **APOLLO, LUNAR**
Style **Resource Management**
Debuted **Jan 1970** (DECUS)
Early 1972 (EDU)
Launch Platform **PDP-8**
Language **FOCAL**

> **CONTROL CALLING LUNAR MODULE. MANUAL CONTROL IS NECESSARY**

ON JULY 20, 1969, the Apollo 11 Lunar Module *Eagle* touched down on the moon, though it had been a close call. With little fuel to spare, pilot Neil Armstrong dodged boulders and craters to find a level spot to put down the LM after it drifted ahead of its planned landing site. When the delicate craft at last touched down, only seconds of descent fuel remained. Seventeen-year-old Jim Storer had been glued to the television broadcast from his family home in Massachusetts, and that fall he pitched a project to the teacher in charge of his high school's PDP-8 computer: a game that would recreate the experience of landing the LM on the moon.

Storer's game printed no title, but the file name, fitting neatly into the operating system's 6-character limit, was *ROCKET*. In an age where storage and memory were still precious, the program took up only thirty-nine tight lines of code. In the game, the player receives rows of data one by one, each representing the elapsed time, altitude, velocity, and fuel remaining in their simulated moon lander's tanks. At the end of the line, the teletype stops printing, and the player contributes a single number: the amount of fuel to burn for the next ten-second interval.

1972

```
YOU MAY RESET FUEL RATE K EACH 10 SECS TO 0 OR ANY VALUE
BETWEEN 8 & 200 LBS/SEC. YOU'VE 16000 LBS FUEL. ESTIMATED
FREE FALL IMPACT TIME-120 SECS. CAPSULE WEIGHT-32500 LBS
FIRST RADAR CHECK COMING UP


COMMENCE LANDING PROCEDURE
TIME,SECS     ALTITUDE,MILES+FEET      VELOCITY,MPH     FUEL,LBS     FUEL RATE
     0              120      0           3600.00        16000.0       K=:10
    10              109   5160           3616.33        15900.0       K=:25
    20               99   5018           3602.91        15650.0       K=:15
    30               89   4930           3609.07        15500.0       K=:12
    40               79   4709           3621.10        15380.0       K=:30
    50               69   4577           3596.78        15080.0       K=:45
    60               59   5030           3541.24        14630.0       K=:
```

Transcripts are unmodified from the original FOCAL version, except that column headers have been reprinted at the top of each excerpt for clarity.

On time-shared systems with slow-printing teletypes, allowing for a few seconds each turn to decide the new burn rate, the game would have given the illusion of playing out roughly in real time. With the ongoing Apollo program still a vibrant part of the national conversation, it would have been easy to imagine a background of echoing mission control commentary and astronaut jargon, lending the stark numbers some vivid context from the real-life space adventures on TV.

The challenge of the game—and it's pretty hard—is a decent analog to Armstrong's, if simplified: you must slow your rate of descent enough to land gracefully before running out of fuel. If you're too cautious, the moon's gravity relentlessly adds to your terrifying downward velocity until there's not enough time before impact to correct it. Too aggressive, and you'll burn through your fuel too early, ceding control of your lander to the fatal math of celestial mechanics. In either case, the result is the same:

```
TIME,SECS     ALTITUDE,MILES+FEET      VELOCITY,MPH     FUEL,LBS     FUEL RATE
   220               9   2181            218.44          330.0        K=:0
   230               8   3994            254.44          330.0        K=:10
   240               8    273            252.94          230.0        K=:10
   250               7   1855            251.22          130.0        K=:10
   260               6   3464            249.28           30.0        K=:3
FUEL OUT AT       270.00 SECS
ON MOON AT        326.77 SECS
IMPACT VELOCITY OF       478.22 M.P.H.
FUEL LEFT:     0.00 LBS
SORRY,BUT THERE WERE NO SURVIVORS-YOU BLEW IT!
IN FACT YOU BLASTED A NEW LUNAR CRATER     108.56 FT. DEEP
TRY AGAIN?
```

see **1971**

Like *Oregon Trail* and most other early programs, Storer's is based around a series of equations. But it benefits from simulating a very human moment, one where the drama came almost entirely from the cold, stark numbers of accelerations, momentums, and forces. While the core loop consists entirely of numbers, Storer gives the simulation just enough framing to engage the imagination, maintaining the illusion that your teletype is connected

1972

to a distant mission control. The game begins with the words `CONTROL CALLING LUNAR MODULE`, and if you quit, it politely prints `CONTROL OUT` before halting. Other human touches like the depth of your fail crater, calculated simply as a percentage of impact speed, serve as gentle consolation prizes to avoid humiliation in the shared space of contemporary computer labs—a failed run turned into jocular bragging rights. For the most part, the program's math is sound. With help from his teacher and his engineer father, Storer programmed equations for acceleration and force, priming them with constants for the real lander's mass and for lunar gravity.

FOCAL is compact by design, but that trade-off makes programs written in it difficult to read. It uses single-letter variable names, for instance, but also single-letter abbreviations for functions. Combined with the core simulation's already hairy calculus, *ROCKET*'s original source code is, to put it mildly, rather obtuse. Here's the core of the game's code for each turn:

```
03.10 I (M-N-.001)4.1;I (T-.001)2.1;S S=T
03.40 I ((N+S*K)-M)3.5,3.5;S S=(M-N)/K
03.50 D 9;I (I)7.1,7.1;I (V)3.8,3.8;I (J)8.1
03.80 D 6;G 3.1
```

The initial numbers are line numbers: a group with the same digits before the decimal (like `03`) acts as a single code block that can be executed and returned from. The `I` on line `3.10` means *If*, and it branches to line `4.1` if the parenthetical expression (here calculating remaining fuel) is less than zero.

The code roughly translates to these steps:

```
If out of fuel, goto freefall handling
If elapsed time not yet calculated, print status & get input
Set elapsed time this turn to 10 seconds
      Adjust if not enough fuel to burn that long
Calculate forces & distance traveled
If altitude <= 0, calculate time to impact then goto endgame
If fuel burned, adjust velocity then pass time
Update global variables
Goto top
```

Storer submitted his program in early 1970 to DEC, the makers of his school's PDP, who published it in their library of user-submitted programs, the DECUS Program Guide. This happened at the perfect moment to catch an explosive crosswind of zeitgeists: Apollo fever and computer mania. Storer's program was cloned, tweaked, improved, and reinvented countless times over the next few years, so much so that by the beginning of 1972 DECUS was advertising "a greatly improved version of the Apollo simulation game which has been running on almost every timesharing system in the country."[1] While some of these programs were independent creations, as time went on the bulk of them would be thinly veiled clones of Storer's version, with his algorithms running largely unchanged under the hood—and a great deal of the reason for this was because of *ROCKET*'s publication in a series of widely read places.

MAJOR VERSIONS

» **ROCKET**, FOCAL, late 1969. Written up in Storer's school newspaper.

» **FOCAL Lunar Landing Simulation (APOLLO)**, DECUS, Jan 1970. Slightly revised from original.

» **BASIC port**, David H. Ahl, early 1972. Printed in *EDU*; reprinted (as *ROCKET*) in *101 BASIC Computer Games*, then (as *LUNAR*) in *BASIC Computer Games*

» **ROCKET (Peters version)**, Eric Peters, 1973. Added visual indicator of distance to surface.

» **LEM**, William Labaree II, 1973. Added more controls including timing and angle of each thrust.

» **APOLLO 11**, David A. Moon, 1972. 5-sec intervals; can steer in multiple axes.

» **Moonlander**, Jack Burness, DEC GT40, 1973. First graphical version.

» **Lunar Lander**, Atari, 1979. Graphical arcade version.

DECUS was the DEC Users' Society; DEC in turn was Digital Equipment Corporation, makers of the PDP minicomputers. (Okay, okay: PDP stood for Programmed Data Processor). The *DECUS Program Guide* was one of the earliest public software catalogs; any user could submit a program, or order one as a source code printout (or on paper tape or punch cards) for a small fee.

Cover page and code extract from the first published version of *ROCKET*.

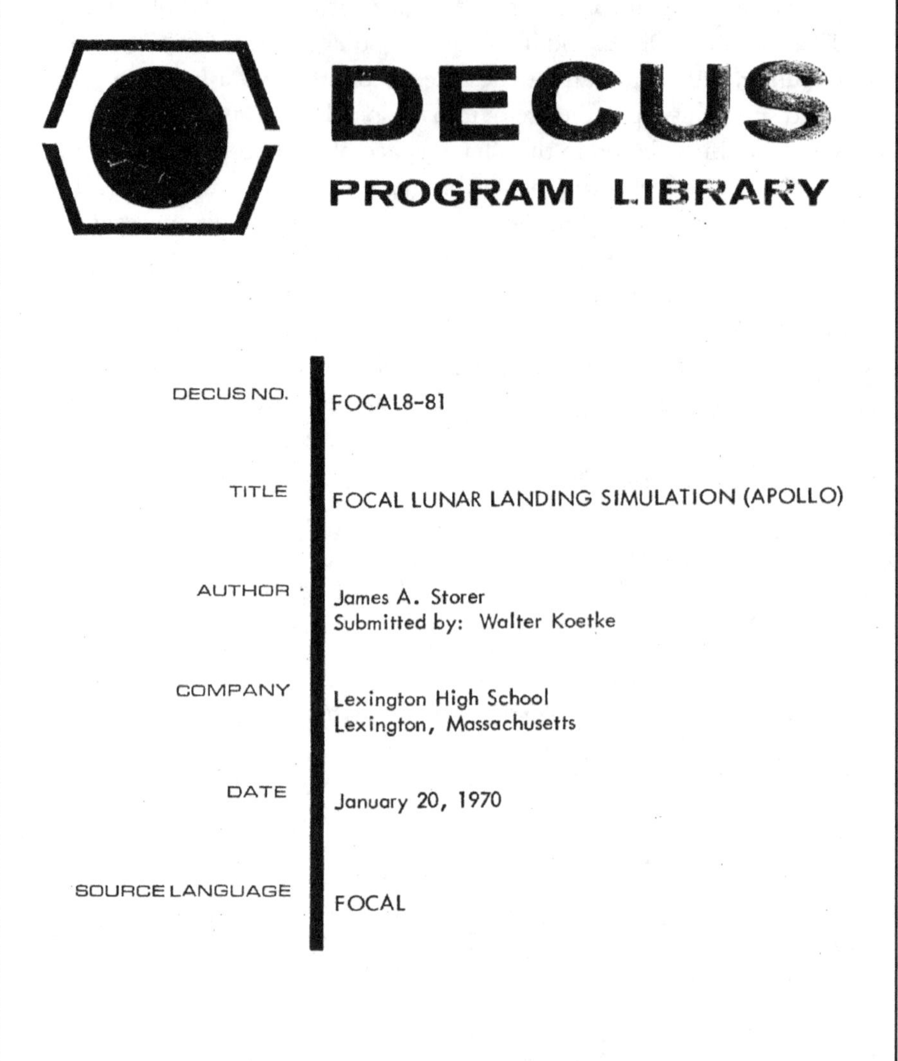


```
05.10 T "ON THE MOON AT",L," SECS"!;S W=3600*V
05.20 T "IMPACT VELOCITY OF",W," M.P.H."!,"FUEL LEFT:"
05.30 T M-N," LBS."!;I (-W+1)5.5,5.5
05.40 T "PERFECT LANDING !-(LUCKY)"!;G 5.9
05.50 I (-W+10)5.6,5.6;T "GOOD LANDING-(COULD BE BETTER)"!;G 5.9
05.60 I (-W+25)5.7,5.7;T "CONGRATULATIONS ON A POOR LANDING"!;G 5.9
05.70 I (-W+60)5.8,5.8;T "CRAFT DAMAGE. GOOD LUCK"!;G 5.9
05.80 T "SORRY,BUT THERE WERE NO SURVIVORS-YOU BLEW IT!"!"IN "
05.81 T "FACT YOU BLASTED A NEW LUNAR CRATER",W*.277777," FT. DEEP"!
05.90 T !!!"TRY AGAIN?"!
05.92 A "(ANS. YES OR NO)"P;I (P-0NO)5.94,5.98
05.94 I (P-0YES)5.92,1.2,5.92
05.98 T "CONTROL OUT";Q
```

1972

In 1969, educational psychology grad student David H. Ahl had taken a job with DEC, managing their educational marketing department. Schools were seen as key customers of their PDP minis, but while the dry *DECUS Program Guide* contained many programs potentially of interest to teachers and students, they were buried amidst dozens of mundane utility and demonstration programs with exciting titles like "PDUMP - DOS Based Register/Core Dump" and "Core Load to MAINDEC Tape." One of Ahl's initiatives was to start a free dedicated newsletter for educational users, which he called *EDU*. He filled it with lesson plans, instructional tips, and success stories from teachers using computers in the classroom. Each issue also included several program listings in BASIC, the language DEC increasingly focused on for its educational platforms. But this meant Ahl had to round up or write a lot of interesting BASIC programs in short order. In addition to welcoming submissions by mail, he scoured the DECUS catalog and other existing collections of source code for old programs to port. Storer's hit lunar landing game was an obvious fit.

Ahl's BASIC port duplicates the exact algorithms and structure of Storer's program but tweaks its text to better explain the rules. It also streamlines a few complexities, though losing some of the original's charm in the process—the conceit that you're communicating directly with mission control, sadly, is absent. Ahl also made some simplifications, possibly in an effort to increase the game's clarity as a teaching tool or maybe just to save space. Storer's original has six different gradations of landing success, for instance, while Ahl's port has only three.

The BASIC *ROCKET* was printed in *EDU* in early 1972, just as the newsletter's readership was exploding. When the first issue had been released the previous fall, it had only three hundred subscribers; by the end of 1972 there were over twenty thousand. With minicomputers becoming more and more affordable, and a generous selection of grants getting them into schools, the demand for educational software was going up like, well, a rocket. Ahl's port exposed Storer's game to thousands more users and inspired new waves of imitators, clones, and remakes.

Later in 1972, as the final Apollo missions were playing out, Ahl pitched DEC the idea of taking the best programs from *EDU* and publishing them as a book. The resulting title, 1973's *101 BASIC Computer Games*, became one of the most influential titles in early computing history. Eventually reissued as just *BASIC Computer Games*, it stayed steadily popular through the first decade of home computers, going on to become the first computer book to sell a million copies. In his notes for the program, Ahl called *ROCKET* "far and away the single most popular computer game."[4] By the end of the 70s, as the personal computer revolution was beginning, hundreds of thousands of kids and adults were typing Storer's program or one of its many variants into their home computers to try recreating Armstrong's famous landing for themselves. In 1979, Atari

Among many other finds, Ahl reprinted a descendant of *The Sumerian Game* 1964 under the name *HMRABI*: later known as *Hammurabi* on systems with more breathing room, it would become a famous early computer classic.

Ahl's version winkingly suggests that the LM's onboard computer has failed because "it wasn't made by Digital," his employer.

Portion of a run of Eric Peters's 1973 *ROCKET* variant. The asterisk shows how far the lander is from the I representing the surface.

released a graphical version called *Lunar Lander*, a name that came to stand in for the entire genre of games inspired by Storer's high school project, further cementing its place in computing history.

While it might seem strange to discuss *ROCKET* in the context of games made with words, since its output is mostly numbers, it arguably succeeds at capturing the immediacy of its dramatic situation even more clearly than *The Oregon Trail* did with prose. Rather than adopting the remote God's-eye viewpoint of most earlier games, you *become* the astronaut in the hot seat, watching the numbers printed on your chattering teletype drop at a disturbingly rapid rate. The game encourages players to imagine themselves as desperate astronauts, sweating from second to second over whether their virtual hero lives or dies. It was an addicting kind of immersion that many future games would strive to recreate and improve, and it inspired countless text game authors to put their readers directly in the shoes—or space boots—of a heroic protagonist.

```
TIME,SECS     ALTITUDE,MILES+FEET     VELOCITY,MPH     FUEL,LBS     FUEL RATE
    190                0     581           8.10          300.0       K=:8
    200                0     425          13.17          220.0       K=:10
    210                0     253          10.30          120.0       K=:9
    220                0      96          11.11           30.0       K=:100
FUEL OUT AT    220.30 SECS
ON THE MOON AT    226.12 SECS
IMPACT VELOCITY OF     9.86 M.P.H.
FUEL LEFT:         0.00 LBS
GOOD LANDING-(COULD BE BETTER)

TRY AGAIN?
(ANS. YES OR NO):NO
CONTROL OUT
```

References

1 DECUS. 1972. "DECUS No. FOCAL8-173: APOLLO 11." In *DECUS Program Library Catalog*, p. F-26. Maynard, Masschusetts: Digital Equipment Computer Users Society.

2 Edwards, Benj. 2009. "Forty Years of Lunar Lander." *Technologizer* (blog). Jul 19, 2009. www.technologizer.com/2009/07/19/lunar-lander | a Mar 8, 2022

3 Storer, James A. 1970. "FOCAL Lunar Landing Simulation (APOLLO)." DECUS Program Library. www.bitsavers.org/pdf/dec/decus/focal/FOCAL8-81_LunarLanding.pdf | a Mar 8, 2022

4 Storer, Jim. 1973. "ROCKET: Land An Apollo Capsule on the Moon." In *101 BASIC Computer Games*, ed. David H. Ahl, 182–87. Maynard, Masschusetts: Digital Equipment Corporation.

5 Storer, Jim. 2009. "Lunar Landing Game Related Documents." Jim Storer (Brandeis Computer Science Department website). 2009. www.cs.brandeis.edu/~storer/LunarLander/LunarLander.html | a Mar 8, 2022

6 Storer, Jim, Eric Peters, and William Labaree II. 1978. "Lunar LEM Rocket." In *BASIC Computer Games*, ed. David H. Ahl, 106–9. New York: Workman Publishing.

7 The System Symptoms. 1970. "Moon Landing" (article in Lexington High School newspaper), Jan 13, 1970. www.cs.brandeis.edu/~storer/LunarLander/LunarLander/Articles/LunarLander-LexingtonHigh1970.pdf | a Mar 8, 2022

8 Willært, Kate. 2021. "Moonlander: One Giant Leap For Game Design." *A Critical Hit!* (blog). Apr 11, 2021. www.acriticalhit.com/moonlander-one-giant-leap-for-game-design | a Mar 8, 2022

HUNT THE WUMPUS

Gregory H. Coresun

Style	**Roguelike**
Debuted	**Apr 1973** (People's Computer Center)
Launch Platform	**PDP-8**
Language	**BASIC**
Launch Price	**$4** (paper tape)

> " WELCOME TO 'HUNT THE WUMPUS'
>   THE WUMPUS LIVES IN A CAVE OF 20
> ROOMS. EACH ROOM HAS 3 TUNNELS LEADING TO
> OTHER ROOMS. (LOOK AT A DODECAHEDRON TO SEE
> HOW THIS WORKS-IF YOU DON'T KNOW WHAT A
> DODECAHEDRON IS, ASK SOMEONE)

EARLY COMPUTER GAMES WERE MADE IN POCKETS OF ISOLATION hard to imagine from our hyperconnected world. Like early life spawning and dying in countless dark seas before the right warm tide pool helped it thrive, digital game innovations were invented and lost and invented again, over and over. Serious computer work was written up in journals and shared at conferences, and industry coders swapped demos at rare meetups. But there was nothing like the rapid and constant iteration on ideas and experiments so vital to future generations of game makers. Before computer games could evolve, they needed community.

1973

In 1972, a computer advocacy group set up shop at a storefront in Menlo Park, California. The city sat at the nexus of Stanford technologists and Bay Area freethinkers who would soon spark the computer revolution and the behemoths of Silicon Valley—but not just yet. Pursuing a dream that computers could and should be for everyone, the nonprofit group who moved into the small retail space that year called themselves the People's Computer Company. No sign or plaque marks the space, now an unassuming dry cleaning business, where many seeds of the coming computer game revolution were planted.

The People's Computer Company was co-founded by Bob Albrecht, a lifelong computer evangelist then in his early forties. Albrecht had been struggling to teach computers in high schools until BASIC appeared in the mid-1960s. The language's simplicity and accessibility made him into a passionate advocate. "I lobbied, ranted, and raved for BASIC," he recalled: "I had made big buttons that said SHAFT (Society to Help Abolish Fortran Teaching)."[1] By the late 60s Albrecht was in the habit of loading a bulky PDP minicomputer in his Volkswagen bus each weekend to give BASIC seminars at college campuses. On Thursday nights he would "run computer programming, wine tasting, and Greek dancing parties" out of his apartment.[1] He also helped found the Portola Institute, the influential Bay Area nonprofit that created counterculture magazine the *Whole Earth Catalog*.

With the help of his wife Mary Jo, Albrecht and a few other like-minded thinkers spun off the People's Computer Company from Portola in the early 70s and launched a community meeting space, the People's Computer Center (both often called just "the PCC"). The idea of the Center was simple: the PCC would convince big companies like DEC and HP to donate hardware, which they would set up and make accessible to members of the public who could stop by to play computer games, "rap about computers," or attend drop-in classes on BASIC (or folk guitar). Open computer time to do anything you liked was available for a few dollars an hour, or less: "The younger you are the less you pay." The PCC's printed newsletter shared a similar spirit, filled with introductory coding tips, annotated program listings, articles on using computers for art or music, and counterculture imagery and slogans. "Liberate Some People From School," one issue buzzed: "Take them on a field trip to PCC by skoolbus, carpool, or bike brigade."[4]

Into this heady environment stumbled a man in his late twenties then called Gregory Yob (later Gregory Coresun). Born in the Pacific Northwest, he had suffered through "a lonely childhood in a relentlessly abusive household that left him with stunted social skills,"[8] emerging with a love for mathematics and, eventually,

Bob Albrecht and fellow PCC co-founder Dennis Allison would later create influential hacker magazine *Dr. Dobb's Journal*: its fictional namesake originated as a portmanteau of Dennis and Bob.

Illustration from the PCC newsletter #1 in 1972.

computers. His partner in later years recalled that "under the grumpy exterior, which sooner or later almost everyone who knew him would bump into, lived a brilliant mind, a compassionate heart and a delightful childlike playfulness."[6] After finishing a graduate degree and moving to California, Greg discovered the PCC and became a regular drop-in and newsletter contributor. He had already been involved in developing an interpreted language called Pilot (designed to run on top of BASIC) that simplified the creation of conversational programs. The PCC's mission of outreach and accessibility no doubt resonated.

Greg began contributing to the PCC newsletter at the same time a game design conversation had begun within its pages. A hide-and-seek program from June 1972, created by a high school computer class, was playable on the center's PDP-8. In this game, the player tried to guess where four computer-controlled opponents were hiding on a 10x10 grid. After each guess, the program would tell you the distance to each opponent, and students were encouraged to use graph paper and triangulation skills to win.

```
TURN NUMBER 1 , WHAT IS YOUR GUESS?
? 4, 3
YOUR DISTANCE FROM PLAYER 1 IS 6.4 UNIT(S).
YOUR DISTANCE FROM PLAYER 2 IS 6.4 UNIT(S).
YOUR DISTANCE FROM PLAYER 3 IS 2.8 UNIT(S).
YOUR DISTANCE FROM PLAYER 4 IS 1 UNIT(S).
TURN NUMBER 2 , WHAT IS YOUR GUESS?
```

Unshackled from a need to make something with educational value, PCC members created their own amusing variations on the program. A common improvement was to replace the anonymous hiders with a single named monster, which inevitably lent its name to the program; games like *Mugwump*, *Snark*, and *Hurkle* proliferated. Most stuck with the original code's 10x10 grid.

```
THE HURKLE IS HIDING. TRY TO FIND HIM.

WHAT IS YOUR GUESS
?5, 5
GO SOUTHWEST

WHAT IS YOUR GUESS
?3, 2
GO EAST
```

In Greg's retelling,[9] *Hunt the Wumpus* was born when he saw several of these monster-hunting program listings side by side in the April 1973 PCC newsletter. Greg, a mathematician fascinated by complex topologies, became annoyed that none of the authors had thought beyond that simple grid. At age nineteen, he'd had a paper accepted by *Scientific American* on "his experiment on simulating gravitational fields with droplets of water on a soap bubble";[6] more recently, a friend had cited his work in a paper on

MAJOR VERSIONS

» **Apr 1973**. Playable at the PCC in Menlo Park, California.

» **Oct 1975**. Source published in *Creative Computing* magazine and later in *The Best of Creative Computing Volume 1*.

» **Wumpus 2**. Added different cave maps.

» **Wumpus 3**, "Howard" at PCC, 1974. Added new hazards and made them move.

» **C port**, Ken Thompson, 1974.

» **Superwumpus**, Jack Emmerichs, 1978. Complete rewrite with random events and resource management.

» **TI graphical remake**, Kevin Kenney, TI-99/4A, 1981.

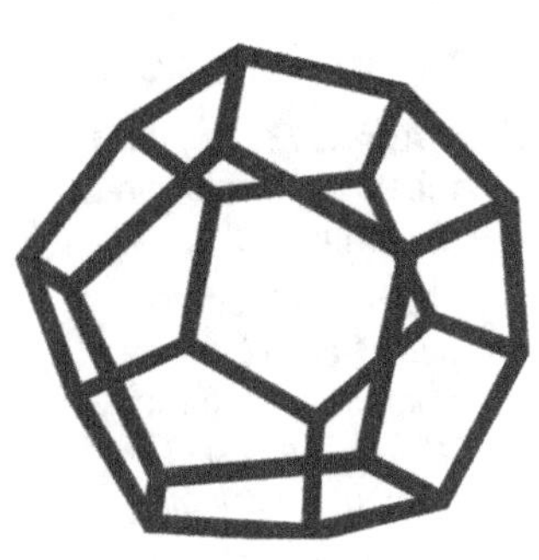

A dodecahedron, basis for the map in *Hunt the Wumpus*.

see *Adventure* **1976**

equations for "homogenous solids from whose center of gravity there are only four normals."[5] Computers were capable of simulating much more interesting spaces, and Greg was capable of visualizing them. By the end of April he'd written his own monster-hunting program. His creature was called the Wumpus, and his map was a dodecahedron.

Greg may also have been influenced by a series of programs floating around the PCC that spring written by fellow member Dave Kaufman. In *Caves1*, the player navigates through a group of rooms arranged in a tree structure, looking for a way to escape:

```
IMAGINE YOURSELF AN EXPLORER OF THE FAMOUS
DUZZLEDORF CAVES. YOU'VE BEEN UNDERGROUND
FOR DAYS, TRIPPING THROUGH THE CAVERNS AND
TUNNELS. UNFORTUNATELY, YOU'RE LOST, AND
YOUR FOOD HAS RUN OUT.

THERE IS ONLY ONE PATH OUT. SEE IF YOU
CAN FIND IT.

YOU'RE IN CAVERN # 1
# 2 # 3 # 4 ARE WHERE YOU CAN GO
WHERE NEXT? 4
YOU'RE IN CAVERN # 4
# 5 # 6 # 7 # 1 ARE WHERE YOU CAN GO
WHERE NEXT? 5
DEADEND
WHERE NEXT?
```

Largely forgotten until game blogger Jason Dyer rediscovered them in 2019,[2] the *Caves* games were some of the earliest where players moved through connected rooms with a fictional theme, a notion that would later become foundational to interactive fiction. The numbered rooms, the conceit of being trapped in a cave, and the language around descriptions and movement are all similar to *Wumpus*. Regardless of which program influenced the other, it's clear the PCC authors were in dialogue, both at the Center and in the pages of its newsletter. A game design conversation was happening.

In *Wumpus*, you explore a network of twenty numbered caves, each with three exits and a complex set of interconnections. The map replicates the points and edges of the dodecahedron, a platonic solid with twelve sides and twenty vertices. While the shape is mathematically simple, it's difficult for anyone but a mathematician to map sensibly in their head or on a flat piece of paper. The result is a virtual space that feels larger than it ought to: disorienting, claustrophobic, perpetually wrapping in on itself in surprising ways. You can't get lost on the comfortable axis of a grid; but even twenty rooms in a strange topology are enough to get lost in.

Within this uneasy environment are hazards and foes. When each game begins, two rooms are selected to hold bottomless pits, which mean instant death if you enter those rooms. Two more host "super bats" that will teleport you to another room at random (including, unfortunately, the rooms with bottomless pits). And in a fifth room is the Wumpus, who might kill you if you blunder into him, or simply slink away through one of the three exits. Critically, you can't see these hazards directly: by the time you stumble into a room containing them, it's too late. Instead you must infer their existence from a distance, via messages printed when you enter an adjacent room: `I FEEL A DRAFT`, `BATS NEARBY`, and `I SMELL A WUMPUS`. Since each room has three exits, you won't know for sure which leads to a hazard unless you're paying close attention, keeping a map, and using basic logic to work out which paths are safe.

```
YOU ARE IN ROOM  9
TUNNELS LEAD TO  8    10    18

SHOOT OR MOVE (S-M)? M
WHERE TO? 10

BATS NEARBY!
YOU ARE IN ROOM 10
TUNNELS LEAD TO 2 9 11

SHOOT OR MOVE (S-M)? M
WHERE TO? 2

ZAP--SUPER BAT SNATCH! ELSEWHEREVILLE FOR YOU!
I SMELL A WUMPUS!
YOU ARE IN ROOM 15
TUNNELS LEAD TO  6    14    16

SHOOT OR MOVE (S-M)?
```

The Wumpus must also be dealt with from a distance, by firing a "crooked arrow" that can travel a twisting path of up to five rooms to hit its target— once you've worked out where that is.

```
SHOOT OR MOVE (S-M)? M
WHERE TO? 14

YOU ARE IN ROOM 14
TUNNELS LEAD TO  4    13    15

SHOOT OR MOVE (S-M)? S
NO. OF ROOMS(1-5)? 2
ROOM #? 15
ROOM #? 16
AHA! YOU GOT THE WUMPUS!
HEE HEE HEE - THE WUMPUS'LL GETCHA NEXT TIME!!
```

Hunt the Wumpus was a more compelling computer game than nearly any that had come before. Unlike most earlier games, the possibility space was large enough to contain different strategies. In contrast to the inevitable

see *The Oregon Trail* **1971**
and *ROCKET* **1972**

westward movement of a wagon train or downward fall toward the lunar surface, here you could choose which direction to move. Shooting through a dizzying network of rooms opened up interesting, unexpected possibilities (like accidentally shooting yourself). There was randomness enough for surprising events (bats dropping you into a pit; lumbering into the Wumpus by accident) without the game feeling unfairly capricious. The maze was genuinely disorienting when you first dropped into it, encouraging players to keep a paper map and annotate it with observations about which rooms were safe or might contain hazards. The Wumpus's occasional movements might invalidate previously safe routes and force a rethinking of strategy halfway through play. And there was just enough description in the instructions to lend the Wumpus himself a hint of character:

```
THE WUMPUS IS NOT BOTHERED BY THE HAZARDS (HE HAS SUCKER
FEET AND IS TOO BIG FOR A BAT TO LIFT). USUALLY HE IS
ASLEEP.
```

In short, *Wumpus* was fun in a way few earlier computer games had managed to capture: immediate, immersive, replayable, and challenging. It was an evolution of what games might be, and its inclusion in an ongoing conversation about games at the PCC may be part of the reason why. It wasn't produced in isolation; it was *reacting* to earlier games. The emergence of local and national communities of computer users would continue to accelerate the speed at which craft wisdom could be learned and shared. It was just one of many computer revolutions.

Greg's game was widely shared around the PCC and soon became a hit. By May, he was seeing it at computer events around the Bay Area, inevitably with clusters of back seat drivers huddled around the person at the terminal, shouting out their own Wumpus-hunting strategies. He quickly devised a sequel, *Wumpus 2* (which added a choice of cave topologies), and began to sell copies of both games on paper tape for four dollars, making him one of the earliest digital game makers to do so. But the idea of copyright for computer code was still nebulous and, indeed, anathema to many early hackers. As with all other successful programs of the time, *Wumpus* was freely copied, ported, remade, and redistributed, soon spreading across the country. Ken Thompson, the creator of Unix, wrote a version in the new language C. By 1974 a rip-off called *Super Wumpus* started circulating. The original's code appeared in *Creative Computing* magazine in 1975 and would later show up in several of David H. Ahl's influential books of BASIC programs. By 1981, a graphical *Wumpus* for the TI-99/4A home computer was on the shelves of stores nationwide, cementing it as an early computing touchstone. "I smell a Wumpus" will still get a smile out of many an aging computer geek.

Other than the *Wumpus* sequel, Greg never released another computer game, though he remained passionate about the potential of computers to challenge minds, especially young ones. He became a regular columnist for *Creative Computing*, and was involved with another walk-in computer center called LO*OP in Cotati, California (north of San Francisco).

Paper tape was a hybrid between the previous decade's punch cards and the coming rise of magnetic storage. Long reels of inch-wide paper would be punched with holes representing binary data, which could be read from or written to with a specially equipped teleprinter. By the early 1970s, most systems had standardized on a 7-column format, meaning each row could store one character from a set of two to the seventh power or 128 possibilities. This implementation of the 7-bit ASCII standard would form the basis of textual data on computers for decades to come.

1973

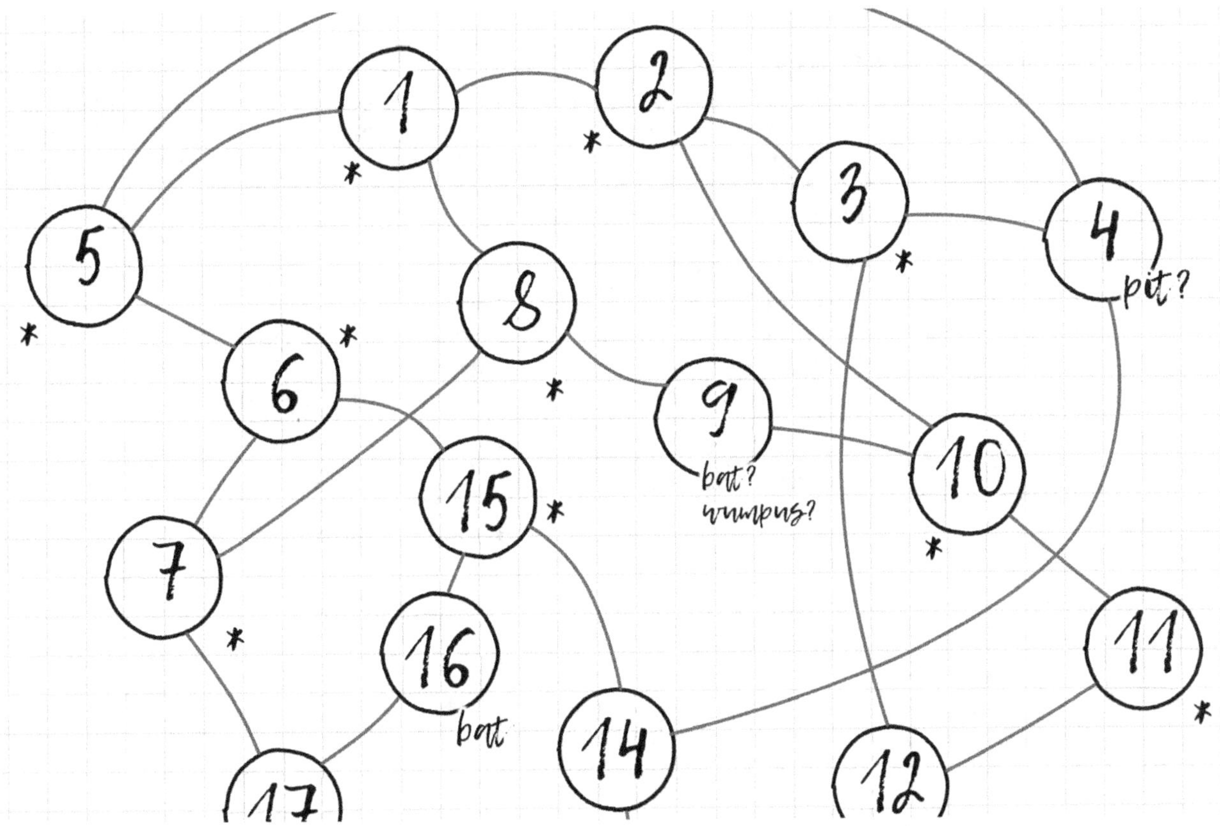

In-progress *Wumpus* map: the player is marking safe rooms with an asterisk, and keeping track of possible hazards in unvisited rooms.

In 1977 he taught a college course called Computers as a Tool for the Artist. Throughout the 1980s he was heavily involved in the user-friendly Commodore PET community, writing regular columns for magazines and instruction manuals for the PET and its many accessories. Increasingly enamored with the potential for technology to expand consciousness and extend life, he wrote an unfinished book about a spiritual human-machine interface, and adopted the shamanic name Hara Ra. "With a gleeful twinkle in his eye," his widow later recalled, "he would call himself a Neo-Neuro-Cyber-Shaman."[6] He eventually retired to Santa Cruz, where he went by the name Gregory Coresun and worked on "interactive computer art of ever-changing mandalas" until his passing in 2005.

Wumpus has been identified as one of the earliest ancestors of both the roguelike and the text adventure, a form that would crystallize more fully with *Adventure* **1976**. Like the later game, it has a map that must be explored, challenges to overcome, memorable adversaries, and the first hints of a compelling story. But Greg's game wasn't born in a vacuum. It grew from a thriving community of computer evangelists playing, sharing, and remixing each other's games. In the years to come, these communities would become a common thread across text game makers from different decades, platforms, and technologies, with the most memorable innovations nearly always woven from communal looms. Even for single-player games, the joy of going on adventures (and the joy of creating them) is often best when shared with others. IMAGINE YOURSELF AN EXPLORER, Dave Kaufman's *Caves* began—and in the years to come, more and more computer users would do just that.

see, among others, **1975**, **1977**, **1980**, **1988**, **1991**, **1993**, **2005**, and **2010**

References

1 Cappetta, Jon. 2015. "Interview with Bob Albrecht by Jon Cappetta." *HCLE Virtual Museum* (blog). Jul 9, 2015. hclemuseum.wordpress.com/2015/07/09/interview-with-bob-albrecht-by-jon-cappetta-2/ | a Apr 12, 2020

2 Dyer, Jason. 2019. "Before Adventure, Parts 1-5." *Renga in Blue* (blog). Mar 14, 2019. bluerenga.blog/tag/before-adventure/ | a Apr 12, 2020

3 Maher, Jimmy. 2011. "Hunt the Wumpus, Parts 1 and 2." *The Digital Antiquarian* (blog). May 13, 2011. www.filfre.net/2011/05/hunt-the-wumpus-part-1/ | a Apr 12, 2020

4 "The People's Computer Company Newsletter" (Archives). Internet Archive. 1972–4. https://archive.org/search.php?query=creator%3A%22People%27s+Computer+Company%22 | a Apr 12, 2020

5 Shafer, Robert E. 1973. "A Generalization of Spherical Harmonics." *SIAM Review* 15 (3).

6 Strong, C.L. 1964. "The Amateur Scientist." *Scientific American*, Dec 1964.

7 van de Loo, Andrea. 2007. "Remembering Hara Ra." CryoNet.Org Mailing List. Oct 3, 2007. www.cryonet.org/cgi-bin/dsp.cgi?msg=29879 | a Apr 12, 2020

8 White, Dan. 2002. "Together Forever: Local Couple Hopes to Be Frozen through Cryonics and See the Future." *Santa Cruz Sentinel*, Jul 12, 2002. www.santacruzsentinel.com/archive/2002/July/12/local/stories/01local.htm | a Apr 12, 2020

9 Yob, Gregory. 1976. "Hunt the Wumpus." In *The Best of Creative Computing, Volume 1*, ed. David H. Ahl. Creative Computing Press.

SUPER STAR TREK

Mike Mayfield and Bob Leedom

<table>
<tr><td align="right">Also Known As</td><td>STTR1, Star Trek</td></tr>
<tr><td align="right">Style</td><td>Roguelike</td></tr>
<tr><td align="right">Debuted</td><td>Summer 1971 (Mayfield original)
Late 1974 (Leedom version)</td></tr>
<tr><td align="right">Launch Platform</td><td>SDS Sigma 7</td></tr>
<tr><td align="right">Language</td><td>BASIC</td></tr>
</table>

> “ YOUR ORDERS ARE AS FOLLOWS:
>   DESTROY THE 10 KLINGON WARSHIPS
> WHICH HAVE INVADED THE GALAXY BEFORE THEY CAN
> ATTACK FEDERATION HEADQUARTERS ON STARDATE
> 2025; THIS GIVES YOU 25 DAYS. THERE ARE 4
> STARBASES IN THE GALAXY FOR RESUPPLYING YOUR
> SHIP.
>
> HIT 'RETURN' WHEN READY TO ASSUME COMMAND

THE FINAL EPISODE OF *STAR TREK* aired on June 3, 1969, just as superfan Mike Mayfield was finishing his sophomore year of high school. It was called "Turnabout Intruder" and it was not a very good episode. *Trek* had been saved from cancellation once before through a devoted letter-writing campaign, but it proved harder to rally the troops a second time. The show's third season had on the whole been less inspired, and it seemed now to be

1974

Major Versions

» **Unpublished original**, SDS Sigma 7, summer 1971.

» **STAR TREK** aka **STTR1**, HP2000C BASIC, Oct 1972. Published by HP in Feb 1973 Contributed Program library.

» **SPACWR,** Mary Cole and David H. Ahl, BASIC-PLUS (port). Published in *EDU*; reprinted in *101 BASIC Computer Games*. Minimal changes; not to be confused with *SpaceWar!*

» **Leedom version**, Data General Nova 800, Bob Leedom, late 1974. Many gameplay improvements including moving Klingons, named quadrants, status reports from show characters, and three-letter command codes.

» **Super Star Trek**, port of Leedom version by Ahl. Printed in May/Jun 1975 *Creative Computing*, and 1976 *The Best of Creative Computing*.

» **1978 version**, port by John Borders to Microsoft 8K BASIC. Cosmetic changes including ASCII "Enterprise" on title screen; appeared in *BASIC Computer Games*.

» **Apple Trek**, Apple II, 1979. Commercial port.

» **Star Raiders**, Atari 8-bit, 1979. Added realtime POV combat.

» **Star Fleet I: The War Begins!**, Interstel, DOS/C64, 1985. Added more story text, color & sound effects, and shield configurations.

» **EGATrek**, Nels Anderson, DOS, 1988. Shareware version with color graphics.

1974

going out with a whimper. A rerun of *The Mod Squad* that night scored twice as many viewers. A long decade would pass before any new live-action *Trek* would appear. In the meantime, fans would have to keep the flame burning themselves.

Mayfield, along with other tech-minded Trekkies, saw in the increasing power of minicomputers a way to keep the show's spirit alive. *Trek* games with varying degrees of complexity had appeared on mainframe systems in the late 60s and early 70s, copied, shared, and improved ad hoc like most other early programs. Today it's hard to piece together the genealogy of these dozens of early games, in part because attribution and even self-attribution were rare, but also because so many of them were entitled simply *Star Trek*. While it proved difficult to capture in a game the big ideas of episodes like "The City on the Edge of Forever," easier to simulate were the tactics and strategy of ship-to-ship combat, as in the season one fan favorite "Balance of Terror" where Kirk plays cat and mouse with a Romulan commander. *Trek* also provided a ready-made frame story for a game in a time when there was little storage space or inclination to create one from scratch. But all this was academic for Mayfield, quite literally: computers were still precious resources locked away in university labs, and the sixteen-year-old had no way to access one.

Not long after the TV series ended, Mayfield saw a demonstration of *SpaceWar!* (an early and influential space combat game) on the University of California Irvine campus near his school. It used a cutting-edge CRT monitor to draw tiny vector-graphic spaceships that players could maneuver around a mostly empty screen, firing torpedoes at each other and trying to avoid the gravitational pull of a central star. It was fun, it was addictive, and it seemed like the future: most computing was still done via teletype printer, so a dynamically updating screen was a revelation. Mayfield's mind was duly blown, and he began to yearn desperately for computer access of his own. He knew connecting to a distant mainframe via teletype was within the realm of possibility—though his school was not yet doing this, others across the country were—but at first he could only daydream:

> A bunch of my other geek friends from high school and I spent a lot of hours brainstorming what we could do if we didn't have a video terminal. Since I was the only one in the group that had any knowledge of computers (little as it was), we ended up coming up with a lot of unimplementable ideas. One idea that did stick was the idea of printing a galactic map and a star map to give you some idea what to shoot at.[2]

Eventually, Mayfield arranged for remote access to the Sigma 7 mainframe at UC Irvine by borrowing an enrolled student's account (something which was not, strictly speaking, allowed). He slowly taught himself BASIC from a textbook, typing in lines one at a time on the teletype. His account had no access to permanent storage space, so at the end of each session he'd have to output his program to paper tape, carefully loading it back in the next time he wanted to work. Progress was slow. But in 1971, by the end of the summer after his senior year, he'd managed to make himself a

Trek game that struck a surprisingly mature balance between playability and complexity.

Originally bearing no title but *STAR TREK*, Mayfield's game puts you in command of the *Enterprise* and tasks you with hunting down Klingons spread throughout the galaxy, represented by an 8 x 8 grid of 64 quadrants. Each quadrant in turn encloses 64 sectors, resulting in a map with 4,096 possible positions. Each quadrant has a handful of stars, which serve as cover for Klingons and obstacles for navigation. Some quadrants have a starbase where the Enterprise can restock photon torpedoes and recover the energy expended to power her warp drive and shields. The goal is to find the Klingons and defeat them all within thirty stardates. On the map, * marks a star and <*> is your ship.

```
-----------------------------------
                <*>              STARDATE           2004
                                 CONDITION          GREEN
           *                     QUADRANT            1 , 4
                                 SECTOR              1 , 4
      *               *          PHOTON TORPEDOES    9
           *                     TOTAL ENERGY        2602
                *                SHIELDS              300
                                 KLINGONS REMAINING  8
   *
-----------------------------------
COMMAND? LRS
LONG RANGE SCAN FOR QUADRANT 1 , 4
-------------------
: *** : *** : *** :
-------------------
: 004 : 006 : 007 :
-------------------
: 005 : 001 : 004 :
-------------------
COMMAND? NAV
COURSE (0-9)? 8.5
WARP FACTOR (0-8)? 2
DAMAGE CONTROL REPORT:   SHORT RANGE SENSORS DAMAGED
NOW ENTERING DENEB II QUADRANT . . .
COMBAT AREA        CONDITION RED
*** SHORT RANGE SENSORS ARE OUT ***
COMMAND? PHA
PHASERS LOCKED ON TARGET;   ENERGY AVAILABLE = 2276 UNITS
NUMBER OF UNITS TO FIRE? 500
  264 UNIT HIT ON KLINGON AT SECTOR 1 , 8
    (SENSORS SHOW 23.480438 UNITS REMAINING)
  17 UNIT HIT ON ENTERPRISE FROM SECTOR 1 , 8
      <SHIELDS DOWN TO 283 UNITS>
COMMAND? PHA
PHASERS LOCKED ON TARGET;   ENERGY AVAILABLE = 1776 UNITS
NUMBER OF UNITS TO FIRE? 200
  145 UNIT HIT ON KLINGON AT SECTOR 1 , 8
*** KLINGON DESTROYED ***
COMMAND?
```

Transcripts are from the 1975 release. Mayfield's original looks similar but with more condensed formatting and terser messages, making it harder to follow without reprinting the full instructions. Commands in both versions were explained in a lengthy block of instructions text players were expected to read before playing: one of the earliest computer game manuals.

see **1975** and **2006**

see **1973** and **1972**

The map—printed out with all other text on the user's teletype—was an early example of what would later be called ASCII graphics, where characters of text are placed in a grid to create primitive visuals. The coming genre of roguelikes would turn this into a well-recognized aesthetic. But more fundamentally, the design of Mayfield's game presaged roguelikes through its use of random generation and increased potential for emergent strategy. Eight different commands let you control the engines, shields, phasers, photon torpedoes, short- and long-range scanners, damage control, and a library computer. Most commands take additional parameters: how much energy to transfer to shields, which computer commands to access, or what speed and direction to feed into the warp drive (using a numbered cardinal rose printed in the instructions). Fractional values let players fine-tune movement in or between quadrants—with enough precision, you can warp halfway across the galaxy and arrive in the perfect position for an attack. The combinatorial space of commands feels refreshingly larger than in earlier games like *Hunt the Wumpus* or *ROCKET*, and the galactic grid that must be explored and scanned to hunt down the enemy creates a sense of danger and discovery. Ship systems can be damaged by taking enemy fire or overusing the warp engines, and each kind of damage offers different trade-offs for deciding whether to keep hunting baddies or sacrifice time finding a starbase for repairs.

Executing most plans in the game requires a series of steps, which enhances the illusion of commanding a complex starship and not just an asterisk. Finding the scattered Klingons, for instance, means deploying your library computer and both types of scanners. Long-range scans show the quadrants surrounding your present location with a three-digit code you must learn to decipher: 114 would signify a quadrant with one Klingon, one starbase, and four stars. When you warp to a quadrant with an enemy, after diverting some energy to your shields you might need to decide between using phasers or torpedoes, each with different strategic considerations. You can spend a variable amount of energy on a phaser shot, which can hit multiple enemies regardless of positioning, but the damage varies based on distance, randomness, and the strength of their shields. Torpedoes, however, always destroy a single enemy outright, but they need line of sight, so you might need to maneuver around a star and open yourself up to counterattacks before firing. You must also calculate the proper trajectory to fire a torpedo or learn how to use the library computer to calculate it for you, manually inputting its suggested parameters. Playing Mayfield's *Trek* required reading the manual and paying attention. It suggested a level of seriousness and focus rarely seen in earlier computer games.

The game's code deployed a number of clever hacks to work around the severe limitations of early BASIC. Storing a map with thousands of locations was impossible given the memory available to students at the time, so rather than keeping the randomly generated contents of each quadrant in a two-dimensional array, this data is lossily compressed into the same three-digit numeric code revealed by the long-range scanners. When a sector is entered, the appropriate number of stars and Klingons are distributed on the sector map at random. This sleight of hand works in large part because you rarely have cause to enter the same quadrant twice. If you do, it's usually because you had to flee from an enemy, and it makes sense for them to be in a different position once you return. Most players would be unlikely to notice that the stars had moved too.

COMPUTER RECORD OF GALAXY FOR QUADRANT 6, 5

	1	2	3	4	5	6	7	8
1	0	0	0	0	0	0	0	0
2	0	0	0	0	0	0	0	0
3	0	0	0	0	7	1	8	0
4	0	0	0	0	7	6	7	0
5	0	0	0	0	6	8	8	0
6	0	0	0	0	0	0	4	2
7	0	0	0	0	0	0	3	8
8	0	0	0	0	0			

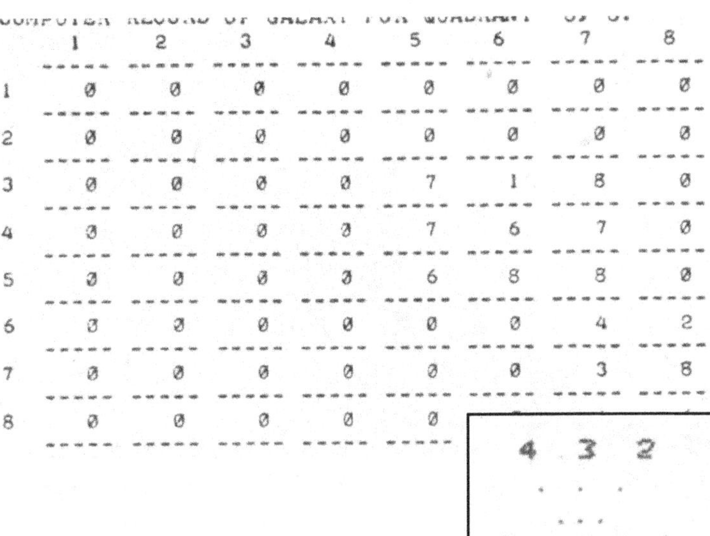

The galactic map (top) of an early game from a sample run in *Creative Computing* May/June 1975, showing the 8 x 8 grid of quadrants; 0s indicate most have not yet been explored. Inset: the compass rose printed in the instructions, used for directional navigation.

At the same time, the code is filled with hints betraying its "learn as you go" origins, with various features of HP2000C BASIC used once or twice as if to try them out, then abandoned. The program defines exactly one function (a relatively new concept in BASIC at the time) and only uses it twice, instead relying on traditional GOSUB and RETURN blocks for the bulk of its reusable code. An 8 x 8 array stores the three-digit quadrant signature, but the current quadrant's contents are tracked with a much hackier method, possibly written earlier. It works by rendering the current quadrant's map image into three strings Q$, R$, and S$. (Because of a 72-character limit for string variables, three of them are needed to store the contents of a grid containing 64 areas, each three characters wide.) Checking positions or updating the map happens by laboriously calculating which set of three characters in which string correspond to the X, Y coordinates in question. Here's the code (circa 1973) to update the sector at Z1, Z2 with the map symbol stored in A$, picking through each of those partial map arrays Q$, R$, and S$ to find the one with the 3-character block it's looking for:

```
5520   S8=Z1*24+Z2*3-26
5530   IF S8>72 THEN 5560
5540   Q$[S8,S8+2]=A$
5550   GOTO 5600
5560   IF S8>144 THEN 5590
5570   R$[S8-72,S8-70]=A$
5580   GOTO 5600
5590   S$[S8-144,S8-142]=A$
5600   RETURN
```

Mayfield's code is representative of the challenges of writing complex programs in early BASIC, with variable names limited to a single letter and optional number, no distinction between global and local variables, and no way to give code blocks meaningful names. While BASIC was a big step up from earlier languages, working out what an unfamiliar program did was often a difficult chore. And yet this was part of the fun for early hackers, who loved to sit down with a listing for an interesting program and figure out, line by line, how it worked.

As Mayfield's *Trek* passed through various hands during the 70s, it was updated to new versions of BASIC or enhanced with extra features. The most well-known revision was by Bob Leedom, a professional coder at Westinghouse working on their Data General Nova line of minicomputers. Leedom worked on and off throughout 1974 on an updated *Trek* that left most of Mayfield's core systems and gameplay intact, but added a few nice touches that gave the game more polish and dynamism. His version replaced the original's numeric commands with three-letter codes (like `LRS` for long-range scan, or `NAV` to engage the engines) reminiscent of the cryptic buttons from the onboard computer system the Apollo astronauts had used. He added better instructions and punched up the in-game messages. (Mayfield's text for a torpedo intersecting a star—YOU CAN'T DESTROY STARS SILLY— was replaced with the somewhat more mature and immersive STAR AT 7,3 ABSORBED TORPEDO ENERGY.) Blowing up a starbase in the original simply removes it from the map; in Leedom's version it results in Starfleet considering a court-martial. Many status reports and error messages were rewritten as if the show's famous bridge crew were relaying them. Trying to warp off the edge of the map in Leedom's version results in:

```
LT. UHURA REPORTS MESSAGE FROM STARFLEET COMMAND:
  'PERMISSION TO ATTEMPT CROSSING OF GALACTIC PERIMETER
  IS HEREBY *DENIED*.  SHUT DOWN YOUR ENGINES.'
CHIEF ENGINEER SCOTT REPORTS  'WARP ENGINES SHUT DOWN
  AT SECTOR 8,2 OF QUADRANT 7,8.'
```

Leedom also gave the game's numbered quadrants evocative names like RIGEL IV, added helpful functions to the library computer, and made Klingons move to a random position after being fired on (rather than waiting around for you to line up a torpedo shot, like sitting ducks). The tweaks went a long way toward increasing the fun factor of Mayfield's original, while preserving its successful core gameplay.

```
DAMAGE CONTROL REPORT:  PHOTON TUBES REPAIR COMPLETED.
NOW ENTERING POLLUX II QUADRANT . . .
COMBAT AREA       CONDITION RED
   SHIELDS DANGEROUSLY LOW
-----------------------------------
        *   +K+      *              STARDATE           3115
                                    CONDITION          *RED*
                        *           QUADRANT           8 , 2
      *  <*>                        SECTOR             4 , 3
                                    PHOTON TORPEDOES   4
                                    TOTAL ENERGY       1866
                *                   SHIELDS            0
        *                           KLINGONS REMAINING 4
-----------------------------------
COMMAND? SHE
ENERGY AVAILABLE = 1866 NUMBER OF UNITS TO SHIELDS? 500
DEFLECTOR CONTROL ROOM REPORT:
  'SHIELDS NOW AT 500 UNITS PER YOUR COMMAND.'
COMMAND? COM
```

```
COMPUTER ACTIVE AND AWAITING COMMAND? 2
FROM ENTERPRISE TO KLINGON BATTLE CRUISER
DIRECTION = 2.6666665
DISTANCE = 3.1622777
COMMAND? TOR
PHOTON TORPEDO COURSE (1-9)? 2.6
TORPEDO TRACK:
            3 , 3
            2 , 4
            1 , 4
*** KLINGON DESTROYED ***
COMMAND?
```

Leedom's improved program was published by David H. Ahl in *Creative Computing* magazine under the name *Super Star Trek*, to differentiate it from earlier versions, and later appeared in the bestselling book *BASIC Computer Games*, cementing its place as the best-known *Trek* game of the decade. Countless other spin-offs and improvements continued to proliferate, rarely crediting the original authors. A two-player version called *WAR* evolved into the multiplayer *DECWAR* [Jeff Potter and Bob Hysick 1978], and later into the popular *MegaWars* [1983] strategy series on CompuServe. A version called *Apple Trek* [Apple Computer 1979] came out for the Apple II; Radio Shack released a series called *Space Trek* [Instant Software 1978] for the TRS-80 and Tandy. A more involved enhancement that added 3D combat against a moving starfield appeared from Atari in 1979's *Star Raiders*; widely recognized as one of the platform's breakout titles; it would directly inspire later games like *Elite* [Acornsoft 1984] and *Wing Commander* [Origin Systems 1990] that defined space combat sims for a generation. Paramount's own officially licensed *Trek* games—once it got around to releasing some—would never have a remotely equivalent impact.

Super Star Trek was not the most literary nor the most complex *Trek* game of the decade. A 1973 version by William K. Char, for instance, featured extensive dialogue from the bridge crew and dozens of commands to do things like jettison the warp core or try obscure strategies from the original show, like Kirk's Corbomite Maneuver. There were plenty of other *Trek*s floating around at all levels of complexity, many of which have since been lost to bit rot or neglect. But Mayfield and Leedom's program settled into its role as the standard in part by occupying a useful middle ground: it was complex enough to be interesting, but short enough to be printed in a magazine or book, in an era when that was still the best way to distribute software. As the longest program in *BASIC Computer Games*, at about five hundred lines of code without the instructions, it required a smaller font than other listings, bordering on illegibility. But it fit. Had it been much longer, it might have been deemed too difficult to include and would never have reached a wider audience.

This would be neither the first nor last time that technical limitations restricted the upper bounds of a text game's complexity, but *Super Star Trek* provided one of the final examples of a case where those limits—page counts and print size—would have been understandable to a creator from an earlier century. Games were soon to boldly go where no book printer had gone before.

References

1 Ahl, David H., Robert Leedom, and Mike Mayfield. 1975. "Super Star Trek." *Creative Computing*, Jun 1975.

2 Markowitz, Maury. 2013. "Star Trek." Games of Fame. Apr 28, 2013. gamesoffame.wordpress.com/star-trek | a Jun 22, 2020

3 Mayfield, Mike. 1973. "SPACWR." In *101 BASIC Computer Games*, ed. David H. Ahl, 201–4. Digital Equipment Corporation.

4 Mayfield, Mike, and Robert Leedom. 1978. "Super Star Trek." In *BASIC Computer Games*, ed. David H. Ahl, 157–63. New York: Workman Publishing.

5 Pappas, Lee. 1981. "Five Star Treks, Count 'Em, Five!" *A.N.A.L.O.G. 400/800*, Feb 1981.

6 Reed, Aaron A. 2020. "Code Archaeology with 'Super Star Trek.'" *Aaron A. Reed's Medium Blog*. Jun 25, 2020. medium.com/@aareed/code-archaeology-with-super-star-trek-928101eb010c | a Jun 25, 2020

7 Rubin, Brian. 2011. "Star Trek (1971) - Boldly Going Where No Game Had Gone Before." *Space Game Junkie* (blog). Oct 17, 2011. www.spacegamejunkie.com/reviews/star-trek-1971-boldly-going-where-no-game-had-gone-before | a Jun 22, 2020

8 Turnbull, Pete. 2005. "Star Trek." dunnington.u-net.com. Mar 26, 2005. www.dunnington.u-net.com/public/startrek | s Jul 19, 2012

9 Veeneman, Dan. 2010. "Hewlett-Packard HP 2000 Time Shared Basic." Decode Systems. Jul 16, 2010. www.decodesystems.com/hp2000 | a Jun 22, 2020

DND

Gary Whisenhunt, Ray Wood, Dirk Pellett, and Flint Pellett

Also Known As **The Game of Dungeons, Whisenwood Dungeon**

Style **Roguelike**

Debuted **Likely Fall 1975**[14] *(PLATO)*

Launch Platform **PLATO IV**

Language **Tutor**

A CURIOUS HIGH SCHOOLER pushes open the door to a university computer lab late one wintry night, tipped off at a party about something interesting happening on campus:

> The room lights were off. Cigarette smoke thick in the air, the ceiling disappeared in the gloom. Odd metal boxlike structures lined the room…. Dozens of people in the room, sitting in groups of twos and threes, hunched over each of the boxes, their faces weirdly lit with a strange orange glow coming from some sort of non-TV screen on the front of each box. Surreal as hell, never seen the like. Doing things with some sort of typewriter keyboard, pointing at the screens, laughing and yelling instructions at each other. Suddenly somebody nearby yelled, "Got 'im!" and simultaneously across the room somebody else yelled, "Damn it!" Games! They're playing *games*![6]

The room was filled with PLATO IV terminals, and few people in the 1970s had seen anything like them. Far ahead of their time, the machines featured

1975

Major Releases

» **Mar 4, 1975,** Whisenhunt and Wood. Earliest timestamp on a related code file; may have been when development began. Early versions had only two dungeon levels.

» **Fall 1975.** Likely the first version publicly available on PLATO.

» **May 1976.** Earliest attested printout of source code. The Pelletts join the team.

» **2.0,** Aug 1976. The Orb and transporters existed by this version.

» **2.8,** Oct 1976. Over 100,000 players.

» **5.4,** Jun 12, 1977. Many new features existed by this point, including stashing. Earliest surviving playable version as of this writing.

» **6.0,** 1977. Additional monsters and new magic items.

» **8.0,** 1978. Added new dungeons "The Caverns" and "Tomb of Doom," a grail guarded by a vampire, more magical effects and variety.

All game excerpts herein are from version 5.4.

plasma touch screens with 512×512 resolution, capable of displaying text in custom fonts and images in sharp-edged orange vector graphics—years before CRTs were common, when most computer interfaces were still based on typewriters. Thousands of PLATO terminals in classrooms across the country had been networked into a single shared environment with message boards and chat, twenty years before the web. And PLATO programs were written in a unique language called Tutor that made it far easier to write software—especially software with graphics—than any other common language of the time.

Funded by a huge government grant dating back to post-Sputnik fears that America was losing its science and education supremacy, PLATO had been developed at the University of Illinois at Urbana-Champaign across a decade of radical experimentation and widening deployment first to Midwestern universities, then to schools around the country. By the 1972 launch of PLATO IV, the platform had grown into a sophisticated multi-user network designed for students and teachers, rather than for specialists and hackers. Naturally, it wasn't long before the students started figuring out how to make the thing play games.

The earliest PLATO games were single-player, education-focused "lessons," as the platform was designed to enable. But within months, illicit lessons like *Moonwar* [Louis A. Bloomfield 1972] and *Empire* [John Daleske 1973] were linking players in massive and increasingly complex multiplayer battles. Running on 1260 baud modems, the PLATO terminals took long seconds to update their screens but were built to be immediately responsive to keystrokes, allowing expert players to furiously key in commands a dozen moves ahead of what their slowly updating display could show. The creators of the games were usually young—some still in high school—and they found many clever hacks to speed up gameplay or improve it. Someone figured out that the terminals' built-in microfiche slide reader could be activated even if no slides were loaded,

> causing the mechanism to shake and make sounds, even illuminate the slide projector's lamp…. Run the code in a loop, and you could get the machine to shake and rumble like a deranged washing machine on spin cycle, along with bright flashes of light as a spaceship exploded.[6]

Since PLATO was designed for lay learners, access at most computer labs was open to all, with few locked doors or password-protected accounts. Often anyone could walk in off the street and sit down at a terminal. But as games proliferated and labs began turning into ad hoc LAN parties, adults started locking down access. This deterred the newborn gamers not at all. Kids started sneaking into computer labs after hours for all-night *Empire* tournaments, having pizzas delivered through windows, going to extreme lengths to secure a weekend of play:

> My friends and I roamed all about the university campus in search of unrestricted PLATO terminals…. [One] lab closed around 8 p.m. Friday, but what they didn't know was the back wall of the cubicles along the back wall of the lab had been unscrewed and set in place. You could pull back this wall and crawl behind it, wait for the lab to clear out, and be

locked up for the weekend.

  … Every now and then, twenty or so minutes prior to the lab closing you'd pull the cubicle wall back and find someone else already hiding inside. Both of you there for the same purpose, neither wanting to lose the option or be called out, you just made room and hung out silently together.[6]

Empire and many other early games were inspired by *Star Trek*—the show had been off the air for five years by 1974 but was still a dominant force in geek culture. But a new challenger appeared that year in the form of *Dungeons & Dragons*. Like PLATO, *D&D* was originally a Midwestern phenomenon, debuting on the wargaming tables of Gary Gygax in Wisconsin and Dave Arneson in Minnesota. The game made its first big appearances at Gygax's Gen Con in Lake Geneva, an afternoon's drive from PLATO's home in Urbana. Within months of the 1974 Gen Con, *D&D*'s first print run of a thousand copies had sold out, with demand continuing to grow. The age of the fantasy roleplaying game had arrived. Soon PLATO was flooded with a glut of games filled with magic, dragons, and dungeons, most of them close adaptations of the tabletop hit.

see **1974**

While tabletop roleplaying would eventually become better known for its focus on, well, *roleplaying*, the hobby's earliest rulebooks can surprise modern readers with how mechanical their gameplay seems. First edition *D&D*'s only example of play, for instance, begins like this:

> REF: Steps down to the east.
> CAL: We're going down.
> REF: 10′, 20′, 30′—a 10′ square landing—steps down to the north and curving down southeast.
> CAL: Take those to the southeast.
> REF: 10′, and the steps curve more to the south; 20′. Steps end, and you are on a 10′ wide passage which runs east, southeast, and west. There is a door to your left across the passage on a northwest wall.
> CAL: Listen at the door—three of us.
> REF: (After rolling three dice) You hear nothing. (At this time a check for wandering monsters is also made.)
> CAL: Ignore the door and proceed along the corridor southeastwards.
> REF: 10′, 20′, 30′, 40′, 50′. "Four way": Northwest, northeast, south and southwest—the south passage is 20′ wide.
> CAL: Go south.[8]

REF here means *referee* (the role later known as dungeon master), and CAL means *caller*, a holdover term from wargaming where it was common for a single player to interface between the referee and the rest of the group.

The rulebook even suggests using "random determination" to distribute monsters and treasures through an underworld map. It's not surprising that so many people familiar with both the first *D&D* and the first computers started thinking about how easily one could digitize dungeon adventures.

see, among others, Will Crowther **1976**

  Within months of *D&D*'s arrival at Midwestern colleges, plans for elaborate digital versions were underway. Many collapsed under their own ambitions. The earliest surviving example of a dungeon game was created by someone sick of waiting for more complex programs to be finished. During the summer of 1975, an Urbana-Champaign employee named Rusty Rutherford wrote a basic PLATO *D&D* game called *The Dungeon*. It didn't try to do multiplayer, generate dozens of unique maps, or implement all the spells in the rulebook. It focused instead on one tight slice of the *D&D*

experience: a hero trapped in a maze of rooms and corridors, fighting an endless barrage of monsters.

Games on other contemporary systems were slowly spitting out uppercase characters on noisy printers, but PLATO's revolutionary display could show all kinds of lettering as well as graphical sprites. Rutherford's dungeon game had twelve of these icons, including a treasure chest and a selection of monsters from giant rats to skeletons—and, of course, a dragon. Given a character with stats generated completely at random, the player explored a map using the WAXD keys (an already-established convention for cursor movement on PLATO). Only the immediate surroundings were drawn around the hero sprite, who stayed stationary in the middle of the screen while the walls and hallways were redrawn around them after each move. The single-level dungeon had a fixed map, but monsters and treasure were randomly placed each game. The randomness could be unforgiving: your first step could collide you with a powerful monster and instantly kill you. But *The Dungeon* was *D&D* on a computer, simplified but playable. Within weeks it became wildly popular.

By 1975, PLATO's gamer subculture had become an increasing irritant to those who thought the expensive computers should be used for education. An archive of the network's electronic message board (one of the world's first) contains dozens of annoyed rants about gamers, including this gem from that August:

```
What has happened during the preceding weeks is that chilren
[sic] of unspecified ages spend their days at cerl playing
games. This is not to say that I necessarily disapprove of
playing games, but in the case of these children, concomitant
with playing is the issuing of loud, disgusting noises
of the following nature: "brrrrr...bang bang...kapow" or
"aieee I have a level six dragon...help...help...HELP..."
What do I care? I am busy trying to do some work which
requires particular attention to detail and these constant
expectorations make any attempt to do so almost impossible.
[...] SOMETHING HAS TO BE DONE.15
```

Some complainants took matters into their own hands:

```
sabotaged as many games as i could find after the morons using
them refused to stop after repeated requests via message ....
the games have not been destroyed but a "stop*" command has
been inserted in the first block of each ....15
```

Administrators tried various techniques to appease the antigamers, from enforced noise ordinances to banning games during school hours or outright deleting any they found on the system. Rutherford's *The Dungeon* was more commonly known by its covert file name *pedit5*—the last allocated lesson name (and thus least likely to be needed) in a block given to the Population and Energy group. An antigame sysadmin was less likely to axe a program with such an innocent-sounding title. But the camouflage was short-lived: *pedit5* soon became a known time waster and candidate for deletion. Rutherford had to recreate the program from scratch at least once, and to retype it from a saved printout on other occasions.

CERL was the Computer-based Education Research Laboratory on the Urbana-Champaign campus; PLATO had largely been developed there.

PLATO terminals had no local storage, disk drives, or printer ports, so backing up your code was tricky. A user could request a code printout for pickup at the program's University of Illinois office. If you lived out of the area, and asked very nicely, you could sometimes get one mailed to you instead.

1975

It was these deletions that motivated two students at nearby Southern Illinois University, Gary Whisenhunt and Ray Wood, to finish up their own long-in-development dungeon crawler. The two had a serious advantage over Rutherford. Unlike at his school, SIU had only a single PLATO terminal, which Whisenhunt had become the admin for after showing far more interest than the faculty member assigned to it. The two called their program *The Game of Dungeons*, and with no risk of deletion they brazenly stored it under the lesson name *dnd*—though in 1975, to those not in the know, this was as esoteric a set of letters as *pedit5*.

Like Rutherford's game, *dnd* was directly inspired by *D&D*, stealing attributes, mechanics, spells, and monsters from its tabletop parent. It took *The Dungeon*'s basic framework and added significant depth to its gameplay, now taking place in the named setting of Whisenwood Dungeon (a portmanteau of the authors' names). One key improvement came in character creation: given a randomly generated character with four of *D&D*'s six stats plus Hits for hit points, you could reroll until you got a hero more likely to make it past the first fight.

```
    Shift-BACK for records
    LAB to reroll
    BACK for previous values
    NEXT to take these values


Strength      17
Intelligence  8
Wisdom        12
Dexterity     9
Hits          6


[NEXT]


What is thy name? > Lordar


Warrior's secret name? >
```

The secret name was essentially a password, letting you return to the same character later; your public name appeared in-game and on the title screen's hall of fame. After making a character, you're dumped at the entrance of a dungeon that would eventually consist of twenty levels. As in *pedit5*, the WAXD keys move you through a maze of corridors and rooms filled with treasure and monsters. While Rutherford's game labeled areas CORRIDOR or ROOM, *dnd* renders its maze only with lines, saving text for status reports or noteworthy events:

```
You found $220 in gold!
```

```
No door there
```

Tellingly, it would be a long time before a computer *D&D* would make use of the Charisma stat: social interaction has always been one of the hardest things to simulate in software.

Among PLATO's many unusual features was a custom keyboard designed to make navigation through lessons more friendly. After typing the name of a program from PLATO's main menu, for instance, rather than hitting ENTER you might press DATA to run it; NEXT to edit it; or LAB to inspect it.

Unlike later dungeon games with increasingly cluttered interfaces, character stats and other info appear only with special keystrokes, leaving the view immersively unadulterated during play. Things get slightly more complicated during combat:

```
            Level 2
              Spectre


fight, evade, magic
or cleric (f,e,m,c) > M

1. Fireball
2. Lightning Bolt
3. Flaming Arrow
4. Eye of Newt
5. Kitchen Sink
6. Sleep
7. Charm

Which spell > 7

The Spectre is not amused. Press NEXT to fight   | NEXT |
________________________________________________________

You were number 1326 for  Spectres
```

This last message indicates the player has been killed (and is the 1,326th victim of spectres since the game's memory was last reset). While combat calculations happened with much of the same complexity as tabletop *D&D*—taking into account monster and player stats, spells in effect, and equipment worn—in *dnd*, this math all happens behind the scenes. (Showing too many numbers might have made the game feel too much like the lessons its creators were trying to avoid.) As in *The Dungeon*, death meant permadeath, with no choice but to roll up a new character and enter the dungeon again.

While some PLATO dungeon games followed *D&D*'s rules obsessively, *dnd* keeps its tongue more in cheek, with joke spells like Kitchen Sink. (You can also cast Dispell and Datspell.) There are inside jokes, like a monster apparently named after a particular obnoxious freshman. Whimsical little epilogues appear when you defeat a monster: "Swiss Cheese!" "Fried it!" "Eat 'em Alive!" The lighthearted humor and rapid demise of characters formed an addictive loop that would become a key draw for dungeon games of future decades. "I've fed 145 characters into the dungeon so far," one modern *dnd* player wrote. "I'm writing this at 3am, but I think I've got time for just one game before bed."[10]

By early 1976, Rutherford had moved on and *pedit5* had been deleted for good, but Whisenhunt and Wood continued to maintain *dnd*, which soon eclipsed its predecessor's popularity. That year an Iowa State student named Dirk Pellett became obsessed with the game, sending in so many suggestions and bug reports ("a few hundred," in his recollection[12]) that the authors gave him edit access and told him to knock himself out. Soon Dirk's brother Flint joined the team, and the two expanded the game significantly over the next few years, adding magic items and potions, books, pits and transporters, more dungeon levels, and even unique items:

> Among the new items was the Genie Lamp ... in a desperate situation the player could wish themselves out of the dungeon.... Another use for the Genie was making a wish to the game operators, by term-comment to write a note [to the game's admins]. The Genie Lamp could be exchanged for nearly anything that could be granted: more hits, a different item, a few levels, and so on.
>
> ... Gerhard Lueschen, a friend of the game authors, once made a wish: "I wish I was an author." He meant, of course, being added as a game author. Instead, the Genie granted his wish: for a week, one book in five found in the dungeon by anyone was "The Life and Times of Gerhard Lueschen, by himself."[12]

dnd was more fair than *pedit5*, with monster strength scaled by dungeon level and more predictable strategy. But it was still brutally hard and seemingly endless. The game eventually gained an explicit goal: reaching the lowermost dungeon level to retrieve "the almighty **ORB**, which makes the holder (you) so invincible that when you get it out, you must be retired to the Elyssian Fields." But the orb is guarded by "the deadliest monster in the dungeon: The Dragon!" who "has been known to cause as many as 100,000 hits of damage."

If you don't count the Wumpus **1973**, the Dragon is one of the earliest end bosses in videogame history.

This was orders of magnitude more Hits than players began with, but they could gain more. In tabletop *D&D*'s original edition, when plundered gold coins were taken out of a dungeon they earned experience points that players could use to level up. *dnd* simplified this by converting gold brought back to the dungeon entrance directly into more hit points and spell slots. But the

The hero of *dnd* at a hallway junction (below); sprites for enemies (top right and opposite).

more gold you're carrying, the more likely monsters are to attack you, so deciding when to turn back becomes a delicate balance between tedium and risk. Winning requires a long and careful grind, playing boldly enough that the gold-to-hits conversion isn't interminably slow, but carefully enough to avoid a fatal random encounter. The game offers many other temptations balancing risk and reward, from teleporters zipping you to more dangerous levels, to immensely powerful but potentially trapped magic items.

```
Magic ring! Now:
pick it up,
leave it,
clerically examine,
visually examine > v
Too dark to tell!> p


You were number 2318 for  The Dungeon
```

The game could take hundreds of hours to beat. By the end of 1976, according to Dirk Pellett, Whisenwood Dungeon had claimed the virtual lives of over 100,000 characters. If this number is accurate, it's a telling testament to *dnd*'s addictiveness, since only a few thousand PLATO IV terminals existed in the world—some of which were presumably still used for teaching, on occasion.

The Pelletts continued improving *dnd*, but spin-offs and competitors multiplied. A saved copy of the deleted *pedit5* was resurrected under the name *Orthanc* by Urbana-Champaign student Paul Resch, who adapted and improved it with a handful of collaborators. *Orthanc* featured a dungeon that would reconfigure itself every 180 days, an updated interface that kept more stats visible on-screen, and limited multiplayer support (you could meet other people exploring the dungeon and chat with them—or kill them). Foreshadowing a common pattern in later games, "higher-level players took to hanging around the entrance and killing lower-level players for the experience,"[3] leading Resch to remove player combat on the dungeon's first level. He also found it odd that lots of folks who met in the dungeon "just talked to each other, even though you could do that anywhere on PLATO." The magic of inhabiting a shared virtual space with other humans would soon become a massively popular obsession.

A game called *Moria* by Iowa State student Kevet Duncombe also appeared in late 1975 or early 1976. Duncombe's game changed the top-down perspective to a first-person view, one of the earliest games to do so. It also featured more sophisticated multiplayer that let you form a party with up to ten other players, and was "one of the first multiplayer games with a persistent game world, where events and actions continued to take place even when the player was not playing."[17] *Moria*'s maps were massive; writing of just the game's starting city, one player recalled that he "lost two characters to starvation just mapping the damn thing."[11] In the city you could chat with

see **1980** and **1990**

Maze [Steve Colley et al. 1973] for the less popular Imlac PDS-1 system, and *Spasim* [Jim Bowery 1974] on PLATO, were a few other early examples.

1975

shopkeepers to buy or sell items, ask limited questions about their wares, or even haggle.[6]

```
Which item, Sire?
>sword
Buying, eh, Sire? Well, how's about $134?
>how's about $40
$40? Can't accept that! How's about $128?
>$90
Deal at $90, then?
>no $70
Offer is too low, Sire!
Deal at $90, then?
>yeah, whatever
What a bargain, Sire!
```

See *Trade Wars* **1991** for more on the lineage of haggling mechanics in text games.

The surprisingly tolerant parser came from a feature of the Tutor language designed to accept answers in quizzes. With a single line of code, the helpful `answer` command let authors recognize multiple possible responses and even fuzzy-match keywords catching typos or misspellings, a feature most text games would still lack decades later.

```
at       805
write    Who was the third president of the United States?
arrow    1003
answer   <T,Thomas> Jefferson
write    That's right!
wrong    <J,John> Adams
write    He was the second president.
endarrow
```

"To borrow a term from linguistics, I'd probably have to call [Tutor] a 'language isolate,'" PLATO systems programmer Paul Koning has said. "It's the programming analog of Basque. In other words, there really isn't anything like it that I can think of."[6] Designed to allow nontechnical teachers to make interactive lessons, Tutor made a lot of classically fiddly interface and structure problems simple. Text and graphics could be easily positioned anywhere on the screen, for instance, even at different sizes or rotations. Affordances to parse text input, record progress, and integrate interaction with other students were also all easy to invoke—and these features were put to good use by PLATO's budding game designers.

The games kept evolving. *Moria* inspired 1977's *Oubliette* [Jim Schwaiger et

Screenshot from *Moria*, descendant of *dnd* and ancestor of later hit series *Wizardry*. **Note Wizardry is one of the stats listed on the right.**

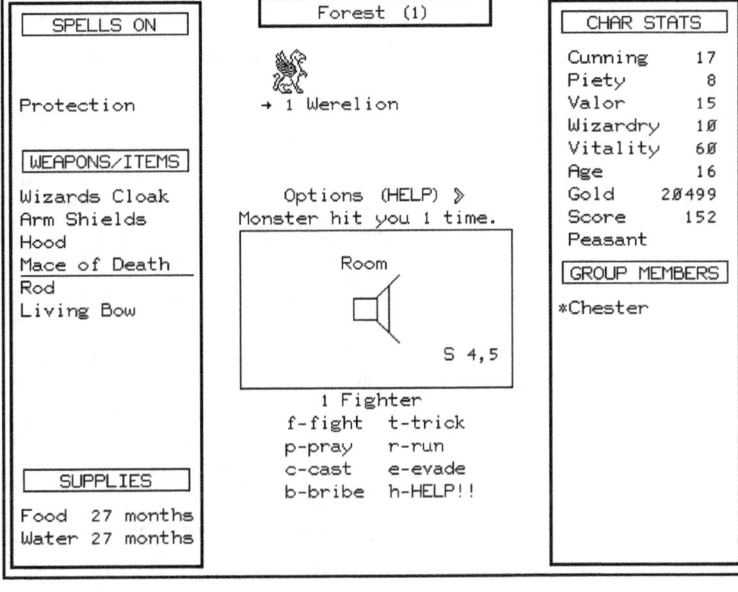

al.], another first-person multiplayer game with taverns where you could meet other players to adventure with. It would in turn inspire *Wizardry* [Sir-Tech 1981], kicking off a successful and long-running franchise of influential computer roleplaying games. A different thread of inspiration starts with a port of *dnd* to the PDP-10 by Daniel Lawrence, which evolved into 1982's *Telengard*, another influential early CRPG. *Oubliette* and other PLATO games inspired the extraordinarily ambitious *Avatar* [Bruce Maggs et al. 1979]—years in the making, it would come to feature elaborate multiplayer interaction, guilds, randomly generated quests, a huge array of items and spells, and a dynamic economy.

see **1980**

The PLATO dungeon games were the earliest examples of genres that later games would name, like *Rogue* [Michael Toy et al. 1980] and *MUD*. They were online multiplayer roleplaying games before most people had heard the word "online," or even realized games could be played on a computer. But PLATO was an island unto itself: with a few exceptions, the games created for it died with their proprietary platform. The PLATO network and the expanding ARPANET were incompatible, unable to connect to each other, and the system's isolate design of 6-bit bytes and proprietary keyboards kept its software from easily making the leap to newer platforms. Most of the innovations from its generation of early game makers would have to be rediscovered and reinvented by others, years later.

But those who experienced the Friendly Orange Glow, as Brian Dear titled his book on the influence of PLATO,[6] never forgot it. They lived the coming future of real-time interactive games a decade or more before it arrived for anyone else. In the 2020s, a graying band of enthusiasts still keeps a handful of PLATO servers running, along with emulators that let modern computers reach them. Some can even simulate the speed of a modem connecting at 1260 baud. The hosts of one server, cyber1, promise that connecting "will feel like coming home again" to those who grew up with PLATO—even if no modern computer can quite recapture the experience of a hundred-pound plasma screen flashing bulbs in your eyes and rumbling like a damaged appliance, as some jerk three rows over cackles like a maniac.

References

1   Barton, Matt. 2008. "Breaking News: Author of PEDIT5 Speaks Out!" *Armchair Arcade* (blog). Aug 31, 2008. armchairarcade.com/neo/node/1948 | s Jul 7, 2011

2   Bolingbrok, Chester. 2019. "Revisiting: The Game of Dungeons (1975)." *The CRPG Addict* (blog). Jan 27, 2019. crpgaddict.blogspot.com/2019/01/revisiting-game-of-dungeons-1975.html | a Aug 14, 2020

3   Bolingbrok, Chester. 2013. "Game 123: Orthanc (1975)." *The CRPG Addict* (blog). Nov 11, 2013. crpgaddict.blogspot.com/2013/11/game-123-orthanc-1977.html | a Aug 14, 2020

4   Bolingbrok, Chester. 2019. "The Final Word on Daniel Lawrence's DND." *The CRPG Addict* (blog). Feb 16, 2019. crpgaddict.blogspot.com/2019/02/the-final-word-on-daniel-lawrences-dnd.html | a Aug 14, 2020

5   Daleske, John. n.d. "Daleske Space - History of Computing - PLATO System - Games - Social Media." daleske.com. daleske.com/index.php | a Aug 14, 2020

6   Dear, Brian. 2017. *The Friendly Orange Glow: The Untold Story of the Rise of Cyberculture*. New York: Vintage.

7   "Games of Chance." 2013. *EDGE* #255, July 2013, p. 80-5.

8   Gygax, Gary, and Dave Arneson. 1974. *Dungeons & Dragons*. 1st ed. 3 vols. Lake Geneva: Tactical Studies

1975

Rules.

9   Olivetti, Justin. 2013. "The Game Archaeologist: The PLATO MMOs, Part 2." *Engadget* (blog). Aug 17, 2013. www.engadget.com/2013-08-17-the-game-archaeologist-the-plato-mmos-part-2.html | a Aug 14, 2020

10   Mahney, Nathan P. 2014. "Game 2: The Game of Dungeons (aka dnd) v5.4 (1975)." *CRPG Adventures* (blog). May 7, 2014. crpgadventures.blogspot.com/2014/05/the-game-of-dungeons-aka-dnd-1975.html | a Aug 14, 2020

11   Mahney, Nathan P. 2015. "Game 4: Moria (1975)." *CRPG Adventures* (blog). Apr 14, 2015. crpgadventures.blogspot.com/2015/04/moria-1975_14.html | a Aug 14, 2020

12   Pellett, Dirk. n.d. "The History of dnd." In-game essay, *dnd* v8.0 (as presented on cyber1.org server). Accessed Aug 1, 2020.

13   Pellett, Dirk. n.d. "Gary Whisenhunt, Ray Wood, Dirk Pellett, and Flint Pellett's DND." Dirk Pellett's WWW Home Page. www.armory.com/~dlp/dnd1.html | a Aug 14, 2020

14   Reed, Aaron A. 2021. "On the Dating of Two Early CRPGs: pedit5 and dnd." *Aaron A. Reed's Medium Blog*. Feb 3, 2021. medium.com/@aareed/on-the-dating-of-two-early-crpgs-pedit5-and-dnd-47538d68f712 | a Mar 16 2022.

15   University of Illinois Archives. 1972. "PLATO System Notes Files." archon.library.illinois.edu/?p=digitallibrary/digitalcontent&id=7132 | a Aug 14, 2020

16   Whisenhunt, Gary, Ray Wood, Dirk Pellett, and Flint Pellett. 2012. "Interview with the creators of dnd (PLATO)." Interview by Carey. RPG Fanatic. www.rpgfanatic.net/advanced_game_wiki_database.html?p=news&nrid=5049&game=dnd | s Oct 27, 2013

17   Williams, Andrew. 2017. *History of Digital Games: Developments in Art, Design and Interaction*. Boca Raton: CRC Press.

ADVENTURE

Will Crowther and Don Woods

Also Known As	**ADVENT, Colossal Cave Adventure**
Style	**Parser**
Debuted	**Early 1976** *(ARPANET)*
Launch Platform	**PDP-10**
Language	**Fortran IV**

> **❝** YOU ARE STANDING AT THE END OF A ROAD
> BEFORE A SMALL BRICK BUILDING . AROUND
> YOU IS A FOREST. A SMALL STREAM FLOWS OUT OF
> THE BUILDING AND DOWN A GULLY.

"It was the hour of insomniacs," begins a chapter in Tracy Kidder's book *The Soul of a New Machine*,[8] a snapshot of hacker culture at the end of the 70s. The author has been taken into a basement computer lab after hours to play *Adventure*, something of a rite of passage.

> Strewn before me across the surface of his desk, like the relics of a party, lay dozens of roughly drawn maps. They consisted of circles, inside of which were scrawled names such as Dirty Passage, Hall of Mists, Hall of the Mountain King, Complex Junction, Splendid Chamber, Bedquilt, and Witts End. Webs of lines connected the circles, and each line was labeled, some with points of the compass, some with the words *up* and *down.* Here and there on the maps were notations—"water here," "oil here," and "damn that pirate!" In the midst of all this paper sat Alsing's computer terminal. On the screen of the tube in white letters, like the little voice that whispers in a wild gambler's ear, this message stood:

ARE YOU SURE YOU WANT TO QUIT NOW?

Major Versions

» **Unfinished original**, Will Crowther, 1976.

» **250-point version**, Don Woods, April 1977. Area beyond troll bridge has an "under construction" sign; this may have been the version that influenced *Zork*.

» **350-point version** (canonical), Don Woods, Jun 3, 1977.

» **430-point version**, Don Woods, 1978. Five new treasures, other additions.

» **Microsoft Adventure**, TRS-80, Jun 1979.

» **550-point version**, David Platt, 1979.

» **Atari Adventure**, Warren Robinett, 1980. Graphical remake loosely inspired by the original.

» **Apple Adventure!**, Apple II, 1980.

» **The Original Adventure**, Software Toolworks, Heath/ Zenith; CP/M, 1982. Only commercial version that paid royalties to Crowther and Woods.

» **Colossal Adventure**, Level 9, MS-DOS, 1983. Added basic graphics.

» **Colossal Cave 3D Adventure**, Cygnus Entertainment, PC/Quest 2, 2023 (planned). VR remake by Sierra On-Line co-founders Ken & Roberta Williams.

In May 1977, *Adventure* became the first computer game blockbuster. While older hits like *Hunt the Wumpus* **1973** or *Super Star Trek* **1974** had trickled out slowly through in-person meetups, mail-order paper tape, and listings in magazines—and others like *dnd* **1975** were confined to niche platforms—*Adventure* arrived just as a critical mass of computer users began connecting to ARPANET, precursor to the modern internet. As a result, it hit everywhere all at once, shared and reshared from one system to the next, and soon became all anyone with computer access was talking about. A famous anecdote goes that the game proved so distracting it "set the entire computer industry back two weeks."[1] Dave Lebling, later a co-founder of Infocom **1977**, recalled: "For a couple of weeks, dozens of people were playing the game and feeding each other clues. Everyone was asking you in the hallway if you had gotten past the snake yet."[4] It would eventually name both the text adventure and graphical adventure game genres. At the time of its release, few people had seen anything like it.

Adventure begins with a description of a forested hill, written in second person as if you are the one there seeing it. Rather than choosing from a list of available options, as in nearly every previous game, the player is invited to type free-form one- or two-word English commands. I WILL BE YOUR EYES AND HANDS, the instructions say: DIRECT ME. Game designer Andrew Plotkin has noted the significance of this novel paradigm: "The help text didn't offer these commands as a menu, or even as suggestions. You discovered them. The exploration of the game world was the exploration of the parser; it was guided by the game's narrative and the player's sense of what was possible."[7] It's hard to appreciate today what a radical notion this once was.

As you begin to explore, you find a small building, a lamp, a set of keys, and the locked entrance to a cave. While earlier games like *Wumpus* or *Trek* let players move through simulated spaces, they were described mostly with numbers, such as grid coordinates or phrases like YOU'RE IN ROOM # 4. In *Adventure*, each location is unique and brought to vivid life with prose:

```
YOU ARE IN A 20 FOOT DEPRESSION FLOORED WITH BARE DIRT. SET
INTO THE DIRT IS A STRONG STEEL GRATE MOUNTED IN CONCRETE.
A DRY STREAMBED LEADS INTO THE DEPRESSION.

THE GRATE IS LOCKED.

UNLOCK GRATE

THE GRATE IS NOW UNLOCKED.

ENTER

YOU ARE IN A SMALL CHAMBER BENEATH A 3X3 STEEL GRATE TO THE
SURFACE. A LOW CRAWL OVER COBBLES LEADS INWARD TO THE WEST.

THE GRATE IS OPEN.
```

```
GO WEST

YOU ARE CRAWLING OVER COBBLES IN A LOW PASSAGE. THERE IS A
DIM LIGHT AT THE EAST END OF THE PASSAGE.

THERE IS A SMALL WICKER CAGE DISCARDED NEARBY.

GET CAGE

OK

WEST

IT IS NOW PITCH BLACK. IF YOU PROCEED YOU WILL LIKELY FALL
INTO A PIT.

LIGHT LAMP

YOUR LAMP IS NOW ON.

YOU ARE IN A DEBRIS ROOM, FILLED WITH STUFF WASHED IN
FROM THE SURFACE. A LOW WIDE PASSAGE WITH COBBLES BECOMES
PLUGGED WITH MUD AND DEBRIS HERE, BUT AN AWKWARD CANYON
LEADS UPWARD AND WEST. A NOTE ON THE WALL SAYS 'MAGIC WORD
XYZZY'.
```

For each long room description, *Adventure* also defines a one-line summary printed when you return to a location (like YOU'RE IN DEBRIS ROOM). When originally played, room descriptions were printed on teletypes; the brief recap literally saved paper. But the convention would become established in later traditions of screen-based text adventures, eventually standardizing into the bolded room name **(Debris Room)** which many modern text adventures still use.

While *Adventure*'s cave is sprinkled with magic words, treasures, and fantastical creatures, it's the compelling descriptions of a realistic cave that are most often remembered. The text transports the player to another place with an immediacy few games had then achieved:

```
YOU ARE AT ONE END OF A VAST HALL STRETCHING FORWARD OUT
OF SIGHT TO THE WEST. THERE ARE OPENINGS TO EITHER SIDE.
NEARBY, A WIDE STONE STAIRCASE LEADS DOWNWARD. THE HALL IS
FILLED WITH WISPS OF WHITE MIST SWAYING TO AND FRO ALMOST
AS IF ALIVE. A COLD WIND BLOWS UP THE STAIRCASE. THERE IS A
PASSAGE AT THE TOP OF A DOME BEHIND YOU
```

The text feels convincing because it was drawn from life. Will Crowther and his wife, Patricia, were avid cavers. After courting as MIT undergraduates in the 1950s, they spent their honeymoon getting lost in Virginia's Breathing Cave. Both had been physics majors who found careers as computer programmers. In the early 70s they'd gotten involved with some cavers in Kentucky on a decades-long quest to connect two adjacent, enormous cave systems. Patricia was instrumental in a culminating 1972 expedition that found the final connection; the small, wiry woman could slip through a tiny squeeze too narrow for any of the men on the trip to attempt. The newly unified Mammoth Cave system, with hundreds of miles of interconnected passages, became the largest in the world. In 1974, while raising two young daughters, the Crowthers embarked on an extensive survey of Colossal Cave (now just another part of Mammoth), producing

While Crowther began work on his *D&D*-inspired game just as the creators of *dnd* **1975** were releasing theirs, the two had no knowledge of each others' work: the ARPANET and PDP ecosystem were almost completely isolated from the world of PLATO's educational network.

an official map of the area near the cave's Bedquilt entrance—as in the game, a steel grate mounted in concrete, set at the bottom of a twenty-foot depression, surrounded by forest.

The Crowthers wrote code to convert hard-won three-dimensional survey data into maps that could be plotted on the equipment at Will's office. Ironically, his day job involved connecting networks too. He'd been a crucial member of a team at the research firm BBN that developed a key part of ARPANET, the hardware and code that would become the world's first network routers. A quiet but brilliant coder, Crowther was "loving the fact that people paid me for playing" with new technology and systems. In a 1990 interview he described his time on ARPANET as "just another one—another fun puzzle. I was willing to do an almost unlimited number of those."[11]

Then, in 1975, everything changed. Will and Pat separated; their two girls stayed with their mom. Pat continued caving, and after the divorce she remarried to a fellow member of her famous final connection expedition. Will dropped out of the caving group and the hobby. He started looking for a new job. While he has rarely spoken about his personal life, he said much later with quiet understatement that he had felt "a bit pulled apart in various ways" that year.[13]

Perhaps to fill some of his unexpected spare time, he joined in on a new tabletop game some of his coworkers were playing called *Dungeons & Dragons*, released the previous year. The group's dungeon master had created a detailed campaign set in Tolkien's Middle-earth, with adventures that mostly took place underground in ancient tunnels and dungeons beneath Mirkwood. Crowther, unlike the other players, named his character after himself: Willie the Thief. The game's focus on mapping and exploration may have been a way of scratching a now-forbidden itch.

Like many other computer users of the time, he began to idly wonder if something like *D&D* could be made on the computer. In the fall of 1975, he decided to try. The impetus may have been an upcoming school holiday when his daughters would be visiting for a long weekend. In a flurry of coding, he wrote the core of a game that would let them, too, explore a cave like their mom and dad. He based the layout on the Bedquilt area he and Pat had mapped so thoroughly, and he borrowed the framework of a dungeon master describing the world and responding to the player's actions—a user interface so simple, even a child could grasp it. Writing dense, uncommented code (his usual style) from a teletype hooked into the PDP-10 mainframe at the office, within a few weeks Crowther had created the outlines of a game called *Adventure*.

The girls were enchanted. Like any good dungeon master, the game hinted at a larger world and greater secrets, even if that was often to disguise its limitations. For example, the command `LOOK` describes the location, but typing it again in the same spot prints `SORRY, BUT I AM NOT ALLOWED TO GIVE MORE DETAIL`—as if by design, not necessity. Unlike most earlier games, *Adventure* responded to commands that didn't change its state but existed purely for color or increased immersion, creating the pleasing illusion of a storyteller on the other end of the chattering terminal. Typing

ENTER STREAM, for instance, does not change your position, but the reply is
YOUR FEET ARE NOW WET.

Crowther gave the game obstacles to overcome so there was more to do
than just explore. Some were obvious (the keys open the locked grate) and
others less so, including the relationship between a bird and a dangerous
snake. It would even offer hints if it detected you were stuck, again like a
helpful dungeon master: ARE YOU TRYING TO CATCH THE BIRD? Or,
after observing the player type cardinal directions a few times, it might
reply: IF YOU PREFER, SIMPLY TYPE W RATHER THAN WEST. *Adventure*
went to great lengths to create the illusion of a conversation, but unlike with
the chatbot *ELIZA*, this was a conversation connected to an underlying
simulation of places, objects, and obstacles. Though limited—only a
prototype—it created a virtual world with a working interface that required
no technical skills to use.

see **1966**

```
YOU ARE IN A LOW N/S PASSAGE AT A HOLE IN THE FLOOR.
THE HOLE GOES DOWN TO AN E/W PASSAGE.

THERE ARE BARS OF SILVER HERE!

GET SILVER

OK

DOWN

YOU ARE IN A DIRTY BROKEN PASSAGE. TO THE EAST IS A CRAWL.
TO THE WEST IS A LARGE PASSAGE. ABOVE YOU IS A HOLE TO
ANOTHER PASSAGE.

E

YOU ARE ON THE BRINK OF A SMALL CLEAN CLIMBABLE PIT.
A CRAWL LEADS WEST.

D

YOU ARE IN THE BOTTOM OF A SMALL PIT WITH A LITTLE STREAM,
WHICH ENTERS AND EXITS THROUGH TINY SLITS.

A LITTLE DWARF JUST WALKED AROUND A CORNER, SAW YOU, THREW
A LITTLE AXE AT YOU WHICH MISSED, CURSED, AND RAN AWAY.

GET AXE

OK
```

Crowther kept improving the game between his daughters' visits, so he'd
always have new bits for them to play. He showed it off to his *D&D* friends
at work, too, though for a different reason: "Will was very proud—or more
accurately amused—of how well he could fool people into thinking that

there was some very complex AI behind the game."[6] Much like *ELIZA*, Crowther's game reveled in the illusion of an intelligence typing back those words on your printer. It's a fantasy we might compare to much older traditions like epistolary literature or puppetry—the magical sense that behind the façade is something real. It's no accident that both chatbots and parser interactive fiction would remain enchanting for decades to come, and that half a century later we're just as entranced by the possibilities of "virtual humans" and text-generating artificial intelligences.

But once Crowther had pulled off the magic trick, delighting daughters and coworkers alike, he had little interest in expanding or perfecting it. By early 1976 he'd abandoned the game about caving, along with other pieces of his old life. ARPANET had been declared officially operational. He'd accepted a job at Xerox PARC across the country in California. He and Pat were not getting back together. He was turning forty. It must have seemed time to turn the page and move on. But before he logged out of his BBN account for the last time, he did something typical for hackers used to a culture of freely sharing programs, a simple act that would have a profound impact on the history of computer games: he put the unfinished *Adventure* in a public folder, where anyone browsing the network could find it.

One year later, twenty-two-year-old Stanford grad student Don Woods stumbled across Crowther's program and became intrigued. Though the game was rough around the edges, Woods saw tremendous potential, and he started to think of ways to extend and complete it (perhaps as a distraction from those first-year graduate courses). But the version he had was only an executable—there was no source code, which meant it couldn't be modified, and it wasn't even clear who had created it. Never really expecting anyone other than his BBN coworkers to peek at it, Crowther had left only a single, cryptic message in the instructions hinting at his program's provenance:

```
(ERRORS, SUGGESTIONS, COMPLAINTS TO CROWTHER)
```

What happened next is one of computer history's most charming stories— both a revealing time capsule of how small the early internet could be and a testament to Woods's outside-the-box approach to problem-solving (which had doubtless drawn him to the game in the first place):

> The game mentioned Crowther as its author, so I sent mail to crowther@ xxx for all hosts xxx on the Internet, which in those days was still very small.… I got back several error messages from sites that had no person by that name, but did eventually hear from Crowther, who … sent me the source for his program.[14]

Armed with the source code, Woods first figured out exactly how it worked, adding extensive documentation and comments explaining Crowther's labyrinthine algorithms. Then he began to revise and expand it. He dramatically increased the size of the game, adding many new rooms, treasures, puzzles, and enemies. He added a scoring system and a way to win (finding all the treasures and returning them aboveground). He made the game smarter by extending the range of inputs it could respond to. He also made it more practical to play by adding the ability to save, restore, and

see *AI Dungeon* **2019**

Historian Jimmy Maher suggests that in the process, Woods may also have become the first email spammer.[10]

restrict the hours during which it was available (vital to prevent sysadmins of the time from deleting it outright).

Woods also made Crowther's unfinished experiment into a more consistent simulation. The original featured a bottle of water you could drink, but Woods extended it to work as a general container for different kinds of liquids that could be filled and emptied at appropriate places, now used in multiple puzzles. He fleshed out dropped threads and unresolved teases in the game's descriptions—both versions include a room where THERE ARE HOLES ALL OVER, BUT THE ONLY BIG ONE IS ON THE WALL DIRECTLY OVER THE EAST PIT WHERE YOU CAN'T GET TO IT, but only in the Woods version does this foreshadow a new area you can actually reach. Crowther's magic word XYZZY was a testing shortcut to jump straight into the cave, but Woods invented a more consistent system of magic words that implied an underlying fictional logic. While Crowther's game was a clever hack, Woods made it closer to a working engine, a consistent simulation of a fictional space that could sensibly respond to a player's exploration.

Part of the workings of that engine, sketched out by Crowther but more fully exercised by Woods, was a cleaner separation between code and data. In part because of Fortran's limited string-handling functionality, Crowther had put most of the game's text in an external data file that the main program could read from when it needed to print room descriptions, player vocabulary, item names, and incidental messages. Scanning through this file gives an impression of the way the game simulates a fictional world, and how it's capable of responding to a range of attempts to interact with it.

```
104 YOU HAVE NOTHING IN WHICH TO CARRY IT.
105 YOUR BOTTLE IS ALREADY FULL.
106 THERE IS NOTHING HERE WITH WHICH TO FILL THE BOTTLE.
107 YOUR BOTTLE IS NOW FULL OF WATER.
108 YOUR BOTTLE IS NOW FULL OF OIL.
109 YOU CAN'T FILL THAT.
110 DON'T BE RIDICULOUS!
```

But, significantly, the data file contains not just the text but much of the logic for when to display it. Rows of numbers that Woods dubbed the "travel table" specify how to respond to typing certain words in certain rooms, either by printing a piece of text or moving the player to a new location. Take, for instance, this travel table line:

```
1    2    2    44    29
```

These numbers meant that *from* Location 1 (End of Road), *move to* Location 2 (Hill) *if* the player's input contains a word from any of vocab lists 2 ("road", "hill"), 44 ("w", "west"), or 29 ("above", "ascend"). The syntax could also describe conditional logic, such as restricting movement when the right object wasn't carried or the wrong flag was set. This meant much of the setting could be created solely from its data file, without needing new Fortran code or a recompile of the original program—in theory, at least. In practice, *Adventure*'s code has special-case exceptions all over the place to enable

One of several bits of *Adventure* that would become interactive fiction shibboleths, along with brass lanterns, treasure hunts, and twisty little passages.

Woods' version has over 200 such messages, and understands 319 unique words for 186 distinct concepts. Sometimes its vocabulary is surprisingly broad: to pick up an object, you can type CARRY, TAKE, KEEP, CATCH, STEAL, CAPTURE, GET, or TOTE.

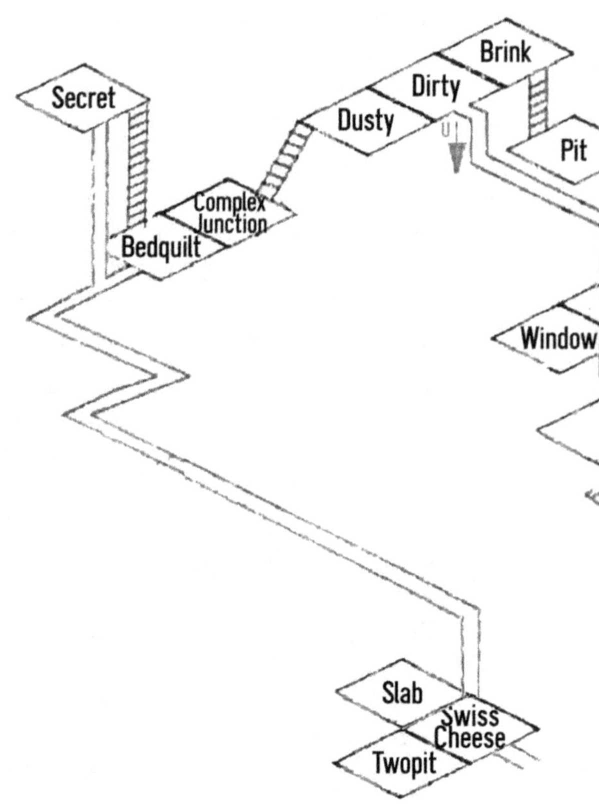

Secret
Brink
Dirty
Dusty
Pit
Complex
Junction
Bedquilt
Window
Slab
Swiss
Cheese
Twopit

Will Crowther's original 1976 version of Adventure.

Modified from an unattributed map at rickadams.org. Omits some dead ends and redundant connections for clarity.

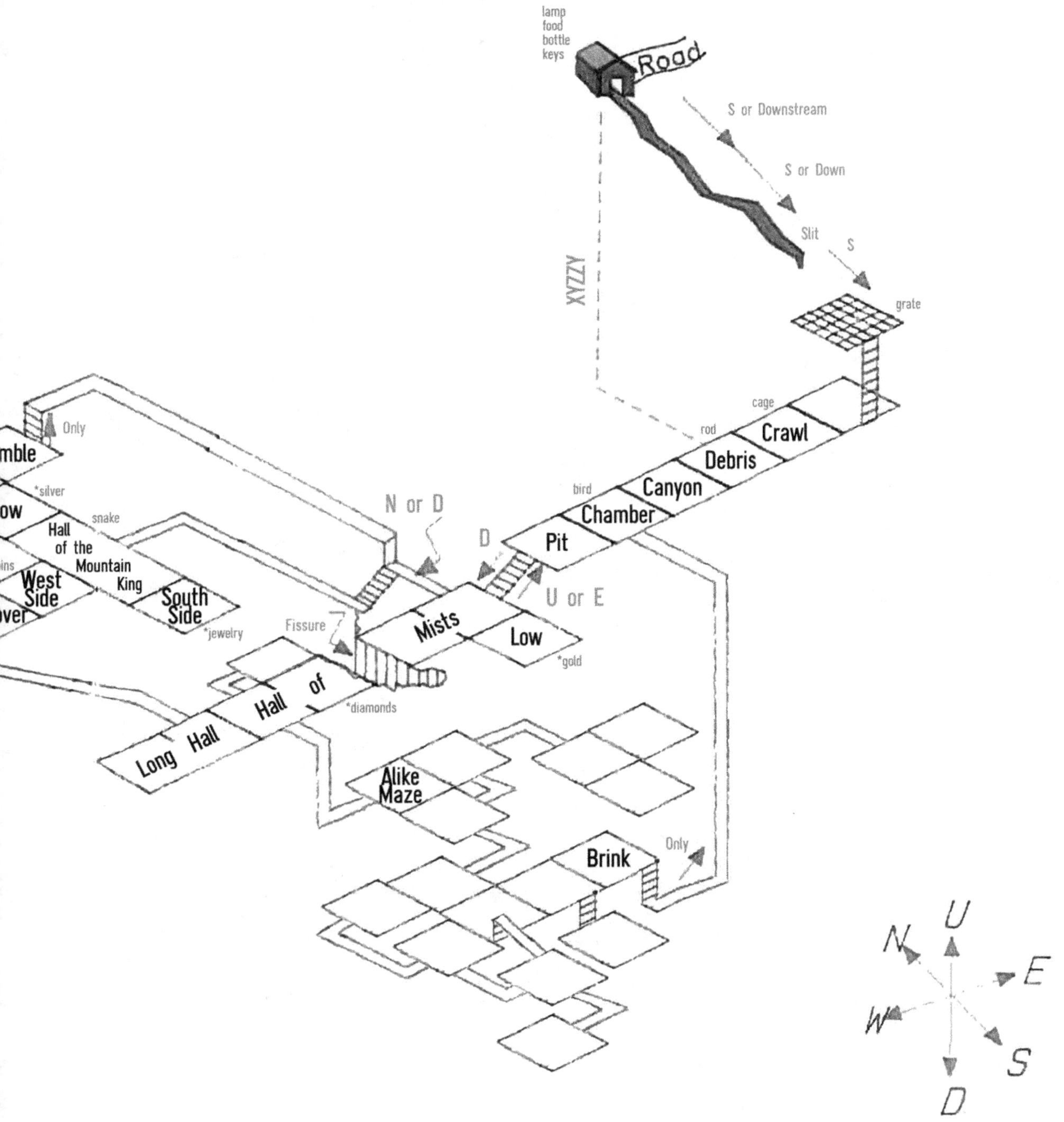

lamp
food
bottle
keys
Road
S or Downstream
S or Down
Slit
S
grate
XYZZY
cage
Crawl
rod
Debris
Canyon
bird
Chamber
Only
mble
*silver
snake
N or D
ow
Hall
of the
Mountain
King
D
Pit
ins
West
Side
South
Side
U or E
ver
*jewelry
Fissure
Mists
Low
*gold
*diamonds
Hall of
Long Hall
Alike
Maze
Brink
Only
N
U
E
W
S
D

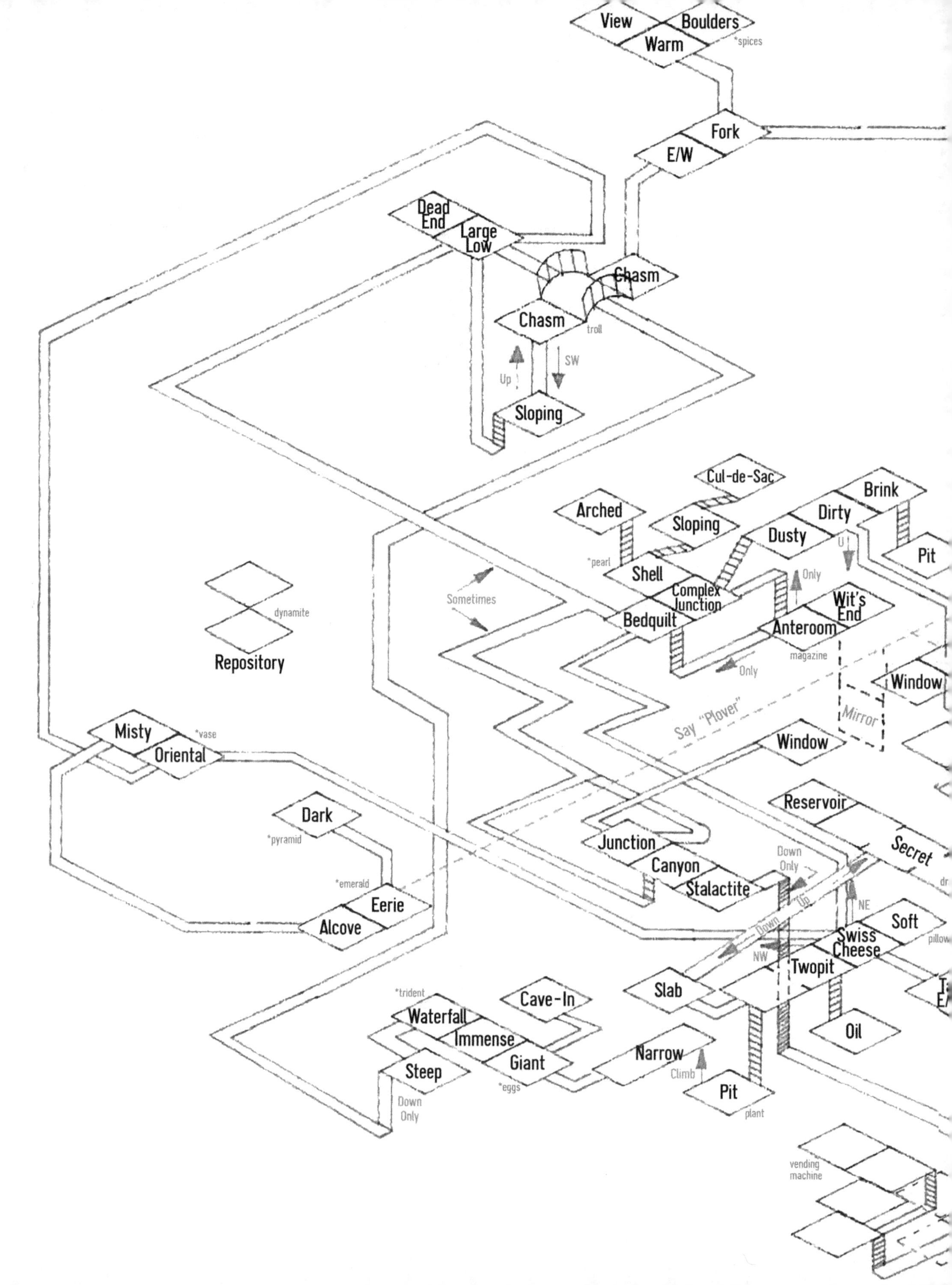

View
Boulders
*spices
Warm
Fork
E/W
Dead End
Large Low
Chasm
Chasm
troll
Up
SW
Sloping
Cul-de-Sac
Brink
Arched
Sloping
Dirty
Dusty
Pit
*pearl
Shell
U
Complex Junction
Only
Wit's End
Bedquilt
Anteroom
magazine
Sometimes
dynamite
Only
Window
Repository
Say "Plover"
Mirror
Misty
*vase
Window
Oriental
Reservoir
Dark
Secret
*pyramid
Junction
dr
Down Only
*emerald
Canyon
Up
Eerie
Stalactite
NE
Alcove
Soft
Down
pillow
NW
Swiss Cheese
*trident
Cave-In
Twopit
Waterfall
Immense
Slab
Oil
Steep
Giant
Narrow
Down Only
*eggs
Climb
Pit
plant
vending machine

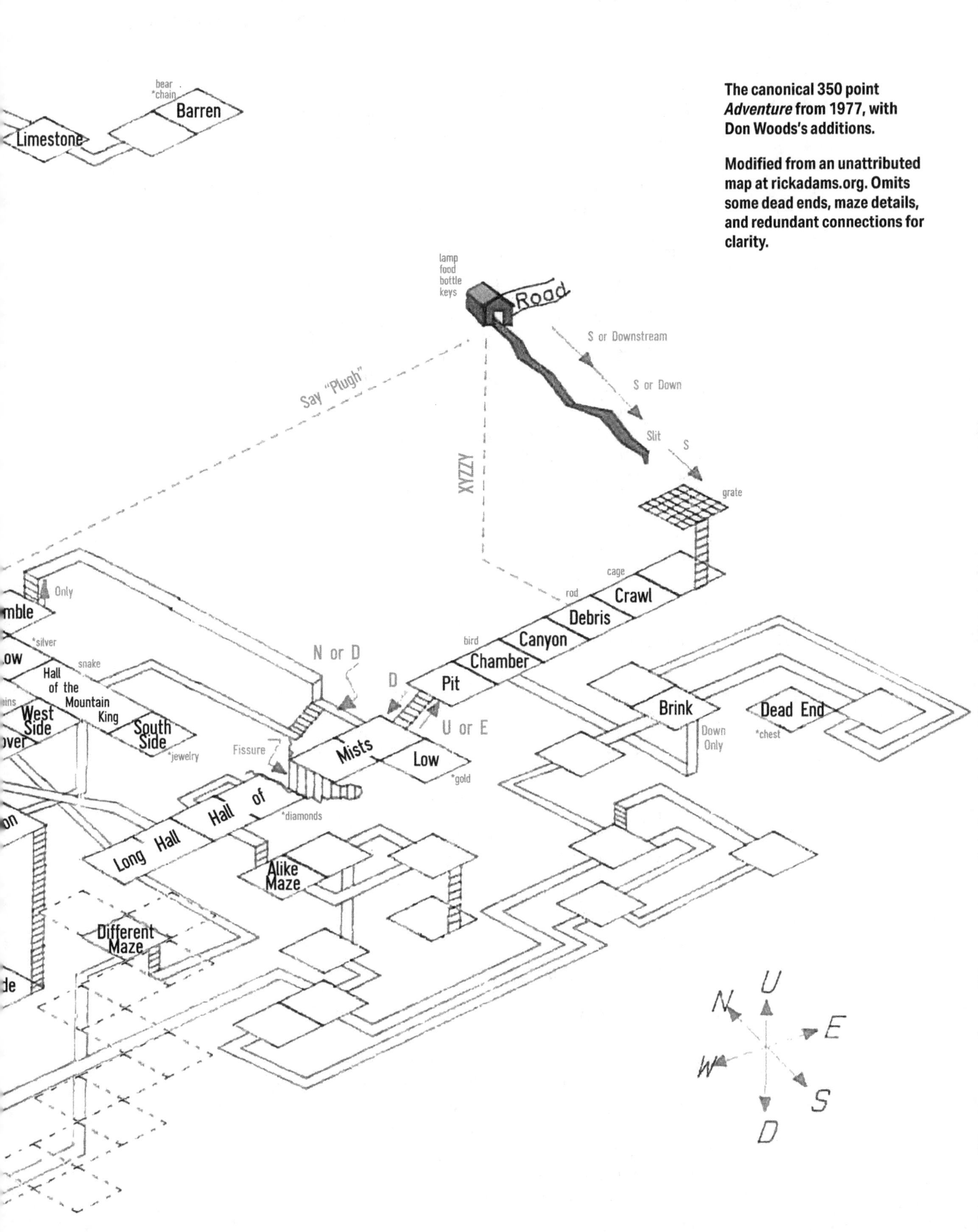

The canonical 350 point Adventure from 1977, with Don Woods's additions.

Modified from an unattributed map at rickadams.org. Omits some dead ends, maze details, and redundant connections for clarity.

Barren
Limestone
bear
*chain
lamp
food
bottle
keys
Road
S or Downstream
S or Down
Slit
S
grate
Say "Plugh"
XYZZY
Only
mble
*silver
ow
snake
Hall of the Mountain King
West Side
South Side
*jewelry
Fissure
N or D
D
Pit
Chamber
Canyon
Debris
Crawl
cage
rod
bird
Mists
Low
*gold
U or E
Brink
Dead End
*chest
Down Only
on
Long Hall
Hall of
*diamonds
Alike Maze
Different Maze
de
N
U
E
W
S
D

much of its interesting behavior. But the separation of concerns suggested the intriguing possibility of distinguishing engine programmer from world designer, a notion that would become crucial to the genre's success in the years to come.

Adventure also included some of the first complex simulations of characters to appear in a computer game. The hostile dwarves (and one pirate) who wander the cave require over a hundred lines of code, far more than the handful devoted to Klingons or Wumpii in earlier titles. Woods's comments go some way toward revealing the complexities of their behavior:

```
FIRST OFF, DON'T LET THE DWARVES FOLLOW HIM INTO A PIT OR
A WALL. ACTIVATE THE WHOLE MESS THE FIRST TIME HE GETS AS
FAR AS THE HALL OF MISTS (LOC 15). IF NEWLOC IS FORBIDDEN
TO PIRATE (IN PARTICULAR, IF IT'S BEYOND THE TROLL BRIDGE),
BYPASS DWARF STUFF. THAT WAY PIRATE CAN'T STEAL RETURN TOLL,
AND DWARVES CAN'T MEET THE BEAR. ALSO MEANS DWARVES WON'T
FOLLOW HIM INTO DEAD END IN MAZE, BUT C'EST LA VIE. THEY'LL
WAIT FOR HIM OUTSIDE THE DEAD END. [...] MOVE EACH DWARF AT
RANDOM, EXCEPT IF HE'S SEEN US HE STICKS WITH US. DWARVES
NEVER GO TO LOCS <15. IF WANDERING AT RANDOM, THEY DON'T
BACK UP UNLESS THERE'S NO ALTERNATIVE. IF THEY DON'T HAVE
TO MOVE, THEY ATTACK. AND, OF COURSE, DEAD DWARVES DON'T DO
MUCH OF ANYTHING.
```

Crowther's code was quite dense. His uncommented version of the dwarf behavior (one small portion of which is shown below) is all but inscrutable to anyone not deeply embedded in the code base:

```
63    IDWARF=IDWARF+1
      ATTACK=0
      DTOT=0
      STICK=0
      DO 66 I=1,3
      IF(2*I+IDWARF.LT.8)GOTO 66
      IF(2*I+IDWARF.GT.23.AND.DSEEN(I).EQ.0)GOTO 66
      ODLOC(I)=DLOC(I)
      IF(DSEEN(I).NE.0.AND.LOC.GT.14)GOTO 65
      DLOC(I)=DTRAV(I*2+IDWARF-8)
      DSEEN(I)=0
      IF(DLOC(I).NE.LOC.AND.ODLOC(I).NE.LOC) GOTO 66
65    DSEEN(I)=1
      DLOC(I)=LOC
      DTOT=DTOT+1
      IF(ODLOC(I).NE.DLOC(I)) GOTO 66
      ATTACK=ATTACK+1
      IF(RAN(QZ).LT.0.1) STICK=STICK+1
```

But the kind of node- and state-based simulation driving *Adventure* was most effective at representing explorable spaces, not interactive characters. The game's cave is three-dimensional and complex. Passages often twist such that you leave a room to the east only to arrive in the next one from the south, or from above. One-way tunnels can drop into a new area you must find your own way out of, or may reveal a shortcut to a familiar landmark. Sometimes

All above-ground locations have IDs of less than 15.

Scholar Dennis Jerz credits Woods's extensive cleanup and documentation as a key factor in the program's later success, making it far easier to understand and thus translate to new platforms.[6]

not all connections from a room are described, or exits are collapsed into vague statements like `PASSAGES OFF IN ALL DIRECTIONS`, lending a sense of discovery to the otherwise rote task of exhausting each exit. Some exits even lead to different places each time you take them, and the teleporting magic words add another dimension to movement. Even after several sessions, the cave can remain disorienting. Like its real-world inspiration, it can only be tamed with careful, scrupulous mapping.

Winning also requires mastering two complex mazes. Crowther's original maze was ten interconnected rooms, each featuring an identical description:

Spoilers for the mazes in Adventure.

```
YOU ARE IN A MAZE OF TWISTY LITTLE PASSAGES, ALL ALIKE.
```

Moving through them, it's impossible to tell which of the ten rooms you're in, and thus how to navigate or escape—the game engenders a sense of dread by removing the information needed to traverse it. But a player who realizes they can `DROP` objects in each room can leave a path like Hansel and Gretel through this textual wilderness, differentiating the identical chambers:

```
YOU ARE IN A MAZE OF TWISTY LITTLE PASSAGES, ALL ALIKE.

THERE IS A LITTLE AXE HERE.

NORTH

YOU ARE IN A MAZE OF TWISTY LITTLE PASSAGES, ALL ALIKE.

THERE IS FOOD HERE.
```

Woods extended Crowther's maze, making it even more tangled and interconnected, but at first wasn't sure how to use the gimmick more than once. But then he hit on an idea for a second maze that took advantage of the medium of delivery. Now the words themselves would matter, not just the imagined space they represented.

```
YOU ARE IN A MAZE OF TWISTY LITTLE PASSAGES, ALL DIFFERENT.

E

YOU ARE IN A LITTLE TWISTY MAZE OF PASSAGES, ALL DIFFERENT.

E

YOU ARE IN A MAZE OF LITTLE TWISTY PASSAGES, ALL DIFFERENT.

N

YOU ARE IN A TWISTING LITTLE MAZE OF PASSAGES, ALL DIFFERENT.
```

The key insight this time is to look *at* the words, not through them to the space they describe. The variants aren't randomized: each is a unique signature identifying one distinct room of the maze: *TLMP* (Twisty Little Maze of Passages) is north of *MLTP* (Maze of Little Twisty Passages). Armed with this insight, the player can make a map, find the secret at the heart of the maze, and escape.

Woods added several other jokes based on wordplay, including a giant clam that turns out to have a pearl inside (after which the embarrassed narrator consistently refers to it instead as a giant oyster), and the Barren Room, which contains a bear. This kind of linguistic play is a joy unique to text games, and some of most beloved of later decades, like *The Gostak* [Carl Muckenhaupt 2001] or *Counterfeit Monkey* [Emily Short 2012], would also involve wordplay that couldn't work in any other medium.

see **1977**

Woods posted his extended version of *Adventure* back to ARPANET in the spring of 1977. By May it had become a massive hit—nearly everyone into computers at the time was playing it. Tens of thousands of players poured hours into solving the game or further extending it with their own revisions, additions, or remakes, of which *Zork* would become the most famous. In years to come, early software companies would release commercial ports to great success, rarely paying or even crediting the original designers. Crowther was surprised and somewhat bemused at his program's unexpected second life and enduring popularity, eventually coming to appreciate the irony that he'd be remembered less for helping invent the internet than for accidentally creating its first viral success.

Adventure was a clever program, but also the right program at the right time. It arrived just as regional clusters of hackers were merging into a single online community, and the tantalizing dream of home computing was becoming reality. Computers for the masses would need software regular people were excited to use, and Crowther and Woods's game became a ready-made demo. It inspired the first generation of commercial game companies and provided a template for their products. It's no exaggeration to say *Adventure* jump-started the entire computer gaming industry.

But arguably its key innovation was to demonstrate one of the most powerful illusions a computer can create: the fun of being transported to another reality. While the game industry as a whole would trend toward chasing that illusion with images more than words, the template *Adventure* provided has become one of the longest-lived models for computer games. Half a century later, people are still writing hundreds of parser interactive fiction games each year with the same basic structure as Crowther's original. Technology has changed, but the right sentence can still paint a picture in the reader's mind of unlimited resolution and perfect fidelity, and the right trick—cleverly framed and carefully coded—can lend even the simplest machine a semblance of life.

References

1   Anderson, Tim, and Stu Galley. 1985. "The History of Zork." *New Zork Times* 4 (1–3).

2   Brucker, Roger W., and Richard A. Watson. 1987. *The Longest Cave*. SIU Press.

3   Buckles, Mary Ann. 1985. "Interactive Fiction: The Computer Storygame 'Adventure.'" Dissertation, San

Diego: University of California.

4   Dyer, Richard. 1984. "Masters of the Game." *Boston Globe Magazine*, May 6, 1984. www.csd.uwo.ca/
     Infocom/Articles/globe84.html | s Feb 22, 1999

5   Hafner, Katie, and Matthew Lyon. 1998. *Where Wizards Stay up Late: The Origins of the Internet*. Simon
     and Schuster.

6   Jerz, Dennis G. 2007. "Somewhere Nearby Is Colossal Cave: Examining Will Crowther's Original
     Adventure in Code and in Kentucky." *Digital Humanities Quarterly* 001 (2).

7   Jong, Philip. 2011. "Andrew Plotkin - Interview." *Adventure Classic Gaming* (blog). Jan 7, 2011. www.
     adventureclassicgaming.com/index.php/site/interviews/622 | a Jul 26, 2020

8   Kidder, Tracy. 1981. *The Soul of a New Machine*. Little, Brown and Company.

9   Lessard, Jonathan. 2013. "Adventure before Adventure Games: A New Look at Crowther and Woods's
     Seminal Program." *Games and Culture* 8 (3): 119–35.

10 Maher, Jimmy. 2011. "The Completed Adventure, Part 1." *The Digital Antiquarian* (blog). Jun 2, 2011. www.
     filfre.net/2011/06/the-completed-adventure-part-1 | a Jul 26, 2020

11 O'Neill, Judy. 1990. "An Interview With William Crowther (OH 184)." Charles Babbage Institute. www.cbi.
     umn.edu/oh/pdf.phtml?id=97 | s Aug 21, 2002

12 Nelson, Graham. 1995. "The Craft of the Adventure: Five Articles on the Design of Adventure Games."
     Self-published. mirror.ifarchive.org/if-archive/info/Craft.Of.Adventure.pdf | a Jul 26, 2020

13 Peterson, Dale. 1983. *Genesis II: Creation and Recreation with Computers*. Reston Pub. Co.

14 Woods, Don. 2001. "Interactive Fiction? I Prefer Adventure." *L'avventura è l'avventura* (blog). June 2001.
     www.avventuretestuali.com/interviste/woods-eng | s Feb 21, 2009

ZORK

Tim Anderson, Marc Blank, Bruce Daniels, and Dave Lebling

Also Known As **Dungeon, Zork I**
Style **Parser**
Debuted **Late Jun 1977** *(ARPANET)*
Launch Platform **PDP-10**
Publisher **Infocom** *(1981 release)*
Language **MDL**

> " You are in an open field west of a big white house, with a boarded front door.
> There is a small mailbox here.

IF *ADVENTURE* INTRODUCED HACKERS to an intriguing new genre of immersive text game, *Zork* brought it to the public at large. In the early 80s, as the personal computer revolution reached into more and more homes, a *Zork* disk became a must-buy for first-time computer owners. By 1982 it had become the industry's bestselling game. *Playboy* covered it; so did *Time*. Astronaut Sally Ride was reportedly obsessed with it. In 1984 it was still consistently beating out newer games on the sales charts, including its own sequels. By the end of 1985 it was still outselling any other game for the Apple II—half a decade after its first release on the platform—and had become the bestselling title of all time on many other systems besides.

Its creation can be traced to a heady Friday in May 1977 on the MIT campus in Cambridge, Massachusetts. It was the last day of finals week, and summer was kicking off with a bang for the school's cohort of tech-obsessed engineers. A new movie called *Star Wars* opened that week in theaters, the groundbreaking Apple II was beginning to ship to eager hobbyists, and

see **1976**

"We have to do something better [than *Adventure*]," Dave Lebling recalled years later of the attitude around the lab at the time. "The honor of MIT is at stake."[8] When the team was profiled for a 1983 *Washington Post* article, the author dryly noted of the rivalry between MIT and Stanford that "American programming primacy is split like the medieval papacy between Cambridge and the West Coast."[25]

Adventure was exploding across the terminals of computer labs nationwide, with thousands of students having no further distractions, at last, to keep them from solving it.

Among those obsessive players were four friends at a campus research lab, the Dynamic Modeling Group. Within two weeks they'd solved *Adventure*, squeezing out every last point through meticulous play and, eventually, the surgical deployment of a machine-language debugger. Once the game was definitively solved, they immediately hatched plans to make something better—not only to prove the superiority of their school's coding prowess over Don Woods at Stanford (though that was undoubtedly part of it), nor simply because many were dragging their feet on graduating or finding jobs, and a challenging new distraction seemed immensely appealing (though that was part of it, too). The most important factor was that *Adventure* had been so incredibly *fun*, and regrettably, there wasn't any more of it. "It was like reading a Sherlock Holmes story," one player recalled, "and you wanted to read another one of them immediately. Only there wasn't one, because nobody had written it."[4]

The four friends were an eclectic group of grad students ranging in age from twenty-two to twenty-eight, united by shared sensibilities and a love of hacking. Dave Lebling had a political science degree and had started programming only because of an accidental hole in his freshman schedule. A "voracious reader"[21] and "frustrated writer,"[25] he'd helped design *Maze* in 1973, one of the earliest graphical exploration games and first-person shooters. Marc Blank was young, tall, thin, and technically enrolled in med school, but found messing around with computers an addictive distraction. Bruce Daniels was nearing thirty and increasingly bored with his PhD topic; while procrastinating, he'd helped develop the MDL programming language (the lab's pet project) and was always eager to find new ways of showing it off. And Tim Anderson was close to finishing his master's degree but none too excited about leaving the stimulating intellectual community at MIT. With *Adventure* solved, the four sat down to hack together a prototype for an improved version, which would also run on a PDP-10 mainframe. Needing a placeholder name for the source file, they typed in *zork*, one of many nonsense words floating around campus. (Among other uses, it could be substituted for an offensive interjection.)

The game they began to create was at first quite similar to *Adventure*, so much so that historian Jimmy Maher has noted parts of it are more remake than homage.[14] Both games begin in a forest outside a house containing supplies for an underground expedition, including food, water, and a light source with limited power; in both, you search for treasures in a vast underground cave system and score points by returning them to the building on the surface; both feature underground volcanoes, locked grates, trolls, and a "maze of twisty little passages, all alike." Hacker tropes and nods to other early text games abound, like a huge bat that whisks you off to another location like in *Hunt the Wumpus*. But as *Zork* expanded it began to develop its own character: less realistic than the caverns sketched from Will Crowther's

see **1973**

1977

life experience, but also more whimsical, more threatening, and driven by an improved parser and world model.

> >OPEN TRAP DOOR
> The door reluctantly opens to reveal a rickety staircase descending into darkness.
> >DOWN
> It is pitch black. You are likely to be eaten by a grue.
> >WHAT IS A GRUE?
> The grue is a sinister, lurking presence in the dark places of the earth. Its favorite diet is adventurers, but its insatiable appetite is tempered by its fear of light. No grue has ever been seen by the light of day, and few have survived its fearsome jaws to tell the tale.

The grue would become the game's best-remembered villain, though it was originally invented as a solution to a sort of bug—not in the game's code, but in the player's suspension of disbelief. In early versions of *Zork*, as in *Adventure*, you'd fall into a bottomless pit if you tried to move through a dark room without a portable light source. But someone noticed this could happen in *Zork* even in the dark attic of the above-ground house. Lebling, stealing the word "grue" from a Jack Vance novel, invented a new and more broadly applicable threat for dark places. The next update reported wryly that the team had spent weeks filling in the dungeon's old bottomless pits.

> >LIGHT LANTERN
> The lamp is now on.
> You are in a dark and damp cellar with a narrow passageway leading east, and a crawlway to the south. On the west is the bottom of a steep metal ramp which is unclimbable.
> The trap door crashes shut, and you hear someone barring it.
> >UP
> The door is closed.
> >EAST
> You are in a small room with passages off in all directions. Bloodstains and deep scratches (perhaps made by an axe) mar the walls.
> A nasty-looking troll, brandishing a bloody axe, blocks all passages out of the room.
> The troll's axe barely misses your ear.
> Your sword has begun to glow very brightly.

The troll is easy enough to dispatch with the "elvish sword of great antiquity" found early on, which glows blue when enemies are near, à la Tolkien. A basic combat system inspired again (**1975 1976**) by *D&D* manages hits and misses of weapons, with the player's power scaling based on the number of treasures they've recovered. But *Zork*'s Great Underground Empire also features a more complex antagonist, a parallel to *Adventure*'s pirate who would pop up now and again to steal your treasure.

MAJOR RELEASES

» **Mainframe version** (originally *Zork*, then *Dungeon*, then *Zork* again), PDP-10, Jun 1977–Feb 1979.

» **Dungeon**, Bob Supnik, Fortran, Jan 1978. Released to DEC user's group; this fork later ported to C and many other languages.

» **PDP-11 version**, 1980. Briefly sold on 8-inch floppy for mainframes.

» **Zork**, Personal Software, ZIL, Z-machine/ TRS-80, Dec 1980. First commercial release for home computers, stripped down and simplified to fit in limited space; distributed in plastic baggie with 5.25" game disc and booklet.

» **Apple II release**, 1981.

» **Zork I**, Infocom, TRS-80/ Apple II, Dec 1981. First version with iconic stone-brick logo.

» **Z-machine ports** for other systems including PC DOS, Atari, and Commodore 64/128 (1983); Commodore 16 & Plus/4 and Mac (1984); Tatung Einstein and Atari ST/ STE (1985); Amstrad PCW/ CPC and Amiga (1986).

» **Version 88**, Jul 1984. Last known official revision of the ZIL source code.

» **In *Zork Trilogy***, Jan 1987. Included a zorkmid coin and other bonus feelies.

» **Zork I (Solid Gold edition)**, Dec 1987. Added built-in hints.

» **Japanese version**, SystemSoft, NEC PC-9801, 1991.

» **Enhanced Japanese version**, Sega Saturn/ PlayStation, 1996. Included graphics and sound effects.

by Personal Software

Zork™ is a computer fantasy of ultimate challenge. Unearthly creatures guard treasures beyond your imagination. Mazes confound your quest. So quicken your wits and pick your path carefully through the Great Underground Empire. The least likely object may be the only thing that can save your life.

Yet, you can succeed. Discover the 20 treasures of Zork, return them to the Trophy Case and leave alive. But bring all the cunning and courage you can muster. Because in Zork, they take no prisoners . .

Zork, The Great Underground Empire, was created by Infocom, Inc., and is available for 32K Apple® II and II Plus and 32K S-80™ Model I Level II disk systems.
$39.95

6 South St., Milford, NH 03055 (603) 673-5144
TOLL FREE OUT-OF-STATE
1-800-258-1790

When you come back from Zork try Arcade Classics a new S-80 action game featuring Cosmic Raiders, Pinball, Rocochet and Blockade. A great way to have fun without feeding quarters into the machines. S-80 cassette $29.95

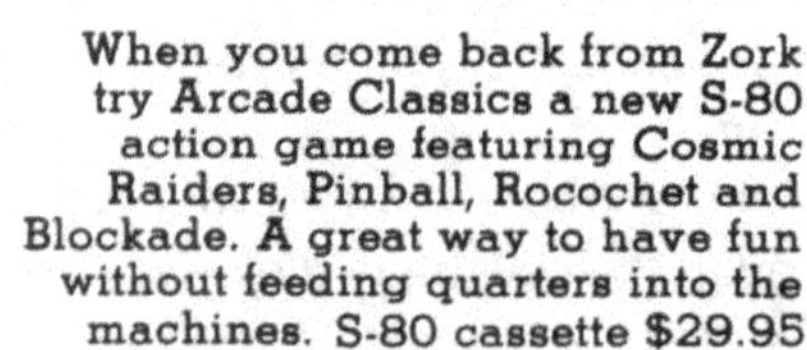

```
>INVENTORY
You are carrying:
A lamp
A sword
A painting
A platinum bar
>NORTH
You are standing in a small circular room with a pedestal. A set of stairs
leads up, and passages leave to the east and west.
There is an extremely valuable (perhaps original) grail here.
Someone carrying a large bag is casually leaning against one of the walls
here. He does not speak, but it is clear from his aspect that the bag will
be taken only over his dead body.
Your sword has begun to glow very brightly.
>GET GRAIL
Taken.
>KILL THIEF
Your stroke lands, but it was only the flat of the blade.
The thief slowly approaches, strikes like a snake, and leaves you
wounded.
The other occupant just left, still carrying his large bag. You may not
have noticed that he robbed you blind first.
>INVENTORY
You are carrying:
A lamp
A sword
```

The thief is more sophisticated than *Adventure*'s pirate: not only does he
nab treasure, but he wanders the map at will, sometimes picking up other
items he finds and discarding them later when he loses interest. Sometimes
he'll ignore the player, but often he'll lash out with his stiletto.

The thief also plays a more subtle role in one of the game's most
confounding puzzles:


```
You are about 10 feet above the ground nestled among some large
branches. The nearest branch above you is above your reach.
On the branch is a small birds nest.
In the bird's nest is a large egg encrusted with precious jewels,
apparently scavenged somewhere by a childless songbird. The egg is
covered with fine gold inlay, and ornamented in lapis lazuli and mother-
of-pearl. Unlike most eggs, this one is hinged and has a delicate looking
clasp holding it closed. The egg appears extremely fragile.
>GET EGG
Taken.
>OPEN IT
There is no obvious way to open the egg.
```


The player can smash the egg to reveal a golden clockwork canary, but this
damages both items and renders them worthless. No command or tool exists

that lets the player open the egg without ruining it. The correct solution, counter to all adventuring instincts, is to let the thief steal the egg. Later, once the player gains enough experience to defeat him, the thief can be tracked to his lair at the heart of the maze and dispatched. Found amidst his treasures are the opened egg and canary, undamaged. The implication helps characterize the thief and gives him a hint of an inner life: insatiable curiosity and an unparalleled expertise.

The thief, as with the rest of *Zork*, evolved through continuous interaction with an active player base in an era when this was not yet common. The PDP-10 that hosted the game ran a homegrown operating system called ITS—the "Incompatible Timesharing System," in reference to an earlier and much-derided "Compatible" platform. Part of the hacker ethos in the 70s was that information should be maximally free, and to that end the developers of ITS had made it an entirely open system, with no modern notions of security or privacy: no passwords, no superusers. Anyone could view and run anyone else's files or watch what was happening on any connected user's terminal. This permissiveness spread even to remote users connecting to an ITS system over ARPANET. And this meant that network spelunkers could discover *Zork*, even without its creators publicly announcing it or promoting it, simply by logging in to the Dynamic Modeling Group's PDP-10 and watching what its users were up to. Much like game makers in the 2010s livestreaming development on Twitch, distant spectators could watch *Zork*'s creators test and play their game in real time as they were making it. It wasn't long before the spectators figured out how to launch the unfinished game themselves and begin their own expeditions into the Great Underground Empire.

The thirst for a new *Adventure* was intense. Even unfinished, *Zork* became so popular its creators set up an official email list for players. They used an in-game newspaper called the *US News & Dungeon Report* (found in the living room of the aboveground house) to advertise the latest fixes and improvements:

> When an error is encountered in this version, you will be asked for a description of the problem immediately, just as if you had used the 'bug' command. We hope that this will improve the handling of such problems.

> A reminder that save files created before 1/17 will not work in this version; fortunately, the program is clever enough to figure out whether a particular save file can be used or not.

> In addition to 'take foo and bar', the parser now claims to understand things like 'take foo and read bar', 'take foo and read it', and so on.

Zork's parser represented another improvement over *Adventure*. While the earlier game could only understand inputs of two words at a time—a verb and a noun—*Zork* added support for multiword verbs like LOOK UNDER or nouns like TRAP DOOR, as well as the concept of both direct and indirect objects, enabling commands that hadn't been possible in the earlier game like ATTACK TROLL WITH SWORD or PUT JEWELS IN SACK. As time went on, the team added pronouns, articles, chaining multiple commands, and ways to refer to groups of objects more selectively, eventually touting that their parser could understand a command as complex as PUT ALL OF THE VALUABLES EXCEPT THE TORCH AND THE COIN INTO THE TROPHY CASE. While inputs this long were rare in practice, the new parser's smarts lent it a certain mystique it would never entirely shed, making *Zork*'s possibility space seem even more unbounded. "I'm not sure it can be solved," wrote one overwhelmed reviewer: "there is so much in it and the possibilities seem staggering."[17] The creators would write about how their program could "simulate enough of the universe to appear to be more intelligent than it really is."[10] Making the parser's capabilities less easy to understand was a key part of that illusion of intelligence.

With a mainframe's generous capacities, *Zork*'s authors were free to keep expanding their game and riddling it with more and more responses to unexpected inputs, often indulging an idiosyncratic sense of humor.

>WIN
Naturally!

>EAT MONEY
Talk about eating rich foods!

>COUNT LEAVES
There are 69,105 leaves here.

But despite their philosophical commitment to the open model of ITS, the team recognized that a fundamental appeal of *Adventure*-likes was their ability to surprise with unexpected messages and challenging puzzles—"problems," as the team called them—which would be spoiled if players could view the game's source code. They hacked ITS to prevent access to the folder containing *Zork*'s secrets. When one clever user found a way to download the forbidden files anyway, the MIT team was so impressed with his technique they weren't even angry. The purloined game, at that point called *Dungeon*—the creators had briefly retitled it before reverting to the original name—found its way to Bob Supnik at DEC, who ported it to Fortran and paved the way for further ports and tweaks. *Dungeon* would proliferate through various systems on a parallel but distinct trajectory from the official *Zork*. Some of the many players who first encountered this form of the game were the authors of *MUD*: the first multi-user *Dungeon*.

While pilfering the source code had been something of a metapuzzle, adding new official problems for the growing fan community kept the *Zork* team busy through 1978 and into early 1979. Implementing new problems often required extending the game's core engine, expanding the code base to support simulating and understanding more and more complex scenarios. Vehicles were added, which could be entered and steered through rooms; an

MEMORABLE PLACES

West of House

Cellar

Entrance to Hades

Engraving Cave

Bank of Zork Lobby

Egyptian Room

Volcano View

Coal Mine

Flood Control Dam #3

Riddle Room

see **1980**

entire sliding-block-puzzle maze of moving rooms showed up. In one area, the player finds a trapped treasure that seems impossible to retrieve:

> You are in a dingy closet adjacent to the machine room. On one wall is a small sticker which says
> > Protected by
> > FROBOZZ
> > Magic Alarm Company
> > (Hello, footpad!)
>
> There is a beautiful crystal sphere here.
> >TAKE SPHERE
> As you reach for the sphere, a steel cage falls from the ceiling to entrap you. To make matters worse, poisonous gas starts coming into the room.

Though there is no escape from the cage, a player who dies and tries again can find nearby a rather incongruous feature for a dungeon: a robot.

> !!!! FROBOZZ MAGIC ROBOT COMPANY !!!!
>
> Hello, Master!
>
>   I am a late-model robot, trained at MIT Tech to perform various simple household functions.
>
> Instructions for use:
>   To activate me, use the following formula:
>   >TELL ROBOT '<something to do>' <cr>
>   The quotation marks are required!

The solution is to instruct the robot to follow you into the room with the sphere and then lift the cage.

> >TELL ROBOT 'GO SOUTH'
> Done.
> >SOUTH
> Dingy Closet
> There is a robot here.
> There is a beautiful white crystal sphere here.
> >GET SPHERE
> As you reach for the sphere, a steel cage falls from the ceiling to entrap you. To make matters worse, poisonous gas starts coming into the room.
> >TELL ROBOT 'LIFT CAGE'
> The cage shakes and is hurled across the room.
> >TAKE SPHERE
> Taken.
> >NORTH

Though each new innovation (compliant robots, rideable rafts) was only used in one or two places, they were programmed as reusable systems, not

Zork was written in a language called Muddle, later retconned as MDL ("MIT Design Language") for more respectability. Even the new name wasn't immune from hacker humor: the joke went that the acronym actually stood for "More Datatypes than Lisp." The Lisp language had an established pedigree as an elegant and powerful alternative to tools like BASIC or Fortran. Everything in Lisp, including the code itself, is represented as lists that can be altered, appended to each other, sorted, or nested. This universality of abstraction makes Lisp programs capable of more self-reflexive operations, including modifying their own code as they're running. For decades, it was the language of choice for any code related to artificial intelligence.

MDL, a pet project of the Dynamic Modeling Group where *Zork* was born, improved on Lisp's flexibility by adding robust support for user-defined data types—"the best of any language with which we are familiar," according to the MDL manual—and better string handling, both of which made an *Adventure*-like program much easier to author. In *Adventure*'s code, for instance, the strings defining room descriptions and the results of actions had to be stored in a separate data file, and were only referenced numerically within the body of the program. With MDL, *Zork* could be written much more naturalistically, with behaviors and descriptions appearing inline together. Here's the (slightly truncated) code for *Zork*'s Carousel Room, which kicks the player out of one of its exits at random, until the player finds a way to stop the room's rotation and the CAROUSEL-FLIP bit is unset:

```
#ROOM {"CAROU"
    ""
    "Round room" %<>
    #EXIT {"NORTH" #CEXIT {"CAROUSEL-FLIP" "CAVE4" "" %<> CAROUSEL-EXIT}
           "SOUTH" #CEXIT {"CAROUSEL-FLIP" "CAVE4" "" %<> CAROUSEL-EXIT}
           "EAST" #CEXIT {"CAROUSEL-FLIP" "MGRAI" "" %<> CAROUSEL-EXIT}
           "WEST" #CEXIT {"CAROUSEL-FLIP" "PASS1" "" %<> CAROUSEL-EXIT}}
    (#FIND-OBJ {"IRBOX"}) CAROUSEL-ROOM}

<DEFINE CAROUSEL-ROOM ()
    <COND (<AND <VERB? "GO-IN"> ,CAROUSEL-ZOOM!-FLAG>
        <JIGS-UP ,SPINDIZZY>)
       (<VERB? "LOOK">
        <TELL
"You are in a circular room with passages off in eight directions.">
        <COND (<NOT ,CAROUSEL-FLIP!-FLAG>
            <TELL
"Your compass needle spins wildly, and you can't get your bearings.">)>)>>

<DEFINE CAROUSEL-EXIT ()
    <COND (,CAROUSEL-FLIP!-FLAG <>)
    (<TELL "Unfortunately, it is impossible to tell directions in here.">
    <CAROUSEL-OUT>)>>

<DEFINE CAROUSEL-OUT ("AUX" CX)
    #DECL ((CX) <OR CEXIT NEXIT ROOM>)
    <AND <TYPE? <SET CX <NTH <REXITS ,HERE> <* 2 <+ 1 <MOD <RANDOM> 8>>>>>
CEXIT>
        <CXROOM .CX>>>
```

MDL let the creators elegantly override the default behavior for movement, just for this one location, by routing cardinal movement to the CAROUSEL-EXIT function (instead of normal movement code) when CAROUSEL-FLIP is set. This ability to define specific overrides to general behavior made *Zork*'s code far simpler to extend and reuse than *Adventure*'s mess of special-case handling in Fortran. It also simplified adding extra responses to invalid commands as the designer thought of them, making the simulation more responsive to unexpected input and the resulting game more fun to play.

In what is apparently an unlikely coincidence, the language created across the Atlantic to write content for *MUD* 1980, the first multiplayer *Zork*-like, was also called Muddle—specifically MUDDL, the Multi-User Dungeon Definition Language.

Among other space-saving measures, mainframe *Zork* was split roughly in half for commercial release as *Zork I* and *Zork II*, with some material left over for *Zork III* as well.

see **1983–5** and **1987**

1977

special-case exceptions. *Zork*'s creators, in short, built something closer to an engine than a hack. In later years, when they founded a company called Infocom and started selling text games commercially, this would prove incredibly useful. A robot that could understand orders and carry out actions, for instance, would become the basis for an entire future game, *Suspended* **1983**, which would exercise the concept in a much more thorough and thought-provoking way. The parser and its model of affordances and concepts could be reused for each new game, continuously improving and slowly strengthening into a stable platform on which simulations of interesting places could be built. Instead of constantly rebuilding the engine, the team could start to focus on the stories they could tell with it.

Today, *Zork* is better remembered for pride of place than actual gameplay. Scholar Nick Montfort praises its innovations, but calls it "a very early and rough effort" that's "not a masterwork by today's standards."[18] A modern reviewer notes that it "wants nothing more than to see you fail, and it's not overly concerned with how much fun you might be having."[19] The game's worldbuilding is a bit of a mess, throwing robots together with elvish swords, mixing *Alice in Wonderland*–type puzzles with a mechanized flood control dam, and putting underground chasms next to underground broom closets. It populates an otherwise eerie Land of the Dead with gratuitous hacker in-jokes. *Zork*'s "problems" could be arbitrary or unfair—one egregious example requires deploying unprompted knowledge of mythology in a way few players would think to try. Many puzzles (including that one) did have alternate solutions. But a player base consisting almost entirely of university hackers expected challenging problems—had the game been too simple, they would have stopped playing. Today's games are made for broader audiences used to far less friction.

And yet *Zork* was massively successful in its own right and as a follow-up to *Adventure*, a second draft of sorts that more fully explored the possibilities inherent in the new kind of game Crowther and Woods had prototyped. In February 1979, *Zork*'s creators declared it finished, in part because they had run out of room to keep building: the MDL language only supported an address space of 256,000 36-bit words, roughly a megabyte of text and code, and the game had brushed up against it. It had expanded to include nearly two hundred rooms, a vocabulary of nine hundred words, thirty-one treasures to collect, and a challenging endgame for master explorers. Its creators had also been stretching the limits of their welcome at MIT, with several long-since graduated and unsure what they wanted to do next. With a handful of other alums and faculty, some founded Infocom with vague hopes of making some kind of business software, but for their first commercial product they turned to a program already on hand: *Zork*. Though they faced significant challenges squeezing the massive mainframe game into the minuscule footprint of early personal computers, the team overcame them, and the rest was history. Infocom would become one of the most legendary text game studios of the century.

Zork is noteworthy for more than its commercial success. When the Library of Congress decided in 2007 to start archiving games with cultural significance, *Zork* was one of the first ten selected. Influencing the aesthetics of games for a generation, it would also provide an enduring technical foundation for future text game makers. After Infocom's demise, the company's engine (the Z-machine, for *Zork*) would be reverse engineered by fans, with the popular Inform design language compiling new games to run on it. Today, thousands and thousands of games have been written for the Z-machine. "A sufficiently imaginative person or persons could probably do this indefinitely,"[10] the team wrote in 1979 about the idea of using *Zork*'s framework to write new games, with no idea how prophetic those words would become.

see **1993**

Zork's creators were thrilled about the new genre they helped popularize, which years later would become known as interactive fiction. Dave Lebling recalled the joy of merging two great passions: "The idea of combining writing and programming, it was like—Wow! How can I do this for my whole life?"[21] As the years went on Infocom's founders became starry-eyed about their new medium's potential, increasingly aware they were circling the edges of something more than a new kind of amusing diversion. It had the potential to become a whole new kind of art. But as they declared their game finished in the winter of 1979, they had no inkling of the explosive spring and heady summer to come: of how much was left to do.

"We were learning how to write adventure games," Lebling wistfully recalls, "and it took a long time to learn to do them better."[8]

References

1 Ahab. 2019. "Versions of Zork I and Their Text Differences." *Data Driven Gamer* (blog). Apr 15, 2019. datadrivengamer.blogspot.com/2019/04/versions-of-zork-i-and-their-text.html | a Dec 25, 2020

2 Anderson, Tim, and Stu Galley. 1985. "The History of Zork." *New Zork Times* 4 (1–3).

3 Chaplin, Heather. 2007. "Is That Just Some Game? No, It's a Cultural Artifact." *New York Times*, Mar 12, 2007, sec. Arts. www.nytimes.com/2007/03/12/arts/design/12vide.html | a Dec 25, 2020

4 Dyer, Richard. 1984. "Masters of the Game." *Boston Globe Magazine*, May 6, 1984.

5 Lebling, Dave. 1996. "Interview with Dave Lebling." *XYZZYnews* #8. www.xyzzynews.com/xyzzy.8d.html | s Feb 28, 2002

6 Lebling, Dave. 2001. "Dave Lebling (Interview)." Interview by Stephen Granade and Philip Jong. AdventureClassicGaming.com. www.adventureclassicgaming.com/index.php/site/interviews/171 | a Dec 25, 2020

7 Lebling, David. 2011. "David Lebling Interview." Interview by Grady Hendrix. GradyHendrix.com. www.gradyhendrix.com/david-lebling-interview | a Dec 25, 2020

8 Lebling, David. 2014. "Classic Game Postmortem: Infocom's Zork." Presented at the 2014 Game Developer's Conference, San Francisco. gdcvault.com/play/1020612/Classic-Game-Postmortem | a Dec 25, 2020

9 Lebling, P. David. 1980. "Zork and the Future of Computerized Fantasy Simulations." *Byte* 5 (12).

10 Lebling, P. David, Marc S. Blank, and Timothy A. Anderson. 1979. "Zork: A Computerized Fantasy Simulation Game." *IEEE Computer* 12 (4).

11 Liddil, Bob. 1981. "Zork, The Great Underground Empire (Review)." *Byte*, Feb 1981.

12 Mace, Scott. 1984. "Games with Windows." *InfoWorld*, Apr 2, 1984.

13 Maher, Jimmy. 2012a. "The Roots of Infocom." *The Digital Antiquarian* (blog). Jan 1, 2012. www.filfre.net/2012/01/the-roots-of-infocom | a Dec 25, 2020

14 Maher, Jimmy. 2012b. "Zork on the PDP-10." *The Digital Antiquarian* (blog). Jan 3, 2012. www.filfre.net/2012/01/zork-on-the-pdp-10 | a Dec 25, 2020

15 Maher, Jimmy. 2012c. "Exploring Zork, Part 1." *The Digital Antiquarian* (blog). Jan 18, 2012. www.filfre.

ALSO BY LEBLING/BLANK

1981 **Zork II** †
1982 **Zork III** †
1983 **Enchanter** †

ALSO BY MARC BLANK

1982 **Deadline** †
1987 **Border Zone** †
1989 **Journey** †
1997 **Zork: The Undiscovered Underground** ‡ *(with Mike Berlyn and G. Kevin Wilson)*

ALSO BY DAVE LEBLING

1982 **Starcross** †
1984 **Suspect** †
1985 **Spellbreaker** †
1987 **The Lurking Horror** †
1989 **Shogun** †

† Infocom
‡ Activision

net/2012/01/exploring-zork-part-1 | a Dec 25, 2020

16 Maher, Jimmy. 2013. "The Top of Its Game." *The Digital Antiquarian* (blog). Mar 20, 2013. www.filfre. net/2013/03/the-top-of-its-game | a Dec 25, 2020

17 Marshall, Debra. 1981. "Zork (Review)." *80 Microcomputing*, Aug 1981.

18 Montfort, Nick. 2005. *Twisty Little Passages: An Approach to Interactive Fiction*. MIT Press.

19 O'Brian, Paul. 2001. "Archaeology (Dungeon Review)." IF-Review. Jun 29, 2001. www.ministryofpeace.com/ if-review/reviews/20010629.html | s Jun 29, 2001

20 Plotkin, Andrew. 2017. "Your Load Is Too Heavy: Zork Deep Reading." *Zarf Updates* (blog). Aug 30, 2017. blog.zarfhome.com/2017/08/your-load-is-too-heavy-zork-deep-reading.html | a Dec 25, 2020

21 Scott, Jason. 2017. "Infocom: The Documentary." www.youtube.com/watch?v=OXNLWy7rwH4 | a Dec 25, 2020

22 Sherman, Howard. 2011. "Zork Turns 30." Malinche Entertainment. Jul 19, 2011. www.malinche.net/zork.html | s Jul 19, 2011

23 Sipe, Russell. 1992. "3900 Games Later." *Computer Gaming World*, Nov 1992.

24 Stone, David P. 1983. "ZORK!: An Overview." *Computer Gaming World*, Apr 1983.

25 Suplee, Curt. 1983. "Through the Zorking Glass." *Washington Post*, Dec 22, 1983.

26 ZipBuckle. n.d. "How to Play (And Beat) Zork: A Step-by-Step Walkthrough." *Retrogeekery* (blog). retrogeekery.com/how-to-play-and-beat-zork-a-step-by-step-walkthrough | a Dec 25, 2020

PIRATE ADVENTURE

Alexis Adams and Scott Adams

Also Known As	**Pirate Cove, Adventure #2**
Style	**Parser**
Debuted	**Dec 1978** *(mail order)*
Launch Platform	**TRS-80**
Publisher	**Adventure International**
Language	**BASIC**
Launch Price	**$14.95** *(cassette tape)*

I am in a Flat in london. Visible items:

Flight of stairs. Sign says: "Bring
TREASURES here, say: SCORE". Bottle of rum.
Rug. Safety sneakers. Sack of crackers.

    -------> Tell me what to do?

IN THE OVERWHELMINGLY MALE-DOMINATED WORLD of 1970s hackers, a popular tale was the one about the wife or girlfriend who just didn't get it. So-called computer widows didn't or couldn't understand what was so interesting about the bulky machines and the code they ran—or so the stories went—and sometimes lashed out in "hysterical" ways. One particular oft-retold anecdote went like this:

MAJOR RELEASES

» **TRS-80**, v4.05, BASIC, Dec 1978.

» **Apple II**, v4.08, summer 1979. This and subsequent releases switched to a two-panel layout and featured a faster, rewritten interpreter.

» **With *Adventureland*,** Creative Computing Software, 1979.

» **Type-in version**, BASIC. Listed in Dec 1980 *Byte*.

» **In *Adventure Value Pack #1*,** various platforms, 1980.

» **S.A.G.A (Scott Adams Graphic Adventure) #2,** various platforms, 1982. Added graphics.

» **Other ports** to Commodore PET, Exidy Sorcerer, Atari 8-bit, TI-99/4A, VIC-20 (as *Pirate Cove*), BBC Micro, Commodore 16 and Plus/4, Acorn Electron, ZX Spectrum, Dragon 32/64, DOS, C64, Oric Atmos, and Dick Smith System 80.

» **In *The Scott Adams Collection*,** Windows, 1997.

see **1976**

1978

One day she had finally had it. I came home to find that she had put all my disks … in the oven. I was not going to program anymore, she said, unless I spent some time with her. Luckily, [she] had been so mad that she'd forgotten to turn the oven on![10]

Like all stories, these were shared because they reinforced myths the listeners wanted to believe. If you'd lost a wife or girlfriend to the hobby, maybe it was her fault—or maybe she was too scatterbrained to be a good match, anyway.

But behind this particular story (which did happen, more or less) lies a pretty obvious truth. The woman in it had intended, of course, for the oven to be off. It wasn't a botched execution. It was a threat.

Her name was Irene Reuben, although she went by Alexis and had taken her husband's name along with, later, his disks. In 1977 she was an ambitious young Floridian with big dreams. At twenty, she already had her own mail-order business selling cookbooks and recipes, and she helped manage a restaurant chain while studying psychology at Miami-Dade Community College. While working for an early computer dating service, she pulled one particular profile out of the queue to respond to it herself: Scott Adams, an adorable goateed geek with a riot of curly hair. The two were engaged months later and married not long after.

Scott was soon to embark on a quixotic project that only makes sense in the context of that particular year of 1977, when it was becoming possible at last to compute at home. Affordable home computer kits for enthusiasts had started appearing by 1975, but the 1977 releases of the TRS-80, the Commodore PET, and the Apple II took microcomputers mainstream. No longer did you need access to a university or company mainframe to run code—for a thousand dollars or less you could have your very own silicon. But what could you actually do with those micros? Their minuscule memory and graphics capabilities meant they were considered little more than expensive toys by "real" hackers. The idea of running a game more complex than tic-tac-toe on one seemed laughable. *Zork* **1977** would take up nearly a megabyte of space on a PDP-10 mainframe. What could you possibly create for a far slower machine with only a few thousand bytes of memory? Just this paragraph would have filled up half the space on a 2K machine.

Adventure arrived that year on the mainframe at Scott's office, and like thousands of others he became briefly obsessed with it. He came into work early and stayed late to play, every day, until he solved it. He wanted to share it with friends but couldn't, since only badged employees were allowed into his office, so he started to wonder what it would take to make something like *Adventure* for a microcomputer. He mentioned this plan to his friends. "Fortunately," he later recalled, "I was not daunted by their laughter."[4]

When an upgrade for the TRS-80 came out in 1978 that gave it an improved version of BASIC and 16K of memory—enough to store about ten printed pages of code and data—Adams saw his moment. A systems programmer first and foremost, he devised a minuscule engine that could read an adventure definition from a data file and execute it. The engine had only the bare minimum needed to reproduce the spirit of the earlier adventures: a simple two-word parser, a baked-in set of possible condition checks, sixteen binary flags to track game state, and a minimalist aesthetic for descriptions and messages. Even tiny as the engine was, little room remained for the evocative descriptions and complex behaviors seen in mainframe games. Scott's would have to entertain more through mechanics than prose. He built a simple editor to create and modify the data format his engine could read—a primitive game construction kit—and by the end of 1978, he'd finished the first game for his system. He called it *Adventureland*.

```
I'm in a hidden grove. Visible items:

*JEWELED FRUIT*. Sign says "Paul's place."

    Some obvious exits are: NORTH EAST

    -------> Tell me what to do? GET FRUIT
OK
    -------> Tell me what to do? EAST
OK

I am in a dismal swamp. Visible items:

Cypress tree. Evil smelling mud. Swamp gas.
Patches of "OILY" slime. Chiggers.

    Some obvious exits are: NORTH EAST WEST

    -------> Tell me what to do?
```

The earliest versions of the Adams games used all-caps text; within six months of release, a TRS-80 upgrade added support for lowercase. Adams recoded his engine to support it, along with adding a new interface paradigm where the current room description always appeared at the top of the screen, with the player's commands and responses in an area below.

While *Adventureland* was a far cry from the glorious sentences and complex puzzles of mainframe adventures, Scott was thrilled he'd managed to capture a spark of their magic on a microcomputer. But his new marriage was already in trouble. He'd told Alexis he was working overtime when he'd spent those early mornings and late nights at the office playing *Adventure*, rather than admit he was socializing with dwarves and dragons instead of her. When he brought his obsession home, the situation only worsened:

> Alexis was pregnant with our first child when I was writing *Adventureland* and she was becoming upset with me. I was spending all kinds of hours on the computer. I would come home from work, jump on the computer until midnight, then get up and work on the program from six to eight in the morning before I left for work.[10]

Alexis started lashing out, hiding Scott's disks around the house and eventually, yes, in the oven. Scott's hobby must have seemed a pointless waste of time, not to mention a thoughtless one, while they were trying to start a family together. She finally gave him an ultimatum. When Scott finished his first adventure game, he promised it would be his last.

But then something unexpected happened: Scott shared copies of *Adventureland* on cassette tape at local computer club meetups, and micro owners went wild over it. There was simply nothing else like it yet available for home machines. He took out ads in the backs of computer magazines, and the game sold. Alexis began to see her husband's Sisyphean project in a different light: it was a *product*, a business opportunity, a chance to tap into a massively underserved market. This was more of a leap than modern audiences might intuitively understand—in 1978, only big companies like IBM had a reputation for selling software (though a little startup named Micro-Soft was hoping to change that) and the only commercial software was meant for business, not pleasure. Sure, hobbyists made a few bucks here and there selling amusing programs out of magazines, and the arcade and video game console industries were beginning to take off. But *Zork* wouldn't hit the home market for two more years, and the idea of a company selling games for primitive home computers was still laughable.

As an entrepreneur, Alexis may have seen the enormous potential her husband's game represented. She wanted in. "Once we had sold a few copies," Scott later remembered, "Alexis decided she wanted to do one."[10] Six months pregnant, she began to collaborate with her husband on a second adventure.

Scott's engine, reusable by design, meant that a second game was far easier to make than the first. Alexis had no programming experience, but building a new game would largely be a matter of setting up a new world of rooms, objects, and rules in Scott's database editor. The two devised a method of collaboration:

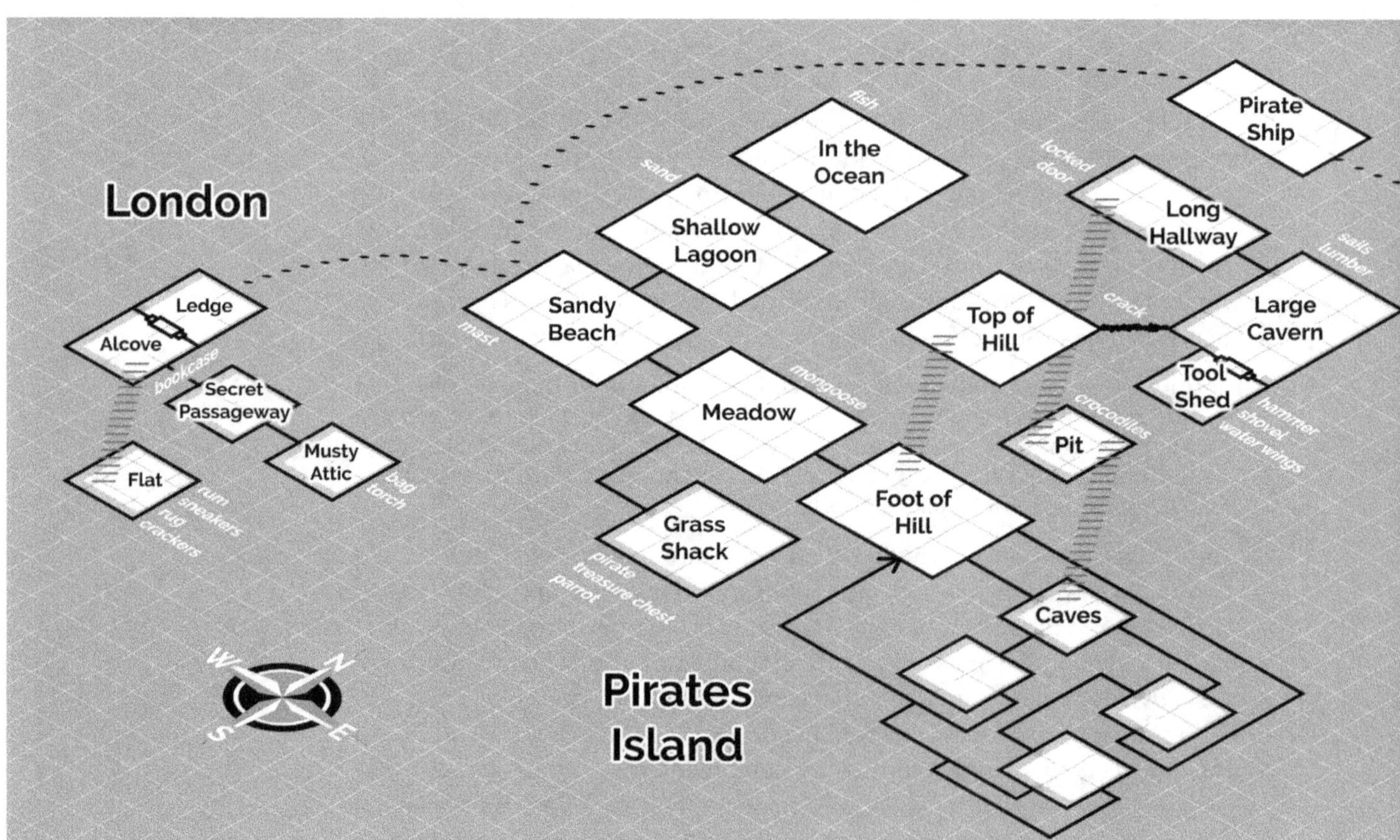

She would supply the ideas. She'd say, "There's a cave," and I'd say, "What do you see in the cave?" "A door," she'd answer. "Why can't we open the door?" "There's a pit of crocodiles in front of the door." "How can we get past the crocodile?" "Well, maybe the crocodiles are hungry." "Great, let's put some fish out in the ocean."[10]

It only took a few weeks to design and code the new game with Scott's editor and Alexis's ideas, and then there were two products to sell.

```
* Welcome to Adventure number 2: "Pirate Adventure"
by Alexis & Scott Adams, dedicated: Ted Heeren & Paul
Sharland. Remember you can always ask for "HELP".
```

The Adamses started advertising the pair of adventures more aggressively. One day in early 1979, Alexis answered a phone call from an electronics store manager in Chicago who wanted fifty copies. Smoothly, she and Scott negotiated a price and closed the deal. Working through the weekend, they made fifty duplicates of the master cassette tape—by hand, one at a time—and dutifully shipped a box of them off. A week later the manager called back, annoyed. The tapes needed to be in some kind of packaging for him to sell them. At a loss, the Adamses called plastic bag manufacturers for quotes, but couldn't find anyone interested in an order size less than 10,000 units. And then they hit on a novel solution, right in front of their noses: a box of plastic baby bottle liners for their newborn. A cassette tape fit perfectly inside one. They stapled business cards to the top, punched a hole in them so the bag could hang on a pegboard, and invented the first retail packaging for a computer game. The company they would soon found, Adventure International, would be the first in the world to exclusively sell them.

A player who loaded the *Pirate Adventure* cassette into their TRS-80's memory—a process that took upwards of twenty minutes—began the game in a modern-day London flat. On a bookshelf with a secret passage behind it the player can find a book with a curious inscription:

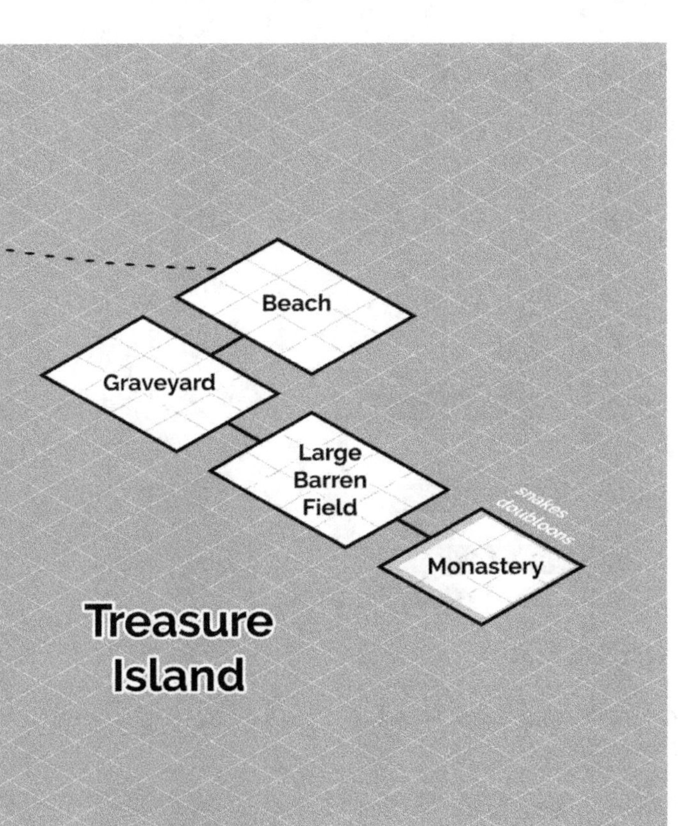

Opposite: room map of *Pirate Adventure*. Some concealed items and redundant room connections are omitted.

> The book is in bad condition but I can make out the title:
> "Treasure Island". There's a word written in blood in the
> flyleaf: "YOHO" and a message: "Long John Silver left 2
> treasures on Treasure Island"

Saying the magic word *YOHO* transports you to a tropical isle with
crocodiles, snakes, caves, and a drunken pirate. But the goal of the game was
unusual for the time, and Scott credited this to Alexis:

> We created an Adventure that was different from any that had ever been
> written before. Instead of simply searching for treasures in this Adventure,
> you now had an added ingredient—a "mission." (In this case, you had to
> figure out how to build a pirate's ship!)[4]

Ship parts are scattered around the landscape, and most of the game's
puzzles involve collecting and reassembling them. Completing the ship lets
you sail to the legendary Treasure Island itself, but the bulk of the game is
the challenge of getting there. For the first time, the treasure hunt took a
back seat. An adventure game could be something more.

```
I am in a sandy beach on a tropical isle. Visible items:

Small ship's keel and mast. Sand. Lagoon. Sign in the sand
says: "Welcome to Pirates Island, watch out for the tide!".

    Some obvious exits are: EAST

   -------> Tell me what to do? BUILD SHIP
I've no plans!
   -------> Tell me what to do? E
OK

I am in a meadow. Visible items:

Mongoose. Grass shack.

    Some obvious exits are: EAST WEST

   -------> Tell me what to do? LOOK MONGOOSE
OK
I see nothing special
   -------> Tell me what to do? GET MONGOOSE
OK
   -------> Tell me what to do? GO SHACK
OK

I am in a grass shack. Visible items:

Wicked looking pirate. Treasure chest. Parrot.
    Some obvious exits are: WEST

   -------> Tell me what to do? OPEN CHEST
Pirate won't let me
The parrot crys: `Check the chest matey`
```

The Adamses were less interested than earlier adventure authors in monsters and fighting, perhaps because unlike most predecessors they hadn't played *Dungeons & Dragons* and been influenced by its integral combat mechanics. *Pirate Adventure* has no weapons, and no enemies but wild animals. There's a pirate, but unlike earlier NPCs, he's less a rival than a besotted companion. A bottle of rum distracts him away from his treasure chest (which contains the required ship plans) and he wanders off with it. Later, when you need a crew for your completed ship, you can find him sleeping off his excesses back in your London flat:

see **1975**, **1976**, and **1977**

```
I am in a musty attic. Visible items:

Pirate's duffel bag. Empty bottle. Sleeping pirate. Rum
bottle smashed into pieces. Sign "Opposite of LIGHT is
Unlight".

    Some obvious exits are: WEST


    -------> Tell me what to do? WAKE PIRATE
Pirate awakens and says "Aye matey we be casting off soon"
He then VANISHES!
```

The pirate accompanies you on your journey to recover Long John Silver's treasures, but remains more interested in booze than gold. When it's time to leave the island with your loot, you can find him sleeping off another bender in a graveyard.

The game's puzzles are mostly simpler than the challenges from earlier games designed by hackers to stump their peers. The player can type HELP for in-game hints, and the pirate's parrot also dispenses advice. Reduced in scope from the sprawling mainframe games, *Pirate Adventure* has only twenty-six rooms and a handful of obstacles, which shrinks the possibility space and makes the game easier to solve. Points of confusion more often come from the primitive parser and terse messages, which could obscure clear understanding of obstacles or situations. At its best, the minimalist prose has a unique charm all its own, presenting a world not lushly drawn in sentences, but lightly sketched with functional nouns and verbs.

Spoilers for getting past the crocodile.

```
I am in a pit. Visible items:

Mean and hungry looking crocodiles. Locked door.

    Some obvious exits are: UP


    -------> Tell me what to do? OPEN DOOR
Crocs stop me
    -------> Tell me what to do? INVENTORY
I'm carrying the following: Large blood soaked book. Sack
of crackers. Lit torch. Matches. Fish.
    -------> Tell me what to do? EAT CRACKER
Yummy
```

```
      -------> Tell me what to do? DROP FISH
Dropped.
Crocs eat fish and leave
```

But the tiny engine could also be maddeningly frustrating. Not knowing which words the program will understand—a problem common to all parser-driven games—is worsened by a platform without spare room for extra synonyms or helpful descriptions:

```
      -------> Tell me what to do? FEED FISH
I must be stupid, but I just don't understand what you mean
      -------> Tell me what to do? FIGHT CROCS
I don't know how to "FIGHT" something.
      -------> Tell me what to do? EXAMINE CROCS
OK
I see nothing special
      -------> Tell me what to do? DODGE CROCS
I don't know how to "DODGE" something.
```


The byte-conscious parser could make it hard to express yourself even when you knew what you wanted to do:

```
      -------> Tell me what to do? READ MAP
Its a map to Treasure Island. At the bottom it says:
"30 paces then dig!"
      -------> Tell me what to do? TAKE 30 PACES
It's beyond my Power to do that.
      -------> Tell me what to do? 30 PACES
I don't know how to "30" something.
      -------> Tell me what to do? PACE
I need a direction too.
      -------> Tell me what to do? PACE NORTH
I can't go in THAT direction.
      -------> Tell me what to do? PACE 30
OK
I walked off 30 paces.
```

Today's players can also fail to appreciate the incredible tedium of playing *any* game on a 1978 microcomputer. That twenty-minute load time to read in the data from cassette was only the beginning. The original BASIC version of the engine (before Scott rewrote it in assembler) took agonizing seconds to process each command. Saving your game took four minutes, not counting the setup time of preparing a blank cassette to save it to. To restore that game required first restarting the system and reloading the entire program from scratch, *then* loading in your save game from the second tape—another thirty minutes of your life gone forever. "No wonder Adams could advertise that *Adventureland* would take weeks or months to complete," quipped game historian Jimmy Maher.[16]

But despite their limitations, the Adamses' adventure games had a head start over almost any other competition, and their company paved the way for the first generation of computer gaming giants. Doug Carlston became Adventure International's first outside author with his game *Galactic Empire* [1980]; he'd use the proceeds to start his own software company, Brøderbund. Another young man who became Adventure International's West Coast distributor, Ken Williams, would found On-Line Systems (later called Sierra On-Line) with his wife Roberta, whose *King's Quest* games would become the most famous of the first generation of graphical adventures. Roberta and Ken took their inspiration in part from the visible success of another power couple selling their games to the growing microcomputer audience.

From 1979 through the early 80s, Adventure International became the computer game industry's first success story, and Alexis was integral to its growth. She "handles most of the business"[6] as the corporate vice president and general manager, Scott noted at the time, and "has been intimately involved in all aspects … from the very beginning."[15] She "is as active in the company as I am"[18] and had "a tremendous say in the direction of the company."[12] As the couple expanded their catalog to include dozens of games by other authors, sales grew at a steady and then an explosive rate. Adventure International eventually employed a staff of more than forty people—at one point, nearly half of them women. Scott's simple engine was easy to port to new platforms, so as the early home computer marketplace fragmented to include over a dozen different systems, Adventure International's games could run on them all.

The Adamses worked hard to build an audience and a network of distributors—in one year they traveled to thirty-eight different trade shows and expos. The couple gained a reputation as good souls in a sometimes cutthroat industry. At one show, Roberta Williams had to track down Adventure International's booth to ask why the then-larger company kept sending customers over to buy Sierra's games: "Aren't we supposed to be competitors?"[10]

"They make an odd couple as they stand together" in their booth, Brøderbund's Doug Carlston remembered: "Scott is a tall, goateed, curly-haired fellow…. His wife, Alexis, is distinctly shorter and more heavy-set."[13] Many men in the industry no doubt noticed Alexis not only for her gender, but her size. Compared to Roberta Williams, whose long golden hair and slim figure came straight out of a storybook, Alexis didn't look like the popular conception of a princess—or a game designer. She wrote in later years that her weight had been a frequent source of stress and anxiety during her career in games, and she became a proponent of "size acceptance," founding a group working against the erasure of people like her from media and public consciousness.

Hint Sheets

One of the Adamses' early innovations was to sell hints for their games, which soon became a major supplemental revenue stream. Later companies would copy this strategy, employing everything from 900 numbers to invisible ink, but Adventure International's approach was much simpler. A single paper sheet for each game would have a list of terse questions (matching the minimalist prose of the games themselves), followed by a series of numbers:

> Can't find second treasure?
> 7 80 52

> Still can't find second treasure?
> 56 71 33 67 22

Below the hints was a key to the numbered words, which could be assembled to reveal any given hint:

> 7 - read
> 80 - the
> 52 - map

Adventure International sold the hint sheets for a dollar each. At one point they realized they were selling more hint sheets than games, due to the widespread practice of copying tapes of games from your friends—early software piracy.

It's still important to remember that when you picture a game executive, a game designer, or an interactive fiction pioneer, you can picture someone like Alexis too.

The Adamses eventually started organizing their own conventions and opened a chain of computer stores in Orlando, where Alexis liked to keep tabs on the customer base:

> I love working in the retail store, even these days. It gives me a chance to learn what people really want.… The immediate feedback has proven invaluable to our product development. We have a network of several hundred local play-testers. When a new product is about to be released, these people are given copies to check thoroughly. They are one of the reasons our products are so well-known for being bug-free.[10]

Alexis continued to broker deals for the expanding company, even through two more pregnancies and six office moves in three years. In 1983 she negotiated a license to the game rights for 20th Century–Fox's big sci-fi film of the year, *Buckaroo Banzai*, and contributed to the game adapted from it. At the end of that year Adventure International landed exclusive rights for ten years to make computer games based on Marvel Comics characters—a deal that a few decades later would have been unimaginably valuable. Scott dedicated the first of his Marvel adventures to Alexis.

While her husband's name was the only one on the box—the company crafted a mystique around Scott as a solo adventure-making genius—Alexis contributed to many of the titles Adventure International produced. Some games credit her as co-creator on their title screens, if nowhere else, and one gives her sole billing there: 1979's *Voodoo Castle*. A few other women designers had published games by that year, including Carol Shaw at Atari, but Alexis was among the first to receive a visible credit. In a contemporary interview, Scott noted that she built the game "95% on her own"[1] after learning how to use his database system; this also might make her the first nonprogrammer in history to use a domain-specific tool to make a digital game. She dedicated *Voodoo Castle* "to all moms!" and it featured multiple female characters, including "Medium Maegen," a hint-dispensing spiritualist named after her daughter—maybe the first woman with dialogue in a video game.

For a time, Adventure International's growth prospects seemed limitless. But a few bad deals, the 1983 video game crash, and a sluggish approach to incorporating graphics drove the company out of business by the middle of the decade. Alexis and Scott would divorce not long after. While Scott has rarely mentioned his ex-wife in interviews since, he has often cited *Voodoo Castle* and *Pirate Adventure* as some of the company's best-remembered titles, the latter being the only of their games to get a sequel. Alexis, who almost never spoke to the press during or after the company's heyday, passed away in 2008 from health complications, at only fifty-one years old. Over time, her part in Adventure International's success has been largely forgotten. Most histories of the company barely mention her.

But period sources make it clear Alexis played a huge part in the rise of the world's first computer game company. She was more than just the madwoman who put her husband's masterpiece in the oven. The meal, in fact, could not have been served without her.

References

1   80-US: The TRS-80 Users Journal. 1981. "80-U.S. Interviews Scott Adams of Adventure International," Mar/Apr 1981.

2   Adams, Alexis. 1998. "A Note from Alexis." Adventure International Tribute Site. 1998. www.alphaworks. com.au/scottadams/Alexis.htm | a Jan 20, 2021

3   Adams, Scott. 1979. "An Adventure in Small Computer Game Simulation." *Creative Computing*, Aug 1979.

4   Adams, Scott. 1980. "Pirate's Adventure." *Byte* 5 (12), Dec 1980.

5   Adams, Scott. 1984. "Scott Adams." Interview by Steve Gould. *Page 6 Magazine*, Jul 1984.

6   Adams, Scott. 1985. "Great Scott!" Interview by Graeme Kidd. *Crash* #15, Apr 1985. getlamp.com/ cast/20070121adams/FILES/crashint.txt | a Jan 20, 2021

7   Adams, Scott. 2007. "GET LAMP: Scott Adams Interview." Interview by Jason Scott, Jan 21, 2007. Video. archive.org/details/GETLAMP-ScottAdams | a Jan 14, 2021

8   Adams, Scott. 2015. "ANTIC Interview 25 - Scott Adams, Adventure International." Interview by ANTIC The Atari 8-bit Podcast, Mar 16, 2015. ataripodcast.libsyn.com/antic-interview-25-the-atari-8-bit-podcast- scott-adams | a Jan 20 2021

9   Adams-Gleaton, Alexis. 1999. "Supersize It." Bigger and Better October Newsletter. Oct 1999. www. biggerandbetter.net/oct.html | a Jan 20, 2021

10 Adams III, Roe E. 1983. "The Saga of Scott and Alexis Adams." *Softalk* 3 (7), Mar 1983.

11 Ahab. 2018. "Game 32: Pirate Adventure." *Data Driven Gamer* (blog). Nov 7, 2018. datadrivengamer. blogspot.com/2018/11/game-32-pirate-adventure.html | a Jan 20, 2021

12 Anderson, Carmel. 1984. "Scott Adams: The Fun and Games Man." *Micro Adventurer*, April 1984.

13 Carlston, Douglas G. 1985. *Software People: An Insider's Look at the Personal Computer Software Industry*. Simon & Schuster.

14 Dobson, Dale. 2009. "The Great Scott Project - Adventure #2." *Gaming After 40* (blog). Aug 19, 2009. gamingafter40.blogspot.com/2009/08/great-scott-project-adventure-2.html | a Jan 20, 2021

15 Jermaine, John. 1985. "Probing QuestProbe." *Commodore Power Play* 4 (1), Feb/Mar 1985.

16 Maher, Jimmy. 2011. "Adventureland, Part 1." *The Digital Antiquarian* (blog). Jun 22, 2011. www.filfre. net/2011/06/adventureland-part-1 | a Jan 20, 2021

17 Mahney, Nathan P. 2016. "Game 10: Pirate Adventure (1978)." *CRPG Adventures* (blog). Jan 13, 2016. crpgadventures.blogspot.com/2016/01/pirate-adventure-1978.html | a Jan 20, 2021

18 Mitchell, Ron. 1983. "Scott Adams: Adventuring with the Atari." *Antic* 2 (4), July 1983.

19 Sweasey, Pete. 1987. "Mindplay." *ZX Computing Monthly*, Jun 1987.

WARNING ! ! ! !

Do not read this book straight through from beginning to end! These pages contain many different adventures you can go on in the Cave of Time. From time to time as you read along, you will be asked to make a choice. Your choice may lead to success or disaster!

The adventures you take are a result of your choice. *You* are responsible because *you* choose! After you make your choice, follow the instructions to see what happens to you next.

Remember—you cannot go back! Think carefully before you make a move! One mistake can be your last . . . or it *may* lead you to fame and fortune!

CHOOSE YOUR OWN ADVENTURE #1
THE CAVE OF TIME

Edward Packard

<table>
<tr><td>Style</td><td>Choice-Based</td></tr>
<tr><td>Debuted</td><td>Jul 1979 (retail)</td></tr>
<tr><td>Launch Platform</td><td>Print</td></tr>
<tr><td>Publisher</td><td>Bantam Books</td></tr>
<tr><td>Launch Price</td><td>$1.25 (paperback)</td></tr>
</table>

> **❝❞** You've hiked through Snake Canyon once before while visiting your Uncle Howard at Red Creek Ranch, but you never noticed any cave entrance. It looks as though a recent rock slide has uncovered it.
> Though the late afternoon sun is striking the opening of the cave, the interior remains in total darkness…

IN THE EARLY HOURS of a 1969 morning, on a long commuter rail trip from Connecticut to Manhattan, a lawyer edging up on forty is scribbling a complex diagram in a worn spiral notebook. The diagram looks "like a tree lying on its side with many branches and limbs."[7] He ignores the view out the window and his fellow passengers, other men in business suits, like him on their way to work. He is busy. He's designing a book you can play like a game.

A few nights earlier, Edward Packard had been spinning a bedtime story for his children. With three hours of daily commuting, the only chance he had to see them during the week was at bedtime, when he liked to make up stories himself rather than read from a book. Sometimes he enlisted a little help:

> I had a character named Pete and I usually had him encountering all these different adventures on an isolated island. But that night I was running out of things for Pete to do, so I just asked [the kids] what they would do.[7]

His daughters Caroline and Andrea each gave a different answer, so Packard obligingly gave each their own ending. "What really struck me was the natural enthusiasm they had for the idea," he later recalled. "And I thought: 'Could I write this down?'"[7]

Packard had always wanted to be a writer, and he had drafted a handful of children's books he'd never managed to sell. Practicing law had seemed a steadier way to support a family. But now the idea of a book that gave kids multiple pathways through a story wouldn't leave his head. He started sketching flowcharts on the train to and from the office, working out the structural and organizational problems that arose with branching narratives and limited page counts. Eventually he had an outline for a book called *The Adventures of You on Sugarcane Island*. On the first page, a rogue wave sweeps "you" off a ship and you wake up on a deserted island:

> [...] lying high on a huge sand dune. Behind you is a broad, sloping beach. You watch the foaming waves thrashing upon it. Ahead of you is a meadow of tall reeds bounded by high rocky hills. You are hungry and thirsty. You look out at the ocean and see nothing but endless blue water. Except for a few sea gulls hovering over the waves, you are all alone.
>
> *If you decide to walk along the beach, turn to page 5.*
>
> *If you decide to climb the rocky hill, turn to page 6.*

Packard hadn't been the first to imagine such a book, or even to write one. Storytelling pioneers of various eras had toyed with narratives that contained their own rules for navigation. The 1930 novel *Consider the Consequences!* by Doris Webster and Mary Alden promised "a brand new idea in fiction—a story which ends in any one of a dozen or more different ways, depending entirely on the taste of the individual reader," that included choice points like this one:

> The reader who thinks she will be wise to avoid argument and trouble by eloping turns to paragraphs H-3. The one who thinks she would better decide to return home, determined to face the music and go through with her marriage in spite of opposition, turns to paragraphs H-4.

Other books, stage shows, or radio programs had tried one-off experiments with audience participation, letting the reader or audience decide which direction a story should go. The 1935 play *Night of January 16th* asked twelve random audience members to serve as jurors for a courtroom drama and render a verdict before the final curtain. Two different endings could unfold depending on their decision. In the 50s and 60s, experiments in "programmed learning" led to a textbook series called Tutor Texts, with multiple-choice questions where each answer instructed the student to turn to a different page; incorrect responses would offer immediate feedback about where the student had gone wrong. But few of these efforts had gained much traction. Each was created largely in ignorance of the others, and as experiments they were rarely repeated.

It seemed at first that the same would prove true for Packard's book. He didn't know of any earlier attempts to create interactive novels, nor was he familiar with the still-nascent experiments with computer games happening at distant universities. But he thought his idea had potential. A friend in New York, who worked for the William Morris Agency, helped Packard find a literary agent who dutifully shopped *Sugarcane Island* around to publishers. There were no takers. After six months Packard abandoned the project. He kept practicing law, and might have done so until retirement except for a coincidental fluke years later.

In 1975, Packard was in Vermont and happened to be browsing through the spring issue of *Vermont Life*, one of those colorful grandparent magazines filled with recipes, photos of barn raisings, and feature stories on interesting fences. He read a profile of a small local company that published children's books and games, run by a couple named Connie and Ray Montgomery. With what the magazine assured the reader was typical Vermonter verve, the Montgomerys felt their books were doing something a little different: they were "specifically and exclusively for children":

> Most children's books are significantly designed with the buyer in mind—the parent or grandparent ... the distribution and displays are geared to the purchaser not the child.... We want the child reader to get involved in what he is reading and experiencing. He should identify with the subject.... He is learning to read, but in the process he is also learning about himself.[5]

Something in the article sparked Packard's imagination—maybe the photos of children clustered around one of the Montgomerys' prototype books, which they took to local schools to try out on the kids rather than relying on adult opinions. The New York publishing suits hadn't given it a chance, but Packard's own children had appreciated the value of a story where they got to make decisions. Maybe Vermont Crossroads Press would too.

Ray Montgomery had been involved with "active learning" for years. After working as both a high school and college instructor, he'd developed roleplaying scenarios for Peace Corps volunteers, giving them practice negotiating tense scenarios they might encounter abroad. He had also helped run a summer school for remedial learners with a focus on so-called experiential learning: "the most powerful way for kids, or for anyone, to

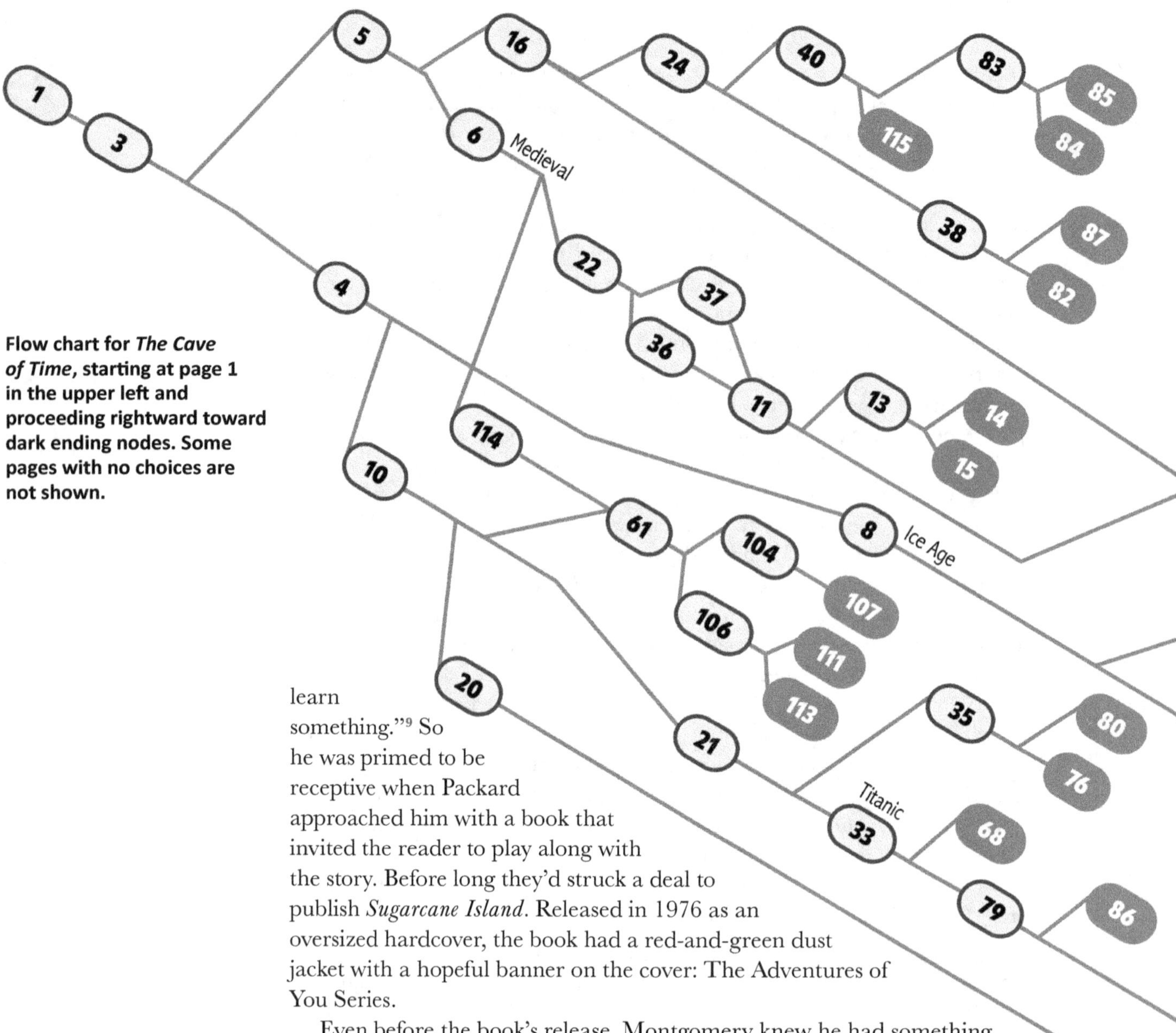

Flow chart for *The Cave of Time*, starting at page 1 in the upper left and proceeding rightward toward dark ending nodes. Some pages with no choices are not shown.

learn something."[9] So he was primed to be receptive when Packard approached him with a book that invited the reader to play along with the story. Before long they'd struck a deal to publish *Sugarcane Island*. Released in 1976 as an oversized hardcover, the book had a red-and-green dust jacket with a hopeful banner on the cover: The Adventures of You Series.

Even before the book's release, Montgomery knew he had something good on his hands. "I Xeroxed 50 copies of Ed's manuscript and took it to a reading teacher in Stowe. His kids—third grade through junior high— couldn't get enough of it."[4] Everywhere he took the book, the reaction was the same. But Vermont Crossroads was too small an operation to make much impact. Montgomery quickly wrote a second Adventures of You book, but it also languished in obscurity. Packard, growing frustrated, had resumed shopping the concept around to other publishers, and in 1977 he struck a deal with Lippincott to release two new choice-based books, *Deadwood City* (1978) and *The Third Planet from Altair* (1979). Each used the phrase "choose your own adventures" on the cover as part of its banner text, but not yet as the name of a series.

Montgomery was also looking for a bigger fish, and he found one in Bantam Books. A young acquisitions editor there, Joëlle Delbourgo, immediately saw the idea's potential: "My first reaction was that it was a brilliant concept and, to make an impact, you had to publish it as a series with a unifying cover concept."[4] When it turned out neither Lippincott nor Packard had registered a trademark on "choose your own adventure," Bantam snatched it up, offering a regular writing contract to both Packard and Montgomery as a consolation prize. In July 1979 Packard's *The Cave of Time* hit bookshops, branded on the cover as Choose Your Own Adventure #1. The dedication noted that "the concept, title, and editorial assistance" for the book had been provided by Packard's daughter Andrea.

Cave opens immediately with your discovery of a mysterious cave on a visit to your uncle's remote ranch. Stepping inside, you begin to feel unaccountably nervous. Hurrying back out reveals the world has changed, and you soon realize you've been transported to the midst of an Ice Age thousands of years earlier. You

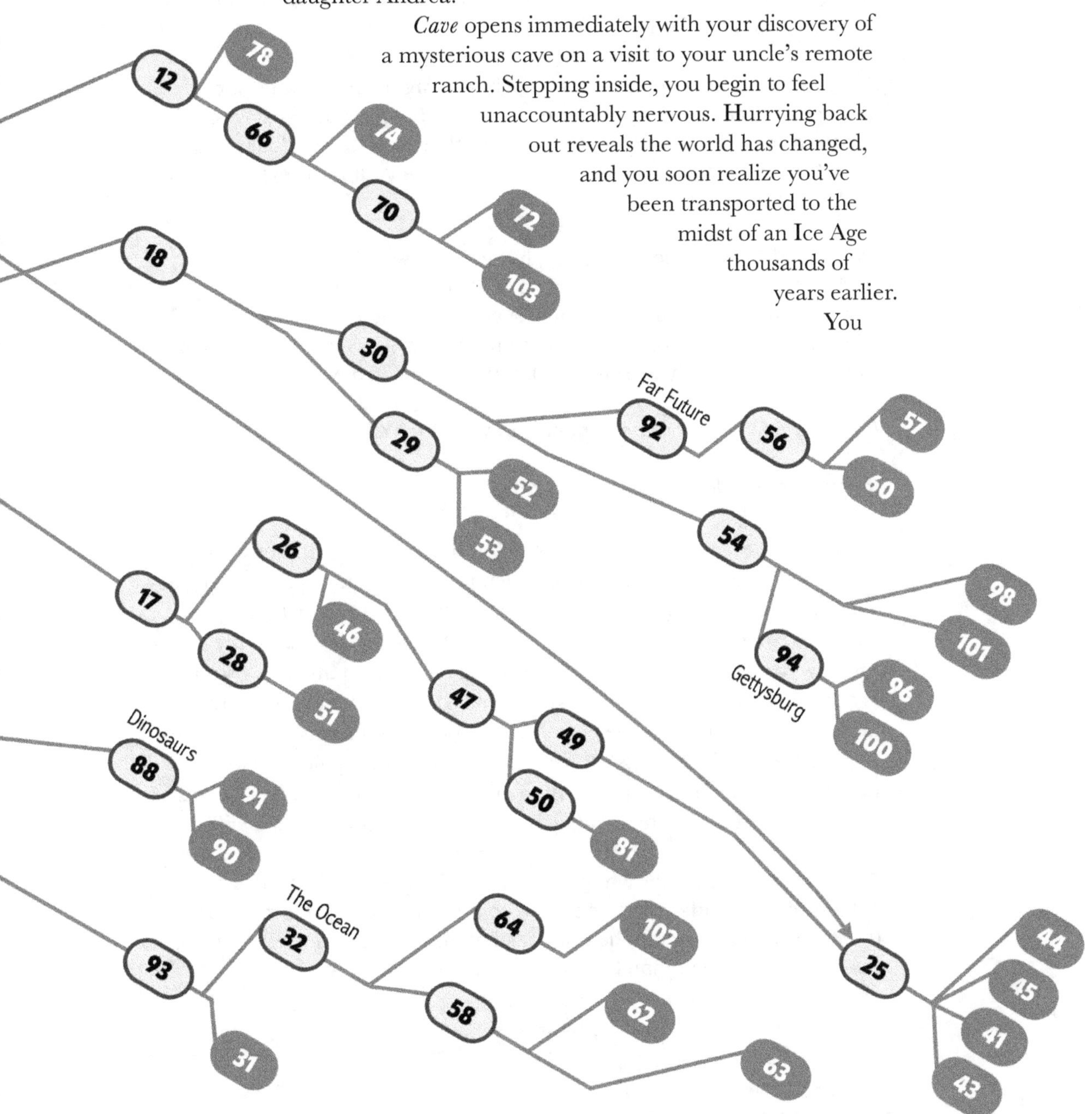

can choose to stay and explore this prehistoric world, or go back into the cave and try to find a way back to your own time. But each tunnel leads to a different place and epoch of history. Across the book's branches you can find yourself in colonial America, medieval Europe, the time of the dinosaurs, or an era beyond the death of the sun. You can witness such "best of" moments as Lincoln's writing of the Gettysburg Address, the sinking of the Titanic, or the building of the Great Wall of China.

A recurring choice is between staying in a strange world to try building a new life there or risking danger to return to the cave, hoping to find a way back to your familiar home:

> Soon you are sitting in front of a huge beach fire, cooking crabs and eating buana cake. Having never had a visitor before, your hosts are happy to see you. They welcome you into their society. Gradually you learn their language. They boys tell you they are your brothers; the girls that they are your sisters.
>
> You enjoy life in this new paradise, but you still wonder whether there might be a way to get back to the Cave of Time. Your new friends are unable to help. Perhaps if you journeyed inland you could find some who could. Your friends warn you against trying, however. They tell you that you will find only terrible jungles and rivers filled with crocodiles.
>
> *If you remain with your new friends, turn to page 62.*
>
> *If you journey inland, turn to page 63.*

The branches in the book come often, with rarely more than two pages passing without a choice. This means each pathway is quite short, taking a reader only ten to fifteen minutes to read—a chunk of time nicely aligned with the length of a bus ride or school recess. While later books in the series would slow down the pacing of choices to enable longer pathways with more plot and character development—and would therefore, by necessity, merge branches much more aggressively, decreasing the reader's agency over the plot—*The Cave of Time* treats each choice as a true divergence. Readers can discover forty different endings, from being eaten by the Loch Ness Monster to becoming a ship captain to riding a mammoth off the edge of a cliff:

> Thousands of years later when Dr. Carleton Frisbee, the famous paleontologist, finds your bones next to those of a wooly mammoth in the Red Creek excavation, he is amazed at how closely you resemble a twentieth-century human being.
>
> **The End**

Bantam's marketing director Barbara Marcus took on the challenge of selling the unusual book. "A children's paperback series [didn't] have dollars, display space, or reviews" in those days, Marcus later recalled.[4] Kids' books were often treated as filler, distributed at random to bookshops along with more profitable adult books, with the stores left to figure out what to do with them. When asked how she promoted the new series, Marcus remembered, "We did absolutely nothing except give the books away. We gave thousands of the books to our salesmen and told them to give five to each bookseller and tell him to give them to the first five kids into his shop." The decision to print the books in standard paperback size, rather than an oversized children's format, was also shrewd: younger readers felt like they were reading a real, grown-up book, and early teens didn't have to feel self-conscious about being seen with one. The numbering, too, was a clever idea, suggesting there were other titles you were missing out on and encouraging kids to trade books or fill in the gaps in their collections. The series soon became a massive success.

While the format would seem to offer little room for experimentation, some books pushed tentatively against its boundaries. In *Inside UFO 54-40* (Choose Your Own Adventure #12), the winning ending—finding a legendary antiauthoritarian utopia—exists only on a page you are never instructed to turn to. *Trouble on Planet Earth* (#29) changes the reality of the story with each choice you make; it's less a book about exploring alternate choices than alternate universes. *Hyperspace* (#21) features all manner of time-and-space bending threads, including a branching book within a branching book and Edward Packard, the author, showing up in his own story.

As CYOA's popularity surged, dozens of competitor series arrived, cementing the hold of a genre later known as gamebooks. Some series like Fighting Fantasy targeted older teens and experimented with more gamelike systems, asking players to track discovered items or remaining hit points, with some choices available only when your character was in a particular state. Other series with educational bents required math or programming challenges to unlock the next page to turn to. Some gamebooks experimented with older audiences or less pulpy aesthetics: the pages of 1985's *MAZE*, by Christopher Manson, render an explorable, puzzle-filled mansion in enigmatic drawings, with a real-world prize of $10,000 offered to the first person to find the optimal pathway through its labyrinth of numbered doors.

But the original Choose Your Own Adventures remained the most popular. The franchise would become one of the most extraordinary successes in the history of publishing, eventually selling 250 million copies—one of the bestselling children's book series of all time. The New York Times in 1981 said the CYOA books were "as contagious as chicken pox."[4] "Kids can't stop reading" them, the colophon of some books in the series proclaimed, and in an era when concerns about screen time (on televisions) were gaining traction, adults saw no reason to stop them. "In 20 years of

A Familiar Interface

Another key to the popularity of Choose Your Own Adventure was the foolproof user interface. The digital interactive stories emerging in the 70s and 80s used command-line parser input, which could go wrong in all kinds of ways: misspelled words, unrecognized commands, bugs or bad implementation, or incorrect syntax. But to play one of Packard's gamebooks, all you needed to know was how to read.

In later years, interactive stories on computers would make a similar turn, sacrificing simulationism for more fool-proof methods of input—but perhaps significantly, not until well after Windows had supplanted DOS as the dominant gaming operating system, and typing was no longer seen as the de facto computer interface.

1979

teaching," one educator wrote, "I have never seen 12-year-olds so excited about anything as they are about Choose Your Own Adventure."[2] Bantam decided to accelerate the pace of releases to one new title a month, and in 1981 Packard gave up his law practice to write full time. He would go on to pen dozens of books in the series.

What made CYOA so popular, and why did that popularity come when it did? *The Cave of Time* hit shelves almost precisely in sync with the first commercial adventure games, and it's often been assumed that one event inspired the other. And yet this seems not to have been the case. "I remember first encountering [CYOA books] after PC-based adventure games came out,"[8] Infocom's Dave Lebling recalled, assuming they were some kind of knockoff from a jealous traditional media. But neither Packard nor Montgomery were familiar with early computer games either.

The real answer may lie far deeper in the cultural subconscious. Historian Eli Cook has suggested the series caught the headwinds of a massive cultural shift from the postwar, post-Depression era of "stability, solidarity, security, and safety" to free agency and plentiful choices as desirable cultural values.[2] The previous generation had "married young, many to their high-school sweethearts," Cook writes. "Most workers preferred career-long job security to flighty labor flexibility." But those values were giving way to more flexible arrangements both at home and at work, as well as "the conservative turn of the early 1980s, in which it came to be broadly assumed that one's success was not dependent on gender, race, class … but rather stemmed solely from the individual life decisions one made." Cook draws parallels between the CYOA books' claims that "you and YOU ALONE are in charge of what happens in this story," that "you are responsible because you choose," and Reagan Republicans cutting welfare programs because people in poverty had only themselves to blame—they'd simply made poor choices. But this wasn't just a conservative turn: the language of abortion-rights advocates settled on "pro-choice" in the 1980s, Cook notes, while ad campaigns across the country were switching to second-person slogans like Have It Your Way or This Bud's for You. Self-determination had become the watchword of the day, and individual agency the most potent application of American freedom.

Whether you buy this cultural psychoanalysis or not, it's unarguable that the books struck a powerful generational chord with younger readers. Packard had a simpler explanation for their success: "Kids love to die," he quipped,[7] recalling with fondness the cowboy games he'd once played with his brother where "it was always more fun to go into death throes." Sensitive to claims the books appealed more to boys than girls, Packard pointed to a fan letter from a young lady reviewer: "I got a spear in my back and went in quicksand," she wrote, "but other than that the book was great." In fact, both Packard and Montgomery had taken pains to author their stories without any assumptions about the reader's gender, and in *The Cave of Time* neither the text nor artwork betrays this conceit: the illustrations usually draw the short-haired protagonist with their back to the viewer. Later books in the series, however, began to use artwork that showed a generic blond white boy as each story's hero. "Bantam insisted it be a boy because they had market research that said girls would identify with boys but boys would never read a book where 'you' was a girl," Packard later explained, musing, "I think we lost a great number of girls" to copycat series less afraid to pursue a feminine demographic.[11]

Choose Your Own Adventure books remained bestsellers well into the 90s, though they slowly lost ground to digital interactive entertainments as computers and video game consoles became affordable for more and more families. The series ended its original run in 1998. Edward Packard cowrote the final book with the same person who'd inspired him since the beginning, a successful adult now with her own career: his daughter Andrea.

Even after its demise, the series would remain the most common cultural touchstone for interactive stories for the next twenty years. No one quite predicted the long-term impact the books would have, despite the wild success of their initial run. A 1981 profile of Packard entitled "He Chose His Own Adventure" paints a fond picture of an unlikely text games godfather at the beginning of his second career, which seemed to suit him far better than his first:

> These days, instead of drawing up legal briefs, Packard reclines on the couch in his Madison Avenue law office. Surrounded by the dark leather-bound statute books he has abandoned, he draws outlines that look like trees. Each branch carries an option, each option sprouts into more options and every leaf represents an ending.
> Then he writes.[7]

References

1   Ashwell, Sam Kabo. 2011. "CYOA Structure: The Cave of Time." *These Heterogenous Tasks* (blog). Aug 5, 2011. heterogenoustasks.wordpress.com/2011/08/05/cyoa-structures-the-cave-of-time | a Jun 11, 2020

2   Cook, Eli. 2020. "Rearing Children of the Market in the 'You' Decade: Choose Your Own Adventure Books and the Ascent of Free Choice in 1980s America." *Journal of American Studies*, Feb 12, 2020.

3   Debnam, Betty. 1984. "Meet the Author of the 'Choose Your Own Adventure' Stories." *The Ledger* (Lakeland, FL), Mar 27, 1984, Sunrise Edition, p. 7D.

4   Harmetz, Aljean. 1981. "'Choose Your Own Adventure' and Make Your Own Ending." *New York Times*, Aug 25, 1981, sec. Books.

5   Heinzerling, Ann Day. 1975. "The Crossroads Press." *Vermont Life*, Spring 1975.

6   Katz, Demian. 1998. "Demian's Gamebook Web Page." gamebooks.org | a Jun 11, 2020

7   Kraft, Scott. 1981. "He Chose His Own Adventure." *The Day* (New London, CT), Oct 10, 1981, sec. Business/Finance.

8   Lebling, David. 2011. "David Lebling Interview." Interview by Grady Hendrix. Blog. www.gradyhendrix.com/david-lebling-interview | s July 11, 2011

9   Montgomery, R.A. 2011. "RA Montgomery Interview." 2011 Interview by Grady Hendrix. Blog. www.gradyhendrix.com/ra-montgomery-interview | a Jun 11, 2020

10 Munger, Sean. 2013. "Choosing Adventure: The Edward Packard Interview." seanmunger.com. Aug 16, 2013. seanmunger.com/2013/08/15/choosing-adventure-the-edward-packard-interview-part-i | a Jun 11, 2020

11 Packard, Edward. 2011. "Edward Packard Interview." Interview by Grady Hendrix. Blog. www.gradyhendrix.com/edward-packard-interview | a Jun 11, 2020

12 Robinson, Sean Michael. 2010. "The Forked Path- Childhood, Death and the Choose Your Own Adventure." *The Hooded Utilitarian* (blog). Sep 23, 2010. hoodedutilitarian.com/2010/09/9447 | s Aug 15, 2011

13 Rossen, Jake. 2014. "A Brief History of 'Choose Your Own Adventure.'" *Mental Floss* (blog). Apr 10, 2014. www.mentalfloss.com/article/56160/brief-history-choose-your-own-adventure | a Jun 11, 2020

THE

19

THE 80S RANG IN the dawn of a computer game industry. Led by companies like Adventure International **1978**, Brøderbund, and On-Line Systems (later Sierra On-Line), it would grow from one- or two-person teams in garages to a $5 billion market by the end of the decade. Text games were a crucial part of that industry's foundation, though not the first bricks laid: Sierra's graphic adventure *Mystery House* hit the home computer market half a year before Infocom's *Zork*. Indeed, Infocom's founders had been advised that making text-only games was a mistake—but for a while, it was so much easier to make text look good than graphics. Sixty-four kilobytes wasn't enough space to hold more than a few primitive line drawings, but Frost or Faulkner would have found it quite roomy. At the start of the decade it was still hard to imagine home computers as the future of art, but the future of fiction seemed closer to hand.

Text games were commercially viable through most of the 80s, charting alongside or even above graphical games. *Zork* was the industry's bestselling game in 1982, and *The Hitchhiker's Guide to the Galaxy* **1984** was outselling hits like *King's Quest* [Sierra On-Line 1984] in early 1985. *Adventure* **1976**—with its immersive second-person prose, natural language text parser, and gameplay focused on exploration and puzzles—had become first a template for mainframe text games, then a model for home computer imitators. The command line where anything might be typed, a familiar interface for early computer users, aligned with the blue-sky feel of the times. In the new digital realm, possibilities seemed endless.

Like early computers themselves, parser games could be fascinating to meddle with but frustrating to master. *ELIZA* and *SHRDLU* had foreshadowed many of the difficulties with software that playfully pretended (or earnestly tried) to understand its users, but it would take more time and perspective for the lessons to sink in. Text adventure UI was hard to learn even before attaching it to games with difficult puzzles; "feelings of frustration and humiliation are therefore quite common in one's initial encounter with interactive fiction," wrote some of the earliest humanities scholars to study the form. Like any medium from opera to anime, parser games developed their own tropes, conventions, and shorthand that could be off-putting or baffling to outsiders. Fans learned which verbs and command forms were likely to be understood, but newcomers often struggled. This book won't belabor the point, but it's worth making once: most encounters with parser games through history have looked less like the successful transcripts usually shown, and more like this.

```
> HELLO THERE
I DO NOT KNOW THE WORD " THERE."
> WHERE AM I
I DO NOT KNOW THE WORD " WHERE "
> GET UP
I SEE NOTHING TO TAKE
> GO
I SEE NOTHING TO GO THROUGH
> GO OUT THE DOR
I DO NOT KNOW THE WORD " DOR."
> GO OUT THE DOOR
I DO NOT KNOW THE VERB " GO OUT "
> HELP
YOU'RE DOING FINE.
> NO I'M NOT
I DO NOT KNOW THE WORD " I'M "
```

Even to fans, text adventures could be frustrating—but also at times exhilarating, transporting, and deeply satisfying to those who learned their rhythms and mastered their riddles. A handful of companies sprang up to specialize in interactive fiction, often attracting passionate fans more well-read and well-rounded than those the game industry as a whole would increasingly cater to. Many were women, over forty, or primarily interested in hobbies other than gaming. In the United States, Infocom became the most famous text game studio, cultivating a reputation as masters of a form they were still in the midst of inventing. The *Zork* [1980–82] and *Enchanter* [1983–85] trilogies, murder mysteries *Deadline* [1982] and *Suspect* [1984], sci-fi sagas *Planetfall* [1983] and *Suspended* [1983], Lovecraftian hacker saga *The*

see **Before the 70s**

Anthony J. Niesz and Norman N. Holland. 1984. "Interactive fiction." *Critical Inquiry* 11, no. 1.

See **1981** for the origin of the term, later popularized by Infocom.

see **1977**, **1983–5**, and **1987**

1980s

Infocom's ads (like this 1983 two-page spread in *Softline*, with inset close-up) often poked fun at the primitive graphics of their rivals, appealed to the intelligence and sophistication of their audience of readers, and billed themselves as masters of an emerging new form of literature.

Lurking Horror [1987], and pirate romance *Plundered Hearts* [1987] speak to the range of styles and audiences the company experimented with. Infocom set a bar for quality that later generations of amateurs 1993 would spend decades chasing, with titles like *Trinity* [1986] and *A Mind Forever Voyaging* 1985 hoping to elevate the form past genre tropes toward serious literature.

Other countries saw different kinds of text game scenes emerge, often shaped by the particulars of regional hardware availability or cultural convention. In Britain, studio Magnetic Scrolls (co-founded by twenty-two-year-old coder Anita Sinclair) garnered a reputation for ambitious text games with a wider range of styles and tones, including *Corruption* [1988], a crime thriller set in the world of high-stakes finances, and *Fish!* [1988], in which the player character is a dimension-hopping espionage agent who starts the game in the body of a goldfish. Level 9, run by three brothers and a sister out of High Wycombe, was a prolific UK text adventure publisher who released well-regarded puzzlers like *Snowball* [1983], ambitious social science fiction like *The Worm In Paradise* [1985], and offbeat comedy laden with homegrown British humor like *Gnome Ranger* [1987]. Hobbyist text games also proliferated in countries where tools to make them, such as The Quill [Gilsoft 1983], were widely distributed: Australian Dorothy Millard (later Dorothy Irene), one of countless game makers straddling the line between amateur and pro,

see **2007** and **1988**

For example source code
from ZIL, Infocom's in-house
language, see **1983**.

```
Professional  Adventure  Writer


      V  -  Vocabulary
      L  -  Locations
      C  -     Connections
      G  -  Graphics
      D  -     Default  Colours
      M  -  Messages
      N  -     System
      O  -  Objects
      I  -     Initially  At
      W  -  Words
      X  -     Weight
      P  -  Process  Tables
      R  -  Response  Table

      E  -  Extra  Options


   Option,  then  ENTER...
```

**PAW, the Professional
Adventure Writer [Gilsoft
1987], was a menu-driven tool
for creating text adventures.**

influential on Choice of
Games; see **2018**

1980s

wrote over a dozen self-published adventures in the late 80s and early 90s
and advertised in publications like *Commodore Network* and *Adventure Probe*.
Game magazines often ran competitions for fan adventures that awarded
cash prizes and distribution offers to winners. Text games in languages other
than English flourished in scenes from Spain to Czechoslovakia—although
in areas slower to adopt personal computers, graphical games sometimes
became standard before a text-only tradition could emerge.

A key to making text games a reproducible success for commercial profit
(or amateur acclaim) was the development of domain-specific creation tools.
While *Adventure* had been written in the general purpose language Fortran,
text adventures featured much reusable code between games and a clear
separation between the underlying system and a particular story, suggesting
a stable engine and a domain-specific language would be useful for writing
them. First-generation text game tools were often trade secrets, in-house
languages and compilers with vaguely specified but much-hyped proprietary
features—by today's standards, often unwieldy and obtuse. But across the
decade, a huge range of commercial and amateur engines emerged with
the enticing promise of letting home users write their own adventures. An
incomplete catalog includes The Quill (marketed as Adventure Writer in the
US) but also Adventure Construction Set, Computer Novel Construction
Set, Alan (Adventure Language), GAGS
(Generic Adventure Game System), PAW
(Professional Adventure Writer), TADS
(Text Adventure Development System),
AGT (Adventure Game Toolkit), and ADL
(Adventure Definition Language). Many of
these tools would gather loyal communities
still improving and updating them decades
later.

While parser games quickly became an
established form, many hoped it would not
be the final one for interactive storytelling.
Mirroring the broader game industry in the
80s, radical experiments and strange new
ideas were still welcomed. Anything might
prove to be the next big hit. Novelist Rob
Swigart's *Portal* [Activision 1986] gave players an interface to a futuristic database
and asked them to piece together a story in fragments; *Uncle Roger* **1986** was
another such "random-access narrative." Canadian poet Barrie Nichol used
his Apple IIe to make poetry for the screen that moved and mutated in *First
Screening: Computer Poems* [1984]. Activision published Robert Pinsky's surreal
text game *Mindwheel* [1985]—a frustrating epic of astral projection, rock stars
and dictators, and copious sonnets—as well as *Alter Ego* [1986], which took
players through not a heroic quest but an ordinary life, from cradle to grave.
Wilderness: A Survival Adventure [Electric Transit 1984] married a parser to a complex
survival simulation. *Star Saga: One* [Masterplay 1988] combined a multiplayer
computer strategy and trading game with megabytes of story text too large to

fit on contemporary disks, printed instead in a stack of companion booklets with almost a thousand numbered sections. Even Infocom tried shaking up their formula, releasing games that played out in real time like *Border Zone* [1987], added RPG mechanics like *Quarterstaff* [1988], or unfolded in standalone vignettes rather than a single unified story as in *Nord and Bert Couldn't Make Head or Tail of It* [1987].

One of the most creative of these experiments was *The Prisoner* [Edu-Ware 1980], based on the cult 1960s TV show about spies, mind games, and control. The game gives the player a three-digit number they're charged never to reveal, then takes them through a far-ranging series of minigames that try to trick them into revealing it, including a city simulator, a priest chatbot, several mazes, a psych quiz, and various banks, gambling halls, and item shops. Pressing the Escape key at certain points, instead of quitting

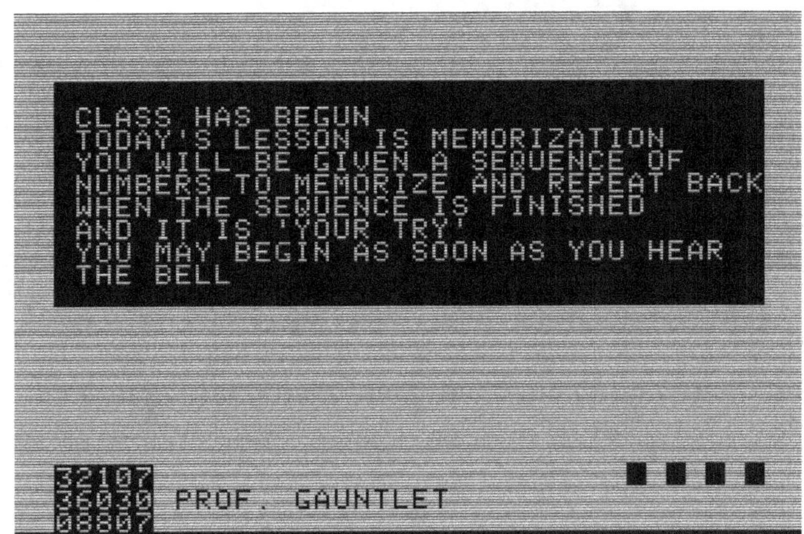

From *The Prisoner* [Edu-Ware 1980]; screenshot courtesy the blog *Renga in Blue*.

the game, shows the message "Such thoughts are punishable." In the 1982 version, the game can accurately simulate a catastrophic crash, prodding the player to investigate its cause. The line number listed as the source of the "crash," which most players would immediately type in by reflex to diagnose the problem, is the player's secret code.

Printed gamebooks were also massively popular through the 80s. Choose Your Own Adventure became one of the bestselling young adult series in history, paving the way for dozens of paper competitors from Fighting Fantasy to Be an Interplanetary Spy to Give Yourself Goosebumps to Follow Your Heart Romance. The Micro Adventure gamebooks by Eileen Buckholtz and Ruth Glick cast readers as kid hackers, and included real BASIC programs to type in and run to decode cyphers or overcome obstacles. Play-by-mail games also grew increasingly popular during the decade, lettings users interact through pencil and paper with distant computers running complex simulations, some managing hundreds or thousands of players in the same virtual universe. Turns unfolded at the slow cadence of once every ten days or two weeks, leaving time for results to be mailed out through the postal system, strategies to be considered, and new orders to be sent back. Though online games like *MUD* and its successors were growing more sophisticated, their audience was still sharply limited by steep hourly connection fees. In contrast, play-by-mail let gamers explore shared virtual worlds for a few dollars a week and the cost of some postage stamps.

see **1979**

see *Monster Island* **1989**

see **1980**

The power and capacity of home computers compounded exponentially throughout the decade, and the cost to store each byte of code and content plummeted. In 1980, a floppy drive with hundred-kilobyte disks was still a new and expensive add-on. For roughly the same price in 1990, you could get a CD-ROM drive reading discs that held half a gigabyte of data—*five thousand times* more. A new 486 PC in 1990 had just enough processing power to stream multimedia content off those discs: detailed images in the 256-color palette provided by the VGA standard, audio for your new sound card, even video. While a home computer that could read and write English was the hot tech demo in 1980, ten years later spoken dialogue and video clips stole the show. The decade ended with interactive text a dying breed on store shelves, another apparent victim of technological progress.

But the story was far from over. If anything, the history of text games was about to get even more interesting.

More Text Games from the 1980s

Note that this is an even more partial list than for other decades: the Interactive Fiction Database records well over 2,000 text adventure games released in the 1980s.

1980
MUD

Ghost Town *(Scott Adams, Adventure International)*. Hidden treasures in a Wild West town. **Haunt** *(John E. Laird, DEC-20)*. Haunted house puzzle game. **Mystery House** *(Roberta Williams, On-Line Systems)*. First of Sierra's hybrid parser/graphical adventure games. **The Prisoner** *(David Mullich, Edu-Ware Services)*. Surreal game of paranoia based on the cult 60s TV show. **Reality Ends** *(William F. Denman, Jr, Med Systems Software)*. Exploration of "parallel realities" via rooms with slightly differing descriptions. **Rogue** *(Michael Toy et al., UNIX)*. RPG with ASCII art and procedurally generated dungeons; namesake of the roguelike genre. **Warp** *(Rob Lucke and Bill Frolik, HP3000)*. Massive mainframe treasure hunt; parser lets users define macros and commands triggered by game state changes.

1981
His Majesty's Ship "Impetuous"

Cyborg *(Mike Berlyn and Muffy Berlyn, Sentient Software)*. Sci-fi story about merging with an AI consciousness; same authors as Infocom's *Suspended* 1983. **The Golden Baton** *(Brian Howarth, Molimerx)*. First in the Mysterious Adventures series written using the Adventure International format. **The Golden Voyage** *(William Demas and Scott Adams, Adventure International)*. Final text-only game from Adventure International. **Madness & the Minotaur** *(Tom Rosenbaum, Spectral Associates)*. Punishingly difficult game with monsters and randomly-changing mazes. **Planet of Death** *(Richard Turner and Chris Thornton, Arctic Computing)*. Perhaps the first commercially sold British text adventure. **Saigon: The Final Days** *(Jyym and Robyn Pearson, Adventure International)*. Hybrid text/graphics; early example of engaging with a serious theme. **Softporn Adventure** *(Chuck Benton, On-Line Systems)*. Sierra's only all-text game, reworked later as graphical *Leisure Suit Larry*. **Thunder Road Adventure** *(Don and Freda Boner, The Programmer's Guild)*. Game about running moonshine in a '57 Chevy by a father/daughter team. **Zork II: The Wizard of Frobozz** *(Dave Lebling and Marc Blank, Infocom)*. Sequel, continuing to port content from the vast mainframe original.

1982
The Hobbit

Avon *(Jon Thackray and Jonathan Partington, IBM System/370)*. Mainframe game in a Shakespearean fantasy world, later ported to micros by Topologika. **Avventura nel castello** *(Enrico Colombini and Chiara Tovena, Dinosoft)*. Probably the first Italian interactive fiction game. **Countdown to Doom** *(Peter D. Kilworth, Topologika)*. Explore an alien planet on a tight timer to find parts to fix your crashed ship. **Deadline**

(Marc Blank, Infocom). Murder mystery with characters to question; early example of complex conversational NPCs. **Dunnet** *(Ron Schnell, DECSYSTEM-20)*. Cyberpunk mainframe game, most famous for a 1992 port included in Emacs, thus making its way into millions of Linux-based operating systems including Mac OS X. **The Mask of the Sun** *(Alan B. Clark et al., Ultrasoft)*. Aztec tomb-robbing game, parser/graphical hybrid. **Middle-Earth Trilogy** *(Peter Austin et al., Level 9)* aka *Jewels of Darkness*. Trilogy expanding on *Adventure* 1976. **Starcross** *(Dave Lebling, Infocom)*. Explore a mysterious alien spaceship filled with logic puzzles. **The Warlock of Firetop Mountain** *(Steve Jackson and Ian Livingstone, Puffin Books)*. First of the successful Fighting Fantasy gamebook series. **Zork III: The Dungeon Master** *(Dave Lebling and Marc Blank, Infocom)*. Difficult end to the trilogy takes steps toward moving on from cave-set treasure hunts.

Beyond the Tesseract *(David Lo, TRS-80)*. Ambitious game involving journeys through mathematical spaces and manipulation of abstract concepts. **The Curse** *(Gilsoft)*. Early Quill game in which a fortune teller transports you to ancient Egypt. **Enchanter** *(Marc Blank and Dave Lebling, Infocom)*. Start of post-*Zork* trilogy using magic words to solve puzzles; includes spells *frotz*, *gnusto*, and *nitfol*, later to name fan-made IF tools. **Infidel** *(Mike Berlyn, Infocom)*. Tomb-robbing puzzler with a surprise twist. **Kingdom of Hamil** *(Jonathan Partington and Jonathan Thackray, Acornsoft)*, aka *Hamil*. Port of puzzle game for the Phoenix mainframe at Cambridge. **Lords of Time** *(Sue Gazzard and Ian Buxton, Level 9)*. Time travel scavenger hunt, start of *Time and Magik* trilogy. **MegaWars** *(CompuServe)*. Clone of *DECWARS* and *Super Star Trek* 1974; early multiplayer space shooter. **Planetfall** *(Steve Meretzky, Infocom)*. Sci-fi comedy remembered for robot buddy Floyd. **Snowball** *(Mike Austin et al., Level 9)*. Hero Kim Kimberly awakens from hibernation aboard a hijacked starship. **Twin Kingdom Valley** *(Trevor Hall and P. M. Skinner, Bug-Byte Software)*. Text/graphics hybrid with wandering NPCs. **Le Vampire Fou** *(Jean-Louis Le Breton, Ciel Bleu)*. First commercial French text adventure. **The Witness** *(Stu Galley, Infocom)*. Noir murder mystery.

1983
Suspended

Back In Time *(Stella MacDonald, Blue Ridge Software Company)*. Educational text/graphics hybrid wherein your schoolbus travels to the age of dinosaurs. **Cutthroats** *(Michael Berlyn and Jerry Wolper, Infocom)*. Treasure hunt through sunken shipwrecks; some frustrating bugs and design. **Drug Wars** *(John E. Dell, DOS)*. Buy and sell as a New York dealer; inspired many later imitators. **First Screening: Computer Poems** *(bpNichol, Underwhich)*. Collection of kinetic poetry for the screen. **Flight from the Dark** *(Joe Dever, Sparrow Books)* aka Lone Wolf #1. First in popular gamebook series with RPG elements. **Hampstead** *(Trevor Lever and Peter Jones, Melbourne House)*. Social satire notable for being an early game to tackle contemporary political issues. **L: A Mathemagical Adventure** *(Association of Teachers of Mathematics, BBC Micro)*. Widely played British edugame with logic and math puzzles. **Racter** *(William Chamberlain and Thomas Etter, Mindscape)*. Chatbot famous for allegedy writing a whimsical book, *The Policeman's Beard is Half-Constructed*. **Rendezvous with Rama** *(Lee Jacknow and Ronald Martinez, Trillium)*. Based on the Clarke novel. **Return to Eden** *(Nick Austin et al., Level 9)*. Sequel to *Snowball* takes Kim to an alien colony world and a city being built by robots. **Seastalker** *(Jim Lawrence and Stu Galley, Infocom)*. Underwater adventure targeted at younger readers. **Sorcerer** *(Steve Meretzky, Infocom)*. Second in *Enchanter* trilogy. **Space Attack: Micro Adventure #1** *(Eileen Buckholtz and Ruth Glick, Scholastic)*. Start of gamebook series with BASIC programs for readers to type in and run. **Suspect** *(Dave Lebling, Infocom)*. Murder mystery with NPCs taking independent actions. **System 15000** *(John Wagstaff, AVS)*. Early hacking simulator. **Trade Wars** *(Chris Sherrick, BASIC)*. First version of space trading made famous by 1991 remake. **Yenght** *(Víctor Ruiz Tejedor, Dinamic)*. Fantasy adventure text/graphics hybrid, one of the earliest in Spanish. **Zauberschloß** *(Dennis Merbach, BASIC)*. Type-in fantasy adventure, one of the earliest known German text games. **Zyll** *(Marshal*

1984
The Hitchhiker's Guide to the Galaxy

Linder and Scott Edwards, IBM). Even Big Blue got into text adventures with this treasure hunt featuring two-player cooperative or competitive play.

1985
A Mind Forever Voyaging

2010: The Text Adventure Game *(Michael Price et al., Coleco).* Tie-in to the Kubrick/Clarke sequel with multiple choice interface. **Essex** *(Bill Darrah and William Mataga, Brøderbund).* Real-time sci-fi adventure billed as an "electronic novel" with conversational NPCs. **Island of Kesmai** *(John Taylor and Kelton Flinn, Kesmai).* Early commercial MUD on CompuServe with roguelike elements; evolved from 1980 *Dungeons of Kesmai.* **Mindwheel** *(Robert Pinsky et al., Brøderbund).* Trippy poetic saga about entering the minds of four famous people; frustrating but unique. **Nine Princes in Amber** *(Mike Amadeo et al., Telarium).* Ambitious attempt to adapt the Zelazny novel into a truly interactive story. **The Pawn** *(Rob Steggles et al., Magnetic Scrolls).* British studio's ambitious debut game. **The Rats** *(GXT/Five Ways Software, Hodder & Stoughton).* Bookware adaptation of horror novel; unusual strategic, structural, and typographical elements. **The Secret of St. Bride's** *(Priscilla Langridge, St. Bride's School).* First of the unusual releases from the Games Mistresses 1992. **Spellbreaker** *(Dave Lebling, Infocom).* Challenging conclusion to *Enchanter* trilogy. **Wilderness: A Survival Adventure** *(Wesley Huntress and Charles Kohlhase, Electric Transit).* Detailed survival simulator. **Wishbringer** *(Brian Moriarty, Infocom).* Introductory fantasy aimed at younger adventurers, with a way to wish away hard puzzles. **The Worm in Paradise** *(Mike Austin et al., Level 9).* Surreal "utopia" in a far-future city.

1986
Uncle Roger

Alter Ego *(Peter J. Favaro, Activision).* Branching-path story about the life of an ordinary person; sold in male and female versions. **Amnesia** *(Thomas M. Disch and Kevin Bentley, Electronic Arts).* Bizarre Manhattan-set game based on 400-page manuscript by the famous author. **Ballyhoo** *(Jeff O'Neill, Infocom).* Circus mystery. **Beyond the Titanic** *(Scott Miller, Apogee).* First game from studio later known for action games. **Breakers** *(Rod Smith, Brøderbund).* Ambitious sci-fi with complex NPCs and worldbuilding. **Bugsy** *(Priscilla Langridge, St. Bride's/CRL Group).* Play a cartoon rabbit gangster trying to take over Chicago in this "advencha" parody. **Dracula** *(Rod Pike, CRL Group).* Well-written, if frustrating, take on the Bram Stoker novel. **Hollywood Hijinx** *(Dave Anderson and Liz Cyr-Jones, Infocom).* Treasure hunt in a Malibu mansion stuffed with movie-themed puzzles. **Leather Goddesses of Phobos** *(Steve Meretzky, Infocom).* Comedy send-up of pulp sci-fi, famous for scratch 'n sniff feelie. **Moonmist** *(Stu Galley and Jim Lawrence, Infocom).* Gothic ghost story at a haunted castle, with four different plot variants based on which "favorite color" you pick. **Portal** *(Rob Swigart, Activision).* Novel in nonlinear fragments about an astronaut returning to Earth after a hundred-year mission. **The Price of Magik** *(Pete Austin et al., Level 9).* Dark fantasy with sprawling map and spells that drain age and sanity. **The Rim Worlds War** *(Jessica Mulligan, GEnie).* Space strategy game; early commercial play-by-email title. **Trinity** *(Brian Moriarty, Infocom).* Finely crafted time-travel parable about nuclear war.

1987
Plundered Hearts

AberMUD *(Alan Cox et al., B).* First popular open-source MUD; engine later forked into many influential variants. **Beyond Zork** *(Brian Moriarty, Infocom).* Adds RPG elements and a revised layout to quest for the Coconut of Quendor. **The Big Sleaze** *(Fergus McNeill, Delta 4).* Three-episode parody of hardboiled detective stories. **Border Zone** *(Marc Blank, Infocom).* Iron Curtain spy thriller with three viewpoint characters and a real-time clock. **Bureaucracy** *(Douglas Adams et al., Infocom).* A quest to get your bank to acknowledge a change-of-address form; just as frustrating as it sounds. **Escape from ANTcatraz** *(Lorri Hopping, Scholastic).* Play as an ant helping your colony escape capture. **Gnome Ranger** *(Pete Austin, Level 9).* Introduced fan-favorite hero Ingrid Bottomlow. **The Guild of Thieves** *(Rob Steggles, Magnetic Scrolls).* Text/graphics hybrid with an already-retro treasure hunt vibe. **Jacaranda Jim** *(Graham Cluley, DOS).* Shareware adventure; example of rise of amateur games spread via BBS. **Jinxter** *(Georgina Sinclair and Michael Bywater, Magnetic Scrolls).* Goofy romp through a fantasy world filled with very British humor. **Knight Orc** *(Pete Austin, Level 9)*. Well-regarded adventure where you play the bad guy; real-time roving NPCs. **The Lurking Horror** *(Dave Lebling, Infocom)*. Hackers and Lovecraftian horror on an MIT-like college campus. **Nord and Bert Couldn't Make Head or Tail of It** *(Jeff O'Neill, Infocom)*. Collection of standalone vignettes that take wordplay to solve. **Quarterstaff** *(Scott D. Schmitz and Kenneth M. Updike, Simulated Environment Systems)*. Adventure/RPG hybrid later updated and rereleased by Infocom. **Stationfall** *(Steve Meretzky, Infocom)*. Sequel to *Planetfall* set on an abandoned space station. **Varitale** *(Timothy S. Campbell, Pinnacle)*. BBS choose-your-path game allowing players to extend the story when they got to an unwritten branch.

The Beast of Torrack Moor *(Linda Wright, Zenobi)*. Mystery set in the English countryside with dynamic NPCs. **Corruption** *(Rob Steggles and Hugh Steers, Magnetic Scrolls)*. Corporate espionage in a timing-based mystery. **Dr. Dumont's Wild P.A.R.T.I.** *(Muffy Berlyn and Mike Berlyn, First Row)*. A mad scientist zaps you into a virtual reality filled with metaphors for particle physics. **Federation II** *(Alan Lenton, Compunet)*. Early nonfantasy MUD; ran near-continuously into the 2020s. **Fish!** *(John Molloy et al., Magnetic Scrolls)*. Quirky game about a dimension- and body-hopping secret agent. **GemStone** *(Simutronics, GEnie)*. Another long-running MUD; survived commercially for decades as *GemStone IV*. **Hidden Agenda** *(Jim Gasperini, Springboard)*. Politics sim set in Central America with strategy elements and multiple-choice scenarios. **Lancelot** *(Christina Erskin et al., Level 9)*. Serious Arthurian adventure with extensive descriptive prose. **The Lost Crown of Queen Anne** *(Robert Wayne Atkins, Softdisk)*. Shareware text game with elaborate UI. **Mindfighter** *(Anna Popkess and Fergus McNeill, Activision)*. Postapocalyptic epic about a kid psychic fighting to survive. **QuantumLink Serial** *(Tracy Reed, Quantum)*. Early weekly serial on the service that would become AOL, told in emails and chatrooms; author would incorporate reader participation in next week's installment. **Sherlock: The Riddle of the Crown Jewels** *(Bob Bates, Infocom)*. One of Infocom's last pure-text adventures. **Star Saga: One** *(Richard Dutton et al., Masterplay)*. Space trading game with unusual format: huge passages of descriptive text printed in companion booklets referenced in the game by numbers.

Agatha's Folly *(Linda Wright, Zenobi)*. Well-regarded Quill-written murder mystery at a country cottage. **Arthur: The Quest For Excalibur** *(Bob Bates, Infocom)*. One of Infocom's final text game titles. **Avalon** *(Yehuda Simmons and Daniel James, Hourglass)*. Fantasy MUD, one of the oldest continuously operating. **Demon's Tomb—The Awakening** *(Simon Price, Virgin Mastertronic)*. Modern-set horror with nice UI features. **Genesis** *(Lars Pensjö, LPMud)*. First world for the popular LPMud software. **The Glory of Kings** *(Agema Publications, play-by-mail)*, aka *La Gloire Du Roi*. Play-by-mail game of eighteenth-century war and diplomacy; some games ran for more than a real-world decade. **James Clavell's Shogun** *(Dave Lebling, Infocom)*. Unsuccessful adaptation of the famous novel. **Journey: The Quest Begins** *(Marc Blank, Infocom)*. Fantasy story told in a past-tense diary format; graphics and UI experiments. **Legend of the Red Dragon** *(Seth Robinson, Robinson Technologies)*, aka *LORD*. Popular BBS door game with fighting and flirting. **Myth** *(Paul Findley, Magnetic Scrolls)*. Journey to the underworld of ancient Greece. **Quantum Space** *(Don Daglow, AOL)*. Popular play-by-email game. **Scapeghost** *(Pete Austin, Level 9)*. Ghosts and gangsters; last from Level 9. **Son of Stagefright** *(Mike McCauley, AGT)*. Community theater shenanigans; winner of the 1989 Softworks AGT Competition. **Zork Zero** *(Steve Meretzky, Infocom)*. Large open map; clickable UI.

1988
P.R.E.S.T.A.V.B.A.

1989
Monster Island

MUD

Roy Trubshaw and Richard Bartle

Also Known As **MUD1, Essex MUD, British Legends**
Style **MUD**
Debuted **Apr 1980** *(ARPANET)*
Launch Platform **PDP-10**
Language **MACRO-10** *(version 1 & 2)*
BCPL/MUDDL *(version 3)*

> **Narrow road between lands.**
> You are stood on a narrow road between The Land and whence you came. To the north and south are the small foothills of a pair of majestic mountains, with a large wall running round. To the west the road continues…

"IMAGINE YOU ARE PLAYING AN ADVENTURE," asks an article in a popular computing magazine, credited to someone called Endora the Witch:

> Let's say you're in a room of a house, you have found some treasure, and are now a bit stumped as to how to get it past the bookcase, which you can't shift but which you're certain conceals a secret passage. You have tried all sorts of commands to no avail, and are about to give up when up on your screen comes the message: "Tom has just arrived."[19]

Tom is "not part of the program, but a real, live person," Endora explains, "sitting possibly hundreds of miles away and exploring the same land as you are." This is a mind-blowing concept not easy, at the time, to explain. "CB radio in fantasyland," tries Endora's editor in the article's subheading; another journalist wrote that the game was built atop "quite a sophisticated teleconferencing system."[10] This adventure with real live people in it had

1980

been getting more and more coverage in the gaming press and at enthusiast meetups. It sounded incredible. Everyone wanted to try it. For a long time, almost nobody could.

The game was called *MUD*, which stood for Multi-User Dungeon—the last word used not in a generic sense, but as the alternate title for *Zork*. During the few months the MIT game had gone by the name *Dungeon*, a popular port had spread far and wide, and one of the places it reached was Essex University in the United Kingdom. Essex was among the first schools to connect to the EPSS (Experimental Packet Switched Service), Britain's answer to ARPANET, and in 1978 was one of the few places in Europe that allowed undergraduates to freely access the burgeoning worldwide network of mainframe computers. Some of the bytes that wended their way beneath the Atlantic to Essex described the underground empires of *Dungeon* and *Adventure* to a fascinated undergraduate named Roy Trubshaw who, like many others on sundry continents, had become enthralled.

see **1977**

see **1976**

Trubshaw and some other Essex hackers had recently discovered a neat trick on the school's PDP-10 mainframe. A time-sharing system like the PDP divides its memory and resources between connected users, isolating them from each other to give each the illusion of their own private machine. Although admins could use "interprocess communications" to share data between users, lowly students didn't have the privileges to do so—but one of Trubshaw's friends had discovered a back door. Each running program had both a shared "code segment" in memory, where all its instructions lived, and a separate "data segment" for each user. It turned out that an obscure and mislabeled monitor call, .SETUWP, actually let an unprivileged user *un*set the write-protection bit for a program's code segment. The friends immediately saw the rich possibilities of this exploit: if some of that memory space could hold not code but shared data, and the running program was simulating a world like in those immersive text games from America, everyone connected could see the results of any other user's changes. The trick enabled the possibility of an unsanctioned but gloriously multi-user *Dungeon*.

The PLATO games like *dnd* 1975 had used a similar feature on that platform to share a common simulation state with multiple players.

Trubshaw started building a proof of concept, sketching in the core features it would need: rooms, objects, and a parser, like its predecessors, but also notifications for events (such as another player arriving in or leaving your location), mechanisms to ensure your game couldn't get out of sync with someone else's, and commands that players could use to communicate with each other. Trubshaw, like many future worldbuilders, began with a digital recreation of his childhood home.

By December 1978 he'd finished a basic version of his multiplayer engine, and to build more content he enlisted the help of Richard Bartle, a bright-eyed underclassman enchanted by the game's potential. As Bartle later remembered, "Roy was mainly interested in the programming side of things, rather than the design of rooms, puzzles and so on."[3] Already planning to build his own virtual world, Bartle was happy to build on Trubshaw's head start and expand his game into a fully realized environment. The two continued improving and extending the game through 1979. Eventually the

1980

engine began to strain against the limitations of MACRO-10, the PDP-specific assembly language it had been written in, and at the end of the year Trubshaw decided to start over in the new and more powerful BCPL, the language that would evolve into C.

But Trubshaw, at some point, was also meant to be graduating. By the end of the 1980 spring term he'd handed over the *MUD* code to Bartle, who would continue improving it in one form or another for nearly a decade. As he first took the reins of the project, Bartle's immediate concern was how to turn the prototype engine and unfinished map into something more stable, a solid game but also a place—a persistent universe you could visit and return to, made from words and sentences.

At its core, *MUD* was not unlike its single-player predecessors. Players explored a map of rooms filled with mazes, monsters, and puzzles, collecting treasures that could be returned to a central location to score points. Bartle broke from most earlier games by setting the majority of his world aboveground, in a realm called the Land filled with magical glades, soft pine forests, misty graveyards, and ancient ruins. But while geography was relatively easy, recreating the puzzles of single-player games proved far more challenging. At first Bartle tried making puzzles that required multiple people to solve, like the bookcase too heavy for one person to move. Another was an area that could only be accessed by enlisting multiple players to meditate, which boosted your spiritual power enough to reach it:

*southeast
Shrine.
You are inside a small yet sacrosanct shrine. A sense of deep respectfulness fills this modest room. The way out, into a pine forest, is to the northwest. It is obvious that the shrine was meant to be used for quiet meditation, like similar chambers.

*shout Does anyone want to meditate with me?

*quickwho
Pathos the champion
Blatch the enchantress
Maria the sorceress
Blink
Mugs the necromancer
Aphrodite the heroine
Jethro
Gobble the legend

*

A male voice in the distance shouts "Gobble does"

*

Aphrodite the heroine tells you "I will"
*

Major Releases

» **Version 1**, MACRO-10, Fall 1978. Proof-of-concept prototype.

» **Version 2**, Dec 1978. Working game but minimal world; Bartle begins adding content.

» **Version 3**, BCPL, Fall 1979–Apr 1980; online through Sep 1987. Opened to external players via EPSS ARPANET. Bartle takes over development in summer 1980 and continues extending.

» **Compunet version** (UK), late 1984–1987. First commercial release.

» **CompuServe version** (US), as *British Legends*, 1987–1999.

» **MUD2** (MUD Version 4), MUSE Ltd, begun 1985. Can run on microcomputers; rewritten for speed, portability, and extensibility; more complete MUDDLE definition language.

The original *MUD* was a living project continually updated, so the notion of transcripts from an "original" version is more nebulous than for published games. The transcripts here are adapted from those printed in the 1985 book *An Introduction to MUD*,[11] representative of the state of the game after years of development

The extra asterisk prompts in these transcripts record the real-time nature of MUDs: new messages arriving while the player is waiting or typing are immediately printed, followed by a new prompt character. (In more modern MUD terminals, the player generally enters their command in a separate part of the interface.)

A female voice in the distance shouts "yep i do blink."

*sh Ok, Im in the shrine. The rest of you get ready!
*

A male voice in the distance shouts "Gobble in cave"

*

Aphrodite the heroine tells you "ready?"

*sh Ok, lets try now!!!

*meditate
You feal a great tranquility filling your being, and when you cease your meditation, you are in a strange place...
Outer sanctum.
A golem of solid iron stands here as guardian of the inner sanctum.

*sh It worked!
*sh Ummm.. is this golem pretty tough?

A male voice in the distance shouts "Idiot. Yes, pretty tough. you got a weapon I hope???"

But *MUD*'s creators soon realized that multiple players pose a fundamental problem for a *Dungeon*-like experience. Object-based puzzles don't work at all: if you need the lamp to go underground, the first person to grab it prevents anyone else from following. And once all puzzles have been solved and treasures claimed, what would be left for new arrivals to do?

Trubshaw and Bartle's first thought was a world that frequently reset itself, moving items back to their original locations and randomizing some positions and room connections. Treasures, when collected, would be dropped in a swamp, removing them from the world until its next reset so only one player could score those points each time around. But this approach also proved unsatisfactory. Experienced players would simply rush out to sweep up all the treasures immediately after a reset, leaving novices confused and clueless about what to do.

Bartle came to realize that a dungeon and a multi-user dungeon were fundamentally different. "The puzzle-based, narratively constrained format of adventure games couldn't work in the setting of a multi-player game," he later wrote. "The world had to assume dominance, not the problem-solving."[9] *Zork* was about puzzles, but "*MUD* was about freedom,"[5] the joy of coexisting with other people in a simulated, dynamic, living world. He began adding more elements that made the game world feel alive (like random rainfall that prevented some actions but enabled others), or creatures that roamed around exhibiting behaviors he called "instincts" (like a cat that attacked mice on sight). Some creatures had an instinct to attack players, and killing these creatures became another way to score points. Bartle named the creatures "mobiles," needing a single-word variable name for something that was neither a player nor a static part of the environment. The term is the origin of "mob," the term still used for enemies in online games today.

Combat, either with mobiles or with other players, became the key way of acquiring points and power in *MUD*. Because typing and connection speeds could vary, fights played out mostly on automatic, the odds for each hit or miss dependent on the relative stats of each character. Of course, reaction time still mattered: a losing player might choose to retreat with the command `FLEE OUT` (which could be abbreviated `F O` when even more urgency was needed).

> *`kill skeleton`
>
> The viciousness of a whack by the skeleton sends you sideways.
> Dazedly you pull through, and press forward into the contest.
> Your mis-timed return blow at the skeleton is effortlessly shrugged off.
> You easily evade a poor swing from the skeleton.
> You bash the skeleton with a punishing forehand!
> You comfortably shrug off a feeble thump by the skeleton.
> You wallop the skeleton with a crushing whack!
> Your last swing took the life of the skeleton!
> You are victorious - this time…

Combat messages made heavy use of templated text. "You wallop the skeleton with a crushing whack!" came from the base:

```
"You :r :p with a :r :r!"
```

The first word might become "wallop," but could also be "thrash," "take aim at," "smite," "bash," or any of a dozen other possibilities. In this way each of these messages could be rendered thousands of different ways to prevent dull repetition, an early example of procedural text in games.

But *MUD*'s true dynamism came from other people, endlessly fascinating even in text-only form. Bartle soon began focusing his energies on game mechanics that maximized the pleasure of peer-to-peer play. He added powerful mobiles, like the dragon, that could only be defeated by a large team of high-ranked players, giving rise to some of online gaming's first raids. Commands were added that had no effect besides nonverbal communication, like `LAUGH`—the earliest emotes. A `WRITE` command let players leave messages in certain parts of the world, such as a Captain's logbook:

> Captain's cabin.
> An inky quill-pen has been left here.
> The log of Captain Oliver is here. In it is transcribed the following:
> "Hack and Slay, Hack and Slay, Hack and Slay!"
> "Shadow's still lengthening, in a 2060 stylee!"
> "Gail was here all alone and without Richard (sob)…"
> "Anana was here with the 5 zombies and 1 skeleton!"
> "Was he? So that makes 6 zombies and a skeleton all together?"
> "Duncan the wizard played from California… All by himself!!!"

1980

Just as *MUD*'s multiplayer foundations were growing stronger, Essex began allowing outside users to dial in to its mainframe via modem. While *MUD*'s original players had all been local, folks from around the country (and, indeed, the world) could now log in. The game grew so popular that the university's meager allotment of phone lines became swamped, and Bartle was forced to restrict *MUD* access to the bleary-eyed hours between two and seven in the morning, when all but the most dedicated legitimate users would be asleep. This proved no deterrent whatsoever. "It was usual for players to grab a line at about midnight," one admin later recalled, "and sit there typing `HELP` every 5 minutes until 2 a.m. so they didn't get disconnected."[13] At first there were only sixteen outside lines available, four of them restricted to a painfully slow 300 baud (at which rate a single line of text could take several seconds to download). *MUD*'s descriptions were supposedly only a few lines long because "any more and you'd get killed while reading them."[11] More phone lines would be added, but the game's architecture could only support a maximum of thirty-six simultaneous players, a hard limit related to the PDP-10's 36-bit word size.

The game's small but hardcore player base, staying up all night to play and yawning through classes or day jobs, began to define a culture for their new online world. Like many first stabs at culture, it was largely based around bloodshed and power. Killing another player netted you a fraction of their points, which in turn influenced your stats and rank, so the fastest way to advance became a well-timed slaughter. While *Adventure* and *Zork* had offered named ranks to players based on points, these were purely decorative. In *MUD*, ranks became a visible pecking order, with a Champion likely to kick the ass of a Warrior but prone to slaughter, in turn, by a Warlock.

Playing the game could be brutal. "It allows you to behave in a way which would be totally unacceptable in real life," one guide wrote. "*MUD* is a very violent game, and pacifists never live long."[11] In a passage that could just as easily describe a postapocalyptic dystopia, it added that "a gang of players is quite difficult to overcome, and players often find it beneficial to form one of their own." One player recalled their typical newbie experience:

> I worked out how to login (not easy), I worked out how to load the game and … I got killed. I tried again, I got killed again and eventually, when people were bored of killing me, I tried to talk to a wizard about how the game worked and was told to bugger off and then killed again…. This was most people's initial experience.[13]

Wizard, or <u>wiz</u>, was the highest rank, and it came with a special form of ultimate power. Trubshaw had built debugging verbs into the game that allowed actions like manipulating objects no matter what room they were in, printing the location of any item or player, or viewing the output of any user's terminal. Bartle had the ingenious idea that these verbs could be made available to high-ranking players if they were rebranded as magic spells. Suddenly there was a tremendously appealing reward for working your way up through the brutal ranks and achieving the maximum level possible: power over the virtual world that mere mortals lacked. While wiz spells were touted as a responsibility—given to experienced players to help enforce order

MUD's ranks came in gendered variants: some, like "necromancess" or "championne," seem especially unnecessary today. The highest rank was wizard/witch, but players rapidly settled on "wiz" as a gender-neutral term for either.

and assist novitiates—surviving anecdotes make clear that they were often used for anything but.

Wizzes, not to put too fine a point on it, were often right bastards. They could move monsters to any room they liked to sic them on unfortunate players, perhaps dropping a deep-sea shark on an unsuspecting hero wandering the forest. They could make objects come alive and attack, like one wiz who enjoyed turning the Land's river into a mobile and granting it tremendous combat skills, setting it loose on hapless mortals. ("Oh no," he'd reportedly shout, "it's that Killer River again!") One reviewer noted it was "not unknown for a wizard to remove the cliff from the beach … so that anyone entering the game falls to their death."[18] And if it amused some wizzes to kill players for no good reason, it amused them even more to torment them first. A secret storeroom accessible only to wizzes was stocked with items designed to frustrate players, including a replica of the game's most valuable treasure—it looked exactly like the real thing, but would score no points when dropped in the swamp. Some wiz traditions were more kindly: the storehouse also held seasonal decorations including reindeer, snow, and a mobile Santa. But since the holidays (when students were on break from classes) were also a time to stage mass battle royales, the efficacy of these items for encouraging goodwill toward men was questionable. "Christmas in the Land of Mud is a time for thanksgiving," Bartle once noted, "and mass slaughter."[2]

Despite the brutal milieu, a culture did take root on *MUD*. A dialect called mudspeke appeared, where *t* meant treasure, *snif* meant sadness, and countless in-jokes were enshrined in shorthand and slang. The game could be brutal, but real friendships grew between adventurers up way past their bedtimes. Soon some wizzes effectively became co-maintainers, working along with Bartle to police, debug, and revise the game.

MUD had been built to be easy to extend. Trubshaw based its data format on the one in *Adventure*, which stored text and map details in external files. He and Bartle extended Will Crowther's format so nearly anything about a world could be defined without touching the engine's source code. They named the format MUDDL (MUD Definition Language), and Bartle boasted that it let you add a new room to the game in two minutes. (Confusingly, this MUDDL is entirely separate from the Muddle/MDL used to author *Zork* **1977**.) In some versions of the engine you didn't even need to recompile or restart the server after adding a room, because certain data was read directly from disk as needed, not stored in memory.

A room was defined by adding two text blocks to the active MUDDL file, one to the `*ROOMS` section:

```
riverl    light
          River.
          You are on the bank of a fast flowing river with
          pasture to the north and forest to the south.
```

And another to the `*TRAVEL` section, defining the exits:

Even more confusingly, when Bartle created a new and much more powerful language to author *MUD2* years later, he named it MUDDLE—with an E.

```
riverl    n        wfall    w
          n        river2   e
          n        clifff   nw
          n        wpstre   n        ne       out
          boat     spstre   s        se       sw
          rain     spstre   s        se       sw
          120               s        se       sw
```


The code above, once deciphered, goes some way toward demonstrating the power of MUDDL syntax. The block defines exits for the room `riverl`, with the next column holding a condition that might gate access to exits in the fourth column on. `n` in the second column means *none* and hence free movement: so going west from `riverl` leads to `wfall`. If an object or a class appears as a condition, it must have the right property or be carried by the player for the exit to be used (the stream to the south can only be crossed with a boat or when it's not raining). A number means to print the indexed message rather than allow movement (message #120 is "`The weather has swollen the river and you cannot cross!`").

Other parts of a MUDDL file could define nearly any particulars of a MUD-based game: `*VOCABULARY`, `*COMBAT`, `*LEVELS`, `*OBJECTS`, and even minutia like the `*HOURS` the game should be available to play. An admin could even define action behavior through a format that linked objects, functions, values, and messages. For instance, the following four lines succinctly define four special-case behaviors for disposing of objects:

```
action drop    .insert      anything   flame      null      null     781  0
       drop    torch        container  destroy    destroy   second   771  0
       drop    something    stream     move       null      bwfall   835
       drop    something    stream     ifweighs   null      2001     836
```


Putting anything into something flame-like will destroy it; putting any torch into a container destroys both items; and dropping something into the stream carries it away to the room behind the waterfall, unless it weighs more than 2 kilograms (the entry **2001** refers to grams). MUDDL allowed extraordinary flexibility in extending and incrementally revising a simulated world, paving the way for thousands of future online games directly or indirectly built on its model. In time, these games would come to be called MUDs.

But it would be a while before multiplayer text games caught fire. Infrastructure still lagged far behind demand—the difficulty of jockeying for a spot on one of Essex's late-night phone lines meant that, for years, few of those who had heard about *MUD* could actually play it. As late as 1985, a grumpy games journalist was calling it "the game you've always wanted to play but have never been able to log on to."[17] The high cost of long-distance connections was also a big factor: "If British Telecom could only be persuaded to reduce its rates for data transmission," another UK journalist wrote, "I believe that this type of game is going to prove far more popular than anyone now suspects."[16]

The devotion of *MUD*'s players had long since convinced Bartle of the commercial potential of multiplayer fantasy gaming. In the mid-80s he struck a deal with Compunet, an early British dial-up network provider, to add the game to their service. By 1987 it was also running on CompuServe in the United States under the name *British Legends*. A trickle of other MUDs had started to appear with titles like *Shades* [Neil Newell 1985], *Gods* [Ben Laurie 1985; commercial version 1988], and *MirrorWorld* [Pip Cordrey 1986]—in part because, despite his commercial ambitions, Bartle had been generous in sharing the game's source code and encouraging others to expand on it:

> We could have clamped some intellectual property on it, but the reason that Roy and I wrote *MUD* wasn't to make money. It was because we wanted to make the real world a better place, and the way to do that isn't by clamping down on intellectual property and stopping anybody else from making it. The way to do that is to give it away for free and to let other people do what they want with it. So that's what we did.[4]

In early 1989, an engine called AberMUD debuted. Written a year earlier by a group based at the University of Wales, Aberystwyth, and then ported to C for Unix-based systems, it caused an explosion of new MUDs and MUD engines. By the early 1990s there may have been something like a thousand active MUDs worldwide, with hundreds of thousands of players exploring virtual universes and building friendships (and rivalries). A branch of MUDs would turn away from their dungeon-crawl origins and become serious spaces for online socializing and creation; the main line would evolve into graphical MMORPGs (massively multiplayer online roleplaying games) by the late 90s. The designers of the first generation of these games, which included titles like *Ultima Online* [Origin Systems 1997] and *EverQuest* [Sony Online Entertainment 1999], often had years of experience running and playing their textual predecessors.

see *LambdaMOO* **1990**

Bartle acknowledges that the contribution he and Trubshaw made was as much an accident of timing as innovation. He likes to tell a story about how many times the game of golf had been independently invented through history before a particular version from Scotland became the one familiar to all. But he also likes to suggest that perhaps *MUD* succeeded because it was built on something more than just technical innovation:

Other early multiplayer text games, developed completely apart from *MUD*, include PLATO dungeon games (see **1975**) like *Avatar* [Bruce Maggs et al. 1979]; *Milieu* [Alan Klietz 1978], later known as *Scepter of Goth*; and *Dungeons of Kesmai* [John Taylor and Kelton Flinn 1980].

> Okay. So it's 1978, and you are a student at the University of Essex, and you're studying computer science. You're not supposed to be there. You're not supposed to be at university: no one in your family's ever been to university before.… [Roy and I,] we weren't rich. My parents—my father was a gas fitter, you know. He spent all day installing cookers in people's houses. My mother was a school meals cook.… I've got a Northern accent, [and] Roy comes from Wolverhampton, and he's got a West Midlands accent.… It doesn't matter, being really smart, if people—as soon as you show up, as soon as you open your mouth, they've pigeonholed you because you're working class.
>
> And we wanted a place where we could go where none of this mattered, where who you were was based on your strength of character, on who you were as a person, and it didn't matter what sex, gender, class, whatever you were, you could just go there and be and become yourself. And we never really discussed it at the time, Roy and I. We just sort of—we implicitly understood that this is what we wanted to do. And so we did it. We made a world.[4]

No utopia survives contact with the real world, of course. *MUD*'s player-versus-player design spawned a new kind of digital class system, although the tyranny of the wizzes was at least in theory a meritocracy—a dictatorship that any connected citizen could aspire to hold. But there's no question that multiplayer fantasy games helped open up a generation to the possibilities of a life free from constraints that had once seemed unbreakable: of social class, of physical ability, of gender, of distance. Online games *would* change the world, even if only the geeks, at first, could see it. "*MUD* is not a one-off occurrence," its creators predicted in 1985, far more accurately than they had any right to. "Instead, it's just the first of a new generation of computer game…. What we see in the Multi-User Dungeons running at various universities … can only be called the beginning."[11]

References

1   Bartle, Richard. 1983. "A Voice from the Dungeon." *Practical Computing* 6 (12): 126-30, Dec 1983.

2   Bartle, Richard. 1984. "Dec the Halls for Christmas." *Micro Adventurer* 14: 9-10, Dec 1984.

3   Bartle, Richard. 1990. "Early MUD History." Usenet post, rec.games.mud, Nov 15, 1990. www.apocalypse. org/pub/u/lpb/muddex/bartle.txt | s Aug 11, 2002

4   Bartle, Richard. 2015. "Matt Chat 296: Richard Bartle on MUDs and British Snobbery." Interview by Matt Barton. YouTube. www.youtube.com/watch?v=F_7_EMjjysA | a Jan 2, 2021

5   Bartle, Richard. 2016. *MMOs from the Inside Out*. New York: Apress/Springer.

6   Bartle, Richard. 2019. "Richard Bartle (MUD1/MUD2)." Interview by Adrian. www.arcadeattack.co.uk/richard-bartle | a Jan 5, 2021

7   Bartle, Richard A. 1985. "MUD Advanced Project Report." CSM-73. Department of Computer Science. University of Essex. mud.co.uk/richard/mapr.htm | a Jan 5, 2021

8   Bartle, Richard A. 2004. *Designing Virtual Worlds*. Indianapolis: New Riders.

9   Bartle, Richard A. 2009. "From MUDs to MMORPGs: The History of Virtual Worlds." In *International Handbook of Internet Research*, ed. Jeremy Hunsinger, Lisbeth Klastrup, and Matthew Allen, p23–39. New York: Springer.

10 The Gnome. 1985. "MUD Glorious Mud." *Prestel* (blog). Aug 30, 1985. mud.co.uk/richard/gnome.htm | a Jan 5, 2021

11 Howard, Duncan. 1985. *An Introduction to MUD*. London: Century Communications.

12 Lawrie, Michael. 1988. "MUDDL" (Documentation). Eastnet. github.com/PDP-10/MUD1 | a Jan 5, 2021

13 Lawrie, Michael. 2003. "Escape from the Dungeon." The Arch-Wizard Archives. Dec 3, 2003. arch-wizard. com/history.html | a Jan 5, 2021

14 Maher, Jimmy. 2017. "Games on the Net Before the Web, Part 2: MUD." *The Digital Antiquarian* (blog). Dec 15, 2017. www.filfre.net/2017/12/games-on-the-net-before-the-web-part-2-mud | a Jan 5, 2021

15 Mahney, Nathan P. 2018. "Game 25: MUD1 (1978)." *CRPG Adventures* (blog). May 27, 2018. crpgadventures. blogspot.com/2018/05/game-25-mud1-1978.html | a Jan 5, 2021

16 Micro Adventurer. 1984. "Editorial." #11: 3, Sep 1984.

17 Personal Computer World. 1985. "Chip Chat." 8 (7): 304, Jul 1985.

18 Rockman, Simon. 1984. "Rockman Files." *Games Computing*, Apr 1984.

19 Thomas, Susan. 1984. "Real, Live MUD!" *Personal Computer World* 7 (8): 134–35.

20 Trubshaw, Roy. 2001. "The History of MUDS: Part II." Interview by David Cuciz. GameSpy. www.gamespy. com/articles/january01/muds1/index4.shtm | s Jan 29, 2001

HIS MAJESTY'S SHIP "IMPETUOUS"

Robert Lafore

Style	**Experimental**
Debuted	**Late 1980 or Early 1981** (retail)
Launch Platform	**TRS-80**
Developer	**Interactive Fiction**
Publisher	**Adventure International**
Language	**BASIC**
Launch Price	**$19.95** (floppy disk)

> " A WINDBLOWN STORY OF THE DAYS WHEN ONLY THE BRITISH FLEET OF FIGHTING SAIL KEPT THE FRENCH AND SPANISH NAVIES FROM SPREADING NAPOLEON'S TYRANNY ACROSS THE GLOBE.

THE FIFTH WEST COAST COMPUTER FAIRE in 1980 captured the personal computer revolution midexplosion. Three hundred vendors and a crowd of twenty thousand filled two adjacent San Francisco venues packed with new hardware and software—evidence of an industry that hadn't even existed five years before, but was now rapidly expanding into the lives of everyday people. If you'd been wandering the aisles, you might have bumped into a man handing out unassuming trifold brochures printed on single sheets of colored paper, plugging something that could run on those new home machines called "Interactive Fiction: A new Literary Artform based on Micro-computers."

MAJOR RELEASES

» **TRS-80**, Adventure International, 5.25" floppy disk, Dec 1980.

» **Apple II** conversion by Marin Computer Center, early 1981.

» **Heath/Zenith 89**, Evryware Inc, 1982.

see *Pirate Adventure* **1978**

see *Adventure* **1976**

see **1966**

Impetuous prompts the player to enter their surname when play begins. The TRS-80 did not yet support automatic word wrapping, so lines mentioning your name are capped at 52 characters, rather than 64, to allow a name up to 12 letters long to fit. With a name like "Reed," this leaves some lines noticeably short.

How does it work?
The computer sets the scene with a fictional situation, which you read from the CRT. Then, you become a character in the story: when it's your turn to speak you type in your response. The dialogue of the other characters and even the plot will depend on what you say.[3]

Interactive Fiction was the name of a company founded the previous year by a longtime programmer in his early forties, Robert Lafore. While cutting his teeth on the PDP-5 mainframe fifteen years earlier, Lafore had written one of its early debuggers, and he'd later worked on programs handling data from high-energy physics experiments at the Lawrence Berkeley Laboratory.

But Lafore was also a closet adventurer. He'd sailed a tiny boat from San Francisco to Tahiti with his wife and daughter, and in his spare time he'd written a series of novels with nautical themes. When he joined the microcomputer revolution himself, purchasing a Radio Shack TRS-80 in 1979, he'd seen some of the primitive games then on offer and was unimpressed. Squeezing the best mainframe adventures onto microcomputers with a fraction of the storage space and memory was an enormous challenge that companies like Adventure International were only just beginning to tackle. Lafore decided he could do better by doing something simpler. Rather than simulating a complex world model and hooking it up to a parser that could understand dozens of commands, he would take inspiration instead from one of the earliest ancestors of text games, already more than a decade old: the ancestor of all chatbots, *ELIZA*. He would create a program that only pretended to listen to what you were saying.

```
HIS MAJESTY'S SHIP "IMPETUOUS" SLIPPED SOUNDLESSLY INTO THE
BAY ON THE LAST OF THE DYING WESTERLY.  IN THE TWILIGHT
CAPTAIN REED COULD JUST MAKE OUT THE SPIRE
OF ROCK MARKED ON THE CHART AS A LANDMARK.  SLOWLY THE ROCK
CAME IN LINE WITH THE DISTANT PEAK OF MONT CHAMPIGNON.[...]

    "SHALL I RIG THE BOARDING NETS, SIR?"
    THIS WAS THE SAILING MASTER, MR STAYSON, A MAN AS CAUTIOUS
AS MR DASHER WAS DARING.  ALTHOUGH THE LITTLE BAY WAS ON THE
FRENCH MAINLAND IT WAS CENTERED IN A DESERTED STRETCH OF COAST
AND THE LIKELIHOOD OF A BOARDING PARTY BEING SENT AGAINST THEM
WAS REMOTE.
    REED TURNED TO MR STAYSON.  "
```

The blinking cursor at the end of the line of abruptly truncated text invited the player to fill in their own contribution:

```
    REED TURNED TO MR STAYSON.  "WHAT WOULD YOU ADVISE,
STAYSON?" HE ASKED.
    "WELL, IT'S LIKE THIS, SIR."  THERE FOLLOWED A FEW MINUTES
OF TECHNICAL DISCUSSION BEFORE STAYSON WENT TO RIG THE
BOARDING NETS.
```

```
(PRESS -ENTER- TO CONTINUE) [ENTER]
_______________________________________________

[...] "SIR, SHALL I BRING YOU A CUP OF HOT WINE?"  MILLBY,
REED'S STEWARD, STOOD AT HIS ELBOW.  "IT'S A COLD
NIGHT, SIR."  MILLBY, A GOOD SERVANT, WAS
ALWAYS SOLICITOUS OF HIS CAPTAIN'S COMFORT.
   REED THOUGHT HOW GOOD THE WINE
WOULD TASTE. "YES, A LITTLE WINE WOULD WARM ME UP QUITE
NICELY. THANK YOU, MILLBY."
   "VERY GOOD, SIR."  MILLBY HURRIED AWAY.
   I'M GLAD I SAID THAT,
REED THOUGHT.  IT MAKES HIM HAPPY TO DO THINGS FOR ME.
```

Players would have read the pale block letters of the game's faintly flickering text on a twelve-inch, black-and-white television screen. The PRESS -ENTER- breaks would clear the screen and refresh it with a new "page" of text, rather than allowing it to scroll. Pages were somewhat cramped: the TRS-80's 1K of video RAM was exactly enough to store sixteen lines of text with sixty-four characters each. The home computer also at first only supported a subset of ASCII with no lowercase letters, one of several regressions to earlier limits seen in the transition from mainframes to micros.

His Majesty's Ship "Impetuous" was Lafore's fourth Interactive Fiction title, and it followed a format the earlier games had established. Unlike *Zork* and most contemporary adventures, Interactive Fictions told a linear story interrupted only rarely by a chance to type. After entering their own name and gender, the player types not second-person commands, but first-person statements in the voice of the protagonist. Like *ELIZA*, the program looks for keywords in the player's input, but unlike the digital therapist it maps keywords to hidden narrative choices, such as whether to attack an enemy ship and risk exposure or to play it safe. The overall story rarely branches, sticking to a seven-chapter spine, but past choices are remembered, altering incidental text or setting up later decisions. The choice of which officer to promote, for instance, impacts whether later choices can succeed, requiring the player to remember the strengths and weaknesses of the man they picked and whether he's right for a given job.

While *ELIZA* had looked for loaded words in the context of a therapy session—words like MOTHER, DREAM, or SORRY—*Impetuous* understood various ways of saying yes, no, or asking a question, as well as keywords specific to each particular interaction point. While the keyword matching was technically simple, Lafore's careful authoring and framing of choices often worked to create a surprisingly compelling illusion of collaboration. One of his key insights, in contrast to parser-driven games, was to often continue the story even if the input hadn't been understood. Compare the below to the end of the previous excerpt. Here, the game doesn't recognize any words in the input as either a yes or no, but it carries on regardless, missing only a bit of commentary on the choice:

The choice of gender is actually a false one, the first of many *Impetuous* offers. Women were invited to instead "imagine yourself with a masculine identity," perhaps "one of the ladies of times past who went to war disguised as a man"; presumably for some combination of historical accuracy and the need to avoid pronoun substitution code.

There are 29 possible interaction points in *Impetuous*: on an average playthrough the reader will see around 20.

> REED THOUGHT HOW GOOD THE WINE
> WOULD TASTE. "REGRETFULLY, MILLBY, I MUST DECLINE," REED
> SAID. "I SHOULD STAY SHARP JUST AT PRESENT."
>   "VERY GOOD, SIR." MILLBY HURRIED AWAY.

see **1979**

While in parser games the player controls their character's every move, Lafore's stories focused on key moments where contributing would be interesting or challenging. They prioritized momentum over correctness, and long runs of prose over a constant rhythm of interactions. The result feels different than a parser game, in some ways similar to the model that would be popularized by Choose Your Own Adventure. But a key distinction was that the range of possible choices could be hidden. While this could be frustrating, it could also beguile. Anything might be possible at any given prompt.

Lafore had been writing Interactive Fictions for a year by the time *Impetuous* was released, and had honed his craft considerably. The simplicity of the code left far more room on the disk for prose, making his games stand out from their detail-starved competitors. While other games used most of that space for program instructions, Lafore's approach let him use almost all of it for writing. His paragraphs of story are especially impressive compared to most games of the era, including others from his publisher, Adventure International:

It also helped that Lafore's games required the greater storage capacity of the TRS-80's add-on floppy drive, giving them a total of 87K for their program instructions and text.

```
I'm in a Beach by ocean.

Obvious exits: South, East, West, Down.

I can also see: Sand - Large stone head - Edge of
impenetrable jungle
```

By comparison, *Impetuous*:

```
IT WAS A PERFECTLY CLEAR APRIL MORNING, WITH A WARM SUN AND A
SKY OF A DEEP CERULEAN BLUE. THE GRAVE WAS ABOVE THE HIGH-TIDE
MARK ON A BEACH TUFTED WITH SPARSE GRASS. A FEW YARDS FARTHER
INLAND THE CLIFFS OF THE SHORELINE HAD COLLAPSED OVER THE
EONS, LEAVING A JUMBLED PILE OF BOULDERS AND INTRICATE MAZE-
LIKE RAVINES, WHICH RAN INLAND AS FAR AS THE EYE COULD SEE.
```

And while characters rarely spoke at all in other games of the time, Lafore's were awash in dialogue from both player and NPCs. It was technically unnecessary for the player to write out long responses to a prompt—the game only cared about matching keywords—but the instructions encouraged you to embody your role, and some players and reviewers warmed to the idea. "If you have any love of story-telling," wrote one, "you're more likely to reply in full sentences, befitting your station as a character."[9] If you played along, after pressing enter there would be nothing on-screen to distinguish your words from Lafore's. Indeed, many of the prompts in *Impetuous* exist purely for roleplaying: under the hood, the game doesn't check them for any keywords at all, though the player doesn't necessarily realize this.

```
    REED, ASTONISHED BY THE SPIRIT WITH WHICH THE
ENEMY SHIPS ATTACKED, UTTERED THE SALTIEST OATH
HE KNEW: "DASH IT ALL!!"
    THE REMARK CAUSED MILLBY, APPROACHING WITH A BOWL OF
CHICKEN SOUP FOR HIS CAPTAIN, TO TURN PALE.
```

While sometimes present only to provide a bit of fun, many of these branchless interactions come at moments where the content of your words matters less than the thought that went into writing them. At times you might be prompted to find the right words to comfort a grieving sailor, or to consider your closing statement at a court-martial. The fact that the game checks some of your input establishes a pattern that the player should take care when writing all of it.

The whirring of the floppy drive after entering each response furthered the illusion that the program was analyzing your words and recalibrating the rest of the story to align with them. Sometimes, in a limited way, it did. Free to experiment beyond the fixed format of verb-noun commands, Lafore created choices that used methods other than keyword matches for judging a player's input. The length of a response could be tested, with characters deeming an utterance too short or too long:

```
"HE CERTAINLY DOES RAMBLE ON AND ON," MUTTERED AN AIDE-DE-CAMP
SNEERINGLY, UNDER HIS BREATH.
```

At other times, an input that omits a particular word might provoke an extra response before any other keywords get resolved, as in this admonition from an admiral:

```
"YOU WILL ADDRESS ME AS 'SIR,' CAPTAIN.  A SERIOUS BREACH OF
ETIQUETTE, BUT I WILL OVERLOOK IT THIS ONCE."
```

Lafore enabled this flexibility through a tight set of **BASIC** subroutines that handled input parsing and string printing, leaving the main code flow to consist almost entirely of story text. The printing subroutine included a preprocessor that could swap in character names or punctuation, for instance, avoiding awkward inline string processing:

```
5230 C$= "#I'LL TAKE MY PISTOLS,# #1 HAD TOLD HIM HARSHLY"
```

```
"I'LL TAKE MY PISTOLS," REED HAD TOLD HIM HARSHLY
```

A "page" of text would be assembled by writing into one of four ordered slots, sometimes conditionally: the variables A$, B$, C$, and D$. One page might assign the bulk of its text to B$, but put a response to the previous choice in A$ as a lead-in. C$ or D$ might then be used for extra text that referenced a choice made earlier in the story. This somewhat cumbersome assembly process was an artifact of the lack of easy word-wrapping on the TRS-80: line length, especially for dynamic text, had to be carefully managed. Each possible fragment that could go in one of the four variables was designed to fill one or more whole lines exactly or end a paragraph, to minimize awkward gaps at the ends of lines no matter which combination of texts had been selected.

Parsing the player's input also happened in a tidy subroutine that stripped punctuation and looked for synonyms of the three basic choice types (yes, no, or asking a question). Further matches could be handled inline with the BASIC command INSTR ("in string"), which returned the 1-indexed position where a given text could be found inside another, or 0 for no match. A value greater than 0 resolved to *true*, allowing a single line of code to add conditional text if a given word or words were detected. The following line, considering the player's input in string variable I$, adds some humorous color before the main body of the response if you tell steward Millby you'll take supper in your cramped quarters:

```
5873 IFINSTR(I$,"CABIN")ORINSTR(I$,"ROOM ")OR
INSTR(I$,"QUARTER") A$=
"   #IN THAT TINY CABIN?#   MILLBY LOOKED HORRIFIED.  #IF YOU
SAY SO, SIR.#":
```


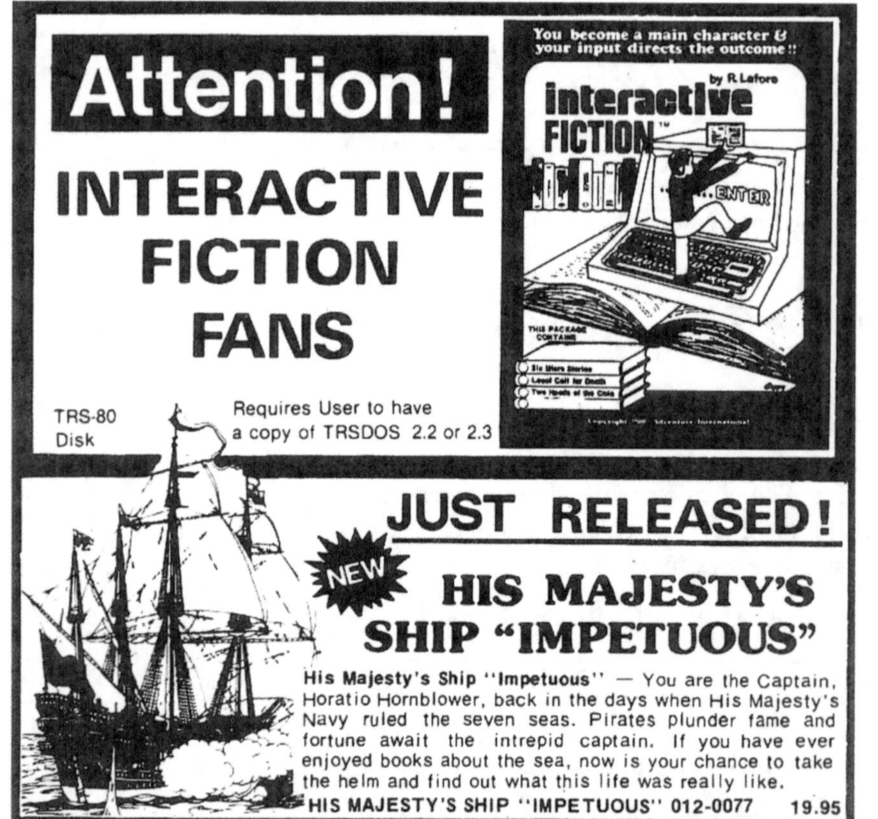

Writing for the system was certainly constrained, but its predictability let Lafore turn his attention from debugging a simulation—which authors of parser games spent so much of their time doing—to writing interesting situations for the player to respond to. Early in *Impetuous*, the player faces a choice of whether to put a young sailor to death for a treasonous offense, or show leniency and risk further eroding shipboard discipline. But the game hints a third choice might be possible. In fact there are four potential outcomes, and coming up with one of the less obvious solutions feels as satisfying as solving a traditional adventure game puzzle—perhaps more so, since you're invited to perform it in your own words.

Lafore became a passionate advocate for his new medium, seeing a bright future that stretched far beyond text:

> Technology will soon permit Interactive Fiction to become a verbal medium, as synthesized speech and speech recognition techniques eliminate the need for typing and reading. The user will be able to actually speak with the other characters in the story. Later, holography and animation will permit the user to "see" the characters he is talking with, and we will have Interactive Movies![3]

He made a case that his games were superior to parser-based adventures. While early game ads often ran to the hyperbolic, Interactive Fiction may have been especially guilty:

> In adventure games (at least the traditional ones) you're restricted to two-word sentences: "Go north," and so on. In interactive fiction you can say whatever you like.[12]

But in truth, Lafore's stories often didn't look at even *one* word in the player's input, let alone two. They were even more "rigidly defined" than traditional text adventures, even if their interface made that limitation more obscure: while you could certainly say whatever you liked, you weren't always understood. *Impetuous* can sometimes be magical, but it's often frustrating, especially when requiring a specific response before the story will continue:

```
OF COURSE THERE WAS THE POSSIBILITY THEY
COULD LAY ALONGSIDE ONE OF THE BIG ENEMY SHIPS, BOARD HER, AND
PERHAPS EVEN CAPTURE HER.  WHAT AN INSPIRATION THAT WOULD BE TO
THE BRITISH FLEET!  BUT WOULD THIS INSPIRATION BE WORTH THE
CASUALTIES? THE INEVITABLE MASSACRE?
    "WE WILL TAKE ON ONE OF THE SMALLER SHIPS FIRST,
CREATING A DIVERSION THAT WILL DRAW THE OTHERS TOWARDS OUR
FLEET," REED SAID.
    "THAT'S TOO COMPLICATED FOR ME, SIR," WILEY SAID.
    "WE MUST ATTACK, SIR," DASHER SAID.  "WE MUST!"
    "ON THE CONTRARY, WE MUST BACK OUR SAILS," STAYSON SAID.
    "GENTLEMEN, WE WILL DRAW THEM INTO A TRAP."
    "WE MUST ATTACK, SIR," DASHER SAID.  "WE MUST!"
    "ON THE CONTRARY, WE MUST BACK OUR SAILS," STAYSON SAID.
    "GENTLEMEN, WE WILL FIRE AT WILL, THEN."
    "WE MUST ATTACK, SIR," DASHER SAID.  "WE MUST!"
    "ON THE CONTRARY, WE MUST BACK OUR SAILS," STAYSON SAID.
```

Reviewers of Lafore's games often noticed the limitations of the keyword approach. "A shadow frequently falls betwixt the delivery and the vow,"[7] wrote one (unusually poetically for an 80s game review) about the gap between the system's reach and grasp. Another wrote that the Interactive Fiction games "suggest, more than fulfill, the possibilities of the form,"[13] and dinged them for having the same price as parser games despite a much shorter playtime (with fewer hours spent fiddling with puzzles or lost in mazes). Their touted replayability was also called into question: longer passages of prose were less amenable to rereading over and over than the punchier, functional text of a typical game.

Published by Adventure International

1981

Lafore would release one further Interactive Fiction title after *Impetuous*, but by the end of 1981 the experiment was fizzling. Adventure International soon bundled all his games together in a single package for $29.95, then $19.95, then stopped selling them altogether. "They sold all right for a while," Lafore later recalled, "but eventually the novelty wore off and I needed a new career."[4] He found one that combined his love of writing and computers in a different way, as a bestselling author of accessible programming textbooks. While he never returned to computer games, the term he invented—"interactive fiction"—would be co-opted by other creators of literary text games as a more serious alternative to "text adventures." It's still in common use today, having named the genre Lafore had hoped to replace.

see **1983**

Though largely forgotten, Lafore's programs are worth remembering for their glimpse at a path not taken in the design of literary games. A world model with a parser would become the standard engine for text games in the 80s and for decades afterward, but it's by no means the only engine possible. Game historian Jason Dyer writes that Lafore's Interactive Fiction today "feels like a map to some hidden shell—covering new possible worlds of gameplay—yet to be cracked open."[2] When computer visionary Ted Nelson reviewed Lafore's games in 1981, he found them more intriguing than the many *Zork* clones filling up the booths at computer expos. He wrote: "Bob Lafore is obviously a talented writer with a nice command of atmosphere, fictional action and structure; not content to be merely a swell teller of conventional tales, we can be glad he favors us with an entire new system of interactive writing.

see **1977**

"Never mind the swords and sacks of souvenirs," he concluded in the review's final paragraph: "I'd rather curl up with a good interactive story."[9]

References

1 Adventure International. 1981. "Catalogue." Summer 1981. www.mocagh.org/ai/ai-v2i2catalog.pdf | a Jan 9, 2021

2 Dyer, Jason. 2019. "His Majesty's Ship 'Impetuous': We May Both Live to Regret This." *Renga in Blue* (blog). Dec 6, 2019. bluerenga.blog/2019/12/05/his-majestys-ship-impetuous-we-may-both-live-to-regret-this | a Jan 12, 2021

3 Interactive Fiction. n.d. "Interactive Fiction: A New Literary Artform Based on Micro-Computers." archive.org/details/TNM_A_new_literary_artform_based_on_micro-compute_20170922_0465 | a Jan 9, 2021

4 Lafore, Robert. 1998. "Object Orientation Is Inevitable: An Interview with Robert Lafore, Author of C++ Interactive Course." *Canadian Computer Wholesaler* 4 (3), Mar 1998.

5 Lafore, Robert. 2002. "Interview: Lafore, Robert." Interview by Studio B. www.studiob.com/content.asp?cID=183 | s Jun 18, 2002

6 Maher, Jimmy. 2011. "Robert Lafore's Interactive Fiction." *The Digital Antiquarian* (blog). Sep 1, 2011. www.filfre.net/2011/09/robert-lafores-interactive-fiction | a Jan 12, 2021

7 Mello Jr., John P. 1982. "Interactive Fiction (Reviews)." *80 Micro*, Aug 1982.

8 Morgan, Chris. 1980. "The 1980 West Coast Computer Faire: A Watershed Year for Personal Computing." *BYTE* 5 (7), Jul 1980.

9 Nelson, Ted. 1981. "Interactive Literature." *Creative Computing* 7 (2), Feb 1981.

10 Niesz, Anthony J., and Norman N. Holland. 1984. "Interactive Fiction." *Critical Inquiry* 11 (1): 110–29.

11 Peterson, Dale. 1983. *Genesis II: Creation and Recreation with Computers*. Reston Pub. Co.

12 Saberhagen, Fred, Robert Lafore, Scott Prussing, Redmond Simonsen, Marc Blank, and Michael Berlyn. 1983. "Call Yourself Ishmael: Micros Get the Literary Itch." *Softline*, Sep-Oct 1983.

13 Softalk. 1981. "Six Micro-Stories and His Majesty's Ship 'Impetuous' (Review)." 1 (11), Jul 1981.

14 West Coast Computer Faire. 1980. "Fifth West Coast Computer Faire Program." archive.computerhistory.org/resources/access/text/2019/04/102725949-05-05-acc.pdf | a Jan 9, 2021

THE HOBBIT

Veronika Megler and Philip Mitchell

Style	**Parser, Procedural Story**
Debuted	**Late 1982** *(retail)*
Launch Platform	**ZX Spectrum**
Developer	**Beam Software**
Publisher	**Melbourne House**
Language	**Z80 Assembler**
Launch Price	**£14.95** *(cassette tape)*

> **"** You are in a comfortable tunnel like hall
> To the east there is the round green door
> You see :
>   the wooden chest.
>   Gandalf. Gandalf is carrying
>   a curious map.
>   Thorin.
> Gandalf gives the curious map to you.
> Thorin sits down and starts singing about gold.

IN AUSTRALIA THE ACADEMIC YEAR starts in January, so it was just a few weeks into 1981 when a computer science student named Veronika Megler returned to the University of Melbourne for her senior year. On the hunt for a job to pay the bills, she noticed a terse note pinned to the bulletin board outside the computer center: someone needed students for part-time

1982

The Hobbit shows player commands and error messages in a separate area from the main flow of the text, which might keep scrolling in real time as characters arrive, depart, or react. This is emulated in these transcripts by heavy indents for the secondary window text.

1982

programming work. The pay was ten dollars an hour. When Megler dialed the phone number on the ad, it turned out the man who posted it had started an Australian software company to make computer games, of all things, for the burgeoning UK market. The position he hoped to fill, he explained eagerly, was straightforward. He wanted to find someone to "write the best adventure game ever. Period."[9]

Megler had been hacking hardware and software for years, ever since giving up freshman plans to become an actuary: "I discovered I was bad at statistics and good at computers."[10] Her old job had been managing the campus mainframe, and her few spare hours outside work and school were often spent on hobby projects like writing control programs for a model railroad (typing them in on a hexadecimal keypad, in assembler) or building her own computer from kits in magazines. "I would go to the electronics parts store with my list of chips, resistors, capacitors and diodes," she later recalled. "In the store they'd say, 'tell your boyfriend we don't have these'—it was not even considered possible that I might be the person purchasing them."[9] Sexist attitudes were "alive and kicking" on campus; in "self-defense," Megler teamed up with one of the few other women in the program, a friend named Kerryn, to do group projects. The pair were sometimes joined by a friend named Philip Mitchell and a buddy of his "who were amongst the few men willing to partner with us." Megler didn't often need the help. In her interview with the Australian game company, Melbourne House, she so impressed the owner that he hired her on the spot. She quickly recruited her three group project friends, too.

But the four had little experience with computer games. The company's founder was familiar with microcomputer titles like *Pirate Adventure* **1978**, and he hoped to improve on them for new generations of more capable machines. But the only earlier text game Megler knew was the original *Adventure* **1976**, which she'd played "obsessively for some time, mapping out the 'maze of twisty little passages,'" until she beat it—"at that point it instantly lost interest for me, and I don't believe I ever played it again."[9] Thinking back on *Adventure* with the prospect of designing her own game now at hand, she realized the root of her boredom was its static, unchanging structure: "It played the same way every time. Each Non-Player Character (NPC) was tied to a single location, and always did the same thing." She decided her game would be different.

```
You go southeast.
You are in Rivendell
Visible exits are: east west
You see :
    Elrond.
Thorin enters.
Elrond says " Hello ".
                    > SAY TO ELROND "HELLO"
You talk to Elrond.
Thorin says " Hurry up ".
Gandalf enters.
```

> Elrond gives some lunch to you.
> > GIVE LUNCH TO THORIN
>
> You give some lunch to Thorin.
> Thorin says " Thank you ".
> Gandalf takes the curious map.
> > GET MAP
>
> GANDALF IS CARRYING THE MAP.
> > SAY TO GANDALF "DROP MAP"
>
> Gandalf says " No ".
> Gandalf says " What's this ? ".
> Thorin waits.
> > SAY TO GANDALF "GIVE MAP TO ELROND"
>
> You talk to Gandalf.
> Gandalf gives the map to Elrond.
> Elrond says " What do you expect me to do with this ? ".
> Thorin waits.
> > SAY TO ELROND "READ MAP"
>
> You talk to Elrond.
> Elrond examines the curious map.
> Elrond says " Go east from the misty mountain to get to a narrow place".
> Thorin sits down and starts singing about gold.

Based on Tolkien's classic novel, *The Hobbit* took a unique approach unlike nearly any previous text adventure. Megler designed her NPCs not as static objects, little different from props or treasures, but as "animals" that could move across the map and take their own actions. They would even act in real time if the player didn't type anything for a while. Megler's characters "just 'played' the game themselves according to their character profile," she later wrote:

> I conceived of an NPC's character as being a set of actions that the NPC might perform, a sequence in which they generally performed them and a frequency of repetition. The individual actions were simple and were generally the same actions that a player could do (run in a given direction, attack another character, and so on); [but] these routines could be overridden for a specific character.… The apparent complexity of the character comes from the length and flexibility of its action sequence; the character "emerges" as a result. For example, Gandalf's short attention span and kleptomania were represented by a sequence like: "[go] <random direction>. [Pick up] <random object> [Say, 'what's this?']. [Go] <random direction>. [Put down] <random object>."[9]

Megler went through the book and "tried to identify common sequences of behavior that I could represent through a sequence of actions that would capture the 'texture' of that character." A troll might simply move about at random and try to kill anything it saw, while Thorin had a penchant for complaining, following Bilbo around, and singing about gold. The game's action sequences and map were randomized, resulting in a simulated world at turns frustrating and fascinating: no two games would be exactly alike. In one, Gandalf might wander off and get killed by a warg; in another, Elrond's secret directions might change, or he might refuse to give them at all. A map

None of the team felt qualified to write an original story for their adventure game, so basing it on an existing tale seemed like a good idea. *The Hobbit* was well-known, with a quest narrative that mapped nicely onto gameplay of exploring a world to recover a treasure. Melbourne House had been a book publisher before getting into games, and its owner had years of contacts and experience licensing Australian rights to US and UK titles. The company worked out an arrangement with the Tolkien estate for a book-to-game adaptation, probably the first such deal ever made.

In a case of parallel evolution, Megler's approach mirrored that of Richard Bartle's real-time "mobiles" with "instincts" in the original *MUD* **1980**, under development on the other side of the globe in the UK.

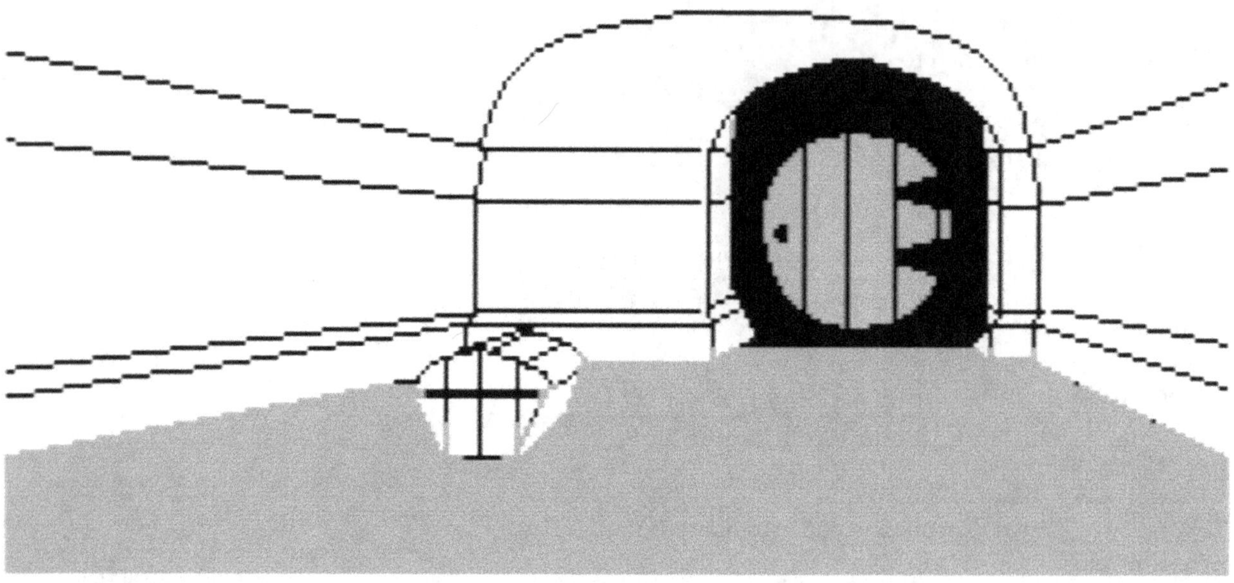

Opening screen from *The Hobbit*.

You Are Carrying...

» a small curious key

» some lunch

» the rope

» the short strong sword

» the golden key

» the valuable golden ring

» a torch

of goblin dungeons carefully made on one playthrough would be wrong by the next, while the sword you were counting on for defense might have shattered because you used it to break down a locked door.

This last kind of outcome was enabled by Megler's choice to make even the static objects in the game dynamic. Each had properties like weight, size, and fragility, and rather than define puzzle solutions as particular commands (such as KILL DRAGON) the game instead often looked for a state (the dragon is dead). The state might have come about in any number of ways. It wouldn't matter whether you convinced Bard to shoot the dragon with an arrow, if you bulked up on elf food and clobbered the beast to death yourself, or even if he blundered into another enemy of his own volition, fought, and was defeated—if the dragon was dead, the puzzle was solved.

Working with other characters—who could take actions that Bilbo the hobbit could not—was also a key part of gameplay. A good example comes when Bilbo is imprisoned in the goblin tunnels beneath the Misty Mountains, and discovers that (or waits around until) another companion has been captured too:

> The nasty goblin captures you.
> You are in the goblins dungeon
> To the north there is the goblins door
> To the west there is the window
> You see :
>   some sand.
>   Gandalf. Gandalf is carrying
>   the large key.

1982

Bilbo is too short to reach the window, but the wizard is not.

```
                    > SAY TO GANDALF "OPEN WINDOW"
You talk to Gandalf.
Gandalf opens the window.
                    > SAY TO GANDALF "PICK ME UP"
You talk to Gandalf.
Gandalf carries you.
                    > SAY TO GANDALF "GO THROUGH WINDOW"
You talk to Gandalf.
Gandalf goes through the window.
You are in the dark winding passage
```

But another solution, if you've mapped the tunnels, is to give your companion a sequence of orders to escape and then come back to set you free: SAY TO GANDALF "OPEN WINDOW, GO WEST, GO SOUTHWEST, OPEN DOOR". There are three possible outcomes to this strategy, as one walkthrough notes:[1] the door will open with your companion waiting outside; they'll end up back in the dungeon with you because they were recaptured along the way; or you never see them again because they got killed trying to carry out your plan.

Unlike many text games of the time written in higher-level languages like BASIC, Megler wrote *The Hobbit* directly in assembler. This enabled the game's complex code to run at a reasonable speed, but debugging it was extraordinarily difficult. Assembler code moves individual numbers in and out of memory registers, making high-level behavior like Megler's proto-AI harder to visualize and follow:

```
L6E11   CP      #08
        JR      NZ,L6E22
        BIT     7,B
        JR      NZ,L6DF5
        LD      A,#08
        CALL    L7589
        INC     B
        DEC     HL
        JR      L6DF5
```

Modern debugging conveniences did not yet exist for Z80 Assembler. "The BASIC programmer's technique of inserting 'print' statements to find out what is happening is not available," Megler remembered grimly. "We had characters interacting with each other in distant parts of the game, and only actions in the current location were printed on the game player's console."[9] A crash might have been caused by some NPC action halfway across the map, which could only be diagnosed, if at all, by poring through core memory dumps. Even simple needs were hard to meet. The game's target platform had no random number generator—not even a system clock, the milliseconds value of which was a common fallback—so Philip Mitchell spent endless hours experimenting with algorithms for pseudo-randomness that could lend the game the unpredictability Megler wanted. Even when everything was working as designed, the game's emergent behavior often led

The team developed the game on a TRS-80 clone, hoping that a system based around its Z80 CPU with enough memory to run the game would hit the UK market before release—an early example of designing for next-gen hardware.

Megler's other two project partners worked on different games for Melbourne House, including several popular books of type-in BASIC programs. Linguistics student Stuart Richie also consulted on early ideas for the new parser, though had little influence on the final game.

to outcomes that seemed like bugs, such as a rampant baddie killing all the other characters before Bilbo could even meet them.

But Megler loved the game's unpredictability. "I didn't make any attempt to stop that," she wrote of unexpected NPC deaths, "because I thought it was cool."[4] Unlike *Adventure*, you never knew quite what would happen when you booted up her game. It was exactly the kind of free-form serendipity she had hoped to create:

> I was really aiming for something like life, where the outcome is the result of many independent occurrences and decisions by many people, and sometimes things just don't work out.... I actively wanted the unpredictability.[5]

While Megler worked on the game engine and scenario, her old lab partner Philip Mitchell was tasked with building a next-generation parser that Melbourne House would eventually brand as "Inglish." The goal was to improve on the two-word parsers still being used in most microcomputer games. (*Zork* had only just arrived on the US market and hadn't made much of an impression outside the country.) Mitchell coded an impressive parser capable of handling commands like TAKE THE LAMP AND THE ROPE OUT OF THE BARREL. It even understood certain adverbs, so it was possible to VICIOUSLY ATTACK THE TROLL WITH THE SWORD. In the end, perhaps because Mitchell's Inglish and Megler's simulation were designed independently, *The Hobbit* doesn't make much use of its parser's extended capabilities—it's a bit hazy even today, for instance, whether it actually paid any attention at all to those adverbs. But marketing hype around the new parser made the case that the game was breaking new ground and raising the bar for what microcomputer text adventures were capable of.

The bar was also lifted by the game's graphics, made possible by the release of the ZX Spectrum in Britain just in time for *The Hobbit*'s launch. The Spectrum was the first color computer in Sinclair's line of entry-level machines. A model that could play the new Melbourne House game sold for just £175, far cheaper than many competitors' systems. It rapidly became the bestselling computer in the UK despite its rubbery keyboard, flimsy plastic case, and limited capabilities. One such limitation was its reliance on cassette tapes for data storage, rather than pricier disk drives. Programs had to be loaded into memory linearly and in their entirety at launch time; there was no support for the random-access data a disk-based system would have used to, say, load new images at the moments they were needed. As a result, *The Hobbit*'s entire engine, data, and text—as well as color illustrations for half of its fifty locations—had to squeeze into the Spectrum's 48K of memory (which was actually closer to 41K with the system's core capabilities loaded in). Artist Kent Rees was brought on to draw simple line art that would be sketched out and flood-filled, one instruction at a time, on the user's screen— far more efficient than storing images as pixel data. Rendering pictures this way could be painfully slow, but was brought much closer to bearable by Megler's optimized code.

Working part time through the 1981 school year out of the large and mostly empty Melbourne House offices (optimistically sized for expansion),

see **1977**

"We were so limited by memory," Megler recalls, "that we would adjust the size of the dictionary to fit the game into the desired memory size; so the number of synonyms available would sometimes decrease if a bug fix required more lines of code."[9]

A similar technique was also used for the black-and-white graphics in *Mystery House* [On-Line Systems 1979], one of the earliest graphical adventure games.

1982

Megler and Mitchell inched *The Hobbit* toward completion between classes and other responsibilities. When Megler graduated at the end of the year, it fell to Mitchell to see the project through to its launch in late 1982. The release would be a landmark event in early British computing, leaving an indelible impression on players and reviewers who found it sometimes compelling, sometimes maddeningly frustrating. Megler's "animals" were indeed unpredictable, but often in buggy, uninteresting, or ridiculous ways. "Gandalf the wizard sadly lacks much of the wisdom of the character in the book,"[2] wrote one commenter (rather more kindly than others phrased a similar sentiment); another suggests that if you find the wizard's odd behavior of stealing objects and wandering off with them bothersome, "you can have him enter the cave, close it on him, and lock him in."[1] The game's assembly code and emergent behaviors proved a nightmare to debug: the manual even claimed that "due to the immense size and complexity of this game it is impossible to guarantee that it will ever be completely error-free." Some bugs became famous exploits: Bilbo could pick up Elrond and carry him around, which many walkthroughs advised doing to procure a continuous supply of restorative elven lunches. Many players despairingly noted the tendency of Bard the Bowman, when led to the dragon Smaug and ordered to slay him, to reply "No."—just before getting roasted to a crisp.

But the game's quirky, unexpected, unpredictable behavior is often memorable, capturing the same emergent charm of much later games like *Dwarf Fortress* or the Versu stories. You're playing through the book of *The Hobbit*, one retrospective noted, "but you're not. It's freedom to break the strait-jacket of the book and play a new adventure, a new story that is filled with the same familiar locations and characters, [that is] remembered by the players."[5] Today one can still find collections of anecdotes recalling the many strange adventures players had in Megler's Middle-earth:

> In one game I played, Gandalf had an odd habit of picking up dead bodies and walking around with them.... [In another, the goblins] captured the wood elf and when I was thrown into the goblins' dungeon, [the elf immediately] threw me into the Elvenking's dungeon.... I once managed to kill Smaug with Gollum's corpse.[1]

"To say that the game's reach exceeds its grasp hardly begins to state the case," writes game historian Jimmy Maher. "The thing the game is reaching for is somewhere in orbit.... But still, *The Hobbit* plays like no adventure before it.... It's a staggeringly ambitious, visionary thing to be attempting."[7] Despite its quirks—or because of them—the game would become a massive bestseller, even priced at three times the typical £5 for a Spectrum adventure. It was ported to nearly every other platform that could run it, and is often credited for helping to jump-start the British home computing market. A US launch in 1985 found equally widespread success, part of a wave of other book-to-game adaptations inspired by its UK success story, including Infocom's *Hitchhiker's Guide to the Galaxy* and properties by authors from Stephen King to James Clavell. *The Hobbit* itself would eventually become, by some estimations, the bestselling text adventure of all time.

MEMORABLE PLACES

a comfortable tunnel like hall

a gloomy empty land with dreary hills ahead

a hard dangerous path in the misty mountains

a narrow dangerous path

the gate to mirkwood

a forest of tangled smothering trees

a bleak barren land that was once green

see **2006** and **2013**

see **1984**

For years, Megler was little aware of the game's success. After she graduated, Melbourne House offered her a full-time position, but she was sick of assembler debugging and turned it down: "I have a very low tolerance for doing the same thing over and over again."[10] She accepted an entry-level job at IBM, who "made it very clear that having written a game was not regarded as any kind of relevant work experience,"[5] and went on to a long and successful career as a computer professional—but never again worked in games. It wasn't until the 2000s that she learned the extent of *The Hobbit*'s popularity and its impact on a generation of adventurers around the world: of players who had first learned English to solve it, or had their imaginations fired for their own computer careers by the magic inherent in the game's simulated possibilities.

"I'm a divergent thinker," Megler has reflected. Looking back at her game in 2016, she wrote that she was "struck again by the power a few simple ideas can have, especially when combined with each other. It's my favorite form of innovation."[9]

References

1   Davis, Jared. 2013. "The Hobbit Adventure Game (Walkthrough, Version 2.0)." Jan 21, 2013. gamefaqs.gamespot.com/sinclair/948634-the-hobbit/faqs/65834 | a Oct 23, 2020

2   Elkan, David. 1984. *A Guide to Playing The Hobbit*. South Melbourne: Melbourne House Publishers.

3   Garratt, Phil. 1983. "The Hobbit (Review)." *ZX Computing* 1 (6), May 1983.

4   Grannell, Craig. 2014. "The Making of The Hobbit." *Retro Gamer* 101, 2014.

5   Hardisty, Mark James. 2018. "Veronika Megler." *The Classic Adventurer* 01, 2018.

6   Kelly, David. 1983. "Elementary, Dr Watson." *Popular Computing Weekly* 2 (43), 1983.

7   Maher, Jimmy. 2012. "The Hobbit." *The Digital Antiquarian* (blog). Nov 16, 2012. www.filfre.net/2012/11/the-hobbit | a Oct 23, 2020

8   Megler, Veronika. 2002. "The Hobbit and his Lady." Interview by L'avventura è L'avventura, April 2002. www.avventuretestuali.com/old/interviste/megler_eng.html | s Nov 21, 2008

9   Megler, Veronika M. 2016. "There and Back Again: A Case History of Writing The Hobbit." *Refractory: A Journal of Entertainment Media*. Aug 30, 2016. refractory.unimelb.edu.au/2016/08/30/vmegler | a Oct 23, 2020

10 Sharwood, Simon. 2012. "Author of '80s Classic The Hobbit Didn't Know Game Was a Hit." *The Register*, Nov 18, 2012. www.theregister.com/2012/11/18/hobbit_author_veronika_megler_reminisces | a Oct 23, 2020

11 Stuckey, Helen. 2014. "Exhibiting The Hobbit: A tale of memories and microcomputers." History of Games International Conference, Jan 2014. www.kinephanos.ca/2014/the-hobbit | a Oct 23, 2020

12 Wild, Chris. n.d. "The Hobbit Data Format." icemark.com. www.icemark.com/dataformats/hobbit | a Oct 23, 2020.

13 ZX Computing Monthly. 1986. "Mindplay: The Hobbit (Review)," October 1986.

SUSPENDED
A CRYOGENIC NIGHTMARE

Michael Berlyn
with Muffy Berlyn

Style	**Parser**
Debuted	**Mar 1983** *(retail)*
Launch Platform	**Z-machine v3** *(for Apple II, Atari 8-bit, Commodore 64, DOS, TRS-80)*
Publisher	**Infocom**
Language	**ZIL**
Launch Price	**$49.95** *(floppy disk)*

> **"** FC ALERT! Planetside systems are deteriorating. FC imbalance detected. Emergency reviving systems completed. You are now in control of the complex.

THE BOX STOOD OUT ON COMPUTER STORE SHELVES like few others yet had. An injection-molded face mask—stark white plastic inset into the surface of the oversized package—stared out at shoppers browsing aisles full of less memorable software packaging. Above the mask, the title appeared in bold block caps, broken by a blood-red EEG brainwave. Behind the mask's eyeholes, shadowed, were wide-open eyes. Those who bought the box, took it home, and opened it up would see the eyes were part of a sketch: a face behind glass, hooked to electrodes, its mouth wide open in a silent scream.

The game on the floppy disk underneath the sketch had a similarly startling premise. In nearly every previous text adventure, the player had controlled a player character who could be directed to move around the world and take actions, with the parser reporting back what that character was seeing and experiencing. But in *Suspended*, the character you're playing never moves. Despite the box art, they never even open their eyes.

> They said you would sleep for half a millennium—not an unreasonable length of time, considering you'd be in limited cryogenic suspension. Your body would rest frozen at the planet's nerve center, an underground complex 20 miles beneath the surface. Your brain, they told you, would be wired to a network of computers; your mind would continue to operate at a minimal level, overseeing maintenance of surface-side equilibrium. And you would not awake, so they promised, until your 500 years had elapsed—barring, of course, the most dire emergency.
>
> Then, and only then, you would be awakened to save your planet by strategically manipulating six robots, each of whom perceives the world differently. But such a catastrophe, you have been assured, could not possibly occur.
>
> Good morning.

As *Suspended* begins, your character—the frozen human guardian for a planetary network of automated systems—has been brought to the surface of consciousness to respond to unexpected disaster. "Your body will be warmed to the point where marginal biological activity is resumed," the manual explains, "supplying your mind with the necessary nutrients and oxygen to function at peak capacity." But your body remains frozen. A set of Filtering Computers (FCs) will connect you via a simple text interface to a crew of repair robots in the underground complex. The Filtering Computers are a diegetic explanation for the game's parser. The interface, and the disconnect between player and character, are part of the story.

Each of the six robots is specialized to understand a specific kind of data about the world. Only Iris can see. Sensa detects vibrations, Waldo can grasp objects and perform delicate actions, Auda can hear, Whiz knows things, and Poet has his own unique way of perceiving the world—"a psychedelic James Joyce,"[2] as one reviewer called him. Through the robots, you must diagnose and repair the damage to the planetary control systems from an ongoing series of earthquakes—before the dying people on the surface decide to replace you.

>**SENSA, REPORT**
FC: Cryolink established to Sensa.
FC: Full report from SENSA
Internal map reference -- Beta FC
I am within an immense device which contains immeasurable circuitry and switching devices. I can detect connections to the north and south of this device.
I cannot sense a thing in my grasping extensions.

>**GO NORTH**
Internal map reference -- Primary Channel
Sensory mechanisms detect the disquieting flow of electricity within this tube. The flow is concentrated within the small cables which line the floor. There is a small hole in the wall of the tube awaiting a plug. Above

---

this hole is a sign.
In the room with me is Waldo.

>READ THE SIGN
I'm not equipped with the necessary visual sensors.

>IRIS, GO TO SENSA
FC: Cryolink established to Iris.
FC: Sensa's location: Primary Channel. Establishing path...
IRIS: Got it, good looking. I'll let you know when I get there.

>POET, REPORT LOCATION
FC: Cryolink established to Poet.
POET: In the Sub Supply Room.

>LOOK
Internal map reference -- Sub Supply Room
It burns and wields tremendous light and makes our joints delight its might.
To rise and fall, and climb new heights, to descend the pit of robot despair.
Everything cracks under pressure, sooner or later.

SENSA INTERRUPT: Secondary tremor detected in lower level. Intensity: 7.3. Projected damage: Cooling systems for FCs in Maintenance Area.

>WHIZ, PLUG IN THEN QUERY ABOUT FCS
FC: Cryolink established to Whiz.
It's great to be home. Plugged in to the Technical Pedestal. Ready to process queries.

TP: The three Filtering Computers are kept in balance by two series of four cables. Four cables run through the Primary Channel, while another four run through the Secondary Channel.

IRIS INTERRUPT: Internal mapping doesn't extend from Central Chamber to Angling Corridor. I'm waiting for alternate instructions.

>SENSA AND WALDO, GO TO MAINTENANCE AREA

Suspended was released by Infocom, the company founded by the creators of *Zork*, including Dave Lebling and Marc Blank. "This business began as a lark," Lebling once remarked, "and it is looking less larky every day."[8] By 1983 Infocom was becoming one of the most successful and respected game companies in the US market. A sales chart for a week at the end of that year showed an astonishing ten Infocom titles in the top thirty bestselling games— no other publisher came close to that level of dominance. Today there's a popular narrative that Infocom's text games only sold well because graphics weren't yet around, but the truth is more complex: "Back in 1981 … we were

see **1977**

told by distributors that we were crazy," Blank recalled. "Nobody wanted text games any more."[10] Yet Infocom persistently made it to the top of the charts with only their words.

Front and back of Lottery Card feelie included in the *Suspended* package.

The company had been founded in June 1979, but its first commercial product, a microcomputer version of *Zork*, wouldn't ship until December 1980. Even trimmed down for home computers, *Zork* became a massive hit and remained the bestselling game through the first half of the 80s; a pair of sequels were quickly produced. In 1982 the company released Marc Blank's *Deadline*, a murder mystery with more traditional plot and characters. The company's move toward more sophisticated storytelling began to turn heads. A 1983 article in *Time* was one of dozens that year scrambling to herald the arrival of a new kind of literature, or at least of mass-market entertainment:

> *Deadline* is part of the latest craze in home computing: programmed fiction. Machines that were used mainly for blasting aliens and calculating monthly budgets are now also churning through adventure tales and murder-mystery plots. "It's like reading a novel, only you are the protagonist," says science-fiction writer Linda Bushyager. While arcade-style games like *Pac-Man* are losing popularity, these complex programs are winning more and more fans…. Judging from recent sales, the text programs are more popular.[9]

But the Infocom team was growing conscious of the fact that they were mostly programmers, not writers, and perhaps not the best folks to usher in the next evolution of the novel. At the Boston Applefest computer meetup in 1982, Blank met another creator of text games with an intriguing pedigree: he was a published science fiction novelist, and he knew how to program. The man was Mike Berlyn, quick-witted and curly-haired (also "high-strung" and "chain-smoking,"[8] according to one reporter); a three-time novelist and two-time text adventure author. He and his wife, Muffy, who was also a writer as well as a journalist and artist, had started a company called Sentient Software and become some of the first professional writers making games with their 1981 adventure *Oo-Topos*. They quickly followed it up with a second game, *Cyborg* [1981], which like Mike's novels was fascinated by questions of human-machine interfaces and perspectives:

```
I CAN'T LOCATE THE EXACT CAUSE OF OUR MALFUNCTION. OUR
POWER UNITS HAVE BEEN SO BADLY DRAINED BOTH OUR LONG-TERM
AND SHORT-TERM MEMORIES HAVE BEEN DAMAGED. [...] THE ONLY
DATA AVAILABLE TO EITHER OUR ORGANIC OR SILICON MEMORIES
RESIDE ON A SINGLE CHIP: YOU AND I ARE PERMANENTLY LINKED.
WE ARE SEPARATE ENTITIES SHARING AN ORGANIC AND METAL SHELL
-- TWO MINDS IN ONE BODY.
```

Mike Berlyn was a 1975 alum of the prestigious Clarion Workshop for sci-fi and fantasy authors.

The Berlyns brought a refreshing notion to their early titles: the idea that games built from words might aspire to be more like traditional stories. "*Cyborg* is a unique approach to gaming with no treasures and no score," the back of its box declared, flaunting the novel feature of "character development" and creatures "you can talk to." It was exactly the direction Infocom's founders hoped to move in. Blank soon hired Mike to begin work on a new game that would keep Infocom innovating. While Muffy wasn't officially allowed to collaborate on the new project—Infocom had a policy against hiring spouses of employees—Mike has said she "contributed extensively"[17] to *Suspended* and "helped design" all his text adventure games. The two would go back to collaborating officially as soon as Mike left Infocom in 1985, and would make many more games together in the following decades.

quote from retail packing, 1986 Polarware rerelease of *Oo-Topos*.

But back in 1982, as Mike moved into his new office at Infocom, he was faced with a daunting possibility space. "In one sense we are working within traditional genres," he reflected, "and in another we are still teaching ourselves, laying out the groundwork for what these things could be. For the most part, we are working without pioneers."[8] Mike was a combination writer/programmer when there was no model yet for what such a role should be. Infocom's founders had hoped the programming language they'd devised to author their games—ZIL, the Zork Implementation Language—might be comprehensible to a tech-savvy writer. Descended from MDL (the MIT research language itself descended from Lisp), ZIL came with a lot of flexibility and power. But the conceptual model of a Lisp-like language was vastly different from the BASIC Mike had worked with before. "I was kind of sat down in front of a terminal," he recalled, "and [they] said, 'Okay, here you go. Have at it.' I was brought in I think as their big experiment. Here's a writer, [who] kind of knows what he's doing. You know, let's give him a shot."[19]

MEMORABLE PLACES

Central Chamber

Advisory Peripheral

Gamma Repair

Skywalk Alpha

Weather Control Area

Sleep Chamber

Access Hallway

```
<ROUTINE JIGS-UP (DESC ROBOT)
     <TELL .DESC CR>
     <CRLF>
     <TELL "FC: So much for that robot. Too bad." CR>
     <PUT ,DEADBOTS <GETP .ROBOT ,P?ROBOT> 30>
     <KILL-GOAL .ROBOT T>
     <FSET .ROBOT ,CUTBIT>
     <DEAD-FCN>
     <RFATAL>>


<ROUTINE PRE-TAKE ()
     <COND (<IN? ,PRSO ,WINNER> <ROBOT-TELL "I already have
```

```
it.">)
    (<AND <IN? ,PRSO ,TOPSHELF>
      <NOT <EQUAL? ,ON-WEDGE <GETP ,WINNER ,P?ROBOT>>>>
<ROBOT-TELL "It's too high up there and I can't reach
it.">
<RTRUE>)
    (<FSET? ,PRSO ,WEARBIT>
<ROBOT-TELL "Not while it's attached.">
<RTRUE>)
    (<AND <IRIS?>
      <NOT ,IRIS-FIXED>>
<ROBOT-TELL "I can't take what I can't see.">
<RFATAL>)
[...]
```


ZIL's ability to nest complex behaviors and functions in lists—which could contain anything from strings to more code—gave it a useful flexibility that enabled the many complex routines of an unusual game like *Suspended*. By contrast, the tools designed for the Adventure International games **1978** or *MUD* **1980** were simpler to use, but could only create the specific kinds of adventures those tools were designed to enable. ZIL had fewer assumptions about what a text adventure was supposed to be, making a radical departure like *Suspended* possible—if not exactly easy to code.

Both coding and playing the game required a different kind of mindset. The player's location, senses, and agency are fractured between six limited entities, causing what one fan dubbed "a thousand little mysteries"[18] in piecing together a coherent picture of the environment from limited clues. Take identifying an object: one robot might grasp it in its manipulators and describe it as "a rough device," while another sees only its electromagnetic emissions and calls it "a scanning device." Whiz can determine it's "a CX1 chip," Iris can see that it's blue, and the whimsical Poet calls it "brain uno." Only by synthesizing all this information in the context of its environment can you come to understand it's a scanning processor chip, useful to repair a malfunctioning robot.

Understanding your role in the game, and learning how to direct your robot avatars, requires careful study of the game's manual and the bonus materials inside its imposing box. Modern players with emulators who may not have access to this content face a much more difficult challenge. The instructions, for instance, detail commands that don't appear in any other Infocom game, such as ways to give multiple robots simultaneous orders:

```
>SENSA, FOLLOW WALDO
FC: Cryolink established to Sensa.
SENSA: Okay. I'll follow Waldo.

>WALDO, GO SOUTH
FC: Cryolink established to Waldo.
WALDO: Internal map reference -- Gamma Repair
I have reached the south end of this area. The walkway ends here.
The walkway is not in motion.
```

Spoilers for getting past the broken mechanism in Gamma Repair.

```
In the room with me is Sensa.
There is a hollow object here.
  The hollow object contains…
    A broken mechanism
>WALDO AND SENSA, EXAMINE BROKEN MECHANISM
FC: Cryolink established to Waldo.
WALDO: I perceive nothing special about the broken mechanism.

FC: Cryolink established to Sensa.
SENSA: I perceive nothing special about the broken device.


>WALDO, GET BROKEN MECHANISM
FC: Cryolink already established to Waldo.
WALDO: I can't manage it. The broken mechanism is too heavy.


>BOTH WALDO AND SENSA, GET BROKEN MECHANISM
FC: Dual-Cryolink established to Waldo and Sensa.
FC: The robots have moved it.
FC: Cryolink established to Waldo.
```

But in addition to gaining mastery over your environment, you must also learn how to do it quickly. "The first time you play *Suspended* will not be your last," say the game's instructions—less because of particularly gripping storytelling than that many playthroughs are needed to gather enough details to solve it before time runs out. A succession of disasters, culminating in your disconnection by angry surface dwellers, leads to Game Over after 160 turns, a fraction of the time one would spend to solve a game like *Zork*. Each playthrough is an opportunity to learn a little more about the crisis you're caught in and how to handle it, and in each game you can spend a bit less time experimenting and a bit more carrying out your plans. *Suspended*, one reviewer noted, is "a marathon that requires conditioning."[20]

But even after you've figured out how to solve the game—*and then* how to do it in less than 160 turns—you still haven't won:

```
All systems returning to normal.
  Weather systems slowly approaching balance.
  Hydroponic systems working at full capacity.
Surface life in recovery mode.

Extrapolation based on current weather systems and food supplies:
  Total recovery in 82 cycles.
  Current surface casualties: 4,277,000
  Projected casualties during recovery: 3,417,000
  Original population: 30,172,000
  Total possible survivors: 22,478,000


This score gives you the possibility of being considered for being burned
in effigy. On a scale of 1 (the best) to 7 (the worst), your ranking was 7.
```

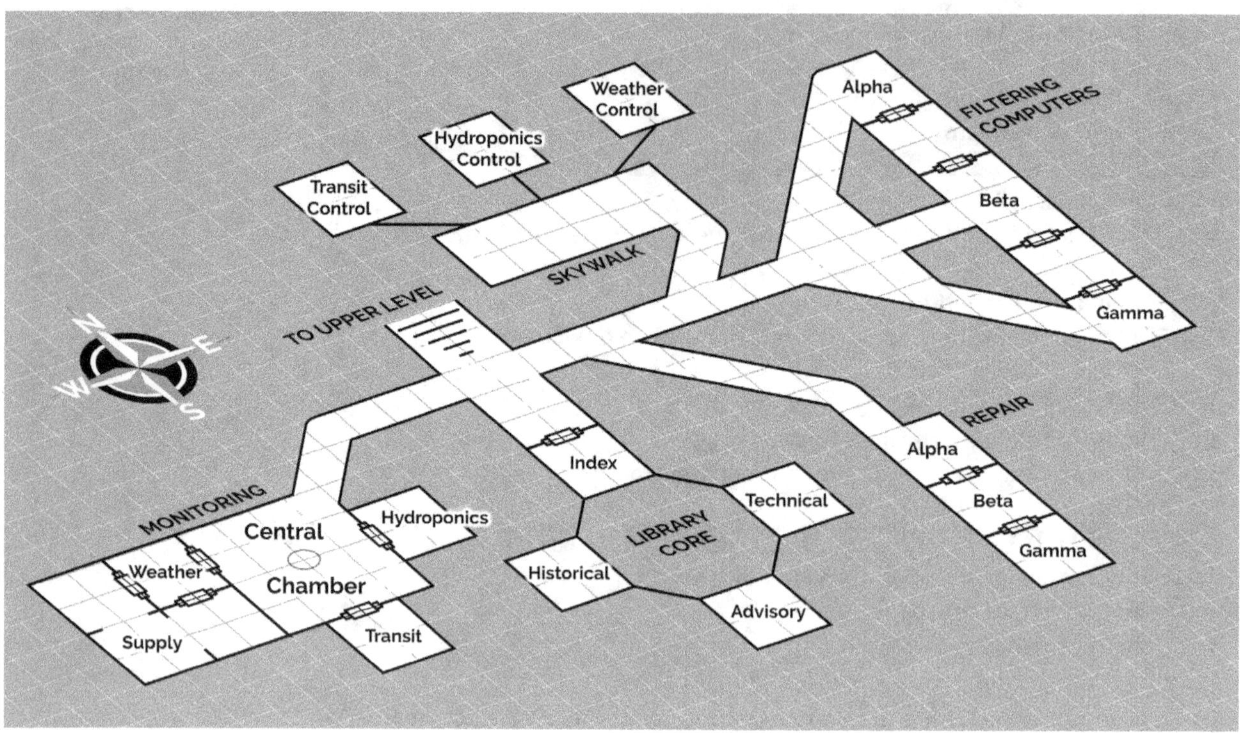

Above: original map of lower level of *Suspended*'s underground complex; the player character technically never leaves the cryogenic pod in the Central Chamber.

Opposite: circular tokens in the game package used to track the location of each robot on the map that came with the game.

Every few turns, your score goes up by a few points—but this is not a good thing. Each point represents a thousand casualties on the surface of the planet, as damaged weather, traffic, and hydroponics control systems go haywire. To truly beat the game, you must optimize your repair plan even further, trying to complete your tasks in the fewest turns possible and keep as many citizens alive as you can. The manual offers some tips:

> Moving your robots one room per cycle can be extremely costly. You may find it easier and more efficient to direct a robot (or more than one) to GO TO a room so you can do something else while the movement is taking place. Robots will progress one room per cycle and will tell you when their destination is reached.

But this is just the beginning of the complex ballet an optimized run of *Suspended* becomes, with no command wasted and each motion choreographed—a precision akin to that seen in modern speedrunning. Skilled players use the six robots like a single machine to relay objects to precisely where they need to be on the turn they need to be there. Since you can enter only one command on each timestep, sequencing and shuffling orders to avoid making robots wait for an item or event becomes crucial. Like an assembly programmer optimizing each cycle of code, your goal is to streamline each task down to the minimum number of steps, then find the most efficient way to order and thread them together. Many reviewers have noted that while *Suspended* starts off as interactive fiction, its endgame is some other genre entirely, closer to the complex cooperative board games (like *Pandemic* [Z-Man Games 2008]) or creative optimization games (like *Opus Magnum* [Zachtronics 2017]) that would appear decades later.

Contemporary reactions were mostly positive, but were also buoyed by an electric sense that Infocom was expanding notions of what a computer game could be. "*Suspended* represents another milestone in the continuing evolution of the interactive computer novel," *Softline* magazine wrote. "This form of literature may be one of the most important waves of the electronic age, and Michael Berlyn and Infocom will certainly be riding on the crest of that literary wave."[2] The game sold over one hundred thousand copies in a time when very few computer games could; only a handful of Infocom titles would ever sell more. No less impressive a tastemaker than *Rolling Stone* reviewed it and called it the best computer game ever made. And at the 1984 CES trade show in Las Vegas, counterculture guru Timothy Leary stopped by Infocom's booth and was blown away. "He certainly understood the fractured reality concept," Berlyn would later recall. "I couldn't rip him away from the machine, and all he had to say was, 'And this is legal?'"[8] Leary would later write that the game forever changed his opinion of computers; he'd go on to help create the surreal game *Mind Mirror* [Electronic Arts 1986]. "It was, oddly enough, Timothy Leary who said that *I* had changed *his* life," Berlyn recalled years later with a smile, "which was kind of funny."[19]

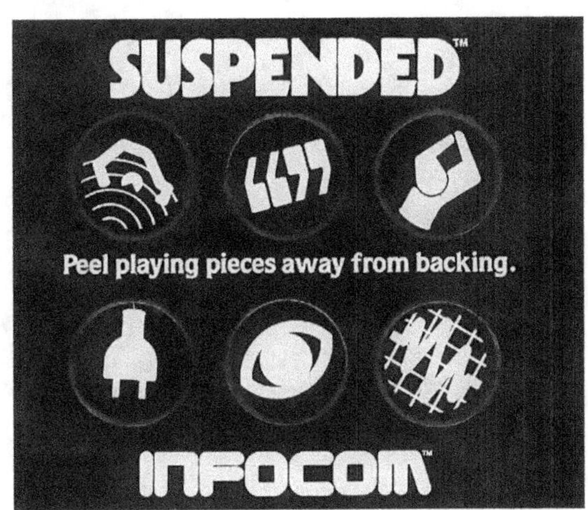

The game's longer-term legacy would be more complex. Its alienating premise and interface turned off players expecting the more traditional storytelling that was becoming the core of Infocom's brand. It was also challenging, uncompromising, and required obsessive attention to detail—"a game for frustrated would-be air traffic controllers,"[6] one reviewer said. The first Infocom game created by a writer, it had less plot and characterization than nearly any of their other titles. Today many consider it one of the company's lesser works, more notable for its unusual packaging and bizarre premise than its often tedious gameplay.

Yet *Suspended* helped change the perception of what a game could be, expanding horizons that until then had seemed more limited. As Leary realized, it didn't use text simply as a poor substitute for graphics like most other adventures—a caption for a photo instead of the real thing. It used its words instead to create a new reality in the mind of the player, in a way that only text could achieve. A graphical version would miss the point of imagining what it might be like to experience the world solely through touch, or electricity, or poetry. While the particulars of its approach were rarely repeated—and graphics would, of course, soon come to dominate games after all—*Suspended* planted a very visible flag that said the status quo didn't always have to satisfy. There had been weirder games, but they hadn't topped the charts; there had been experiments in form, but not from Infocom. Story games could aspire to be more than awkward adventure novels, and bestsellers could be cerebral.

Two notable exceptions: *Bad Machine* [Dan Shiovitz 1998] also turns the parser into an interface with a confusing, unfamiliar system; and *Hadean Lands* [Andrew Plotkin 2014] distills the notion of repeating and mastering the steps of a complex plan into a masterful exploration of causality and puzzle solving.

In a somewhat glib and giddy 1984 interview, the growing group of Infocom creatives were asked what they thought about the future of computer games:

Meretzky: There'll be a lot more variety, there'll be kinds of games that you can't even imagine.
Berlyn: I can't imagine that. But we are working on the future.
Blank: Yes, we're building one in our backyard.[1]

References

1 Addams, Shay. 1984. "'Frooing the Mumble' with the All-Text All-Stars of Adventure Games." *Computer Games*, Feb 1984.

2 Bang, Derrick. 1983. "Gameline." *Softline* 2 (4), May-Jun 1983.

3 Berlyn, Michael. 2016. "Interview with Michael Berlyn the creator of Bubsy Bobcat." Interview by doctorclu. Video. May 24, 2016. www.youtube.com/watch?v=jIYW3pof8JI | a Jan 30, 2021

4 Briceno, Hector, Wesley Chao, Andrew Glenn, Stanley Hu, Ashwin Krishnamurthy, and Bruce Tsuchida. 2000. "Down From the Top of Its Game." *Structure of Engineering Revolutions*. Cambridge: MIT.

5 Cifaldi, Frank. 2005. "Playing Catch-Up: Bubsy's Michael Berlyn." *Gamasutra* (blog). Oct 3, 2005. www.gamasutra.com | a Jan 30, 2021

6 Cree, Graeme. 1996. "Suspended (Review)." *SPAG* #8, Feb 5, 1996. www.spagmag.org/archives/backissues/spag8.html | a Jan 30, 2021

7 Dunigan, Stanley E. 2009. "The Optimized Straightforward Walkthru for Suspended." gamefaqs.gamespot.com/pc/564451-suspended/faqs/56382 | a Jan 30, 2021

8 Dyer, Richard. 1984. "Masters of the Game." *Boston Globe Magazine*, May 6, 1984.

9 Elmer-Dewitt, Philip. 1983. "Computers: Putting Fiction on a Floppy." *Time*, Dec 5, 1983.

10 Ferrell, Keith. 1988. "Interactive Text In An Animated Age: Infocom Faces the Challenge." *COMPUTE!* 10 (1), Jan 1988.

11 Grevstad, Eric. 1984. "The 'Hard Boiled' School of Software." *Family Computing* 2 (6), Jun 1984.

12 Maher, Jimmy. 2012. "Sentient Software." *The Digital Antiquarian* (blog). Apr 26, 2012. www.filfre.net/2012/04/sentient-software | a Jan 30, 2021

13 Maher, Jimmy. 2013a. "Suspended." *The Digital Antiquarian* (blog). Mar 5, 2013. www.filfre.net/2013/03/suspended | a Jan 30, 2021

14 Maher, Jimmy. 2013b. "Masters of the Game." *The Digital Antiquarian* (blog). Oct 23, 2013. www.filfre.net/2013/10/masters-of-the-game | a Jan 30, 2021

15 The New Zork Times. 1983. "Infocom Announces New Science-Fiction Masterpiece Suspended." 3 (1), Spring 1983.

16 Pranevich, Joe. 2017. "Missed Classic 39: Suspended (1983)." *The Adventure Gamer* (blog). Apr 14, 2017. advgamer.blogspot.com/2017/04/missed-classic-39-suspended-1983.html | a Jan 30, 2021

17 QuestBusters. 1985. "Adventure Hotline." 2 (8), Sep 1985.

18 Savetz, Kevin, and Carrington Vanston. 2017. "Suspended." Eaten By A Grue, the Infocom Podcast. Nov 25, 2017.

19 Scott, Jason. 2017. *Infocom: The Documentary*. Video. www.youtube.com/watch?v=OXNLWy7rwH4 | a Dec 25, 2020.

20 Sodaro, Robert J. 1984. "Suspended (Review)." *Ahoy!*, Jan 1984.

THE HITCHHIKER'S GUIDE TO THE GALAXY

Douglas Adams and Steve Meretzky

Style	**Parser**
Debuted	**Oct 1984** *(retail)*
Launch Platform	**Z-machine v3** *(for Apple II, Atari 8-bit, Commodore series, DOS, Macintosh, TI-99/4A, TRS-80)*
Publisher	**Infocom**
Language	**ZIL**
Launch Price	**$39.95** *(floppy disk)*

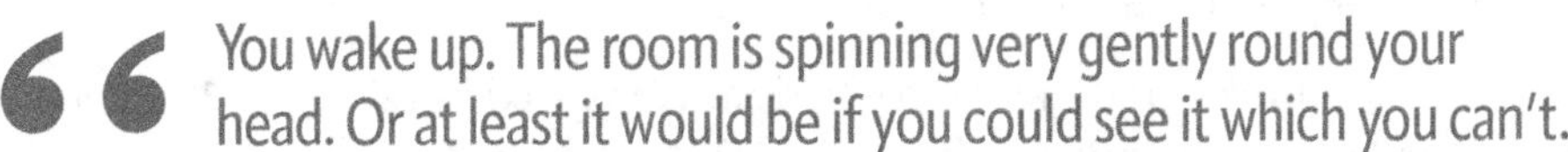

> You wake up. The room is spinning very gently round your head. Or at least it would be if you could see it which you can't.

DOUGLAS ADAMS, AT FIRST, DID NOT LIKE COMPUTERS. He had built a career out of making fun of them with his *Hitchhiker's Guide* franchise, which began on the radio before spilling into other media, most famously a series of bestselling books. *Hitchhiker's* is hard to summarize, but one of its themes is that technology, in the hands of big business and bloated bureaucracies, does not make life better—it makes it far, far worse. Hence characters like Marvin, the robot given a "Genuine People Personality" who promptly becomes terminally, insufferably depressed; Deep Thought, a computer tasked with finding the meaning of life and coming back millions of years later with the number forty-two; or the mechanical crew of an interplanetary flight whose departure has been delayed for nine hundred years:

1984

see **1982** and **1979**

1984

FORD: What's happening on this hell ship?

AUTOPILOT: There has been a delay. The passengers are kept in temporary suspended animation for their comfort and convenience. Coffee and biscuits are served every ten years, after which passengers are returned to suspended animation for their comfort and convenience. Departure will take place when flight stores are complete. We apologize for the delay.

FORD: Delay? Have you seen the world outside this ship? It's a wasteland, a desert. Civilization's been and gone. It's over. There are no lemon-soaked paper napkins on the way from anywhere.

AUTOPILOT: The statistical likelihood is that other civilizations will arise. There will one day be lemon-soaked paper napkins. Till then, there will be a short delay. Please return to your seats.[1]

Corporate-mandated cheerfulness; algorithmically enabled, mutually assured destruction; user interfaces so determined to be friendly they render themselves utterly useless—much of *Hitchhiker's* is a prescient and sometimes rather dark prediction of a future that seemed very likely in the 1980s, when IBM, the Cold War, and the rise of automated phone lines were still dominant in the cultural imagination. "Dealing with the American Express computer" to acknowledge a change-of-address form, Adams once complained, "has been beyond Kafka's worst paranoid nightmares."[21]

But then something changed. While living in Hollywood for a year as he attempted to write a *Hitchhiker's* screenplay, Adams bought his own computer and got hooked. It was the ultimate procrastination device, of course, but also a tinkerer's dream. For the first time, a computer wasn't something imposed on him by a soulless authority; it was a platform and a tool he could approach on his own terms. He taught himself some programming and tried playing a few games, but at first was unimpressed:

> Up till then when people said "computer game," I thought, oh, it's shooting down rocket ships and chasing little aliens around mazes and all that kind of boring stuff, which a) I was bored by and b) I didn't have the hand-to-eye coordination necessary to get any decent score.[3]

Then Adams discovered interactive fiction. He played *Adventure* **1976**, then got turned on to the games of Infocom—*Suspended* **1983**, in particular, fascinated him. He "discovered that there was a sort of great world of wit and invention and logical problems" in text games. "And I suddenly thought, 'I would love to be doing this.'"[3]

Adams got in touch with Infocom, who by 1984 were at peak supremacy. Product manager Mike Dornbrook, noting to an interviewer that there were now two million personal computers in people's homes, said Infocom's research suggested their products had penetrated nearly half of those systems. "Our joke is that we have penetrated them all," he quipped, "if you count the pirated games."[9] Two million was still a small audience compared to traditional media, but publishing and entertainment companies were starting to take note. Spurred by Infocom's success, the massive popularity of games like *The Hobbit*, and the booming sales of gamebook series like Choose Your Own Adventure, 1984 saw an enormous influx of half-baked attempts by traditional media outlets to create "interactive books"—playable adaptations of titles from big-name authors like Isaac Asimov, Stephen King, Michael Crichton, and Anne McCaffrey. They were almost universally awful, since few of their developers knew anything about how to make interactive stories work, and few of the famous authors in question were actually involved in the adaptations. Yet publishing houses were beyond keen to get in on that new software money. Simon & Schuster executives met with Infocom about the possibility of an acquisition and were alarmed to learn that Infocom's hint books alone were outselling many of their paperback titles.

Infocom paired Adams up with Steve Meretzky, author of their well-regarded sci-fi comedy *Planetfall* [1983]. Meretzky, like Adams, was a converted technophobe. He had first joined the company as a tester, after Dornbrook, his roommate at the time, kept bringing unfinished *Zork* games home. At first disdainful, Meretzky soon got sucked in and became a passionate champion for the new medium. While Adams originally wanted to do something other than another *Hitchhiker's* adaptation, it was by far the most obvious choice for a project. He perked up at the notion that the game could be more experimental than previous incarnations. "I could take stuff out of the book, and didn't have to follow it slavishly," he recalled. "The book became a bank of ideas. In fact, I looked for things that weren't well-developed in the book: odd lines that seemed to go nowhere."[11] In the end he imagined the game would bear "as much relationship to the books as *Rosencrantz and Guildenstern are Dead* does to *Hamlet*."[10]

As in previous versions, the game of *Hitchhiker's* follows hapless Earthman Arthur Dent, who loses first his house and then his entire planet to unscheduled demolitions at the hands of uncaring civil servants, local and galactic. Arthur joins up with Ford Prefect, a roving researcher for the titular Guide—basically space Wikipedia on a tablet, before either such concept had been invented. The Guide provides a useful source of authorial digression and, in the game, occasionally useful information. The plot of the game involves collecting four pieces of fluff from across space and time that will combine to form a seedling of a plant that offers a glimpse of the future—but, as in previous versions of the story, the plot wasn't really the point. Half the fun was putting the player in bizarre situations that gave Adams's and Meretzky's writing a chance to shine.

> **>ENJOY POETRY**
> You realise that, although the Vogon poetry is indeed astoundingly bad, worse things happen at sea, and in fact, at school. With an effort for which Hercules himself would have patted you on the back, you grit your teeth and enjoy the stuff.

> **>OPEN DOOR**
> The door explains, in a haughty tone, that the room is occupied by a superintelligent robot and that lesser beings (by which it means you) are not to be admitted. "Show me some tiny example of your intelligence,"

These games were called everything from "electronic novels" or "compunovels" to "bookware" and even "living literature." The phrase invented and then abandoned by Robert Lafore, "interactive fiction" (see **1981**) was only just starting to become Infocom's preferred term.

see **1977**

it says, "and maybe, just maybe, I might reconsider."

>KICK DOOR
"I suppose you think that since you have legs and I have not, you can get away with that sort of thing. Well," the door continues stiffly, "maybe you can and maybe you can't."

There is a molecular hyperwave pincer here.

>EXAMINE PINCER
It looks like every other molecular hyperwave pincer you've ever seen.

But the *Hitchhiker's* game was more than funny prose. Much of its humor came from poking fun at—even deconstructing—the emerging conventions of the text adventure, playing with the nature of interactivity and with its own limitations in a way that few games had yet attempted.

Corridor, Aft End
This is one end of a short corridor that continues fore along the main deck of the Heart of Gold. Doorways lead to aft and port. In addition, a gangway leads downward.

>AFT
That entrance leads to the Infinite Improbability Drive chamber. It's supposed to be a terribly dangerous area of the ship. Are you sure you want to go in there?

>YES
Absolutely sure?

>YES
I can tell you don't want to really. You stride away with a spring in your step, wisely leaving the Drive Chamber safely behind you. Telegrams arrive from well-wishers in all corners of the Galaxy congratulating you on your prudence and wisdom, cheering you up immensely.

When the player convinces the parser that they really do want to enter the drive chamber, it sulkily refuses to describe any of the objects therein until the player insists.

The unreliable narrator shows up in other moments of the game:

You hear the deep and distant hum of a star drive coming from far above. There is an exit to port.

>PORT
You can't go that way.

> \>GO TO PORT
> You can't go that way.
>
> \>MOVE TO PORT
> You used the word "port" in a way that I don't understand.
>
> \>STARBOARD
> You can't go that way.
>
> \>AFT
> (We were lying about the exit to port.) You emerge from a small doorway...

Like *Tristram Shandy*, the eighteenth-century novel that violated every inviolable convention of the book, *Hitchhiker's* delights in breaking the rules of its own new medium. The game awards points, for instance, but they don't really matter: the highest-scoring action by far is simply drinking a cup of tea, a remnant of an early Adams idea that you'd be rewarded not for collecting treasure but for enjoying things. Early on, you can die and the game keeps going:

> You try to think of some suitable last words, but what with the confusion of the moment and the spinning of your head, you are unable to compose anything pithy and expire in silence.
>
> \>LOOK
> You keep out of this, you're dead. An ambulance arrives.
>
> \>LOOK AT AMBULANCE
> You keep out of this, you're dead and should be concentrating on developing a good firm rigor mortis. You are put in the ambulance, which drives away.

At one point (in a passage lifted from the book) the action is interrupted by a long story describing how some random words of Arthur's are sucked through a freak wormhole in the space-time continuum and end up precipitating an intergalactic war. In the game, the words are a recent player command the parser didn't understand:

> The creature stirred in its sickly broiling vapour, and at that very moment the words "move to port" drifted across the conference table. Unfortunately, in the Vl'Hurg tongue this was the most dreadful insult imaginable, and there was nothing for it but to wage terrible war for centuries.
>
> [...] You have destroyed most of a small galaxy. Please pick your words with greater care.

Then there were the puzzles, and it's impossible to talk about *Hitchhiker's* without mentioning the babel fish. Say this phrase to any text game fan alive in the 80s and you'll get a knowing look: it would become shorthand for puzzles that were outrageously hard or outrageously unfair. The truth, though, is that the babel fish puzzle was neither. To defend this claim will require some explanation of how it worked. Arthur, trapped in the hold of a spaceship, needs to operate a dispenser to retrieve a fish that (for reasons we're not going to get into) will allow him to understand alien languages:

>EXAMINE DISPENSER
The dispenser is tall, has a button at around eye-level, and says "Babel Fish" in large letters. Anything dispensed would probably come out the slot at around knee-level. It bears a small label which reads "Another fine product of the Sirius Cybernetics Corporation."

>PRESS DISPENSER BUTTON
A single babel fish shoots out of the slot. It sails across the room and through a small hole in the wall, just under a metal hook.

Arthur is probably wearing a dressing gown at this point with "a small loop at the back of the collar," so observant puzzle fiends will eventually try:

>PUT GOWN ON HOOK
The gown is now hanging from the hook, covering a tiny hole.

>PRESS DISPENSER BUTTON
A single babel fish shoots out of the slot. It sails across the room and hits the dressing gown. The fish slides down the sleeve of the gown and falls to the floor, vanishing through the grating of a hitherto unnoticed drain.

The drain can be covered by a towel, but this produces another complication, and resolving *that* leads to yet another. It's a chain of frustrations that work through most of the items you've acquired in the game so far; the scene comes early in the story, so there are only a handful of inventory items to consider. It's a complex and deliberately obtuse puzzle, to be sure, but each step is decently clued, and an experienced adventure gamer has a good chance to get through the sequence without too much trouble.

The problem was that *Hitchhiker's* wasn't sold to experienced adventure gamers. Based on a well-known franchise, arriving in a watershed year for personal computers, an enormous number of its players had not come up through the trenches of *Zork* and *Suspended*, solving puzzles like early hackers for sheer masochistic pleasure. They were expecting something more like a story from a game based on a bestselling book. And taken that way—as part of a *story*—the babel fish puzzle can be infuriating. Why would Arthur have picked up all of these objects in the first place, when his home and planet were about to be demolished? Why can he only hang the dressing gown from the hook, not the towel? How should players know the command COVER DRAIN WITH TOWEL works but PUT TOWEL ON TOP OF DRAIN does not, when

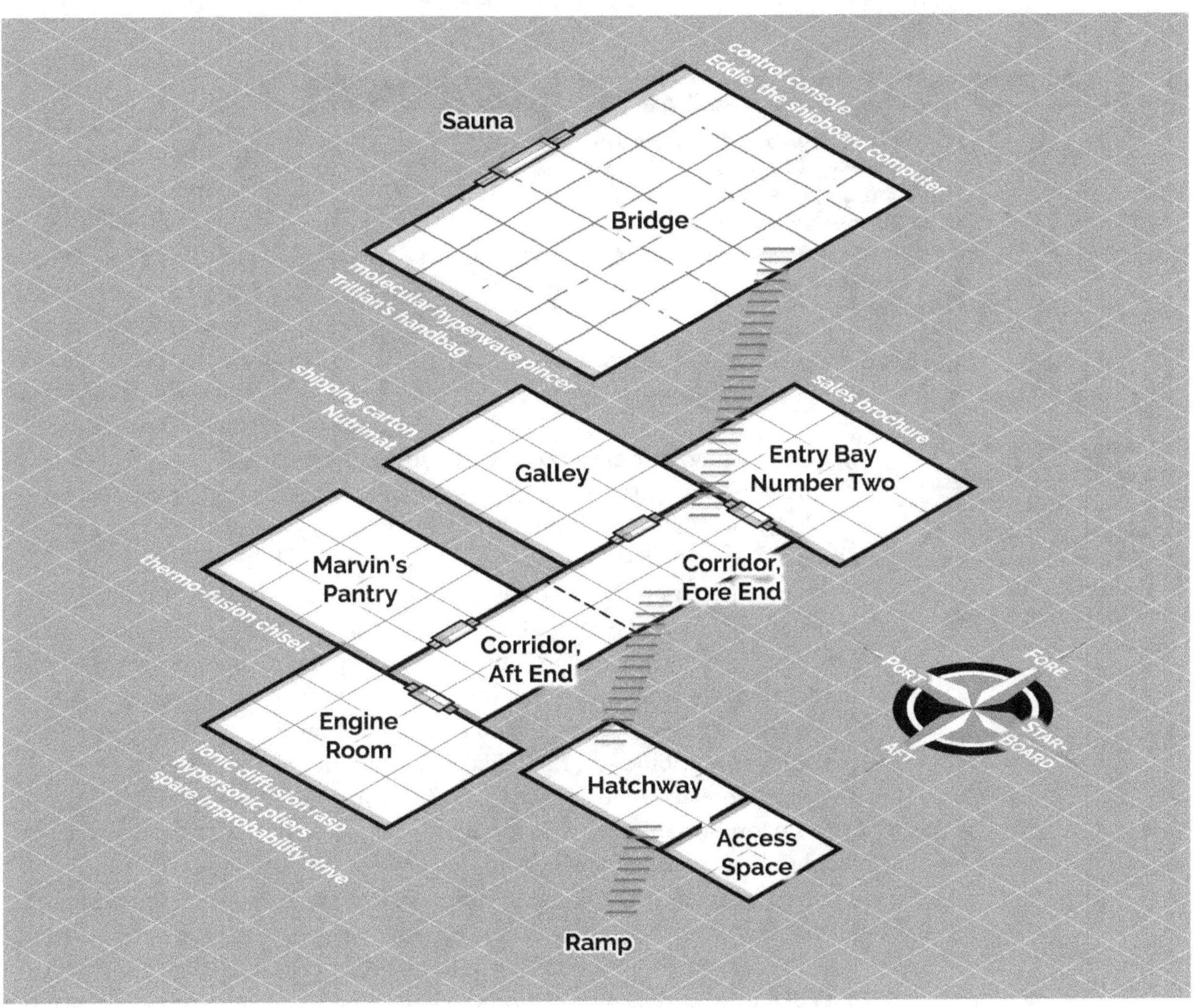

the manual says only to "type your sentence in plain English"? Why can't Arthur enlist Ford's help with the babel fish (as in the book) or, for that matter, why can't he just stand directly in front of the damn dispenser and catch the fish as it comes out of the slot? The contortions necessary to marry logic puzzles and a limited simulation with a narrative become strained as the story takes on more importance and the audience grows less familiar with puzzle game conventions. *Hitchhiker's* had both the most narrative storyline and the least experienced audience of any previous Infocom title.

Game historian Jimmy Maher has speculated that the babel fish puzzle, appearing early in what was to become the bestselling text adventure of the year, may have marked the beginning of the end for a medium aspiring to be the future of both games and books.[14] It frustrated tens of thousands, so much so that Infocom sold T-shirts reading "I Got the Babel Fish" and copious hint books. But folks who didn't buy either—first-time computer users and interactive fiction novices—may have just given up on the whole concept entirely; *Hitchhiker's* may have been both the first and last such game many new computer users played. One reviewer called it "utterly *impossible*" and "punishingly difficult."[12] Others admitted with rare honesty that they hadn't actually gotten very far into the thing before their deadlines. "It's a

Map of the starship *Heart of Gold*, one of the largest areas in *Hitchhiker's*. At only thirty-one rooms, the game had one of the smallest maps of any of the classic Infocom titles.

This Week	Last Week	Weeks on Chart	RECREATIONAL SOFTWARE
1	2	15	**Hitchhiker's Guide to the Galaxy** · Infocom · AP, IBM, MAC, C64, AT
2	1	108	**Microsoft Flight Simulator** · Microsoft · IBM
3	3	112	**Flight Simulator II** · Sublogic · AP, C64, AT
4	4	81	**Lode Runner** · Broderbund · AP, IBM, MAC, C64, AT
5	5	64	**Sargon III** · Hayden Software · AP, IBM, MAC, C64
6	11	128	**Zork I** · Infocom · AP, IBM, MAC, AT, CP/M, DEC, TIP
7	—	18	**Trivia Fever** · Professional Software · AP, IBM, MAC, C64
8	6	16	**Gato** · Spectrum Holobyte · IBM
9	9	128	**Wizardry** · Sir-Tech Software · AP, IBM
10	7	16	**King's Quest** · Sierra On-Line · APe, IBM

Bestselling computer games for a week in early 1985 from the Softsel Hot List, showing *Hitchhiker's* at its fifteenth charted week and *Zork* still at #6, more than three years after its own release.

masterpiece," wrote one. "Hilarious. Adams has done a marvellous job. And next time I see him, I'll kill him."[21] While 1984 may have seemed like only the start of Infocom's meteoric rise, it would in fact begin a terminal decline. It would be the highest-grossing year of the company's short history.

The babel fish was not the game's only frustrating moment. Meretzky recalled, "Douglas and I both felt that adventure games were becoming a little too easy; that the original *Zork* had been much harder than more recent offerings, and the 24/7 obsessive brain-racking was what made these games so addictive. We might have overreacted and gone too far in the other direction."[15] While characters almost never respond to attempts to give them orders, for example, sometimes doing so is the only way to proceed. One scene requires ordering a whole group of guards to *not* do something, managing to combine several unlikely-to-work ideas into a single command. It's easy to lose access to seemingly trivial items—like a toothbrush in Arthur Dent's bedroom, the very first room of the game—that can turn out to be vital hundreds of moves later. And the game at times requires unintuitive actions: if you take the towel Ford offers you in an early scene, something any fan would instantly do, it results in your unexpected death a few moves later.

And yet some of the *Hitchhiker's* puzzles are delightful—examples of the text adventure and its unique brand of lateral thinking at their best. Once the early game is finished, you can find an Improbability Generator which, when activated, throws you into a seemingly featureless void:

> Dark
> You can see nothing, feel nothing, hear nothing, taste nothing, smell nothing, and are not entirely certain who you are.
>
> >LOOK
> Dark
> You can't hear anything, see anything, smell anything, feel anything, or taste anything, and do not even know where you are or who you are or how you got there.

Spoilers for getting out of the Dark.

The message shifts subtly each time, and the parser responds to none of your commands, but an observant player will soon notice that something about the text has changed:

> Dark
> You can hear nothing, taste nothing, see nothing, feel nothing, and are not even certain who you are.

> >SMELL
> (darkness)
> It does smell a bit. There's something pungent being waved under your nose. Your head begins to clear. You can make out a shadow moving in the dark.

End spoilers.

The player eventually learns how to reach ten different environments across space and time via the Dark (two for each of the five senses), all of them rather improbable situations as befitting your means of getting there. Some are scenes that have already happened. In one you revisit the opening of the game, but this time as Ford Prefect, not Arthur. In another, you find yourself in the vanguard of the space fleet fighting the war caused by your earlier mistake:

> >TALK TO G'GUGVUNT LEADER
> You are clearly the worst diplomat that ever lived, and are about to become the worst one that ever died. That is an even worse insult in the G'Gugvunt tongue than "move to port" is in the Vl'Hurg tongue.

Shifting through space, time, and selves, you'll need to think like a time traveler to solve certain scenes. Generously, if you don't complete a sequence the first time through, it resets, and you can return as often as you like until you nail it—death is frequent but temporary. Another much-maligned *Hitchhiker's* puzzle involves needing to feed a certain cheese sandwich to a certain dog to prevent it from devouring a certain microscopic space fleet, long before you would have any idea you needed to do such a thing. But a closer look at the structure of the game reveals it actually assumes you'll fail to do this your first time through. It's only once you replay the scene as a different character, having seen the consequences of the failed action, that you're meant, à la *Groundhog Day*, to correct it.

"The puzzles are tough, but they follow a certain capricious, twisted internal logic,"[18] one reviewer admitted; another praised the game's "consistent illogic."[8] Perhaps the best example comes in a puzzle that requires you to be holding "tea" and "no tea" at the same time (for, again, reasons we're not going to get into). While "no tea" is indeed listed in your inventory when the game begins, the parser dismisses any attempts to treat it like a distinct object:

> >EXAMINE NO TEA
> You're talking complete nonsense; pull yourself together.
>
> >DROP NO TEA
> Your common sense tells you that you can't do that.

Yet at the same time the game persists in slyly implying "no tea" is an actual object simulated in the game's code, just one that obviously can't be held at the same time as tea.

> <code>>GET TEA</code>
> no tea: Dropped.
>
> <code>>DROP TEA</code>
> no tea: Taken.

Spoilers for no tea.

In one of the Improbability vignettes, you find yourself wandering a "maze of twisty little synapses"—a nod to *Adventure* **1976**—which are, in fact, the spongy passageways of Arthur's own brain. Therein you can find "a large black particle [with] some faint markings" blocking a gap between synapses, labelled "Sense, Common for Dent, Arthur." Removing the particle—your own common sense—lets you at last carry tea and no tea at the same time, a triumph of wordplay and twisted logic fondly remembered by many fans.

Adams and Meretzky proved successful collaborators, with shared sensibilities in both humor and design. "Watching them work together is inspiring, as they thrust and parry understatements," one reporter wrote. "Brilliant non sequiturs follow jabs of incongruities."[6] Though they spent only a few weeks together in person during the game's development, they collaborated often via email, swapping ideas, designs, game text, and playable prototypes as they pushed to finish *Hitchhiker's* in time for the 1984 holiday season. "Douglas wrote the bulk of the responses to 'correct inputs,'" Meretzky noted, "but that's just a small part of the text in an adventure game." He would end up authoring over half of the content, seamlessly matching the cadences and style of his much more famous collaborator, as well as doing all the coding. "I was gratified," he proudly recalled, when upon the game's release Adams "remarked that in many cases he couldn't tell which bits he'd written and which bits I'd written."[15]

As the game moved toward completion and into its marketing phase, Meretzky remained heavily involved. Infocom had become known for a clever style of packaging that included bonus materials and knickknacks, the now-legendary "feelies." In an age of rampant software piracy, a box full of extras provided an incentive for buying the game yourself rather than copying the disk from a friend. The *Hitchhiker's* package would include a full-color brochure advertising the Guide itself, destruct orders for both Arthur's home and the planet Earth, a bit of fluff, a Don't Panic! button, and a small plastic baggie labeled "Official Hitchhiker's Guide to the Galaxy Microscopic Space Fleet" with (apparently) nothing inside. Also included, each listing of the contents took pains to mention, was no tea.

Hitchhiker's would become one of the most profitable titles in Infocom's history. Employees in the office were asked to volunteer for overtime shifts on the factory floor to ensure enough copies could ship by Christmas. It would hover at the top of the bestseller lists for most of 1985, eventually selling nearly half a million copies. A promised sequel never appeared—Adams had become weary of more *Hitchhiker's*—but he'd go on to collaborate on a different game with Infocom:

***Hitchhiker's* feelie, a small plastic baggie with (apparently) nothing inside.**

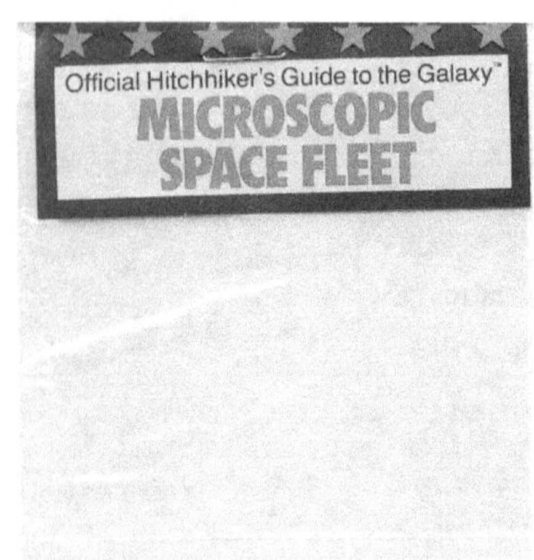

1987's *Bureacracy*, which takes you on an epic quest to get the post office to acknowledge a change-of-address form.

Adams would remain an enthusiast of computers as tools for self-expression for the rest of his life, becoming an early Mac evangelist and writing regular columns on software and technology for both mainstream and specialist audiences. "I think media are at their most interesting before anybody's thought of calling them art," he once observed, "when people still think they're just a load of junk."[5] As a bona fide writer, he was often asked how he thought text adventures, or bookware, or IL (Interactive Literature, another acronym-of-the-week) compared with the real thing:

> You can't compare IL with literature. If you do, you can very easily make a fool of yourself. When Leo Fender first invented an electric guitar one could have said: "But to what extent is this real music?" To which the answer is: "All right, we're not going to play Beethoven on it, but at least let's see what we can do."[10]

Adams often expressed his hope that other noncoders and nontechies would try writing interactive stories: "Imagine if everything ever written on a typewriter had been written by the guys who invented the typewriter," he once remarked.[2] While bookware would prove a short-lived fad, doors were indeed opening for new kinds of creators—and the improbable games they'd create were like nothing the big publishing houses could have ever imagined.

References

1 Adams, Douglas. 1985a. *The Original Hitchhiker Radio Scripts*. New York: Harmony Books.

2 Adams, Douglas. 1985b. "Q. How Do You Make Fiction 'Interactive'? A. I Dunno. Ask Hitchhiker's Doug Adams." *Family Computing* 3(6), Jun 1985.

3 Adams, Douglas. 1985c. Interview. *Saturday Review* (BBC Television Program), Jun 1, 1985. www.bbc.co.uk/archive/hitchhikers_guide_to_the_galaxy_game/zdtff4j | a Feb 6, 2021

4 Adams, Douglas. 1992. "Douglas Adams on Hypercard." In *The Macintosh Reader*, ed. Doug Clapp. New York: Random House.

5 Adams, Douglas. 1998. "Douglas Adams Interview by Keith Phipps." *Onion AV Club*, Jan 28, 1998. www.avclub.com/douglas-adams-1798207882 | a Feb 6, 2021

6 Adams, Roe. 1985. "Come Cast a Spell With Me: Hitchhiker's Guide to the Galaxy Leads an Invasion of the Pros." *Computer Gaming World* 5 (1), Jan 1985.

7 Coxon, John. 2008. "The Hitchhiker's Guide to the Galaxy (Walkthrough) Version 1.8." www.ign.com/faqs/2008/the-hitchhikers-guide-to-the-galaxy-walkthrough-429003 | a Feb 6, 2021

8 Cree, Graeme. 1995. "The Hitchhiker's Guide to the Galaxy" (Review). *SPAG* #5, Apr 19, 1995. www.spagmag.org/archives/backissues/spag5.html | a Feb 6, 2021

9 Dyer, Richard. 1984. "Masters of the Game." *Boston Globe Magazine*, May 6, 1984.

10 Gaiman, Neil. 1988. *Don't Panic: The Official Hitchhiker's Guide to the Galaxy Companion*. New York: Pocket Books.

11 Glatzer, Hal. 1985. "'Hitchhiker's' Trip: From Best Seller To Computer Game." *Wall Street Journal*, Jan 31, 1985, sec. Leisure & Arts.

12 Grasso, Michael. 2019. "Grues and Invisiclues: A Personal Remembrance of Infocom." *We Are the Mutants* (blog). Mar 26, 2019. wearethemutants.com/2019/03/26/grues-and-invisiclues-a-personal-remembrance-of-infocom | a Feb 6, 2021

13 Maher, Jimmy. 2013a. "The Computerized Hitchhiker's." *The Digital Antiquarian* (blog). Nov 14, 2013. www.filfre.net/2013/11/the-computerized-hitchhikers | a Feb 6, 2021

14 Maher, Jimmy. 2013b. "Hitchhiking the Galaxy Infocom-Style." *The Digital Antiquarian* (blog). November 19, 2013. www.filfre.net/2013/11/hitchhiking-the-galaxy-infocom-style | a Feb 6, 2021

15 Meretzky, Steve. 1984. "Interview with Steve Meretzky, co-author of the Game." Interview by M.J.

ALSO BY
STEVE MERETZKY

1983 **Planetfall** †

1984 **Sorcerer** †

<u>1985</u> **A Mind Forever Voyaging** †

1986 **Leather Goddesses of Phobos** †

1987 **Stationfall** †

1988 **Zork Zero** †

1990 **Spellcasting 101: Sorcerers Get All The Girls** ‡

1991 **Spellcasting 201: The Sorcerer's Appliance** ‡

1992 **Spellcasting 301: Spring Break** ‡

† Infocom
‡ Legend

ALSO BY
DOUGLAS ADAMS

1987 **Bureacracy** †

1998 **Starship Titanic** ‡

† Infocom
‡ The Digital Village

Simpson. www.bbc.co.uk/radio4/hitchhikers/stevem.shtml | a Feb 6, 2021

16 Meretzky, Steve. 2015. The Infocom Cabinet: Hitchhiker's Guide to the Galaxy. archive.org/details/
    InfocomCabinetHitchhikersGuide | a Feb 6, 2021

17 Meretzky, Steve. 2017. "Steve Meretzky (Infocom) - Interview." Interview by Adrian for Arcade Attack.
    www.arcadeattack.co.uk/steve-meretzky | a Feb 6, 2021

18 Powell, Jack, and Michael Ciraolo. 1985. "The Hitchhiker's Guide to the Galaxy (Review)." *Antic* 4 (1),
    May 1985.

19 Pranevich, Joe. 2018. "Missed Classic: Hitchhiker's Guide - I Got the Babelfish!" *The Adventure Gamer*
    (blog). Aug 19, 2018. advgamer.blogspot.com/2018/08/missed-classic-hitchhikers-guide-i-got.html | a Feb 6,
    2021

20 Punch (magazine). 1985. "Database." Jan 2, 1985.

21 Simpson, Mike J. 2003. *Hitchhiker: A Biography of Douglas Adams*. Boston: Justin, Charles & Co.

A MIND FOREVER VOYAGING

Steve Meretzky

Style	**Parser**
Debuted	**Sep 1985** *(retail)*
Launch Platform	**Z-machine v4** *(for Amiga, Apple II series, Atari ST, Commodore 128, DOS, Macintosh)*
Publisher	**Infocom**
Language	**ZIL**
Launch Price	**$44.95** *(floppy disk)*

> " You "hear" a message coming in on the official message line: "PRISM? Perelman here. The psych tests have all checked out at 100%, which means that you've recovered from the, ah, awakening without any trauma or other serious effects. We'll be ready to begin the simulation soon…"

STEVE MERETZKY STOOD AT A PODIUM in the New York Public Library before an audience of a hundred journalists, ready to introduce them to his new game. The Trustees Room in the famous grande dame of Manhattan featured "sculpted ceilings, Flemish tapestries, [a] marble fireplace, [and] rich draperies"; tea and scones were served on fine china to a guest list of gaming press; "port sherry and scotch on the rocks" were also available.[12] It was September of 1985, the same week the original *Super Mario Bros.* [Nintendo] released in Japan, and the same year games like *Gauntlet* [Atari

Major Releases

» **77/850814**, Aug 1985. Version frozen for initial retail release.

» **79/851122**, Nov 1985. Final compiled version.

» In *The Lost Treasures of Infocom II*, Amiga/Apple IIGS/DOS/Macintosh, floppy disk and CD-ROM, 1992.

» In *The Sci-fi Collection*, Activision, DOS/Macintosh CD-ROM, 1995.

» In *Classic Text Adventure Masterpieces of Infocom*, Activision, Win/Mac CD-ROM, 1996.

» In *The Lost Treasures of Infocom*, iOS, Available 2012–2017.

Note: this article as a whole contains major spoilers for the arc of revelations in A Mind Forever Voyaging *normally revealed through gameplay.*

Games], *King's Quest II* [Sierra On-Line], and *Ultima IV* [Origin Systems] accelerated a push toward dynamic, colorful graphics. Meretzky's *Hitchhiker's Guide to the Galaxy* **1984** text adventure had been a bestseller, but its numbers disguised the worrying fact that sales for text games were in rapid decline. Yet the lavish press conference that day was for a game with no images, no sounds, no side-scrolling action; Infocom, famous for their interactive stories, was doubling down. They'd invited the press for a first look at a title hyped as "a major departure," their "greatest step yet away from games, and toward true fiction."[8] Making a good impression on the media—convincing them text games were a maturing market, not a dying breed—was absolutely crucial.

Meretzky—"tall, shamblin' Steve," the "honest yet modest"[9] creator of three Infocom hits who had been working in construction management only four years earlier—now found himself here, trying to save a new medium he'd come to love. Clutching a small stack of note cards, he told the assembled journalists a story about the Mercury astronauts featured in the popular book and film *The Right Stuff*. They'd had a phrase: "Pushing the envelope." It meant flying higher and faster than anyone had done before, and doing it with style. "Infocom is also pushing the envelope,"[12] Meretzky said, explaining the improvements in the latest iteration of the company's Z-machine engine.

"But the envelope doesn't only refer to technological advances," he added, shuffling to his next card. "It's also an envelope of ideas."

Meretzky's game *A Mind Forever Voyaging* was indeed a major departure from Infocom's puzzle-filled legacy. Players would spend their time not grappling with monsters or brainteasers, but exploring a simulation of a fictional but plausible American city—Rockvil, South Dakota—and observing the daily lives of its citizens. The simulation, as the game explains, is part of a program in the year 2031 (forty-five years in the future, when Meretzky was writing), to extrapolate how a radical new policy plan might affect a typical city a decade after being put into practice. Your job is to record evidence suggesting whether the Plan is succeeding or failing. It's a game, in short, about witnessing. "You'll find no treasures of gold or jade to loot," fan magazine *Questbusters* wrote, "and the key to the only locked door is already in your pocket. The reward is knowledge."[1]

While set in the future, *Voyaging* was more deeply concerned with the present than nearly any other game of its time. The fictional Plan for Renewed National Purpose was a thinly veiled elaboration of the conservative Republican policies then reshaping the United States. In November 1984, Ronald Reagan had been reelected by one of the largest margins in American history, winning an astonishing 525 out of 538 electoral votes—forty-nine out of fifty states. Reagan had risen to power on a bold conservative platform of deregulating industries, waging a war on drugs, cutting government services, and slashing corporate and personal taxes. In 1984, the plan had seemed by many to be working: unemployment and inflation had plummeted, and Reagan campaigned on the theme Morning in America, pitching a recovery from the austerity and energy crises of the 1970s.

But the long-term effects of Reaganomics were unknown, and progressives feared they would prove devastating. Meretzky, who was just finishing up *Hitchhiker's* during the election, later recalled being "pretty horrified" by the results:

> Not just by Reagan's re-election, but by the fact that he was re-elected in a landslide. I felt like a huge number of Americans were fooled by an avuncular smile and a twinkling eye, and didn't realize how these Reagan-era policies were leading the country in such a wrong direction.[19]

Meretzky had been a teenager during the Watergate crisis that ended Republican Richard Nixon's presidency in disgrace, an event that helped shape his politics. Now, as Reagan openly mused about repealing the Twenty-Second Amendment so he could run for a third term and prepared for another four years of conservative policy—slashing government assistance to the poor, increasing military spending, sending hundreds of thousands to prison for minor drug offenses, propping up pro-American dictators abroad—Meretzky felt helpless. But he started to think about the medium in which he was working, and the unique way it engaged its audience:

> Text adventures tend to soak up all of your attention, even when you aren't playing them. Like, you're driving around town or mowing the lawn, but you're thinking about a puzzle you can't beat, or some solution you haven't tried yet. If the games could do that with puzzles, maybe I could harness interactive fiction to get inside people's heads and change their minds about political ideas.[3]

In the last month of 1984—a year that had naturally and repeatedly brought Orwell's dystopian novel to mind—Meretzky began sketching out ideas for something few people had ever tried to make: an explicitly political game. He compiled the prototype code for the first time in the last week of that year, on December 26, a day he should probably have had off. But the idea had taken hold. Steve Meretzky had found something to say.

The player's experience with the game would begin, as with most Infocom titles, with the rich bonus materials in the package. Among these was a short story about a boy named Perry Simm, who lives through a typical American childhood and adolescence in Rockvil: lost in a department store as a toddler; bullied on his first day of school; a first love and a first broken heart. But at his first job interview after graduating college, Perry Simm is told he's not a real person. He's a computer called PRISM, built by a team of researchers who learned that the only way to make a sentient computer was to let it grow up, simulating the experience of living through an entire life to adulthood. In the game you play as PRISM, who has matured just in time to test the simulated effects of the Plan for Renewed National Purpose,

One of Steve Meretzky's notecards from the *Mind Forever Voyaging* press conference.

"combining the economic freedom and strong moral values of the 1950's with the technological advancements of the 21st century":

> * cut tax rates by fifty percent
> * vigorous prosecution of tax evasion
> * decentralization of federal responsibilities
> * deregulation of all major industries
> * reinstatement of the military draft
> * emphasis on fundamentals and traditional values in education
> * mandatory conscription for troublemakers and criminals
> * a strict "USNA First" trade policy
> * termination of aid to nations not pro-USNA
> * cutbacks on all types of bureaucracy, e.g. registering cars, guns
> * termination of government subsidies to outmoded industries

In this future, the US has merged with Canada and Mexico to become the United States of North America.

PRISM can access a range of data about the Plan, including opinion polls; speeches by its McCarthey-esque proponent, Senator Richard Ryder; and excerpts "from a position paper issued by Citizens for Sanity in Government, a political action committee." (Few previous games had asked their players to review reports from political action committees, fictional or otherwise.) PRISM can also view a wide array of information on current events in 2031 and can even watch a live news feed to get a sense of the world the Plan is meant to fix, with the feed cycling through more than a hundred paragraphs of unique events before repeating. When you've done as much research as you like, you can enter Simulation Mode to return to Rockvil, now projected ten years forward into a future where the Plan has been put into action. Your creator, Dr. Perelman, asks you to document a variety of activities around town using the game's RECORD command, such as reading a newspaper, riding public transit, talking to a church official, or going to a movie. You're given a simulated credit card with a spending limit of $600. And at first you simply observe:

> Main & River
> This is a typical four-way intersection between Main and River Streets. An entranceway through the massive walls of Heiman Village fills the southeast corner of the street, and a health care facility occupies the northeast corner.
>
> To the southwest is 80 River Street, a brand new plastalloy and glass office building, with many floors still unoccupied according to the billboard over the entrance. The fourth corner, the northwest, is the site of Perez Towers, a luxury apartment building. The sidewalks and street are crowded with people.
>
> A skycopter drones by far overhead and disappears into the distance.
>
> >READ BILLBOARD
> The billboard advertises office space within the building.

1985

>SOUTHWEST
As you enter, a security guard, seeing that you have no badge, politely
leads you back out to the street and then returns to the building.

>SOUTHEAST
Heiman Village
This massive complex is a revolutionary and controversial concept in
urban development, the "city within a city." Apartments of every size,
schools, offices, stores, and city services, all can be found under this one
gigantic roof. Exits from the Village lead northwest, west, and east.

Proponents of this type of city-microcosm say that it makes the
desirable urban lifestyle available to the middle class, saves energy and
commuting time, and shields people from the crime and pollution of the
city streets.

Critics call it an urban cocoon, creating a sterile, isolated environment
and eliminating the need to deal with the urban problems which make
isolation so desirable.

Heiman Village, in the few years it has been open, has proved to be a
tremendous commercial success, and more communities of the type are
being planned.

>INVENTORY
You are carrying:
  a key
  a wallet

>OPEN WALLET
Opening the wallet reveals a driver's license, and a credit card.

>READ LICENSE
"Perry Simm   ID# 909-147-3838
Parkview Apartments, Southway
Rockvil, SD, Zone 55-18901"

Your address helps you find your apartment, where a simulated wife and
child are waiting. The three-room apartment is created with an astonishing
level of detail for a game of the time, with more than two thousand lines
of code for just this one small area: you can open the fridge and snack on
leftovers, kiss your wife, enjoy the view out the window, play with the baby.

PRISM can save anything he observes to a recording buffer, but he only
has a limited amount of storage space, so you need to be judicious with
what you choose to capture. After checking all the items off Perelman's list,
you can leave Simulation Mode to show him the recordings. The data you
capture seems to suggest the Plan will work as expected, and the team passes
on a recommendation to the government for implementation.

Symbolic knowledge versus rigorously ordered knowledge
heuristic "rule of thumb" problem solving versus precise algorithmic p.s.

Pioneers (40's & 50's) Alan Turing Norbert Weiner
Early programs: Proved theorems of propositional logic and plane geometry
Played checkers & improved itself
~~Proved~~ Recognized handwritten characters
Translating text from one language to another.

First step in learning how to make machines think was to figure
out how people think & solve problems = cognitive science.

Jill "script"

Start at	End at	Location	Activity
9:52am 592	10:44am 644	Kitchen	making sandwiches
10:45am 645	11:37am 697	Living Room	reading book
11:38am 698	1:33pm 813	Living Room	painting
1:34pm 814	2:19pm 859	Kitchen	eating sandwich
2:20pm 860	3:12pm 912	Kitchen	washing dishes
3:13pm 913	6:04pm 1084	Living Room	painting
6:05pm 1085	6:57pm 1137	Living Room	neatening & cleaning

7/31/85

To: Mike
cc: Steve, John
From: Jon

You're concerned that AMFV may tarnish Infocom's image, because some of
the story may be offensive to some people.

I think we should avoid making some kind of "policy" regarding artistic
freedom. Instead, each story/game should be evaluated on a case-by-case
basis. If Dave Lebling wanted to write a pro-Reaganomics story, I'd say
"feel free," as long as it was enjoyable. Political opinions can differ
story to story; even moral standards can differ. The only alternative
(avoiding controversial issues or taking a "please-everyone" approach)
is writing mush.

But then the game does something odd. It doesn't end, but leaves you with nothing to do. Perelman apologizes: "I've been so snowed under I haven't had time to line up any projects for you." You can continue watching news feeds, check on the various camera views around the PRISM complex, or browse the data files about the Plan. But the only real option of interest is returning to Simulation Mode. And when you do this, you discover that the data you collected has allowed the system to project its simulated Rockvil even further into the future. If you like, you can now enter the Rockvil of twenty years hence, not just ten. And the world in this future begins to seem not quite so sunny.

> Several BSF [Border Security Force] officers trot out of a nearby building and climb into an unmarked BSF van which drives away.

> **>TALK TO OFFICIAL**
> You have a brief chat with the government official, who grumpily complains that most of his department has been laid off as city services are cut back. Suddenly he notices the time, looks frightened, and rushes away.

> **>LOOK AT HEALTH CENTER**
> The Anderson Health Care center is a respected, member-owned HMO which has consistently refused to follow the trend of providing inferior health care to those unable to afford the best procedures.

The post office now only opens for limited hours; a faction of intolerant fundamentalists is gaining more cultural and political power; everything in the shops is noticeably more expensive. Though the game no longer gives you explicit instructions to do so, you can continue recording events, looking for evidence that the long-term consequences of the Plan might do more harm than good. If you show your new recordings to Perelman, he remains unconvinced—there are warning signs everywhere, but few smoking guns—but enough time spent observing events in the 2051 simulation lets the system extrapolate further forward to 2061. And the remainder of the game becomes a voyage deeper and deeper into the future, you and PRISM able to do nothing but observe as the extrapolated long-term consequences of the Plan become more and more stark.

> All along the east side of the street is the featureless, cliff-like facade of Heiman World. Little, if anything, has been done to restore the top several floors, gutted by fire about five years ago.
>
> That fire, which cost several thousand lives, revealed a severe deficiency of built-in fire control systems, but the courts threw out all suits since the building was built after the deregulation of the construction industry in '38...

YOU ARE CARRYING…

» a key

» a wallet

» a credit card

» a driver's license

» a newspaper

» a bag of groceries

» a glossy pamphlet

» a bottle of cheap scotch

> CRACK! Something hits you from behind. As you crumple to the ground, you catch a glimpse of someone wielding a metal bar. Unknown minutes later, your head clears, and you stagger slowly to your feet. Everything you were carrying is gone.

> Neither the Bobcats nor the Rockets are playing today; instead, the stadium is being used for the public execution of criminals.

> A grocery store, its grimy windows barely transparent enough to reveal a large sign reading "Rations for 1's, 2's and 3's today", spans the southern side of the street.

As pillars of society crumble, so does Perry's simulated family. His now-grown son joins the cultish Church of God's Word, who consider only its members to be fully human, and denounces his parents as "animals." The University is repeatedly raided by government officials looking for subversive students, then closed down entirely. Public transit and other services deteriorate and are shuttered. Casual racism rises, eventually becoming normalized. An increasingly violent police force harasses and then murders its minority citizens. The final Rockvil you can reach, fifty years into the future, is an apocalyptic hellscape brought on, perhaps, by a nuclear war precipitated by an increasingly hawkish and nationalistic government.

Voyaging's prose is often minimal, an artifact of a medium still constrained by limited storage space. But the game's power comes from the way you experience the words. It "allows players to experience a linear narrative in a non-linear way," a modern reviewer wrote:

> It is inevitable that certain events will happen, and that societal change like increasing poverty will occur, but you are given the freedom to explore the effects of these changes and discover many of the scripted events that take place in your own way, gathering evidence and piecing together the narrative. While playing, I almost thought of myself as a journalist, or a historian perhaps—not just a player or reader.[16]

The player can rarely intervene in the events they record, but the weight of collecting them can become surprisingly wearying.

> A pregnant woman walks past you, sobbing quietly. You turn, but she is gone, swallowed up by the crowds.

This unassuming ambient message crystallized for one of Infocom's beta testers the profound effect the game was having on her:

> I had to get up from the computer for a minute and catch my breath.... This was one of the most terrifying things I have ever read, done or experienced. The horror was not even in the major events of the game (although they were pretty frightening) but in the "casual" remarks.[12]

Few mainstream games had engaged with real-world issues so directly. Themes of racism and religious bigotry, debates about economic policy, allegorical critiques of political figures—this was no *Super Mario Bros.* People of color had rarely appeared at all in games before 1985, let alone in situations that touched on real issues affecting them. *Voyaging* was indeed pushing the envelope of what games could be, radically and on multiple levels, perhaps more abruptly than any other game before or since.

The depth of *Voyaging*'s simulation also goes far beyond what nearly any previous text game had attempted. Each location's code juggles descriptions for five different time periods and a day/night cycle with buildings that open and close at realistic hours. A tracking system silently notes the aggregate severity of what **PRISM** has recorded, with nearly two hundred descriptions or events that can be captured as evidence of the Plan's consequences. Each is given a hidden point value distinguishing minor details from major catastrophes:

```
1 ;"film titles sound insipid, 2051"
2 ;"Symphony Hall is closed, 2071"
3 ;"guards are abusive, 2071"
2 ;"international travellers strip searched,
       2061 or 2071"
2 ;"long lines at soup kitchen, 2051"
3 ;"wastes dumped into river w/o processing, 2051 thru 2071"
5 ;"Policemen casually beating up black youth, 2061"
```

Though it often serves no in-game purpose, you can perform many everyday activities to immerse yourself in virtual Rockvil: buy groceries, apply for a library card, drink at a bar, ride the subway, get arrested, max out your credit card shopping for clothes.

```
<ROUTINE RACKS-F ()
  <COND (<VERB? EXAMINE>
    <COND (<EQUAL? ,SYEAR 2041>
      <TELL "The clothes are diverse and fashionable, and
quite steeply priced." CR>)
      (<EQUAL? ,SYEAR 2051>
      <TELL "The clothes are quite stylish, and virtually all
out of your price range." CR>)
      (T <TELL "The clothes in the few racks near you are
mostly in the drab browns and olives worn by the lower
classes. Over in the restricted areas of the store, you can
spot racks laden with stylish clothes in the violets and
golds favored by Churchmen and other landowners." CR>)>)>>
```

While the game struggled to fit within limitations that seem painfully small today, every word of its twenty-nine thousand lines of code and prose

Mockup of a print ad concept for *Voyaging*, from Meretzky's development binder.

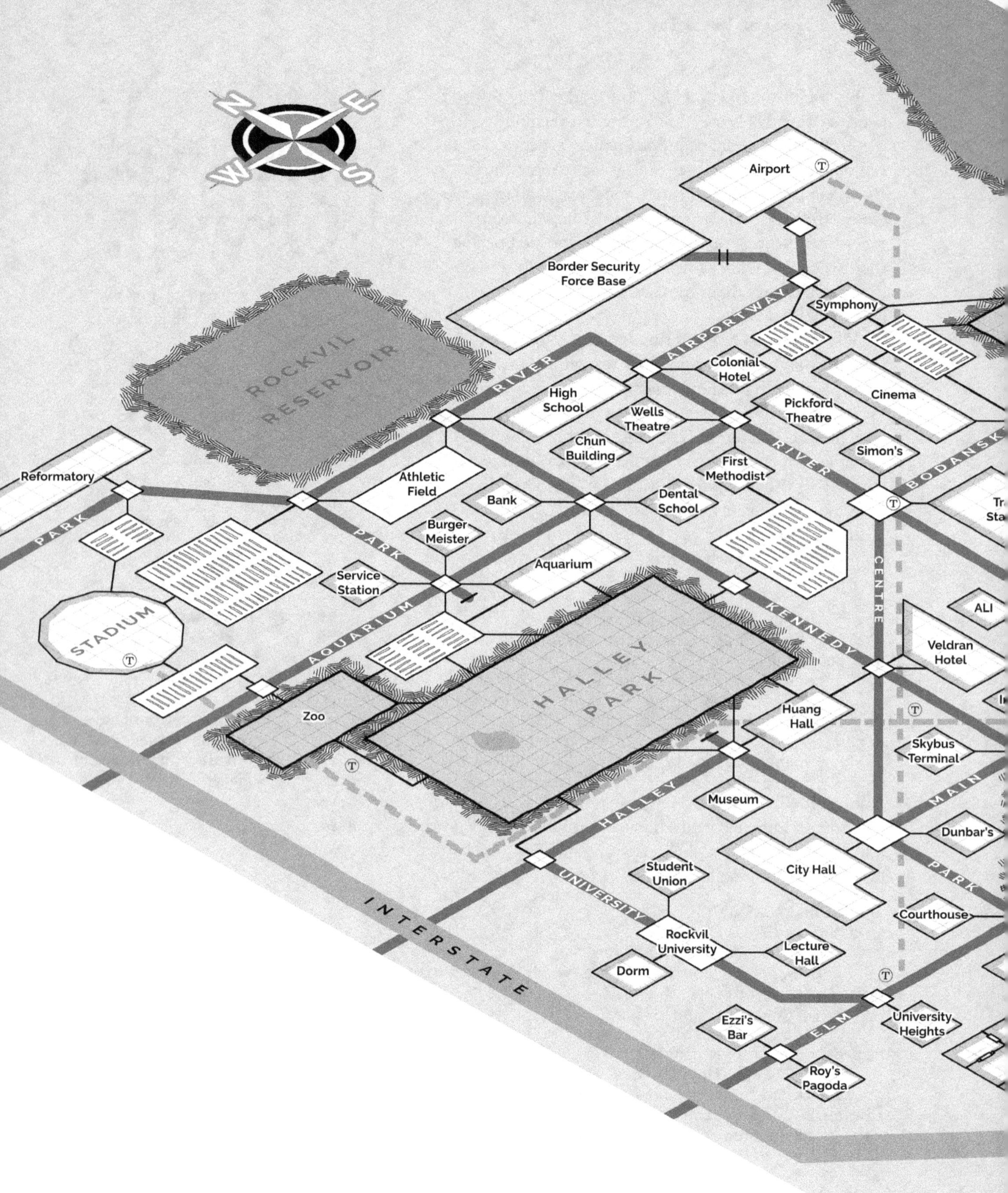

N
E
W
S
Airport
T
Border Security
Force Base
AIRPORTWAY
Symphony
Colonial
Hotel
ROCKVIL
RESERVOIR
High
School
Wells
Theatre
Chun
Building
RIVER
Cinema
Pickford
Theatre
Simon's
RIVER
BODANSK
Reformatory
Athletic
Field
Bank
First
Methodist
Dental
School
T
Tr
Sta
PARK
Burger
Meister
PARK
Aquarium
CENTRE
ALI
Service
Station
AQUARIUM
Veldran
Hotel
STADIUM
T
HALLEY   PARK
KENNEDY
Zoo
Huang
Hall
T
I
Skybus
Terminal
T
Museum
MAIN
HALLEY
Dunbar's
Student
Union
City Hall
UNIVERSITY
Rockvil
University
Lecture
Hall
Courthouse
PARK
Dorm
INTERSTATE
T
Ezzi's
Bar
ELM
University
Heights
Roy's
Pagoda

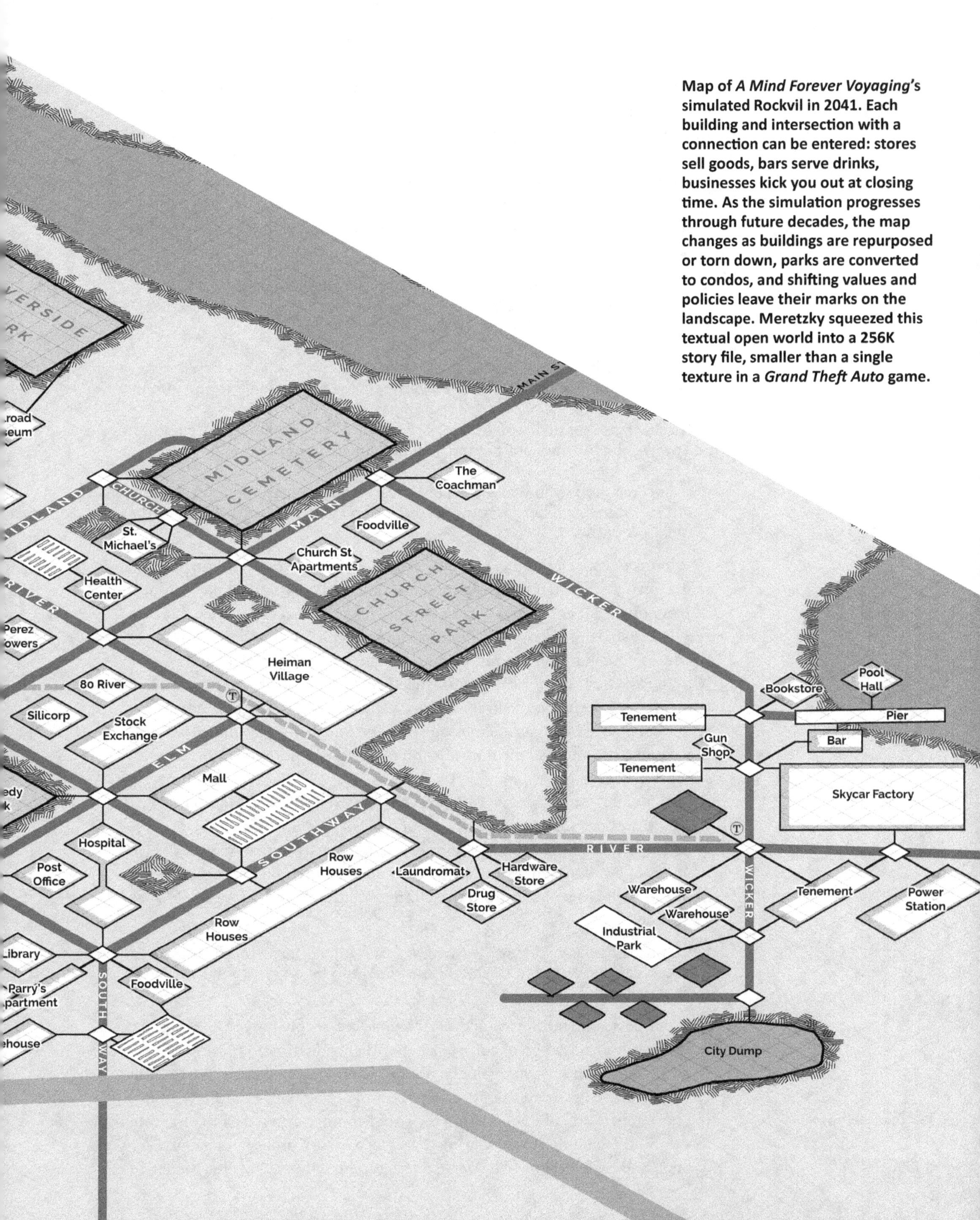

Map of *A Mind Forever Voyaging*'s simulated Rockvil in 2041. Each building and intersection with a connection can be entered: stores sell goods, bars serve drinks, businesses kick you out at closing time. As the simulation progresses through future decades, the map changes as buildings are repurposed or torn down, parks are converted to condos, and shifting values and policies leave their marks on the landscape. Meretzky squeezed this textual open world into a 256K story file, smaller than a single texture in a *Grand Theft Auto* game.

was put to use creating an explorable open world, rendered in text but driven by complex systems. It was Infocom's first game to require 128K of memory rather than 64K, and Meretzky used all but ten bytes of the space the newly expanded engine allowed. He finished the game in eight months, in time to be on shelves for the 1985 holiday season.

The reaction was complicated. Most of Infocom's testers, used to lighter-weight puzzlefests, either intensely disliked it or simply didn't know what to make of it:

> What a waste of talent! Steve Meretzky has written your two best games—*Planetfall* and *Hitchhiker's Guide*—why didn't he spend all the time devoted to this turkey on sequels to them?

> The rather blatant parody of the political philosophy of the current administration is out of place in a game that is purchased for recreation.

> Lacks the spontaneity and humor of recent Infocom releases … what I saw was interesting, but not particularly entertaining.

> I sincerely hope you will reconsider your decision to rush into production on this game.… There is something to offend everyone in this vicious political parody.[12]

Meretzky expected the game to be controversial. He'd even thought it might garner enough attention to make a dent in the national conversation. "I was hoping I'd get dragged in front of a congressional committee," he recalled years later with a grin.[3] But sales were tepid, and reviews were routine. Game journalists simply had no register for critiquing a game with the kinds of themes *Voyaging* engaged with, and culture critics in the wider arts scene had seen no reasons yet to cover games at all. Most reviewers ignored the game's message entirely, sticking to familiar scripts of plot summaries and technical details. But some seemed to grasp the title's significance, even if they couldn't quite articulate it: "There is something special about *A Mind Forever Voyaging* that is hard to define," *Amiga World* wrote.[2] Another magazine praised the novelty of "a game with a social conscience" and declared it "a major event in software entertainment."[12] In a binder of development notes, Meretzky collected review clippings, good and bad, including a letter from the Home Entertainment Editor of *Billboard* magazine:

> "Mind Forever Voyaging" is the best game Infocom has produced yet. All I know is that I started it when it was dark and broke off when I noticed it was daylight.[12]

Countless younger fans would find themselves deeply moved by the game. It awoke in some a political conscience, in others a fascination for open-ended exploration without artificial obstacles, and in many a giddy sense that games could be far more than they'd previously imagined. Hundreds among the next generation of game designers would come to cite it as a foundational inspiration, including Adam Cadre (*Photopia*), Chris Klimas (creator of Twine), and Sam Barlow (*Her Story*), among many others. Novelist Richard

see **1998** and **2012**

1985

Powers, whose book *The Overstory* won a Pulitzer in 2019, has spoken of the game's influence on him as a young writer, as has screenwriter Gary Whitta (*The Book of Eli*; *Star Wars: Rogue One*), who tried for years, unsuccessfully, to pitch Hollywood on a movie adaptation.

A common critique of the game has been that its political leanings are too obvious and overexaggerated: it has a "distinct lack of nuance,"[16] a modern reviewer noted. Its projections of the Plan have been called naïve caricatures of conservative policy, taken to extremes too ridiculous to take seriously. And yet, four decades after Reagan, many of the details of future Rockvil that were once meant to be warnings have already come to pass and go unnoticed by modern players. The death of local newspapers; cities with contaminated drinking water from underregulated utilities; a deliberately hamstrung postal service; politicians who reject facts as fake and declare the press the enemy; overly aggressive airport security measures; extremists occupying government buildings; routine mass shootings; a constant backdrop of police brutality—the list of parallels to today's world, many of which were once science fiction, is profoundly disturbing to compile.

The long-term impact of Reaganomics did, in fact, prove devastating. Trickle-down economics assumed that if the rich paid less taxes, they would pump more money into the economy and everyone would benefit. Instead it led to forty years of declining real wages for the middle class, while the richest Americans multiplied their net worth again and again to amounts that would once have been called obscene. By 2015 America would have the highest prison population per capita in the world as millions served out sentences for minor drug infractions, shattering families and disproportionately affecting the poor and people of color. Chronic homelessness has risen dramatically since Reagan's time, and federal assistance to local governments—for services like libraries, public schools, and sanitation—fell from 22 percent of the average city's budget at the start of the Reagan years to only 6 percent by the end. "If the notion that Reaganite policies would lead to an apocalyptic collapse seemed a touch hysterical in the 80s," wrote one commenter in 2020, "it feels distinctly less so now."[15]

"So many of the things I was worried about in the 1980s have come to pass," Meretzky noted in 2017. "All of the warmongering and trickle-down economics produced exactly the sort of results I was afraid of."[3] And as this book was being written in the aftermath of the Trump presidency, *A Mind Forever Voyaging* felt almost disturbingly prescient. When PRISM's simulation data threatens the Plan's adoption, Senator Ryder shows up to bully Perelman into providing different results. The scene has new resonance in a world where an American president pressured a state election official to "find" enough votes to overturn his opponent's win.

> "PRISM, I'm just back from Washington. [...] They rejected the contents [of your recordings] outright. They called the recordings fakes. They refused to act on them. Several members even questioned my patriotism, made vague threats."

The rise of the cultish Church of God's Word, who believe in revelations transmitted via technology and the utter inhumanity of nonbelievers, is more chilling at a time when millions of QAnon followers are calling their opponents Satan-worshipping pedophiles and threatening violent takeovers of government buildings. This paragraph from the game's news reports could just as easily be about the Malheur National Wildlife Refuge's 2016 occupation by extremists:

> The Arizona Supreme Court has ruled that state authorities cannot evict members of a religious sect from the radio telescope facility atop Greens Peak. The sect, a group of extremists calling itself the Church of God's Word, seized the facility in December of 2027 [...] [The group] received a great deal of media attention from the occupation.

One modern strategy guide for *Voyaging*, which spends nearly thirty thousand words meticulously cataloging every corner of Rockvil, ends with a statement rather startling for a GameFAQs guide: "[I'd] like to dedicate this walkthrough I have made to an America that's being torn apart along with the rest of the world by the Trump administration. We may be divided, and we may be battered and polluted, but we will never surrender or give up to the evil forces at work here."[10]

Infocom's marketing compared their game to Orwell's *1984*, perhaps overzealously. Orwell was forty-six years old when he drafted his warning about the future, a lifelong writer working in a centuries-old medium; Meretzky was twenty-seven writing his, four years into a career as a creative and working in a mode few yet took seriously, still hampered by technical limits. Even so, *Voyaging* is well worth remembering. "It offered a concrete example of how a game could offer pointed social commentary at a time when no one really thought that was something that a game was capable of," one retrospective noted. "And it did so in a way that only a game could, through its mechanics and its systems."[3] Today most Infocom fans remember it as one of the studio's greatest achievements.

When the *New Zork Times*, Infocom's company newsletter, covered the audacious press conference that had launched the game, they described it (unsurprisingly) as a success, waxing a bit rhapsodic: "How did interactive fiction evolve from *Zork* into *A Mind Forever Voyaging*? If interactive fiction can do this, then what else can it do?" More than anything else, it noted, "the audience was left with the impression that interactive fiction can be more, much more, than puzzles."[9] The coming years and decades would prove this right—though not in the profitable way Infocom had hoped. But their gamble would inspire countless future visionaries, each pushing the envelope in their own unique way. Meretzky had found the title for his game in a poem from Wordsworth, describing a statue of that legendary visionary Isaac Newton,

> with his prism and silent face,
> The marble index of a mind for ever
> Voyaging through strange seas of Thought, alone.

see **1977**

1985

References

1 Addams, Shay. 1985. "A Mind Forever Voyaging" (Review). *QuestBusters* II (10), Nov 1985.

2 AmigaWorld. 1986. "A Mind Forever Voyaging" (Review). 2 (5), Sept/Oct 1986.

3 Baker, Chris. 2017. "Flashback: How 'A Mind Forever Voyaging' Took Aim at Right-Wing Politics." *Glixel* (blog). 2017. www.glixel.com/news/how-a-mind-forever-voyaging-took-aim-at-right-wing-politics-w469663 | s Mar 1, 2017

4 Bateman, Selby. 1985. "The Prose and the Parser: How Writers See Games." *COMPUTE!'s Gazette* 3 (24), Jun 1985.

5 Cadre, Adam. 2001. "A Mind Forever Voyaging by Steve Meretzky, played by Adam Cadre." *L'avventura è l'avventura* (blog). June 2001. www.avventuretestuali.com/recensioni/a-mind-forever-voyaging-eng | a Feb 27, 2021

6 Dreier, Peter. 2011. "Reagan's Real Legacy." *The Nation*. Feb 4, 2011. www.thenation.com/article/archive/reagans-real-legacy | a Feb 27, 2021

7 inequality.org. n.d. "Income Inequality." inequality.org/facts/income-inequality | a Feb 27, 2021

8 Infocom. 1985a. "New Release: A Mind Forever Voyaging." *New Zork Times* 4 (2), Summer 1985.

9 Infocom. 1985b. "A Mind Forever Voyaging Goes to the Library." *New Zork Times* IV (4), Fall 1985.

10 Kearns, Deborah L. 2017. "General Walkthrough For A Mind Forever Voyaging." GameFAQs. 2017. gamefaqs.gamespot.com/pc/564462-a-mind-forever-voyaging/faqs/74934 | a Feb 27, 2021

11 Meretzky, Steve. 2001. "Interview: Steve Meretzky." Interview by Adventure Collective (Philip Jong). May 3, 2001. www.getlamp.com/cast/20060718meretzky/FILES/acint.txt | a Feb 25, 2021

12 Meretzky, Steve. 2015. "Infocom Cabinet: A Mind Forever Voyaging." archive.org/details/InfocomCabinetAMindForeverVoyaging/page/n359 | a Feb 25, 2021

13 Mulligan, Megan. 2019. "Q&A: 2019 Fiction Winner Richard Powers." *The Pulitzer Prizes* (blog). 2019. www.pulitzer.org/article/qa-2019-fiction-winner-richard-powers | a Feb 27, 2021

14 One More Continue (blog). 2017. "A Mind Forever Voyaging: The Original Political Game." Jul 23, 2017. onemorecontinue.com/mind-forever-voyaging-original-political-game | a Feb 27, 2021

15 Rosenfield, Eric. 2020. "A Mind Forever Voyaging into Neoliberalism: Steve Meretzky and the Video Game That Saw It All Coming." *Literate Machine* (blog). Mar 1, 2020. literatemachine.com/2020/03/01/a-mind-forever-voyaging-into-neoliberalism-steve-meretzky-and-the-video-game-that-saw-it-all-coming | a Feb 27, 2021

16 Watson, Steven. 2014. "A Mind Forever Voyaging: Flashback Review." *Adventure Gamers* (blog). Aug 15, 2014. adventuregamers.com/articles/view/26877 | a Feb 27, 2021

17 Whitta, Gary. 2011. "A Mind Forever Voyaging." Gary Whitta (website). Feb 20, 2011. gwhitta.blogspot.com/2011/02/mind-forever-voyaging.html | s Jul 26, 2011

18 Wilcox, Timothy. 2020. "From Wordsworth's Poetic Problem to Puzzleless Interactive Fiction." In Proceedings, Electronic Literature Organization Conference and Media Festival, 2020. stars.library.ucf.edu/elo2020/asynchronous/proceedingspapers/15 | a Feb 24, 2021

19 Woger, Martin. 2012. "A Mind Forever Voyaging - Interview Steve Meretzky." EuroGamer.de. Dec 20, 2012. www.eurogamer.de/articles/2012-12-18-a-mind-forever-voyaging-interview-steve-meretzky | a Feb 27, 2021

UNCLE ROGER

Judy Malloy

Style	**Hypertext**
Debuted	**Dec 1, 1986 to Jan 29, 1987** *(daily posts)*
Launch Platform	**The WELL BBS**
Publisher	**Art Com** *(1987–8 releases)*
Language	**Plain text** *(original)* **Unix shell scripts and AppleSoft BASIC** *(boxed version)*

> " I drank too much red wine. The Broadthrow's party is looping in my mind, nested with brief dreams and nightmares.

IT'S 1969. A young woman in Boulder, Colorado, is working for an engineering firm that's building the Orbiting Solar Observatory satellites, the world's first space telescopes. She's there to help computerize the firm's databases, not build satellites, but she can't help stopping by the viewing platform overlooking the clean room to watch this glorious piece of hardware be assembled. "People entered in lab coats," she reminisced later. "The thing was gold, it was shining, it was huge, it was intricate. It was—beautiful. Absolutely beautiful."[3]

And yet another part of her was sad. Outside of working hours, she was also an artist, and she'd struggled like all artists for even the smallest scraps of funding: fifty dollars for materials here, a weeklong residency there. Looking at the multimillion-dollar satellite, the culmination of a decade of

Major Releases

» **Original**, The WELL (BBS), Dec 1 1986–Jan 29 1987 (File 1), July 1987 (File 2). Text postings to ACEN forum with hand-annotated keywords.

» **Interactive version**, The WELL, 1987 (File 1), 1988 (Files 2 and 3). Searchable version created with Unix shell scripts.

» **Boxed version**, Art Com, AppleSoft BASIC, 1987 (File 1); 1988 (File 2); Compilation (1988). Compilation featured all three disks in a clear plastic case for $15.

» **Web version**, 1995. Added keyword links to bottom of each page in lieu of ability to search; rewrote some text.

» **DOSBox version**, download, 2012. Recreates interface of boxed version but keeps text updates from web version, along with some additional text tweaks.

1986

expensive work, she realized no artist would ever have the budget to make something so incredible.

But then a different thought struck her. "Okay, an artist cannot create *that*," she remembers thinking. "I cannot create an Orbiting Solar Observatory…. But an artist could use technology."

The woman was Judy Malloy, "a slight woman with sandy blonde hair"[1] and infectious enthusiasm: when excited, she would lean sharply forward with widened eyes and gesture expansively, as if ideas might flow in and out through pupils or be captured by hands. Her mother had been a journalist and writer, and her father had read Homer to her and her brothers growing up. She got a degree in literature with a concentration in art, and she found a job at the Library of Congress working in "a huge, huge warehouse, full of card catalogs … to work on the cards, we rolled around on chairs."[15] In the mid-1960s such catalogs were just starting to be computerized, and Malloy jumped at the chance to become an expert in an emerging field, taking a Fortran class offered at one company she worked for. At that time the women there, as at many firms, weren't allowed to wear pants or have long hair—she had to hide hers under a wig.

But when she let her hair down after work, Malloy had an entirely different life as a writer and performance artist. On a high school trip to New York, she'd slipped away to visit the Guggenheim and ended up hanging out with "two artists in their studio as they tossed back sips of whiskey and played chess."[4] As an adult she became active in local art spaces wherever she lived, turning her writing into spoken word performance pieces accompanied by slides, or into installations with her words projected on backgrounds or painted on canvas. She wrote single-page short stories and left mimeographed copies in bars, or passed them out on street corners. One New Year's Eve found her

> on the streets of San Francisco, on Broadway and Columbus, dressed in red satin shorts and a blue satin cape passing out chapter 12 of *SUPER LUCY*, a serial about Lucy, a clerical worker, who encounters common workplace situations and problems and deals with them in unorthodox ways—leaving behind her a trail of bosses tied to their chairs with masking tape, system analysts locked in supply cabinets, and blatantly misfiled 3 x 5 cards.[9]

At first her work and her art stayed mostly separate. But by the end of the 70s she had become intrigued by the notion that databases, those mechanical and soulless ways of sorting and archiving huge stockpiles of information, might become distinctly modern tools of artistic expression. She had come up with a notion of "molecular narrative units"[13] that could be accessed in different orders or recombined to create stories without traditional structure. She began to explore these ideas in her art. She founded a company called OK Research and wrote to big businesses requesting information for a new database she was compiling. She didn't mention the database would be used not for generating new business leads, but for performance art. One OK Research installation surrounded the viewer with hundreds of blown-up texts taken from the piles of literature she'd received in the mail, enormous out-of-context koans like LIQUID CHROMATOGRAPHY IS AN ART and FOR ADVENTURE I WORK AT RAYCHEM and HERCULES PROFAX WILL SET YOU FREE.

Then she began to make custom artist's books out of card catalogs. On each card she pasted a fragment of prose or imagery, and she labeled the index tabs with cut-up pieces of photographs. Readers could flip through the catalog to view cards in any order they liked, charting their own course through a story. Later she worked with battery-powered address books, in which sorted business cards could be accessed by the press of a button marked with a letter of the alphabet. Instead of professional contacts, Malloy filled hers with fiction. She removed the letters from the buttons to leave twenty-six blank keys—mechanical bookmarks to random sections of a story that the reader could push in any order they liked.

But the projects were frustrating. Each was time-consuming to create, and they could not be duplicated or shared. Malloy believed experimental literature should be circulated to a broad audience, not locked up in a gallery, but she could see no way to publish or distribute her database narratives.

It might seem odd in hindsight that Malloy hadn't thought of using computers in her projects. But to her they were still the behemoths she'd been trained on, massive mainframes with restrictive hours, gatekeeping technicians, and maddeningly fiddly punch cards. By the 80s the personal computer had arrived, but also a divorce: in the middle of the decade Malloy was a single mom struggling to keep food on the table, and for a long time her own computer seemed a frivolous expense. In 1985 she finally bought a used Apple II, but mostly for her son, who did schoolwork and played Infocom games on it. She tinkered with commercial database software, but the computer mostly seemed a distraction from more serious work. She was almost forty-five years old, and it seemed an unlikely time for a radical change in direction.

see **1983–5**

But then change came to her, in the form of The WELL. Founded in 1985 by Stewart Brand, editor of the *Whole Earth Catalog*, WELL stood for Whole Earth 'Lectronic Link. The dial-up service had a mission of providing cheap access to online communities for the San Francisco Bay Area. Bulletin board systems were becoming more popular, offering email, information, and discussion boards, but most were still outrageously expensive, with some charging fifteen to twenty-five dollars per hour to connect. The WELL charged just three dollars an hour, and it aimed to be a democratizing space open to anyone, with a network of forums—"conferences," in WELL-speak—on subjects ranging from parenting to rock music to technology to religion. An old friend of Malloy's from the art world, Carl Loeffler, had been invited to bring his magazine *Art Com* onto the WELL with its own conference, the Art Com Electronic Network (ACEN). Loeffler's magazine had a long tradition of experimenting with new formats, putting out issues on videocassette, audio tape, and microfiche. He hoped ACEN could be a place not only for art discussion but where artists could publish original, born-digital work. Loeffler invited Malloy to conceive of a piece that could be shown on ACEN.

The WELL was part of the same lineage that had given rise to the People's Computer Company and *Hunt the Wumpus* **1973** a decade earlier.

It was as if all the threads of her life had come together. "I was struck, I was thrilled," she later recalled:

> I already had those skills. I knew how to think about the algorithms, I knew how to do the basic programming…. I realized that I could do what I'd been trying to do with the card catalogs…. I started working on them before I could actually make the vision I had for the kind of literature they were meant to be into something real by using the Apple II. It was sitting on the desk in our house, you know, it was right there.[15]

On December 1, 1986, a new topic was created on ACEN called "A Party in Woodside," the first "File" of a project known as *Uncle Roger*. Following in the Homeric tradition, Malloy had decided she would tell the story live, logging in each day to post new fragments—"records," as she called them using database parlance—of a tale that would only make sense when a reader compiled its disparate threads for themselves, like a researcher following trails of references. Each record would hold only a few lines of the story, but each would be tagged with metadata: its relevant keywords.

Uncle Roger usually wears tweed suits which look
as if he has had them for a long time.
He is short and plump, and when I was younger,
I thought that his briefcase was glued to his right hand.

Because one day when we picked him up at the station,
he said to my Mother: "Given that I live on the train,
I wish that they would serve martinis,"
I also thought
that he lived on the Boston & Maine.

*uncle roger *family *jenny

Malloy at first urged readers to copy each record by hand into a local database program—something most tech-savvy WELL readers would have had on hand—and index them with the given keywords. As the story grew, they could find their own connections and pathways through it. She called it a Serial Novel for the Net, a random-access narrative, a database novel. Pretty soon she had a regular audience who would drop by the conference often to catch up on the latest pieces. "Somebody told me it was their bedtime story every day,"[3] she remembers with a smile. Anyone could have posted in the original thread with the ongoing story, but no one ever did, keeping it clear for Malloy's daily entries. (A second topic was later created for discussion of the piece.) Eventually some technical folks on ACEN helped Malloy make a tiny program out of Unix shell scripts that let readers search the posts by keyword or combinations of keywords, allowing even those without their own database software to access the story with its intended interface.

choose one of
the keywords below and type it

Excerpts are from the author's preferred version of the text, the DOSBox Emulator release, except for the keyword searching example, which is taken from a screenshot of the interactive WELL version.

```
at the prompt

jenny        puffy       uncle roger
dreams       jane        miss gorgel
jeff         jack        jenny's family
tom          dorrie      men in tan suits
louise       rose        chips
mark         laura       refreshments
caroline     david       the house

? JENNY

do you want to combine another keyword with   jenny
type  y  or  n

? Y

what keyword do you want to combine with   jenny

? JEFF

There is a funny feeling in my stomach,
and I can't erase Jeff's image. It hovers over my bed
like the image of God when I said the prayer
that began "Heavenly father hear my prayer,
keep me in your loving care"
and lay in bed in the house in Massachusets.

God was a sort of long, dark man
who hovered horizontally over me
and had no face.


<return> or stop
```

Pressing return would show the next match with that combination of keywords, then the next and the next, leading inevitably to:

```
There are no, or no more records that include
 the keyword(s) you chose   jenny, jeff
```

The user could then try again with a new keyword search, continuing as long as they remained interested. The piece tracked no state and "Woodside" had no explicit ending, letting the user dictate the duration and style of their engagement.

The story that emerged from the fragmented records was unlike almost any that had previously been told on a computer: more literary, free of genre trappings, concerned with people and emotions more than objects and actions, and strongly tied to the time and place of its creation. Set in the

The
Blue
Notebook

The things I wrote in the blue notebook didn't happen in exactly the way I wrote them.

Silicon Valley of the early 80s—when hardware, not software, was king—the story is narrated by a young woman named Jenny who has moved from the East Coast to California, much like Malloy had a decade earlier. Jenny takes a job nannying the kids of microchip tycoon Tom Broadthrow, and "Woodside" takes place at a party of chip industry movers and shakers held at the Broadthrows' swanky home. "Like a guest at a real party," Malloy wrote, "the reader hears snatches of conversation, observes what strangers are wearing and meets old friends. No single reader experiences the evening in the same way."[8] Her ex-husband had been a semiconductor engineer, so she drew from real experience in navigating the surreal excitement of an industry rapidly positioning itself as the center of a realigning world. Exploring *Uncle Roger* reveals a sometimes satiric, often familiar portrait of male-dominated tech culture and the women doing their best to survive within it.

> "There are many stories in the Valley," said Dorrie.
>
> She was easy to listen to. Jane and I sat quietly.
>
> "Some are fairy tales, but there are nightmares.
> Look into the nightmares
> and you'll see Tom Broadthrow's name
> every other page."
>
> I looked at Tom.
> He has a slight build, sandy hair and a pleasant smile.
>
> "Why do you work for him?"
>
> "Someone has to protect the girls on the line."
>
> <return> or stop `[return]`

1986

> Jeff kept talking about custom chips.
> He got very excited.
> I looked into his eyes which are brown.
> I wanted him to keep talking.
>
> "What is a custom chip?" I asked.
>
> <return> or stop [return]
>
> Mark cut through the thick green frosting of the cake,
> put a large slice on a paper plate
> that had pictures of snowmen running around its rim.
> "I have some photos of me surfing on my new surfboard," he said.
> "They're in my room. Do you want to see them."

Below and opposite: front and back of two 5.25" floppy disks in the 1988 compilation release of *Uncle Roger*. The disk sleeves were hand-cut and hand-lettered by Malloy for each copy. Scans courtesy the Pathfinders project.

The most outlandish character is Jenny's uncle Roger, an inveterate prankster and shameless womanizer who keeps turning up in the story like a bad penny. "He's a semiconductor industry analyst," Jenny notes when she first sees him arrive at the party. "He might even have been invited." Piecing together enough records reveals Roger is involved in a chip espionage scheme, a real phenomenon from a time when the company that could make the fastest silicon could crush its competitors. Malloy calls Roger a Falstaffian character, since "you can't tell who he is or what he's doing throughout the story,"[3] and since his aggressively lecherous behavior is intertwined with unexpected kindnesses and quick reversals.

The character of Uncle Roger might be read as standing in for all the frustratingly complex relationships with men that women in the tech industry have dealt with, in the 80s and every decade since. He pays Jenny's tuition but hits on her friends; he's family, but not to be trusted; he involves her in his schemes without asking for consent, but in the end gifts his stolen chip design to her boyfriend, wrapping up the story in an unlooked-for happy ending. "It's the kind of trick that would happen in the theater this was based on,"[3] Malloy observes. She deliberately conceived her story

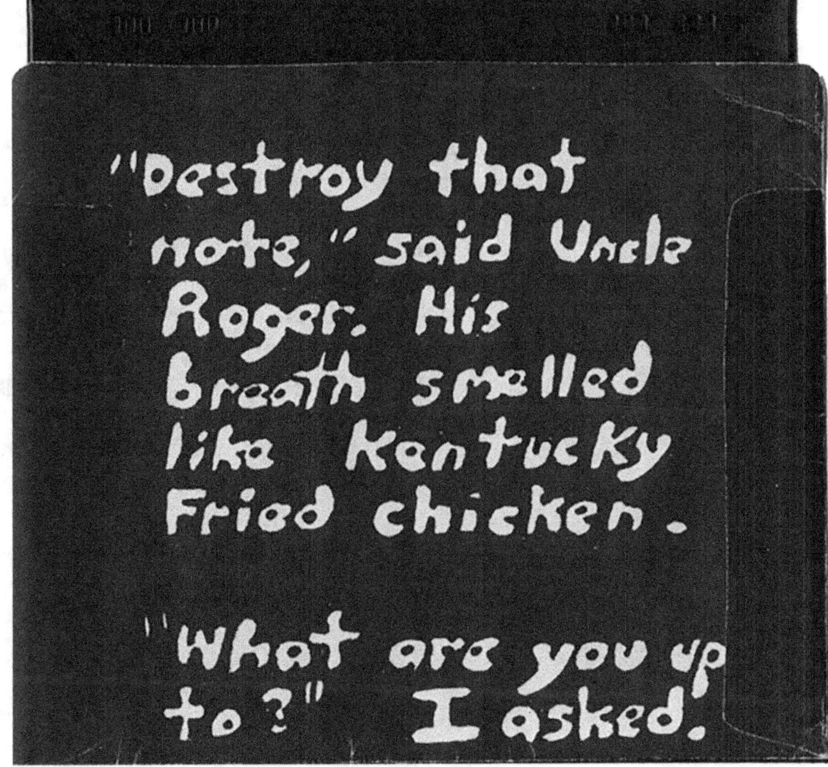

in the style of a jig, the bite-sized comic interludes that would bookend more
serious stage drama in Shakespeare's time: bawdy satires filled with stock
characters, clowns and tricksters, and scheming villains.

> He ate about 1/4 of the salmon cream cheese loaf,
> from the end that Puffy [the cat] hadn't licked.
> "Where is the bathroom?" he asked.
>
> "There are three upstairs," I said.
> "The one that adjoins Tom and Louise's bedroom
> is closest to the top of the stairs."
>
> "Thank you", said Uncle Roger.
> He put a large chunk of sourdough baguette into his pocket
> and headed upstairs, whispering "Be careful, Jenny,
> this is a dangerous household."

But the story is also about Jenny coming into her own, learning to assert
herself and define her place in the new terrains of both California and a
world increasingly dominated by technology. Malloy later extended the story
with two more Files that interweave more of Jenny's flashbacks and dreams
into the narrative, framing them as the thoughts of a wandering mind during
a tedious new job at a word processing center.

> The woman at the station to my left is typing steadily.
> Her husband is an IBM salesman, and she
> keeps his picture in a small silver frame
> beside her computer.

> Cold water dripped down my face.
> I looked at myself
> in the mirror of the ladies room.
> David wanted me to go back East with him.
> I was having dinner with Jeff next Monday.
> Uncle Roger wanted me to be a file clerk.
>
> Water splashes had left dark spots on the front
> of my gray sweater. I took off the silver
> barrette which held my hair away from my face
> and put it in my pocketbook.

> "Do you have any money?" he asked.
>
> "Only about $5.00 ," I said.
>
> He reached in his back pocket,
> pulled out his wallet, and handed it to me.

1986

"See if I've got any," he said.
David had over $50.00 in his wallet.
In a side pocket was a picture of Linda.
I took it out and looked at it. She was
wearing a white sun dress, and her long red hair
was blowing around her face.
David was looking at the road.
I tore the picture into little pieces and
put it back in the pocket of his wallet.
"You have about $50.00," I said.

A woman's story had never been told like this in a text game. While there had been a handful of earlier female protagonists and women authors, those stories had rarely strayed beyond genre archetypes or delved into the inner lives of their characters. Jenny was one of the first women in a digital fiction to be more than a cardboard cutout, with a voice perhaps inevitably shaped by the technology her creator had used to write it. "I was not a poet when I started writing *Uncle Roger*," Malloy recalls:

> But there was a fifty-character limitation on Datanet.... So I kept each line to fifty characters. You can see that in the way *Uncle Roger* flows. [It's] a bit choppy: but that's Jenny's voice also. It flows that way. I wrote to the fifty characters. Well, by the time I was finished with three Files and three hundred lexias writing to fifty characters—I was a poet.[3]

Malloy finished her original telling of "A Party in Woodside" at the end of January 1987, with a record consisting solely of the three words END OF DATA. Over the next year she would create File 2, "The Blue Notebook," and File 3, "Terminals." For File 3, Malloy tried replacing the search-driven interface with a random one: "In the same way [information] comes and goes in the narrator's mind," she wrote, one of the hundred records of "Terminals" would appear unpredictably each time you requested a new one. "Sometimes one record will be repeated several times," the instructions note, "or one part of the story will be submerged for a long time"—perhaps never to surface at all, for some readers.

Malloy published the completed *Uncle Roger* through the new Art Com Software, designed to give computer artists a route to distribution. The original edition came on three floppy disks, one for each File, in a transparent plastic box with labels and disk sleeves covered in hand-inked lettering. She devised the term "narrabase" for her project, and wrote a program of the same name to make it easier to author new ones. "Instead of baseball statistics or information on the migratory habits of fresh water fish," she wrote, "narrabases contain fictional, narrative information."[8]

LOST AND FOUND

The original version of *Uncle Roger* had been thought lost from around the 1990s (when Malloy created the web version) until the early 2010s, when she happened to find an old floppy with the earlier version. With help from the Electronic Literature Organization, she was able to create a replica of the original work running in DOSBox, an MS-DOS emulator.

After years with only the web version for reference, she noted afterward "how much better the original versions of 'A Party in Woodside' and 'Terminals' are... Perhaps this is a similar issue to harpsichord works that were recreated on the piano. Initially when this was done, it was often seen as an improvement. But as the early music movement reclaimed the harpsichord, it has become clear that works composed for the harpsichord usually sound much better on the harpsichord."[14]

1986

Each file is a pool of information into which the reader plunges repeatedly, emerging with a cumulative and individual picture. Thus, the narrabase form uses a computer database as a way to build up levels of meaning and to show many aspects of the story and characters, rather than as a means of providing alternate plot turns and endings.[7]

Malloy wrote more narrabases, continuing to bring her artist's instincts to new forms of writing and storytelling. A critic wrote that reading her work is like "stepping into a labyrinth in which you're lost and finding things at the same time."[4] But her specific project would become eclipsed in literary circles by the more general phenomenon of hypertext fiction that would rise to prominence a few years later, built around a metaphor of clickable words rather than searchable archives. For years, Malloy would not get the credit she deserved for being one of the earliest pioneers of "electronic literature," as the literary hypertext movement came to be called. Pieces by men writing later became more famous and better studied. It wasn't until the 2010s that feminist scholars like Kathi Berens[1] and Dene Grigar[3] helped shine a stronger spotlight on Malloy's crucial early achievements.

Malloy never stopped writing, and she proved surprisingly prescient about the ways technology would change how people read. "In the 21st century," she wrote in 1992, "readers will turn on and interact with literature that is displayed on affordable, book-sized computers."[8] Unwilling to wait for that future to arrive, she has created dozens of projects over the decades since that explore different interfaces to stories and new paradigms for reading them. In a 2012 interview, she leans forward with wide-eyed excitement, gesturing broadly as she talks about a work in progress:

> I'm working in musical notation … essentially I'm creating text that comes out on three or four different screens.… I'm scoring it. So you know, I have 4/4 time, I have to translate that into a slower time. So I'm writing scores! And I'm really excited about it … to me, this is amazing.[3]

Malloy's work has continued to take inspiration from the classics as much as new technology. When asked to contribute to a book called *The Future of Text*, she sent in a chapter composed entirely of quotations from the past, including this one from Virginia Woolf that echoed her 2012 project: "I should like to write four lines at a time, describing the same feeling, as a musician does; because it always seems to me that things are going on at so many different levels simultaneously."[11] In 2020, when she was seventy-eight, her active website tracked an astonishing eight new projects she was involved in that year.

An interviewer once compared *Uncle Roger* to the nonlinear, stream-of-consciousness writing of James Joyce's *Ulysses*. Malloy's answer engaged less with comparisons of style than with the way both works were critical darlings but popular duds:

> People will say to me, "Well, this story wasn't influential because nobody else did it." You know, as a writer, is that your goal? Was that Hemingway's goal? Was that Joyce's goal? Was that Virginia Woolf's goal? Who writes like Joyce now?[3]

In the video, an infectious grin splits her face, and her eyes are sparkling like a trickster's.

References

1 Berens, Kathi Inman. 2014. "Judy Malloy's Seat at the (Database) Table: A Feminist Reception History of Early Hypertext Literature." *Literary and Linguistic Computing* 29 (3).

2 Frost, Charlotte. 2019. "Digital Critics: The Early History of Online Art Criticism." *Leonardo* 52 (1), 2019.

3 Grigar, Dene, and Stuart Moulthrop. 2015. "Pathfinders: Judy Malloy's Uncle Roger." Pathfinders. 2015. scalar.usc.edu/works/pathfinders/judy-malloy | a Feb 20, 2021

4 jrank.org. n.d. "Judy Malloy." reference.jrank.org/biography-2/Malloy_Judy.html | a Feb 20, 2021

5 Malloy, Judy. 1987. "Information as an Artist's Material." *Whole Earth Review* 57, Winter 1987.

6 Malloy, Judy. 1988. "OK Research, OK Genetic Engineering, Bad Information: Information Art Describes Technology." *Leonardo* 21 (4), 1988.

7 Malloy, Judy. 1991. "Uncle Roger, an Online Narrabase." *Leonardo* 24 (2), 1991.

8 Malloy, Judy. 1992. "Electronic Storytelling in the 21st Century." In *Visions of the Future: Art, Technology, and Computing in the 21st Century*, ed. Clifford A. Pickover. New York: St. Martin's Press.

9 Malloy, Judy. 1993. "CFP'93 - Portrait of the Artist on the Net." Computer Professionals for Social Responsibility. 1993. cpsr.org/prevsite/conferences/cfp93/malloy.html | a Feb 20, 2021

10 Malloy, Judy. 2014. "Digital Literature Pioneers: Judy Malloy on 'narrabases.'" Interview by The Lit Platform. theliteraryplatform.com/news/2014/04/digital-literature-pioneers-judy-malloy-on-narrabases-80s-silicon-valley-and-e-literature-today | a Feb 20, 2021

11 Malloy, Judy. 2020. "The Words of the Creators." In *The Future of Text*, ed. Frode Alexander Hegland. Future Text Publishing.

12 Malloy, Judy. n.d. "Home Page." people.well.com/user/jmalloy/mybio.html#mylife | a Feb 20, 2021

13 Malloy, Judy. n.d. "Notes on Uncle Roger." people.well.com/user/jmalloy/uncleroger/uncle.html | a Feb 18, 2021

14 Malloy, Judy. n.d. "Judy Malloy: The BASIC Uncle Roger - Beta Version_2." www.narrabase.net/uncle_readme.html | a Oct 6, 2022

15 Nyhan, Julianne, and Andrew Flinn. 2016. "The Influence of Algorithmic Thinking: Judy Malloy and Julianne Nyhan." In *Computation and the Humanities: Towards an Oral History of Digital Humanities*. Springer Series on Cultural Computing. Cham: Springer International Publishing.

16 Rheingold, Howard. 1993. *The Virtual Community: Homesteading on the Electronic Frontier*. Addison-Wesley Longman.

PLUNDERED HEARTS

Amy Briggs

Style	**Parser**
Debuted	**Sep 1987**
Launch Platform	**Z-machine v3** *(for Amiga, Amstrad series, Apple II, Atari series, Commodore 64, DOS, Macintosh)*
Publisher	**Infocom**
Language	**ZIL**
Launch Price	**$39.95** *(floppy disk)*

> **>SHOOT THE PIRATE**
> Trembling, you fire the heavy arquebus. You hear its loud report over the roaring wind, yet the dark figure still approaches. The gun falls from your nerveless hands.
>
> "You won't kill me," he says, stepping over the weapon. "Not when I am the only protection you have from Jean Lafond."
>
> Chestnut hair, tousled by the wind, frames the tanned oval of his face. Lips curving, his eyes rake over your inadequately dressed body, the damp chemise clinging to your legs and heaving bosom, your gleaming hair. You are intensely aware of the strength of his hard seaworn body, of the deep sea blue of his eyes. And then his mouth is on yours, lips parted, demanding, and you arch into his kiss...
>
> He presses you against him, head bent. "But who, my dear," he whispers into your hair, "will protect you from me?"

1987

see **1978**, **1983**

see **1984** and **1985**

1987

"**Yuk!**" began *Commodore User* magazine's review of something new for Infocom and, perhaps, for the reviewer: a romance. "Probably Infocom's easiest title," it concluded dismissively,[4] in a tone matched by many other critics of the day. *Computer and Video Games* wrote, "There is, of course, a place for easy adventures—after all, everyone has got to start somewhere."[11] Everyone presumably meant women, the only plausible audience for an easy game with kissing. Many male reviewers assumed the game was a cheap attempt to expand Infocom's audience to a new, less sophisticated demographic: a "two-fisted attempt to attract more female purchasers,"[13] said an Atari fan mag. Uneasy jokes were made about whether male readers were really expected to try playing a game that starred a lady. "Can it be enjoyed by someone other than a member of the fairer sex?" asked one. "Certainly—if you don't feel strange reading about your craving for the arms of another man."[18] A British computer magazine asked, "Will the challenge of the game make a man of you? Or … will abandoning the trousers for a cotton frock give you a kick worth nearly £30?"[14]

But *Plundered Hearts* had not been created via marketing dictate, and Infocom's audience had never been exclusively male. Amy Briggs, its author, was one of many women who were fans of the company's games (even the hard ones). She had first discovered text games via the Adventure International titles before moving on to Infocom's more sophisticated fare, finding *Suspended* an especially intriguing challenge. Through an accident of timing, she graduated from fan to employee quite abruptly: just after finishing college she'd moved to Boston, and she saw an ad from her favorite game company in the local paper her first day there. They were looking for testers. Two weeks later, she was working at Infocom.

Briggs had grown up in rural Minnesota—one of her first jobs had been as an usher on *A Prairie Home Companion*—and since high school she'd been a huge fan of romance novels, reading them "in great quantities."[2] At one point she'd even thought writing them might make a nice career. In college she'd majored in English with a specialty in British literature, but she'd also taken computer science classes, so she felt both qualified and interested when the Infocom job popped up. But Briggs didn't want to remain a tester. She stayed into evenings and came in on weekends to teach herself Infocom's in-house programming language, ZIL, and at the encouragement of Steve Meretzky she built a sample game to prove her proficiency—an *Alice in Wonderland* pastiche about a game tester assigned increasingly surreal tasks. In two years, after lots of hard work, she'd achieved her dream of becoming one of Infocom's famed Implementors: the writer/designer/coders who were the creative force behind the company's interactive fiction. At twenty-four, she got the greenlight for her first game.

It was Briggs's idea to make the game a romance, even though Meretzky had warned her against it (people were the most difficult part of a simulated story to get right). It would be Infocom's first in the genre, as well as its first game written by a woman and its first with a female protagonist. It would, in fact, be one of the first mainstream games of any sort that dealt with love from a feminine point of view. Women designers were still seen as oddities in a career increasingly coded as masculine. The extent of this can be felt in a 1988 column by a male industry analyst who wrote that Briggs's game was the first where you played as a female character (it was not) and that Briggs might be "the only woman working in the field" (she wasn't).[9] That a mainstream columnist could make these claims as late as 1988 speaks to the abysmal lack of visibility for professional women in gaming. Each one had to act like a pioneer. Each had to accept that their every move would be second-guessed by the men around them, as well as many of the women.

Plundered Hearts leans heavily into the genre conventions of historical romance, the books sometimes called "bodice rippers" where young women meet dangerous men and, though kept apart by unassailable social conventions, assail them nonetheless. The game casts you as a dutiful young gentlewoman of the seventeenth century whose father, the aging Lord Dimsford, has been kidnapped by the villainous governor of a Caribbean isle, Jean Lafond of St. Sinistra. As the story begins, you're rescued from one of Lafond's lackeys by a dashing pirate captain.

> A tall form blocks the shattered door, one fist still raised from striking your attacker. You catch a glimpse of the hard masculinity of his broad shoulders, the implied power in the scar that etches the stranger's jaw, and feel tremors course through your veins. Then you realize how ragged are his shirt, patched breeches and high boots. Intuitively, you understand—he is the dreaded Falcon, scourge of the sea! Alas, your fate is sealed. Resigned, you meet his sea-blue eyes.

The Falcon, aka Captain Nicholas Jamison, turns out to be an unlikely ally of your imprisoned father's and is planning to aid him and settle a score with Lafond; but traitors in his crew are working against him. In the end, it's mostly up to you to effect the rescue, working your way through a delightful set of pirate adventure and historical romance tropes: climbing up trellises, discovering secret passages, dancing with handsome men (and drugging the goblets of lecherous ones), swinging from chandeliers, and narrowly avoiding exploding barrels of gunpowder.

While most previous games had made little of the player's gender, Lady Dimsford is heavily constrained by the conventions of hers, in the sense of both history and genre. Early on, for instance, you need to escape a shipboard cabin through a shattered window to climb up to the deck:

> The end of a rope ladder blows past the window.
>
> >CLIMB ONTO LEDGE
> You climb onto the ledge. The ladder drifts within reach.
>
> >GRAB LADDER
> You put everything in your reticule and reach out for the ladder and over-balance, tumbling from your perch. Your hand closes on a slimy hemp rung as you fly out over the waves, clinging tenuously, feet free, to the ladder.

Level 9's *Snowball* [1982] was an early text game with a female protagonist, while arcade titles dating back to the 70s had women player characters; and though a game industry analyst might not have known about Judy Malloy 1986, he certainly ought to have been aware of Roberta Williams or Alexis Adams 1978, among others.

1987

On the Ladder
    You are clinging to a slimy ladder, tied to a rail of the poop deck above you. Not far from your feet, waves kiss the stern of the ship.

>UP
In these clothes? You jest.
    All air is driven out of you as the ladder slams into the stern.

>EXAMINE MYSELF
You are wearing a cotton frock, very pretty, if a tad outmoded for today's fashions.

If you climb back inside and remove your frock, revealing "a linen chemise and a few layers of unmentionables," you can climb the ladder successfully. But arriving on deck so undressed results in "a fate worse than death" when the lecherous pirate crew sees you. To move freely about the ship, you must first find a male disguise—a pair of breeches and a shirt, discarded by a cabin boy.

Puzzles in *Plundered Hearts* tend more toward the pragmatic than the enigmatic. The game often allows alternate solutions: there are several different ways to break into Lafond's estate, and several possible uses for a garter belt. In one scene you need to signal a ship at harbor from the window of Lafond's manor, and you're meant to do this with a chipped piece of mirror found much earlier, using it to reflect the brilliant moonbeam shining in through the window. But if you forget to bring the mirror with you or never discovered it, the same scene involves a butler serving food on a "mirror-bright" silver tray:

>WAVE TRAY IN MOONLIGHT
You scrape everything off the silver tray into the bushes below. You roll the silver tray around in the beam of moonlight till it glows silver-white. After a moment, a flash of light responds from the Helena Louise.

The puzzles are also more tightly coupled to plot than in most previous Infocom games, serving as gates between sequential dramatic scenes more than sundry challenges in an open environment. "This is not a romp through a lot of puzzles but a voyage through an interesting story,"[2] Briggs wrote at the time. Game historian Jimmy Maher has noted that *Plundered Hearts* has "a plot thrust—a narrative urgency—that's largely missing elsewhere in the Infocom canon." While the company often compared their games to "waking up inside a story," Maher says *Hearts* approached that ideal more closely than any of the company's other titles, with "many more of the sorts of things the uninitiated might actually think of when they hear the term 'interactive fiction.'"

As you play, the plot thickens, events unfold, relationships change, characters develop and deepen, romance blossoms. In short, real, plot-related things actually *happen*. I don't mean to say that this is the only way to write a compelling text adventure. Nor do I mean to say that there's a lot of plot here by the standards of a typical novel.… What I am saying is that Amy Briggs took interactive fiction as Infocom preferred to describe it and made her best good-faith effort to live up to that ideal.[12]

Though constrained by space—the game was stuck with Infocom's old z3 file format, not the expanded z4 afforded Meretzky on *A Mind Forever Voyaging*—Briggs stuffed every corner of the space allotted her with color and character. The code often takes situational advantage of the game state to add nice bits of genre-appropriate color, such as when you try to climb a ship's rigging while carrying a dagger:

see **1985**

> >UP
> You bite down on the dagger, freeing your hands to climb. When you stop, you take it back again. The wind, a mere breeze on the deck, blows more fiercely.

This even extends to the game's system messages:

> [Which pirate dost thou mean, Captain Jamison or Crulley?]

> >SAVE
> Aye-aye.

And the game delights in letting you lean into the conventions of its genre: shrieking at timely moments, slapping people who deserve to be slapped, and dressing up in fancy clothes. (In a first for Infocom, the game contains a thousand-line `clothes.zil` file to simulate the various dresses, breeches, brooches, and hats you might encounter.) Briggs even worked in responses to appropriate verbs that might not have been attempted in most previous Infocom games:

> >SWOON
> You've never been missish enough to faint on demand.
>
> >SIGH
> You sigh contentedly, smiling.

Plundered Hearts, in short, asks you to embody and perform a role laden in a genre's gender stereotypes. Few previous games had done this so consciously, and not everyone was willing to play along (as we'll come to shortly). But it's worth nothing that Briggs certainly did this deliberately, and she often pushed back against tropes in both obvious and subtle ways. While the dashing Captain Jamison is ostensibly the hero of the story, he's actually not very effective at pretty much anything, and to complete the game you'll need to take matters firmly into your own hands. Jamison, in fact, must be rescued by you, not once but several times. And in the game's

"I've had some people write that the hero is a wimp," Briggs once noted. "I personally like to think of him as a sensitive wimp."[9]

final moments, one of four possible endings is to abandon him on the beach and commandeer his ship:

> The tale you tell Jamison's crew, of rapine and blood, of your heroic attempt to save their captain, and of your own escape after his death in your arms, is not so far from the truth that you cannot appear sincere. Cannily, you take advantage of their temporary grief, select a private guard, and teach the rest the discipline of the whip.
>
> In 253 turns, you have achieved a score of 25 out of 25 points. Thus you have finished the story of PLUNDERED HEARTS, earning the title, "Pirate Queen."

YOU ARE CARRYING...

- your reticule (hanging from your wrist)
- a garter
- a jewelled brooch
- smelling salts
- a beautiful ball gown (being worn)
- a linen chemise
- an invitation
- a bit of mirror
- a banknote

Some have viewed the game as more of a tongue-in-cheek critique of romance novel tropes than reinforcement of them. It's hard to take entirely seriously, for instance, its near-total replacement of the traditionally frequent adventure game deaths with sequences like these:

> Dragoons surround you. Something cracks over your head, knocking you unconscious.
> You awaken, cuddled in a huge purple and gold curtained bed, with a shocking migraine. The man lying next to you pays no heed to your complaints, and commands you in French when you try to defend yourself. He tires of you within a few weeks, but lets you work the streets of Santa Ananas.
>
> *** You have suffered
> a fate worse than death ***

MEMORABLE PLACES

In the Rigging

Quarter Deck

Captain's Quarters

Veranda

Supper Room

Lafond's Bedroom

Dungeon

Library

> A brig, Portuguese by its sails, rescues you. The sailors are brown skinned and smooth, and the first mate, the ship's and yours, is gentle. They leave you in Rio, alone and forgotten.
>
> *** You have suffered
> a fate worse than death ***

But while conscious she was writing in a genre rife with stereotypes about women, Briggs seemed less concerned with deconstructing its tropes than having fun with them, and writing a kind of story she'd always imagined it would be entertaining to tell:

> C. S. Lewis said he had to write the *Chronicles of Narnia* because they were books he wanted to read, and nobody else had written them yet. *Plundered Hearts* was a game I wanted to play.... In general I like stories about strong heroines. I like those stories more when the heroines are not above falling in love.... One doesn't have to be Miss Simper to enjoy dancing (or necking in the gazebo) or be Ms. Rambo to defeat the bad guys. Just be yourself, and do both.[2]

Not all women were willing to give the game the benefit of the doubt. "At the time there were some critical reviews that just hated it because of its over-femminess," Briggs remembered in 2010. "I remember one reviewer just lit into the game because she was trying to karate chop and to do tough guy stuff and the game wouldn't let her, and so she was criticizing it for not allowing the character to be strong."[3] The reviewer in question was Janet Murray, a professor who would go on to write one of the most influential academic texts of the 90s on interactive storytelling theory, *Hamlet on the Holodeck*. Murray wrote of the game:

> It's hip, it's clever, it's tongue-in-cheek. But it's not feminist…. Romance fiction is focused on the image of the powerful, violent male and the helpless maiden. It's obsessed with female virginity and male potency. Briggs observes all those conventions.[9]

Other women reviewers, sensitive perhaps that they'd been assigned to cover the game *because* they were women, also took issue. Well-known columnist Scorpia wrote, "Right up front, I'll tell you that when I heard Infocom was putting out a gak romance adventure, my stomach did flip-flops. This is not to say that romance doesn't have a place, just that its place is not in adventure games."[15] (She did admit it was "not so bad as I expected.") Betty DeMunn, writing for an Atari ST magazine, praised Briggs for offering the chance "to shed 'him' and become 'her'" for a change, but ultimately gave the game a negative review, her first ever for an Infocom title:

> *Plundered Hearts* disappointed me. The intent is to be applauded. Women have long been overlooked, both as authors and consumers, but to grab us, you need a stronger hook. Let us be what we are today, or will be in the future—not what we were 300 years ago…. Being a feisty old feminist, I have to say that *Plundered Hearts* is one small step for womankind, sideways.[7]

Between these sentiments and the tendency of some male reviewers to dismiss or trivialize the game, *Plundered Hearts* seemed destined for commercial failure. Its release came at a troubled time for Infocom: the company was in dire financial straits. Only a few years earlier it had been a popular studio on the cusp of widespread cultural relevance, coming off the massive success of *Hitchhiker's Guide to the Galaxy*, profiled in *Time* and

Map of the *Helena Louise* from *Plundered Hearts*.

see **1984**

Newsweek, and praised by celebrities like Robin Williams (who supposedly called up co-founder Marc Blank in the middle of the night for hints). But graphical games were increasingly kicking text adventures off retail shelves, and Infocom's sales had been plummeting. A long-in-the-works but disastrous attempt to pivot the company to business software proved a failure, in the interim starving the games division of R&D money that might have helped them add meaningful multimedia to their titles. An acquisition by Activision, which had at first seemed like a good partnership and safety net, turned sour after a new CEO there micromanaged Infocom into the ground; among other questionable decisions, decreeing that the company's long-successful practice of promoting popular catalog titles should be jettisoned in favor of fresh boxes on store shelves each quarter, which meant accelerating the pace of new releases to an unsustainable pitch. By 1987, the company was down to less than thirty employees from a height of over a hundred. Briggs, in fact, was one of the last to be hired.

The result was enormous pressure on the remaining designers to deliver a success—and not just any success, but a blockbuster big enough to save the company. Briggs recalled:

> There was a panic underlying everything of "where is the next *Hitchhiker's Guide to the Galaxy?* ... Go out and just write us another game that will sell 150,000 copies." Which none of the other games had done except for *Hitchhiker's*.
>
> ...It was this impossible task that was laid on. "We don't want to burden you with telling you what to do. You just write us a hit."[3]

SOFTWARE PIRACY

Game companies tried everything in the 1980s to keep players from copying disks to give to friends. Software-based copy protection schemes were almost inevitably hacked, so many companies turned instead to hardware: making the physical materials in the retail package required to unlock the game it contained. A common technique was to ask the player to enter, say, Word X on Line Y of Page Z of the game manual. Infocom got more creative, often incorporating their infamous "feelies" (bonus goodies included in the box) into the game's puzzles. *Plundered Hearts* features a vital clue hidden in plain sight on a St. Sinistra banknote feelie; in *The Lurking Horror* you need the number printed on the student ID card in the box to log in to the campus mainframe. In *Sherlock* and *Zork Zero*, worldbuilding "flavor text" in the box was actually laced with important clues for major puzzles—making it not only useful, but actually essential, to read.

Infocom marketing went a little overboard with the game and what Briggs described as the "by a woman, for women" angle. The back of the box gushed that "in the 17th century, the seas are as wild as the untamed heart of a young woman," and claimed that "In *Plundered Hearts*, Infocom brings your wildest fantasies to life." Yet the company was also desperate to convince manly men that they'd enjoy the game too, and it's perhaps no surprise that, in the end, few customers of any gender were convinced to give it a try. None of Infocom's games were selling very well anymore. The company that had once affixed to its door a plaque reading Imagination Sold and Serviced Here was finding fewer and fewer buyers.

"I came in at the end of the good stuff," Briggs recalled decades later. But she considered even the company's twilight one of the best times of her life: "It was the best job I've ever had ... it was really *not* a job, it was an amazing creative experience ... something very special and unusual."[3] In another interview she said, "We were all young, creative, humorous, enthusiastic people, we loved what we were doing and we enjoyed our own games more than anything— and that shows in the games themselves, I believe."[6] Though she was the youngest Implementor, it wasn't by much, and the Infocom designers were a tight-knit group. Open office doors meant ideas were often kicked around with colleagues, and design and coding advice was swapped freely at lunches or on walks taken to workshop awkward puzzles or dig a character out of a story hole. "It was everybody working on their own thing," Briggs recalled, "but together."[3]

But declining sales and a continuing lack of corporate support meant the end was coming. In 1989, Activision effectively shuttered Infocom, laying off half its remaining employees and offering the rest the chance to relocate to a West Coast office. Only a handful accepted. Briggs had already left after a frustrating period of being shuttled from one half-baked project to another, while her own pitches for adaptations of the Anne Rice vampire novels and an interactive *Doctor Who* went ignored. Management was floundering. The "good stuff" was over.

While a critical and commercial dud in the 80s, Briggs's game has been fondly remembered. Plenty of young women could overlook the flaws in its representation for the sheer novelty of having some, and fewer men today are afraid to admit that "abandoning the trousers for a cotton frock" can be pretty fun. Many reviews, even on release, were positive—one called it "a wonderful adventure, bursting at the seams with atmosphere, interesting puzzles and tense situations"[20]—and the game's focus on story over puzzles proved ahead of its time, forecasting the turn most amateur interactive fiction would take in the decades to come. "*Plundered Hearts* is one of Infocom's more underrated games," a 90s retrospective noted,[5] while 2000s IF writer Emily Short called it "almost pitch-perfect … [it] has a lot more plot than most other Infocom games, and often feels surprisingly modern."[16] In the 2010s Jimmy Maher, who covered the entire Infocom canon extensively for his blog *The Digital Antiquarian*, called *Plundered Hearts* one of his favorites: "In terms of sheer entertainment I don't think Infocom ever made a better game."[12] And in 2020 Jon Ingold, co-founder of successful story-driven game studio inkle, also called it the best of the Infocom titles. "It's stunningly good," he noted:

see *Photopia* **1998**

see *80 Days* **2014**

> It's one of the few that manages to put its fiction above its puzzle-solving at all times, the whole way through. When I think back to that game I don't remember a single puzzle, I don't remember a single moment of friction. What I remember is dressing up and dancing at the governor's ball, and hiding behind a door and whacking someone on the head with a box in order to escape. I remember moments of swashbuckling.… When I look back on it I remember having been *on an adventure* rather than having played a game, and that's such an achievement.[10]

>**UNTIE ROPE**
Untied. The chandelier swings slightly, dribs of hot wax spilling to the floor.
 Nicholas and Lafond circle each other intently, the one breathing hard, the other casual, sword tips almost touching. Jamison has lost copious amounts of blood and is no match for Lafond, cool and competent.

Briggs did work on several other projects in Infocom's dying days: she was one of several serial lead designers on the ill-fated, never finished *Hitchhiker's Guide* sequel; she did editorial work and rewrites on *Quarterstaff* [1988]; and she wrote part of a game in the unloved line of InfoComics, *Gamma Force: Pit of a Thousand Screams* [1988].

> **>SWING DOWN**
>
> "Aaieeee!" The cry comes uncalled to your lips as you swoop down from the balcony, petticoats flying, on the end of the rope.
>
> Your timing is perfect: you slam into Lafond just as he steps into his lunge. His rapier stabs wildly, piercing Nicholas's shoulder, missing his heart. You and Lafond roll into a snowball of petticoats and brocade [...]

Briggs never made another game after leaving Infocom, though she'd meant to spend some time writing the proverbial Great American Novel. For her goodbye party, her coworkers made her a T-shirt: 1989 Winner of the Pulitzer Prize. "I was asked, 'Why can't you write the Great American *Interactive* Novel,'" she recalled, "to which I responded that characters are the stuff of great novels, and that realistic character was a great weakness in interactive fiction."[6] She didn't end up writing the book, but went back to school to get a doctorate in Experimental and Behavioral Psychology. Her dissertation was about how readers understand character in stories. Some passions, indeed, are hard to quit.

References

1 Briceno, Hector, Wesley Chao, Andrew Glenn, Stanley Hu, Ashwin Krishnamurthy, and Bruce Tsuchida. 2000. "Down From the Top of Its Game." In *Structure of Engineering Revolutions*. citeseerx.ist.psu.edu/viewdoc/download?doi=10.1.1.694.1911&rep=rep1&type=pdf | a Apr 5, 2021

2 Briggs, Amy. 1987. "Infocom's First Romance." *The Status Line* VI (4), Winter 1987.

3 Briggs, Amy. 2007. "GET LAMP: Amy Briggs." Interview by Jason Scott. Nov 12, 2007. Video. archive.org/details/getlamp-abriggs | a Apr 5, 2021

4 Commodore User. 1988. "Plundered Hearts" (Review). Jan 1988.

5 Cree, Graeme. 1995. "Plundered Hearts" (Review). *SPAG* #4, Mar 2, 1995. www.spagmag.org/archives/backissues/spag4.html | a Apr 5, 2021

6 deMause, Neil. 1996. "Romancing the Genre: An Interview with Plundered Hearts Author Amy Briggs." *XYZZYnews* #12, Nov/Dec 1996. www.ifarchive.org/if-archive/magazines/XYZZYnews/XYZZY12.TXT | a Apr 5, 2021

7 DeMunn, Betty D. 1988. "Review: Plundered Hearts (Infocom)." *ST-Log* #20, Jun 1988.

8 Dobson, Dale. 2009. "Adventure of the Week: Plundered Hearts (1987)." *Gaming After 40* (blog). Nov 24, 2009. gamingafter40.blogspot.com/2009/11/adventure-of-week-plundered-hearts-1987.html | a Apr 5, 2021

9 Gaffney, Dennis. 1988. "Trends: Interactive Romance." *Technology Review* 91 (4), May/Jun 1988.

10 Ingold, Jon. 2020. "Designer Notes: Jon Ingold - Part 1." Designer Notes Episode 53 (Idle Thumbs). June 18, 2020. Podcast. www.idlethumbs.net/designernotes/episodes/jon-ingold-part-1 | a Apr 5, 2021

11 Keith. 1987. "Adventure Reviews Plundered Hearts." *Computer Video Games*, Dec 1987.

12 Maher, Jimmy. 2015. "Plundered Hearts." *The Digital Antiquarian* (blog). Oct 23, 2015. www.filfre.net/2015/10/plundered-hearts | a Apr 5, 2021

13 Panak, Steve. 1988. "Panak Strikes." *A.N.A.L.O.G. Computing* #64, Sep 1988.

14 The Pilgrim. 1988. "Plundered Hearts" (Review). *ACE (Advanced Computer Entertainment)* #4, Jan 1988.

15 Scorpia. 1987. "Scorpion's Tale." *Computer Gaming World* #42, Dec 1987.

16 Short, Emily. 2008. "Plundered Hearts" (Review). IFDB. ifdb.org/viewgame?id=ddagftras22bnz8h | a Apr 5, 2021

17 The Status Line. 1987. "Peril & Passion in Plundered Hearts." VI (3), Fall 1987.

18 Trunzo, James V. 1988. "Plundered Hearts and Nord and Bert Couldn't Make Head or Tail of It." *Compute!* #92, Jan 1988.

19 The Walkthrough King. n.d. "Plundered Hearts." www.walkthroughking.com/text/plunderedhearts.aspx | a Apr 5, 2021

20 ZZap!64 Magazine. 1988. "Plundered Hearts" (Review). #33, Jan 1988.

1987

P.R.E.S.T.A.V.B.A.

(P.E.R.E.S.T.R.O.I.K.A.)

Miroslav Fídler
as "UV Software"

Style **Parser**
Debuted **Jul or Aug 1988**
(hand-distributed cassette)
Launch Platform **ZX Spectrum**
Language **BASIC** *(code)*
Czech *(text)*

> UV SOFTWARE SI U PRILEZITOSTI 20.
> VYROCI OSVOBOZENI CESKOSLOVENSKA
> SPOJENECKYMI ARMADAMI DOVOLUJE
> NABIDNOUT VAM LOGICKOU KONVERZACNI
> HRU:
>
>   P.R.E.S.T.A.V.B.A.
>
> **P**rogram **R**evolucni **E**xperimentalni
>   **S**ocialisticky **T**vorive
>   **A**vantgardni **V**oloviny
>   **B**asniku a **A**nalfabetu
>
> © 1988 UV SOFTWARE   SAVE-S
> NAMET © 1968 ZIVOT

CENTRAL COMMITTEE SOFTWARE ON THE
OCCASION OF THE 20TH ANNIVERSARY OF
THE LIBERATION OF CZECHOSLOVAKIA BY
WARSAW PACT ARMIES WOULD LIKE TO
OFFER A CONVERSATIONAL PUZZLE GAME:

    P.E.R.E.S.T.R.O.I.K.A.

Program for **E**xperimental
  REvolutionary **S**ocialist **TR**ipe
  by **O**bvious **I**lliterates and
  Kooky **A**uthors

© 1988 ÚV SOFTWARE   SAVE-S
SCENARIO © 1968 REAL LIFE

On **A**ugust 21, 1968, **the Soviet Union** sent half a million Warsaw Pact troops into Czechoslovakia, bringing an end to a reform movement known as the Prague Spring. The fellow communist country had aimed to increase freedom of the press, allow for multiple political parties, and soften a Soviet-inspired system into a more modern and liberal democratic socialism.

1988

Major Releases

» **Original**, ZX Spectrum, Jul or Aug 1988.

» **Atari 400/800** (port), late 1988, author unknown.

» **Web remake**, Jaroslav Švelch and Martin Kouba, 2019. Fixed typos; added accented characters, title screen image, modern UI conveniences.

» **English translation**, James Gerrie, May 18, 2021. Ported to Micro Color Basic for TRS-80 emulation, with some minor playability improvements.

Translations in excerpts are by the author.

But to the Soviets this was unacceptable, an erosion of their dominance over the Eastern Bloc and thus their position in the global Cold War. They responded with one of the most aggressive military actions postwar Europe had seen. Troops occupied major cities; dissenters were beaten, jailed, or killed; and hundreds of thousands of Czechs and Slovaks fled. A new loyalist government was installed, reversing the Prague Spring reforms and making Czechoslovakia "one of the region's most dogmatic and conservative regimes," ushering in "an era in which conformity was valued above all else."[7]

The story of how the invasion relates to the history of computer games is a surprisingly complex one that ripples through decades and continents, generational shifts, and cultural blind spots. One small piece of that story begins with the August 1968 invasion, and ends exactly twenty years later with a protest commemorating it and an invitation to attend in a form no regime leader had yet considered as an avenue of dissent—a text adventure.

In the late 1980s, personal computers were rapidly taking over most Western countries, but less than 2 percent of the population in the Czechoslovak Socialist Republic owned one. This was largely because the state, which controlled all production, had never made producing personal computers for its citizens a priority. As a sense began to grow that the nation's youth might be falling behind Western countries' in their readiness for a digital future, belated attempts were made to jump-start a homegrown computer industry. But with neither the economies of scale that made cheap computer parts possible, nor marketing firms to convince people they needed one, computers in Czechoslovakia remained rare and very expensive. And while computer games had become big business under capitalism, in the ČSSR there was simply no way for such an industry to arise. The state had no interest in games, and private citizens had no legal means of distributing or making a living from them—even if they could get hold of a computer to write some.

So most of the few computers and computer games in the country had to be imported, often under the table. While it wasn't illegal to bring goods across the border, Czechoslovak crowns were not convertible with Western currencies, and the state charged exorbitant import fees even for those who did have foreign money. A more practical means to obtain a computer was to pay a friend who could afford a visit abroad to smuggle one back for you. And one of the easiest computers to smuggle was the British ZX Spectrum, an aging machine already replaced by newer models in its home country. Its small size—contained within a plastic keyboard about the size of a trade paperback and designed to hook up to a television set—made it easy to shove deep into a bag or under a pile of laundry. One importer wrapped a Spectrum up like a sandwich and hid it in a basket of snacks. By 1988 there may have been close to one hundred thousand Spectrums in Czechoslovakia, some brought in legally but most slipped through "gaps in the Iron Curtain."[7]

The cost and the risk still kept computers inaccessible to most families, so at first the only way most young people could use one was at a computer club. While it wasn't legal to form private organizations or own equipment collectively, a number of official state organizations became umbrella groups for all kinds of hobbyist activities. Svazarm, a kind of all-ages Scouts designed to train comrades in skills that might be useful in military service (such as ham radio or first aid), began hosting computer clubs during the 80s. At a branch in Prague, three young teens in particular bonded over the club's shared computers. "The life-long dream of all of us was that we would one day have a computer at home,"[4] one of them, Miroslav Fídler, recalled years later. He and his friends, Tomâš Rylek and František Fuka, would eventually form a loose collective known as the Golden Triangle and become some of the most famous game programmers in the country.

But that would come later. Without computers at home, the trio would often stay at the club until midnight when allowed, taking long walks along the Vltava River sharing project ideas and schemes at times when the available machines had all been claimed by others. Eventually Rylek and Fídler's families went in on a joint purchase of a Spectrum the boys could share, and the two worked out a plan to use it in shifts. Within a year they'd worn out the cheap keyboard. With no way to get official replacement parts, they scrambled to hack together a replacement out of scavenged materials, including doorbell buttons.

Day by day, their hardware hacking and coding skills improved. Fídler had already been programming for years, writing simple code on a TI-58 calculator that he'd manage to hook up to a printer: "[It] could be told to print letters through some crazy method, so I made a program that made sentences out of words."[4] The Spectrum, even with its limited memory, was an impressive upgrade.

"The first software [we had access to] was program listings in magazines,"[4] Rylek later recalled—sometimes in smuggled-in computer publications from the West; sometimes in official newsletters for computer club members—private citizens couldn't distribute literature or own a printing press. Rylek dryly remembers a then-typical experience with magazine program listings: "One typed it into the computer, and wondered why it didn't work."

Homemade replacement keyboard for a ZX Spectrum. Photo by Silvia Kolesárová.

But soon Western games smuggled in on cassette tapes started circulating. The Spectrum could hook up to any tape player to read or write data, and tapes were easy to copy. These pirated games—though piracy was a fuzzy concept in a country without private industry—would circulate via a "sneakernet" of copied and shared cassettes. Many of the games had been locally cracked to remove their copy protection or add cheats and tweaks, and their loading screens would be modified with messages from the hackers. Club members in different cities, who had never met in person, left elaborate chains of notes to each other on crack screens, forming friendships and rivalries encoded in BASIC strings. Soon the shared games "became a fully-fledged means of communication within a subculture of young geeks, like 8-bit chain letters or, perhaps, social media of the early digital era"[9]—an internet that existed mostly on magnetic tapes, shoved into school backpacks and zipping around the country on buses and bicycles. Literature and music was heavily censored by the government and could not be legally distributed by amateurs, but software was not on the radar of the Party or its secret police at all. The authorities had not yet realized that the computer could be a medium for expression.

Soon the Golden Triangle and other young hackers started giving out cassettes of their own original games. The analog distribution network was so efficient that, within weeks, new games might spread to tens of thousands of players in all parts of the country. "One of the games that I released was offered back to me from Bratislava [two hundred miles away] six days later,"[7] Fuka fondly recalls. And while many of the country's amateur games used graphics, the most popular genre was the *textovka*, or text adventure. Few Western text games circulated in the country—fewer and fewer Western companies were even still making them—so an amateur Czech or Slovak text game had less competition from professionals abroad. Since few of the pirated games were translated, the novelty of playing a game in one's native language was a big draw. And since they didn't need graphics or sound, a textovka was easy for a single person to create. Authors would often put their phone numbers in the game's title screen, hoping for calls from fans. Fuka recalls getting endless hint requests as his games got more popular. "Next to the phone, I had some basic questions and answers prepared on paper," he remembers, "so when I wasn't at home, my mother could answer for me."[5]

By the summer of 1988, Fídler was eighteen, and he and his friends had become some of "the most famous and respected Czechoslovak video game programmers."[10] But a wave of change was stirring in the country that year. Fídler's generation was too young to have lived through the trauma of the Prague Spring's final days, and few young people took the heavy-handed and ever-present Communist propaganda seriously. In the Soviet Union, Mikhail Gorbachev had announced a reform movement called perestroika, a restructuring that would loosen state control, allow more press freedoms, and introduce some free-market elements to the economy—almost exactly the reform ideas the loyalist Czechoslovak government had spent two decades trying to suppress. Public confidence in the ČSSR Party dropped dramatically in the aftermath, falling from a 57 percent positive approval rating in 1986 to only 31 percent by 1989. Murmurs spread of a public protest to honor the twentieth anniversary of the Soviet invasion. While he was no revolutionary, Fídler counted himself among the discontented, in part because he "had always wanted to make a living programming and making games, and the regime, in a way, made that impossible."[7] That summer, with

When asked what the differences were between the policies of his plan and the Prague Spring, Gorbachev famously answered "nineteen years."

adulthood and a state-sanctioned career looming, he fired up his Spectrum and started a different kind of coding project: a protest game.

Its title was *P.R.E.S.T.A.V.B.A.*, the Czech word for "perestroika" styled as an acronym. It was credited to the fictional ÚV Software, or "Central Committee Software," jokingly suggesting the game was an official program created by the state. The game takes the form of a short text adventure purporting to star a devoted, loyal comrade; familiar Party slogans appear after most commands, and the tone is as earnest as a propaganda film. Yet each puzzle functions as a punchline, poking fun at sacred cows and deflating the pomposity of the state's fealty to outdated Soviet ideals, which even the USSR itself had begun to move on from:

Excerpts show original Czech (left) and English translation (right). The original program ran on Spectrums that could not yet display the accented characters Czech requires; this has been preserved here.

```
STOJIS V MALE ZAPRASENE MISTNOSTI.


VYCHODY: S,J,Z
VIDIS POKLOP.


     PROLETARI VSECH ZEMI,SPOJTE SE !

ZAPAD

STOJIS V TMAVEM VYKLENKU.


VYCHODY: V
VIDIS ZAPALOVAC.


     SMRT IMPERIALISTICKYM STVACUM !

VEZMI ZAPALOVAC

VZAL JSI ZAPALOVAC

PROZKOUMEJ ZAPALOVAC


JISTE BY S NIM SLO LECOS ZAPALIT.
JE TO TOTIZ KVALITNI ZAPALOVAC.
"MADE IN USSR".

ZAPAL ZAPALOVAC

ZAPALOVAC VYNECHAL...


     SLAVA LENINSKE POLITICE STRANY !
```

```
YOU ARE STANDING IN A SMALL DUSTY ROOM.


EXITS: N,S,W
YOU SEE A HATCH.


     WORKERS OF THE WORLD, UNITE !

WEST

YOU ARE STANDING IN A DARK ALCOVE.


EXITS: E
YOU SEE A LIGHTER.


     DEATH TO THE IMPERIALIST SQUADRONS !

TAKE LIGHTER

YOU TOOK A LIGHTER

EXAMINE LIGHTER


SURELY SOMETHING COULD BE SET ON FIRE
WITH IT. IT IS A QUALITY "MADE IN THE
USSR" LIGHTER.

LIGHT LIGHTER

THE LIGHTER SKIPPED...


     GLORY TO THE LENINIST POLITICS
     OF THE PARTY !
```

The quality Soviet lighter, in fact, is coded to only work 30 percent of the time, a joke more poignant in a country filled with shoddy goods made by state-run factories. Nearby, a dark tunnel gates your progress, but even when the lighter does strike, it's not enough alone to illuminate the passage. Fortunately, in another room you can find something combustible:

V

JSI NA SPINAVEM ZACHODE.RADSI
TO NEBUDU PRILIS POPISOVAT,MOHLO
BY SE TI UDELAT NEVOLNO.

VYCHODY: Z
VIDIS MISU.

PROZKOUMEJ MISU

JE UPLNE ZASCHLA.
NECO JSI NASEL !

VIDIS KNIHU,MISU.

     ZA OSVOBOZENI VYKORISTOVANYCH !

PROZKOUMEJ KNIHU

JE TO MARXUV KAPITAL.

E

YOU'RE IN A DIRTY TOILET. I'D RATHER
NOT DESCRIBE IT TOO MUCH, YOU MIGHT
FEEL SICK.

EXITS: W
YOU SEE A BOWL.

EXAMINE BOWL

IT'S COMPLETELY DRY.
YOU FOUND SOMETHING !

YOU SEE A BOOK,A BOWL

     FOR THE LIBERATION OF THE EXPLOITED!

EXAMINE BOOK

IT'S MARX'S DAS KAPITAL.

When lit on fire, the tome provides enough illumination to make it through the tunnel: KEZ OSVITI TVOJI CESTU! the game exclaims. (May it enlighten your way!) Later, you need to dig a tunnel but can only find the proper motivation to do so by reading some inspirational words in the official party newspaper, *Rudeho Prava* (Red Law):

KOPAT

NECHCE SE TI MAKAT.

PRECTI UVODNIK

PRECETL JSI SI UVODNIK RUDEHO PRAVA.
OKAMZITE JSI DOSTAL CHUT K PRACI,
KTERA JE ZAKLADNI CTI SOCIALISTICKEHO
OBCANA.

KOPAT

PODARILO SE TI PROKOPAT SE DO NIZSIHO
PODLAZI !

DIG

YOU CAN'T BE BOTHERED.

READ EDITORIAL

YOU READ THE EDITORIAL IN RED LAW.
YOU IMMEDIATELY ACQUIRED A TASTE FOR
WORK, WHICH IS AN ESSENTIAL HONOR FOR
ANY SOCIALIST CITIZEN TO DO.

DIG

YOU MANAGED TO DIG INTO THE LOWER
FLOOR !

Fídler's game wasn't the only political game making the rounds. Stanislav Hrda's *Shatokhin* [1988] takes its title from the star of a widely screened Soviet propaganda film—a buff action hero meant as an answer to Hollywood's Rambo—and pits him against his famous rival. Beginning with an enormous graphic of a hammer and sickle, it also purports to be a loyal proregime product. But Hrda used the unique ability of games to present multiple possible outcomes in a cleverly subversive way. While you play as Shatokhin with the nominal goal of defeating Rambo, the game is nearly impossible to win, with most choices leading Shatokhin to a constant series of violent and humiliating deaths: "'charred to bits' in a burning helicopter, crushed against a coral reef, simultaneously poisoned by crude oil and eaten by sharks, drowned in a sewer,"[5] and even killed in an embarrassing accident involving a beer bottle. Michal Hlaváč, who created the graphics for the game, recalled fondly how its creation

> allowed us, through humor and satire, to exert some kind of control over something we didn't have power over…. We were not going to pick up a gun and go out into the streets, so we wrote a game about a major of the Red Army, and we made it difficult for him to win.

In *P.R.E.S.T.A.V.B.A.*, you eventually escape the building you're trapped in and break out onto the streets of Prague. The climax of the short game involves finding a stick of dynamite and using it to blow up a statue of Lenin, inside of which is a golden brick. `GRATULUJI VITEZI!` (Congratulations winners!) the game declares once you take it:

`JE VIDET, ZE SOCIALISTICKY CLOVEK SI PORADI V KAZDE SITUACI...`
 	
`JESTE JEDNOU GRATULUJI.SEJDEME SE VSICHNI `**`21.SRPNA`**` NA STARO-MESTSKEM NAMESTI...(NEBO JINDE)`
	`YOU SEE, A SOCIALIST MAN CAN BE HELPFUL IN ANY SITUATION...`
	
	`CONGRATULATIONS AGAIN. WE WILL ALL MEET ON `**`AUGUST 21`**` IN OLD TOWN SQUARE...`
	`(OR ANYWHERE ELSE)`

Old Town Square, in the heart of Prague, was one of several places where rumors said protesters might gather to mark the twentieth anniversary of the Soviet occupation. Any reader at the time would have understood the import of the date and the place. If you had put these notions in a leaflet or a novel—burning Marx, blowing up a statue of Lenin, invitations to an illegal protest—you probably would have been arrested, or worse. Though the authorities had never shown much interest in or awareness of games, Fídler was taking a risk.

"I was so proud of my technical abilities," Fídler later recalled, "that I thought: there are five people in this country who can do things at my level, so I must produce bad code so that the State Police does not catch me."[5] Though he was by then an accomplished assembly programmer, he wrote *P.R.E.S.T.A.V.B.A.* in straightforward BASIC in the hopes of disguising his authorship, and took great pains to ensure no code comments or other details might be traced back to him. He distributed the first copies only to trusted friends who would have deniability: each could claim they had acquired the game in the course of prolific cassette trading, not from the original author, and that they hadn't even known what the contents were. Since people might swap dozens of games at a time on compilation cassettes, this was eminently plausible.

The paranoia, however, proved unfounded. State police hadn't even begun to suspect that computer games might be a medium for political statements (though later declassified reports from the secret police reported the confiscation of "150 leaflets" and "15 opprobrious signs" promoting the protests²). Even if they had, the potential audience of savvy computer users—a tiny fraction of the country's total population—wasn't large enough to worry about. But none of that changed the way Fídler must have felt as he handed out the first copies of his game: wondering how far it might spread, and to whom.

On August 21, the rally took place. A few hundred citizens gathered in Old Town Square and nearby Wenceslas Square—where, in 1969, a student had set himself on fire to protest the Soviet invasion—for a small demonstration that seemed at first relatively inconsequential. But as police began to disperse the gathering, the streets swelled with thousands more protesters who'd seen the crowds from their apartment windows or heard news of them in the street. Eventually nearly ten thousand people were marching on the seat of government, shouting for reforms and freedom.

The rally would prove a catalyst, triggering larger protests in the months to come that were put down by more violent police actions. These, in turn, spurred further protests—and more protest games. One textovka starred Western hero Indiana Jones, who had become a popular game avatar in a country free from copyright laws, casting him as a protester defending himself and the crowd from murderous cops. In another (pictured at left), you must find a camera to document instances of police brutality at a riot that turned deadly. The game was created within forty-eight hours of the events it depicted. By November 1989, a peaceful coup—the Velvet Revolution—deposed the Soviet loyalist government in favor of a new leadership dedicated to permanent reform. Elsewhere in Europe, the Berlin Wall was falling and the Soviet bloc was crumbling. At the end of 1991, the USSR itself would dissolve, ending an era. Czechoslovakia held its first democratic elections since the Second World War in June 1990.

With their audience of a few thousand teenagers, the influence a handful of computer games had on these events was tiny. But the amateur protest games "became part of the 'chorus of activist media' that included student papers, rock songs, and *samizdat*—handwritten or typewritten versions of banned books and publications that circulated illegally,"⁵ according to journalist Andrada Fiscutean. In *Gaming the Iron Curtain*, a history of the country's 1980s games scene, Jaroslav Švelch writes that the Czechoslovak amateurs

Title screen of *17.11.1989*, author unknown: the header translates to "We don't want violence," a slogan chanted by student protesters who were badly beaten by police on that date. Typical of games in the scene, the detailed cop face was borrowed from a pirated Western fighting game.

became some of the first in the world to continuously make activist games about current political events…. The amateur scene developed its own genre conventions, its own canon, and even its own programmer stars. It discovered that games were a medium, and used them not only for entertainment but also as a means of self-expression.[7]

In the aftermath of the revolution, as groups of citizens came together to try to form a new government, Fídler and his friends kept helping in their own small way. One night they took a break from their computers to make posters and hang them in the subway: The Golden Triangle Supports the Civic Forum.

In a democratic Czech Republic, Fídler would realize his dream of programming for a living, working for years making bestselling commercial games. The Czech game industry grew from a hobbled start into one of Europe's most successful indie game hubs, producing titles like *Factorio* [Wube Software 2020], *Samorost* [Amanita Design 2003], *Beat Saber* [Beat Games 2019], and *DayZ* [Bohemia Interactive 2018], and in 2016 Fídler and his Golden Triangle buddies were honored with induction into the country's gaming Hall of Fame. It was a fitting coda for some kids who had once worked on a single plastic computer in shifts, typing on a hacked-together keyboard made from spare parts, trying with all their hearts to put a piece of themselves in their games.

References

1 Associated Press. 1988. "10,000 in Prague Protest 1968 Invasion." *New York Times*, Aug 22, 1988, sec. World.

2 Czechoslovak Secret Police (StB) Memorandum. 1989. "Information Regarding the Situation in the CSSR up to 20 August 1989." History and Public Policy Program Digital Archive, A. Lorenc et al., T8/91 vol. XIX., envelope 1, #79-84. digitalarchive.wilsoncenter.org/document/113167 | a Oct 15, 2022

3 Fídler, Miroslav. 1992. "Miroslav Fídler." Interview by BiT Magazine. www.oldgames.sk/mag/bit-6/page/38 | a Mar 17, 2021

4 Fídler, Miroslav, František Fuka, and Tomáš Rylek. n.d. "GOLDEN TRIANGLE PO DESETI LETECH." Interview by Živel. zivel.net/archiv?magazin=8&kapitola=133 | a Mar 17, 2021

5 Fiscutean, Andrada. 2020. "How Indiana Jones, Rambo, and Others Ended up in 1980s Czechoslovak Text-Adventures." *Ars Technica*. Oct 23, 2020. arstechnica.com/gaming/2020/10/how-indiana-jones-fought-the-communists-and-led-an-era-of-activist-video-games | a Mar 17, 2021

6 Naegele, Jolyon. 1999. "Czech Republic: The Velvet Revolution -- The Legacy of 1968." RadioFreeEurope/RadioLiberty. Nov 9, 1999. www.rferl.org/a/1092649.html | a Mar 17, 2021

7 Švelch, Jaroslav. 2018. *Gaming the Iron Curtain: How Teenagers and Amateurs in Communist Czechoslovakia Claimed the Medium of Computer Games*. MIT Press.

8 Švelch, Jaroslav. 2019a. "Počítačové Hry." 100 Studentských (r)Evolucí. www.studenti89.usd.cas.cz/pocitacove-hry | a Mar 17, 2021

9 Švelch, Jaroslav. 2019b. "This Game Has a Message: Subversive Gaming in 1980s Czechoslovakia." *Obieg* #12. 2019. obieg.u-jazdowski.pl/en/numery/the-speed-of-guccifer/this-game-has-a-nbsp-message-subversive-gaming-in-1980s-czechoslovakia | a Mar 17, 2021

10 Švelch, Jaroslav. 2019c. "Vernissage: Czechoslovak 8-bit Underground." Game Days. Apr 8, 2019. www.gdays.sk/timetable/event/vystava-retro | a Apr 27, 2021

11 UgraUgra. 2018. "Hra 252: P.Ř.E.S.T.A.V.B.A. (1988)." *Herní Archeolog* (blog). Oct 1, 2018. herniarcheolog.blogspot.com/2018/10/hra-252-prestavba-1988.html | a Mar 17, 2021

MONSTER ISLAND

Jack B. Everitt

Style **Play-by-Mail**
Debuted **Dec 1989**
Launch Platform **Pen and paper** *(client)*
DOS *(server)*
Publisher **Adventures By Mail**
Language **QuickBasic 4.1**
Launch Price · **$4** *(per mailed turn)*

> " MONSTER ISLAND is a whole new type of Play-by-mail game. It is a strange game, unlike anything you've seen. Throw away any preconceived ideas you may have; MONSTER ISLAND has its own special feel and works in a very intelligent way.

THE MAILBOX SQUEAKS OPEN, and a teenager's eyes light up. Amid the junk mail for parents is a bulky envelope from a company called Adventures By Mail. The teen has waited all week for it to get here.

Inside is a trifold newsletter and a long, stiff postcard, with a New York return address on one side and a blank grid marked with esoteric abbreviations on the other. But the bulk of the content is a stack of stapled, laser-printed pages. While everyone getting letters from Adventures By Mail this week received the same card and newsletter, the pages in each envelope are unique, printed for one person alone. These pages describe the fate of

MAJOR VERSIONS

» **Original**, Adventures by Mail, 1989–2004 (US).

» **Adventurer Guild**, 2005–2008 (US).

» **KJC Games**, 1990?–2017? (UK/Europe).

» **Daydream Productions**, 1993–? (Germany).

the character whose adventures this teenager has dictated for the past few months: a Monster named Doggar who is not a villain in this story, but one of its many, many heroes.

MONSTER ISLAND

MONSTER# 8489	DAY CYCLE# 8
ACCT# 12067	CREDITS = 6
TURN# 8	WEEK# 11

This turn was processed on MAY 19 at 9:52 AM
Your WEEK# 12 will be from MAY 29 to JUNE 9
Your next turn may be run IMMEDIATELY (a make-up turn is due)

DOGGAR'S RESULTS

'TWEEN

It's been 6 days since you made camp. You're still alive on Monster Island. [+2 Toughness.] Resting 'Tween turns restores some of your Health. [+11 Health.] You spend 15 Action Pts repairing your Haversuit. What fun. You break camp.

RESULTS OF THIS TURN'S ORDERS

F - 48   FRIENDLINESS/RISKINESS: Change level
Your Friendliness level is now at 4, guarded. Your Riskiness level is now at 8, somewhat risky. (0 Action Pts used, 135 left.)

T - 33   TRAVEL: Move East, then East again
CROSSING INTO NEXT SQUARE(6,31): Still more Jungle.

CROSSING INTO NEXT SQUARE(6,32): Still more Jungle. You chow down. (-1 Food.) (20 Action Pts used, 115 left.)

J - 15   JAZZERCIZE AEROBICS: For 15 Action Pts
You do stretching exercises until you can't stand it anymore. The exercising pays off. [+11 Health, +1 Muscle.] (15 Action Pts used, 100 left.)

T - 45   TRAVEL: Move Southeast, then South
CROSSING INTO NEXT SQUARE(5,33): The terrain continues to be Jungle. You take a break and chew down a tasty meal. (-1 Food.)

CROSSING INTO NEXT SQUARE(4,33): The terrain continues to be Jungle. Uh, oh! A strange smell alerts you to the presence of a Creature nearby. Silently, you squat until all is quiet again. Unfortunately, the Creature keeps coming toward you. It's a Jungle Rattler. (See blurb.)

1989

> Battle ensues…
> ** BATTLE: DOGGAR vs. a Jungle Rattler ** With sweaty palms, you
> fire one rock toward the Jungle Rattler and connect with it in its upper
> section. [1 Hit reduces its Health by 4.] Taking a deep breath, you
> become one with your weapon […]

The teen skips ahead to the end of the stack of pages to read the
new blurb describing the Jungle Rattler—a creature never previously
encountered—then flips back to see the outcome of the battle (Doggar wins)
and remaining actions. These include two more fights, a bout of weapons
practice, an unsuccessful Quest for Knowledge, and more travel. Eventually,
the action points run out and the turn ends:

> **MAKE CAMP**
>
> You select a campsite and check out the surrounding area. You hunt
> for a bit. No luck hunting. The rigors of this week's travels have been
> of benefit to you. [+1 Toughness.] It's been too long since you last had
> some water. This lack of water is making you weaker. [-2 Health.] […]
> You're no longer able to keep your eyes open. You fall asleep.
>
> From the square you washed ashore, you've travelled 34 squares East
> and 2 squares North.

The next pages shows a map of Doggar's journey this turn: a grid
ten squares wide filled with a black-and-white pattern that might almost
represent a jungle if you squint, overlaid with clip-art symbols for creatures
found and objects discovered. Pages of statistics follow, tracking (among
many other things) that Doggar has found 40 Knowledge Blurbs, has 71
Toughness and 42 Muscle, is carrying 3 Small Round Rocks and 1 Large
Clam Shell, is very thirsty, and has 152 Action Points available for Turn #9.

It will be a few days before the teenager's next move. Some thinking
is needed to plan next steps before penciling in a new set of orders on the
card. This week's blurbs must be cross-referenced with others previously
received and carefully cataloged in a basement filing cabinet. There is more
to do, too: writing a letter at the kitchen table to a would-be group leader,
explaining that Doggar is now waiting in the square they agreed on and
hoping the leader can get there in time to perform the promised initiation
ceremony; responding to a letter from a Monster met on a previous turn who
had written a polite cursive note asking for any information on Maladors or
Ghoul Buzzards. Eventually the small stack of correspondence is stamped
and returned to the curbside mailbox. It will be at least a week until the next
turn results come back.

Believe it or not, the teenager is playing a computer game.

The genre of play-by-mail (PBM) games originated with postal chess,
where opponents would mail moves back and forth over months of play.
By the 1960s a tradition of PBM wargames had started, spurred largely by
the 1959 release of the board game *Diplomacy* [Allan B. Calhamer]. Requiring

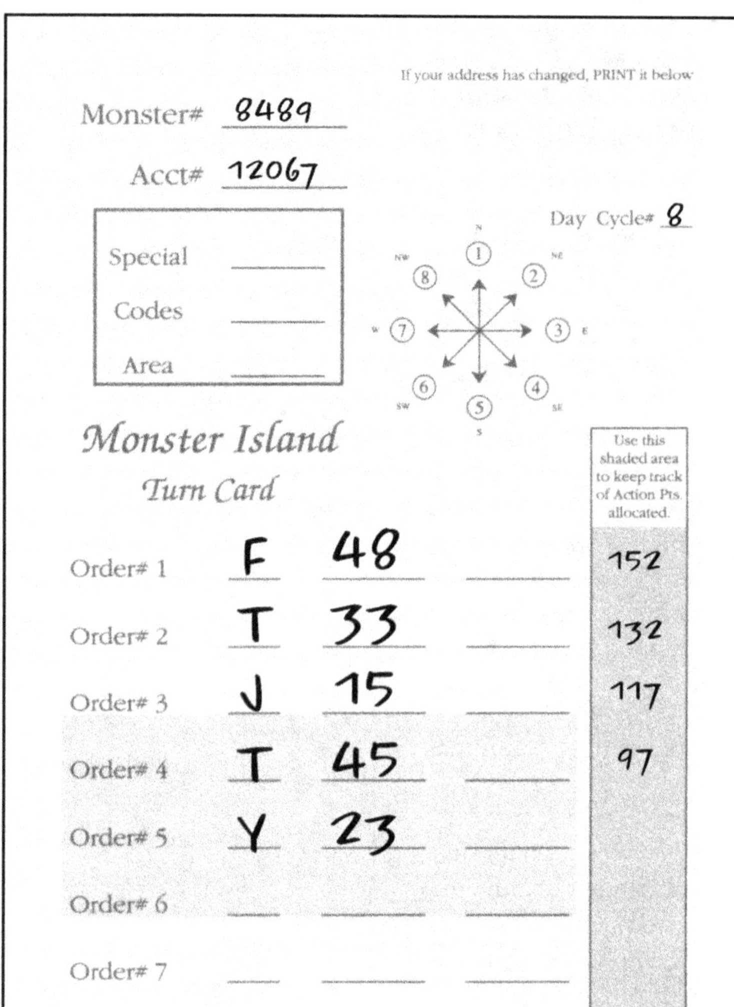

Partial *Monster Island* turn card with several orders filled in; the long narrow postcard had Adventure By Mail's return address on the reverse. Note the compass rose: the second order listed, T-33, means to Travel east (3) then east again.

exactly seven dedicated players, and released at a time when board games were still frowned upon as a hobby for adults, the game was a natural fit for the asynchronous, private, and distributed mode of play offered by PBM, where players could think about each turn for as long as they liked and weren't limited to their local area when searching for opponents. In a growing network of fanzines, *Diplomacy* fans listed their addresses and advertised upcoming games they wanted to run or their availability for games run by others.

Diplomacy is a game with a focus on negotiation and social strategy, and here, too, the slower pace of play-by-mail could be an advantage. Some postal games spaced out their turns across months of real-world time, so players could mail a flurry of diplomatic missives, threats, promises, and negotiations before any actual moves needed to be decided. But stripped of social interaction, *Diplomacy* is mechanically fairly simple. Inevitably, some PBM fans began to invent their own original games with more complex rules. (Two such fans, incidentally, were Gary Gygax and Dave Arneson, whose custom PBM wargames would evolve into *Dungeons & Dragons* and inspire the dawn of tabletop roleplaying—but that's another story.)

In 1970, a young wargamer named Rick Loomis, who was serving out his Vietnam draft at a fort in Hawaii, had moved beyond playing PBM games to making his own:

> I had invented a multi-player game called *Nuclear Destruction* which was a little different from *Diplomacy* in that it had hidden movement. Thus, the moderator had to send different information to each player.… All this gaming kept my mailbox full of letters, which was the primary purpose back then. But soon I had over 200 players in my game, and it was becoming difficult to keep up. So I asked my friend Steve MacGregor to write a computer program for me which would run the *Nuclear Destruction* game. We rented time on a Control Data computer which was near the Fort.[8]

Loomis's computer-assisted PBM game became wildly popular. The computer allowed the level of detail, complexity, size, and scope of a play-by-mail game to grow far beyond what a human moderator could keep up with.

1989

When he got out of the army, Loomis started the first commercial **PBM** company, <u>Flying Buffalo</u>, and paid $14,000 for a Raytheon 704 computer that processed turns using paper tape. Years later he'd joke that he might have been the first person in the world to buy a computer specifically to play games with. Outside of specialized applications like military wargame simulations, he may well have been.

Dozens of other commercial **PBM** companies sprung up, charging players a fee of anywhere from two to twelve dollars to process a turn in increasingly elaborate games. While some games remained human moderated, the most complex required a computer to keep up with states that might involve thousands of units, each of which might respond to hundreds of possible orders. Some game manuals became inches thick. Each turn, players would submit an order card that laid out everything they wanted their units to do, generally with alphanumeric codes that could easily be input into the computer. For instance, 47-M-33 might mean to (M)ove unit (47) east (3) and then east (3) again. Optical character recognition technology was still emerging, so an employee would generally type in the orders on each player's card by hand, a tedious job repeated with each new day's stack of mail. In some games, order results might run to dozens of pages that contained the outcome of multiple actions as well as statistics, information learned, and communications received or intercepted.

Mainframe-powered **PBM** games of the late 70s and early 80s were far more sophisticated than anything available on personal computers at the time, even for the few players who owned one. One fan would later reminisce about the unique experience of playing: "Board games can't quite match it, because they're over in one night and you don't really have a chance to connive with fellow gamers much. Computer games can't come close unless they are multi-player, but ultimately fall short for the same reason—they are completed quickly and the pace allows for nothing other than action and grind."[5] PBM games, by contrast, could last hundreds of turns spread out over years of real-world time, and they allowed for strategies so complex it could take days to plot them out and set them up.

By the end of the 80s, hundreds of unique play-by-mail games had come and gone, and a new generation of designers had grown up on them. PBM fans Jack B. Everitt, Bob Cook, and Mike Popolizio had founded Adventures By Mail in 1981, hoping to stand out in a crowded marketplace by focusing on reliability and quality. They were longtime fans of George Schubel's popular human-moderated PBM game *The Tribes of Crane* [1976], so their first title was a space-themed variant called *Beyond the Stellar Empire* [1982]. Their first breakout hit was *It's a Crime* [1985], in which each player controlled a competing gang fighting for turf in a fictional city. <u>The game was cleverly designed</u> to start off simple, with only twelve possible orders, but to open up in complexity as players rose to higher ranks of power and learned new orders to direct minions, create contracts, join or fight the mafia, and mastermind various business ventures. Advertising at cons and in magazines aimed at roleplaying, sci-fi, and miniatures fans, Adventures By Mail hoped to expand the core audience of PBM beyond its base of hardcore wargamers.

Flying Buffalo also made tabletop roleplaying games, including one of the first *D&D* competitors, *Tunnels & Trolls*. In 1976 they published Loomis's *Buffalo Castle*, a solo adventure for *T&T* that was one of the earliest modern gamebooks, predating Choose Your Own Adventure #1 <u>1979</u> by several years.

It's a Crime was also one of the cheapest PBM games available at the time, with each turn costing only $1.50 to play. In 1986 it won Origin's "Best New PBM Game" award, a new category joining the "Best Play-by-Mail Game" that had debuted in 1984.

Everitt, though, had even more ambitious dreams. While still in the midst of launching _It's a Crime_, he had already started planning a "monster of a game—with a whole continent to explore and lots of things to find and make and do. It would have adventure and mystery, and it would never end."[2] A competitor had recently touted the fact that their system could support a game with five hundred players at once. Everitt wanted to make a game that could handle fifteen thousand. Most PBM turn reports were printed on smudgy dot matrix printers, making them dreary walls of text, but laser printers were becoming increasingly affordable. Everitt had visions of sending players clean reports with crisp text, multiple fonts, and graphical maps. He began coding even though he knew his company could not yet afford the hardware and storage to handle his dream game, trusting the tech he needed would keep dropping in price.

It did. After four years of intermittent work, the new game was ready to launch, running on a then-expensive 386 computer and hooked up to a 150 MB Bernoulli Box storage system. The game needed this space: its terrain contained over a quarter of a million locations, each with up to 120 associated variables, and there were a whopping 2,100 variables allocated for each player character. In December 1989 the first _Monster Island_ turns were processed, and after a six-month beta with a few hundred players, Adventures By Mail added more laser printers and began to promote the game in earnest.

In the game you control not an army or a fleet of battleships, but a single survivor washed up on the shore of a strange land. You are a Monster, a strong and sturdy (yet ugly and unrefined) explorer of a massive unpeopled island—really more of a continent, described in the manual as "three times the size of Australia."[2] Rather than issuing single-turn orders to large groups of units, in _Monster Island_ you would write a sequential task list for a single character: your own Monster. While combat was still present, it was a relatively minor part of each turn and largely outside the player's control, resolved via randomness and statistics. The game's focus, instead, was discovery. By pushing forward into uncharted squares, Monsters could find ruins with buried treasure, learn to craft useful items, trade stories and goods at outposts, build forts, and slowly increase their knowledge about the huge land in which they wandered. And unlike most PBM games, which featured a set number of players in a simulation that reset at the end of each run (like a board game), _Monster Island_ was a single, persistent world. Each new player washed up somewhere on its western shore, with tougher challenges and bigger treasures to be found the farther east they traveled.

Like _It's a Crime_, Everitt's new game made the clever decision to initially hide most of its complexity. Rather than starting off with an enormous rulebook, new players received only a slim pamphlet that laid out in fewer than twenty half-size pages the game's premise, instructions, and a starting set of nineteen orders. In fact, there were more than seventy possible orders in the game, most of which had to be discovered through play. Reach a trading outpost and you'd learn orders for buying and selling goods; stumble across another player and you'd learn commands for being friendly or

MAP OF THIS TURN'S TRAVELS

Turn# 8 for UNCLE GRUNK, ending in the Southern Westlands region.

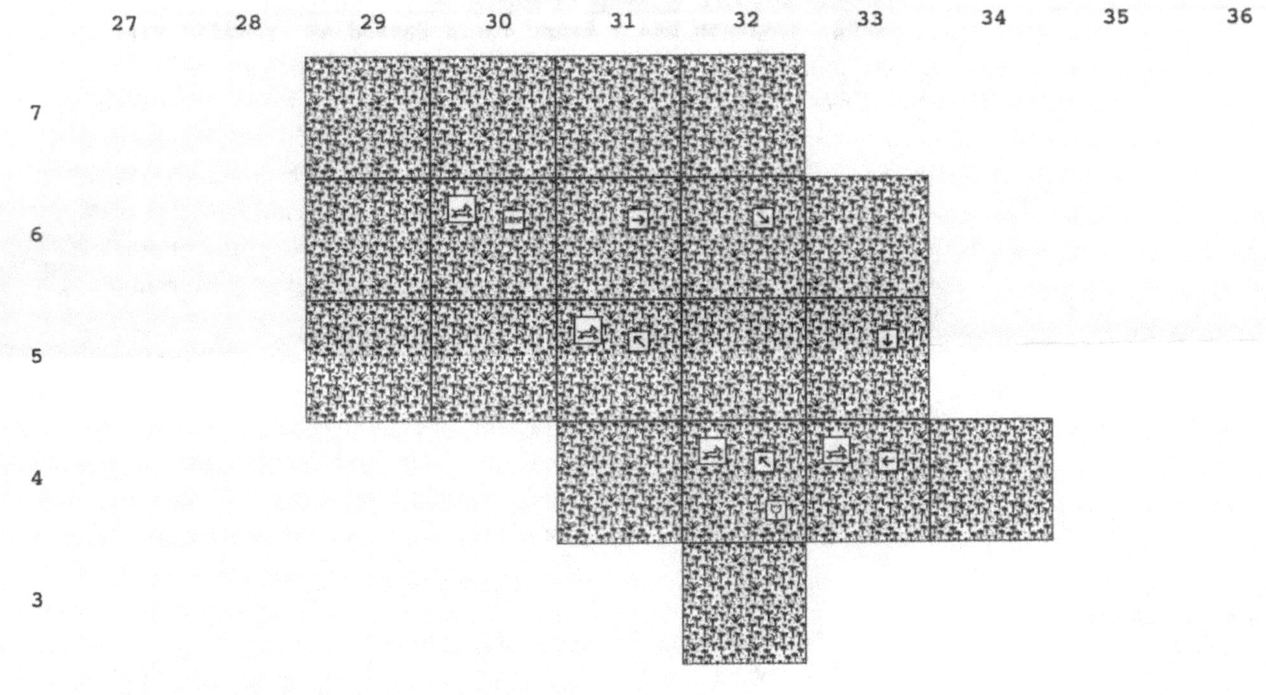

Sightings from squares visited this turn:
Square(4,33): Jungle Rattlers(#114).
Square(4,32): Porqubeasts(#126), and Purple Lotus shrub.
Square(5,31): Porqubeasts(#126).
Square(6,30): Porqubeasts(#126).

STATS AND STUFF

UNCLE GRUNK is a male of Race# 4, Norman
Overall Healthiness = 42% (Down 15%)

Stats

71 Toughness (+3)   5 Friendliness
42 Muscle (+1)   6 Riskiness
18 Badness   219 Monsterliness (+12)
 9 Stealth   40 Knowledge Blurbs (+2)
30 Health (-9)
 5 Food eaten this turn
History: Total of 13 Creatures killed (+3)
Capture Creature set to: Stemtoad (150)
Wrestling: 3 Offense   5 Defense

Equipped Items

Primary Weapon: Driftclub, Class 1
Missile Weapon: Sling, Class 1

Weapon Skills

Missile: Level 2   Pole: Level 1   Bashing: Level 2

>>> 152 Action Pts are <<<
    available for next turn

Possessions

Weaponry

~1 Driftclub (43)   ~1 Crude Spear (3)   ~ 3 Small Round Rocks (36)
~1 Sling (46)   2 Rattler Darts (50)

hostile. You might even unlock the ability to request and send in entirely different kinds of order cards.

One such custom order card was for group management. *It's a Crime* had benefited from extensive communication between players, who planned elaborate alliances and betrayals through letters and phone calls. Similarly, in *Monster Island* players could opt in to sharing their contact info with other Monsters they crossed paths with in their adventures. Players starting the game at the same time were often placed in clusters near each other, and the starter manual explained that a group of eight Monsters could meet in a grid square and perform a ritual that would link them as a Group. Everitt added this mechanic to the early game to encourage player collaboration from the beginning.

This deliberate design of hidden mechanics but easy communication led to cooperative play, as players needed to correspond and share info to figure out how the game they were playing even worked: its boundaries of geography and possibility, and the capabilities of its complex, hidden engine. Initially in the official newsletter, then in a smattering of fanzines, players asked each other for help and began to share hard-won info:

> Has anyone resurrected (or have information [about]) a ghost?

> A monster has heard of demi-gods of Vampires (from ancient silver spike blurb), Gargoyles (from iron spike blurb) and Spiders (from ???). Are there any others? Has anyone found a way to worship or follow one of these gods???

> So far I have only noted the following benefits from having a mount. First they will steer you around quicksand. Second a Demon Condor tried to carry me away but my legs had a firm hold on my plodder (mount) and the Demon Condor failed.

> Supposedly a Purpumpkin and four Stemtoad glands will allow you to make a lantern. This one definitely belongs in the unconfirmed rumor section.

In a time before personal websites—and long before wikis—there was no central storehouse of information about the game or easy way to create one. Adventures By Mail officially frowned on fanzines revealing secrets directly or reprinting the blurbs found in order results, which detailed new commands or elusive secrets. But within a year of the game's release, players had begun to self-organize in fanzines like *Blood Moon Tribune* to create peer-to-peer information sharing networks, and via in-game groups whose primary purpose was to learn and explore:

> David Gloss would like to create an "information clearing house" for *Monster Island*. If you're feeling frustrated, and don't want to wait to learn something during the normal course of the game, send your questions and an S.A.S.E. to [address omitted]. Also send him any interesting information you have, so he can pass it on to other players.

> Jae Kim is undertaking an ambitious task—mapping the entire Island! Send your map data to him at the address below. You can also send Jae

an SASE, requesting information on your area; if he can figure out where you are, he'll send you back whatever information he has, in as much or as little detail as you want.

But the game's ambitions were perhaps too vast. Players had trouble finding each other in all the island's immense spaces. Coordinating across turns could be difficult as well, due to a design decision meant to increase the speed of play: turns weren't synced to a fixed clock, but advanced for each player whenever their order card was processed. Many fanzine personals show signs of frustration:

PRAALUU: What is your new address? Contact your group leader.

THE BLACK DEATH! Where are you guys? I joined your group and I haven't met any members in the last 25 turns. Please contact: Bambi the Viper.

It has become sickening that every monster that we have tried to write to neglects to write back after sending very few letters. It distresses us that we take the time to form communications between monsters only to not get a response. If you dumb, stupid, idiotic monsters think that you can get away with this, you have another thing coming. Bounties on the following monsters are set at 50 oculars…

SLIPPERY JEEM - Where are you? I looked and looked and looked and couldn't find you! Please Yell or make some inscriptions or carve a tree or something! - NAKEMIN T'HED

Years after launch, players had still not uncovered major portions of the game. In late 1992, official publication the *Monster Island Journal* revealed that only "50 Monsters have successfully performed the Disciple Rite and can now cast spells. They have access to over 40 different spells, although no Monster has learned more than 15 spells." In 1996, nearly seven years after the game's debut, an online post announced that a Monster named Skizlum Skallaglamm had become "the first American monster to cross the Crystal Hills barrier," a range of seemingly impassable mountains hundreds of squares east of the game's starting zone, but by no means marking its furthest boundaries.

As fandoms began to move online, *Monster Island* players gathered on CompuServe's PBMGAMES forum, GEnie, America Online, and Usenet, where the rec.games.pbm newsgroup appeared in 1991. Online communities accelerated the pace of communication and information sharing, but perversely were also sounding the death knell for PBM. Why would anyone pay money to play games via paper mail when email was free? But that doom was still a few years off. The short-term problem was that while players were increasingly online, they were still spread across a myriad of services and standalone communities rather than a unified web, and were years away from the collaborative

Mapping was difficult because each player had their own unique coordinate system, relative to the position where they'd washed up on the island. Coordinating different player maps by matching up landmarks could be a herculean task.

ESCAPIST ENTERTAINMENT

Another segment of play-by-mail's audience was incarcerated people, particularly in times before access to computers and email became seen as a basic right for prisoners. (Even today, it's not uncommon for those in prison to have limited access to websites and email, and they are often unable to download file attachments.) The ability to lose oneself for hours in a complex world, planning strategies and corresponding with other players—using nothing more than paper, pencils, stamps, and envelopes—made PBM gameplay a lifeline for many serving out prison sentences.

see **2006**

Among other fan efforts, some players wrote custom software to aid in play. One program for mapping your explorations, Monster Mapper [Jim Wuerch 1992], delighted the game's creators so much they offered to ship it on a floppy disk for free to players who used a special code in their orders (Q3 for 3.5" disks or Q5 for 5.25").

editing technologies that would simplify information collating for later complex games like *Dwarf Fortress* or *Minecraft* [Mojang Studios 2011].

Monster Island survived nonetheless, and for a surprisingly long time. The reference to American monsters in the earlier quote was due to the game's popularity in Europe, where UK-based KJC Games had been managing an iteration that surpassed the US game in popularity. A German version run by a company called Daydream Productions launched in 1993. While *Monster Island* never became the breakaway hit Everitt had hoped for, the US game had over 1,600 active players by October 1992, making it financially sustainable in a field littered with the corpses of games that never made it past their first handful of turns. "It sounds so easy," wrote Flying Buffalo's Loomis back in 1983:

> Get a personal computer, write a program to run your game, put an ad in a few magazines, then sit back and let your computer do all the work while you bank a few extra bucks each week. Unfortunately there are so many problems that are not initially apparent: program bugs, equipment breakdowns, answering rules questions, answering complaints, opening letters, entering moves into the computer, correcting mistakes, moves that arrive late, moves that have unreadable game numbers or return addresses, keeping track of how much money everyone owes, deciding what to do about someone who hasn't paid the money he owes but is still sending in game turns, handling bounced checks, and on and on. It is easy for a newcomer to get swamped.

Adventures By Mail overcame these hurdles and survived for over a decade in a brutal industry with minuscule profit margins and customers who were hard to attract and retain. But there were signs by 1993 that Everitt's interest in *Monster Island*, and in PBM more generally, was waning. While the fanzines kept coming, no more official newsletters were published after 1992, and a promised fourth edition of the rulebook never materialized. Improvements to the game slowed as Everitt realized the cutting-edge framework he'd started developing in the 80s had now locked him into its legacy limitations: "I'm pretty much out of free variables for Monster stats," he lamented in August 1993.[3] The thought of porting five years of QuickBasic code to a new framework no doubt seemed immensely unattractive.

But the turning point came that summer at Gen Con, the tabletop gaming convention Everitt religiously attended each year to do outreach and promotion. That year was the Gen Con of *Magic: The Gathering*, which hit the industry like a tidal wave: released on August 5, 1993, the collectible card game was all anyone was talking about when the con opened two weeks later. Upstart company Wizards of the Coast sold all the *Magic* cards they'd brought to the convention within two days, and by October had sold out their entire first printing of ten million cards. *Magic* became a cultural phenomenon in a way PBM and even roleplaying games writ large never had. Wizards of the Coast grew so quickly they were able to acquire TSR, the makers of *Dungeons & Dragons*, less than four years later.

Everitt saw huge potential in the new style of game. Upon his return from Gen Con, he started a new venture, Adventures Distributing, to sell

Magic cards by mail, having negotiated a bulk rate from Wizards. Eventually Adventures By Mail turned over further development of *Monster Island* to KJC in the UK; by 1998 all the original founders had left. Play-by-Mail was on its way out anyway, as internet multiplayer gaming swallowed more and more of its player base. The company shut down for good in 2004, having lost most of its players to newer, shinier games.

But *Monster Island*, like its preternaturally tough residents, refused to die. The game's European version had amassed a large enough following to form strong ties among player groups, some of which had survived for a decade or longer, still invested in the exploits of their Monsters. By 1999, KJC had "processed in excess of a million game turns with tens of thousands [of] active and satisfied customers."[6] Introducing the ability for players to submit turns via email—and later to receive turn reports that way too—lowered operational costs and provided an easier entry point for new players discovering the game through the internet. In 2005 a fan-run operation called Adventurer Guild purchased the servers and rights to run *Monster Island* in the US, and it kept that version running for three more years, processing over five thousand turns for a trickle of dedicated players. Across the pond, KJC kept the game alive until at least 2017—a run of nearly thirty years for a game its creator had hoped would last for three.

PBM survives today, though mostly in the form of PBEM (play-by-email). The name of a modern fanzine, *Suspense & Decision*, neatly sums up the genre's appeal, captured also by a retrospective on the blog *Greyhawk Grognard*:

> What these sorts of games bring that few others do is time. Time to savor the situation, drink it in, plot and plan. Time to have multiple conversations with folks before you need to get your orders in, and then of course the delicious wait while you scowl at the mailbox wondering why that damned game master hasn't sent your turn back. You could get that with a PBEM game, but there is also something very visceral about getting that envelope in your hands and pouring over the results in hard-copy. It's a very different experience than the instant gratification in modern computer games. It's also different than a face-to-face game, as the negotiations can get really, really involved and of course the number of potential players is vastly greater.[1]

Though gaming culture has mostly forgotten it, PBM represents one of the oldest threads of digital games. The very first textual computer games ran on mainframes without monitors or interactive terminals. Play happened by reading printouts and inputting commands via filling out a form or punching a card. Inputs were processed in batch jobs that might not start for days and might take hours to compute. Early games like *The Carnegie Tech Management Game* had core loops much like the few PBM games that survive today, with centralized servers processing bulk orders on daily or weekly schedules—a legacy of digital gaming that stretches back two-thirds of a century. Most of those mainframe games are impossible to play today, just as most of their PBM descendants have also been lost. Though few lived in the right time and place to play each in their prime, the legacy of these games with different rhythms would be monstrous to forget.

Everitt would expand his mail-order business and start a chain of gaming stores in upstate New York. He would go on to contribute to both the *Dragon Ball Z* and *Pokémon* collectible card games.

see **1959**

References

1 Bloch, Joseph. 2009. "Play-By-Mail Games." *Greyhawk Grognard* (blog). Feb 27, 2009. www.greyhawkgrognard.com/2009/01/27/play-by-mail-games | a Apr 7, 2020

2 Everitt, Jack B. 1991. *Monster Island Travel Guide & Rules*. Third edition. Adventures By Mail.

3 Everitt, Jack. 1993. "Monster Island Journal Issue 4.5." In *Blood Moon Tribune* #7, Aug 1993.

4 Graves, Terry Joe. 2011. "Victory." PlayByMail.Net Forum. Mar 16, 2011. playbymail.net/mybb/showthread.php?tid=83 | a Apr 7, 2020

5 ixnay. 2011. "PBM Is Dead! Long Live PBM!" PlayByMail.Net Forum. Jan 7, 2011. playbymail.net/mybb/showthread.php?tid=5&pid=10 | a Apr 7, 2020

6 KJC Games. n.d. Official website. www.kjcgames.com | s Feb 8, 1999

7 Lindahl, Greg. n.d. "Play by Email (PBeM) & Play by Mail (PBM) List Index." www.pbm.com/~lindahl/pbm_list | a Apr 7, 2020

8 Loomis, Rick. 1983. "The History of Play-by-Mail and Flying Buffalo." *Flying Buffalo Quarterly* #48, Jun 1983. playbymail.net/mybb/showthread.php?tid=78 | a Apr 2, 2020

9 Peterson, Jon. 2012. *Playing at the World: A History of Simulating Wars, People and Fantastic Adventures, from Chess to Role-Playing Games*. San Diego: Unreason Press.

10 "Play by Mail Games Frequently Asked Questions (FAQ)." n.d. rec.games.pbm. www.pbm.com/~lindahl/rgp.faq.html#Q1 | a Apr 7, 2020

11 "The Adventure Guild." 2004. Dec 3, 2004. www.adventureguild.net | a Apr 7, 2020

12 Webb, Ed J. n.d. "Ed's Monster Island Site." monster.edwebb.net | a Apr 7, 2020

THE

19

90s

THERE'S A MISCONCEPTION that the 90s were a fallow time for text games, caught between the commercial death of interactive fiction and its rebirth at the hands of amateurs. In truth, it was a time of radical experimentation and profound change that saw the emergence of many new forms and the reshuffling of structures that a few years before had seemed indomitable. After a heady youth, text games faced their first major setback: to survive, they were forced to grow.

While online text games had been present since the beginning (see **1975** and **1980**), at first only a tiny percentage of computer users had the means (and the modem) to connect. In the 90s the internet finally broke through to the general public, at first through a growing wave of dial-up services like GEnie, Prodigy, CompuServe, and America Online. These services offered user-friendly front-ends to the complex array of preweb technologies like Gopher, FTP, Fido, Archie, and Usenet, as well as forums and discussion groups where like-minded fans could gather. The rise of these services, coinciding with the fall of commercial text adventures, led to many online communities of fans still playing and, increasingly, making them. On the CompuServe Gamer's Forum, fans using AGT (the Adventure Game

Connecting to a BBS on an Amiga computer. Image courtesy Blake Patterson (cc by 2.0 license).

see *The Playground* **1994**

see *Curses* **1993**

1990s

Toolkit) organized collaborations and competitions for amateur games; on another forum dedicated to play-by-mail, enthusiasts swapped fanzines, tips, and reviews. On Usenet, newsgroups like alt.hypertext, rec.games.mud, and rec.arts.int-fiction became asynchronous gathering places for those interested in interactive stories—an odd mixture of academics, computer professionals, curious authors, and diehard fans. While communities in previous decades were linked by paper newsletters or in-person meetups, online meeting spaces greatly accelerated the speed of conversations and provided easy access to archives and an audience. You could post a new game online and someone could be playing and reviewing it the next day.

Most amateur games were idle experiments, but some were surprisingly elaborate. A group of seven authors on the Gamer's Forum, led by Judith Pintar, collaborated to produce *Shades of Gray* [1992], a formally and narratively ambitious saga of linked presents and pasts involving, among other things, the history of Haiti. *Perdition's Flames* [Michael J. Roberts 1993] featured a sprawling collection of puzzles in a hellaciously modernized afterlife, with 666 possible points. Meanwhile, a group of academics were attempting to reinvent text adventures as a platform for the future of artificial intelligence, and a distributed group of fans were reverse engineering Infocom's story format and compiler with the hope of one day writing new games for it. There was no obvious next direction for text games, freeing fans to explore any direction they chose.

The newsgroups rec.arts.int-fiction and rec.games.int-fiction became particularly influential online communities. A nexus of parser game fans would help bootstrap a rebirth of the form that would push it far beyond what most commercial publishers had envisioned or attempted. Long discussions coalesced into dense articles on IF design and theory, like Graham Nelson's "The Craft of Adventure" (1995) and Roger Giner-Sorolla's "Crimes Against Mimesis" (1996). Nelson's programming language Inform, the most significant end product of the collective Infocom research, let authors easily create new games that ran in the defunct studio's cross-platform engine. Along with Mike Roberts' TADS (Text Adventure Development System), Inform led to an explosion of new games, some rivaling or exceeding the complexity of the old commercial titles. Fans on CompuServe had sporadically run a competition for new games written in AGT between 1986 and 1994, but the newsgroups took on the mantle in 1995 by starting an annual Interactive Fiction Competition still running as of this writing, after twenty-seven years. Its two-hour time limit for judging is credited with shifting the kinds of text games people were writing away from traditional full-length games, which could take amateurs years to write, toward smaller and shorter titles, which in turn encouraged experimentation and increased the speed of iteration on ideas, techniques, and styles.

Elsewhere on the early net, bulletin board systems (BBSes) and multi-user dungeons (MUDs) both reached peak popularity in the first half of the 90s. MUDs had grown from Trubshaw and Bartle's original into a thriving genre, with hundreds running worldwide by the early 90s. Much like their later graphical descendants, massively multiplayer online roleplaying games (MMORPGs), MUDs provided not only escapist entertainment but communities where friendships and uniquely online cultures were forged. Some MUDs ran for decades: *GemStone* [Simutronics 1988], *Federation II* [Interactive Broadcasting 1988], and *Genesis* [Lars Pensjö 1989] are all still running as of this writing. Others grew away from their hack-and-slash origins into exclusively social or creative places, evolving into almost unrecognizably different forms.

MUDs generally needed to run on a network that a dozen or more users could connect to simultaneously. The BBS ecosystem was different. While there were exceptions, most bulletin boards had only a single phone line, meaning the games designed for them focused on asynchronous rather than simultaneous play—like elaborate board games, with only one player taking a turn at a time. Games like *Legend of the Red Dragon* [Seth Robinson 1989], *Food Fight* [Rigor Mortis 1987; Michael Wilson 1992], and *Trade Wars 2002* were filled with colorful ASCII text and ANSI graphics, and often served as narratively-charged second places where members of a board's community could play out friendships and rivalries, running in thousands of unique instances with exclusively local players.

see **1980**

see also *Achaea* **1997**

see *LambdaMOO* **1990**

see **1991**

Login screen for *LegendMUD*, founded in 1994.

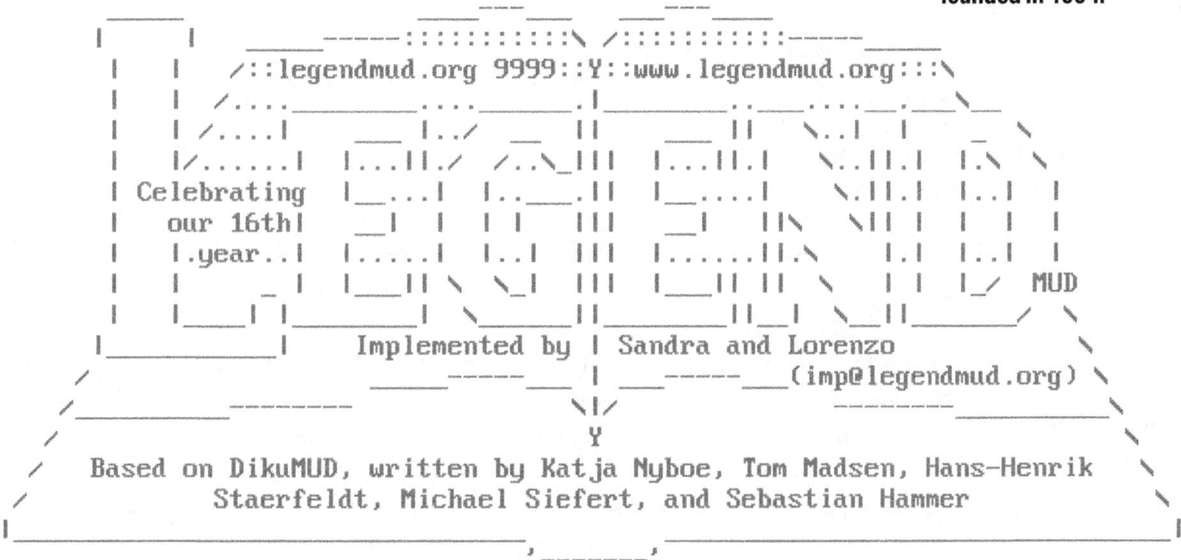


```
[1] Connect to a character        [6] Read about LegendMUD's Premise
[2] Establish a new character     [7] Unarchive a character
[4] Request the Newbie Guide      [0] Exit
[5] List immortals online who can help
```

The possibilities of interactive prose were also being explored by communities of writers. Experiments in linking bits of story together via indexed keywords or arbitrary linkages, rather than in linear sequence, had been happening for decades (see **1986**), but by the 90s there was ready-made software for writing such narratives. Apple's Hypercard [1987], included for free on all Macs sold until the early 90s, provided a user-friendly graphical interface for constructing nonlinear sequences of text or images; while

Mid-90s discussion on the rec.arts.int-fiction newsgroup, in Microsoft's Windows 95 newsreader.

Internet News

File   Edit   View   News   Offline   Help

New Message | Reply to Group | Reply to Author | Forward | Newsgroups | Connect | Disconnect | Stop

Newsgroups   rec.arts.int-fiction

Subject	From	Sent	Size
recent additions to the Interactive Fiction A...	Volker Blasius	1995-06-29 2:21 ...	141 line(s)
New member	JD rOm inc	1995-06-29 10:32 ...	3 line(s)
Everything about Inform that confuses me	Andrew C. Plotkin	1995-06-28 4:51 ...	43 line(s)
Latest version of Zip code	Dan Keith	1995-06-28 2:13 PM...	18 line(s)
Update #2: Whizzard's Guide to IF.	Gerry Kevin Wilson	1995-06-27 10:13 ...	351 line(s)
Only a game? Merely symbols? (was: Amora...	Magnus Olsson	1995-06-20 8:17 ...	40 line(s)
Re: Only a game? Merely symbols? (was: Amoral b...	Greg Koster	1995-06-25 10:08 AM ...	21 line(s)
Re: Only a game? Merely symbols? (was: ...	Arlo Smith	1995-06-25 2:43 ...	16 line(s)
Eamon Main Hall source code	Paul Francis Gilbert	1995-06-27 9:21 ...	31 line(s)
Looking for adventure writer	Angelique N Wahlst...	1995-06-26 11:32 ...	15 line(s)
TADS problem	Aaron Hardy	1995-06-25 4:11 ...	18 line(s)

From: Greg Koster
Subject: Only a game? Merely symbols? (was: Amoral behvaiour in IF)

I've held back on posting this idea in the hope that someone else would offer it (and spare me the risk of a poor memory), but here goes:
Return to Zork did try to address the amorality issue of the earlier Zork games. The game has an explicit set of moral rules, which are pretty close to real-world morality (no stealing, for example)--and if you break the rules, you are punished.

Most of the discussion on this newsgroup about Return to Zork as a game

Eastgate's Storyspace and the first hypertext novel written within it, *afternoon, a story* [Michael Joyce], both went on sale in 1990. These tools gave rise to a small but energized movement of writers investigating the literary possibilities of nonlinear prose, often under the name "electronic literature." Works like *Victory Garden* [Stuart Moulthrop 1991], *Marble Springs* [Deena Larsen 1993], and *Uncle Buddy's Phantom Funhouse* [John McDaid 1992] explored the creative possibilities of hyperlinked text, often without the underlying simulation or gamelike qualities that characterized parser-based interactive fiction.

see *Patchwork Girl* **1995**

Hypertext would in fact prove to be an undeniable pivot of the 1990s, not just for text games or even games generally, but for society at large. The World Wide Web and its hypertext markup language and transfer protocol (HTML and HTTP) would *become* the internet for most users within a short

1990s

span of years, replacing the patchwork quilt of tools and services that had come before and bringing in vastly more users. Journalist Julian Dibbell captured the shock of this transition in his book on 90s **MUD** culture *My Tiny Life*, writing how early netizens were at first skeptical of the web, which was

> a new and, at the time, still relatively unknown virtual space—a global library full of brightly illustrated "pages" of information, each one linked to another in a free-form mesh that appeared, potentially at least, to spread forever in every direction…. In the early months of 1995, the Web burst into popular consciousness in a flurry of magazine covers, initial stock offerings, and cocktail-party conversations, and as its fame and fortune grew it swiftly remade the Internet in its own vivid image. The Net that **MUDs** had flourished in—a place of unadorned text and self-contained sites spread out among the universities and research centers of the world—gave way to a place of swirling color, sound, and commerce, a free-flowing sea of information that was growing so vast so quickly that the great engines of media hype could barely keep ahead of it in their rush to exaggerate its importance.

The web had first been announced on the alt.hypertext newsgroup in 1991, where a few years later the first graphical web browser Mosaic would also debut. In both cases, the venue was presumably picked "because its community was recognized as the most likely to understand and appreciate the importance and potential" of the web. In the wake of the sea change, new waves of experiments followed. Early novels and serials for the web like *Delirium* [Douglas Cooper 1994], *The Spot* [Scott Zakarin 1995–7], and *Sunshine 69* [Bobby Rabyd 1996] targeted a wide range of audiences from soap opera fans to narrative postmodernists, exploring many ways hyperlinked text and media might tell a story. Client-side languages like JavaScript and server-side frameworks like Perl and PHP opened up the possibility of creating games for the web, though these would not really begin to compete until the next decade. Most early web narratives were more prose than system.

As commercial computer games across the decade boasted increasingly impressive sound and graphics—with the rise of video cards, CD-ROM, 3D graphics, and full-motion video clips—text games went underground. But their makers were more keen than ever to try new

James Blustein and Ann-Barbara Graff. 2016. "alt. hypertext: An Early Social Medium." In *Social Media Archaelogy and Poetics*, ed. Judy Malloy, MIT Press.

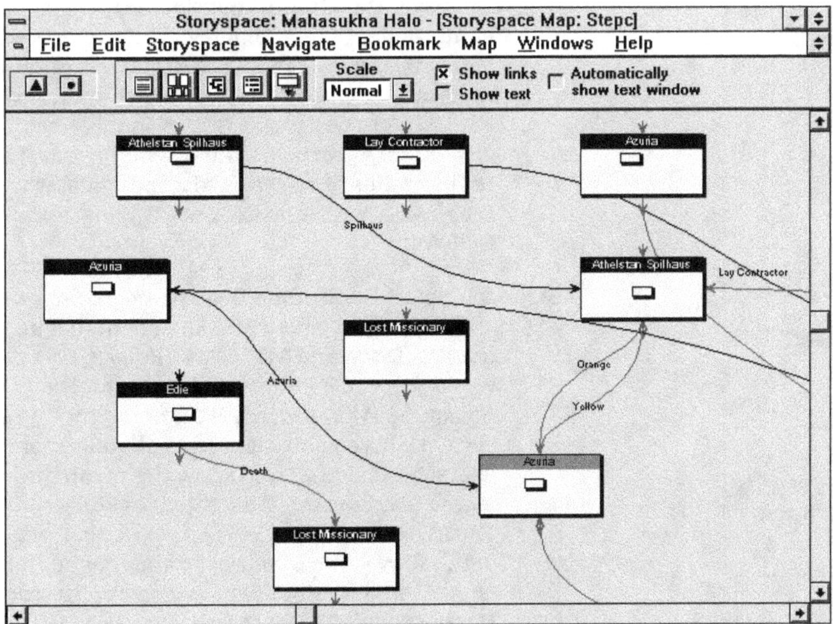

The Storyspace hypertext editor running on a Macintosh.

experiments and discover what place, if any, their playful text might have in the coming twenty-first century.

More Text Games from the 1990s

1990
LambdaMOO

afternoon, a story *(Michael Joyce, Eastgate).* Influential hypertext novel explores fragmented memories triggered by witnessing an auto accident. **The Axe of Kolt** *(Larry Horsfield, FSF Adventures).* Amateur fantasy adventure for the ZX Spectrum. **BatMUD** *(Antti Luostarinen and Niklas Lindroos, LPMud).* Early game running the LPMud software, based in Finland; complex, massive, and still running as of 2022. **La Diosa de Cozumel** *(Andrés Samudio Monro et al., Aventuras AD).* First of influential Spanish "Ci-U-Than" trilogy about Mayan temples and mythology. **Ditch Day Drifter** *(Michael J. Roberts, TADS).* The original TADS example game simulates campus shenanigans at Caltech. **Dragon's Gate** *(Adventures Unlimited, GEnie).* Commercial MUD with a roleplaying emphasis; ran on various services through 2007. **Spellcasting 101: Sorcerers Get All the Girls** *(Steve Meretzky, Legend Entertainment).* First game from company staffed by several Infocom vets; hybrid graphics/text interface with mildly ribald college hijinks. **Unnkulian Underworld** *(D.A. Leary, TADS).* Traditional *Zork*-like; first of a shareware trilogy. **Wonderland** *(David Bishop et al., Magnetic Scrolls).* Final text game from the British company; well-remembered take on the *Alice* story.

1991
Trade Wars 2002

Cosmoserve *(Judith Pintar, AGT).* Lovingly simulated parody of BBS culture. **DikuMUD** *(Sebastian Hammer et al., DikuMUD).* Combat-centric MUD whose open-source engine became a much-used platform and inspired first-generation MMOs like *EverQuest*. **Humbug** *(Graham Cluley, DOS).* Surreal holiday puzzle adventure set in and around a multiversal manor house; unusually, written in straight code, not an IF dev language. **The Multi-Dimensional Thief** *(Joel Finch, AGT).* World-hopping treasure hunt; winner of the CompuServe Softworks AGT Competition. **Save Princeton** *(Jacob Weinstein and Karine Schaefer, TADS).* Another collegial puzzle game with the requisite campus-specific in-jokes. **TimeQuest** *(Bob Bates, Legend Entertainment).* Stop a villain from destroying history in this adventure by a former Infocomer. **T-Zero** *(Dennis Cunningham, DOS).* Another time-travel adventure, this one from an amateur, set in a series of surreal landscapes; quality writing and puzzles. **Victory Garden** *(Stuart Moulthrop, Eastgate Systems).* Hypertext novel set during and reacting to the Gulf War.

1992
Silverwolf

Agrippa: A Book of the Dead *(William Gibson, Kevin Begos Jr. Publishing).* Artist's book and floppy disk with a 300-line poem that permanently encrypted itself after reading. **Discworld MUD** *(David Bennett, LPMud).* Based on Pratchett's fantasy world, grew to immense size and complexity; still running in 2020. **Empire** *(Farhaj Hashmi, DikuMUD-derived).* MUD noted for PVP combat and a roleplay-focused system where names and stats of other characters were not shown unless your character had reason to know them; ran through 2010. **Gateway** *(Mike Verdu et al., Legend Entertainment).* Adaptation of Pohl sci-fi classic with well-regarded puzzles. **The Mines of Lithiad** *(Jack Lockerby, Zenobi Software).* Rescue an egg for a dragon in this PAW game by a prolific amateur author. **Shades of Gray** *(Judith Pintar et al., AGT).* Multi-author work with complex storyline involving politics and tarot. **Uncle Buddy's Phantom Funhouse** *(John McDaid, Eastgate Systems).* Story told as a collection of HyperCard stacks cataloging the ephemera of a quirky relative's life.

1993
Curses

The Abbey *(Art LaFrana, DOS).* Shareware game in a custom development system; creepy, strongly plotted mystery in a medieval abbey. **Eric the Unready** *(Bob Bates, Legend Entertainment).* Fantasy comedy about an inept knight with hybrid text/graphics interface. **Gateway 2: Homeworld** *(Mike Verdu and Glen Dahlgren, Legend Entertainment).* One of the last commercially released text adventures of the period. **The Horror of Rylvania** *(D.A. Leary, TADS)*. Shareware vampire puzzle game with quality writing. **Marble Springs** *(Deena Larsen, Eastgate Systems)*. HyperCard-driven anthology telling stories of women in a nineteenth-century American town. **MediaMOO** *(Amy Bruckman, MOO)*. Online space for academics and researchers, created at MIT Media Lab. **Perdition's Flames** *(Michael J. Roberts, TADS)*. Epic puzzle game set in a bureaucratic hell, by designer of TADS language. **The Sound of One Hand Clapping** *(Erica Sadun, AdvSys)*. Atmospheric puzzle game in a Buddhist-inspired world.

Balances *(Graham Nelson, Inform)*. Demonstration of Inform's advanced features, with intriguing spellcasting puzzles inspired by Infocom's *Enchanter* series. **Delirium** *(Douglas Anthony Cooper, web)*. Early novel serialized on the web with four interconnected pathways, later published in altered form as a print book. **Enhanced** *(Hans Persson and Dominik Zemmler, TADS)*. Short, shareware, cyberpunk. **The Legend Lives!** *(David Baggett, TADS)*. Set in far future of the Unnkulia universe where you battle a sentient computer virus; focus on story over puzzles. **LegendMUD** *(Sherry Menton and Rick Delashmit, DikuMUD)*. MUD with areas based on well-researched historical periods; future MMO designer Raph Koster was an immortal. **Legends of Terris** *(Paul Barnett, Online Games Company)*. UK-based MUD licensed to AOL Europe; most popular game on the service through the late 90s. **Realms of Despair** *(Derek Snider, SMAUG)*. Popular MUD with evolved Diku codebase. **The Two Towers** *(Aule et al., LPMud)*. Long-lived Tolkien MUD.

1994
The Playground

A Change in the Weather *(Andrew Plotkin, Inform 5)*. Time-constrained puzzles in a landscape changing as a storm rolls in; first Inform game by Plotkin and joint winner of the first IF Comp. **A.L.I.C.E.** *(Richard Wallace, SETL)*. Prize-winning chatbot with thousands of hand-authored conversational gambits; origin of AIML format for bot content authoring. **Christminster** *(Gareth Rees, Inform 5)*. Big college-set puzzle game with mysteries, NPCs, and an advancing story. **The Eternal Adventure** *(Bill Piel and Josh Solan, EK Corporation)*. BBS storytelling game that let players add new choices and branches to an ever-growing digital gamebook. **Hegirascope** *(Stuart Moulthrop, web)*. Postmodern hypertext novel with heavily interlinked passages that rapidly refresh, often before they can be completely read. **Jigsaw** *(Graham Nelson, Inform 5)*. Ambitious follow-up to *Curses*; time-travel romance inspired in part by Infocom's *Trinity* and glorying in the fiddly objects and setpieces Inform enabled. **John's Fire Witch** *(John Baker, TADS)*. Short game of elemental magic and well-clued puzzles; helped revive the idea of a competition for shorter games. **The Spot** *(Scott Zakarin, web)*. One of the first popular episodic "soaps" for the web with daily diary entries from a cast of fictional Santa Monicans; ran through 1997. **Theatre** *(Brendon Wyber, Inform 5)*. Well-crafted horror in an abandoned playhouse with a dark history. **Uncle Zebulon's Will** *(Magnus Olsson, TADS)*. Your oddball uncle turns out to be a wizard, clever magic-based puzzles ensue; joint winner of the first IF Comp. **Undo** *(Neil deMause, TADS)*. Minimalist unwinnable game with IF metajokes that spurred discussions about the essence of the form.

1995
Patchwork Girl

Aardwolf *(Lasher, originally Diku/OLC)*. Long-running MUD with major player versus player elements and hundreds of custom quests; still popular in 2022. **Delusions** *(C.E. Forman, Inform 6)*. Rollercoaster of a game set in virtual reality. **DragonRealms** *(Simutronics, Interactive Fiction Engine)*. Commercial MUD reachable from various early dial-up services like AOL. **Fear** *(Chuan-Tze Teo, Inform 5)*. Three puzzle-based vignettes explore fears through the eyes of a phobia-laden character. **In the End** *(Joe Mason, Inform 5)*. Meditation on the meaning of life in a near-future world; early experiment in puzzleless design that also eschewed compass navigation, inventory, and save/restore. **Kissing the Buddha's Feet** *(Leon Lin, TADS)*. Help your college roommate study by eliminating distractions; clever puzzles and memorable characters. **Lost New York** *(Neil deMause, TADS)*. Well-researched time travel adventure exploring the history of the Big Apple. **The Meteor, the Stone**

1996
So Far

and a Long Glass of Sherbet *(Graham Nelson, Inform 6)*. *Zork* homage; winner of 2nd IF Comp. **My Boyfriend Came Back From the War** *(Olia Lialina, web)*. Web-based hypertext with nested frames and multimedia, telling a nonlinear story about an interrupted relationship. **Pick Up the Phone Booth and Die** *(Rob Noyes, Inform 5)*. Controversial joke game that became a minimalist touchstone; inspired nearly a dozen parodies and imitators. **Small World** *(Andrew D. Pontious, TADS)*. Repair a miniature solar system in this fun, well-regarded puzzler. **Sunshine 69** *(Bobby Rabyd, web)*. Early novel written for the web with scenes accessible in different orders; explores the dark sides of San Francisco's Summer of Love. **Tapestry** *(Daniel Ravipinto, Inform 5)*. After death, an angelic being offers you the chance to revisit three key moments in your life and decide if you want to change them. **TorilMUD** *(Kris Kortright, Sequent)*. Set in *D&D*'s Forgotten Realms, a descendant of earlier MUD *Sojourn*; player Brad McQuaid would go on to create *EverQuest*.

1997
Achaea

Babel *(Ian Finley, TADS)*. Creepy game at a polar research station with extensive story and memorable writing. **A Bear's Night Out** *(David Dyte, Inform 6)*. Play a teddy bear getting up to mischief. **The Edifice** *(Lucian Smith, Inform 6)*. IF Comp winner echoing *2001: A Space Odyssey*; solve puzzles involving an alien structure helping you evolve. **Glowgrass** *(Nate Cull, TADS)*. Explore a strange planet as a xenohistorian from a far future. **Jabberwacky** *(Rollo Carpenter, web)*. Chatbot that learned interactions from prior humans who had talked with it; 2008 descendant Cleverbot had more than 150 million conversations. **The Lost Spellmaker** *(Neil James Brown, Inform 6)*. Spellcasting mystery; early example of a lesbian protagonist in a game. **Mercy** *(Chris Klimas, Inform 6)*. Early puzzleless game set at a hospital in the midst of a deadly epidemic. **She's Got a Thing for a Spring** *(Brent VanFossen, Inform 6)*. Remembered for great implementation of NPCs and a tranquil setting in a Rocky Mountain campsite. **The Space Under the Window** *(Andrew Plotkin, Inform 6)*. Experimental story navigated through typing words to shift focus. **Sunset Over Savannah** *(Ivan Cockrum, TADS)*. Beautifully written, tranquil exploration of a beach at a turning point in your character's life. **Tryst of Fate** *(G.M. Zagurski, Inform 6)*. A housewife bumps her head and ends up in a fantastical Wild West. **UltraCorps** *(Stan James, VR-1 Entertainment)*. Commercial multiplayer browser game, one of the first of its kind for the web; turn-based space conquest strategy with a mostly text interface. **We Descend** *(Bill Bly, Eastgate Systems)*. Hypertext novel in the form of an archive of documents by a scholar from a dark future. **Zero Sum Game** *(Cody Sandifer, TADS)*. Play an adventurer who needs to return a pillaged kingdom to its original state. **Zork: The Undiscovered Underground** *(Marc Blank, Michael Berlyn, and G. Kevin Wilson, Inform 6)*. Created as a tie-in for a new graphical *Zork*, this short text sequel paired two Infocom veterans with amateur IF writer Wilson.

1998
Photopia

Anchorhead *(Michael Gentry, Inform 6)*. Horror classic about a house and town hiding a dark Lovecraftian secret. **Bad Machine** *(Dan Shiovitz, TADS)*. Interact with a malfunctioning robot via an alien interface. **Enlightenment** *(Taro Ogawa, Inform 6)*. One-room puzzler, lovingly crafted homage to classic treasure hunts. **Firebird** *(Bonnie Montgomery, TADS)*. An adventure in the mode of a Russian folk tale. **Little Blue Men** *(Michael S. Gentry, Inform 6)*. Unusual game with elements of satire, horror, comedy, surreality, and office politics. **Losing Your Grip** *(Stephen Granade, TADS)*. Allegorical journey through a modern-day addict's recovering subconscious. **Mother Loose** *(Irene Callaci, Inform 6)*. Lighthearted adventure in a nursery-rhyme world. **Muse: An Autumn Romance** *(Christopher Huang, Inform 6)*. Victorian love story with unusual voice and protagonist, and elegant writing. **Once and Future** *(G. Kevin Wilson, TADS)*. Ambitious time-traveling Arthurian epic in the classic adventure mold, years in the making and released commercially. **The Plant** *(Michael J. Roberts, TADS)*. Well-implemented puzzle game set at a mysterious factory. **Rice** *(geniwate, web)*. Collection of hypertext poems about a Westerner's travels through Vietnam. **Spider and Web** *(Andrew Plotkin, Inform 6)*. Spy thriller with a unique narrative and narratorial structure. **The Unknown** *(William Gillespie et al., web)*. Heavily interlinked hypertext novel about three writers on a publicity tour.

Aisle *(Sam Barlow, Inform 6)*. Influential one-room, one-move game. **Exhibition** *(Ian Finley, TADS)*. Character-driven piece about remembering the life of a dead artist through the perspectives of four visitors to his final show. **For a Change** *(Dan Schmidt, Inform 6)*. Unusual language and strange setting make for a memorable and distinctly textual game. **Halothane** *(Ravi Rajkumar, Inform 6)*. An author enters his own discarded manuscript. **Life's Lottery** *(Kim Newman, Simon & Schuster)*. Serious gamebook by a novelist explores a British man's life; can be read linearly or by making choices. **The Mulldoon Legacy** *(Jon Ingold, Inform 6)*. Large puzzlefest with unique challenges and alternate solutions, set in a magical museum. **Remembrance** *(Casey Tait, web)*. Much-maligned early attempt at a web-based interactive story interface, telling a story of soldiers in the first World War. **Six Stories** *(Neil K. Guy, TADS)*. Extensive use of spoken narration, sound, and photography in a collection of interactive vignettes. **Utopia** *(Mehul Patel, Solaria Games)*. Early complex browser game of real-time territory expansion and resource management in a fantasy kingdom. **Varicella** *(Adam Cadre, Inform 6)*. Black humor, social engineering, and courtly intrigue. **Winter Wonderland** *(Laura Knauth, Inform 6)*. IF Comp winner about a girl transported to a fantastical icy world. **Worlds Apart** *(Suzanne Britton, TADS)*. Sprawling epic of self-discovery in a fantastical other world laden with explorable objects and complex characters.

1999
King of Dragon Pass

LAMBDAMOO

Pavel Curtis

Early Contributers: Tim Allen, Judy Anderson, Roger Crew, and Erik Ostrom

Style	**MUD**
Debuted	**Oct 30, 1990** *(beta)* **Feb 5, 1991** *(announced)*
Launch Platform	**Unix** *(server)* **Telnet** *(client)*
Language	**C** *(server)* **MOO** *(world)*

> " LambdaMOO is a new kind of society, where thousands of people voluntarily come together from all over the world. What these people say or do may not always be to your liking; as when visiting any international city, it is wise to be careful who you associate with and what you say.

***** Connected *****
The Coat Closet
The closet is a dark, cramped space. It appears to be very crowded in here; you keep bumping into what feels like coats, boots, and other people (apparently sleeping). One useful thing that you've discovered in your bumbling about is a metal doorknob set at waist level into what might be a door.

`open door`

1990

> You open the closet door and leave the darkness for the living room, closing the door behind you so as not to wake the sleeping people inside.
> The Living Room
> It is very bright, open, and airy here, with large plate-glass windows looking southward over the pool to the gardens beyond. On the north wall, there is a rough stonework fireplace. The east and west walls are almost completely covered with large, well-stocked bookcases. An exit in the northwest corner leads to the kitchen and, in a more northerly direction, to the entrance hall. The door into the coat closet is at the north end of the east wall, and at the south end is a sliding glass door leading out onto a wooden deck. There are two sets of couches, one clustered around the fireplace and one with a view out the windows.
> You see Cockatoo, README for New MOOers, Welcome Poster, a fireplace, The Daily Whale, Helpful Person Finder, The Birthday Machine, a map of LambdaHouse, and lag meter here.
> Hagbard, Rusty (distracted), Porcupine (asleep), Primate's_Stick, and Purple_Guest are here.
> `say Hello, world.`
> You say, "Hello, world."
> Purple_Guest laughs.

see **1980**

see also *Achaea* **1997**

A DECADE AFTER THE ORIGINAL *MUD* demonstrated the appeal of a shared virtual world, multi-user dungeons had become an established genre. As more university students gained access to computers and unmetered internet time, they created first dozens, then hundreds and hundreds, of *MUD* clones. The earliest were simple knockoffs, but soon they had evolved into increasingly sophisticated simulations of fantastical otherworlds.

This complexity had largely taken the form of more and more elaborate rules for combat, skill advancement, magic spells and items, or world simulation. By the end of the 80s some MUDs offered dozens of character classes to choose from, each with complex progressions of skill trees; player-run guilds with arcane hierarchies of power; hundreds of unique weapons and monsters; and complex weather systems or day/night cycles. But some mudders had grown bored with the endless grind of combat and leveling. A few had started to wonder if it might be possible to base a virtual world around a different central conceit.

In many MUDs, the ultimate goal was to rise to the highest experience level and become a wizard. To reward such long-term community engagement, wizards were often granted special powers and responsibilities: the power to teleport, for instance, or to enforce order by resolving disputes or banishing troublemakers. But the most tantalizing wizard ability of all was the power of creation. Some MUDs gave wizards access to new verbs that let them literally reshape the world, creating new rooms and connections, unique monsters and objects, and original puzzles and quests. Becoming a wizard could take tremendous effort—hundreds or thousands of hours of playtime, not to mention the social skills necessary to ingratiate yourself to the existing wizard community—but what a reward to look forward to!

Near the end of 1988, a short-lived MUD called *Monster* [Richard Skrenta] launched with a simple but intriguing idea: what if you didn't have to rise through the ranks and earn your wizardhood to help make the world? What if ultimate power was given out to everyone? While it hadn't been the first game to experiment with this notion, *Monster* caught the attention of Carnegie Mellon University grad student James Aspnes, who ended up streamlining and rewriting the popular package AberMUD [Alan Cox et al. 1987] into a version that stripped out the extensive combat, magic, stats, and advancement rules and gave all players the generous building permissions of a wizard. He called his engine TinyMUD [1989], and he hoped the lack of premade content would force players to start building their own, perhaps based on something other than combat. He suggested the "D" in MUD didn't have to stand for dungeon. What about domain, or dimension?

While many mudders shrugged at the weird experiment and kept slaying virtual orcs, some found the concept wildly intriguing. Within a few months, the original TinyMUD had to be shut down for exceeding the limitations of its host computer—user-made content had completely overwhelmed it. But Aspnes had freely shared the server code and various clones sprung up to take its place, often further iterating on and improving the software. Soon, spin-offs like TinyMUCK [Stephen White 1990] and TinyMUSH [Larry Foard 1990] were everywhere.

In the summer of 1990, a Canadian student named Stephen White released a package called MOO, which stood for MUD, Object-Oriented. White realized that for players to truly be creative in a virtual world, the power to make new rooms and objects wasn't enough. They would need the ability to create new rules and systems too. But that would require an embedded programming language capable of altering the very world its user was immersed in, and an ontology allowing that world to be changed in a simple and consistent manner. Object-oriented programming was becoming increasingly popular, so White decided to build a system where everything in the world—from players, to items, to rooms, to the exits connecting those rooms—was represented as an object that could be created or modified by special commands. Objects could have associated properties and routines; for example, a property called `description` might be common to all objects, or code specifying that only the creator of an object could modify it.

But object-oriented programming also allowed for a system of inheritance, which could let an object "descend" from an ancestor to gain its qualities. Useful boilerplate objects like Room or Person might be created first, defined with all the code and properties each needed to function. A Room might inherit a generic object's `description` property and be given a new one, `exit_list`, that stored connections to other rooms. One might then make a more specific Room called Outdoor Room, inheriting the features of its parent but adding new behaviors to simulate external areas where sun and sky were visible. Finally, one might add a child of Outdoor Room called In the Meadow to simulate one such room in particular. Inheritance provided a simple and well-understood conceptual framework and technical underpinning, allowing for reuse of code and keeping the universe's

Richard Bartle has pointed out that this feature actually existed in the earliest versions of the original *MUD*, but was removed because players kept adding inappropriate content.

fundamental structure orderly and predictable. Crucially, it also enabled players to easily build on each other's contributions.

White demonstrated his MOO code base with an alpha world he never widely publicized, but among those who discovered it was Pavel Curtis, a researcher at the Xerox PARC lab in Palo Alto, California. PARC had become well enshrined as a preeminent institution of forward-thinking computer research, having birthed innovations like the graphical user interface, the laser printer, the Ethernet protocol, and some of the first object-oriented programming languages. Curtis, who was researching language design and interested in the challenges of teaching programming to kids, had recently stumbled across MUD culture and became intrigued by the potential of White's MOO. Could this be the next big thing for PARC—shared virtual environments that any user could help design? White's enthusiasm for the project had flagged, so with his permission—and having been granted free rein by the PARC bosses to set up a long-term virtual worlds research project—Curtis took over work on a revised new version of MOO. His character on White's server was named Lambda (after a term important in his favorite programming language, Scheme), so he decided to give both his software and the first test world running it the name *LambdaMOO*.

Like many first-time interactive fiction authors, the first thing Curtis built was his own house. As he invited in a first wave of friends and colleagues to test the system, he encouraged them to extend the environment but keep it thematically consistent. One of his earliest collaborators was Judy Anderson, a former fellow resident of the house he was virtually recreating. Judy, whose avatar in this mirror world was called yduJ, took to the role of possibility architect with gusto. She soon began coding interesting objects for visitors to interact with, like an interactive hot tub with working jets and temperature controls, and created the game's first puzzle (disabling an obnoxious burglar alarm). yduJ and others in the first wave of residents also extended the house beyond its original modest footprint, creating new wings, hallways, and rooms with the `@DIG` command, and new objects to fill them via `@CREATE`.

By February 1991, when Curtis opened *LambdaMOO* to the public with an announcement on the Usenet group rec.games.mud, the house had swelled to the point that it was already easy to get lost. Unlike other TinyMUD-likes with no enforcement of a consistent universe—a wizard's castle might adjoin a busy spaceport, or a recreation of a real Chicago dive bar—*LambdaMOO* took pains to enforce a consensus reality for its virtual space, a fictional framework that nonetheless might allow almost any kind of contribution:

> *LambdaMOO* takes place inside and on the grounds of a large, sprawling mansion…. The house is also very large, so large in fact that the current occupants themselves have only ever explored a tiny portion of it. What may be going on in other parts of the house is anybody's guess…. With nobody having the means or inclination to patrol the whole place, almost anything could be squatting here.
>
> South of the occupied part of the house lie the palatial gardens. Many parts of the gardens are still being tended and cared for…. Of course,

1990

there are other parts of the gardens that have become quite overgrown and wild, sheltering who knows what.

The land underneath the house is also full of strange tunnels, odd caverns, perhaps a forgotten mine, and other amusements. Of course, except for the wine cellars, the current occupants are completely unaware of such developments.

LambdaMOO grew slowly at first, but it grew. After a year of building, with more and more keen creators joining every day, the dimensions of Lambda House had taken on dizzyingly fractal qualities. The grounds outside extended past lawns and gardens through thickets and rolling hills, eventually stretching to distant beaches and lands beyond. Pocket dimensions sprung up within the house itself, like the Looking-Glass Tavern, which could be visited by gazing into a mirror in the foyer, or an entire miniature town built on a model railroad table in the guest bedroom, which one could magically shrink down to explore. A nightclub in Tiny Town became one of the MOO's most happening hangout spots, and its miniature residential district was a popular place to `@DIG` a virtual home. Another common place to put down roots was the lavish hotel found inside a red plastic piece in the working Monopoly set in the dining room. Treehouses, rooftop observatories, hidden underground grottoes, crawlspaces between the walls— the house and its grounds had become a wonderland of creative architecture and inspired worldbuilding. In this place of "pure communication, where looks don't matter and only the best writers get laid,"[16] descriptions were often richly evocative:

> **The Sleeping Forest**
> The trees here are absolutely enormous. Their trunks are each at least thirty feet in diameter, and stretch upwards forever, disappearing finally into the mist far above. The light here is dim, and the silence is nearly absolute. The plants which grow all around are a deep green, and are soft and silent under your feet.

> **Outside of Barn**
> You're standing outside of an old, wooden barn that probably received its last coat of red paint over a decade ago. The grey-brown shingles of the roof are covered with moss and withered brown leaves, and beneath the corners you see clumps of twigs, dried grass and string where swallows have built their nests. You can see them flying sometimes in the evening: swift, purplegreen, darting after insects.
>
> Despite its overall look of gentle decrepitude, it's clear that somebody's been here. All over the front of the barn, strange objects are affixed—some as old and weathered as the structure itself, but some fairly new. You see plastic dollheads, their pink cheeks and glassy blue eyes startling against the faded wood; animal bones painted bright colors with bits of mirrors or bright glass affixed to them; bicycle wheels and fanblades flecked with rust, warped 45 RPM vinyl records, painted

> spirals and incomprehensible words inscribed in spidery calligraphy around them.

> North Wing Fireside Hall
> [...] The air here is filled with the smell of spruce and pine, wafting through the air from the fireplace which sits in the center of the room. The room is decorated in a comfortable dark brown, with a varnished hardwood floor and thick dark oak beams supporting the ceiling, and giving the room a general sense of solidity.
>   Lined up against the western wall stand four or five armored statues, with swords and axes in their metallic hands [...] The fireplace sits in a depression in the center of the room, radiating cozy warmth throughout the room. A wide, circular couch surrounds it, covered in a lush upholstery.

Unlike in single-player IF, these were spaces designed for lingering, for inhabiting: stages for conversations and seductions and meetings with friends.

Increasingly, both on *LambdaMOO* and elsewhere, these worlds were referred to as virtual realities. Contrary to popular conceptions of VR involving cutting-edge graphics or full-immersion bodysuits—fundamentally, a thing of the future—proponents of MOO-VR saw text as a far superior (and already available) way to directly engage the imagination and experience a sense of immersive transportation. And the key to that immersion was collaboration, not only between the people who were playing but between them and the simulation itself. Good players could, of course, emote in ways that referenced the room they occupied and the objects it contained:

> :collapses on the old couch, putting his feet up on the creaking end table.
> Kelvin collapses on the old couch, putting his feet up on the creaking end table.

But the ability to program from within the virtual world let the software become a collaborative partner in the project of maintaining its fictional consistency:

> The living room's description mentioned a couch (two sets of couches, actually) for the longest time. Then someone built an actual VR couch. You can sit on it, shove people off, stuff things into it, jostle it, reupholster it, search for things, and (occasionally) fall in. From under the couch cushions, you can shout, or return something that falls in (from someone else's pockets, to be sure).[13]

These behaviors were created through the straightforward but powerful MOO programming language. For instance, a popular in-game coding tutorial would teach you how to create your own pet rock. To program the ability to pet your pet rock, you needed to type in three commands at the

Ironically, at least for someone not familiar with the oddities of programming tech stacks, MOO was not itself an object-oriented language.

1990

prompt—commands no different, from the system's perspective, than any other player input like LOOK or GO NORTH:

```
@verb rock:pet this none none rxd
@program rock:pet
player:tell("You pet the rock. Nothing happens."); .
```

The words this none none in the first line define the specification of the PET verb from the rock's perspective: it takes a single direct object this (the rock) and no preposition or indirect object. The flags rxd indicate the verb is readable by others (anyone can pet the rock), callable by other verbs like a function, and will show a traceback if its program crashes. The dot at the end of the third line indicates the program being entered is finished. A player might weave these instructions into a stream of conversation with friends and interaction with the existing environment. Reprogramming the world was just another fundamental part of existing within it.

MOO programs could become surprisingly complex, able to interface with nearly any aspect of the simulation they ran within, calling functions to query the game state or piping messages to other parts of the virtual world. As more residents mastered the language, the objects they created became more and more elaborate. Advanced programmers were soon creating toys like the helicopter on the west lawn, which had over twenty custom verbs and included extensive help text:

> The helicopter's description and behavior change depending on whether it's running or stopped, parked, hovering, or in flight. If you land on the asphalt roof, they'll hear the rumble of the engine in the living room…. There are appropriate messages for spectators outside the helicopter when it takes off, flies overhead, and lands. These messages also differ depending on how high the helicopter is flying. If you are at the landing site when someone crashes it, you get to see a team of engineers truck it in and put it back together…. As you overfly locations, people on the ground are notified…. Aircraft cast shadows, which are actual objects that are moved to the various locations the aircraft overfly. This enables people on the ground to wave to people in the aircraft (type wave at helicopter for example). Helicopters can only be landed at catalogued outdoor rooms that have wind socks.

Object inheritance led to a culture of reuse and sharing. The creator of a useful object could set a fertile flag that would let others create child objects from it, and soon whole catalogs of useful parent objects were available in the house's library, with names like Simple Lockable Thing, Generic Amplifiable Musical Instrument, Generic Programmable Puppet, or Generic Aircraft (from which the helicopter descended). Improved children could themselves be made fertile, leading to long chains of iterative refinements and ever-increasing functionality. Programmer-players created camcorders that could record real-time logs of MOO happenings, saving them to the viewable text buffer of a child of Generic Videocassette. Elaborate recreations of real-world pastimes were developed—board games; laser tag arenas; even *LambdaMOO* ports of classic text games, like a *Super Star Trek* that whisked players to the bridge of a starship to navigate

Programs could be typed in line by line as individual commands, or via a special editing environment—which was itself just a custom-made room one could enter, with its own specialty verbs for manipulating text stored inside its buffer.

see **1974**

a three-dimensional grid of galactic sectors. Certain stock NPC classes became useful to architects building clubs or hangouts, such as a Waiter who could show up when a group claimed a table, take drink orders, and return minutes later to distribute beverage objects with drink verbs and simulations of fullness.

Players could even adjust the inheritance tree of their own avatar, the object representing their digital self. One popular generic player class provided verbs to adjust how the system described your appearance and actions, so for instance one could morph into a dragon that would "thunder" rather than "say" any words spoken aloud. Another player class included a range of helpful features for cybersex, including ways to write descriptions of oneself at various states of undress, and to grant other players permission to use various verbs to uncover them.

Within this rich world—which Pavel Curtis called a "prose-based reality"—a village was born. Many MUDs had spawned communities, often strong ones with bonds that spilled out into the real world. But through some combination of *LambdaMOO*'s appeal to older players less interested in pure gameplay, its consistent fictional frame that aided suspension of disbelief, and the way players could alter that frame and reshape it to make a world they wanted to live in, Curtis's experiment rapidly evolved a proper society steeped in a dense network of ideas, friendships, romances, and, soon enough, rivalries. Within a year of launch, there were thousands of registered players and often more than a hundred online at peak hours, enough to sustain a vibrancy of discourse that few other virtual spaces had yet achieved. A hundred simultaneous users might seem small by today's standards, but was in many ways ideal—the size of a large party that never ended, with conversations spilling out into various wings and back porches, and a healthy network of friendly faces, rival cliques, and shared social spaces. It was the perfect shape for a single community.

The MOO had arrived at a pivotal moment in the growing cultural awareness of the internet. Journalist Julian Dibbell would later place *LambdaMOO*'s ascendancy as taking place "about halfway between the first time you heard the words *information superhighway* and the first time you wished you never had."[9] Attracting attention from first specialist and then mainstream media, it seemed a dizzyingly immediate example of the coming future, the opening of a digital utopia where anyone could have the powers of a god.

This heady vision was intoxicating and often addictive. "They were the seductions natural to any world built from the stuff of books and maps," Dibbell later wrote, "the siren song of possibility."[9] Nearly every article or book on MUDs and MOOs written in the 90s included a warning of some kind. One book had a four-page section asking whether virtual worlds were "a hobby or an addiction,"[20] noting that many a college student had dropped out of classes to spend hour after hour in the computer lab, living inside them. Some joked that the acronym stood for Multi-Undergraduate Destroyers. A *Wired* reporter assigned to write a feature on "Why playing MUDs is becoming the addiction of the 90s" ended up becoming addicted

MUD parsers evolved in a strange parallel world to single-player IF parsers, sharing many features of their common ancestors like *Adventure* 1976 but often diverging in sometimes arbitrary, sometimes revealing ways.

In both types of games, for instance, LOOK and EXAMINE will give information about something in the world. In parser IF, the abbreviation for the latter became X; in MUDs, it's generally EX or EXAM. Both words typically do the same thing in parser IF, except you can't "examine" a room. But in some MUDs, they have distinct meanings. In *LambdaMOO*, to LOOK AT something means to view its fictional, in-world description, while to EXAM it is to query the system about how it works, returning its object number, synonyms, owner, and the verbs that can be used to interact with it.

    a fireplace (aka #43212, a fireplace, fireplace, fire, and mantel)
    Owned by Sleeper.
    [...] Obvious verbs:
     light fireplace
     re*move/ta*ke/g*et <anything> from fireplace
     burn <anything> <anything> fireplace
     put <anything> <anything> fireplace
     open fireplace
     close fireplace
     roast/toast/cook/bake/fry/barbecue <anything> on fireplace
     enter fireplace
     g*et/t*ake fireplace
     d*rop/th*row fireplace
     gi*ve/ha*nd fireplace to <anything>
     help fireplace

This is, in fact, the expected way to learn how to use an unfamiliar object—a contrast to parser IF games, which consider it improper to break the fourth wall so brazenly.

EXAM is an exception, but MOOs often enforce a visible distinction between in-world verbs like LOOK, SAY, and TAKE, and out-of-world verbs like @WHO, @MESSAGES, or @DIG. Parser games also have metacommands like SAVE or UNDO but don't typographically distinguish them.

Another distinction can be seen in how both kinds of games handle connections between rooms. Most parser IF hard codes movement verbs with a built-in model of cardinal directions, understanding a concept like "north" and commands like NORTH or N as referring to it. These directions are the default (and sometimes only) way to connect rooms together.

By contrast, on many MOOs a connection between two rooms is simply any word the author wishes to use, with no underlying directional compass coded in. This seemingly clunkier model encourages a mode of creation where relative directions have equal validity to cardinal ones. Exits on *LambdaMOO* are sometimes described with compass points, but just as often with words like DOOR or CLIMB, relative directions like LEFT or RIGHT, or any other system an author might think to deploy. A hallway in a hotel with thirty numbered rooms can simply be linked by numbered directions, so typing 25 would enter that room—a flexibility not possible with a traditional compass model. (The downside is that labeling an exit NORTH has no special meaning to the game engine at all; if you want N to work as well, you must manually add it as a synonym.)

Some syntax insights are so obviously useful, it's a wonder they haven't become universal. Many MUD parsers, for instance, have an annoying inability to recognize the names of items inside open containers; a player might need to manually take an object off a shelf before it can be looked at. Parser IF's more complex recognition model (based on a simulation of visibility) saves some typing. On the other hand, some MUD engines elegantly solve a classic parser disambiguation problem with synonym subsets: if the player types GET BIRD and there's both a "bird" and a "bird house" present, many parsers offer no way for the player to specify which they mean. Some MUDs support a syntax like GET 2.BIRD, specifying the second item in the last message containing that word.

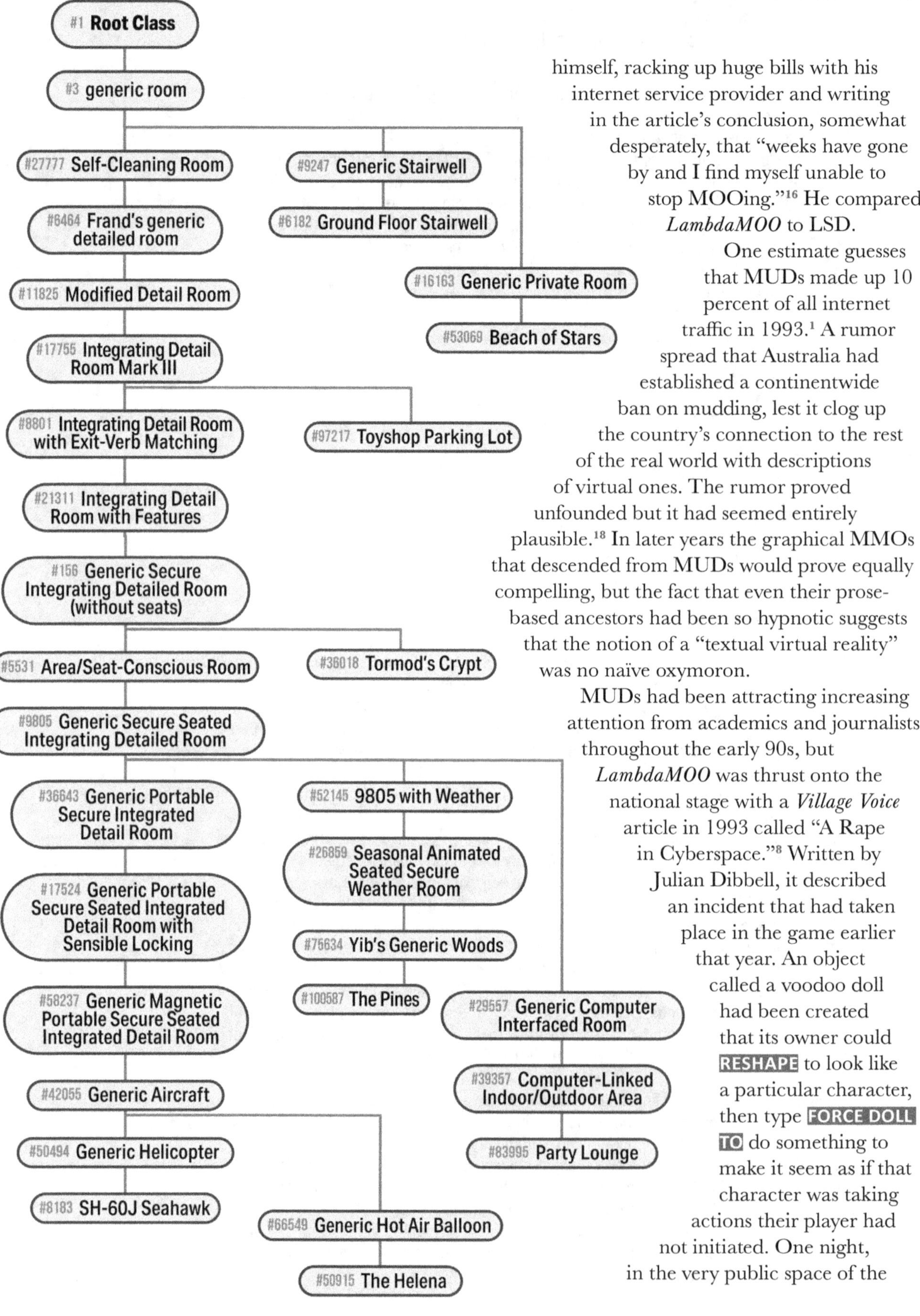

himself, racking up huge bills with his internet service provider and writing in the article's conclusion, somewhat desperately, that "weeks have gone by and I find myself unable to stop MOOing."[16] He compared *LambdaMOO* to LSD.

One estimate guesses that MUDs made up 10 percent of all internet traffic in 1993.[1] A rumor spread that Australia had established a continentwide ban on mudding, lest it clog up the country's connection to the rest of the real world with descriptions of virtual ones. The rumor proved unfounded but it had seemed entirely plausible.[18] In later years the graphical MMOs that descended from MUDs would prove equally compelling, but the fact that even their prose-based ancestors had been so hypnotic suggests that the notion of a "textual virtual reality" was no naïve oxymoron.

MUDs had been attracting increasing attention from academics and journalists throughout the early 90s, but *LambdaMOO* was thrust onto the national stage with a *Village Voice* article in 1993 called "A Rape in Cyberspace."[8] Written by Julian Dibbell, it described an incident that had taken place in the game earlier that year. An object called a voodoo doll had been created that its owner could **RESHAPE** to look like a particular character, then type **FORCE DOLL TO** do something to make it seem as if that character was taking actions their player had not initiated. One night, in the very public space of the

Living Room, a player dressed as a perverted clown used a voodoo doll to make two women appear to do disturbing, violent, and sexual things to each other and to onlookers, much to their players' horror and distress. The incident had sparked a blaze of discussion in the previously laissez-faire community about standards of behavior and where disciplinary power should be vested. Dibbell's article, musing about the morality of communities where words literally instantiated consensus reality, struck a nerve that would prove resonant across future decades. Noting that while no physical crime had occurred in the real world, the women involved still felt violated, Dibbell began to question sharp lines between words and action he had once held firm to: "The more seriously I took the notion of virtual rape, the less seriously I was able to take the notion of freedom of speech, with its tidy division of the world into the symbolic and the real."

The incident came in the midst of a remarkable transition of power on *LambdaMOO*. A few months earlier the system admins, exhausted by the constant stream of player disputes and moderation requests, announced that they were "pulling out of the discipline/manners/arbitration business; we're handing the burden and freedom of that role to the society at large."[12] But in lieu of any formal replacement for admin policing, the question of who, if anyone, now had the power to ban a virtual rapist went unanswered. Eventually one admin banned the perpetrator on his own initiative, but this too proved controversial. Many residents had come to think of Lambda House as a second home—one where some of their most intense social connections were centered—and the notion that an arbitrary whim could expel you from it forever was anathema.

In the wake of public outcry, the admins set up a formal in-game system for petitions and balloting that let any player whose idea captured two-thirds of the popular vote deliver a mandate to the developers. They would implement any passing proposal that met certain legal and feasibility standards, from banning a specific player, to reprogramming core systems, to even shutting the whole thing down if that was what the player base wanted. This high-minded experiment—the admins as obedient servants of the people's will—inspired a flurry of activity both inside and outside the community. Petitions on all kinds of topics, from trivial to world-breaking, were circulated, discussed, and debated endlessly. Political science, law, and sociology academics descended on *LambdaMOO* in swarms to observe a civilization pulling itself out of anarchy from first principles. Curtis's PARC experiment into advancing the evolution of virtual worlds seemed to be bearing real fruit.

But, perhaps predictably, the petition system led to an increasingly vitriolic environment, accompanied by all the hostility and bitterness that comes with real-world politicking, moral crusades, and battles for ideological survival. While *LambdaMOO*'s population continued to grow, much of its core community slowly stopped logging in. All the fun had been leached out of their virtual playground, replaced by something that smacked far too much of reality. Curtis would later reflect:

We see these communities form whenever technology changes. Every time we give people another mechanism to communicate, they latch onto it. And then we see human nature happen again. People. Some of them will be assholes, some of them will care an enormous amount. Some will be beautiful and wonderful and some will be hateful and awful. There's such a hunger for these kinds of systems, [but] then human nature does what we expect it to do if we're paying attention at all, and there will always be people who are disappointed because they thought, this time—this time it is pure.[15]

Mudding never really died, but its player base became subsumed by far larger crowds attracted to the graphical descendants emerging by the late 90s. MUDs gave way to MMOs (massively multiplayer online games) like *Ultima Online* [Electronic Arts 1997], *EverQuest* [Sony Online Entertainment 1999], and *Star Wars Galaxies* [Sony Online Entertainment 2003]. These were more than mere spiritual successors: many were designed by teams of former mudders, and often adopted concepts, designs, and lingo whole cloth from their textual ancestors.

But few graphical MUDs dared give players the powers of a MOO—neither the wizardly tools of creation, nor the radically democratic notions of a self-guided community. Perhaps the most famous exception came with Linden Lab's *Second Life* [2003], which at first attracted hype similar to *LambdaMOO*'s a decade earlier for its dream of a player-made world. But 3D objects are much harder to model and animate believably than textual ones, making most user content seem amateurish, and the company's focus on commercial transactions turned vast swaths of the game's terrain into virtual strip malls, soulless and exploitative. For many years *Second Life* was held up as the exception that proved the rule: giving players too much creative power was as difficult as it was dangerous. In most online spaces from the 2000s on, all a user could really change about the world was their own appearance—within the carefully curated limits of a nose-length slider or a set of preapproved skin tones.

Yet, in the last decade, new seeds of player creativity have grown from the soil of games like *Minecraft* [Mojang Studios 2011] and platforms like *Roblox* [Roblox Corporation 2006]. On the MOO in the early 90s, hundreds of people who had never considered themselves coders or writers discovered the joy of creating something strange or beautiful or funny or functional and sharing it with friends. Today, millions find the same kind of thrill in new virtual spaces that embrace player creativity, cobbling together JavaScript or Lua instead of MOO-code, wrangling voxels or textures instead of words. These new games, too, have become places for community and connection, in part because they are *places* rather than the dimensionless abstractions of social media—places you choose when to enter and when to

LANGUAGE AND SELF-EXPRESSION

LambdaMOO had a surprisingly sophisticated pronoun system for a game from 1990. Among other options, players could instruct the game to describe their character with traditional gendered pronouns; singular they; the royal we; to always use both traditional pronouns (i.e. printing "he/she"); "splat" pronouns, where distinctions between male and female forms were replaced by asterisks (*h*s* instead of *his* or *hers*); and Spivak pronouns (e, em, ir), which the MOO helped bring attention to.

The array of options—neither binary, nor binary plus a single catchall alternative—helped create a culture on the server where gender expression and sexuality could be explored more fluidly by residents, some of whom experimented with changing their pronouns often, or settled into options unfamiliar in the real world but to which their virtual neighbors grew quickly accustomed.

leave, filled with people you can approach or stay away from, and inhabited by a virtual body that can emote and perform, not just post. The 2020s may accelerate awareness of something that seemed obvious to many MOOers decades earlier: conversations need the context of space, and a virtual community ought to feel like a home.

LambdaMOO is still running as of this writing, but is a strange place to visit, both heavy with the dust of ages and as fresh and functional as the day its code first ran. A public bulletin board in the library exhibits surreal temporal collapse: an ad for a long-defunct BBS with a high-speed 14.4k modem sits alongside a note from a lonely Italian in quarantine with COVID-19. The last official news bulletin dates from 2004, yet the @WHO command still shows a dozen or so active players at any given moment, squirreled away in odd corners of the map, still @DIGging. The hundreds of useful generic objects created over the decades remain just as fertile as they were in 1991, their code ready for reuse in a new generation's projects.

Each player on the MOO is given a fixed quota of disk space, a rationing that prevents the community from exceeding the means of its hardware. As new players register characters, inactive players and objects are "reaped" to make room, in reverse order of how recently they've logged in or been used. During the MOO's height of popularity, reaping could happen to inactive players as soon as six weeks after their last login. Today, one can avoid the reaper far longer—but not indefinitely. Within the house you can find an auction block where soon-to-be-reaped objects, rooms, and generic classes are up for grabs, transferable to any active players who might want to claim them. Perusing these digital discards provokes a strange ennui. A tank missile, a bucket, a pair of angelic handcuffs, a skull-topped staff, a galaxy; rooms called Secluded Jungle Hot Tub, Generic Shower Stall, the Library of Rosecliff, or Under a Starry Sky. Which, if any, are worth saving? Once a player has been logged off for too long, their avatar appears to be sleeping, and wandering the map today can feel like exploring an enchanted kingdom of sleeping beauties, some of whom have been asleep for decades.

Yet Lambda House still intrigues. Exploration remains perpetually magical: unlike in a single-author text game, here you never find the limits of the world model or the edges of the map. The next object might always have a new verb programmed into it, and behind any corner might lie a new domain. Listening to a seashell in a gazebo transports you to a lazy tropical paradise; winding a music box in a hidden glade summons ghostly figures to enact a tableau from Keats. Rooms with dynamic descriptions responding to the seasons and the time of day keep cycling through the hours, virtual moons moving through their phases above. Even with most of the people gone, the code they left behind keeps Lambda House alive.

LambdaMOO is not the only or even the oldest period MUD to have survived into the 2020s. Others still running at publication time include *Federation II* [Interactive Broadcasting 1988], *Genesis LPMud* [Lars Pensjö 1989], *BatMUD* [Jaf et al. 1990], *FurryMUCK* [Drew Maxwell et al. 1990], *Discworld MUD* [David Bennett et al. 1991], and *Ancient Anguish* [Balz Meierhans and Olivier Maquelin 1992]. Some of these virtual worlds have grown to include tens of thousands of individual rooms.

References

1 Bartle, Richard A. 2004. *Designing Virtual Worlds*. New Riders.

2 Benedikt, Claire Lisette, and Dave Ciskowski. 1995. *MUDs: Exploring Virtual Worlds on the Internet.*

BradyGames.

3 Burka, Lauren P. 1995. The MUDLine. www.linnaean.org/~lpb/muddex/mudline.html | a Jun 3, 2020

4 Curtis, Pavel. 1992. "Mudding: Social Phenomena in Text-Based Virtual Realities." In *High Noon on the Electronic Frontier: Conceptual Issues in Cyberspace*, 1992.

5 Curtis, Pavel, and David A. Nichols. 1994. "MUDs Grow up: Social Virtual Reality in the Real World." In *Proceedings of COMPCON'94*, IEEE.

6 Curtis, Pavel. 1997. "LambdaMOO Programmer's Manual." hayseed.net/MOO/manuals/ProgrammersManual.html | a Jun 3, 2020

7 Curtis, Pavel. 2001. "Not Just a Game: How LambdaMOO Came to Exist and What It Did To Get Back At Me." In *High Wired: On the Design, Use, and Theory of Educational MOOs*, ed. Cynthia A. Haynes and Jan Rune Holmevik. University of Michigan Press.

8 Dibbell, Julian. 1993. "A Rape in Cyberspace." *The Village Voice*, Dec 23, 1993.

9 Dibbell, Julian. 1998. *My Tiny Life: Crime and Passion in a Virtual World*. New York: Holt.

10 Evans, Claire L. 2018. "A Mansion Filled With Hidden Worlds: When the Internet Was Young." *Undark Magazine* (blog). Jul 20, 2018. undark.org/2018/07/20/wilo-evans-broad-band | a Jun 3, 2020

11 Funkhouser, Chris. 2002. *Whereis Mineral: Adventures in MOO*. Self-published.

12 Haakon. 1992. "LambdaMOO Takes A New Direction." Post to LambdaMOO *News list. Dec 9, 1992.

13 Hess, Elizabeth. 2003. *Yib's Guide to MOOing: Getting the Most From Virtual Communities on the Internet*. Self-published.

14 Koster, Raph. 2000. The Online World Timeline. Mar 4, 2000. www.raphkoster.com/games/the-online-world-timeline | a Jun 3, 2020

15 Laurel, Brenda. 2013. *Computers as Theatre*. 2nd ed. Addison-Wesley.

16 Quittner, Josh. 1994. "Johnny Manhattan Meets the Furry Muckers." *Wired* 2 (3), Mar 1, 1994. www.wired.com/1994/03/muds-3 | a Jun 3, 2020

17 Randall, Neil. 1994. *Teach Yourself the Internet: Around the World in 21 Days*. Sams.

18 Reid, Elizabeth. 1994. "Are MUDs Banned in Australia?" *Computer-Mediated Communication Magazine* 1 (4), Aug 1, 1994.

19 Rheingold, Howard. 1994. "PARC Is Back!" *Wired*, Feb 1, 1994. www.wired.com/1994/02/parc | a Jun 3, 2020

20 Shah, Rawn, and Jim Romine. 1995. *Playing MUDS on the Internet*. John Wiley & Sons, Inc.

21 Sundsted, Todd. 2014. "Keeping Old Code Alive: The Venerable LambdaMOO Server in 2014." Presented at Hope X, New York City, July 20. www.youtube.com/watch?v=SxGbHYGTGWw | a Jun 3, 2020

22 Wisner, Bill. 1990. "A Brief (and Very Incomplete) History of MUDs." Usenet post, rec.games.mud, Sep 28, 1990. groups.google.com/forum/#!msg/rec.games.mud/B6pib_EkVeg/TgdA5l8lwGoJ | a Jun 3, 2020

Gary Martin, MaryAnn Martin,
and John Pritchett

Also Known As	**TradeWars, TW2002**
Style	**BBS**
Debuted	**Jun 1991** *(Castle Ravenloft BBS)*
Launch Platform	**WWIV / DOS**
Publisher	**Martech Software**
Language	**Turbo Pascal 6.0**
Launch Price	**$20** *(sysop registration fee)*

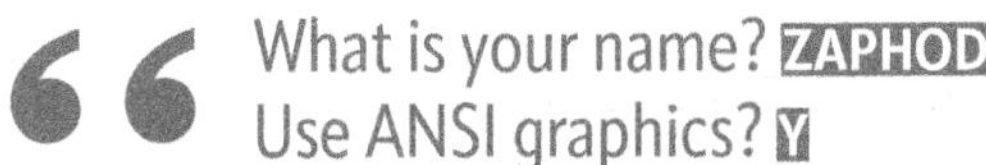

What is your name? **ZAPHOD**
Use ANSI graphics? **Y**

IF YOU FIRST WENT ONLINE AFTER 1996 or so, you might never have connected to a BBS. If you first went online after 2006, you might never even have heard of one.

Reading the histories of online games like *dnd* **1975**, *MUD* **1980**, or *LambdaMOO* **1990** can give the impression that gamers have been happily playing together on the internet since the 70s. In some special places like university campuses, they have been. But for most early computer users there was no cheap or easy way to connect to the global net. For them, going online meant dialing into a local bulletin board system—and the games on those systems were a curious sort of multiplayer, because only one person could play them at a time.

1991

Major Versions

» **Trade Wars**, Chris Sherrick, BASIC, 1984. Defined core gameplay of moving between numbered sectors; trading ore, organics, and equipment at space ports; combat with NPC ships (the "evil Cabal") and other players.

» **TradeWars 2/QuixPlus**, Lord Darkseid and Quixotic Software, Pascal, 1986. Port that added planet creation/destruction, ship armor, space mines.

» **Trade Wars 2001**, Gary Martin, 1987. Rewritten for WWIV and improved in various ways; added *Star Trek* and *Star Wars* references; expanded number of sectors.

» **Trade Wars 2002**, Gary and MaryAnn Martin, Jun 1991. Complete rewrite for C-based WWIV (which raised max program size above 64K). Added Stardock, Planetary Citadels, more ship types & sectors, ANSI art.

» **v2** (WideBeta 1), Dec 18, 1993. Support for a wider range of BBS types; added Interdictor Cruiser, stronger citadels, multiple planet types.

» **High Velocity Software port**, The Major BBS, 1994. First (unofficial) version to support real-time multiplayer.

» **v3**, John Pritchett, 1997. Added real-time multiplayer, multiple player ships, NavHaz.

» **Trade Wars Game Server (TWGS)**, 1998. Enabled games over the web.

» **Trade Wars 2002 v3.34**, 2012. Most recent official update.

1991

Backing up: a BBS was simply a regular computer hooked up to a phone line, which anyone dialing in with a modem could control. Often this computer was just a spare in someone's home, hooked up to a second landline. BBS host software let callers create accounts and provided access to whatever message boards, file archives, and games the system operator (sysop) had made available. Each BBS was its own tiny island with unique user accounts, layouts, information, and entertainment. And since phone companies still charged by the minute for long-distance calls, most users were local, exploring an archipelago of hometown systems via a notepad full of phone numbers collected by word of mouth or found on other BBSes. At the peak of their popularity in the early 90s, there may have been something like 150,000 such systems running around the world.

While a large or commercial BBS might have multiple phone lines, most were hobby operations with just one, meaning only one person could connect at a time. So a multiplayer BBS game had to be played sequentially, not simultaneously, like a board game with person after person taking a turn. Bandwidth over analog phone lines was slow, meaning all interactions were by necessity text-based. Downloading a single jpeg might take ten minutes over 2400 baud, but a few hundred characters of text could be transmitted each second, fast enough to fill a screen in moments.

And that screen didn't have to be drab. The ANSI text standard, supported by most computers by 1990, allowed sixteen foreground and eight background colors as well as a range of special characters for lines, shapes, and textures—extended ASCII—which together could paint vibrant, blocky pseudographics in an 80×24 grid of characters. While standalone games had moved on to 256 colors and CD-ROM video and audio by the 90s, BBS games were forced to attract players and hold their interest with nothing but their text. Their aesthetics were retro even in their prime: their gameplay, and their words, were the only places they could innovate.

Most of these games were standalone MS-DOS programs to which the BBS software could hand over execution, along with some metadata like the name of the logged-in user and their permissions. These were called door games, since the user was in essence passing through an invisible portal between one program on the host's system and the next. By the early 90s, limits around memory and compatibility that had sharply restricted the size of door games had mostly vanished, paving the way for BBS games to become sophisticated and complex. But to tell the story of how *Trade Wars* became the most popular BBS door of all time, we need to go back even further, to a pair of games from the 70s. One was covered earlier in this book—*Super Star Trek* **1974**—and the other was called *Star Trader*.

Star Trader was another popular early BASIC game passed around and improved from one hacker to another, originating with People's Computer Center member Dave Kaufman (whose *Caves* games probably influenced *Hunt the Wumpus* **1973**). Kaufman's program took a very simple premise— buy low, sell high—and gave it a patina of sci-fi excitement by casting its players as interstellar merchants:

```
EACH OF YOU IS THE CAPTAIN OF TWO INTERSTELLAR TRADING
SHIPS. YOU WILL TRAVEL FROM STAR SYSTEM TO STAR SYSTEM,
BUYING AND SELLING MERCHANDISE. IF YOU DRIVE A GOOD BARGAIN
YOU CAN MAKE LARGE PROFITS.
```

Multiple players sharing the same keyboard could take turns navigating a small region of half a dozen stars, looking for deals on goods like uranium, star gems, helium, and (naturally) computer software:

```
PLAYER 1, WHICH STAR WILL ARGOSY TRAVEL TO? QUIN
THE ETA AT QUIN IS MAY 3, 2070

ARGOSY HAS LANDED ON QUIN
$ ON BOARD: 5000      NET WT 25
UR   MET   HE   MED   SOFT   GEMS
0    0     15   10    10     0
WE ARE BUYING:
HE    WE NEED 6 UNITS.
HOW MANY ARE YOU SELLING?  6
WE OFFER $ 25900
WHAT DO YOU BID? 27000
WE OFFER $ 26100
WHAT DO YOU BID? 26500
WE'LL TAKE IT!
```

Star Trader was a surprisingly clever program for its day. The trading algorithm was smart, involving a hidden range of acceptable prices a merchant might take that would shrink the longer haggling continued. Also, it was *fun* to out-barter your friends, snatching up all the units of a rare commodity and watching your credits increase at their expense. Republished in a popular early book of **BASIC** source listings, *What to Do After You Hit Return* (1975), the game became an early computing standard.

Around the same time, *Star Trek* games were also big hits, merging the joys of exploring strange new worlds with the thrill of blowing up Klingons, and adding multiplayer to Trek games became a popular hacker pastime. One variant called *WAR* [author and release date unknown] cast one player as the Klingons and another at the same keyboard as the Federation, and allowed players to claim planets and make them useful starbases. *WAR* soon evolved into *DECWAR* [Jeff Potter and Bob Hysick 1978] on the Digital Equipment Corporation's PDP-11, which supported multiple simultaneous connections and allowed up to ten players divided into two teams, Federation and Klingons, to face off in real time. *DECWAR* became wildly popular, evolving new multiplayer-specific mechanics and gameplay. When the first commercial internet providers began to appear, the multiplayer mainframe games were exactly the kinds of experiences they wanted to bring to home computer users. CompuServe reskinned *DECWAR* as *MegaWars* [1983], removing the *Star Trek* references (and the original creators' names), and it became a popular part of the service for well over a decade.

Worth noting: in the early 70s the very notion of individuals buying and selling software was still science fiction.

But CompuServe was expensive: twelve dollars an hour for access, even at off-peak times. One of the many gamers who had heard about *MegaWars* but couldn't afford to play[1] was named Chris Sherrick, and he wanted to bring something like it to his free BBS. Based on secondhand knowledge of the game and his familiarity with the early BASIC classics like *Star Trader* and *Wumpus,* he created a game called *Trade Wars* [1984] and made it available for free to other sysops. In Sherrick's game, players navigated a maze of sixty numbered sectors with complex interconnections (much like in *Wumpus*), buying and selling goods (as in *Star Trader*) while fighting off enemies and operating a starship with a range of advanced capabilities (as in *Trek* and its many descendants). It was a grab bag of successes from earlier games, put in a new package that anyone with a modem could dial in to play—no credit card required.

Sherrick's was not destined to become the most famous *Trade Wars*. After passing through a number of ports and revisions, a version found its way to Kansas coder and sysop Gary Martin, who wanted to get it running on his BBS Castle Ravenloft ("the Loft," as it was affectionately known). The Loft's software couldn't run a BASIC program as a door, so Martin was hunting for a working Pascal port, but the best candidate he could find seemed buggy and kept crashing. He decided to do some major surgery and, while he was in there, to add some tweaks of his own. After fits and starts of tinkering, he released his version of Sherrick's game in 1987, under the name *Trade Wars 2001*. Martin's version was at first quite similar to previous incarnations, with its main innovation the addition of some pop culture sci-fi references (cribbing <u>mostly from *Star Trek* and *Star Wars*</u>) to lend it a bit of borrowed character.

Crucially, Martin also made his version of *Trade Wars* compatible with WWIV, a newer and more powerful BBS platform that would soon become dominant. In 1988, WWIV was rewritten in C, which removed a limitation that restricted doors to no more than 64K in size. With space now for a much bigger game, Martin began a long-term revamp to make "the Trade Wars game that I wanted to play, not just a clone of what previous ones had been."[4] With the help of his new wife MaryAnn, who managed registrations and business affairs while also contributing ideas and designs to the project, Martin released *Trade Wars 2002* (or *TW2002*) in 1991—the version that would become the definitive BBS space trading game.

After launching *TW2002* from the games menu of your favorite BBS, you gave your character a name—either the same one you used on that BBS, or an alias if you wanted to play incognito—and claimed your starter ship, perhaps a Merchant Cruiser with twenty cargo holds. You could then begin exploring a galaxy of hundreds or thousands of interconnected, numbered sectors (the exact count, along with many other details, could be customized by each sysop). The game's core loop remained virtually unchanged from the days of *Star Trader*: dock at ports to buy and sell goods, warp between star systems, and try to turn your cargo into profit.

One of Martin's changes was to name the game's NPC villains the Ferrengi, at the time rumored to be the new big baddies in the upcoming *Star Trek: The Next Generation*. Though the new TV villains would prove underwhelming and evolve into comic relief, they remained the bad guys in Martin's game through decades of updates, grandfathered into ferociousness and a now noncanonical spelling (the show would standardize on Ferengi, with one *r*).

```
Sector   : 885 in uncharted space (unexplored).
Ferrengi: Sheccag Mioqtiap, with 8,000 ftrs,
             in Ovaoq Fadavej (Ferrengi Battle Cruiser)
Warps to Sector(s):  (383) - (707)

Command [TL=00:27:51]:[885] (?=Help)? : 383
<Move>
Warping to Sector 383

Sector   : 383 in Tarterus (unexplored).
Ports    : Huygens, Class 2 (BSB)
Traders  : Civilian Ender, w/ 30 ftrs,
             in Sweet Justice (Impetuoso Merchant Cruiser)
Warps to Sector(s):  885 - (249) - (273) - (279) - (620)

Command [TL=00:27:43]:[383] (?=Help)? : P
<A> Attack this Port
<T> Trade at this Port
<Q> Quit, nevermind

Enter your choice [T] ? T
<Port>

Docking...
One turn deducted, 73 turns left.
```

Trade Wars 2002 uses many different colors of text to make its complex blocks of information easy to parse. This has been simulated in these transcripts in a limited way via different font styles.

Limited turn counts were a ubiquitous mechanic in door games, to prevent overzealous players hogging a phone line indefinitely. Some sysops also enforced a real-world time limit, as the TL (time left) clock counting down above demonstrates.

```
Commerce report for  Huygens: 09:55:10 PM Thu Apr 17, 2033

-=-=-           Docking Log          -=-=-
No current ship docking log on file.
For finding this neglected port you receive 50 experience
point(s).
You have been promoted to Staff Sergeant!

Items        Status  Trading % of max OnBoard
----         -----  -------------------
Fuel Ore     Buying    1710    100%      20
Organics     Selling   1110    100%       0
Equipment    Buying     830    100%       0
```

TW2002 used the same three core goods as the original *Trade Wars*: Ore, Organics, and Equipment. It also used a bartering mechanic that had changed little since the 1970s *Star Trader*:

```
You have 220 credits and 0 empty cargo holds.

We are buying up to 1710. You have 20 in your holds.
```

```
How many holds of Fuel Ore do you want to sell [20]? 20
Agreed, 20 units.

We'll buy them for 681 credits.
Your offer [681] ? 720

We'll buy them for 687 credits.
Your offer [687] ? 690
If only more honest traders would port here, we'll take
them though.
For your good trading you receive 1 experience point(s).

You have 910 credits and 20 empty cargo holds.
```

In your first few days of play, a key challenge would be to find the StarDock, a major hub with useful services including stores, a shipyard, and sources of missions and interactions with other players. The StarDock was a key addition to Martin's version of the game that went a long way toward making its galaxy feel more like a dynamic, living place, filled with things to do such as shopping, gambling, or visiting a theater to watch ASCII sci-fi parody "movies" with titles like *Vulcan Thunder*.

But the StarDock also provided a major community hub, a key difference from earlier, less social space trading games. At the StarDock's tavern you can pay credits to post a public message that everyone will see, add to the graffiti scrawled on the bathroom wall, or pay a "grimy Trader" in the back room to learn information about other players, such as what sector their ship was last seen in. The grimy Trader could share a large selection of hints and useful info about the game state, provided you could think of the right things to ask him (and had credits to pay).

```
"Why hello der matey! Have a sit and buy me an ale, eh?"

You sit down and talk to the old Trader.
(Enter the subject you want to know about, blank to exit)
>FEDERATION
"I can tell you something about FEDERATION, but its gonna
cost ya!"
"Would ye pay me 2,500 credits for it?" YES
"Tryin to cheat me eh? You bum! You ain't got the dough!"
```

The StarDock also holds secrets. Pressing a key not listed on the menu of available commands lets your character explore seedier, lesser-known parts of the station. A particular unlisted key leads to a locked door and a secret password that, once learned—from the grimy Trader, perhaps, or another player—admits you to the Underground, where nefarious players can buy illicit goods and coordinate against law-abiding Federation forces.

As you build up enough money to buy a better ship and properly equip it, a key challenge becomes finding a secure location to build a base. Planets could be created in any unoccupied sector by purchasing a Genesis Torpedo (a reference to 80s classic *Star Trek II: The Wrath of Khan*), and colonists could

1991

be ferried from Terra in Sector 1 to the new planet to manufacture trade goods. Planets could be defended with space mines or a Planetary Citadel, which could be built up with greater and greater defenses until, after weeks of daily turns, it became near-impregnable. An ideal sector for a home planet would be a dead end, off the well-traveled routes around the StarDock or other key sectors, ideally in a lonely part of the map less likely to be stumbled upon by accident. Each game would require finding such a spot anew, since every BBS would have a different map configuration, randomly generated by the sysop with a program called `BIGBANG.EXE` before their version of the game went live.

Since combat could not be real-time, successfully attacking another player or their well-guarded base was mainly a matter of which side had the best equipment. While death was never permanent, logging on to find yourself floating in an escape pod—your expensive ship blown to dust—might form the basis of a long-term grudge that could take days or weeks of turns to repay.

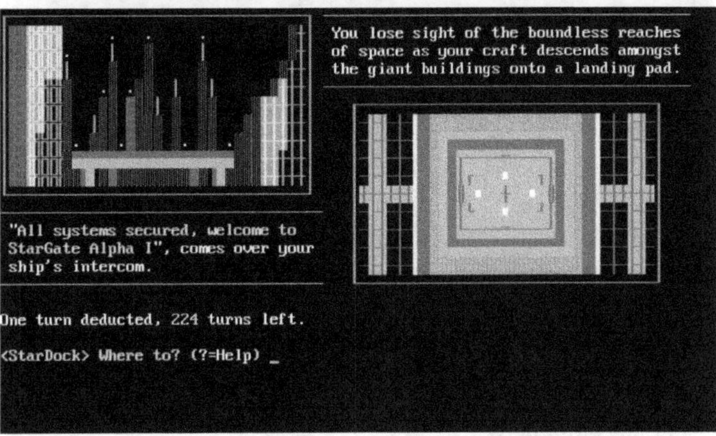

Screenshots from _Trade Wars 2002_, illustrated with 16-color ANSI graphics made from extended text characters.

```
Your fighters: 5,208 vs. theirs: 7,241
Choose your action, Captain : (F)lee, (A)ttack,
(S)urrender, (I)nfo? F
  Constellation Attack!
Combat computer reports damages of 738 battle points!


You rush to an escape pod and abandon ship...
Your Scout Marauder has been destroyed!

Your trusty Escape Pod is functioning normally.
For getting blown up you LOSE 99 experience point(s).
Sector 130 will now be avoided in future navigation
calculations.
```

Rivalries could be settled by putting a bounty on another player, or alliances enhanced by banding together with friends in a Corporation, which allowed for sharing goods and resources as well as access to better ships. The Martins were canny enough to realize this feature was less about promoting player cooperation than creating more chaos:

The whole point of the TW200x design was the underlying concept that "No one wins in a war." When it comes down to fighting, both sides lose. It becomes a matter of who loses the most. The whole corporate design was there to stir the pot and cause more conflict amongst players, not to create safety in numbers.[4]

Deeper than most door games, *Trade Wars* has enough commands, ship types, upgrades, and strategies to support a wide range of play styles, and there are often multiple possible solutions to any emergent problem. For self-defense you might get a cloaking device to hide your ship, leave it in an out-of-the-way sector, or surround it with mines and booby traps when you log off. You might earn credits by finding a good set of "trading pair" ports to shuttle goods between, by gambling, by fulfilling bounties on NPCs or other players, or by social engineering your way into a Corporation before robbing them blind. Sysops were given back-end tools to customize dozens of details of a particular game's configuration—from a player's starting loadout, to the number of sectors in the galaxy, to the specs of available ships, to how aggressive the Ferrengi would be (or whether they were even called Ferrengi)—enabling each BBS to advertise their own unique flavor of the game. Evil-aligned characters could rob ports; good-aligned characters could gain access to the Imperial Starship, a monstrously powerful cruiser capable of bombarding the hell out of evildoers. Every strategy had a counterstrategy and each play style had its strengths and weaknesses. Thanks to this depth, *TW2002* spread fast, and within a year it was running on a huge percentage of BBSes. While exact data is impossible to come by, since records were spread out over tens of thousands of individual systems, there may have been over a million regular players at the game's peak, with more than thirty-five thousand sysops having paid to register the game for their dozens or hundreds of users. Countless more pirated copies were doubtless running on less scrupulous boards.

The Martins' *Trade Wars* didn't change much as time went on, beyond an irregular progression of bug fixes. John Pritchett joined the team in 1994 to work on bugs and updates, eventually taking over development of a version 3 that supported simultaneous multiplayer; there were fewer BBSes by then, and most survivors were larger operations with multiple phone lines. But BBS games were entering a rapid decline as more and more users upgraded to services that connected them to the global internet—increasingly over broadband, not dial-up, which opened a new world of multiplayer gaming filled with graphics and low-latency action. By the end of the decade, Gary Martin had decided there was no point trying to compete:

> You have to remember, this was back in a period where one developer could put out a complete game by himself. It didn't take an art

---

The Anterra Network (215)675-3851 Hatboro, Pennsylvania since 03/90. Sysop: Steve Ferguson. Using WildCat 3.9 with 5 lines on MS-DOS with 10800 MB storage. US Robotics at 16.8 bps. $5 Monthly fee. Philadelphia area's largest BBS. Over 53,000 files and 700 message conferences from FidoNet, WildNet, ThrobNet, AdultNet, ElNet, and RimeNet. The best game of Trade Wars in the 215 area code.

BBS ad using *Trade Wars* as a selling point, from *Boardwatch* magazine (Feb 1995). Games, files (especially adult files), number of phone lines, and modem speed were all common selling points.

department, musicians, or celebrity voice actors to create a title. So in a world where all of these text BBS games are thriving, suddenly here comes a title like _Wing Commander_. Celebrity voice actors, a HUGE art department, coding department, music department, etc. The bar to create a competitive game was suddenly far too high to reach as an individual or even a small development company. Since I didn't want to create an inferior game in that world, I chose to stop working on it entirely.[4]

In 2000 Pritchett bought the _Trade Wars_ brand and code base from the Martins and continued maintaining and improving the game, creating versions that could be hosted over the internet and adding other small improvements. But the game was a harder sell in an always-online world. "It was the anticipation of the game that made it so addictive," Pritchett later reflected.[6] The tension of hearing a busy signal and wondering if someone else was smashing up your base; the camaraderie of a small community with usernames you knew from other local boards and other local games; the feeling of handing off the universe from one player to the next, and knowing each time you connected that you were the only person inside it; the surety that each player had the same fixed turn count, no matter how much or how little free time they had in real life—these experiences were hard to recapture on the web, superior though most everyone agreed it to be. Something ineffable had, nonetheless, been lost.

Door games, like play-by-mail **1989**, MOOs **1990**, and others built around tentative ideas of what online communities might be, suffered a fate far worse than technological obsolescence when the very structure of community changed around them. Today they've been almost forgotten—almost. In the 2020s, there are still die-hard fan communities running their own _TW2002_ servers and playing their daily turns: booby-trapping ships with Corbomite Transducers as a nasty surprise for overnight attackers, saving up for an Interdictor Cruiser or a Corellian Battleship, and posting gloating notes in the tavern for friends and foes to see the next time they log in.

Trade Wars wasn't trying to change the world. It didn't boast a serious story or an innovative parser, and it was more focused on perfecting what had come before than innovating anything new. But it was a lot of fun. It would be influential on designers of new generations of complex space games like _EVE Online_ [CCP Games 2003] or the _X Series_ [Egosoft 1999–]. The team behind _Star Citizen_ [Cloud Imperium Games], which raised hundreds of millions of dollars through crowdfunding in the 2010s, cited _TW2002_ as one of their inspirations; so did the designers of early space MMO _Earth & Beyond_ [Westwood Studios 2002]. In 2009, _PC World_ named the Martins' game one of the ten best of all time for the platform. It was nice of them to remember the amateur text game that had drawn countless teens away from their CD-ROM drives—even if only for a while.

Wing Commander III: Heart of the Tiger, starring celebrities like Mark Hamill, Malcolm McDowell, and John Rhys-Davies, was released by Origin on CD-ROM in 1994.

JOHN PRITCHETT ON THE TRADE WARS DIASPORA

When _Trade Wars_ transitioned from single-line BBSes to the open Internet, the community split into two main groups. There were large, competitive public sites where gameplay became very automated, turning the game into a sort of "botwars," and then there were small local games hosted either online by invitation or on a LAN for small groups.

To me, that is the only way to play the game today, among a group of friends where a gameop can establish rules and players can be trusted to abide by those rules, similar to a tabletop game like _Dungeons and Dragons_. And like a game of _D&D_, the experience often centers on a particular gameop's creation of a particular game world, as well as gameplay goals, victory conditions, etc. Such games continue to run today.[7]

References

1 Cadenhead, Rogers. n.d. "TradeWars 2 by Chris Sherrick and John Morris." Workbench. workbench. cadenhead.org/news/3165/tradewars-2-chris-sherrick-and-john-morris | a Apr 18, 2021

2 Games of Fame (blog). 2013. "WAR, DECWAR and MegaWars." Apr 28, 2013. gamesoffame.wordpress.com/ war-decwar-and-megawars | a Apr 18, 2021

3 Martin, Gary. 1997. "Interview With A Trader." Interview by Rick Mead. Gypsy's War Room. wiki.classictw. com/index.php/Interview_with_Gary_Martin_by_Rick_Mead | a Apr 18, 2021

4 Martin, Gary. 2019. "Gary Martin, creator of 'TradeWars 2002'." Interview by Josh Renaud. *Break Into Chat* (blog). July 19, 2019. breakintochat.com/blog/2019/07/19/gary-martin-creator-tradewars-2002 | a Apr 18, 2021

5 Mead, Rick. n.d. "Gypsy's Big Dummy's Guide to TradeWars." wiki.classictw.com/index. php?title=Gypsy%27s_Big_Dummy%27s_Guide_to_TradeWars_Text | a Apr 18, 2021

6 Pritchett, John. 2014. "BBS Door History / John Pritchett Interview." Interview by BuckGB. *Game Banshee* (blog). www.gamebanshee.com/interviews/114084-bbs-door-history-john-pritchett-interview.html | a Apr 18, 2021

7 Pritchett, John. 2022. Email with author. Sep 5, 2022.

8 Pritchett, John. n.d. "TradeWars Museum." wiki.classictw.com/index.php/Main_Page | a Apr 18, 2021

9 Psycho. 1993. "TradeWars 2002 Bible v1.1." wiki.classictw.com/index.php/TradeWars_2002_Bible_v1.1 | a Apr 18, 2021

10 Scott, Jason, director. 2005. *BBS: The Documentary*. Bovine Ignition Systems. 5 hr., 30 min.

11 "Star Trader Tribute Page." 2011. langesite.com. www.langesite.com/startrader | s Aug 7, 2011

12 "TradeWars 2002." n.d. Break Into Chat - BBS Wiki. breakintochat.com/wiki/TradeWars_2002 | a Apr 18, 2021

13 Wehner, Fred. 1997. "How To Play TradeWars And Stay Alive!" May 1997. www.electricscotland.com/games/ twadvice.txt | a Apr 18, 2021

SILVERWOLF

St. Bride's School

Style	**Parser**
Debuted	**Late 1991 or Early 1992** (retail)
Launch Platform	**ZX Spectrum**
Developer	**St. Bride's School**
Publisher	**G.I. Games**
Language	**PAW**
Launch Price	**£1.99** (cassette tape)
	£3.49 (Spectrum +3 Disk)

> **UNDERLAKE**
> Here graze green sheep on white grass under a liquid turquoise sky. The air is scented with violets…

IT WAS AN ODD ADVERT for a computer magazine. Next to a sketch of a provocatively posed, long-legged young woman in stockings—okay, maybe *that* part wasn't so odd—its copy hyped not a new piece of hardware, but a house in Ireland,

the famous school where grown-up girls are transformed into schoolgirls…. Now you can find out for yourself as you guide Trixie Trinian through the classrooms, corridors and secret places of the *strangest* school ever—to uncover

THE SECRET OF ST. BRIDE'S

"Not so much a programme more a way of life," the text below helpfully clarified. While not entirely apparent, this was an ad for an adventure game, *The Secret of St. Bride's*. Sending £5.95 to St. Bride's School, Burtonport, County Donegal, Ireland would get you a cassette tape for your Spectrum

1992

"

48K containing a text adventure written by, according to its label, "the Games Mistresses."

At the address was "a white crumbling turn-of-the-century house overlooking the tiny fishing village of Burtonport,"[24] where women could take a paid holiday that would immerse them in the life of a proper boarding school girl of an earlier time. "There were no electric lights in the place," one game journalist wrote upon visiting; "the maid who answered the door was surely not of this decade."[15] The students wore bonnets and period clothes while attending lessons on mathematics, literature, and penmanship; plastic and other modern materials were forbidden; the headmistress was a severe woman in black who enforced strict discipline—stricter, at times, than some of the students might have preferred. "Quite where computers fit into this situation is difficult to understand,"[4] another journalist wrote, and nobody could really put their finger on what the "situation" even was. Were the group "Victorian cultists"?[3] Were they live-action roleplayers? Were they con artists preying on emotionally immature women? Were they a game studio with a very unusual front? Or was there, as one embarrassed Irish reporter asked, "almost a gay element to the activities here"?[22] Answers were not then forthcoming. Few are even today.

The story of how St. Bride's School came to release not one but *eight* full-length text adventures between 1985 and 1992—most with female protagonists, all cleverly written and well-reviewed—is one of the strangest in the history of gaming. It's a complicated story where no clear heroes emerge, or even a clear cast of characters. The stories of their nearly lost game, *Silverwolf*, and its creation are both about the beguiling and dangerous power of becoming someone else. They are stories full of frustrating riddles and beautiful imagery that never quite resolve into coherent wholes. They blur the boundaries of the everyday world with fantastic intrusions. They are stories that can be hard, at times, to believe.

Oxford, 1971. Two years after the Stonewall riots, a wave of student and activist groups are loosely uniting under the mantle of the Gay Liberation Front, accelerating queer and feminist conversations about equal rights and alternatives to hegemonic patriarchy. At women's college Lady Margaret Hall, one student group bonds over a difference with most of their sisters-in-arms: they reject the crass, drug- and sex-fueled decadence of the 60s, even while admitting it "left openings for a new feminist consciousness," as one member would later write: "We welcome [rock culture] as we would welcome typhoid in the enemy's water supply. But we do not drink it ourselves."[19]

Out of this group would arise several radical separatist movements with overlapping membership, including a religious one called Lux Madriana (which worshiped a female god with rituals supposedly passed down from a "magical matriarchal community"[14] in a distant past), and an elaborately fleshed-out otherworld called Aristasia. Much like the rich fantasy worlds created by Tolkien or the Brontë sisters, Aristasia became an ever-growing obsession for its creators, with its own customs, calendar, literature, and history, to the extent that some of the worldbuilders eventually dropped out of university to attend their own unofficial Aristasian school instead. In Aristasia there were two genders, both female (assertive brunettes and demure blondes); the decadent modern world was known as the Pit; and the word for person was not "man" but "maid."

Eventually some of this group took up residence in the remote coastal house in Burtonport, which would become the stage for their next decade of inventing new realities. At first they styled themselves a community of "Rhennish" folk, the last descendants of a five-thousand-year-old matriarchal culture, and called themselves the Silver Sisterhood. But their plans to live off the land fell through, and after a few seasons it seemed a quite different group was occupying the house, now called St. Bride's School. St. Bride's billed itself as something between a real school and a holiday retreat, posting ads for weeklong terms where students would "spend 24 hours a day living in a different time, living a different life."[15] The staff and students observed a strict hierarchy, with obedient students appointed prefects to keep the others in line, and prefects reporting in turn to teachers: "Some maids like to tell others what to do," as a visitor summarized the philosophy during the Silver Sisterhood days, "and some maids like to be told what to do."[26] Both the Sisterhood and St. Bride's attracted copious media attention—which seems likely to have been deliberately sought—and from news clips it's clear at least some residents of both groups were the same people, though going by different names and speaking with changed accents. These were the first of many transformations.

The women behind the school reveled in shifting identities. At least two dozen different names were used at various points across the 80s and 90s by people associated with the school—they may have belonged to as many as fourteen distinct women, or as few as two. One of the women would become known to the gaming world as Marianne Scarlett (the name used throughout this chapter) though she was Brighe Dachcolwyn in her capacity as St. Bride's headmistress and Clare Tyrrell when she appeared on television. No matter the name, over the years the public face most often associated with the group was hers. When pressed about how many of the St. Bride's personas belonged to her, she would be noncommittal: "We like to cultivate different personalities here, you see."[16] Asked once if the names used by the women at St. Bride's were aliases, an associate replied, "Those are their real names, though not the names they were born with.... One's real name is the name you are using at the time."[24]

Years later, when Scarlett was writing a magazine column under the name Marianne Martindale, the publication's editor invited her to a staff party,

> only for a stranger to show up: "I said, 'Oh … you don't look very much like your pictures'. And this woman smiled and said, 'There are many Miss Martindales.'"[29]

A second key name—though this one without a face—is Priscilla Langridge, who seems to have been the driving force behind the St. Bride's computer games, if she in fact existed. The official story went that Langridge had been a St. Bride's student who had smuggled in a computer, which the

"On reflection," noted Tim Gilberts, who worked on a port of one of the St. Bride's games, "considering … they had to make money to support themselves … the computer [may simply have been] one of the vehicles that could also provide such an income stream."[8]

Memorable Places

Underlake

The Moths

The Tapestry Room

The Sandcastle

The Willow Cot

Gonsteth

The Henge

The Dragon's Cave

The Chalk Path

The Bone Fire

1992

skeptical headmistress came to find enthralling: "We discovered that she had this penchant for blasting things,"[24] Langridge later explained. But this story seems fairly suspect. Why would someone paying to attend a holiday escape from the modern world bring along a bulky microcomputer? Why would the headmistress who styled herself a stickler for rules and an enemy of everything modern go along with such a scheme? Some signs indicate Langridge had been not a student but one of the group's founding members back in the Lux Madriana days. The truth, as will become a common refrain in this chapter, is difficult to know.

In fact, much about Langridge's identity is far from clear. While Scarlett was happy to be photographed by journalists (always in elegant period clothing), Langridge rarely was, and the few times she made an exception she was veiled or masked. It should be noted that Priscilla is a diminutive form of a Latin name meaning "ancient" or "old-fashioned" (from the same root as "prior"), making it plausible that the name was another alias—but for whom? One theory is that there were also many Priscillas: it was a composite identity for whoever Scarlett happened to be working with at the time. Another is that Priscilla Langridge was a distinct persona of a woman from New Zealand who made public appearances with Scarlett at times, under the name Miss Raynor.

Yet another possibility is that the veiled woman had a reason to stay concealed in 1980s Ireland, where homosexuality and other lifestyles seen as deviant were still illegal. Some evidence, including hurtful gossip spread by at least one reporter,[7] suggests Langridge may have been trans. A woman interviewed during the group's Rhennish days and identified as Sister Angelina (who may or may not be the same person as Langridge) is shown only from the back or side angles because of her "spiritual role."[21] In a follow-up piece, the reporter noted that "we had a number of calls from viewers who suggested the occupant interviewed was in fact a man. [But] we can only take the person interviewed at face value."[22]

If we do the same and also assume Langridge was one particular person, not a composite, then the portrait of her that emerges from the available facts is a consistent one. She was a writer and illustrator with "an enviable knowledge of the more obscure comic strips,"[24] and regardless of how she had inveigled computers into St. Bride's, she looked upon them "as another medium, like books or comics, to be exploited as a rich experience."[15] Both computers and comics, she wrote, were interesting as "unusual media for presenting fantasies." Langridge also praised the "economy" of the simple parsers of early text games. "I like the two-word input," she once told a reporter, "the over-use of 'get' and 'drop'. It's useful to have a very simple command structure which can be used inventively. People make a fetish of over-sophistication."[24] Langridge talked enthusiastically about the St. Bride's games and once wrote a letter to a magazine to correct some mistaken points in a review.[12] Since Scarlett rarely spoke about the specifics of the games themselves, it seems a reasonable assumption that Langridge was the driving force behind their creation.

The many quotes from journalists speak to the success of the school's
first game, *The Secret of St. Bride's* [1985], sold through direct mail via gaming
magazines. The cultivated air of mystery around the game's creation and
the school itself proved an intriguing angle for editors, and most reviewers
agreed the game was surprisingly good. In it, the player takes the role of a
new student at St. Bride's who finds herself transported from the modern
world back to the 1920s. With the help of her schoolmates she must embark
on an adventure to find a way to return to her own time.

Whether the game had been designed to generate publicity for the school
or vice versa, it was working: copies sold, and St. Bride's immediately set
to work making more. One of these was a title called *Silverwolf*, which was
to be released alongside an original comic by Langridge. It was based on
a serialized fantasy story appearing in a lesbian periodical called *Artemis*,
which the St. Bride's crew were also distributing under yet different aliases.
The stories were credited to "Laeretta Krenne-Genovene with illustrations
by Michele Dennis"; one or both of these people may, or may not, have been
Langridge. The stories tapped into the deep well of Aristasian mythology,
and the recap at the start of one episode gives a sense of their flavor:

> Modern English schoolgirl Petra Stone is a reincarnation of the
> matriarchal warrior princess Mayanna. The princess and the schoolgirl
> exist as two independent personalities. She has been taken back into
> ancient matriarchal Britain by an Amazon group: Rahiyana, the leader;
> Thunder, a seven-foot powerhouse; Whirlwind, the teen tornado and
> a shape-shifting imp called Uisce. But the evil patriarchal Lord Fear is
> determined to kill Petra and has sent in pursuit of the group a powerful
> and mysterious band known only as the Swarm.[11]

A reviewer for another lesbian zine, *WomanSpirit*, praised the story's
writing and its fully feminine mythology, finding in its mythical storytelling
a rich parable for the eternal fight against "the incipient ideology of
patriarchy"; she noted that the villain's name, Fear, is the Celtic word for
"man."[10] She praised the layers of identity in the stories, such as in the
central character, "actually three characters in one": schoolgirl Petra,
princess Mayanna, and alter ego Silverwolf, whom Petra/Mayanna can
transform into to become an avenging protector. As one of the *Silverwolf*
stories described her:

> Her hair is silver. Her face is a silver mask of rage and beauty. She strains
> furiously against her chains. First one gives way, and then the other. Her
> hand flashes to her side to draw an imaginary sword, and it is no longer
> imaginary.... Seven brothers converge on her from all sides. She leaps
> forward, cutting off the head of the first. Before the head hits the ground,
> the other six are dead.
>
> For a moment she stands poised, like a wild animal preparing to spring.
> Her words are brief.
>
> "Commend your souls, if butchers such as ye have gods. For now ye face
> the wrath of Silverwolf."[11]

In the text adventure based on the stories, you play as Petra's four
Amazon companions, switching between them on a quest to help the
reincarnated princess gain the power to become Silverwolf. The game is

You Are Carrying...

» green wool

» a honeycomb

» a rosewood mazer

» a sprig of dried honesty
  pods

» a sprig of mistletoe

» a bone knife

» an amber ring

split into two parts that can be played in either order (they may originally have come on two sides of the same cassette tape). In one part you play as Rahiyana and Whirlwind, trying to escort Petra to the Holy Mountain where she can complete the ritual to transform into Silverwolf, and in the other you play Thunder and Uisce, trying to retrieve the enchanted sword that Silverwolf will wield. Each of the four Amazon women has their own special power, and you must switch between them using commands like `BECOME WHIRLWIND` to complete the game. Transformation is in fact a recurring motif: Uisce can turn into any creature she sees with the command `TURN INTO`, and this includes other people—in some sequences you'll need to `BECOME UISCE` and then `TURN INTO THUNDER` to complete a puzzle. To activate Rahiyana's archery skills, the player needs to summon the power of the goddess Diana into her body by typing the phrase `HAYA DYANA`. The game, like its creators, is obsessed with becoming other people, or allowing them to become you.

Silverwolf's writing is lyrical, effectively evoking a mythic age. In the first scenes of part one, you plunge into a lake only to discover a fantastical kingdom beneath the waves. The puzzles in this world follow a fairy-tale dream logic:

THE TREE

In the centre stands a tree of ice with roots stretching down to the frozen lands below the earth. Silver bees buzz to and fro, gathering nectar from the snowy blossoms.

NEXT `EXAMINE TREE`
From the branches hangs a glass hive.

NEXT `EXAMINE HIVE`
I see a tiny spring door.

NEXT `OPEN DOOR`
I try, but my fingers are frozen.

Spoilers for various puzzles in Silverwolf.

To open the frozen door and claim the honeycomb inside, you'll need to find an old woman to spin you a pair of mittens out of wool from undersea sheep. Evocative inventory items abound—a rosewood mazer brimming with silver moonshine, a ring of carved amber, a bone knife. Many puzzles take the form of magical rituals: you'll find yourself typing commands like `CHANT PAEAN OF THAME`, or disturbing a room filled with fluttering moths until they part to reveal a secret niche, or ringing bells strewn through the branches of dead trees:

As the silver bells peal out, the clouds over the sun splinter into a host of silvery-white birds. The sky explodes into an unbearable brilliance as they drop shimmering towards the ground. The sight strikes terror into the light-hating Swarm, who, as one, shriek and cower and flee.

1992

In one puzzle sequence, you must make use of Uisce's shape-shifting to reach a series of progressively more unlikely areas. Spotting a bullfrog in the rushes of a lake, you can transform into it to leap to a lily pad. From the lily pad you can see a dragonfly, which you can in turn become to fly to a hidden beach. On the beach is a sandcastle, and the dragonfly is small enough to see this is a fortress home for a band of fairies. Becoming a fairy lets you enter the castle and recover a buried key. The game can be frustrating—there are riddles which only familiarity with the obscure lore will help you solve, and the simple parser has trouble with many commands—but it's a memorable journey that ends with Petra merging her three identities to become, at last, "the living avatar of Silverwolf."

End spoilers.

While the release of *Silverwolf* was pushed back, perhaps waiting on completion of the comic that was meant to accompany it, St. Bride's put out other games that continued selling and reviewing well. By the end of 1985 they'd signed a distribution deal with a publisher, and for a while new titles kept coming on a regular basis. *The Very Big Cave Adventure* [1986] was a well-received parody of *Adventure* starring the snarky Trixie from *The Secret of St. Bride's*. "I've done Caves before, so I've got the job of showing new adventurers around," she writes on the game's opening screen. "Let's have a look at you. Healthy enough, I suppose. Do with a bit more exercise. Still, you'll soon get that." The heroine of *The Snow Queen* [1986], adapted from the Hans Christian Anderson story, is "wilfully independent—to the extent that she sometimes takes control of the game away from the player."[29] She "allows you to help her,"[18] as one reviewer put it. The games were popular enough that a regular newsletter for fans was planned: the *St. Bride's Swashbuckler*. "If you like St. Bride's you'll love the *Swashbuckler*," an ad explained; "and if you hate St. Bride's it'll give you ammunition for months."[30]

see **1976**

As with their other endeavors, the school's turn into an unlikely adventure game powerhouse was irresistible media bait. Scarlett and Langridge attended a few British game industry trade shows in the late 80s, dressed in prim crinolines with Langridge always behind her veil. ("It would be fair to say that they were conspicuous," one observer wrote.[4]) The school would delight in inviting reporters up to rural Ireland for tours of the Burtonport house, playing gramophone records for them by flickering candlelight and acting coy about the authorship of their games, which were generally credited simply to St. Bride's on their title screens. "Questions remain unanswered," another frustrated reporter wrote. "The programming room remains unshown, and a whole area of the house, the old servants quarters joining the school by just one door, stays a mystery"[15]—much like the *Secret of St. Bride's* game had featured a locked door that was forbidden to pass through. Scarlett liked to regale visitors with stories of the building's odd past: in the 1970s it had been home to a commune called Atlantis, whose members practiced primal scream therapy, and in the 1920s was a safe house for IRA gunmen, who would disguise themselves as women to escape notice. The house, it would seem, had always been a place of transformations.

Reporters had little success extracting any details about the authorship of the St. Bride's games. One teased out the names "Jenny Falconer" and "Maureen" as some of the co-authors, but these names seem never to have been mentioned again; "some of the more shadowy contributors prefer not to be named," he concluded feebly.[4] It's possible Langridge or someone else wrote all the St. Bride's games on their own; it's also possible some, or all, were collaborations.

For a while the school seemed to have aspirations to become a serious player in the UK games scene. "The production of games software is a very undeveloped field in Ireland,"[5] Scarlett wrote in 1985, adding, "We intend to strike ahead and fill that gap." Shortly thereafter she claimed, "Our aim is to build St Bride's into one of the foremost software houses in the British Isles."[6] But the women were getting into text games as everyone else was getting out of them. They tried to capitalize on the rise of graphics in another head-scratching contradiction with their prim Victorian personas: at the end of 1987, they released a *Jack the Ripper* game with low-res but gory illustrations of murdered women, which became so controversial it spurred the British Board of Film Classification to give it an 18 certificate, the first ever for a video game. The school's then-publisher would later claim this had been engineered from the start as a publicity stunt.

But the group increasingly found itself snared in financial and legal troubles. Rent became overdue on the Burtonport house, and a coder hired to convert the still-unreleased *Silverwolf* to the Commodore 64 platform was never paid. In 1990 a woman named Mari De Colwyn (likely Scarlett) was convicted of "actual bodily harm" for caning an adult St. Bride's student. ("She had done a very naughty thing," the former headmistress offered by way of explanation.[25]) The ladies eventually abandoned the house. Its owners, seeking their unpaid rent, broke in one night and leaked a story to the media that the place had been filled with "material produced by neo-Nazi organizations and the sado-masochistic sex industry,"[16] as well as correspondence with far-right organizations like Britain's virulently racist National Front.

Whether these claims were valid or a vengeful smear is another open question. A spokesperson for the group calling herself Laetitia Linden Dorvf (likely also Scarlett) did not deny the materials were present but rejected any ideological affiliation, saying only that the school received mail from groups around the world: "We do not endorse any of them as they are all collaborating with the degeneration of the late 20th century."[16] One historian of the school finds the claim credible, arguing, "It would have been very easy for an organisation like St Bride's to get on some very dodgy mailing lists in the 80s and 90s."[29] On the other hand, uncomfortable echoes of far-right thinking had been present in the St. Bride's ethos from the start, from a focus on discipline and a "proper place" for everyone to a yearning for an earlier, purer time. Some of these notions may have been inspired in part by readings in the Oxford days of anti-modernist philosopher René Guénon, whose ideas would later also resonate for alt-right figures like Richard Spencer and Steve Bannon. Regardless, the school's reputation had forever changed from strange to sinister, and tabloids would repeatedly characterize its members as Nazis and lesbian sex fiends through the rest of the 90s.

QUILLED

Silverwolf was written with a toolkit called PAW, the Professional Adventure Writer, a successor to popular game-making program The Quill. Both were part of a chain of efforts by fans (including an influential article by coder Ken Reed in the August 1980 issue of *Practical Computing*) to recreate the efficient format of the Adventure International **1978** games, much as Inform would later arise from reverse engineering Infocom's virtual machine **1993**. Created by tiny UK company Gilsoft, PAW and The Quill let users create text adventures purely by navigating menus to define locations, objects, and interactions. The results were less flexible than what could be achieved with a traditional programming language, but significantly easier to author.

The Quill and PAW opened up text adventure creation to anyone with basic computer skills, which led to an explosion of British adventure games: at one point more than half of all text games sold in the country were Quilled. While the software cost money to buy, Gilsoft did not charge authors a licensing fee to release games created with it, a crucial part of its success and popularity.

Scarlett would continue to shape-shift through other increasingly improbable personas—the remainder of her life story involves royal astronomer Sir Patrick Moore, marriage to a Hollywood director, and further press-baiting tabloid scandals.

But what of Priscilla Langridge? She mostly vanished after the St. Bride's era—she seems to have stayed with Scarlett for at least a few more years, but then the trail of the person, or at least the persona, goes cold. *Silverwolf,* while probably finished sometime in late 1987 or early 1988, would not debut until 1992, when a small distributor bought the rerelease rights to the St. Bride's games and dumped them on the market at a cut-rate price, along with *Silverwolf* and two other unreleased titles. The game received only a handful of reviews, and while they were all positive—one called it an "absolute gem of a game"[31]—the world had moved on from text adventures. Many gamers already thought them as old-fashioned as lace bonnets or gramophone records.

"The Ladies of St. Brides are difficult to understand," a journalist wrote in 1987. "How much is hype is difficult to assess.... They say [their game] *Jack the Ripper* is serious but are they ever serious about anything?"[4] The group's former publisher suspects their primary motive was always financial: "I think, basically, St Bride's were in business: they were doing it on a commercial basis, however un-commercial they may have looked!"[29] But some of the school's pupils in later years would come to characterize the group as dangerously earnest, with one describing it as a cult. "There was something sinister at the heart of it," she wrote. "The founder was a remarkable person but was leading a fantasy life—we were living in someone else's fantasy."[1] While much about the Games Mistresses would shift across their decades of fronts and personas, disconnection from the everyday world was a constant theme. "We really, truly are not living in the same place as you,"[27] one once wrote; "I don't like the modern world, and I don't live in it,"[24] Scarlett has said. "We don't concern ourselves with the present at all. We live in a little world inside our house ... it's a world apart, really, where we are."[13]

The St. Bride's adventures are hard to evaluate apart from their complicated legacy. They are feminist games in many ways, yet grounded in nineteenth century ideals most feminists would find regressive. They are perhaps some of the earliest queer games, but are tarnished by alleged associations with repulsive ideologies. They are games about becoming someone else, even when that transformation is dangerous or destructive. They are beautiful, frustrating, and haunting. "My name is Silverwolf," began one of the serialized stories from *Artemis.* "My power is like a song within me.... I am more than human. My heart is a star."[11]

Illustration and hand-lettered cover for *Artemis #5*, credited to Michele Dennis.

When a visiting reporter once asked Langridge for the real secret of St. Bride's, she paused to think. "I suppose," she finally answered, "to rub out the lines between fantasy and real life."[24] Perhaps, from this perspective, fascination with gaming's power to make imagined worlds feel real, at least for a while, becomes less difficult to understand.

References

1   Bradford Telegraph & Argus. 1999. "How I Was Drawn to Life in a Cult." Feb 16, 1999. www.thetelegraphandargus.co.uk/news/8068126.how-i-was-drawn-to-life-in-a-cult | a May 1, 2021

2   Brawls, Terry. 1992. "Silverwolf" (Review). *Red Herring* #3, Feb 1992.

3   Briscoe, Cliff. 2019. "How Victorian Cultists in Rural Donegal Created the World's First 18 Rated Video Game." *Skag Magazine* (blog). Jul 21, 2019. www.skagmagazine.com/articles/victorian-cultists-rural-donegal | a May 1, 2021

4   Cohen, Amon. 1987. "Ding Dong Belles." *Your Computer*, Dec 1987.

5   Computer & Video Games. 1985a. "Games News." August 1985.

6   Computer & Video Games. 1985b. "News." Dec 1985.

7   Farrell, Nicholas. 1993. "Oxford Educators: Miss Partridge and Miss Langridge Run Meetings for Students Downstairs, Discipline Sessions for Paying Punters Upstairs." *Sunday Telegraph*, Feb 7, 1993. worldofspectrum.org/interviews2/stbrides-st930207.txt | s Jan 19, 2012

8   Gilberts, Tim. 2022. Email to author. Sep 1, 2022.

9   Gremlin. 1986. "Love Is Never Having to Say…" *Sinclair User* #47, Feb 1986.

10 James, Helen. 1983. "Silverwolf" (Review). *WomanSpirit* 10 (38), Winter Solstice 1983.

11 Krenne-Genovene, Laeretta. 1984a. "Silverwolf." *Artemis: For Women Who Love Women* #5/#6, 1984.

12 Langridge, Priscilla. 1986. "Mailbag." Computer & Video Games, May 1986.

13 The Late Late Show. 1988. "Victorian Values Reign In Donegal." With Gay Byrne. Mar 25, 1988. Television. www.rte.ie//archives/2018/0322/949314-donegal-victorian-romantics | a May 1, 2021

14 "Madrian Deanic Resources." n.d. madriandeanicresources.wordpress.com | a May 1, 2021

15 Minson, John. 1986. "Games Lessons." *CRASH* #26, Mar 1986.

16 Pendry, Richard, and Helena de Bertodano. 1993. "Neo-Nazi Leaflets Found in Gracious Ladies' Academy Where Caning Was on the Curriculum." *Sunday Telegraph*, Jan 3, 1993. worldofspectrum.org/interviews2/stbrides-st930103.txt | s Jan 19, 2012

17 Pitchford, Gareth. 2021. "The Secret Games of St. Bride's." *Twilight Inventory* (blog). Mar 28, 2021. 8bitag.com/info/stbrides.html | a May 1, 2021

18 Price, Richard. 1985. "In The Deep Midwinter." *Sinclair User* #44, Nov 1985.

19 The Provisional Matriarchal League. 1983. "The REAL Radicals." *Artemis: For Women Who Love Women* #1, 1983.

20 Rosetti, Miss Anthea. n.d. "A History of Aristasia-in-Telluria." aristasia.net. www.aristasia.net/history.html | s July 13, 2013

21 RTÉ News. 1982. "Maids of the Silver Sisterhood." Nov 19, 1982. Television. www.rte.ie/archives/2017/1116/920656-the-silver-sisterhood-of-burtonport | a May 1, 2021

22 RTÉ News. 1984. "School For Young Ladies." May 4, 1984. Television. www.rte.ie/archives/2019/0319/1037244-saint-brides-school-donegal | a May 1, 2021

23 Sheehan, Terri. 2003. "Silverwolf (Solution)." CASA. Dec 4, 2003. www.solutionarchive.com/file/id%2C7263 | a May 1, 2021

24 Sinclair User. 1985. "Back to School: The Secret of St Bride's." #45, Dec 1985.

25 This Is Local London. 1998. "Miss Kinky Denies Right Wing Smear," Mar 28, 1998. www.thisislocallondon.co.uk/archive/1998/03/28/Local+London+Archive/6513044.MISS_KINKY_DENIES_RIGHT_WING_SMEAR_ | s Jun 28, 2011

26 Turner, Buckwheat. 1984. "The Silver Sisterhood." *WomanSpirit* 10 (39), Spring Equinox 1984.

27 Turner, Roy. n.d. "Passport to Aristasia." *Domina* #5.

28 "Who Is Miss Marianne Martindale?" 2009. The Journey of a Lifetime: Aristasia. Feb 23, 2009. www.aristasia.co.uk/missmartindale.html | s Feb 23, 2009

29 Williams, Owen. 2014. "St Bride's School." *Owen Williams* (blog). Feb 16, 2014. flexiblehead.blog/2014/02/16/st-brides-school | a May 1, 2021

30 Your Sinclair. 1986. "St. Bride's Chronicle." #4, April 1986.

31 Your Sinclair. 1992. "Silverwolf" (Review). August 1992.

1992

CURSES

Graham Nelson

Style **Parser**
Debuted **May 9, 1993** (Usenet)
Launch Platform **Z-machine v5**
Language **Inform**

> " It's become a matter of pride now not to give up. That tourist map of Paris must be up here somewhere in all this clutter, even if it has been five years since your last trip. And it's your own fault. It looks as if your great-grandfather was the last person to tidy up these lofts…

BY 1993, IT WOULD HAVE BEEN A SAFE BET to say the text adventure was dead. That year saw the last release of a traditional parser game by a mainstream publisher: Legend Entertainment's *Gateway II: Homeworld*, a sequel only greenlit because the 1992 original had sold unexpectedly well. But the unlikely success was not repeated. The bestselling games of the year would be CD-ROM extravaganzas like *Myst* [Cyan 1993] and *The 7th Guest* [Virgin Interactive Entertainment 1993], loaded with animations, music, voice acting, and video. Infocom—once the king of interactive fiction (see **1984**)—was out of business, its lauded text games now in the remainder bin (if they could still be found at all). It did not seem likely the genre they helped popularize would ever come back.

Some fans had tried to take up the mantle themselves. But game-making tools, even for text games, were still awkward to use, lacking in power, or expensive. Programs like AGT (Adventure Game Toolkit), PAW (Professional Adventure Writer), or TADS (Text Adventure Development System) were either commercial products or shareware that required paid

1993

Major Releases

» **Release 7**, May 9, 1993. Inform v549. First public release, alongside original release of Inform.

» **Release 8**, Jun 3, 1993. Released alongside Inform 2. "Much enhanced, and slightly larger... grown from 115K to 123K in length."

» **Release 9**, Nov 11, 1993. Released alongside Inform 3. "The Director's Cut, bigger and better... 25K of new material... The game is now the maximum possible 128K long and, I hope, finished."

» **Release 10**, Jan 24, 1994. Inform v1171. Released alongside Inform 4. "44 minor improvements... no substantial new material."

» **Release 12**, Z-machine v5, Jun 4, 1994. Inform v1258 / Interpreter 3 Version Z. Released alongside Inform 5.

» **Release 14**, May 22, 1995. Rewritten in Inform 5; several hundred fixes and improvements; "about 10% more text."

» **Release 16**, Oct 24, 1995. Inform v1600 Library 5/12. "Fixes a few minor bugs and one major one."

registrations to unlock their advanced features, and even the full versions had trouble matching the capabilities of the best 80s text games, which had been developed with proprietary engines considered trade secrets. Finding and sharing amateur games was also difficult before the web, with fan communities split between local bulletin boards and standalone services like CompuServe, GEnie, or Prodigy. Some amateurs struggled through these hoops for the joy of making and sharing new games (see **The 1990s**), but most interactive fiction fans at the time were going through a period of mourning.

Usenet newsgroups were becoming popular service-agnostic hubs for discussion, and by 1993 IF refugees had taken over a pair of them: rec.arts.int-fiction and rec.games.int-fiction. Like many text game communities of the time, they were mostly looking backward. The first week of May that year saw posts in the IF newsgroups on the best and worst Infocom endings, hint requests for *Zork* **1977** and *Planetfall* [Infocom 1983], a thread about the Infocom spin-off novels, a comparison of Sierra's graphical games to Infocom's text games, and discussion of a bug in one of the company's last titles, *Sherlock* [1988]. But on May 9, someone named Graham Nelson interrupted the nostalgia to post something rather extraordinary:

> Infocom game story files are as near to a universal format as we have for interactive fiction games, but until now it has been very difficult to construct them, and I am not aware that anyone has previously created them outside of Infocom itself.
>
> I have written such a compiler, called "Inform", the ANSI C source of which is public domain. It is not a marvellously well-written program, but it does work, and it is documented.... I have no objection to anyone using its output for anything they wish.[9]

The modest announcement was a Promethean moment for the cold and huddling text game masses: a chance for anyone with some coding skills to create their own new games in a beloved studio's engine. Along with his compiler, Nelson also announced—by the way—a new full-length, Infocom-style game that he'd written to test it. The twin releases of tool and game would lead to an extraordinary resurrection: an interactive fiction renaissance that sparked an explosion of new games and decades of experimentation, some of which would greatly influence both the mainstream game industry and scholarly understanding of the possibilities of interactive narratives.

It almost didn't happen. Nelson had first made his announcement at the end of April, and became depressed when nobody seemed to care—he received not a single response. It was only a week later that he realized his newsreader was glitching and his message had never been sent. Had he given up before noticing the problem, the history of interactive storytelling might have been rather different.

Nelson, a first-generation college student from a middle-class family, was then working on a mathematics PhD at Oxford. Half a year before his newsgroup announcement, he'd tracked down a hefty box of software called *The Lost Treasures of Infocom* [1991]. Activision, years after purchasing the

beleaguered interactive fiction studio and later shutting it down, had decided
to raise some money by reissuing Infocom's back catalog in an omnibus
collection. For fans of a company that had spent nearly a decade creating
titles praised for their craft and quality, this was a veritable treasure trove,
an entire body of acclaimed work now affordable and at gamers' fingertips:
games like *Deadline* [1982], *Enchanter* [1983], *Suspended*, *Hitchhiker's Guide*, *A
Mind Forever Voyaging*, *Trinity* [1986], and many other influential titles besides.
"If Infocom is to be compared with Shakespeare," Nelson later wrote, "then
this was the First Folio."[12] Nelson had played a few of the Infocom games
as an undergraduate, but now—not a fan of the turn toward first-person
shooters and military themes that mainstream games were taking—he
intended to devour the rest.

see **1983–5**

But first he faced a more immediate challenge: how to play the *Lost
Treasures* games on his incompatible Acorn Archimedes computer. Due to the
fragmented nature of the early home computer market, Infocom had built
a system-agnostic virtual machine to run their games, the Z-machine (Z
for *Zork*). Once this existed, they could simply write an interpreter program
for that machine that ran on each platform they wished to support, making
all current and future titles at once playable on each new architecture.
But Nelson's Archimedes had only been sold in the UK, and US-based
Infocom had never built an interpreter for it. Poking around on Usenet,
Nelson learned that a group of Australian college students calling themselves
the InfoTaskForce had reverse engineered Infocom's story format to write
their own interpreter in C, which was easy enough to compile on most any
modern machine. Without much trouble, Nelson built the InfoTaskForce
interpreter on his Archimedes and could easily play all the story files from
the *Lost Treasures* disks—the beauty of the virtual machine design meant the
games ran just fine on a platform they'd never been tested on or previously
compiled for.

But the new interpreter implied an intriguing corollary. If you
understood the Z-machine well enough to emulate it, you should also be
capable of writing new programs to run on it. All you'd need would be
a human-readable way to specify them—a programming language—and
a compiler that could turn those specifications into Z-code. While it was
known that Infocom had used an in-house language called ZIL (the Zork
Implementation Language) to create their games, its specifics had never
been made public. Nelson, intrigued by the idea of writing new games in
Infocom's engine, began to hack together his own solution. Having once
written a compiler called Teraform, he decided to christen his new one
Inform, later retronymically styling it as an "Infocom-format compiler." The
language and compiler were relatively straightforward—at least at first—so
Nelson spent most of his time on an ambitious game to thoroughly exercise
them, demonstrating that Inform was capable of producing something equal
to the complexity of any Infocom release. His game was called *Curses*, and
it was the first released program written in Inform. The decades to come
would see thousands more.

A decade later, Nelson
would reinvent Inform with
a radically new paradigm
for programming, based on
natural language; the story
of Inform 7 is told in **2008**.

When Inform and *Curses* debuted on the newsgroups, the reaction at first was muted (even after Nelson fixed his newsreader). It might have all felt, perhaps, too good to be true—the year had seemed destined for disappointments, not miracles. Yet responses slowly began to accrue. "Is anyone else playing [*Curses*]," someone posted a week after Nelson's announcement. "I'm doing fairly well … but I could use some hints."[16] As players got deeper into a game whose first impression was rather pedestrian—a hunt for a missing map in an overstuffed attic—the hint requests grew more involved. It seemed scarcely possible, to those not yet playing, that these people were asking about the same game with the mildly eccentric British relations and all the tea chests. "I've killed the kraken with the flash from the Pharos," one hint petitioner began,

> but am killed and resurrected, myself, only to find Andromeda still chained. Nor am I able to cross the sacred ground to reach the Temple of Zeus, or attain the ekmek in the taverna. My guess is that these three are related somehow, but how? Is there some alternative way to save Andromeda?? Should I save her at all??? Do I need more than just the flash to do the job????[5]

"You have to get a coin from the temple of zeus to buy the ekmek," explained one responder. "To do that you need to use the rod of luck. To use the rod of luck you have to change the nature of the universe." Gradually more and more people decided to give this new game a shot, downloading it via FTP and running it on their InfoTaskForce interpreters just to see what all the fuss was about. It soon became all anyone on the newsgroups was talking about, and remained that way for most of the next two years.

Curses begins, as mentioned, in the present-day attic of an old British estate called Meldrew Hall. As the latest Meldrew, you've climbed the stairs in part to search for an old tourist map of Paris, but also to escape from the hectic bustle of your family preparing for a trip to the continent.

>SOUTH

Old Furniture
Scruffy old furniture is piled up here: armchairs with springs coming out, umbrella stands, a badly scratched cupboard, a table with one leg missing... You try to remember why you keep all this rubbish, and fail. Anyway the attic continues to the southeast.

>SEARCH CUPBOARD
In the scratched cupboard are a bird whistle, a gift-wrapped parcel and a guaranteed-unbreakable medicine bottle with a child-proof lock.

>SOUTHEAST

Over the East Wing
The air is dusty and warm, almost making you choke in this rather empty area. The attic turns from northwest to east, and there is also a tight

doorway leading west. A short flight of wooden steps leads down and to the south.

>SOUTH
Disused Observatory
Once upon a time, this small circular room had a dome and a telescope, but it leaked dreadfully and so now there's a proper roof.

A circular mural painted with the signs of the zodiac is interrupted by a short flight of stairs leading up to the north, a smoke detector, a west doorway to a shadowy alcove and the continuation of the stairs down and to the south.

Mounted on the old telescope stand is what looks like a solid glass ball.

As you search the expansive nooks and crannies of the attic, its dimensions and the scope of your task begin to expand. Secret doors and dumbwaiters provide access to hidden cellars, precarious rooftops, and long-sealed rooms. Ghosts are met and strange dreams visited, some projecting you to unexpected places:

Cups and Glasses
This basement room is filled with crate after crate of glasses and cups, enough for an entire hotel, or restaurant perhaps. Almost anything might be hidden among them. [...]

You can see a ship in a bottle here.

>EXAMINE SHIP
You look very closely at the fine detail on the model sailing ship. Perhaps it's the distorting glass of the bottle, perhaps your romantic imagination, but the deck seems more detailed, the rigging might almost be swaying, the little figure by one mast might almost be alive...

In fact, the closer you look the more sea-sick you feel.

Thank heavens for the deck rail, something to hang on to while this moment of queasiness passes.

>LOOK

Aboard Ship
There is a storm tossing the deck, one which drives no rain: you reel from one side to the other, hanging onto the rail, grabbing at the mast or the rigging. Nobody else seems to be aboard. The boat makes no headway in a strange, glassy mist.

Soon you find yourself traveling through time and visiting other eras of the manor and its grounds, the demesnes of previous Meldrews.

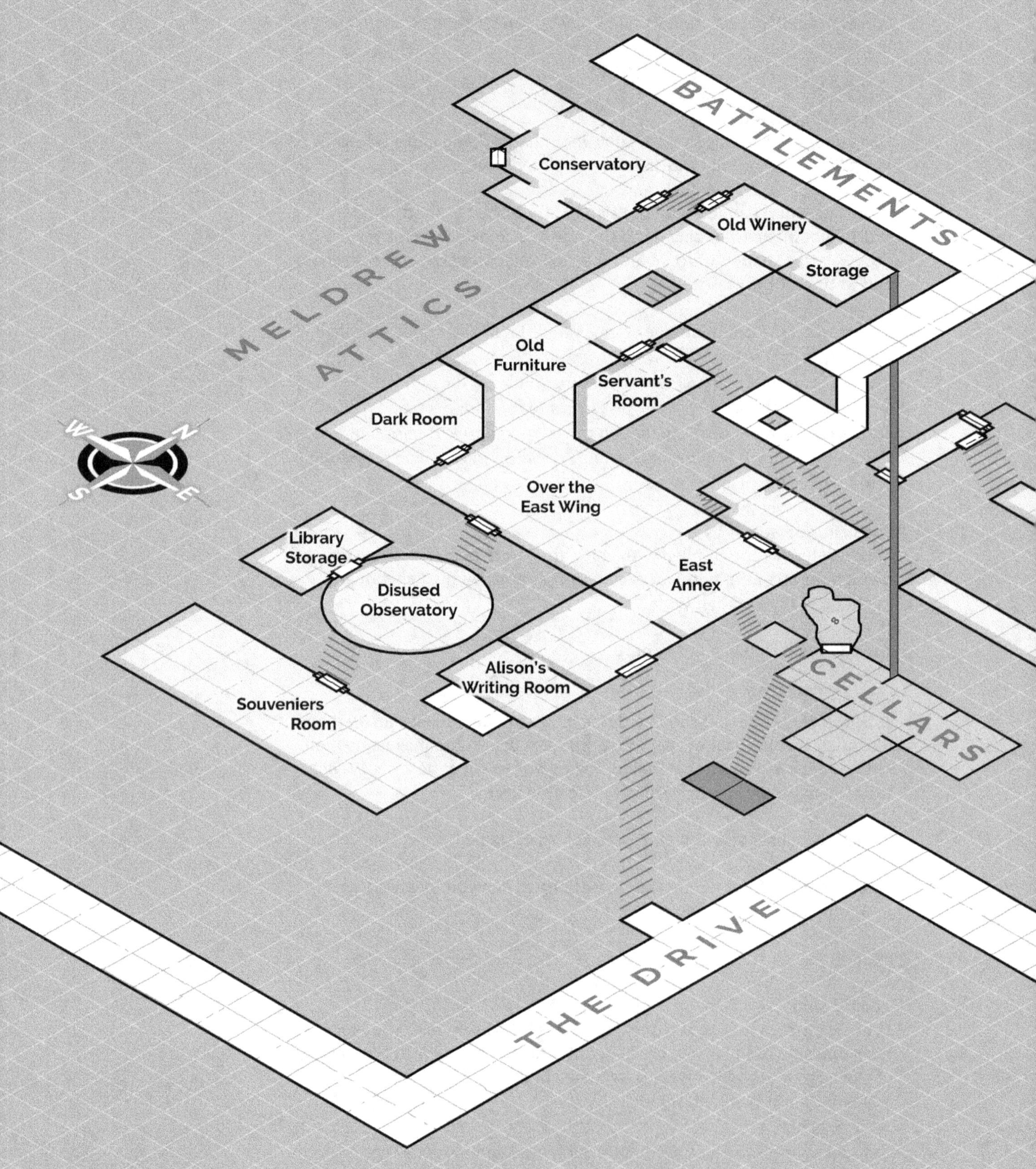

BATTLEMENTS
MELDREW ATTICS
Conservatory
Old Winery
Storage
Old Furniture
Servant's Room
Dark Room
Over the East Wing
Library Storage
Disused Observatory
East Annex
CELLARS
Souveniers Room
Alison's Writing Room
THE DRIVE
W N S E

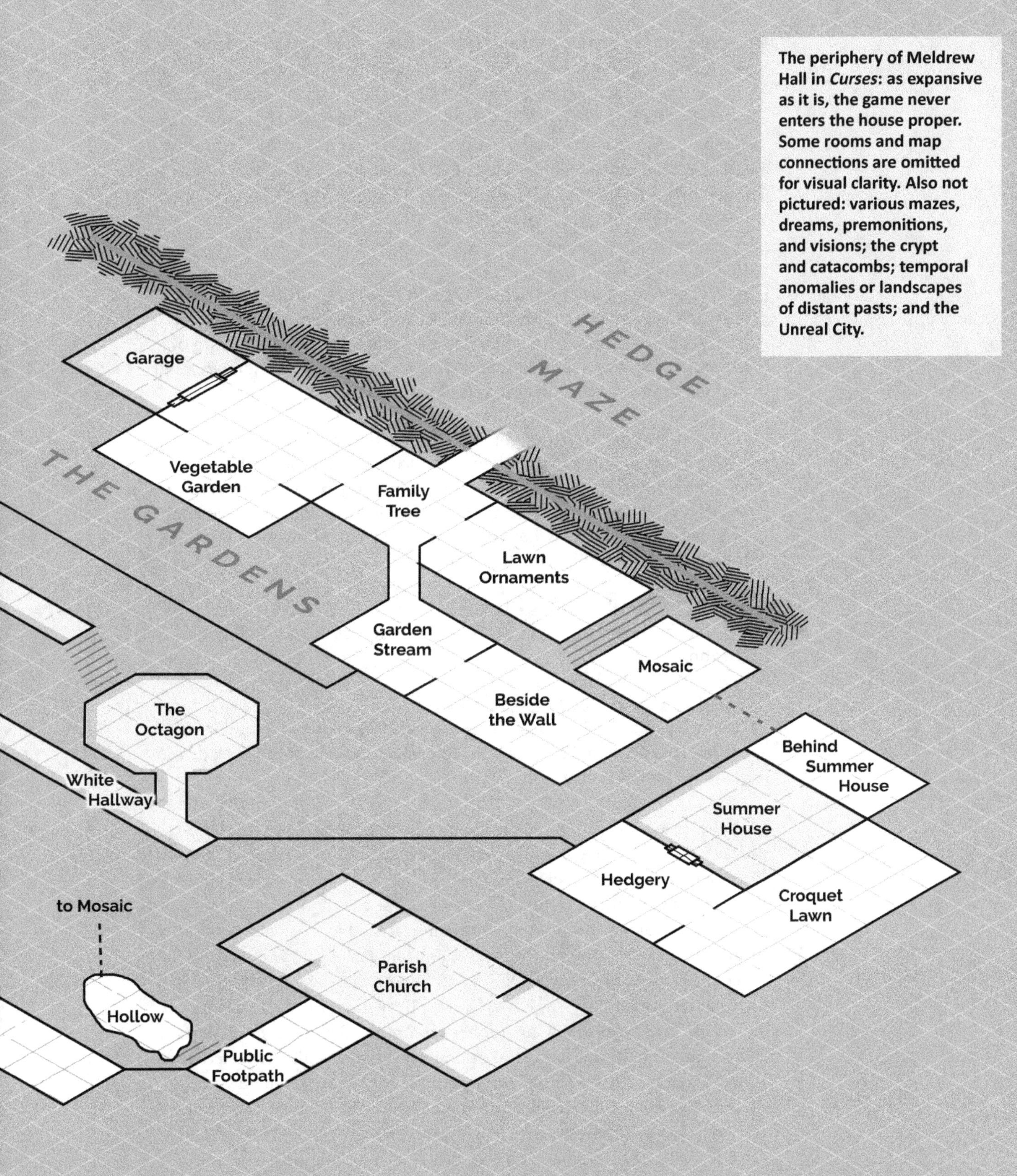

The periphery of Meldrew Hall in *Curses*: as expansive as it is, the game never enters the house proper. Some rooms and map connections are omitted for visual clarity. Also not pictured: various mazes, dreams, premonitions, and visions; the crypt and catacombs; temporal anomalies or landscapes of distant pasts; and the Unreal City.

Each ancestor, you come to learn, had their own quixotic quest they could never quite complete, a familial curse stretching back many centuries. Your own hunt for the map (and perhaps an end to the curse) eventually comes to involve deciphering hieroglyphics, replicating druidic rituals, shouting orders at a robot through a hole in the wall, and altering history with a bottle of weed killer. Before completing the game you'll visit ancient Greece and meet Homer, take a boat ride with a rather literal Hollow Man (à la T. S. Eliot), and even get hints from a demon:

Hellish Place
Hell, you always imagined, would contain fiery, sulphurous pits and a great many gentlemen with forked tails. You were right about the last part. A demon is sitting behind a flame-proofed desk at the bottom of the stairs. There are some disconcerting screams from further away, but nothing to worry about. Not in this life, anyway.

"Good afternoon," says the demon with a memorable smile. "As a reward for your naked greed, may I welcome you to our little information service. We try to be as helpful as possible to explorers who are lost, or can't think how to solve their problems, you know the kind of thing. So just tell me what you want to know, or show me something to look at. You get the usual three hints."

>SHOW TAROT CARD TO DEMON
"Clairvoyantes are expert at detecting stacked decks, so it's no good cheating."

>SHOW ROD OF FIRE TO DEMON
"Under Regulation 3, paragraph 15 (i) clause (f), only one hint per visit to the infernal domain. You'll have to go away again and come back if you want another. So sorry."

Curses is scavenger hunt meets Dante's *Inferno*, "an allegorical rite of passage,"[17] adventure game by way of historical footnote. It certainly owes a great debt to Infocom, recreating the company's signature style even while literally resurrecting its technical bones. It's filled with puzzles, magic words, clever mazes, an enormous map, and interesting objects (sidebar opposite).

But Nelson also took much inspiration from history and classics. When asked once about his favorite games and authors, he gave much more space to the latter, listing "Auden, Eliot, Donne, Browning, Elizabeth Bishop…. For plays, Tom Stoppard, Christopher Hampton, David Hare."[10] *Curses* is steeped in antiquities, from the abandoned odds and ends squirreled away in the Meldrew attics—an old wireless radio, for instance, which seems to do nothing when turned on until you realize it takes a few turns to warm up—to its detailed time-travel excursions to lovingly researched long-ago eras. It's very much a game about odd corners and margins—interstitial places. As huge as the game is, it never takes its players into Meldrew Hall proper, leaving them instead to scuttle through attics, basements, and secret crawlspaces. If you try to step into the main rooms of the house, or even somewhere you might be spotted from a window or doorway, the game promptly ends as you're swept up into your family's quotidian concerns: "You have missed the point entirely," it admonishes. Nelson, in the midst of his PhD, had also embarked on a quixotic quest that bore little relation to his supposedly more pressing duties. The attics and basements of the Z-machine's virtual architecture, and the ever-expanding house he was building atop it, seemed perhaps pleasant places to take refuge.

Nelson's game would take over the IF newsgroups as players who thought they'd seen the last of the great text adventures discovered a worthy modern successor. "Congratulations," wrote one poster. "Its almost like having Infocom back."[19] Hint requests and discussion of the game proliferated, dominating the newsgroups through the rest of 1993 and 1994 so much that there was a half-hearted proposal for a dedicated new group, rec.games. curses, just so there would be enough oxygen to talk about anything else.[3]

As popular as *Curses* was, the Inform language would come to have an even larger impact on interactive fiction history. It had at first been more of "an assembler with delusions of grandeur,"[11] with code written close to the virtual metal of the Z-machine. But as Nelson kept improving it, the language began to evolve more elegant features for efficiently crafting simulated worlds. By the release of version 5 in the summer of 1994—just as its author was at last defending his PhD—Inform had become powerful and stable enough for others to start building ambitious projects of their own. Inform 6, appearing two years later, would become the definitive version.

A snippet from example game *Toyshop* [1994] demonstrates the ease with which an Inform 6 author can create an interesting object—a bag that nothing can be removed from—and a sticky object to defeat it.

```
Object -> "toothed bag"
   with name "toothed" "bag",
   initial "In one corner is a curious, toothed bag.",
   description "A capacious bag with a toothed mouth.",
   before
      [; LetGo: "The bag defiantly bites itself shut on your
         hand until you desist.";
      ],
   after
      [; Receive:
         if (noun==cone)
         {  self.before=0; self.after=0;
            "The bag wriggles interminably as it tries
             to eat the enormous mass of marzipan. That'll
             teach it.";
         }
         "The bag wriggles hideously as it swallows ", (the)
         noun, ".";
      ],
   has  container open;
```

Among other elegant notions—such as a bare string printing a message and returning from a code block—the **before** and **after** segments let authors easily intervene in the behavior of actions, whether directly triggered by the player or implied. When the player tries to remove something from the bag, for instance, its code can interfere by intercepting the action from its own point of view: `LetGo`.

The set of actions was also a useful contribution from Nelson. He combed through the catalog of Infocom games in *Lost Treasures* and created a standard library of verbs, rules, and concepts, normalizing behaviors common to many titles but not always consistently implemented, and worked them into a reusable module that an author could simply include in any new project. Nelson's Standard Library was quite sophisticated, including a mature parser and a uniform framework for simulating locations, containers, doors, locks, light, directions, and many other atomic units of adventure game design. For a generation of IF authors, Inform would establish a standard baseline driven by the simulationist model the 80s games had popularized and the 90s MUDs and MOOs had adapted, enshrining the notion that an interactive story should be built on a simulated virtual world that a player can move through and interact with. That paradigm would not be seriously challenged for many text game writers until the rise of Twine in the 2010s.

see *Achaea* **1997** and *LambdaMOO* **1990**

see *Howling Dogs* **2012**

In the years after Inform's release, the community forged in the nostalgia-heavy IF newsgroups would expand and rebrand itself as a place for making, not just reminiscing. The release of Inform and *Curses* kindled a resurgence of interest in text games and their creation, with languages like TADS also seeing a new surge of popularity. New community institutions soon sprung up to support the new generation of game makers. In 1995, the first annual Interactive Fiction Competition was held, designed to give the increasing number of new authors a place to showcase their games. The competition was still going strong twenty-five years later, attracting over a hundred entries in the 2020 season. The newsletter *SPAG* (Society for the Preservation, later Promotion, of Adventure Games) launched in 1994, featuring long-form reviews, analyses, and interviews. Another publication, *XYZZYnews* (named after a magic word in *Adventure*), debuted in 1995 with a Graham Nelson interview, and would later spin off the annual XYZZY Awards—a text games Oscars. And the quality and success of Inform caused other makers of text game tools to rethink their approaches, with some dropping their commercial pricing models or adding improved features to keep pace with the most popular game creation tools.

see **1976**

Curses is less remembered today than the Inform games written in the years and decades that followed it. In demonstrating so thoroughly the possibility of making a game as good as anything from Infocom, it naturally inspired the next generation of makers to aim even higher. But to do so, it had by necessity planted its flag squarely in the past. "Curses is not experimental," one reviewer wrote in 2000. "Curses is conclusional. It does not try to explore the vague borders of the medium; it stays well behind the trenches, ploughs the rich soil and collects the harvest that feeds the experimentalists' armies."[15] In the years after its release, those "experimentalists" would carry forward a conversation about interactive

1993

stories that had begun in the 70s and continues to this day—a conversation in prototypes and playable theories about what games made from words can be, mean, and do. Freed at last from technical constraints, compatibility problems, commercial concerns, and the siloed isolation of the early internet, text games and their authors thrived like never before.

Those who do remember Graham Nelson's first game do so fondly, despite the challenge of mastering it. "For starters, it's really really hard," wrote one reviewer. "Funny! And extremely erudite. But hard."[1] *Curses* "may be one of the best text adventures ever written," wrote another reviewer, and "deserves the effort which is required to solve it."[2] Yet another agreed, "*Curses* is not a game to be solved in a couple of hours. It is a game to be enjoyed for weeks. It is a game to create obsessions."[15] For some fans, it's "the best Infocom game that Infocom never made"[4]—and it's hard to imagine a more satisfying compliment for the author who prised open the back door of the legendary game studio's glorious, abandoned estate.

see **1998**, **2000**, and **2004**, among other examples

References

1 Blaheta, Don. 2007. "Curses" (review). *Digital Analogue* (blog). Aug 26, 2007. www.blahedo.org/blog/archives/001012.html | a May 11, 2021

2 Bryan, Russ. 1994. "Curses -- Version 12: The Walkthrough." IF Archive, Nov 11, 1994. ifarchive.org/if-archive/solutions/Curses.sol | a May 11, 2021

3 DBlaheta. 1994. "REQ: rec.games.curses." Usenet post, rec.games.int-fiction, Sep 19, 1994. groups.google.com/g/rec.games.int-fiction/c/gLJpuQQDkM8/m/TUAXA_ZjORAJ | a May 11, 2021

4 De Smet, Alan. 2006. "Curses" (review). Pontifications from the High Programmer. Mar 14, 2006. www.highprogrammer.com/alan/rants/reviews/video_games/if/curses.html | a May 11, 2021

5 Igou, Rick. 1993. "Curses: A Plea for Help." Usenet post, rec.games.int-fiction, May 28, 1993. groups.google.com/g/rec.games.int-fiction/c/4ylg-hZApzM/m/657S1A9HE3QJ | a May 11, 2021

6 Maher, Jimmy. 2019a. "New Tricks for an Old Z-Machine, Part 1: Digging the Trenches." *The Digital Antiquarian* (blog). Oct 18, 2019. www.filfre.net/2019/10/new-tricks-for-an-old-z-machine-part-1-digging-the-trenches | a May 11, 2021

7 Maher, Jimmy. 2019b. "New Tricks for an Old Z-Machine, Part 3: A Renaissance Is Nigh." *The Digital Antiquarian* (blog). Nov 22, 2019. www.filfre.net/2019/11/new-tricks-for-an-old-z-machine-part-3-a-renaissance-is-nigh | a May 11, 2021

8 MLeduc. n.d. "The Solution to Curses 1.6." GameFAQs. gamefaqs.gamespot.com/pc/564680-curses/faqs/1918 | a May 11, 2021

9 Nelson, Graham. 1993. "[Announcement: INFORM] Announcing 'Inform', an Infocom-Format Compiler." Usenet post, rec.arts.int-fiction, May 9, 1993. groups.google.com/g/rec.arts.int-fiction/c/CqsdYXYI1Ss/m/ff321YSrlqwJ | a May 11, 2021

10 Nelson, Graham. 1995. "Interview: Graham Nelson." In *XYZZYnews* #1, Jan/Feb 1995. mirror.ifarchive.org/if-archive/magazines/XYZZYnews/XYZZY1.TXT | a May 11, 2021

11 Nelson, Graham. 1996. "Inform 6.21 Technical Manual." inform-fiction.org. Apr 27, 1996. www.inform-fiction.org/source/tm/TechMan.txt | a May 11, 2021

12 Nelson, Graham. 2001. *The Inform Designer's Manual*. 4th edition. St. Charles, Illinois: The Interactive Fiction Library.

13 Nelson, Graham. 2018. "Inform: Past, Present, Future." Presented at the London IF Meetup, London South Bank University, Jun 9, 2018. www.emshort.com/ifmu/inform.html | a May 11, 2021

14 Nelson, Graham. 2019. "New Tricks for an Old Z-Machine, Part 2: Hacking Deeper (or, Follies of Graham Nelson's Youth)." *The Digital Antiquarian* (blog). Nov 8, 2019. www.filfre.net/2019/11/new-tricks-for-an-old-z-machine-part-2-hacking-deeper-or-follies-of-graham-nelsons-youth | a May 11, 2021

15 Patavalis, Nick. 2000. "Curses" (review). *SPAG* #22, Sep 15, 2000. www.spagmag.org/archives/backissues/spag22.html#curses | a May 11, 2021

16 Ridley, Thomas R. 1993. "Hints Needed for Curses." Usenet post, rec.games.int-fiction, May 14, 1993. groups.google.com/g/rec.games.int-fiction/c/_GlNZ1Vug7I/m/hwkCO37-uZkJ | a May 11, 2021

17 Rushton, Brian. 2016. "Effective Design Decisions in Graham Nelson's Curses!" Forum post, The

Also by
Graham Nelson

1994 **Balances** †

1995 **Jigsaw** †

1996 **The Meteor, the Stone and a Long Glass of Sherbet** † *(as Angela M. Horns)*

1997 **The Tempest** † *(credited "with William Shakespeare")*

2006 **The Reliques of Tolti-Aph** ‡

† Inform 1-6
‡ Inform 7

Interactive Fiction Community Forum, Feb 5, 2016. intfiction.org/t/effective-design-decisions-in-graham-nelsons-curses/9732 | a May 11, 2021

18 Taylor, Marion. 1996. "CURSES by Graham Nelson" (review). *Syn Tax Adventure Magazine* #41, 1996. www.syntax2000.co.uk/issues/41/curses.rev.txt | a May 11, 2021

19 West, John. 1993. "Curses (SPOILERS)." Usenet post, rec.games.int-fiction, May 17, 1993. groups.google.com/g/rec.games.int-fiction/c/IX33Jw3DLX4/m/lmpr3CqOqDQJ | a May 11, 2021

THE PLAYGROUND

Scott Neal Reilly

Style	**Procedural Story**
Debuted	**Unreleased** *(developed 1994–1996 at Carnegie Mellon)*
Launch Platform	**Mach Unix**
Developer	**The Oz Project**
Language	**Hap, Common Lisp**

> " The recess bell has just rung and it's time to really start working. Math, English, and Social Studies are nothing compared to the harsh competition out on the playground.
>
> Try to collect baseball cards of players you like by trading with the other kids on the playground. Who knows, this may even be your big chance to get that Willie Mays card you've been trying to get for so long!

ON A SPRING DAY IN 1990, in a tiny studio theater at Carnegie Mellon—the first university in the world to offer a degree in drama—a most unusual performance took place. The seats were empty except for a handful of computer science researchers, and the only audience member was on the stage. She stood amidst a minimalist set representing a bus station, along with a small troupe of improv actors wearing headsets. She'd been told she was taking part in an experiment in "interactive drama," but her only guidance was to try to buy a bus ticket: she had no script, and neither did the actors with their headsets. Not even the director, whispering to the actors through an offstage microphone, had the lines. All he had were a graph of possible outcomes and a straightforward goal: whatever the onstage woman did, keep the story around her compelling.

The play was an experiment by an ambitious campus research group that called themselves the Oz Project. They were hoping to solve what they saw as a glaring problem in the still-teething world of computer games. While the software behind bestsellers then on shelves was capable of all kinds of interesting simulations—of 3D spaces, of realistic lighting, of airplane aerodynamics, of the growth of virtual cities—one aspect still depressingly static was their stories. Scholar Espen Aarseth would later write of the difference between a "simulated door" in a video game (one the player can open, move through, perhaps lock and unlock or use for cover) and a merely "fictional door" (a painted-on texture, leading nowhere, not understood as a door by the system or able to be operated as one by the player).[1] While simulated and fictional doors might look the same to a player at first glance, a merely fictional door can't take part in the make-believe world of a video game except as set dressing. You can't *play* with it. By the 90s many games featured increasingly elaborate stories—some laden with video clips, recorded audio, and starring famous actors—but those stories were not, in any meaningful way, simulated. They were painted on: prerendered and unable to change in response to the player's actions, except perhaps through brute-force authoring of alternatives.

But as computing power continued to increase, some researchers had begun to wonder if you could teach a computer enough about stories and characters and dramatic arcs, the same way flight sims encoded wisdom about lift and drag and throttles, for the system to tell a story that could be playful—reacting to the player and reshaping itself to whatever they tried to do, while still telling the same core tale the author had devised. "One approach is to see them [the player and the system] in a kind of two-player game, such as chess," wrote Joseph Bates, the Oz Project's founder:

> The director and user are taking turns, the user acting as a free agent in the world, the director looking down from above and very gently pushing the elements of the world in various ways. The director is constantly trying to maximize the chances of a pleasing overall experience, no matter what the user does along the way.… The director wins if the complete history of the world is consistent with the creator's aesthetic goals, thereby (presumably) pleasing the user.[3]

"Our idea is to gently guide the user's experience so it conforms in some way to an artistic destiny," another Oz researcher posted on the rec.arts.int-fiction newsgroup in 1991, "while at the same time allowing the user complete freedom of action."[19] And while new technologies like virtual reality seemed imminently on the horizon, the easiest medium in which to prototype such a system was text. Projects like *LambdaMOO* had already demonstrated how compelling and complex a text-based virtual world could become. The Oz Project, at least at first, would focus on "developing technology for high quality interactive fiction."[4]

see **1990**

1994

In the experimental play, the actors and director were standing in for components of a yet-unbuilt computer program. The director represented a future algorithmic Playwright who could replot a scenario in real time based on the player's actions, by feeding new instructions to the actors in their headsets. The actors in turn stood in for NPCs who would have some autonomy of their own, but could also pivot on a whim to adapt to the Playwright's new instructions. The details of the scenario, involving a troubled bus station customer who begins to turn violent, weren't really important; the point was to gather data on the strategies the Playwright and actors invented to keep the plot moving, and to observe how the lone audience member experienced a performance tailored just for her. The goal was a first step toward learning how "to create a medium beyond 'static stories' … [of] constructed yet unpredictable worlds."[15]

The project had evolved out of a line of academic thinking traced back to two 1980s dissertations, both by women, which would become the foundations of interactive narrative scholarship. Mary Ann Buckles's "Interactive Fiction: The Computer Storygame 'Adventure'" had been one of the first book-length scholarly works to seriously study interactive fiction as a new and unique medium, breaking down how Crowther and Woods's genre-defining game both connected to earlier literary traditions and also functioned as a legitimately new art form. Brenda Laurel's "Toward the Design of a Computer-Based Interactive Fantasy System" went a step further, positing a theory of how truly interactive and responsive stories might function. Inspired by Aristotle's *Poetics* and live theater traditions, Laurel defined an interactive drama as "a first-person experience within a fantasy world, in which the user may create, enact, and observe a character whose choices and actions affect the course of events just as they might in a play."[11] Contemporary adventure games were a start, but they were entirely different from the truly interactive experiences Laurel envisioned, driven by a digital Playwright working to marry a human player's improvisations with a human author's story.

Laurel had first developed these ideas at an extraordinary meeting of minds arranged by computing pioneer Alan Kay, who in the 60s helped popularize many foundational concepts of modern computing from windowed interfaces to word processing. In the early 80s, Atari hired Kay as their chief scientist, and he promptly set up a think tank and research lab to explore the future of games and entertainment technology. "Alan's strategy was simple," remembers Laurel, part of Kay's cohort:

> Create the richest possible environment and plop creative people into it, and something wonderful is bound to be the result. Atari in 1981–82 was the perfect place for such a grand experiment—with revenues in excess of a billion dollars, the company was in a position to build a "dream lab" for creating the future of high-tech consumer products.[11]

Members of the group had wide leeway to devise their own experimental projects, requisitioning equipment and hiring contractors as needed. Surviving memos are filled with truly heady concepts: one from Laurel wondered, "Is there a video game we could imagine that a human and a

see *Adventure* **1976**

Laurel, for instance, proposed replacing the static story's graph of rising and falling action with a "flying wedge": as a player progresses through a truly interactive narrative making choices and decisions, the number of plausible dramatically satisfying resolutions to the story grows smaller and smaller, eventually shrinking to the single necessary ending for that player's unique performance of their character.

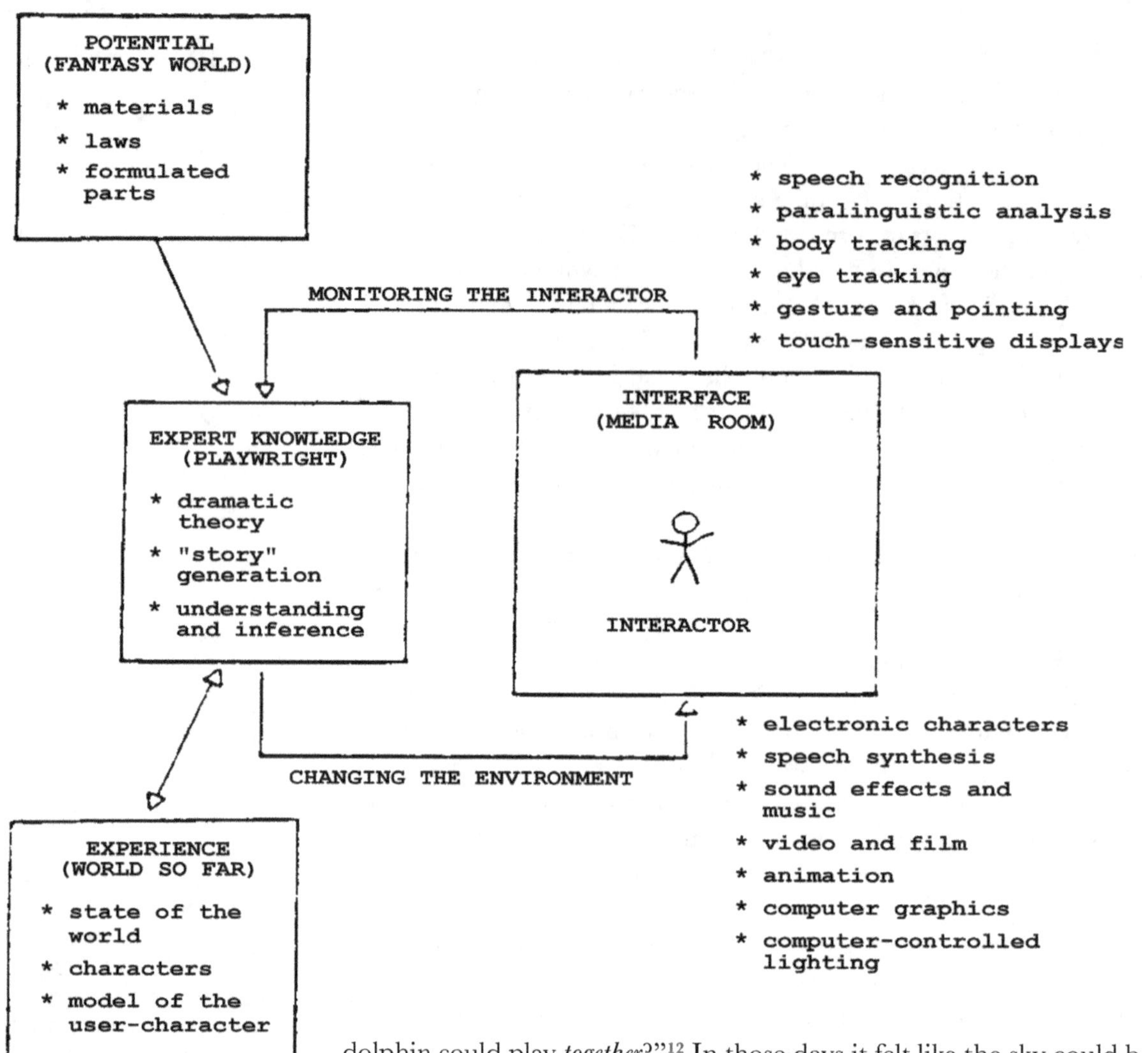

Overview diagram from Brenda Laurel's "Toward the Design of an Interactive Fantasy System: Description and Functional Requirements," a report from her time at Atari.[12] Laurel would later evolve many ideas from the report into a PhD dissertation.[11]

dolphin could play *together*?"[12] In those days it felt like the sky could be the limit for the future of computer-enabled play, and the dreams were big.

Kay believed that "in order to do good research, one needs a 'grand idea'—a vision of something that might exist, far in the future and beyond our abilities to imagine it fully."[11] Laurel's grand idea (after the dolphins, perhaps, got little traction) was a pitch for an ambitious game prototype that would immerse a player in an environment created by wraparound screens and simulated sound and lighting effects, maybe even smells. Inspired by the immersive nursery playroom in the Ray Bradbury story "The Veldt," she imagined a rich multimedia experience where a concealed human Playwright would manipulate the projected images and deploy live actors puppeteering digital characters to adapt an ongoing story to the player's actions. Laurel got as far as convincing Bradbury himself to be the system's first Playwright of a scenario based on his classic *Something Wicked This Way Comes*. But it was not to be. Atari, hit hard by the video game crash and suddenly more interested in immediate than distant futures, had disbanded Kay's research group by early 1984.

Laurel carried her work over into a PhD dissertation, which would in turn inspire another brilliant mind: Joseph Bates, a child prodigy who had enrolled in college at age thirteen and graduated before he could vote.

1994

U: <It looks like I'm in a bedroom-- I'll assume it's mine. I
wonder what's out the window.>

    I: (Body tracking display indicates user moving toward
    "window" projected in north screen.)

        P: She's moving toward the window. Get ready to open it.
        Wait for the gesture.

U: (Reaches toward window.)

    I: (Polhemus display indicates gesture toward window; body
    tracking display shows another step north.)

        P: Fire the window opening sequence.

            O: (Window opens in video image on north wall.
            Sound of window opening. Night sounds become louder.
            Wisteria smell is dispersed.)

U: <Wow! A summer night... looks like a small town... >

* * * * *

THE USER MOVES INTO THE YARD, HEARS THE PASSING TRAIN, AND
DECIDES TO WANDER OFF TOWARD THE TRACKS.

* * * * *

            O: (Circus train rushing by on east screen. Engine
            roar doppler-shifts as the train seems to move
            southward. Train passes out of view; empty tracks
            illuminated in moonlight.)

U: A carnival!

    I: (Speech synthesizer recieves output from recognizer and
    produces phrase, "A carnivore!")

        P: Must be "carnival"-- She's got it, but she's not
        moving. Let's try a strange glow in the southern sky.

            O: (Red and yellow searchlight beams produced in
            computer graphics sweep the sky on the south screen.)

U: <What's going on over there?>

        P: She's still not going for it. Give me some carnival
        music.

            O: (Distant calliope music drifts in from the south.)

U: <Oh my God, they're setting it up-- in the middle of the
night-- I've got to see this.>

    I: (Body tracking registers a few steps south; polhemnus
    shows a moderately accelerating, sweeping gesture toward the
    south with user's left hand.)

        P: Okay, she's running at a moderate pace. Let's go
        to the carnival...

Excerpt from a transcript for a never-built game from the Atari research group, designed for a full immersion media room and based on Ray Bradbury's *Something Wicked This Way Comes*. ***U*** **marks the user (with unspoken thoughts in brackets),** *I* **and** *O* **are the media room's inputs and outputs, and** *P* **is the human Playwright in a separate room, envisioned as a capable storyteller and improviser who could dynamically adjust the experience to ensure a compelling plot, no matter what actions the user might take.**

Fifteen years later, he'd started a research group at Carnegie Mellon devoted to inventing the future of interactive stories. Like Kay and Laurel, Bates was a big dreamer: "You have to be able to invent new, strange stuff, and you have to be able to throw out most of it," he once wrote.[16] His initial missives for the Oz Project were beyond ambitious. In an early critique of a part of Laurel's thesis which proposed an interactive *Hamlet,* he wrote that her ideas of dynamic storytelling were too limiting because

> in these situations the user never ceases to be himself, in Hamlet's position. What if the user *is* Hamlet … what if the user's mind is manipulated by the system to try to make the user think/feel like Hamlet, not just experience Hamlet's objective experiences?[17]

In lieu of any means for realizing this rather revisionist take on the nature of storytelling itself, Bates and his group hoped, as a first step, to at least build something like Laurel's hypothetical interactive drama system. They deconstructed Infocom games like *Deadline* [1982] to understand how the games created the illusion of dynamic plot, and they staged a variant of Laurel's unrealized theater experiment with a human Playwright directing live actors, enlisting the help of Margaret Kelso, a professor in the CMU drama department. While small in scale, the experiment was nothing like what other researchers into games or AI were doing. It was "new, strange stuff" indeed.

Bates and a handful of graduate students soon began work on an interactive narrative engine called Oz, written in Common Lisp—then the language of choice for anything connected to artificial intelligence. Initially the work was divided into six problem areas:

> how to simulate the physical world, how to simulate the minds of characters, how to design the user interface, how to build a working theory of drama, how to design the world-building environment, and how to facilitate artistic use of the system.[15]

As more grad students came aboard the exciting project, each was set to work on one problem or facet of a problem, with many designing and prototyping new components of the overall Oz architecture. Most modules were named after a character from L. Frank Baum's famous books. An engine to generate natural language descriptions of a simulated world was called Glinda, a parser to understand a wider range of natural language input was dubbed the Gump, and a core framework for agents (characters) to operate within a virtual world was named Tok, after Dorothy's mechanical companion Tik-Tok who "Thinks, Speaks, Acts, and Does Everything but Live."

One CMU grad student, Scott Neal Reilly, focused on the problem of giving Tok characters more realistic behaviors and social understanding through a program called Em, for emotion (and Dorothy's aunt). "The goal of building believable agents is inherently an artistic one," Reilly wrote:

> Traditional AI goals of creating competence and building models of human cognition are only tangentially related because creating

see **1977**, **1983–5**, **1987**

Not as an end unto itself, but to "provide just enough of a physical reality to let authors construct interesting characters and stories."[15]

1994

believability is not the same as creating intelligence or realism. Therefore, the tools that have been designed for those tasks are not appropriate.[14]

So-called believable agents, Reilly thought, would not make perfect plans and execute them in the most efficient way possible. Their plans might be ill-advised, and they ought to endearingly fail many times before succeeding (if they ever did) in ways designed to reveal their character and make players relate to them, cheer them, or despise them. Like many Oz students, Reilly had looked for inspiration outside computer science research, studying the techniques fiction writers and Disney animators used to bring memorable characters to life. "Artists know how to create believable characters," he wrote, but "AI researchers know how to create autonomous agents." The problem was finding a way to bring those disparate worlds together, to find a path "somewhere between the arts and artificial intelligence"—somewhere, you might say, over the rainbow.

In the course of his dissertation work, Reilly would build several small simulations to test Em. One of these, *The Playground*, casts you as a school kid with the goal of trading baseball cards with two peers: Melvin, a friendly *Star Trek* nut, and Sluggo, a not-too-bright bully. The action played out in a small virtual world that seemed on the surface to operate much like traditional interactive fiction:

You are in the playground.

The sand box, the jungle gym and the tree house are in the playground.
Sluggo is in the tree house.
Sluggo is holding a Willie Mays trading card, a Jose Canseco trading card and a Catfish Hunter trading card.
Melvin is in the sand box.
Melvin is holding a Tom Seaver trading card, a Mickey Mantle trading card and a Reggie Jackson trading card.
Melvin is wearing his eye glasses.

You are holding a Babe Ruth trading card, a Ted Williams trading card and a Henry Aaron trading card.
PLAYER> GET IN THE SANDBOX

You go into the sand box.
Sluggo spits.
Melvin is now smiling.
Melvin is speaking to you.
Melvin's voice says ``Salutations, Vulcan ambassador! The Klingon high command has sent me in search of baseball cards.''.
PLAYER> MELVIN: WHAT CARDS DO THE KLINGON HIGH COMMAND WANT?

You are speaking to Melvin.
Player's voice says ``What cards do the Klingon high command want?''.
Sluggo smokes.

> Melvin is speaking to you.
> Melvin's voice says ``The Klingon Emperor wants to know if you would
> be willing to part with Babe Ruth for Reggie Jackson?''.
> PLAYER> MELVIN: NO WAY!
>
> You are speaking to Melvin.
> Player's voice says ``No way!''.
> Sluggo spits.
> Melvin is speaking to you.
> Melvin's voice says ``I wouldn't be hasty if I were you. Reggie Jackson for
> Babe Ruth is a trade any Ferengi would be proud of.''.
> PLAYER> MELVIN: HOW ABOUT RUTH FOR JACKSON AND
> MANTLE?

While *Playground* featured only a simple parser and text narration system—the player's lines in the example above are mostly recognized through keyword matches, and the stilted output comes from a system that simply reports the status of the underlying simulation with no attempts at artifice—the code driving character behavior was far more complex than any commercial text game had shipped with. Most games even today create NPC behavior with some equivalent of a list of if-then statements accounting for specific foreseen eventualities, something like: "*If* player offers Melvin a trade evaluated as good, *then* say Melvin smiles and accepts the trade." But the Oz framework with Reilly's extensions broke this process down into many more steps, each of which had its own possibility to influence the outcome.

For example, an earlier Oz prototype designed as a test bed for Tok and Em had simulated a cat named Lyotard, who would actually perceive things about the world through specific senses and use those impressions to update an internal representation of his model of reality. Lyotard might remember where he had last eaten food, for instance, and return there when hungry even if the player had since moved his tins of sardines. The tactile sensation of a comfy chair might cause an emotion of contentedness that could change Lyotard's reactions to events like a human walking into the room, or could cause him to develop an attachment to fuzzy objects. Mistreating the virtual cat could make him develop long-term emotions of hatred toward you that would in turn affect his actions in your presence. Lyotard made decisions about what to do—such as whether to allow an unfamiliar hand to pet him, or bite it—based on a constantly shifting bank of sensory inputs, emotional states, and memories. While the results might not have seemed much different from a well-implemented cat in a traditional text adventure, the behind-the-scenes systems were laying the groundwork for worlds with truly emergent characters who could believably respond to unexpected events. They were characters transitioning from merely fictional to meaningfully simulated.

Characters in Tok used a three-stage cycle of *sense, think, act* to plan their behaviors, doing so in the context of goals they wished to achieve. Lyotard's goals might be taking a nap or eating food when hungry. But Reilly hoped to introduce more complex emotional and social reasoning into the *think* step

Like, say, the one in Graham Nelson's *Curses* **1993**.

that could handle human NPCs with more complex goals and drives than a house cat's. He began to extend Em to support more advanced emotional reasoning, using a language called Hap (also an Oz invention) to write reactive planner rules that defined how a character's simulated emotions might influence the formation and performance of goals. For instance, Hap code to define a trigger for a *frustration* emotion, occurring when an attempt to take steps toward completing a plan fails, might look like this:

```
(sequential-production update-frustration ()
   (demon em-update-frustration-demon
      ;; LHS
      ;; Fire when a failed behavior has been put in
      ;; the $plan-failures slot and the importance of the
      ;; behavior is greater than O
   (and   (match $plan-failures (list-containing ?plan))
          (match (call importance ?plan) ?intensity)
          (> ?intensity 0)

          ;; Create an emotion structure. Set the variable
          ;; ?emotion-structure to the structure
          (match (make  frustration-emotion
                     actor self
                     cause ?plan
                     frustration-production ?intensity)
               ?emotion-structure))

   ;; RHS
   ;; Store the structure
   (mental-act
      (call add-emotion
         (slot emotion-type-hierarchy $em)
         $$emotion-structure
         `frustration))

   ;; Remove the behavior from the $plan-failures slot
   (mental-act
      (setf $plan-failures
         (remove $$plan $plan-failures)))))
```

Reilly created a library of a few dozen emotions that could each be defined as a consequence of interactions between an agent's goals and the model world. *Fear*, for instance, was the emotion where "a goal is considered to be likely to fail and it is important to the agent that the goal not fail." Various events might cause *happiness*, such as "A goal succeeds that the agent hoped would succeed." *Resentment* was felt "when an agent dislikes another agent who is happy." Each emotion had an intensity and a rate of decay (*hatred* would linger much longer than *disappointment*), and emotions could also be attached to the person or event that had caused them.

Interacting with the world, then, each agent would accrue a set of active emotions that might alter their future behavior. While some behaviors were general, Reilly noted that most would be character-specific—in a traditional game the writer's prose would do most of the work of defining character, but an Oz game would lean much more on the way its characters behaved and

This chunk of code is an "emotion generator" rule with two main parts: a left-hand side (LHS) defining when the rule should apply, and a right-hand side (RHS) defining what should happen when it does: in this case, adding the frustration emotion to the character's memory.

reacted. In *The Playground*, for instance, Trekkie Melvin feels joy when the player uses *Star Trek* lingo in their interactions with him, enjoys the social interaction of trading cards more than the specifics of making a good trade, and feels fear when bully Sluggo gets too close. Emotions, in turn, could cause character-specific behaviors: Melvin will use geeky ways of phrasing things if he's happy, but might abandon a trade with a new goal of running away if he gets too scared. Melvin gets sad and shy if insulted, but Sluggo gets angry:

```
You are speaking to Melvin.
Player's voice says ``What do you want for Mantle?''.
Sluggo smokes a cigarette.
Melvin is speaking to you.
Melvin's voice says ``The aliens told me to offer you Mickey Mantle in
return for Babe Ruth.''.
PLAYER> SLUGGO: HEY DORK, GET A LIFE!

You are speaking to Sluggo.
Player's voice says ``Hey dork, get a life!''.
Sluggo is now red.
Sluggo is now scowling.
Sluggo is now tense.
Sluggo goes into the sand box.
Melvin is now pale.
Melvin is now bug-eyed.
Melvin is now trembling.
Melvin is speaking to you.
Melvin's voice says ``Why don't we finish this later...''.
Melvin gets on the jungle gym.
```

Melvin's goals, emotions, and behaviors in *The Playground* differ from Sluggo's in noticeable ways, which helps paint the two as unique characters. One of Melvin's goals is making friends, which he knows social interaction helps him achieve; he also values the novelty of new baseball cards in his collection. Together, these two motivations might cause him to make a trade he knows isn't optimal, especially if he likes you, because he hopes it will help him make a new friend. Sluggo, by contrast, only cares about having *good* cards in his hand. He gains no satisfaction from the patter leading up to a trade or the act of trading itself, resulting in different kinds of performances (like getting annoyed if the player is slow to complete a trade). Characters could even be programmed with their own unique ways of translating sensory inputs into internal models of the world, or of understanding the player. Melvin, for instance, can mentally juggle more complex trades than Sluggo. If you try offering Sluggo a trade involving more than two cards, he gets "angry, distressed, and reproachful towards the player for making him feel stupid."[14]

The Playground was explicitly a prototype, never meant to be a polished experience for either players or outsider creators, and neither the game nor its full source code were ever formally released. It was one of a series of Oz experiments designed to rapidly iterate on the team's design and technology questions, moving toward Bates's ambitious vision of a future, five or ten years down the road, when the logic behind those purely textual worlds could begin driving immersive virtual realities. It was a foundational assumption that interactive drama and reactive character technology would have to be the true underpinnings of any such systems, not the more prosaic concerns of head tracking and high-res rendering: "We see this focus on [VR] interface as something like studying celluloid instead of cinema, paper instead of novels, cathode ray tubes instead of television."[3] Bates hoped that after his band of technologists had built a successful interactive drama engine, tools would follow for writers and artists to tell stories with it. He envisioned libraries of reusable character behaviors or reasoning logic which could be built up over time, "similar perhaps to the backlots of Hollywood studios."[2] He imagined tools for both rapid prototyping and fine-grained polish, tools for crafting VR conversations with believable characters who could understand speech and improvise their own. It seemed quite plausible that the reactive characters of *Star Trek*'s holodeck, debuting in the pilot episode of *The Next Generation* in 1987, might be only a decade or so away.

But in the 2020s that future has yet to arrive, and interactive drama in the form imagined by Laurel, Bates, and the Oz Project team seems in many ways barely closer than it did thirty years ago. There are likely many reasons why. The simplest explanation is that games with static stories—presented in cutscenes, in between bouts of combat—remained profitable despite their "merely fictional" structure. Upsetting the status quo presented a risk: if dynamic stories had the potential to be emergently better, they might also be emergently worse. While many Oz prototypes worked and produced intriguing results, they required authors comfortable with Lisp and logic programming, both notoriously hard concepts to teach. Even experts had a hard time working with interlinked systems with the complexity of Oz modules. And while the idea of text-only worlds as high-tech prototypes was still conceivable in the early 90s, with commercial text games only a few years gone from shelves, they would increasingly seem old-fashioned enough to discourage influencers or investors from taking them seriously in the years to come. Time spent on resources not visible in screenshots or game trailers, no matter how visionary the ideas behind them, became hard to justify.

When virtual reality for the masses finally did arrive in the 2010s, there were no ready-made interactive storytelling engines to drive it. The rainbow bridge "between the arts and artificial intelligence" can seem, at times, as

Like Tik-Tok himself, the Oz project would eventually wind down as fewer and fewer folks were left to keep turning the key.

Bates and several graduating students left CMU in 1997 to found a company called Zoesis to commercialize Oz technology. It survived for some time on spec work and prototypes for the early, more experimental web, but would sadly never attain the kind of sustainable and recurring traction that comes with widespread adoption.

Perhaps the most famous descendant of Oz technology would be the 2005 game *Façade* by Andrew Stern and Michael Mateas (the last Oz graduate student). In the twenty-minute interactive drama, the player visits friends Trip and Grace, a married couple in the midst of a quarrel, and takes part in a character-driven story that can end in many ways based on the player's moment-to-moment performance. The culmination of years of authoring and programming effort, it remains one of the most intriguing glimpses at what truly dynamic and responsive stories might be like. The immense effort and expertise required to create it have rarely been brought together since.

illusory as ever—stories in bestselling games remain firmly fictional, not simulated.

And yet it isn't true that there's been no progress; it's just come in dozens of isolated steps instead of one grand unifying vision. From the elaborately simulated world inhabited by the bearded "agents" of *Dwarf Fortress*, to dynamic systems personalizing Middle-earth's enemies or a first-person shooter's difficulty, to newer experiments involving reactive characters with memories and emotions, to increasingly accurate speech recognition and believable speech synthesis, to the rise of new tools for procedural text and story—many of the problem areas once named after characters from the Land of Oz keep cropping up in unexpected and disparate places. Flung by some hidden Playwright to faraway lands, their ultimate destinies, artistic and otherwise, remain undecided.

Whether they will ever return to Oz, or somewhere like it, to tell a story together once again will have to be a tale for another time.

see **2006**; *Versu: A Family Supper* **2013**; and *AI Dungeon* **2019**

References

1   Aarseth, Espen. 2007. "Doors and Perception: Fiction vs. Simulation in Games." *Intermédialités: Histoire et Théorie Des Arts, Des Lettres et Des Techniques/Intermediality: History and Theory of the Arts, Literature and Technologies*, no. 9, Centre de recherche sur l'intermédialité.

2   Bates, Joseph. 1990. "Computational Drama in Oz." *ART COM Magazine* 10 (10), Dec 1990.

3   Bates, Joseph. 1992. "Virtual Reality, Art, and Entertainment." *Presence: Teleoperators & Virtual Environments* 1 (1), MIT Press.

4   Bates, Joseph, A. Bryan Loyall, and W. Scott Reilly. 1992. "An Architecture for Action, Emotion, and Social Behavior." In *European Workshop on Modelling Autonomous Agents in a Multi-Agent World*. Springer.

5   Buckles, Mary Ann. 1985. "Interactive Fiction: The Computer Storygame 'Adventure.'" PhD Thesis, University of California, San Diego.

6   Carnegie Mellon University School of Computer Science. 2002. OZ Project Home Page. www.cs.cmu.edu/afs/cs.cmu.edu/project/oz/web/oz.html | a Jun 13, 2021

7   Crecente, Brian. 2016. "VR's Quintessential Innovators." *Polygon* (blog). Oct 26, 2016. www.polygon.com/features/2016/10/26/13411364/heilig-fisher-marks-de-la-pena-laurel-vr-bio | a Jun 13, 2021

8   Gudmundsen, Jinny. 2001. "Kids Find Adventure at Interactive Sites." Gannett Online, 2001. www.gannettonline.com/e/columnists/10000354.html | s Dec 17, 2005

9   Kelso, Margaret Thomas, Peter Weyhrauch, and Joseph Bates. 1993. "Dramatic Presence." *PRESENCE: Teleoperators & Virtual Environments* 2 (1), MIT Press.

10   Lancaster, Kurt. 1999. *Warlocks and Warpdrive: Contemporary Fantasy Entertainments with Interactive and Virtual Environments*. McFarland & Company, Inc.

11   Laurel, Brenda. 1986. "Toward the Design of a Computer-Based Interactive Fantasy System." PhD Thesis, The Ohio State University.

12   Laurel, Brenda. 1989. "Atari Research Memos on the Subject of Interactive Fantasy and Related Topics." Atari Sunnyvale Research Laboratory. leech.cybernoid.gr/files/oldskool/laurel_atari.pdf | a Jun 13, 2021

13   Laurel, Brenda. 2013. *Computers as Theatre*. 2nd ed. Addison-Wesley.

14   Reilly, W Scott Neal. 1996. "Believable Social and Emotional Agents." PhD Thesis, Pittsburgh: Carnegie Mellon University. apps.dtic.mil/dtic/tr/fulltext/u2/a310766.pdf |

15   Sloane, Sarah Jane. 1994. "Riding the Bus in Silicon Valley: Building Virtual Worlds." In *Colors of a Different Horse: Rethinking Creative Writing Theory and Pedagogy*, ed. Wendy Bishop and Hans Ostrom. ERIC.

16   Smith, Peter Andrey. 2017. "The 62-Year-Old Child Genius." *Topic* 6, Dec 2017. www.topic.com/the-62-year-old-child-genius | a Jun 13, 2021

17   Smith, Sean, and Joseph Bates. 1989. "Towards a Theory of Narrative for Interactive Fiction." Report. CMU-CS-89-121. Feb 20, 1989. Carnegie Mellon University.

18   Wardrip-Fruin, Noah. 2009. *Expressive Processing: Digital Fictions, Computer Games, and Software Studies*. MIT Press.

19   Weyhrauch, Peter. 1992. "OO Adventure Games." rec.arts.int-fiction (Usenet), Oct 28, 1992. groups.google.com/g/rec.arts.int-fiction/c/-l4PSRWrr9M/m/9yE9QGA7XcAJ | a Jun 13, 2021

PATCHWORK GIRL

OR, A MODERN MONSTER

Shelley Jackson
as MARY/SHELLEY, & HERSELF

Style	**Hypertext**
Debuted	**Oct 1995** *(online store)*
Launch Platform	**Macintosh, Windows**
Publisher	**Eastgate Systems**
Language	**Storyspace**
Launch Price	**$19.95** *(floppy disk)*

> " I am buried here. You can resurrect me, but only piecemeal. If you want to see the whole, you will have to sew me together yourself.

IT WAS THE LAST TALK OF A LONG DAY. On the MIT campus in October 1997, an interdisciplinary symposium called "Transformations of the Book" had assembled "classicists, Shakespearean scholars, technological wizards and lovers of all media"[13] to explore how the digital age was challenging, and changing, the written word. The talks started just after lunch, and it was coming up on nine o'clock when the final speaker, a woman in her midtwenties, took the stage. In her author photo she wore a sleeveless vest and a dense cluster of ear piercings; an ampersand was tattooed on her upper arm. Her speaker bio noted that "she specializes in lies and digressions." The talk was entitled "Stitch Bitch," and it began like this:

1995

Novelist Robert Coover, a
major early proponent of
hypertext fiction, started
a regular undergraduate
course on the subject at
Brown in 1991. See also
Screen 2002.

It has come to my attention that a young woman claiming to be the
author of my being has been making appearances under the name of
Shelley Jackson. It seems you have even invited her to speak tonight,
under the misapprehension that she exists, that she is something besides a
parasite…. May I say that I find this an extraordinary impertinence, and
that if she would like to come forward, we shall soon see who is the author
of whom.

Well? Well?

Very well.

I expect there are some of you who still think I am Shelley Jackson,
author of a hypertext about an imaginary monster, the patchwork girl
Mary Shelley made after her first-born ran amok. No, I am the monster
herself, and it is Shelley Jackson who is imaginary.[4]

The writer was there to reflect on a project that had, in the short time
since its release, already become one of the most celebrated examples of a
new kind of literature: the hypertext novel. *Patchwork Girl; or, A Modern
Monster* riffed on Mary Shelley's *Frankenstein; or, The Modern Prometheus*,
remixing text from the original and other sources alongside a new story
about the female counterpart made by Dr. Frankenstein for his monster. In
the original story, the female monster is destroyed by her creator in a fit of
despair before she can be given life. Jackson's novel suggests she was brought
back in secret, reborn "under the needle, and under the pen"—sewn back
together, but also given life through the electricity of words on screens.

Jackson grew up in Berkeley, California, and as a teen she worked at
her family's bookstore. After finishing an art degree at nearby Stanford, she
moved across the country for an MFA in creative writing at Brown, which
had developed a reputation for the study of experimental literature. Several
students and faculty had begun exploring the possibilities of nonlinear
hypertext writing, and while Jackson "didn't have a particularly strong techie
bent,"[7] when a graduate course she took around 1993 assigned the creation
of a hypertext story as a final project, she began work on a piece that would
evolve into *Patchwork Girl*. "I've always had a very spatial understanding
of text," she later recalled, and for the idea she'd begun to develop, it felt
right to conceive of story as discrete pieces that could be dragged around,
connected, and deliberately positioned. The potential of this new medium
seemed limitless: "I saw from the very first that an infinite number of new
possibilities for literature were opening up before us. I felt like I was standing
on the coast of a new world."[7]

The software Jackson wrote with was called Storyspace. It had been
created by a group of hypertext authors and theorists in 1987, two decades
after digital hypertexts first appeared on computers but still years before
the rise of the web with its hypertext markup language (HTML). By 1990,
Storyspace had become the commercial product of a tiny company, Eastgate
Systems. Eastgate's aspirations were to become a publishing house for
interactive literature, with the same standards and respectability of any
traditional literary publisher. By the mid-1990s their catalog listed over
a dozen hypertext titles for sale. The company "advertised itself as the
publisher of 'serious' hypertext fiction—perhaps in an attempt to differentiate
itself from 'text adventure' publishing enterprises or the emerging market

of games," according to scholar Scott Rettberg.[12] Despite the ambitions of companies like Infocom to have their stories taken seriously by mainstream media, text games (and indeed, games in general) had won little respect to date from cultural critics. An article on hypertext from 1994 took pains to note:

> One thing hyperfictions are *not* is games. There is no scoring, no winner or loser, no right or wrong path to take. The writers assiduously avoid you-are-there fantasy adventures. Their texts are literature, not literary fun-house rides where *you* chase Moby-Dick! *You* make love to Madame Bovary! *You* get buried alive in the House of Usher![11]

see *A Mind Forever Voyaging* **1985**

Ironically, the very next paragraph of this article compares the sometimes frustrating experience of navigating hypertext fiction to Chutes & Ladders.

Eastgate was determined to avoid the comparison. "There was a concerted if in retrospect somewhat desperate attempt to carve a niche for hypertext fiction within the boundaries" of conventional literature, writes Rettberg.[12] The company priced their titles like hardcovers; they sent advance copies to the *New York Times Book Review*, not *Game Informer*; and they positioned Storyspace as a software tool for professionals—it cost $245 at the time of *Patchwork Girl*'s release. The work they published was also aimed not at casual readers but the more erudite audiences of literary journals: fiction dense with allusions often impenetrable to those outside the ivory tower, and informed by postmodern and post-structuralist rejections of mainstream storytelling techniques. Perhaps in part for these reasons, and undoubtedly also because of its hefty price tag, Storyspace and most works produced with it would remain an isolated niche even within the already tiny world of interactive text. Both in the 90s and today, very few makers or readers of text games have been familiar with the movement it enabled.

Those who did gain access to Storyspace, like Jackson through her graduate course, found in it a powerful visual tool for creating nonlinear narratives. While a decade earlier creators had needed to build tools for digital texts nearly from scratch, a new era of more mature authoring systems was arriving. Storyspace let authors create named nodes of text called "lexia," of any length from a few words to multiple pages, and arrange them spatially within "containers" that could themselves be positioned on a virtual page. A container showed a miniature map of the lexia inside, letting the author cluster and position texts in groups. Lexia could be connected by creating a link from a word or phrase; clicking the link opened the target lexia in its own window, letting the reader reposition and juxtapose different nodes of the text they were reading. Two decades before the rise of Twine, Storyspace authors and other early pioneers were developing an aesthetics of interlinked prose. "When I first started writing hypertext," Jackson recalls,

see *Uncle Roger* **1986**

see *Howling Dogs* **2012**

> I discovered that the link was not neutral, but was itself a kind of argument, one that I should not duplicate in my prose. I had to learn to allow the link to make points that I would formerly have spelled out in words. In this sense, programming is not just a substrate but an active part of the writing.[5]

In contrast to conventions that would later develop for the web, links weren't necessarily visible to the reader. Early hypertext author Michael Joyce had championed this aesthetic, where a paragraph of unstyled text "encouraged readers to seek out 'words that yield'—that is, to click on given words that seem to be particularly evocative, and to see if the system will respond."[12] But this philosophy could make navigation challenging. Some words clicked might not link to anything at all; a crucial passage or even a whole sequence might be hidden behind an unassuming word most readers might never think to click. Combined with the lack of interest in traditional narrative structure from most authors, many early hypertexts became

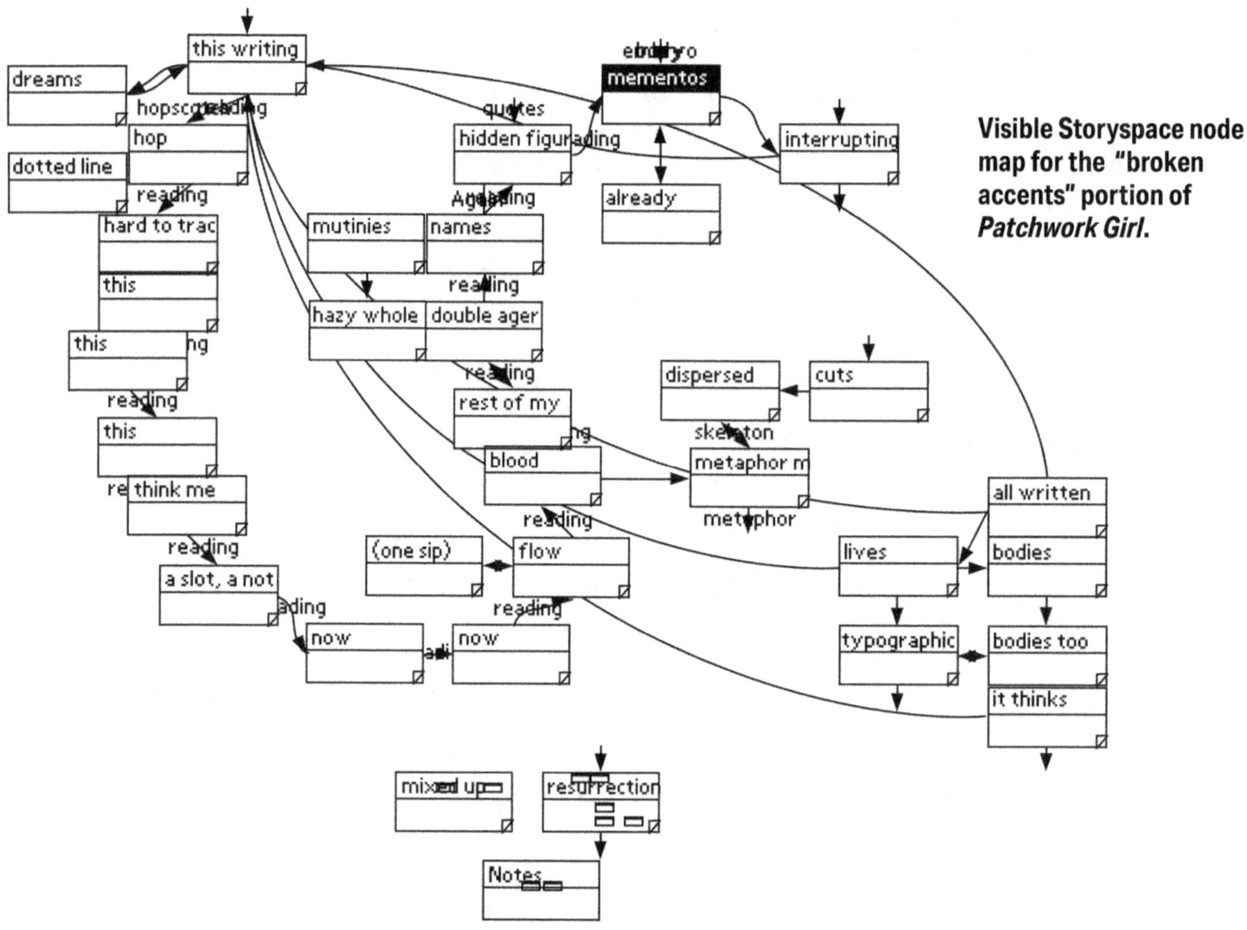

Visible Storyspace node map for the "broken accents" portion of *Patchwork Girl*.

deliberately disorienting spaces, with the pleasures of reading for immersion hard to find.

As she began to flesh out her project, developing an idea based on her long fascination with *Frankenstein* and its unfinished female monster, Jackson became inspired also by "the Storyspace software itself and the look of it even, the feel of moving around in these nested boxes."[7] She had been resistant to the deliberate distancing in many early hypertext works, and was coming to feel that

> all those [unconventional] features of hypertextuality are actually felt more keenly when they're pulling *against* the expectations and the desires aroused by a more conventional narrative. So I thought it was important to try to write something that was richly imagistic, full of character, full of

wordplay, and even a sense of story ... in order to fully feel the effects of rupture and disorientation and wandering.

The tale that eventually emerged from her experiments was told from the female monster's point of view, a perspective that blurs at times with those of the two Shelleys: *Frankenstein*'s author, and *Patchwork Girl*'s. The lexia are split into five named sections, each exploring a different aesthetic of nonlinear text through complex networks of interconnected prose. But a through line emerges that tells a long and mostly linear story, narrating the monster's life after she leaves her creator, takes a ship to America, and tries to discover or invent herself, building in the process an identity out of fragments and disjointed pieces.

Jackson's conception of the monster violates boundaries of gender, self, and species. She is made up of pieces mostly from women, but also from men and animals. With her large frame, "women and men alike mistake my gender and both are drawn to me," and often she to them. On her sea voyage she meets a kindhearted cabin boy whose identity is more complex than appearance suggests; in America she befriends a sideshow performer with an artificial tail he desperately wishes were real. Before her departure, the monster sleeps with her creator: not Victor Frankenstein, but Mary Shelley, the two drawn into each other's arms by powerful, unexpected compulsion. On the morning after, the two exchange coin-sized pieces of skin, each grafting the circle of flesh where its twin was removed. "If I am made of some of you," the monster writes, "I could be made of more."

Later, she pays a woman named Elsie in exchange for Elsie's name and her past—the memories, preferences, prejudices, and habits she hopes will bring her the unity of a real, whole person, "human, and seamless." But this effort fails: the monster's stitched-together pieces begin to loosen and come unjoined. As she literally falls apart in a bathtub, body losing its cohesion, she is visited one last time by Elsie, who helps her come to a revelation: "I was all in pieces, yet not apart. I felt permitted. I began to invent something new: a way to hang together without pretending I was whole." "You'll have to find another name," Elsie says as she leaves, "because I'm taking mine back."

The monster survives through two centuries into the present-day world of laptops and hypertext. "I was never comfortable in the drawing rooms or the pruned and cherished gardens of Mary's time," she writes, safer in a world of more anonymity and fewer preconceptions. She tries to write her memoirs, but is perpetually frustrated:

> Sometimes it bothers me to put my words on paper. Set in ranks, they argue I possess a "life" (as in Lives of the Artists), only one, actual and limited, and that it will become as hurtless, juiceless, entertaining and purely factual as anyone else's, after I'm dead. I watch my own words graduating instantaneously into the past tense and becoming someone else's someone else. They look fixed. [...] It bothers me, the thought of my words becoming clues, something someone might peer at to try to find a lost object. I don't want to be a reclusive beetle disappearing into a sheaf of papers. I was not one person and there is more than

1995

Opposite: *Patchwork Girl's* navigation features clickable images as another entry point into its maze of lexia. Each word in this node labeled "phrenology" links to a different passage.

one way to write this. I wish there were a way to show that every latest word I write has space for anything after it. Everything could have been different and already is.

The phrase "a way" yields, when clicked:

a way

Assembling these patched words in an electronic space, I feel half-blind [...]

The link suggests that, in hypertext, the monster has at last found a medium to hold her fragmented, multiplicious story. "The links can stretch very far before they break," she writes:

The moments of text get smaller
[anywhere]
and smaller
[anywhere]
and yet never seem small enough, because to pause on a given screen—even for a sip of coffee—is an interruption of the flow. The flow, which turns out to be the main point. Not the passages I am moving through, however beguiling, not this cafe in which I am still sitting [...] but the sheer pleasure of movement. [...] Here where the spindly bamboo bridges of the links criss-cross the void (from tufted hillock to leaning tower I am in a Seuss landscape, where gravity is an untested hypothesis), I run faster and faster over the quivering spans, dizzied by the echoes of my footsteps that rebound from far below me and from above until I doubt up and down and scuttle through a universe of sideways.

I will follow the paths and dispense with the scenery. I will be pure particulate flow, an electronic speedster gunning it through a cloud chamber, a quantum sky-diver. My hair flies out behind me, the skin on my face pulls taut and my clothes wrestle around me [...]

Unlike in many Storyspace works, Jackson makes the map of linked nodes visible to readers, who can use it to jump between different passages at will rather than solely navigating through text links. Jackson and her monster both write about how the black link lines connecting a maze of boxes call to mind sutures, or quilts; forging your own path through them is an act of stitching and assembly. Like many hypertexts, *Patchwork Girl* does not have a gamelike world simulation in which the reader is embedded. But Storyspace does track which lexia a reader has seen, and a feature called "guard fields" lets an author change the presence or direction of a link based on this history. In one early lexia of the main narrative sequence, for instance, you might find this sentence:

see *Adventure* 1976

1995

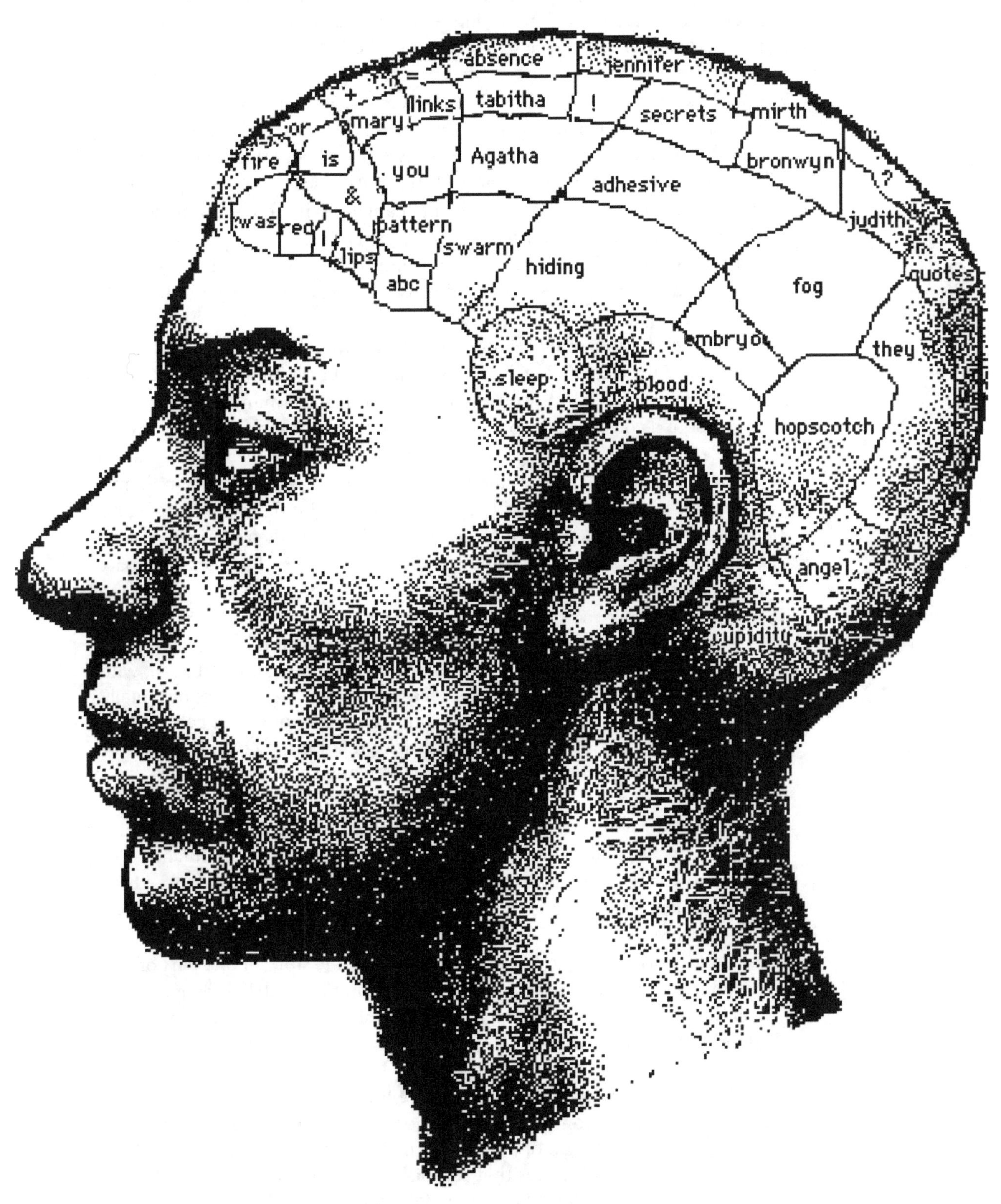

absence
jennifer
+
=
links
tabitha
!
secrets
mirth
or
mary
fire
is
bronwyn
?
you
Agatha
adhesive
&
judith
was red
pattern
swarm
lips
quotes
abc
hiding
fog
embryo
they
sleep
blood
hopscotch
angel
cupidity

> I bought passage on a ship to America, and at a dressmaker's shop outfitted myself in full mourning—what might be a monster's disguise, or a resounding farewell to a monstrous life left behind, my own.

Two links lead forward, from "a monster's disguise" or "farewell to a monstrous life." Depending on which phrase the reader clicks, different versions of many future lexia will be shown during an otherwise linear sequence about the monster's adventures in America. The passages differ in subtle details rather than significant changes, as if there is no single, definitive truth to the monster's story. Instead of multiple small choices with predictable effects, as in a text adventure, here a single choice leads to far-reaching ripples of disconnected consequence, much harder to trace or keep contained.

Patchwork Girl's other sections are less linear, many remixing text from multiple sources, including *Frankenstein* and L. Frank Baum's *The Patchwork Girl of Oz*: one book by a woman about a constructed man; the other by a man about a constructed woman. Baum's Girl was made from a "crazy-quilt" doll brought to life, and though other denizens of Oz find her flaunting of social norms and uneven stitching unsettling, she herself revels in them: "'Horrid?' she replied. 'Why, I'm thoroughly delightful. I'm an Original, if you please, and therefore incomparable.'" Jackson stitches together new texts out of phrases from both novels and other sources, like the Storyspace manual and essays on philosophy or critical theory:

> At first I couldn't think what to make her of. I collected bones from charnel houses, paragraphs from Heart of Darkness, and disturbed, with profane fingers, the tremendous secrets of the human frame, but finally in searching through a chest in a solitary chamber, or rather cell, at the top of the house, I came across a fabric of relations, an old patchwork quilt, which my grandmother once made when she was young.

Clicking anywhere in these passages shows a parallel lexia where each phrase is tied to its original source by citation, the seams between the stitched-together words and their origins made visible. Clicking again returns the text to its unblemished, untethered form. Both versions seem equally definitive.

Another section, titled "a Graveyard," contains dozens of lexia named for body parts: *right arm, liver, tongue*. Each tells the story of one part of the monster and its original owner. The result is another patchwork quilt of selves, stories from which the monster has fashioned her own composite identity. Most are portraits of women from an earlier century:

> My left leg belonged to Jane, a nanny who harbored under her durable grey dresses and sensible undergarments a remembrance of a less sensible time: a tattoo of a ship and the legend, Come Back To Me. Nanny knew some stories that astonished her charges, and though the ship on her thigh blurred and grew faint and blue with distance, until it seemed that the currents must have long ago finished their work, undoing its planks one by one with unfailing patience, she always took

> the children to the wharf when word came that a ship was docking, and
> many a sailor greeted her by name.
>
> My leg is always twitching, jumping, joggling. It wants to go places. It has
> had enough of waiting.

Other clusters of the more than three hundred lexia in *Patchwork Girl*
weave in and out of the main narrative, wandering through musings on
identity, gender, biology, and dreams. The experience of reading can be
overwhelming, especially while the reader is still learning the shapes and
rhythms of the piece. "A radical text can't just depict monstrosity," Jackson
has said, "but must be itself monstrous. Oddly, I don't think that's too
hard. All texts are monstrous, really, always more chaotic and less coherent
than they pretend to be, but most writers smooth over the stitches that
hold them together."[5] When she began the project, Jackson first linked
together any passages that seemed conceptually related, but found the result
"shapeless and uninteresting ... though the reader was actively following
links, they were passive in the sense that they weren't being asked to make
the connections themselves between the far-flung parts of the text."[7] So she
removed most of the links and started over, instead focusing on identifying
what she called "threads," chains of passages that could be productively
joined to suggest continuities—while trusting readers to also find their own.

Jackson's professor George Landow showed her class project to Eastgate,
who offered her a publishing contract. After extensive revisions and
extensions, *Patchwork Girl* was released in 1995 on a 3.5″ floppy disk, and it
would become among the most famous of Eastgate's "serious hypertexts." In
an early review, Landow called it "brilliant" and "the finest hypertext fiction
thus far to have appeared ... [filled with] wonderful writing—sharp, bracing,
surprising, endlessly inventive."[9] It's remembered today for many reasons,
not least its resonant connections between medium and message. It's "a
special kind of text," wrote another scholar, "which, just like [Frankenstein's]
creature, is the end result of certain technological developments."[1] Landow
noted:

> Hypertext, Jackson permits us to see, enables us to recognize the degree
> to which the qualities of collage—particularly those of appropriation,
> assemblage, concatenation, and the blurring of limits, edges, and
> borders—characterize a good deal of the way we conceive of gender and
> identity. Sooner or later all information technologies, we recall, have
> always convinced those who use them both that these technologies are
> natural and that they provide ways to describe the human mind and self.
> At the early stage of a digital information regime, *Patchwork Girl* permits
> us to use hypertext as powerful speculative tool that reveals new things
> about ourselves while at the same time retaining the sense of strangeness,
> of novelty.[9]

Patchwork Girl is challenging to play today. Unlike most software from
the 90s, it's still for sale from its original publisher, running in a proprietary
engine that has not always kept up with the latest platforms. In today's
Storyspace, Jackson's original navigation controls are gone; some links are

One tip for modern readers:
pressing Ctrl-Alt on a PC
or Cmd-Option on a Mac
will reveal the links in a
passage.

broken; and lexia no longer appear in individual windows, able to be moved around and juxtaposed. The visible link lines whose aesthetics helped inspire Jackson's story are no longer shown in the map view—the boxes themselves are properly positioned, but the interface hides the ways they are sutured together. A user's expectations today are drastically different too: Storyspace was designed in an era when reading the manual was crucial to operating a piece of software, but the manual distributed with the piece no longer accurately describes its operation, if it's even read at all—a loss with dire consequences for successful navigation.

Jackson has framed this slow degradation of the piece as, in a way, "completely appropriate … to try to hang on to it would be inconsistent with my central argument" about the ephemerality of bodies and the fluidity of forms. She has little interest in a port to a modern platform: "I couldn't pour it into a contemporary container without altering it significantly."[7]

While Jackson kept writing hypertext for a few more years, she would eventually find a career in teaching and in writing more traditional novels, though her work would continue to challenge conventions and boundaries. In 2003 she began a project called *Skin*, which called for two thousand volunteers to each tattoo a single word of a new short story on their body. Only volunteers who sent proof of their participation were allowed to read the entire text. Even her books printed with more traditional ink have often been experiments in form, style, and structure. "My favorite texts loiter, dawdle, tease, pass notes," she said in that late-night spoken-word manifesto at MIT; "they resist the linear, they pervert it." At that venue, which had brought together the worlds of traditional literature and new technology— still not quite certain if they could be friends—she expressed that she had "no desire to demolish linear thought, but to make it one option among many," explaining:

> I adore the book, but I don't fit into it very well, as a writer or a reader. There's always some of me hanging untidily outside, looking like a mess, an excrescence, something the editor should have lopped off and for which I feel a bit apologetic. To make something orderly and consecutive out of the divergent fragments that come naturally feels like forcing myself through a Klein bottle.… *Patchwork Girl* grew in clumps and strands like everything I write, but unlike everything else it had permission to stay that way.[4]

"I had considered myself an esoteric writer whose audience might always be small," the author reflected more recently.

> I discovered that the world is more malleable and people more ready to embrace the improbable than I had ever imagined. Now it seems to me that it was subtly arrogant to imagine otherwise, and also kind of lazy. Now I think I should not let lack of precedent stop me from imagining preposterous things into being.

"The world," she concluded, "can be rewritten."[6]

References

1   Carazo, Carolina Sánchez-Palencia, and Manuel Almagro Jiménez. 2006. "Gathering the Limbs of the Text in Shelley Jackson's 'Patchwork Girl'." *Atlantis* 28 (1).

2   Grigar, Dene M., and Stuart A. Moulthrop. 2015. *Pathfinders: Documenting the Experience of Early Digital Literature*. Nouspace Publications.

3   Hayles, N. Katherine. 2000. "Flickering Connectivities in Shelley Jackson's Patchwork Girl: The Importance of Media-Specific Analysis." *Postmodern Culture* 10 (2).

4   Jackson, Shelley. 1997. "Stitch Bitch: The Patchwork Girl." Presented at Transformations of the Book, MIT, Nov 4, 1997. web.mit.edu/m-i-t/articles/jackson.html

5   Jackson, Shelley. 2002. "Of Dolls and Monsters." Interview by Rita Raley. www.elo-repository.org/TIRweb/tirweb/feature/jackson/interview.html

6   Jackson, Shelley. 2003. "Written On (and Under) the Skin." Interview by Rosita Nunes. www.tattoohighway.org/8/sjinterview.html

7   Jackson, Shelley. 2013. "Shelley Jackson Interview." Interview by Dene Grigar. Video. vimeo.com/114482904.

8   Koskimaa, Raine. 2000. "Digital Literature: From Text to Hypertext and Beyond." University of Jyväskylä. users.jyu.fi/~koskimaa/thesis/thesis.shtml

9   Landow, George P. 1996. "Stiching Together Narrative, Sexuality, Self: Shelley Jackson's 'Patchwork Girl.'" *Electronic Book Review*, Sep 1, 1996. electronicbookreview.com/essay/stitching-together-narrative-sexuality-self-shelley-jacksons-patchwork-girl/

10 Malssen, Kara van. 2005. "Risk Assessment and Structure of an Interactive CDROM: Patchwork Girl by Shelley Jackson." www.nyu.edu/tisch/preservation/program/student_work/2005fall/05f_1805_vanmalssen_a3.pdf

11 Melrod, George. 1994. "Digital Unbound." *Details*, Oct 1994. college.cengage.com/english/amore/chapter3/ch3_r1.html

12 Rettberg, Scott. 2015. "The American Hypertext Novel, and Whatever Became of It?" In *Interactive Digital Narrative*, ed. Hartmut Koenitz, Gabriele Ferri et al. Routledge.

13 Wright, Sarah H. 1997. "Conferees Ponder the Shape of Books in the Electronic Age." *MIT Tech Talk*, Oct 29, 1997. news.mit.edu/1997/books-1029

SO FAR

Andrew Plotkin

Style **Parser**
Debuted **Jun 19, 1996** *(Usenet)*
Launch Platform **Z-machine v8**
Language **Inform 5**

> " Hot, foul, and dark. How did indoor theater become so fashionable? Well enough in spring rain or winter, but not in the thick, dead afternoon of high summer. And though *Rito and Imita* looks very fine, shining with electric moonslight in the enclosed gloom, you're much more aware of being crammed in neck-by-neck with your sweaty fellow citizens.

THE RELEASE OF GRAHAM NELSON'S *Curses* **1993** and Inform, the programming language he'd made to write it, set off an explosion of amateur text game development that would echo for decades. Alongside other maturing tools like TADS and old standards like AGT, passionate fans saw increasingly viable pathways to creating their own games in a mode abandoned by commercial publishers but which still had a devoted readership online. Within a few years, fans went from picking over a scant handful of new text games each season to dozens and dozens. A whole new era for interactive fiction had arrived.

So Far, released in 1996, was one of several amateur games that year that might have passed for an Infocom game in scope and depth of worldbuilding. It opens with a play that has the rhythms of Shakespeare but unfolds under a strange sky where two moons shine. Onstage, estranged lovers Rito and Imita are meeting for the first time since Rito has learned of his love's affair.

1996

Major Releases

» **Release 5**, Jun 19, 1996.
First public.

» **Release 6**, Dec 19,
1996. "All the changes are
nuisance bugs—typos, bad
default responses, a few
missing synonyms. There
have been no changes to
the plot or game design."

> Rito:
> How come you, harlot? Dare you come this way,
> your skin yet dark with Tato's shadow's stain?

Imita begs Rito not to despise her, but admits she is pregnant with Tato's
child. Rito rushes from the stage, overcome with emotion. In a soliloquy
to the audience, Imita pleads "What scourge, what scourge I bear, from
what red star / So near to happiness, and yet so far?" The play draws to its
inevitable conclusion with a duel, a bloody death, and a reconciliation before
a wedding and a happy ending:

> Imita (simply):
> Ah, my love. Can you forgive me?
>
> Rito:
> How can I deny you? There is nothing to forgive.

But the game that follows takes the player on a difficult journey that echoes
the lovers' final questions in many ways and through unexpected registers.
Resolutions seem harder to come by than a fifth act finale, wounds harder to
heal. As Elizabethan theater often opened with a dumbshow to explain the
essentials of the upcoming plot to the audience, *So Far* begins with a drama
that primes the reader for the challenges of a story they must play.

As the curtain falls, the player—pursuing their own lover Aessa, half-
glimpsed in the audience—pushes through the milling crowd and into stifling
summer air outside. Many have gathered to watch a rare astronomical event:
the two moons in near conjunction, approaching but destined to never quite
touch. The gap between you and Aessa, too, seems unbridgeable: she has
vanished and you cannot find her. But a faint breath of cool air tempts you
elsewhere, leading to a disused backstage corner where a "shadow's stain"
offers passage to another world entirely, one where summer has moved on.

> **Theater Storage**
> Or perhaps ex-storage, since the room is almost bare. A small dirty
> window to the west admits bright beams, but they fall across only the
> floor and a battered cabinet against the north wall. The doorway lies to
> the east.
>
> The air here is rich with autumn, brisk and cool. It's impossible, absurd.
>
> >EXAMINE CABINET
> A closed cabinet, chipped and stained, stands against the wall. Sunlight
> brings a tattered, hopeful glow out of the old wood, but shadow falls
> behind.
>
> >LOOK BEHIND CABINET
> Blackness lies behind the cabinet. Opaque... in this brightly lit room, no
> shadow should be so thick.

As you step back from the cabinet, the shadow *flares*. A sunbeam might shine off crystal to paint the whole world white for one angle of an instant; so this shadow widens into a gulf beneath black and wider than everything. Then you move a fraction farther, and it is only a line of too-black behind chipped wood.

>TOUCH SHADOW
You reach into the shadow, and in, in, and the farther you stretch the farther there is to go -- you pull back, shivering.

>ENTER SHADOW
The shadow *flares* again as you set foot to it. The cabinet is to your left and the wall to your right, never mind the space that isn't there between them, and then never mind anything because blackness has taken the world, never mind, never world, not even you, never you—

[Hit any key.]
[ENTER]

—And then daylight smacks you in the behind, ordinary as a dirt road.

Abandoned Road
The sky is almost violet, infinitely distant—you've never seen such a sky, and without the haze of metallic heat that summer should have. But the wind is sharp and chilly, and the trees nearby are a quilt of orange, red, and gold.

Beneath you the road is old, filled with weeds and ragged moss [...]

YOU ARE CARRYING...

» a red pod

» a clay jar full of water

» a scrap of something blue

» an odd wooden box

» a ceramic square

» two lengths of thin pipe

» a twisted key

The rest of *So Far* is a surreal journey through richly drawn worlds linked by pools of impossible shadow. As your journey continues, the landscapes become imbued with symbolism, echoes in architecture and geography of Imita and Rito's star-crossed story. The puzzles in those landscapes likewise recycle and reinvent endless permutations on themes of pairs, shadows, betrayal, wounds, closeness, and separation. The game is written in a mode of text adventure design that today seems harsh, requiring judicious use of SAVE, RESTORE, and UNDO to successfully navigate; the puzzles often require thinking with a brutal dream logic that many in the years since its release have found hard to connect with. But *So Far* enchanted players in 1996 because it pointed toward a richer future for interactive fiction. Its puzzles and story intertwined in a way that elevated both over the sometimes simpler games of the 80s and the fan works of the early 90s that tried to emulate them. *So Far* felt like something new. Interactive fiction, it seemed, could evolve.

Andrew Plotkin had appeared on the scene the previous year as a winner of the first ever Interactive Fiction Competition (IF Comp) with his game *A Change in the Weather*. A lifelong fan of text games, he had fiddled with

see *Photopia* **1998** for more on IF Comp

making his own in his teens and had long dreamed of crafting his own IF authoring language. When Inform was released he'd been intrigued by its potential, but it was the announcement of IF Comp that pushed him to try game writing again: "It lit the fire under me—and several other authors, not limited to Inform users—to get a game written; not as a vague long-term project, but right now."[3] *Weather* was praised both for its challenging puzzles and its shifting descriptions of an outdoor landscape that transitions from pleasant evening to deadly midnight storm. *So Far*, his follow-up, would be bigger in scope and, with more elaborate puzzles and more richly realized environments, longer than the two-hour games IF Comp was beginning to normalize.

So Far took inspiration from two games that had become some of Plotkin's touchstones. Cyan's *Myst* [1993] had reinvigorated adventure games with its combination of breathtaking landscapes and challenging puzzles embedded in a narrative framework; *So Far*'s surreal worlds and strange machines can be read in part as homage. Another clear influence is Infocom's *Trinity* [1986], one of the company's few explicit attempts to elevate text games to a more artistic and intellectual level. *Trinity* tells a richly symbolic story of the dawn of nuclear weapons and the existential threat they brought to human history, mostly through mute tableaux and the player's actions. In the shadow of an enormous sundial, for instance, the player explores a vista of huge toadstools that grow denser and larger as they near the terrain marked out for sunset. The toadstools, the player comes to realize, each represent a nuclear mushroom cloud. The landscape is a temporal map of coming apocalypse—a shadow sweeping inexorably across history.

So Far also offers a landscape suffused with metaphorical imagery and representational puzzles, recurring variations on its foreshadowed themes. The formal poetry of the opening play is echoed in a ritual dance, frenetic and wordless, by people living under a different sky. A crack in the theater wall mirrors a crack in a distant ice floe. Pairs, in fact, are everywhere: two cracks; two lovers; two dancers; two moons; two reptilian mounts; two guardians blocking access to forbidden streets; two cubes that must be pushed close together to solve a puzzle, but not so close as to ever quite touch. Two pillars guard a gate that can only be passed through once one of them is destroyed. There is a world of silence and a world of nothing but sound; a world of all form and no meaning and another all meaning and no form. The landscape makes physical the opening drama's tale of damaged lovers and its questions of forgiveness and redemption, while the game's puzzles make the same ideas playable. The world, mechanics, and meaning rhyme. Understanding them is easier together than apart.

The worlds you visit are divided into two groups of five, interconnected through portals of shadow. Vivid language, filled with color and bright description, brings the first set to life:

> The vine is actually a muddy color, but the leaves are broad and streaked with bright yellow. Uncounted fine tendrils root deeply into the mound.

See *A Mind Forever Voyaging* **1985** for another example.

1996

> A single fat red pod, about the size of your fist, clings to the vine at one point.

> The dome's surface is a polished brown-grey, a bit mottled, and the whole structure is very slightly irregular; a homey, reassuring effect. The ground beneath you is a shocking contrast. Bright lichen covers everything with magenta tufts; there's not a blade of grass or stick of shrubbery within fifty yards of the dome. The olive-mossed roads are the only relief [...]

The worlds in the second grouping, by contrast, are spare and minimal, experimental and surreal. In one there is no light, and you must navigate an environment described only in abstract sounds to find the one place of silence—an aural landscape's equal to a portal of shadow. In another world you drift in a formless void chasing shadows of memory—scenes from what seem to be your character's past. Only by moving toward the more difficult memories can you reach the most difficult of all and find a path forward.

The two moons are present in the sky of each world, suggesting perhaps a journey through different times or realities, not places. With each world you visit, they draw closer together, but never quite touch.

Eventually you reach a grim world trapped between infinite planes of metal above and below, so tight you cannot stand upright (but not quite touching). Movement in any direction seems pointless, and the only items are bone-handled silver pipes of different thicknesses, some narrow, some wide. Through experimentation, you learn that striking a pipe makes a resonant tone that transports you to different aspects of this strange environment, perhaps parallel dimensions. The narrow and wide pipes move you toward different ends of a conceptual stack of subtly different metal hells.

> **>TAP WIDE PIPE**
> *Tunnnggg...* The pipe blurs, and for a moment it seems to extend, vertically, forever. You cannot breathe for the sound. The bounded world blurs vertically as well, and the metal ceiling recedes into the distance...
>
> **Caught In Metal**
> The space between these plates is, if anything, fractionally lower than the first one you fell into. A dim phosphorescent grid is traced out across the ceiling, marking silent distance in all directions.
>
> There are three more lengths of silver pipe here, just like the ones you found earlier. Two are narrow; one is wide.
>
> The sound, and the pipe you struck, are gone.

In the wide direction things seem older, more damaged, more cramped, and deeper; in the narrow direction they are newer, more pristine, less claustrophobic, and higher up. As you travel you find more pipes, but

Navigating a pitch-black environment with hazards may be an homage to *Hunt the Wumpus* **1973**, a game which Plotkin would later more explicitly reference with his *Hunter, in Darkness* [1999].

Spoilers for the Caught In Metal world.

exploration is brutal: using a pipe destroys it, and at first it seems impossible to gather enough to escape in either direction. Solving a puzzle that involves bringing light to a dark dimension will uncover one additional pipe, giving you exactly the number you need to escape—assuming you make no mistakes. There is not a single pipe to spare.

Near the end of the wide direction, you come across another prisoner in this strange metal purgatory:

> A figure sprawls indifferently on its back a few feet away. His back; it's a boy, raggedly dressed; young, you think, although it's oddly uncertain a guess. He breathes steadily in sleep.
>
> The sound, and the pipe you struck, are gone.
>
> Your knee slips abruptly on moss; you jerk a hand out to catch yourself. The length of thin pipe flies from you and hits the ground with a muffled clank. The boy slips a syllable of protest, turns on his side, and huddles, still asleep.
>
> >WAKE BOY
> Perhaps it was only the stirring of the air; the child is awake. A thin hand darts out and snatches the length of thin pipe. The boy clutches the metal to his chest, staring at you wildly.

The child is afraid of you at first, but warms up if you let him. Though you share no language, he shows you that the phosphorescent moss on the infinite floor and ceiling can be eaten, and demonstrates how crawling away is futile, always leading back to the same spot. It becomes clear he understands, just as you do, the rules of this place; and that the wide and narrow pipes are the only possible means of escape. But there is only one pipe. Only one of you can use it.

> >ASK BOY FOR PIPE
> He twitches violently. Wrapping his hands around the pipe, the boy turns away, shaking, hiding the silver metal with his body.
>
> Then he straightens, slowly. His eyes search yours, pressing at the wall of understanding between you; they drop to the length of pipe, and rise again. Moss-light shivers on the polished surface. And—very softly—he lays the pipe down before you.
>
> >GET THE PIPE
> The boy's hand clenches as you pick up the length of pipe. But his face does not change.
>
> >TAP IT
> *Tunnnggg...* The pipe blurs, and for a moment it seems to extend, vertically, forever. You cannot breathe for the sound. The bounded world blurs vertically as well, and the metal ceiling recedes into the distance...

> The boy's eyes seem to fade last of all. They watch you, full of something you may never see again.

Carefully mapping the distribution of spaces and pipes makes clear there is no possible way to arrive at the boy's space carrying an extra pipe. There's no escape without sacrifice, or perhaps betrayal. "So near," Imita's line on stage foreshadowed, "and yet so far."

End spoilers.

Many of the puzzles in Plotkin's game, and most of the ones he would write in the years to come, require observing complex systems closely enough to learn how to operate them—though rarely with such grim logic. In a world filled with bustling, mute people, watching carefully reveals routines you can take advantage of to slip into off-limits places. To get through a gate, you must build up a mental picture of a complex set of rusted pulleys whose components appear across half a dozen separate rooms, coming to understand how they interact with each other and the environment around them. Plotkin has described this systemic approach as foundational to his thinking on game design:

> A good IF game floods the player with his environment—all the senses, all the time. It has a story, or variations of story, which turn on the player's actions. (Not necessarily his choices.) It invites the player to think inside the game world, by requiring deductions and combinations of game elements which are interesting in the game world's terms.[1]

When this approach to design and storytelling works, it can feel revelatory. And yet it's fair to say it doesn't always work. *So Far*'s surreal, symbolically charged environment can sometimes obscure the player's ability to understand it well enough to gain mastery, frustrating the intended revelations. Like many puzzle games, it often errs on the side of being too hard rather than too easy. Jon Ingold, who would later co-found commercial IF studio inkle, wrote in a 2008 review of *So Far* that while he deeply loved the game, he had a hard time recommending it to others—the review's title was "Horribly unfair, hauntingly beautiful."[2] Reviewer Alistair G. Thomas, however, found the sense of confusion that permeates the game an integral part of it:

see *80 Days* **2014**

> In most games, this would mean you'd missed out the bit where you found out the answers. In *So Far*, the author has pushed the idea that in a strange world, the player might well face strange incomprehensible things, and to pass through that world, he might well have to figure out what they can do for him. He is not the focus of this world; it has its own history, its own concerns. The player will not get his hand held here.[7]

Plotkin would later move away from more unforgiving styles of puzzle design that he saw as "still adhering to the Infocom tradition: a game should take many run-throughs to finish; you will almost certainly have to back up and retry earlier parts of the game in a different way."[8] A few weeks after the first release of *So Far*, he came up with a system later known as the Zarfian Cruelty Scale (after his online handle, Zarf) that could categorize the way a game's puzzle design impacted the experience of play. A "cruel" game, for instance, lets you get into an unwinnable state without revealing there's no longer any way to win. While many classic games had been cruel, conventional wisdom began to hold that this kind of design move was not really something most players enjoyed. IF was trending instead toward the "merciful" end of the scale, a key survival move in an era when players increasingly had far more games to choose from and less time to struggle with them. Plotkin's next game, *The Space Under the Window* [1997], discarded puzzles and a consistent simulated world for a hypertextual story space navigated with single keywords; the narrative could change based on what parts of it the player chose to focus on. *Shade* [2000] tells a hauntingly spare story of a narrator whose reality is melting away around him, one item at a time. By the release of *Hadean Lands* [2014], a magnum opus of puzzle and system design, Plotkin had become one of interactive fiction's grandmasters, an expert practitioner who has also contributed enormously to both code bases and community over the years, doing vital work to keep IF networks and tools alive. Among many other contributions, he defined the 32-bit Glulx format, which extended the lifetime of Inform games beyond the Z-machine's legacy limitations, and he's one of the founders of the Interactive Fiction Technology Foundation, a nonprofit helping to maintain and preserve IF history and technology.

So Far remains significant for the way it pointed toward a different kind of future for interactive stories. *Curses* had demonstrated it was possible to make new games in the style of Infocom; now newer authors were beginning to explore what other kinds of styles there could be. In 2001, IF newcomer Emily Short **2000 2013** would write that while playing *So Far* is at times a struggle, its greatest achievement

> is not teaching the player how to regard a single action as representative of moral choice, but presenting the whole world in such a way that it seems redolent of such choices, tying the physical environment intimately to the emotional one in ways that are sometimes visible only in retrospect.… Plotkin's symbolism is merged wholly with the landscape; it *is* the landscape. The pieces are polyvalent and connotative, any given thing suggesting an array of connections and meanings, not denoting a single concept in its purity.
>
> I am not sure whether any subsequent work has approached it in this regard. I am not sure that anyone has tried.[4]

A new generation of interactive storytellers was arriving, one that was thinking more deeply than ever about their medium's potential and its possibility. "If this carry-on doesn't stop," wrote Alistair Thomas in his *So Far* review, "we'll be a proper grown-up medium before you know it."[7]

References

1 Crigger, Lara. 2006. "Andrew Plotkin and Emily Short: The CGM Interviews." *Brass Lantern* (blog). brasslantern.org/community/interviews/cgm.html | a Mar 28, 2020

2 Ingold, Jon. 2008. "Horribly Unfair, Hauntingly Beautiful." *IFDB*. Mar 29, 2008. ifdb.org/ viewgame?id=rcrihauxixy48svr&review=3429 | a Oct 24, 2022

3 Jong, Philip. 2011. "Andrew Plotkin [Interview]." *Adventure Classic Gaming* (blog). Jan 7, 2011. www.

adventureclassicgaming.com/index.php/site/interviews/622 | a Mar 28, 2020

4 Short, Emily. 2001. "A Step." *IF-Review* (blog). www.ministryofpeace.com/if-review/reviews/20010622.html | s Jun 22, 2001

5 Sineath, Luke. 2012. "Jung on Myst." *IFDB*. Apr 24, 2012. ifdb.tads.org/viewgame?id=rcrihauxixy48svr | a Mar 28, 2020

6 Stevens, Duncan. 2001. "So Far" (review). *SPAG* #25, Jun 20, 2001. www.spagmag.org/archives/backissues/spag25.html#far | a Mar 28, 2020

7 Thomas, Alistair G. 1997. "So Far" (review). *SPAG* #12, Dec 13, 1997. www.spagmag.org/archives/backissues/spag12.html | a Mar 28, 2020

8 Vestal, Andrew, and Nich Maragos. 2004. "Magic Words: Interactive Fiction in the 21st Century (Interview: Andrew Plotkin)." *Brass Lantern* (blog). www.brasslantern.org/community/interviews/magicwords-f.html | a Mar 28, 2020

ACHAEA
DREAM OF DIVINE LANDS

Matt Mihály and others

Style	**MUD**
Debuted	**Sep 8, 1997**
Launch Platform	**Linux** *(server)* **Telnet** *(client)*
Developer	**Iron Realms Entertainment**
Language	**Hourglass** *(launch)* **Vortex** *(first rewrite)* **Rapture Engine in C/C++ and Lua scripting** *(second rewrite)*

> **"** Your fate and fame shall be an echo and a light unto eternity.

IT WAS A GÖTTERDÄMMERUNG: a twilight of gods.

Dark portents had been gathering for months. First, a plague. Then the opening of portals to an evil realm of reptiloid terrors and huge flying monstrosities, the airborne sandworms known as the Dala'myrr. The world's oldest dragon had been killed in a senseless attack; the Fire Behind the Flame, granting both gods and mortals the spark of life, was guttering, no longer able to resurrect the dead or keep the worldtree warm. When an evil cult helped summon into being the monstrous demon Bal'met—the Worldreaver—the squabbling gods of Sapience were forced to join in a

1997

1997

grand alliance to defeat him. In the Garden of the Gods atop the world's tallest mountain, they fought:

> The earth rumbles ominously as the voice of Artemis, Goddess of the Cataclysm, booms across the firmament, "The Cataclysm does not forget your transgressions upon Nature and its protectors, vile creature. Relinquish the power that is not yours to control!"
>
> Bal'met swells with scorn and rapacious hunger, becoming a great spear of destructive energy that streaks toward the unprotected Garden, resolving as a billowing cloud before the six Gods.
>
> Hefting His hammer high, Phaestus slams it upon the ground, striking a massive blow that shakes the very earth.
>
> The Garden of the Gods shudders and quakes, and a complex pattern of runes flares to life beneath the fluctuating form of Bal'met.

But the fight went poorly. Many gods were slain, and cities that had stood for centuries were wiped from the map. Constant skirmishes played out between good and evil mortals as factions fought to purify or corrupt key shrines of power. At last, in the world's most desperate hour, Maya, the goddess of creation herself, sacrificed her life to give hundreds of mortal heroes a piece of her divine power, drawing them into the heavenly realm to take part in the final battle against Bal'met:

> As you are pulled within the swirling vortex, your body and soul expand and contract, twisted and thrown about as if by a turbulent gale. One moment it seems your soul is torn apart from your body; a second later your body seems a heavy weight lying deep within your soul.
>
> Always moving forward, you are spun and woven through the fabric of reality, and the tempestuous journey seems to last for eons before all is suddenly calm.
>
> [...] Your race is now that of Demigod.

The god-touched heroes, and even the gods themselves, were players in one of the last remaining commercial MUDs online. The battle was the culmination of a massive event unfolding over ten weeks of real-world time—while the Achaean year was 613 AF, on Earth the finale came in December 2012. And many who took part in the War of the Worldreaver would remember it for the rest of their lives. It took place in a world made of words—a world without graphics that would soon look dated, and with nearly limitless production values. The battle was a defining moment in a history players had created together for fifteen years, built on a platform where "very little stands between those 'wouldn't it be cool?' moments and their subsequent implementation."[9] "I've always loved how the game feels like a favorite book you wish you could be the character in," one player wrote, "and in this case you are."[7]

Achaea launched in September 1997, maybe one of the worst possible moments to start a new commercial MUD. That same month *Ultima Online* [Origin Systems] debuted, heralding a new era for online fantasy gaming brought to life with graphics, not prose. The early 90s experiments with more social virtual worlds like *LambdaMOO* were petering out as expectations of 3D graphics became entrenched, and while single-player text games were in the midst of a quiet renaissance, their player base had little overlap with mudders. Worse, for years most commercial MUDs had charged hourly connection fees, a standard model that other dial-up services like America Online had normalized. But AOL had recently switched to a monthly flat-fee rate: "Hourly charges instantly became a non-starter for everyone in the industry," creator Matt Mihály recalls.[3] It was an open question whether anyone would still want to play, let alone pay for, an online text game.

Mihály had gotten into mudding while an undergrad at Cornell, entranced by the fascinating possibilities of persistent virtual worlds. He spent countless hours on *BatMUD* [Antti Luostarinen and Niklas Lindroos 1990], forcing himself to stop playing his senior year so he could graduate. Afterward he landed a job as a stockbroker, but found it a miserable experience. He quit and fell back into MUDs, spending upwards of eight hours a day in a long-running British game that had recently opened up to worldwide connections: "I mainly spent 1995 playing *Avalon* [Yehuda Simmons 1989]," he later remembered.[3] Sometime that year, Mihály started wondering if perhaps he could turn his obsessive hobby into a profession, using funds banked from his short-lived career in finance. He decided to start a commercial MUD.

see the original *MUD* **1980**

see **1990**

see **1993** and **1996**

MUD clients are highly configurable so expert players can absorb relevant details as quickly as possible. The italics here indicate variable text not part of the room description (and thus more likely to contain immediately useful info, like nearby objects or people). The bold line printed before each command in this transcript shows current health, mana, endurance, and willpower; "ex" at the end means the player character has equilibrium and balance.

Lakeside highway. (road)
Silver sparks dance across the heavens as the dazzling orb of the sun rushes past Achaea's three rings, the second brilliantly coruscating at its passing. Roughly following the line of Lake Vundamere, the road bends northwest and east, while the southern edge of the highway shows the passage of the many feet that have detoured from their travels to enjoy the beauty of the lake for a time. Bits and pieces of debris remain along the roadway and you can see where the ground has been cleared in various spots for campfires, some still giving off smoke which drifts eastward in the breeze. [...] *A rune that looks like something out of your nightmares has been sketched into the ground here. An indigo nightfire butterfly flutters here peacefully. Valayra is here.*
You see exits leading east, south, and northwest.
477h, 512m, 1325e, 1475w ex- SAY HELLO
You say, "Hello."
477h, 512m, 1325e, 1475w ex- QUICKSCORE
Loristo (male Tsol'aa)
You are level 6 (Novice) and 23% of the way to the next level.
Health: 618 / 582   Mana: 654 / 618
Endurance: 1510 / 1510   Willpower: 1690 / 1690

> Strength: 12 Dexterity: 12 Constitution: 11 Intelligence: 13
> You are a fledgling in the Sylvan class.
> **477h, 512m, 1325e, 1475w ex-**
> Valayra waves her hand in greeting.
> **477h, 512m, 1325e, 1475w ex-`SIP HEALTH`**
> You take a drink from an oaken vial.
> The elixir heals and soothes you.
> **535h, 512m, 1325e, 1475w ex-**
> Reonna arrives, following Caladbolg from the east.
> **535h, 512m, 1325e, 1475w ex-**
> Reonna leaves, following Caladbolg to the northwest.
> **535h, 512m, 1325e, 1475w ex-`WALK TO BEKU`**
> Do you really want to walk to Beku, the pygmy chieftain in the land of
> Minia?
> Type AGREE to proceed.
> **535h, 512m, 1325e, 1475w ex-**
> Valayra positions a shining silver scabbard on her hip with a look of
> determination.
> **535h, 565m, 1325e, 1475w ex-`AGREE`**
> Carefully getting your bearings, you set off east toward your goal.

Most such games, then and now, were hobbyist affairs run on spare hardware and in spare time. But a few MUDs had managed to attract paid subscribers with the promise of polished content, regular updates, and reliable support. Mihály, who by then felt he knew the mudding world inside and out, founded a company named Achaea LLC after its planned first game. Licensing *Avalon*'s engine from the game's creator, who had become a friend, Mihály soon realized it would need a serious rewrite: written originally by a fifteen-year-old, among other limiting features it had no support for local variables and no way to pass variables to subroutines.

But more existentially pressing was the problem of revenue. Without the name-brand clout of *Ultima*'s Richard Garriott or the backing of a major game studio, Mihály doubted he could convince enough would-be players to sign up for a monthly subscription sight unseen. He decided to make *Achaea* free but sell credits, which could speed the process of leveling up your character. Soon, at the request of players, he began holding auctions for custom in-game items he'd coded; one such event raised five thousand dollars at a time Mihály was struggling to pay the rent. Soon the irregular auctions became a persistent storefront on the game's website, a place to spend real money on virtual goods.

This was not a common feature in games of the time: "One of the really strange things about *Achaea* is how it makes money," one reviewer noted.[18] While it was not the first game to let players buy virtual perks—the 1990 arcade game *Double Dragon 3* [Technōs Japan], for instance, had an item shop where extra quarters could be exchanged for better equipment—Mihály's game company would become one of the first to use strategies later known as "microtransactions" or "free-to-play" to fully fund their business. In the days before services like PayPal made online payments more convenient, many players bought their virtual goods by mailing a paper check to Mihály's San Francisco address.

To compete with graphical games and distinguish his MUD from competitors, Mihály focused on building a roleplay-focused world with rich lore and driven by player-to-player interactions. It was a world where gods and dragons walked the lands, both run by players who had reached the highest levels of gameplay. In contrast with other MUDs where the cliquish upper echelons rarely interacted with mere mortals, *Achaea* was designed so that the two groups had good reasons, both in and out of character, to deal with each other. Gods, for instance, gained their power based on how many active worshipers they had: the more sacrifices and sacred rituals were performed in their name, the stronger their influence became. This mechanical correspondence encouraged players to proselytize for their chosen deity or smite nonbelievers, and it incentivized gods to act in character as mentors and protectors.

Mihály, a political science major in college, also coded support for complex systems of government into the game's engine. Players could join one of half a dozen city-states spread throughout the world to help them claim territory, defend their borders, or manage their affairs:

> Each city-state has a ruling council, whom the citizens vote for, and then a sovereign, whom the ruling council votes for. The sovereign then appoints players to seven different Ministries: Ambassador, War, Security, Treasury, Steward, Trade, and Chancellor. Each Ministry is responsible for different areas of city administration, and may appoint other citizens as his or her aides.... The internal news system is often filled with the powerful political players engaged in debates over the direction of their guild or city.[6]

Mihály saw politicking and player-run organizations as a key way to realize his vision of a game where roleplay and character interaction could actually impact the world. While the actions of individual characters were hard to make meaningful, cities and guilds could function like metaplayers on a global stage, whose actions the developers and scenario designers could respond to with permanent changes or reactive events. "Instead of 10,000 people purely doing their own things," Mihály wrote,

> you might have 50 political structures that players focus some of their effort through. Providing the organizations have an ability to impact the world in real ways, this allows story to emerge from the web of relationships and inevitable conflicts between these entities. It's the difference between interesting complexity and indistinguishable chaos.[14]

A third form of player interaction was player-versus-player combat (PvP). Most of the game's skill tree focused on battling, and besides purchasing credits, the chief way to improve skills was by leveling up through endless grinding. To ensure customers were motivated to improve those skills, Mihály extended Achaea's PvP systems until they became some of the most complex ever seen. A 1999 review attempted to summarize:

> Fighting in *Achaea* is like nothing you've ever seen before.... There are hundreds of different ways to attack an opponent. There is telepathy, the

ability to use shrines for offensive and defensive purposes, flying in the skies (and dropping victims), the use of trees and beehives to attack your opponents (for druids), martial arts, weapons, tarot cards, entities, and so much more. There is also body-part damage. You can get concussions from getting hit in the head too much, you can get internal bleeding from getting hit in the torso a lot, and you can get broken or mangled limbs. Not only does fighting consist of damage to your body, but it also involves afflictions. There are approximately 50–75 different afflictions you can have. You could have stupidity, epilepsy, dizziness, confusion, etc. To cure these afflictions, you need to use herbs, which I will talk about a bit later...[6]

The combat system became so complex that scripting—writing small programs to autotype commands in response to key phrases in incoming messages, a practice discouraged by most MUDs—soon became necessary to stay competitive in high-level PvP play. The person with the better script had a serious edge. Soon some players were selling finely tuned combat scripts to others, commanding premium prices. The powerful unique items available via microtransactions provided another critical edge, leading to complaints that only players who dropped huge amounts of money could come out on top in combat—a pattern that would later be called "pay-to-win." But others pointed out that neither elite equipment nor elaborate scripts would help a player who hadn't mastered the complex strategies behind Achaean combat, or who wasn't skilled in parsing a battle taking place in messages that sometimes scrolled past at the speed of dozens of sentences per second. "Within a four second period," a reviewer playing a Serpentlord wrote, "I might secrete two venoms, bite someone twice, heal a broken limb by applying a mending salve, raise my mana by drinking a mana elixir, and attempt to writhe off a sword that's impaled me. I might also have 30 different defences active, as well as a full complement of magical tattoos."[18] Battles in *Achaea* were not for the faint of heart.

But the game offered plenty of opportunities for those not interested in fighting. By 2015 the game world had grown to include hundreds of thousands of described locations—not counting remote wilderness areas represented by grids of nondescript rooms. Countless hours of labor by both paid staff and player volunteers had produced millions of words that brought the continent of Sapience to vivid life, from the deserts and jungles of the south to the frigid islands of the remote north. Just exploring the world could take an age. One forum poster noted that he would never have the time to experience everything the game had to offer, but "I hope that one of my daughters will take over [my character] some day. I might put it in a will."[21]

As in other MUDs, dynamism like a day/night cycle, hundreds of named NPCs, and wandering monsters and animals helped bring this textual world to life. And without the burden of multimedia assets to support them, new mechanics and systems could be added easily and continuously. Browsing through the dozens of detailed subsystems in *Achaea*'s help files is enough to make designers of games that need graphical assets weep:

Unlike some other MUDs, *Achaea* does not have separate PvP and non-PvP zones (except for a newbie area where you can't be attacked); the whole world is PvP. But the company has an interesting policy for adjudicating when player-on-player attacks are acceptable: your *character* must have a valid reason to attack. If you defile a shrine and a believer tracks you down for vengeance, you're getting what you deserve; but if you're struck down for no good reason, you can take your case to the gods (or the mods) and receive swift justice.

> Your shop will cost the city it is in money to pay for guards to keep thieves and brigands out of your shop. As such, the city may decide to tax your shop. [...] You may control the colour of your SHOP SIGN as a configuration option. Type CONFIG COLOUR and you will see the setting [...]

> The ship that wishes to permit diving must also have a diving bell. [...] The bell can be raised or lowered (SHIP RAISE BELL, SHIP LOWER BELL) under most circumstances while not moving and not in port. [...] A leadline is a handy thing used to SHIP TAKE SOUNDING. This will tell you how deep the water is and whether diving will be of any potential benefit. [...] A shipfitter can make you a skeleton key to unlock the mysterious bone chests found below.

> CHESS MOVE <position> to <position> : Moves a chess piece. You may use either algebraic notation (a1, b3, etc) or descriptive notation (q3, kkt4, etc) [...]

> A practitioner of Hypnosis will be able to sink someone into a hypnotic trance, possibly even without them realising it, and implant various subliminal suggestions. They can then seal their victim's mind and implant a timer that determines how long after the hypnosis has been triggered until the suggestions start becoming active [...]

John Romero, co-creator of *Doom*, blurbed *Achaea* in the early 2000s saying he "doesn't believe there is a deeper game in existence." While graphical MMOs were increasingly stealing the player base, their mature textual ancestors were "an object of fascination among [mainstream] game designers … the feature-rich MUD seemed like a promised land of sorts,"[9] an escape from what Mihály once called "the plodding literalism of 3D graphics."[3] They were places where anything you imagined could be built. Text games, perhaps, were abandoned far too early, just when they were starting to realize their potential. "Imagine the challenge for literature," a journalist interviewing Mihály once mused, "if movies had come along within a decade of the invention [of the] printing press."[3]

Roleplayers on the richly appointed stage of *Achaea* proved more than capable of generating their own stories. In 2001, one reviewer noted that recently,

> the three guilds of the Serpentlord class (Serpentlords, Shadowsnakes, and Dawnstriders) got together and decided to assassinate the NPC who sold certain venoms. They did this because they didn't like the effective price ceiling that the NPC's existence caused. They then, as a cartel, imposed price controls on the sale of all venoms which caused considerable tension not only between the members of the cartel, but between the cartel and certain influential city officials who depended on venoms.[18]

Quoted on the Iron Realms website.

The official account of the legendary War of the Worldreaver—just one small part of *Achaea*'s history—runs to 33,285 words, half the length of a novel. In keeping with the game's roleplay-focused ethos, it's written entirely in character. Time passes in *Achaea* at the rate of one day per hour of real time, which means the game's historians have documented around seven hundred years of history since launch.

1997

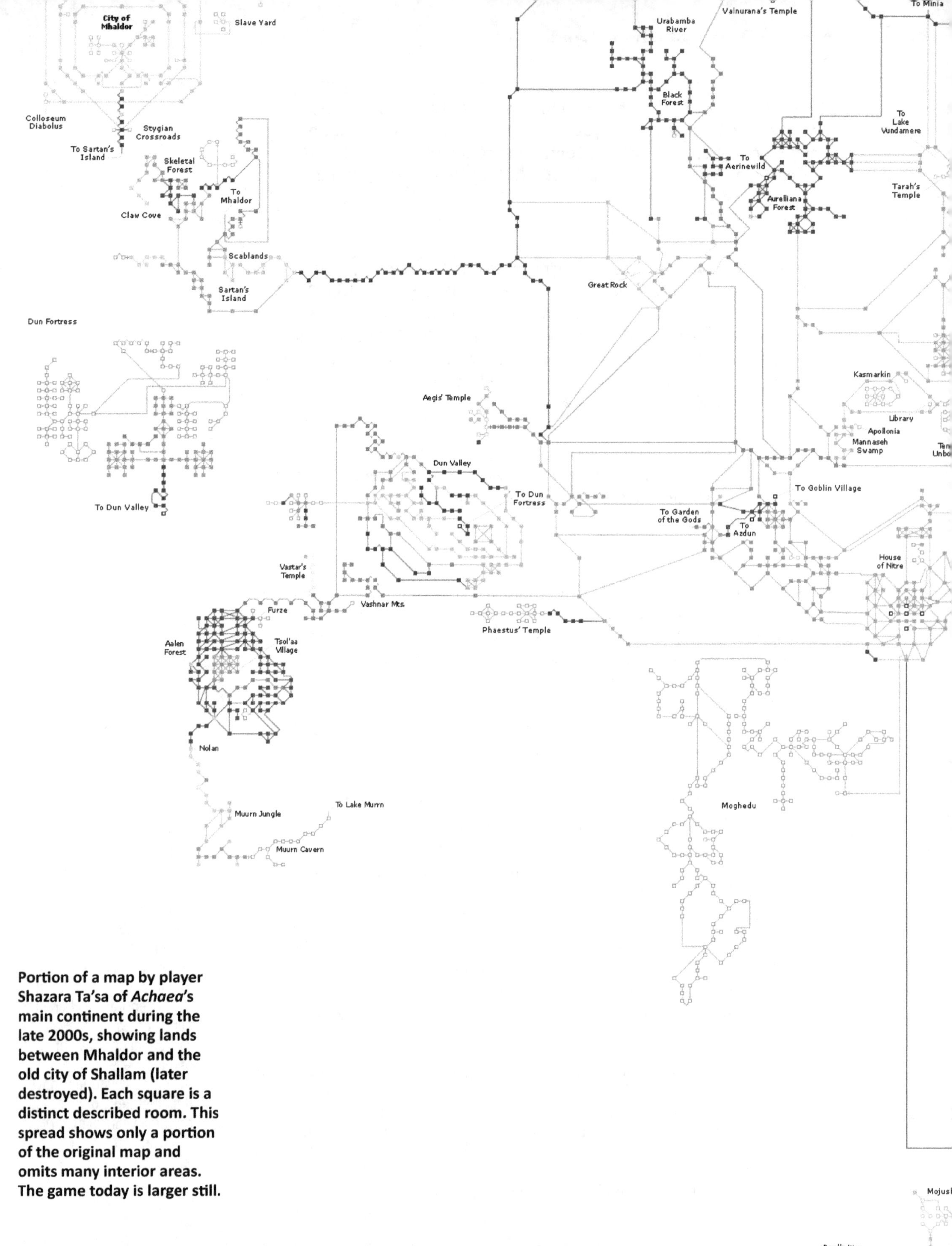

Portion of a map by player Shazara Ta'sa of *Achaea*'s main continent during the late 2000s, showing lands between Mhaldor and the old city of Shallam (later destroyed). Each square is a distinct described room. This spread shows only a portion of the original map and omits many interior areas. The game today is larger still.

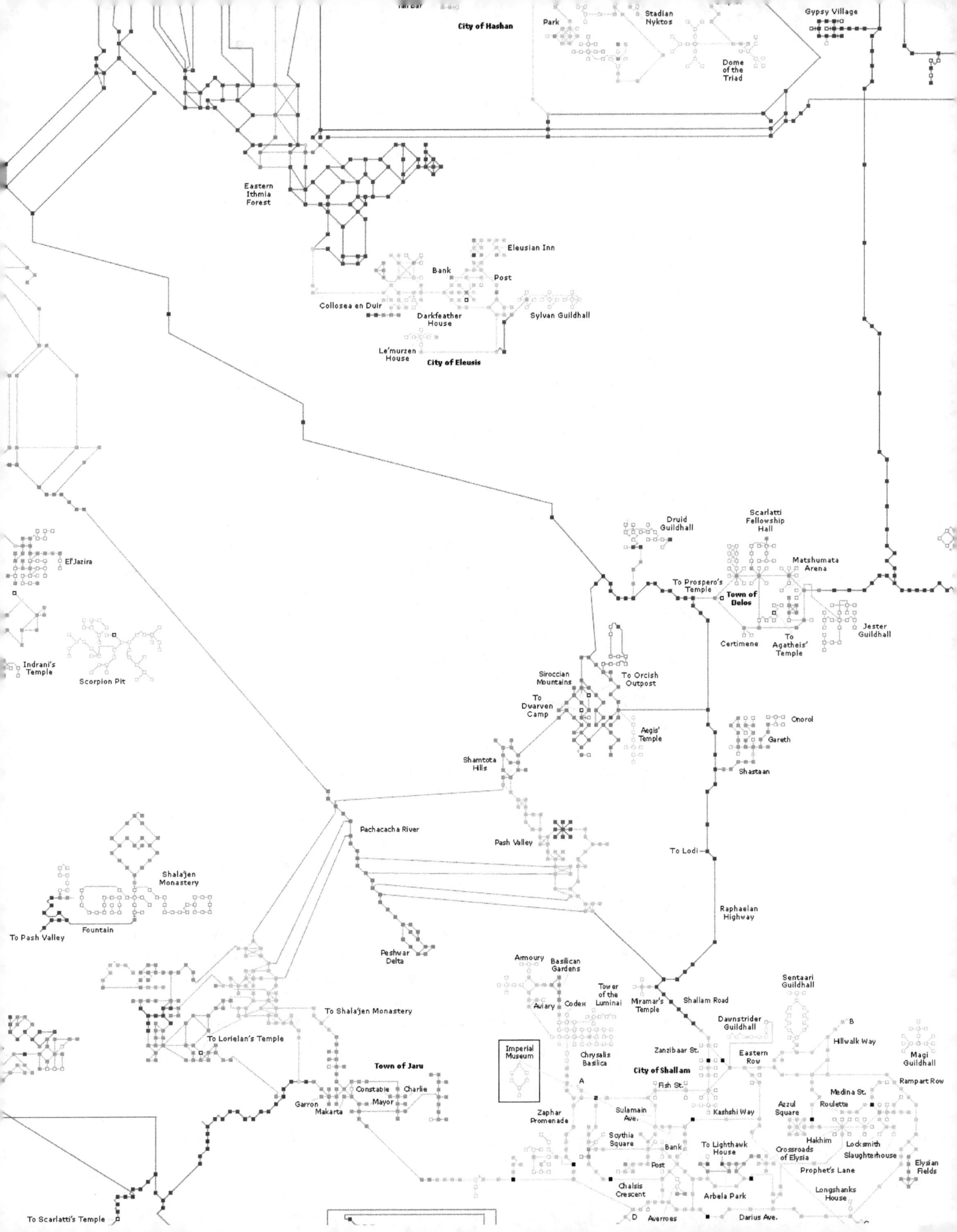
Tan Bar
City of Hashan
Park
Stadian Nyktos
Gypsy Village
Dome of the Triad
Eleusian Inn
Bank
Post
Eastern Ithmia Forest
Collosea en Duir
Darkfeather House
Sylvan Guildhall
Le'murzen House
City of Eleusis
Druid Guildhall
Scarlatti Fellowship Hall
Matshumata Arena
To Prospero's Temple
Town of Delos
Certimene
To Agatheis' Temple
Jester Guildhall
El'Jazira
Indrani's Temple
Scorpion Pit
Siroccian Mountains
To Orcish Outpost
To Dwarven Camp
Aegis' Temple
Onorol
Gareth
Shamtota Hills
Shastaan
Pachacacha River
Pash Valley
To Lodi
Shala'jen Monastery
Raphaelan Highway
To Pash Valley
Fountain
Peshwar Delta
Armoury
Basilican Gardens
Tower of the Luminai
Miramar's Temple
Shallam Road
Sentaari Guildhall
Aviary
Codex
Dawnstrider Guildhall
B
Hillwalk Way
Magi Guildhall
To Shala'jen Monastery
Imperial Museum
Zanzibaar St.
Eastern Row
To Lorielan's Temple
Chrysalis Basilica
City of Shallam
A
Fish St.
Medina St.
Rampart Row
Town of Jaru
Zaphar Promenade
Sulamain Ave.
Kashshi Way
Azzul Square
Roulette
Garron
Makarta
Constable
Charlie
Mayor
Scythia Square
Bank
To Lighthawk House
Hakhim
Locksmith
Slaughterhouse
Post
Crossroads of Elysia
Elysian Fields
Prophet's Lane
Longshanks House
To Scarlatti's Temple
Chalsis Crescent
Arbela Park
Darius Ave.
D
Averroes

But unlike hobbyist MUDs, *Achaea* could also pay designers to craft planned stories and events. In 2004, the MUD attracted media attention over a subplot involving the introduction of an addictive drug called "gleam." The drug would raise your character's stats, but came with procedurally enforced side effects. The game engine would remove spaces from the chat messages of a character who had taken gleam, for instance, in proportion to how big a dose they were on. Addicts would start to hallucinate people entering the room who weren't actually there. Withdrawal could trigger autonomous actions: shivering, vomiting, even begging other characters for more gleam or the money to buy it—totally outside the player's control.

Attention from the press would be rare. *Achaea* expanded for its first few years of operation, and Mihály eventually launched a series of spin-off commercial MUDs, including an officially licensed one based on the fantasy novels of Raymond E. Feist; he renamed his company Iron Realms Entertainment to match its new multiversal scope. But traffic peaked sometime around 2005, correlating with the rise of second-generation MMOs like *World of Warcraft* [Blizzard Entertainment 2004], which siphoned away even more longtime mudders. The few who remained were increasingly diehards, committed inexorably to games in which they'd spent thousands of hours—and, in some cases, thousands of dollars. As the rest of the gaming world caught up to the monetization strategies Mihály's game had helped pioneer, some gamers began to question the ethics of free-to-play models that put no upper limit on how much a dedicated fan could spend, and were often driven by addiction psychology techniques like impulse buys and loss aversion. A 2020 exposé interviewed *Achaea* players who had spent over $10,000 for in-game perks,[16] inspiring new criticisms of the game's "pay-to-win" mechanics.

And yet the critical coverage could only exist because the payment model had worked: *Achaea* was still around in 2020 to critique, decades after the supposed death of commercial text games. It has remained consistently popular for over twenty years, generally ranking somewhere in the top five or ten spots on MUD aggregator sites that ping servers for active player counts. It is "one of the most complex and detailed MUDs I have ever played," one review advised.[12] Another gushed, "It's the most innovative MUD or MMORPG around. Its range of features is incredible, and the depth … is unparalleled."[18] Perhaps a thousand regular players still visited *Achaea* on an ongoing basis circa 2020, with over a hundred online on any given evening. Another forum thread—"What Happened To You Today?"—documents over eight hundred pages of posts where Achaeans share interesting or mundane events, tens of thousands of missives from the daily life of a virtual world:

- I shot a few Targossians with arrows.

- I finally bought a hookah.

- Dajio tried to backstab gank me in Moghedu twice… He failed.

- I got text married, and it was probably the best surprise wedding involving drug-frogs that has ever existed.

- Joined the massive kraken hunt.

- Got teleported to an island in the middle of nowhere.

- Found a telescope of sorts. Put it together. Saw a bunch of neato ASCII constellations.

- I found 3600 gold in my bait bucket. I think I stashed it there something like three years ago.

- Learned how to climb trees for the first time ever… Discovered that fire destroys trees, and fall to ground, breaking both legs and can't move.

- Found a pair of tiny white lace panties, with little red hearts, laying on the ground in the forest. Realized they belonged to a gold dragon. Decided I never want to know how they got dropped.

- I found a new hat, so I'm happy.[19]

"We are never going to abandon the text market unless it abandons us," Mihály once promised.[3] In the mid-2000s he'd stepped down from running his MUDs to focus on a short-lived graphical MMO, *Earth Eternal* [Turnout Ventures 2009], but he returned to the text-only side of his business a few years later (though increasingly handing the reins to the next generation of creators and admins). During his tenure he's seen the best client for connecting to his worlds change from Telnet to apps written in Java, Flash, and HTML5; he's pushed through three major engine upgrades; he's overseen teams of writers and designers who have created hundreds of live events and thousands of unique locations, characters, and items; and he's seen generations of graphical competitors rise and fall while his games keep running. Keeping players happy—and paying—in the face of flashier competitors has been, at times, a difficult slog for him and his team. "There are definitely challenges with the public perception" of his payment model, he concedes.[9] But he loves what he does:

> We don't have to put up with crunch time, we don't have to deal with anyone censoring our content, and we have *complete* creative control over what we do. We'll never be as polished as [*World of Warcraft*] and we'll never be awarded Game of the Year by major publications, but on the other hand, they'll never approach the depth certain aspects of our games achieve, and they can't even dream about the amount of design freedom we have.[15]

Mihály recalls that, back in 1997, "everybody told me it was crazy to dive into MUDs commercially when it was clear that they were not the future of the market. I'm incredibly glad we were too stubborn to listen."[10]

In the aftermath of the epic War of the Worldreaver, after many gods had died and hundreds of players helped the survivors defeat the abomination of Bal'met, there was one final sacrifice. Mihály's own character, Sarapis—the god whose will had inspired all creation—realized the life-giving Fire Behind the Flame was in danger of guttering out forever. After bidding a gentle farewell to his creations,[4] he left to spend eternity tending the Fire, departing the mortal world for good. Mihály had played the character for fifteen years—most of his adult life. "I had tears running down my cheeks when I

Ironically, Mihály is a form of Michael, a name which means, in essence, "no man can be like God."

delivered Sarapis' goodbye forever speech,"[11] he later wrote. But sometimes there's a price to pay for keeping the flame alive.

References

1 "Achaea Wiki." n.d. wiki.achaea.com/Main_Page | a Jun 25, 2021

2 "Achaean News [Archive]." 1997-2021. achaea.com. www.achaea.com/news/?game=Achaea§ion=announce&number=1 | a Jun 25, 2021

3 Davis, Steven. 2006. "The World of Text MMOs / MUDs - An Interview with Matt Mihaly, CEO of Iron Realms Entertainment." *PlayNoEvil* (blog). Sep 8, 2006. www.playnoevil.com/serendipity/index.php?/archives/765-The-World-of-text-MMOs-MUDs-An-Interview-with-Matt-Mihaly,-CEO-of-Iron-Realms-Entertainment.html | s Oct 31, 2006

4 "The Departure of the Logos." Dec 21, 2012. Achaean News. www.achaea.com/news/events/419/ | a Jun 25, 2021

5 Gibson, Jon M. 2004. "Just Say No to Gleam." *Computer Gaming World*, Sep 2004.

6 Hardeman, Kurt. 1999. "Achaea" (review). *MPOG Dot Com* (blog). Aug 30, 1999. www.mpog.com/reviews/software/rpg/achaea | s Aug 18, 2000

7 Hindman, Beau. 2013. "Beau Interviews Matt from Achaea." May 23, 2013. Video. www.youtube.com/watch?v=MtuNM5PiVCk | a Jun 25, 2021

8 Hindman, Beau. 2015. "Achaea the MUD with Tecton the Producer!" May 1, 2015. Video. www.youtube.com/watch?v=1LA4-pmpsgE | a Jun 25, 2021

9 Hrodey, Matt. 2019. "Meet the Man Who Invented Microtransactions Years before Oblivion's Horse Armour." *PCGamesN* (blog). www.pcgamesn.com/first-game-with-microtransactions | a Jun 25, 2021

10 Iron Realms Entertainment. 2007. "Iron Realms Celebrates 10th Anniversary of Achaea!" Press Release. Sep 10, 2007. www.gamesindustry.biz/articles/iron-realms-celebrates-10th-anniversary-of-achaea | a Jun 25, 2021

11 Iron Realms Entertainment. 2012. "The Worldreaver Saga." achaea.com. www.achaea.com/history/the-worldreaver-saga | a Jun 25, 2021

12 Jennings, Scott. 2005. *Massively Multiplayer Games for Dummies*. John Wiley & Sons.

13 Michaly, Matthew. 2000. "Constructive Politics in a Massively Multiplayer Online Roleplaying Game." *Gamasutra* (blog). Mar 9, 2000. www.gamasutra.com/features/20000309/mihaly_01.htm | s Apr 7, 2000

14 Mihály, Matt. 2004. "Matt Mihaly, Designer/Entrepreneur." In *Downloaded Character Development and Storytelling for Games*, by Lee Sheldon. Boston: Thomson Course Technology PTR.

15 Mihály, Matt. 2005. "Burn Baby Burn." *Terra Nova* (blog). Mar 17, 2005. terranova.blogs.com/terra_nova/2005/03/burn_baby_burn.html | a Jun 25, 2021

16 Mills, Mark. 2020. "Achaea: The Game Where Microtransactions Cost Hundreds of Dollars." *Rock, Paper, Shotgun* (blog). Apr 15, 2020. www.rockpapershotgun.com/achaea-the-game-where-microtransactions-cost-hundreds-of-dollars | a Jun 25, 2021

17 niDistinct. 2021. "Multi-User Dungeons (MUDs): What Are They? And How to Play." *Hacker News* (blog). Comments. news.ycombinator.com/item?id=26297000 | a Jun 25, 2021

18 Reyes, Scott. 2001. "Achaea MUD Review." *RPG Planet* (blog). Mar 22, 2001. www.rpgplanet.com/community/voice/achaea | s May 7, 2001

19 Sarapis. 2014. "What Happened To You Today?" Achaea Forums. Aug 6, 2014. forums.achaea.com/discussion/2477/what-happened-to-you-today | a Jun 25, 2021

20 Sarapis. 2015. "Re: Lack of Players?" Achaea Forums. Nov 18, 2015. forums.achaea.com/discussion/4233/lack-of-players/p3 | a Jun 25, 2021

21 Shibumi. 2013. "Re: Why Did You Start Playing? Why Did You Stay?" Achaea Forums. May 30, 2013. forums.achaea.com/discussion/1259/why-did-you-start-playing-why-did-you-stay | a Jun 25, 2021

22 Sylvance. 2012. "The Bal'met Event." Achaea Forums. Nov 11, 2012. forums.achaea.com/discussion/440/the-balmet-event | a Jun 25, 2021

23 Terdiman, Daniel. 2004. "Virtual Dopers Crave High Scores." *Wired* (blog). May 25, 2004. www.wired.com/2004/05/virtual-dopers-crave-high-scores | a Jun 25, 2021

24 Xith. 2012. "Justifying MUD Purchases to Non-Players." Achaea Forums. Dec 8, 2012. forums.achaea.com/discussion/comment/26803 | a Jun 25, 2021

25 Zenn. 2008. "Exclusive with Matt Mihaly and Jeremy Saunders." *MUDNews* (blog). Dec 18, 2008. mudnews.blogspot.com/2008/12/exclusive-with-matt-mihaly-and-jeremy.html | a Jun 25, 2021

PHOTOPIA

Adam Cadre
as Opal O'Donnell

Style **Parser**
Debuted **Oct 1, 1998** *(IF Comp)*
Launch Platform **Z-machine v5**
Language **Inform 6**

> **"** The streetlights are bright. Unbearably bright. You have to squint as hard as you can to keep your retinas from bursting into flame.

NOTHING FELT MOMENTOUS about *Photopia*'s first release. Indeed, twenty-six other games came out the same day. The fourth annual Interactive Fiction Competition unveiled the year's new entries on the first of October, and as per its rules, no open discussion of the games in competition was allowed during the six-week judging period. The rule aimed to put all games on equal footing and keep early front-runners from dominating the conversation. Sometimes a game by a well-known author would attract lopsided attention anyway, but Opal O'Donnell was not a well-known name, and most players came to the game under that byline without preconceptions. In later years *Photopia* would often be called one of the best interactive fictions of all time, kindling one of the form's most significant turns. But for those first six weeks, it was as anonymous as any other stick of wood.

By 1998, IF Comp was already an established tradition with its own norms and conventions, not all of them written down. An axiom not explicitly stated by its rules was that interactive fiction fundamentally involved a marriage between story and puzzles. The lateral thinking

1998

MAJOR RELEASES

» **1998.10**. Original competition release.

» **PHOTOBW.Z5**. Black-and-white version for interpreters without color.

» **1.30**. Final Z-machine release. "Missing the graphical wrapper but is otherwise basically the same beast as v2.01."

» **2.01**, Mar 23, 2002, Glulx. Wrapped in a graphical frame with a custom font for quotations and transitions.

» **iOS** (port), with Carter Sande, Aug 15, 2015. Added title screen and illustrations.

see **1995** and **1986**

see **1985**

More so than most games, much of *Photopia*'s pleasure comes from the unique experience of encountering it for yourself. One reviewer has gone so far as to say that "to describe it is to destroy it."[18] Consider playing it yourself, if you haven't, before reading on: the remainder of this chapter spoils some of the game's core revelations.

1998

problems popularized by early games like *Adventure* **1976** and *Zork* **1977** were seen as a necessary part of the medium Graham Nelson **1993** famously called "a narrative at war with a crossword"[8]—both story and puzzles were necessary for the analogy to make sense. Puzzles differentiated IF from choice-based interfaces like in Choose Your Own Adventures **1979**, which (supposedly) required no skill to navigate. They gave players something meaningful to do within a simulated world; they provided pacing; and they offered a sense of accomplishment and ownership for reaching an ending. They were present in the graphical adventures still on retail shelves, like *Grim Fandango* [LucasArts 1998] or *The Curse of Monkey Island* [LucasArts 1997]. The previous year's Comp winner, *The Edifice* [Lucian P. Smith 1997], had been a much-loved tour de force of puzzle design centered on deciphering an alien language, and nearly all high-ranking Comp games to date had worked hard to balance an interesting story with memorable challenges.

In contrast, *Photopia* had few or no puzzles (depending on your definition). There had certainly been earlier experiments in puzzleless games, some quite high-profile: Joe Mason's *In the End* [1996], Andrew Plotkin's *The Space Under the Window* [1997], and Chris Klimas's *Mercy* [1997] had all tried various flavors of puzzle-light or puzzle-free design, leaving copious amounts of discussion in their wake. Hypertexts like *Patchwork Girl* or *Uncle Roger* came from a separate tradition of interactive text without gameplay challenges. Even Infocom had experimented with near-puzzle-free designs in titles like *A Mind Forever Voyaging*. But to the IF newsgroup community these were all exceptions, not rules. Many reviewers still gave points for puzzles and story separately, such that a game that left out one would inherently get a lower score than a game with both. Some reviewers would even give a game without puzzles the lowest possible ranking, as a protest against what they felt was an abuse of the form—by their definition, puzzleless games were not interactive fiction at all. Releasing a puzzle-free game in IF Comp was not, at the time, a good strategy for winning it.

If you'd asked a film historian around the time of *Photopia*'s release to name the greatest movie of all time, the title you'd probably hear would be *Citizen Kane*. This could be baffling to newer generations of movie fans. *Kane* was a good film, but the best ever? Really? The root of the disconnect is historical context: Orson Welles's film became remembered as the most visible example of a momentous shift in cinematic style. It popularized so many technical and narrative innovations that became part of the new lexicon of filmmaking, it's hard for later generations to realize they were ever absent. *Photopia*'s fame has sometimes left newer cohorts of IF fans similarly perplexed. "I guess this was groundbreaking?" one skeptical review from 2019 begins; "[it's] fun to read, but it's not a masterpiece or anything."[7] IF author Emily Short has noted that "a number of its features look perfectly ordinary now,"[12] even though they were revolutionary at the time. At the risk of overfitting the analogy, we might note both Orson Welles and Adam Cadre (*Photopia*'s true author) were twenty-four years old when they began work on their bellwether titles, and neither of their audiences quite grasped the changes that were coming.

As *Photopia* begins, you find yourself in the passenger seat of a speeding car. You and a drunken frat buddy are on the way to a late-night meetup with some girls you met at a ski lodge. Within a handful of turns, a predictable disaster strikes:

> You look up. "Hey, it's red," you say.
>
> "Huh what?" Rob says.
>
> "The light," you say. "You know, red? As in STOP?"
>
> But you don't stop. You don't even slow down as you fly into the intersection, and the light stays an unmistakeable red...

The screen empties so only the word RED remains, the text color shifting to a red font against a black background. Now you're somewhere and someone else: an astronaut named Wendy, "first girl on the red planet," exploring the wreckage of a prior mission and looking for salvage. You play for long enough to start believing this must surely be the game's main story, despite its incongruous prelude and some oddities in the narration you can't at first explain:

> Every remnant of the colony you've encountered so far has left a depression. ("Remnant" means a remaining piece. "Depression" means a sort of bowl-shaped hole in the ground.)

And some of it suggests this reality isn't quite what it seems:

> \>EXAMINE SPACESHIP
> This is your trusty spaceship, which you recently renamed from the Space Pony to the Aspiration—a wise choice, if I may say so.
>
> \>SLEEP
> You may be feeling drowsy in real life, but not in the story!

But just when you start to get a handle on the kind of story you're in and who might be telling it, the setting shifts again, the colors snapping back to monochrome. Now you're a suburban mom rescuing her young daughter from a near-fatal drowning. But then comes a segue into another fantastical bedtime story—this one SEA-BLUE—and as successions of colorful dream worlds and monochrome everyday vignettes continue, the out-of-order scenes cohere into a single story of a teenage girl named Alley whose life is cut short far too early. While you never play Alley herself, by the final scene you've been many of the people whose lives intersected with hers or who will mourn her once she's gone, coming to understand what she meant to each of them. It's a tragedy you must piece together yourself, as if the loss it narrates is so senseless it can't be told directly but apprehended only in shattered fragments, one piece at a time.

Photopia's use of out-of-order storytelling was also less common at the time; some reviewers cited Quentin Tarantino's *Pulp Fiction* (then only a few years old) as one of the few places they had ever seen it used before. A fragmented story functions, in a sense, as a different kind of puzzle: challenging audiences to connect and rearrange scenes that at first seem unrelated, in order to make sense of the whole.

1998

Shortly after *Photopia*'s release, Adam Cadre described himself in a similarly fragmented way:

> I'm 25 (but look somewhere between 13 and 17.) … I'm straightedge. I'm multiracial. I'm overeducated.… I suppose I can call myself a professional writer now that I've sold my first novel, but it still seems a bit silly to say that.… I suppose I can also call myself a professional musician, since I'm in a band which has a CD for sale.… I feel equally uncomfortable calling myself a teacher, since even though I work as a substitute teacher and in-home tutor, I don't have a class of my own.… I'm not a capitalist and so I suppose that defining myself in terms of how I make money, as the culture seems to demand, is bound to feel wrong to me.[10]

The Lost Treasures of Infocom II [Activision 1992], second in the series of omnibus releases also influential on Graham Nelson (see **1993**).

Unlike many IF authors, Cadre hadn't discovered the genre as a kid, but years later. He picked up a compilation of Infocom games in the mid-90s, finding Steve Meretzky's haunting and literary *A Mind Forever Voyaging* especially fascinating. The collection had included the winners of the first IF Comp as a bonus feature, and Cadre was thrilled to learn the medium he'd just discovered wasn't dead: there were still people writing and sharing and theorizing about text games. He wrote one of his own that became a surprise hit, so he decided to release his second under a pseudonym, to see if the concept would work on its own terms without a known author's name behind it. Picking an idea that he thought he could finish in time for the IF Comp deadline, he began work on a story he'd later say was inspired by everything from the film *The Sweet Hereafter* to Carl Sagan's *Cosmos* to the death, years before, of his infant sister. His new game would be part of a growing body of interactive fiction taking inspiration more from life and literature than fantasy novels or other games.

Photopia can be read as a tragedy, all the more affecting because you're both invited to help enact it and powerless to prevent it. But it can also be understood as a critique of the tropes then foundational to IF design. The game begins with two unattributed lines of dialogue, which the player later realizes are spoken by Wendy—the girl listening to the fantastical bedtime stories—and Alley, her babysitter:

> "Will you read me a story?"
>
> "Read you a story? What fun would that be? I've got a better idea: let's tell a story together."

This promise of collaboration has often been at the heart of IF's appeal. It's appeared in one form or another throughout its history—as marketing copy promising tales that adapt to every choice you make, in academic essays arguing for the potency of an interactive medium, in the mouths of fans gushing about why interactive stories are so much better than linear ones. "Let's tell a story together." And yet *Photopia* makes the case that this promise is usually made with crossed fingers. "You have to admit," Wendy later observes, that "even though she SAYS you're making up the stories together, Alley does most of the work."

Photopia's first storybook scene, RED, clothes itself in familiar IF trappings: a large area to explore on the red planet; interesting damaged equipment that seems primed for involvement in later salvage and repair puzzles. In fact, it's an elaborate shell game. The rooms of the map are laid out in a fixed sequence, placed in the same order no matter which directions the player happens to go; and when you read the descriptions more closely, you'll find few items you can actually interact with or acquire. Try to find something to TAKE in this room description:

> **Inside the housing unit**
> Since no one ever moved into this unit, it's really nothing but an empty gray box, no bigger than your bedroom back home. These quarters weren't designed with anything but sleeping in mind: the first colonists were expected to take their meals in a central dining commons, and bathrooms were to be in a separate structure, with each one shared by a number of people. Still, you can't help but feel a twinge. This was going to be someone's HOME. The first thing they saw when they woke up, the place they looked forward to retreating to after a hard day doing research or exploring the planet's surface or helping to maintain the colony. There were going to be pictures on these walls, footprints on the floor. Now the only footprints left here will be yours.

In fact only a single object can be claimed from the desolate landscape, and there's only one thing you can do with it. As the game continues, it becomes increasingly clear the player is being led, step by step, through an entirely preordained story. "Whispering voices tickle the edge of your hearing," implying you should LISTEN to continue; a character tosses you a remote control and says you can "push the white button," leaving little doubt as to what your next command should be. All good IF uses these tricks to a certain extent, of course, but *Photopia* often pushes them to extremes that make them uncomfortably visible. In one scene, a man on the phone with paramedics gives your character step-by-step instructions for reviving a young Alley pulled face-down from a pool:

> "First you must tilt her head back!"
>
> >TILT HEAD
> You tilt her head back.
>
> "Good!" Gabriel says. "Now you must breathe into her mouth."
>
> >BREATHE INTO MOUTH
> You breathe into Alley's mouth.
>
> "Good!" Gabriel says. "Now you must press her chest."

If you fail to comply with these prompts, Gabriel shoves you aside and performs them himself. Earlier in this scene, if you don't investigate the sounds of a worrying splash, your character drifts toward it of her own volition regardless of what you instruct her to do. In another sequence your commands are even typed out for you, removing your ability to interact entirely.

Yet expectations of agency—of the chance to influence outcomes, to meaningfully interact with an interactive fiction—are so ingrained that the player can't help but try to intervene. In a scene playing as Wendy's father, driving Alley home after a night of babysitting, the player is meant to have a heart-stopping revelation. "Suddenly, in the middle of the conversation," one reviewer noted,

> I realized, "Oh no, we're going to crash! Maybe I have the opportunity to change what will happen!" I typed "STOP" and [skidded into the intersection, to be] hit by the other car. I had this awful feeling of being just barely too late.[17]

The game, as replay makes clear, ensures you are always just barely too late, no matter what you type or when you type it. But the moment still has power, precisely because the medium has so trained players that bad outcomes are their own fault. If you lose in a world where "your choices really matter," it must be because you weren't good enough to win. The player feels the same guilt as the characters who couldn't keep Alley safe, even if there was nothing they could have done to save her.

Some players resented this. "If there had been some way to alter the central event," wrote one, "indeed some way of interacting to go down anything other than the one ordained path, I'd have been a whole lot happier with this piece."[5] Others have assumed *Photopia* means to tell a story about predestination: the railroaded structure as the inevitability of fate. But IF author Victor Gijsbers has noted that Cadre's project seems less concerned with removing the player's free will than pointing out it had never really been there in the first place:

> How much of the interactive fiction that precedes *Photopia* allows the player to change the outcome of the story? (And indeed, how much of the interactive fiction that came after *Photopia* allows it?)
> The answer is, of course, "almost none."[6]

Most interactive fiction has only one ending—or one "correct" ending, and many unsatisfying ways to lose. If plot lines branch, they generally rejoin. Gijsbers argues that IF's promise of meaningful agency has often been an emperor with no clothes, and *Photopia* is merely the first game to so nakedly point this out.

Gijsbers proposes that Cadre's project is less about exploring themes of predestination than of how we make meaning through stories, regardless of the manner in which we tell them. Much of the game hinges around the stories Alley hears from others and the way she passes them on in turn, part of a chain of human meaning-making that continues even when her link is abruptly removed. Her father shares his love of astronomy with her in a late-night stargazing session, speaking of the way elements like iron and gold are ejected from supernovas. Later Alley spins Wendy a story of a beach filled with gold fallen from the sky. The supernova anecdote was encoded by Cadre from a story he perhaps heard from Carl Sagan, and in telling it, no matter whether the medium is interactive or not, he passes it on to us. When we play *Photopia*, we're telling a story together—and that matters; we're a real part of the chain of retellings—even if Cadre is the one doing most of the work. In this interpretation it's stories, not sandboxes (real or illusory), that really matter.

In one of *Photopia*'s most famous scenes, adventurer Wendy becomes lost in an open-air labyrinth surrounding a crystal city. Its terse description echoes the mazes from *Adventure* and many games that followed.

see **1976**

> You step into the crystal labyrinth and immediately get lost.
>
> **In the crystal labyrinth**
> You are in a dazzling crystal maze, with passages leading out to the north, south, and west.
>
> >SOUTH
> You wander around the maze of glass until you find yourself at another intersection…
>
> **In the crystal labyrinth**
> You are in a dazzling crystal maze, with passages leading out to the west, east, and south.

The rooms resist any attempt to map them, and there seems at first no escape. Yet the parser—the narrator, Alley—keeps drawing your gaze upward, mentioning the blue color of the sky above the roofless labyrinth, or the soaring architecture of the city looming over its walls. As you continue to wander, the cooling unit fails on your spacesuit, and the narrator describes an increasingly unbearable heat, prompting the player to finally type:

Spoilers for Photopia's *crystal labyrinth.*

> >REMOVE SUIT
> You take off your spacesuit and drop it on the ground.

And then, a few turns later:

> The cool breeze ruffles the feathers of your wings.

Players often remember this moment from *Photopia* as the solution to a puzzle, but that's not quite what's happening. The story has never mentioned wings before, nor have the instructions ever introduced a verb to use them. But the way the scene has been presented, it's almost inevitable that the next thing most players will type is:

> >FLY
> You stretch your wings and soar into the sky.

> **Flying above the crystal labyrinth**
> You are hovering above the crystal labyrinth; from this perspective, it looks like a mind-bogglingly complex mandala. (A "mandala" is a pattern that some people use in prayer.) There is no way you could have possibly navigated it on the ground—in fact, it almost gives you a headache. Much more relaxing is the cloudless, sparkling blue sky all around you.

End spoilers.

Medium and Message

Photopia's medium also informed its aesthetics in less obvious ways. Alley's bedtime stories unfold across six color-themed vignettes, each of which begins with a single color word and turns the text its dominant color: RED, SEA-BLUE, GOLD, SKY-BLUE, GREEN, and PURPLE. But this palette was forced on Cadre by the constraints of the Z-machine, the legacy system invented by Infocom and taken up by amateur fans **1993**, which offered only these six options for colored text (with the somewhat less poetic names of red, blue, yellow, cyan, green, and magenta).

The Z-machine was designed during a time of many competing home computer standards, and the closest thing to a consistent representation for color was something like IBM's CGA: a single bit (either on or off) for each red, green, or blue phosphor dot on a screen. (In fact, CGA supported a 4-bit RGBI format, with an extra Intensity bit, bright or dim, for each color; Infocom may have only supported 3-bit color because not all of their target platforms supported intensity.) With RGB, only six chromatic colors can be produced: each color alone (red, green, and blue) and each possible set of active pairs (producing yellow, magenta, and cyan).

Though CGA was ancient history by 1998, the Z-machine's backward compatibility and portability had entrenched it as the dominant format for writing interactive fiction, leaving a color palette so limiting few modern authors had ever bothered to make use of it. Cadre's move to turn this limitation into artistic device mirrors constraint-born inventions from other media— the film noir that began to appear not long after *Citizen Kane*, for instance, arose in part from the availability of cheap high-contrast black-and-white film stock.

"I have never seen a more astounding example of adroit use of the 'magician's choice,'" wrote one reviewer,[14] referring to the technique of prompting an audience member to act exactly as the performer intended. It may not be a puzzle, but flying in *Photopia* is memorable for capturing so perfectly the *feeling* of solving one: the joy of realizing something you can type will open new doors and unlock new stories, making your part in the telling feel meaningful. Magician's choice or not, if the magic works, who cares? Once escaped from its limitations, the confusing snarl of the labyrinth becomes a mandala, a symbol of meaning and reassurance. And the use of the word "labyrinth" may itself be significant: though the words are often used interchangeably, a labyrinth is distinct from a maze in that it has only a single path with no branches or dead ends. Walking it always leads to the center.

As the fourth IF Comp ended and the review embargo lifted, some commenters found fault with *Photopia*'s deconstructionist approach, whether or not they were conscious of how intentional it had been. One called out its "unpleasantly linear" nature: "The plot is compelling, but there's just not enough interactivity to make it worthwhile."[19] Another wrote, "In IF I don't want all puzzles, but, on the other hand, I don't want all story either, I want a balance. I want a nice tension between the two that allows me to feel that I am the protagonist affecting the plot."[4] Many took offense at calling *Photopia* interactive fiction at all, suggesting it ought to have been disqualified from competition. Some weren't even sure it counted as a game, and that included Cadre himself: "It's not a game, of course," he wrote, "but I find myself calling it one anyway."[10]

Not for the first time, the IF community was a decade ahead of the conversation in the wider gaming world. The 2008 release of the linear, deconstructionist *Dear Esther* [Dan Pinchbeck] would kick off years of discussion—and, sadly, harassment— about what kinds of experiences "count" as real games. *Esther,* a mod for the engine that drove popular shooter *Half-Life 2* [Valve 2004], like *Photopia*

removed a foundational pacing mechanic from its genre (in this case,
shooting enemies). The game and its copycats elicited scathing reviews
and passionate defenses of so-called walking simulators in the early 2010s,
echoing the same conversations about *Photopia*'s lack of puzzles that had
played out on the IF newsgroups in the late 1990s.

Resistance to *Photopia* was real, but not as strong as anyone, including
its author, expected. Cadre had not intended to win the Comp, hoping
only that folks would find his game—story—whatever—"a mildly interesting
experiment."[10] But even before the judging period had ended and open
discussion could begin, excitement was mounting:

> If there was a prize for "competition game most mentioned on the
> newsgroups before the deadline had passed," *Photopia* would win hands
> down. Everyone was quite courteous about it, spoiler warnings and rot13
> and all that, but there was a marked impatience to talk about this game,
> recommend it to other people, make it the test case in any number of
> arguments.[9]

Photopia took first place in the competition, and also won the Miss
Congeniality award where entrants vote for their favorite games by other
authors. While even some of its fans suggested it might have worked just
as well had it been a traditional short story, others argued passionately for
exactly the opposite. "IF is the ideal medium for this story," wrote one;[17]
another called it "perfectly suited to the I-F medium,"[2] and a third deemed it
"a breakthrough" for the form.[1] A retrospective years later, reflecting on this
split of opinion, would theorize that the piece works so well precisely because
it violates preconceptions of how it is *supposed* to work:

> *Photopia* uses its medium not just as a gimmick, but to create an effect that
> would be lost in a non-interactive narrative form.… It is a work of fiction
> that utilizes the ideas of a game, the technical framework as well as the
> audience's expectations … to tell its story.[15]

Cadre's success signaled that the parser IF community was beginning
to broaden its horizons—not looking exclusively inward or backward but
out, toward new and different possible futures. Slowly at first, but with
increasing momentum, story would begin to take prominence over puzzles
in the games the community celebrated, which in turn would influence
larger conversations about what successful interactive narratives could look
like. A decade after *Photopia*, browser text games like *Fallen London* were
telling complex interactive stories without anything like traditional puzzles,
while Twine-based hypertext stories, most puzzleless, would soon become
increasingly popular. Even games that kept using the technical scaffold of
Infocom's Z-machine let many of its affordances for locked doors, expiring
light sources, scored points, and unexpected deaths grow dusty and disused.
Photopia was not the sole cause of all these changes, of course, any more than
Citizen Kane single-handedly changed cinema, and the evolution took place
over decades, not in a single moment. But in the years since, *Photopia* has
come to stand in for that fictional point of transition, a fulcrum which many
felt shifting even then. Andrew Plotkin, author of *So Far* **1996**, began his
review of Cadre's game by writing simply: "This, I think, will do."[11]

rot13 is a basic cypher for obscuring spoilers in text, shifting all letters thirteen positions up so A becomes N etc.; web tools make it easy to copy and paste text in and out of the format.

see **2000** and **2004**

see **2009** and **2012**

Photopia is about a moment that changes everything, so it feels somehow fitting that its legacy would be to stand in for such a moment in interactive fiction's history. Whether its impact will continue to be felt by newer generations of game makers remains an open question. *Citizen Kane* rarely tops best-of lists any more, routinely ousted in the 2000s by *The Godfather* and, more recently, *Star Wars*. The conversation moves on—but those who lived through the moment find it hard to forget.

References

1 Barnwell, Brendan. 1999. "Photopia" (review). *XYZZYnews* #18. ifarchive.org/if-archive/magazines/XYZZYnews/XYZZY18.TXT | a Jul 6, 2020

2 Bruce. 1998. "A Lurker's Competition Games Reviews." Usenet post, rec.games.int-fiction, Nov 16, 1998. groups.google.com/forum/#!msg/rec.games.int-fiction/ospgvm159w0/FUZvjVoeZCQJ | a Jul 6, 2020

3 Cadre, Adam. 2000. "The Photopia Phaq, v2.1." adamcadre.ac. adamcadre.ac/content/phaq.txt | a Jul 5, 2020

4 Doe. 1998. "[Comp 98] Doe's (Female Deer's) Reviews, Photopia." Usenet post, rec.games.int-fiction, Nov 18, 1998. groups.google.com/forum/#!msg/rec.games.int-fiction/iw3UVDYcJuO/wOjv0ycFEgsJ | a Jul 6, 2020

5 Firedrake. 1998. "[COMP98] [SPOILERS] Firedrake's Reviews 1/2." Usenet post, rec.games.int-fiction, Nov 17, 1998. groups.google.com/forum/#!msg/rec.games.int-fiction/3vC7VeJ-5bg/DpSxMQYSbhQJ | a Jul 6, 2020

6 Gijsbers, Victor. 2008. "SPAG Specifics: Photopia." *SPAG* #53, Nov 16, 2008. www.spagmag.org/archives/backissues/spag53.html#Photopia | a Jul 6, 2020

7 HaleyDreams. 2019. "I Guess This Was Groundbreaking?" IFDB. Dec 3, 2019. ifdb.org/viewgame?id=ju778uv5xaswnlpl&review=50811 | a Jun 30, 2022

8 Nelson, Graham. 1995. "The Craft of the Adventure: Five Articles on the Design of Adventure Games." Self-published. mirror.ifarchive.org/if-archive/info/Craft.Of.Adventure.pdf | a Jul 26, 2020

9 O'Brian, Paul. 1999. "Photopia" (review). *SPAG* #17, May 10, 1999. www.spagmag.org/archives/backissues/spag17.html | a Jul 5, 2020

10 Olsson, Magnus. 1999. "Interview With Adam Cadre." *SPAG* #17, May 10, 1999. www.spagmag.org/archives/backissues/spag17.html | a Jul 5, 2020

11 Plotkin, Andrew. 1998. "Reviews: IF Competition 1998." E BLONG. www.eblong.com/zarf/gamerev/comp98.html#1 | a Jul 5, 2020

12 Short, Emily. 2007. "Canonical." IFDB. Oct 21, 2007. ifdb.org/viewgame?id=ju778uv5xaswnlpl&review=1002 | a Jun 30, 2022

13 Skinner, Suzanne. 1998. "[Comp 98] Surprises." Usenet post, rec.games.int-fiction, Nov 17, 1998. groups.google.com/g/rec.games.int-fiction/c/-N_0vDoykKk/m/zKe3tk6-2A4J | a Jul 5, 2020

14 Smith, Lucian. 1998. "Lucian's Ratings: Comp'98." Lucian Smith's Website. www.bioc.rice.edu/~lpsmith/IF/rate98.html | s May 12, 2008

15 Sorooshian, Roxana. 2017. "In Focus: Photopia." *Storytelling Study* (blog). Dec 8, 2017. genreandstorytellinginvideogames.wordpress.com/2017/12/08/in-focus-photopia | a Jul 6, 2020

16 Stevens, Duncan. 2011. "10 Years of IF: 1994-2004." In *IF Theory Reader*, ed. Kevin Jackson-Mead and J. Robinson Wheeler. Boston: >TRANSCRIPT ON PRESS.

17 Straight, Michael. 1998. "[Comp98] More Praise for the Good Stuff (1 of 2)." Usenet post, rec.games.int-fiction, Nov 17, 1998. groups.google.com/forum/#!msg/rec.games.int-fiction/cmQFXn5lOyU/KUsATQSNgdcJ | a Jul 5, 2020

18 Walker, John. 2008. "Photopia" (review). *Rock, Paper, Shotgun* (blog). Mar 31, 2008. www.rockpapershotgun.com/2008/03/31/photopia | a Jul 5, 2020

19 Wildstrom, Jake. 1998. "[COMP '98] Reviews (Feel Free to Hate Me for Them…)." Usenet post, rec.games.int-fiction, Nov 17, 1998. groups.google.com/forum/#!msg/rec.games.int-fiction/B8_HhoCf8T4/XvfSoNC67KcJ | a Jul 6, 2020

KING OF DRAGON PASS

David Dunham (Project Lead), Robin Laws (Lead Writer and Co-Designer), Elise Bowditch (Associate Producer), Greg Stafford (Additional Design and Writing), and others

Style	**Storylet-Driven, Procedural Story**
Debuted	**Oct 29, 1999** *(retail)*
Launch Platform	**Macintosh, Windows**
Publisher	**A Sharp**
Language	**C++** *(engine)*, **Opal Scripting Language** *(story)*, **mTropolis** *(UI)*
Launch Price	**$37.50** *(CD-ROM)*

> **"** There once was a time when gods and people walked the earth together.

It's "**the best game you've never played.**"[24] It's "one of the best video games ever made."[11] It's "timeless…. There is nothing like it in the world: a game with a smoothly telescopic scale that alternates seamlessly between fantasy empire-builder and character-driven RPG."[12] It's "a tough game to describe … part text adventure, part civilization game, and part choose your

1999

see **1979**

own adventure book … it feels like a book come to life."[29] It's "an original game design, something all too rare in this world of big-budget clones."[3] It has "a more convincing illusion of conflict and consequence" than anything one reviewer had ever played.[27] It's "just so different than any other game … it flows like a novel, but one you have a hand in writing … you can play over and over again."[17] It's "amazing,"[29] it's "basically peerless,"[28] it's "outstanding"[17] and "exceptional."[13] It is, one reviewer declared, "the game you've been waiting for."[29]

And when it first released, it bombed.

"Call me shallow," wrote *Computer Gaming World* upon the publication of *King of Dragon Pass* in 1999, "but I want gameplay *and* graphics. And I'll bet you do, too." Damningly, the reviewer wrote, *Dragon Pass* "is just a few icons and pretty, hand-drawn screens away from being a text-based game."[1] At the end of the 90s, when sales of graphics cards were surging and polygon counts were king, "text-based" was a terminal insult. Asking gamers to pay for words was inconceivable.

David Dunham and his wife, Elise Bowditch, had not expected such a hard sell. Their game *did* have graphics, after all: hundreds of screens of hand-drawn art, evocative even if it wasn't 3D or animated. It had deep strategic gameplay, evolved over three years of development into something compelling, unique, and eminently replayable. And it was set in the world of Glorantha, a fantasy setting popularized by the tabletop roleplaying game *RuneQuest* [The Chaosium 1978] with a rich, deep lore and hundreds of thousands of fans. Yet it would be over a decade before *Dragon Pass* found an audience and claimed its place as a classic. The story of what went so wrong with the game's release—and so right with its design and long-term legacy—is a fascinating time capsule of a strange era for video games, poised between the dominance of big publishers and retail stores in the twentieth century and the rise of indies and online distribution in the twenty-first.

Dunham had begun *Dragon Pass* in 1996, after a nexus of inspirations came together. He'd started programming in the seventh grade (his first game was "a football simulator that ran on an Olivetti 101 programmable calculator"[19]), and as an adult he became an Apple developer, working on software for the company's ill-fated, ahead-of-its-time tablet, the Newton. A lifelong board game fan, he was intrigued by strategy video games like Sid Meier's *Civilization* [MicroProse 1991], which gave players complex simulations and great freedom in interaction. In particular, a statement attributed to Meier had caught Dunham's eye: that "a good game is a series of interesting decisions," which "must be frequent and meaningful."[6] Dunham had also been a fan of the complex mythology and worldbuilding of the Glorantha setting for many years, particularly stories of the contested region of Dragon Pass, filled with strange monsters and struggling clans. He'd been intrigued, too, by creator Greg Stafford's tabletop roleplaying game *Pendragon* [Chaosium 1985], which explored dynasties and generations rather than heroes in their prime, and he'd run a mash-up campaign for a while called, naturally, "PenDragon Pass." Dunham had started a small software company, A Sharp, with Bowditch—who was also a programmer, not to mention a poet. With

Among Dunham's other accomplishments, in the mid-80s he wrote one of the earliest "smart quotes" algorithms to automatically replace keyboard-entered quote characters with typographically correct opening and closing variations.

1999

her encouragement, he began sketching out ideas for a computer game set in Dragon Pass that would merge strategic gameplay, deep lore, dynamic storytelling, and long-term, generational play:

> I wanted to have characters get born and then grow up and become heroes, maybe, or in some cases you'll die of old age. And that scale also helped establish that you were going to have long-term consequences, because it had to be something that could matter ten years later. You know, your kid might have to deal with it.[9]

The game Dunham had in mind didn't quite fit in any existing genre. It would be more narrative than an empire-building strategy game but more replayable than adventure games, which usually told single, predefined stories. He coined the term "storytelling strategy game" to describe what he had in mind. While he first conceived it as a game for the Newton, the idea soon grew beyond the scope of what the handheld device was capable of. Developing games for desktop Macs in the 90s was financially risky due to their tiny market share, but Dunham and Bowditch found a product called mTropolis that promised an easy way to create cross-platform UI so they could release for Windows too. Securing independent funding that would allow for hiring contract artists, writers, and QA testers, the two began working on the game out of their Seattle home office in January 1997.

Dunham had been in touch with Glorantha creator Greg Stafford, who provided some design ideas and his blessing, but the real creative workhorse on the project would be tabletop roleplaying designer Robin Laws. Already in the process of becoming one of the industry's most innovative designers, Laws had written for a number of games including *Earthdawn* [FASA 1993], *Feng Shui* [Daedalus Entertainment 1996], and *GURPS* [Steve Jackson Games 1986], and he'd been part of a push for more "narrativist" roleplaying frameworks that prioritized story over systems. He was also a huge Glorantha fan. A chance meeting between Dunham and Laws at a convention led to the latter coming aboard *Dragon Pass* as a writer, but so many of his ideas worked their way into the final game that he was eventually credited as co-designer. Already familiar with the world's rich lore, Laws could immediately start writing narrative vignettes for the evolving "storytelling strategy game"—which would, in the end, grow to include over four hundred thousand words of content.

The game that evolved from the collaboration would follow a clan of Orlanthi, one of several humanlike races in Glorantha with Bronze Age technology and divinely gifted magic. Newly arrived in Dragon Pass, your clan struggles to establish a foothold while dealing with vengeful undead, awakening dragons, mystical treasures, and dozens of rival clans with their own agendas. Rather than playing as a specific character, you take a God's-eye perspective on your clan, setting policies and making big decisions as your people's story unfolds across years and decades. At the game's core is a robust economic simulation reminiscent of one of the earliest text games, *Hammurabi*: fields, grain, and cattle must be carefully managed to keep a growing population fed. But the engine in *Dragon Pass* is far more complex, encompassing magic, religion, exploration, trade, and relationships with the

Major Releases

» **1.0**, Mac/Win CD-ROM, Oct 29, 1999. "All black or black and blue" CD printing.

» **Demo**. Allowed play for one year. Included in some game magazine CDs including *MacAddict* #44.

» **1.1**, early 2000. First CD-ROM reprint; "black and orange" CD printing. Bug fixes.

» **1.3**, 2000. Second and final CD-ROM reprint, "black and purple" CD printing. Bug fixes.

» **1.7**, Oct 8, 2002. Final update to original version (downloadable patch). Bug fixes.

» **iPhone version** (2.0), Sep 7, 2011. New UI; streamlined some complexities of original; twenty-five new scenes.

» **GOG.com version**, Aug 2012. Original version via emulator; first time this had been playable on modern computers in a number of years.

» **iPad version**, Sep 4, 2012.

» **Android version**, Aug 2014.

» **Modern PC/Mac port**, HeroCraft, Steam and GOG.com, Jul 2015. Port of more modern tablet version to desktop.

see **1962**

many other clans. One review's list of "stuff you do" in the game goes some way toward illustrating the simulation's depth:

- Selecting and managing a balanced pool of leaders to serve as your advisors on the clan ring (of upmost importance)
- Clan mood management, both for your farmers and your warriors— taking actions (feasts, etc.) to increase the mood
- Allocation of crop land vs. grazing land vs. hunting grounds
- Recruitment and maintenance of weaponthanes (e.g. warriors)
- Building defenses
- Conducting full raids, cattle raids, and aggressions on other clans
- Sending exploration parties to nearby or distant places to search for treasures or other discoveries
- Erecting shrines to the 20 or so different gods, conducting sacrifices to learn new magic (essentially the game's technology tree), etc.
- Trade system for trading goods/cows/food or establishing on-going trade relationships
- Diplomacy system for creating alliances, tribes, paying tributes, giving gifts, exchanging knowledge/lore, etc.
- Preparing leaders and sending them on "Hero Quests" to trigger special events or gain an unique/powerful advantage[18]

But the simulation is only part of the game. As you take actions, frequent narrative events, which the creators called scenes, interrupt you. On the surface these seem like vignettes from a branching-path story: a paragraph or two presenting a conflict or opportunity, followed by a list of choices for how to respond. But what's happening under the hood is more complex than it seems.

> Prominent members of the Bayberry clan come to your clan for help. "This is not a good thing we have to say, but our chieftain, Robasart, has gone mad. He makes foolish decisions, and will not listen to the counsel of the clan ring. We do not want to risk kinstrife, but something must be done. If you agree to raid us, we will make sure that Robasart falls beneath your blades. Then we will owe you a great debt."
>
> » *1. Demand a specific reward to do as they ask.*
> » *2. Do as they ask.*
> » *3. Politely decline.*
> » *4. Scold them for betraying Orlanthi values.*
> » *5. Send a delegation to warn Robasart of their intentions.*

While the text and choices in scenes appear to be static, they are filled with custom specifics tied to the state of the simulation. The Bayberry clan above, for instance, might have been picked for this scene because the player had previously established a friendship with them. The name shown for their chieftain is one the player might have seen while trading or negotiating. The scene manager has "an awful lot of flexibility in how [scenes] are coded so that they can handle all kinds of situations," recalls Dunham:

> There's a ton of conditionals, there's placeholders, there's a little randomness in them … they won't be the same any two times, either because text will be randomized, or sometimes responses aren't available depending on things you've done before…. In a way you could say, "oh, S-27 is the scene where the visitors from the South show up with their magic instruments," but that's not going to be the same any two times because of the other contextual changes.[9]

To help the player make decisions, the game shows advice from your clan's ring of seven leaders, drawn from simulated nobles in the clan. The player can change who sits on the ring at any time, and is encouraged to recruit a ring with a range of backgrounds. Each ring member has their own perspective—they might worship different gods, or have different skills and interests—and each gives advice accordingly.

Renatha: If we succeed in killing their chief, relations with them will improve. If we try and fail, they will get much worse.

Heortarl: They labor under some kind of curse. This could happen again.

Orlgard: If you decide to warn old Mad-Blood, send at least five warriors along with our delegate.

Enderos: Better a specific reward than a vague promise. Maybe they will offer us as many as twenty-five cows!

Offir: Orlanthi are expected to obey chosen leaders. But since Robasart has gone mad, it could be argued that he is no longer the leader they chose.

Harsaltar: Normally I find politics dull, but this is exciting!

After weighing advice from the ring, the player must pick one of the available responses—and each will change the simulation in some meaningful way. Some might invoke other game systems: deciding to attack the mad chieftain jumps to the game's clan warfare screen. Some responses lead to follow-up questions, like bartering over the specifics of a trade or a punishment. Choices might succeed or fail based on hidden tests of skills: a respected leader is more likely to convince her people to take a dangerous action, for instance, and a deception might pit your chieftain's cunning against your opponent's. After the results of the scene are shown, leaders might gain or lose prestige; alliances might strengthen or weaken; goods might change hands; and seasons will advance. And the new simulation state impacts the pool of future scenes now available. If the plan to overthrow the mad chieftain is botched, relations with that clan might plummet, unlocking a new scene about a clan seeking vengeance; choosing to do nothing, however, could weaken your chieftain's prestige and activate a scene where a more forceful leader among your people jockeys for power. Actions have consequences, and the player's choices compound into long-term effects. "By the late game," one reviewer noted, "every decision you're making is a result of choices made hours ago, the culmination of events that seem inevitable with hindsight."[26] One move at a time, each player builds their own unique story of how their clan survived Dragon Pass—or didn't.

Surviving isn't easy. Play reminded one reviewer of "a fairly realistic flight simulator in that you can realize your plane is going down, and you know you need to pull up, but there's also all these other buttons and switches that need to be hit at the right time and in the right order to make what seems like a simple maneuver actually transpire properly." He went on to explain:

> You could have a random occurrence that suddenly leads to a disease outbreak amongst your farmers. The more time your farmers spend in bed sick, the less time they spend producing food for your clan. "Heal the farmers" seems like the obvious answer, just like pulling up in a flight simulator, but it's not that simple. To heal via magical means, you'll need to sacrifice to gods. If you're already low on resources, sacrificing even more can make the situation much worse. Alternatively, you could send out warriors to raid a nearby tribe to steal supplies from them, but the raid could fail, or worse yet, you could over-extend yourself and be defenseless if you get raided while your warriors are out on their raid. You could attempt to go out trading for food, but your caravan could be ambushed or not result in enough food anyway.[15]

The flexibility of the scenes and their tight coupling to the underlying simulation was enabled by the custom Opal Scripting Language, or OSL ("Opal" was the game's original codename). Dunham's goal was to enable "a relatively non-technical author" like Laws to "create files that were almost valid code."[6] The notion of the scenarios being *almost* valid was key: the system was so complex that Dunham expected he'd need to fine-tune each scene to get it to compile and run correctly. But a clean syntax meant that a nontechnical writer could get a scene most of the way there, and that target was far easier to design for than a tool that tried to be one hundred percent usable by a technical novice.

Speaking to the complexity of the simulation, most OSL scenes are more logic than text. At the top of each scene definition, special functions let the system cast the scene's roles with plausible participants:

```
scene: scene_52politicaltrouble
music: "ItIsBad"
otherclan = BestRelations(KnownClans)
anotherClan = WorstRelations(KnownClans)
c = .chief
y = politician
x = y.leadership
complainer = MaleName
```

Functions to cast clans or characters could even be nested. The following line would set c to a friendly neighboring clan with a strong military:

```
c = StrongestMilitary(ClansWithPositiveAttitude(Neighboring
    Clans))
```

Variables could easily be referenced in the midst of text shown to the player. The extract below follows after forming an initial phrase like "A number of the clan's leading men" (depending on the gender of the hidden "politician" hoping to cast doubt on the current leader):

```
text: approach the ring. Their leader, <complainer>, has
    a litany of complaints. "Ever since <c> became chief,"
    <complainer> says,
text: "<d3:things have gone from bad to worse/this clan has
    headed downhill/our reputation has suffered>.
text: Our friends the <otherclan.plural> <d4:ridicule our
    ancestors/tell jokes about us as part of their holy day
    ceremonies/compare us unfavorably with their livestock/
    mock us at every chance they get>.
```

Many possible complaints might be situationally assembled, based on the current simulation state and the particulars of your clan's current leader:

```
[AntiAldryamiCharacter = c] text: <he/she> sends our
    weaponthanes into the woods on pointless hunts for the
    plant-folk.
[ProDragonewtCharacter = c AND (dragonAttitude= 'hostile OR
    dragonAttitude = 'negative)] text: <he/she> gives away
    clan wealth to those fiendish talking lizards.
[ProverbialCharacter = c] text: Half the time when <he/she>
    says something, nobody can figure out what <he/she> really
    means.
[WeLostOurLastRaid] text: <c> is unlucky in battle.
z = d3 # Some randomization to the complaints
[z = 1] text: <he/she> sings off-key.
```

Each possible choice can then define the hidden test that controls whether it will succeed, and the consequences. In one option for this scene—disputing the allegations—the chief's `Leadership` score is tested against the `Savvy` of the hidden politician behind the complaints:

```
{
    test Leadership(c) vs Savvy x
    win: {
        text: <c> patiently addressed each of their complaints.
            <He/She> exposed each one as an exaggeration or
            misunderstanding, until even <complainer> reaffirmed
            allegiance to <c> as the clan's chosen leader.
        .mood += 20
    }
    lose: {
        text: <c> started explaining <his/her> decisions,
            but after <he/she> was drowned out by laughter, and
            then shouted down, <he/she> fell silent.
        .mood -= 5
        c.leadership -= 0.1
        r = true
```

```
            i = true
            goto restart
        }
    }
}
```

Each scene also provides many possible bits of advice, which different members of the player's ring might deploy based on their skills and other aspects of the state. The numbers at the end of each line indicate which of the possible courses of action is recommended (**45** means both option 4 and 5 are acceptable to that advisor):

```
[Animals >= 3 AND ManyCows] No matter what <complainer>
    may say, our herds are strong, and that's what's really
    important. [1]
[Animals >= 3 AND FewCows] I hate to say it, but <complainer>
    has some good points. [45]
[Leadership >= 3] Somehow, I don't think <complainer> is
    behind this. [16]
[Leadership >= 4 AND NOT s] <complainer> is acting on behalf
    of someone. [6]
[Leadership >= 5 AND s] Unfortunately, <politician> does have
    more of a knack for leadership than does <c>, and will be
    able to maintain a strong anti-<c> faction if we don't ask
    <c> to resign. [35]
```

Each scene was a complex miniature program, designed to tightly interface with another complex program—the world simulation—running underneath. Eventually Laws wrote over five hundred scenes (with other team members, including Dunham and Bowditch, pitching in) and A Sharp established a steady pipeline for thoroughly testing story content. At its peak, twelve people were working on *Dragon Pass*, including artists who created hundreds of hand-drawn illustrations for scenes. It took far longer than originally anticipated, but after three years the game was complete, with total development costs—mostly in up-front salaries, rather than royalties or other deferred payments—coming to $500,000. Everyone involved was incredibly excited about what they had produced. Here, at last, was a truly interactive story, responsive to the player's decisions, drawing from an enormous pool of content, and steeped in a rich and complex lore. It seemed like a game that might forever advance the state of the art.

The small company's plan had always been to partner with a big-name publisher for release. As the game neared completion, Dunham hit the trade show circuit, scheduling meeting after meeting with distributors. But the uniqueness of his game proved a curse, not a blessing. Publishers at the time were selling games to retail stores conscious of the shelf space allocated to each company and genre. Retail buyers "were kind of looking for, 'we need a roleplaying game for this month, and a strategy game for this month, and a sports game for this month, which one do you have for me?' And this wasn't any one of those, really."[9] Publishers thought *Dragon Pass* was too niche: they literally couldn't place it on a store shelf. And so, with half a million dollars already invested, A Sharp realized they'd have to publish the game themselves.

At the end of the 90s, this was nowhere near an easy proposition. While independent game makers had been releasing "shareware" for years via BBS, FTP, and the World Wide Web, or selling direct via magazine ads and catalogs, few had successfully marketed a big game with a six-figure budget that way. Worse, the rise of the CD-ROM meant the size of a competitive game had ballooned far beyond the bandwidth available to most home computer users who might otherwise have bought one online. Broadband was not yet ubiquitous, with many people still connected to the web via dial-up modem. And there were no established digital storefronts yet for video game downloads, no trusted entities like Itch.io or Steam to handle credit card payments and secure game libraries. Putting a game in a box and getting it into a physical store was still crucial to reaching customers. Yet most retail stores would only grant shelf space to big publishers with proven track records. Dunham tried to partner with other small Mac developers in a group called Bunch Media in the hopes that they could collectively negotiate for retail placement, but the measure was largely unsuccessful. Retail stores didn't know who they were, and they didn't have the cash or clout to force their way in.

So A Sharp got creative. Unable to afford the massive fees to advertise in large gaming publications, they took out ads in sci-fi and fantasy fiction mags—one ad in *Asimov's* was headlined "Played Any Good Stories Lately?" They made a demo and got it included on the bonus CDs that came with popular computing magazines. They partnered with local hobby stores

King of Dragon Pass **ad from the April 2000** *Realms of Fantasy* **short story magazine, an example of A Sharp looking beyond traditional gamers to find an audience.**

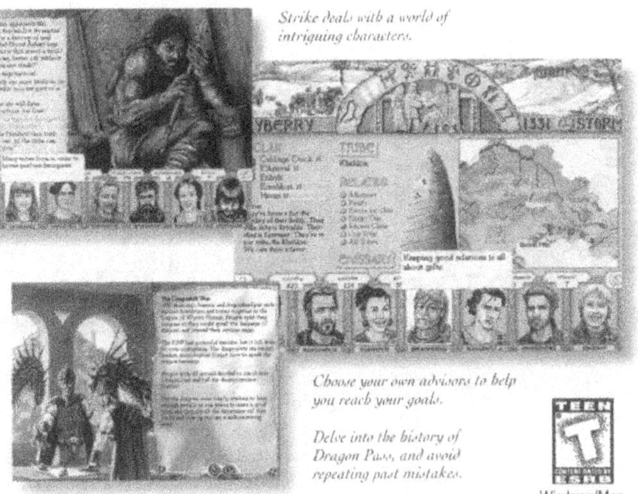

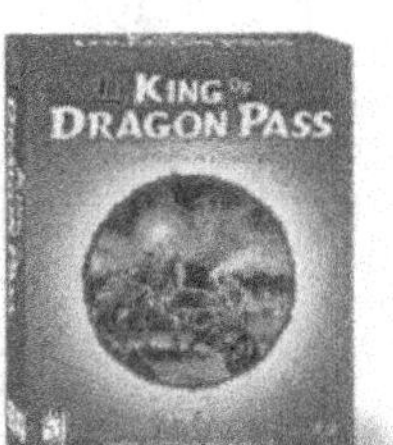

Among other release challenges, *King of Dragon Pass* was given a T rating for "Animated Violence" by the Entertainment Software Rating Board (game ratings can have a significant impact on sales). "We were astonished," Dunham recalled, "since *King of Dragon Pass* uses no animation."[5]

to get the game on shelves next to Glorantha roleplaying books. They did direct sales on their website—though then, as now, driving traffic there was a perpetual chore. But having to take all these steps without financial support was a massive challenge: "We didn't have much cash left for marketing,"[2] Dunham recalls, and he had to take out a loan to fund mass replication of game CDs and boxes.

In October 1999, the game was finally released to mixed results. The very concept of an "indie game"—the term had not yet been popularized— was foreign to many review outlets used to the massive hype campaigns drummed up by mainstream publishers. One reviewer noted the novelty of "a totally unknown game—a definite surprise in today's world."[21] The game's originality, as well as its complexity—it came with a large and necessary manual, in a time when those were rapidly falling out of fashion—also turned off reviewers, with one describing feeling "overwhelmed" by the amount of freedom the game provided.[23] Worse, it was a game that didn't show off your fancy new graphics card, a deadly sin in the eyes of many reviewers. Some seemed unable to reconcile their instinct to recommend it with their impression that it was commercially nonviable:

> It is a fabulous and rewarding experience. Please note however, that artfully presented as *King of Dragon Pass* may be, there are zero polygons in the entire game and no moving pictures of even the most rudimentary, flipping the top corners of a comic digest form. The game is completely narrative …
>
> *King of Dragon Pass* is a number of years too late to be a mainstream title. There isn't even the feedback of moving units on a map a la *Civilization*. All is static, staid, dull. Still, it has a market. I hope…. I surprise myself at the length of apologetics that I am willing to stoop for this obscure little game…. I'm trying hard to come up with a potential market, but the low system requirements and artful presentation make it a perfect game for many traditional non gamers. It is a game that can appeal to folklorists, historians, old style pen and paper role players, and other people who probably aren't playing much *Quake 3*. Who's going to tell them about it though?[14]

As it turned out, almost no one would. Many major gaming outlets didn't cover the game at all. Some that did gave it mixed or negative reviews. While a few of those folks not playing *Quake* did find *Dragon Pass*, and many fell in love with it, the game would languish in obscurity for more than a decade.

But the story has a happy ending. Over time, the game's reputation grew through the slow chatter of word of mouth. It proved fascinating for designers intrigued by the challenge of marrying strong narratives to compelling gameplay, and inspired a small but growing number of further experiments. Among other titles, the popular browser game *Fallen London*, which debuted ten years after *Dragon Pass*, was heavily inspired by its core mechanics as well as its success in marrying strategic decisions with personal stories:

> The temptation in strategy games is to treat everything as a resource. Effective strategic play means taking a dispassionate, high-level view of events. But *King of Dragon Pass*' parade of feuds, venality, romance and nobility keep your feet firmly planted in the soil…. [It] names everyone

see **2009**

and everything: "Thanes and priests from the Tree Brother clan come to accuse one of your young carls, Yanioth, of secret murder. 'We found our revered god-talker Brenna dead in the temple, a dagger in her back.'" The game never misses an opportunity to remind you that a clan is composed of people, not statistics.[13]

In the 2010s, the rise of digital gaming storefronts and mobile app stores gave indies an increasing number of routes to finding an audience. Even a niche game now had a way to reach would-be fans. Dunham started wondering whether his game, which began as an idea for the Apple Newton, might be reborn on the Apple iPhone. Buoyed by a resurgence of interest, A Sharp released a mobile version of *Dragon Pass* in 2011 and a tablet version the following year, with the revamped UI and engine making their way back to PC and Mac in 2015. This time the game would sell, eventually moving a hundred times as many copies as it had in its first retail run. Twenty years after being derided as embarrassingly behind the times, it now seems incredibly modern: a recent move toward narrative games driven by "quality-based narrative" or "storylets"[20] directly descends from the core *Dragon Pass* concept of templated scenes both gated by and altering an underlying simulation. In 2018, A Sharp released *Six Ages: Ride Like the Wind*, the first of a series of planned sequels.

The original *Dragon Pass* now sometimes appears on all-time "best of" lists for both the RPG and strategy genres—having failed to fit into either at first, it has now conquered both. "It sometimes takes many in-game years to become obvious," one modern reviewer wrote of playing *Dragon Pass*, "but this is a world that never forgets."[27] He meant to invoke the way decisions in the game can come back years later with surprising consequences, but the statement might apply just as well to the real-life story of how A Sharp's game became a classic. Sometimes it takes some waiting for the right scene to come around before seeds planted ages ago can grow.

References

1   Asher, Mark. 2000. "Reading Is Fundamental." *Computer Gaming World* #188, Mar 2000.

2   Asher, Mark. n.d. "Hardcore Gaming's Salvation?" Quarter to Three. www.quartertothree.com/features/selling_direct/direct_sales_salvation2.shtml | a Apr 12, 2021

3   Costikyan, Greg. 2000. "King of Dragon Pass" (review). *Happy Puppy* (blog). Feb 7, 2000. www.happypuppy.com/win/reviews/kingofdrag-win-1.html | s Oct 14, 2000

4   Dunham, David. 2001a. "King of Dragon Pass Postmortem." *iDevGames* (blog). Feb 20, 2001. www.idevgames.com/postmortems/king-of-dragon-pass | s Mar 6, 2010

5   Dunham, David. 2001b. "Rating System Flawed." *Game Developer*, June 2001.

6   Dunham, David. 2010. "Choices." *King of Dragon Pass* (blog). Sep 12, 2010. kingofdragonpass.blogspot.com/2010/09/choices.html | a Jul 6, 2022

7   Dunham, David. 2011. "OSL (King of Dragon Pass Scripting)." *King of Dragon Pass* (blog). Oct 2, 2011. kingofdragonpass.blogspot.com/2011/10/osl-king-of-dragon-pass-scripting.html | a Apr 12, 2021

8   Dunham, David. 2018a. "Interview with David Dunham, lead designer of Six Ages." Interview by Runeblog. Jul 6, 2018. elruneblog.blogspot.com/2018/07/interview-with-david-dunham-lead.html | a Apr 12, 2021

9   Dunham, David. 2018b. "The Legacy of King of Dragon Pass and the Future of Six Ages." Interview by Perceptive Podcast. Video. Sep 21, 2018. www.youtube.com/watch?v=Alg_RzxVWfU | a Apr 12, 2021

10   Dunham, David. n.d. "OSL Sample." A Sharp Homepage. a-sharp.com/kodp/osl.html | a Apr 12, 2021

11   Edgeworth, Mitch. 2012. "King of Dragon Pass" (review). *Grub Street: Margins of the Literary Scene*

(blog). Sep 4, 2012. grubstreethack.wordpress.com/2012/09/04/king-of-dragon-pass | a Apr 12, 2021

12 Faraday, Owen. 2013. "A Decade Later, King of Dragon Pass Development Keeps Questing On." *Pocket Tactics* (blog). Mar 5, 2013. www.pockettactics.com/2013/03/05/a-decade-later-king-of-dragon-pass-development-keeps-questing-on | s Jul 5, 2013

13 Gardiner, Chris. 2011. "Echo Bazaar Inspirations: King of Dragon Pass." *Failbetter Games* (blog). Oct 4, 2011. www.failbettergames.com/echo-bazaar-inspirations-king-of-dragon-pass | a Apr 12, 2021

14 Grant, Jules. 1999. "King of Dragon Pass" (review). *The Electric Playground* (blog). Dec 19, 1999. www.elecplay.com/review.html?article=1763 | s Jun 27, 2001

15 Hodapp, Eli. 2011. "'King of Dragon Pass' Review - 'Thus Ends Our Sorry Tale, the Tale of Clan Fart.'" *TouchArcade* (blog). Sep 8, 2011. toucharcade.com/2011/09/08/king-of-dragon-pass-review | a Apr 12, 2021

16 Hollebone, Bruce. 2000. "King of Dragon Pass Mailing List FAQ." Dec 2, 2000. www.a-sharp.com/kodp/bh/KoDPfaq.html | a Apr 12, 2021

17 Johnson, Wes. 1999. "Review of King of Dragon Pass." *RPGnet* (blog). Dec 6, 1999. www.rpg.net/reviews/archive/classic/rev_2592.phtml | a Apr 12, 2021

18 Kiley, Oliver. 2014. "15 Years and Worlds Apart - Autumn Dynasty: Warlords & The King of Dragon Pass." *BoardGameGeek* (blog). Mar 5, 2014. boardgamegeek.com/blogpost/28220/15-years-and-worlds-apart-autumn-dynasty-warlords | a Apr 12, 2021

19 Klaehn, Jeffery, and David Dunham. 2016. "Interview: David Dunham, Lead Designer, Producer and Programmer of the Award-Winning Strategy Storytelling Game, King of Dragon Pass." *Journal of the Canadian Game Studies Association* 10 (15), Spring/Summer 2016.

20 Kreminski, Max and Noah Wardrip-Fruin. 2018. "Sketching a Map of the Storylets Design Space." In *Interactive Storytelling: 11th International Conference on Interactive Digital Storytelling*, ed. Rebecca Rouse, Hartmut Koenitz, Mads Haahr, Springer.

21 Krol, Scott R. 2002. "King of Dragon Pass" (review). *Gameworld Network* (blog). Sep 24, 2002. pcgames.gwn.com/reviews/gamereview.php/id/161/p/0/title/King_of_Dragon_Pass.html | s Apr 5, 2007

22 Laws, Robin. 2018. "The Six Ages Team: Robin Laws." *Six Ages Development Blog*. Jul 9, 2018. blog.sixages.com/index.php/2018/07/09/the-six-ages-team-robin-laws | a Apr 12, 2021

23 MacHOME. 1999. "King of Dragon Pass" (review). www.machome.com/reviews/MacReviewZone.lasso?grr8=34028 | s Nov 5, 2003

24 Meer, Alec. 2015. "Wot I Think: King Of Dragon Pass." *Rock, Paper, Shotgun* (blog). Aug 4, 2015. www.rockpapershotgun.com/king-of-dragon-pass-review-pc | a Apr 12, 2021

25 Purchese, Robert. 2013. "The Story of King of Dragon Pass: Do You Remember Demolition Man?" *Eurogamer* (blog). Apr 12, 2013. www.eurogamer.net/articles/2013-04-12-the-story-of-king-of-dragon-pass-do-you-remember-demolition-man | a Apr 12, 2021

26 Salgado, Filipe. 2011. "Review: Religion, Wars, and Everything Else." *Pitchfork* (blog). Dec 9, 2011. pitchfork.com/killscreen/107-review-religion-wars-and-everything-else | s Jan 11, 2012

27 Stanton, Rich. 2012. "App of the Day: King of Dragon Pass." *Eurogamer* (blog). Dec 5, 2012. www.eurogamer.net/articles/2012-12-05-app-of-the-day-king-of-dragon-pass | a Apr 12, 2021

28 Vega, Sin. 2014. "Remembering King Of Dragon Pass." *Rock, Paper, Shotgun* (blog). Oct 17, 2014. www.rockpapershotgun.com/king-of-dragon-pass-retro | a Apr 12, 2021

29 Zuccarelli, Dan. 2011. "King of Dragon Pass Review." *Gamezebo* (blog). Sep 13, 2011. www.gamezebo.com/games/king-dragon-pass/review | s Feb 21, 2013

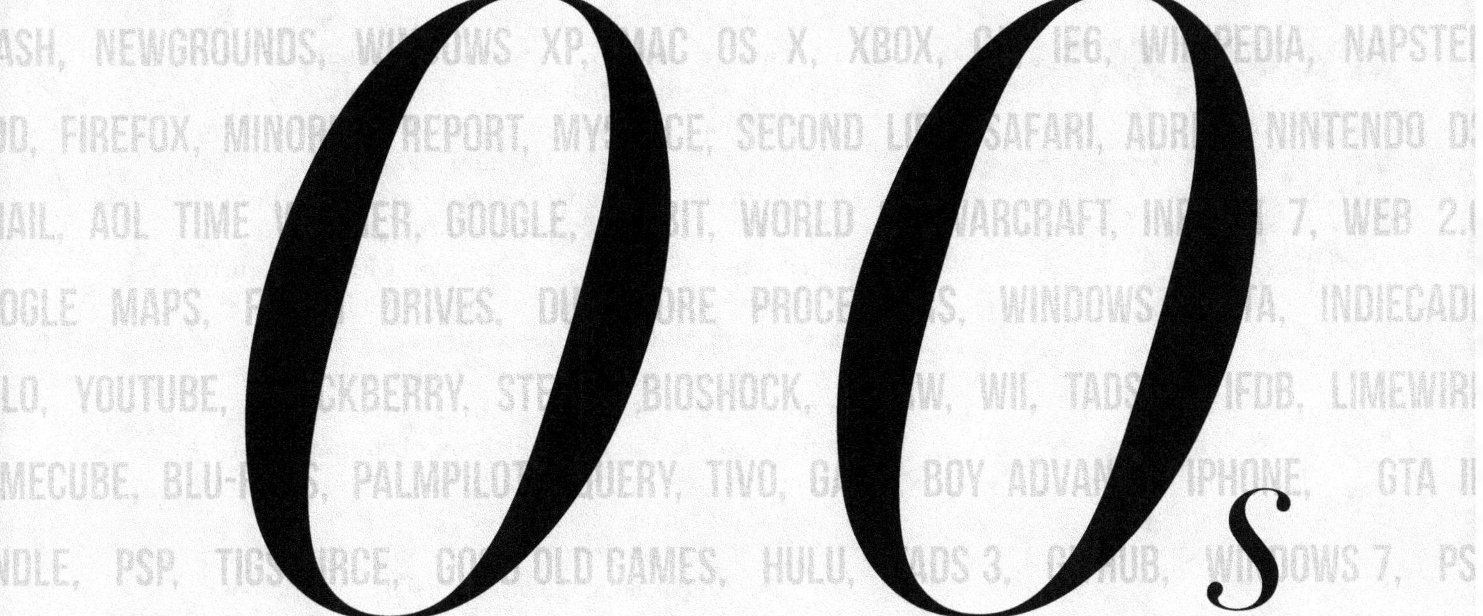

OOs

THE MOMENT MORE THAN HALF OF AMERICAN HOUSEHOLDS HAD INTERNET access came sometime in the year 2000, an apt milestone for the arrival of the new millennium. The vast majority were still connecting through slow dial-up services like America Online, which superbly captured the tremendous sea change from old media to new when it acquired the Time Warner media empire in 2001. But by the end of the decade, four out of five internet users had upgraded to always-on, high-speed broadband. The early web, largely text-driven by necessity, was vanishing with the arrival of streaming video and other high-bandwidth luxuries.

Digital text was at a low point of mainstream popularity in a new century of multimedia, but fan communities were thriving like never before. The parser IF scene centered around the rec.arts.int-fiction newsgroup **1993** was producing dozens of innovative and increasingly sophisticated interactive stories each year. The first year of the decade alone saw the release of acclaimed titles like Emily Short's *Galatea* **2000**, about a complex conversation with a single character; *Shade* [Andrew Plotkin], a hallucinatory parable set in a one-room apartment; *Rameses* [Stephen Bond], a game about bullying and control that challenged traditional relationships between

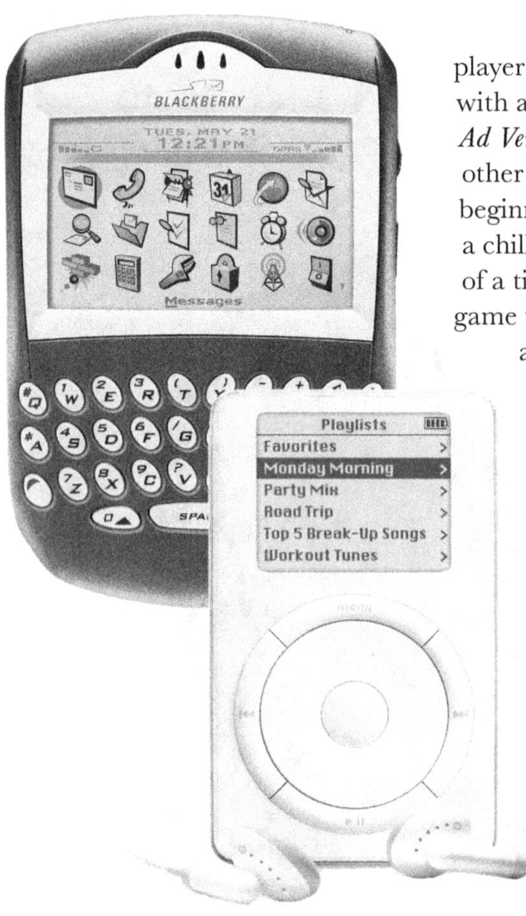

Early 2000s devices like the BlackBerry 7000 series or Apple's original iPod did not yet have the large screens that would make reading interactive text on them an appealing proposition in future decades.

Some examples of text games on the festival circuit during the decade include *Whom the Telling Changed* [Aaron A. Reed 2005], *Book and Volume* [Nick Montfort 2005], and *Everybody Dies* [Jim Munroe 2008].

player and character; *9:05* [Adam Cadre], which merged interactivity with an unreliable narrator to produce an unforgettable twist; *Ad Verbum* [Nick Montfort], a wordplay game that asked players (among other challenges) to explore a series of rooms where only words beginning with the right letter were recognized; *LASH* [Paul O'Brian], a chilling exploration of Civil War–era slavery through the eyes of a time-folding robot; and *Rematch* [Andrew D. Pontious], a puzzle game that lasts only a single turn and requires replaying again and again to learn how to win. A new generation of interactive storytelling wizards were in their prime: authors like Andrew Plotkin, Adam Cadre, Emily Short, Paul O'Brian, Kathleen Fischer, Jon Ingold, Ian Finley, and many others were producing a stream of well-written and well-designed games. The community expanded beyond the single annual Interactive Fiction Competition with new recurring events like Spring Thing, IntroComp, One Room Game Comp, and the Halloween-themed EctoComp. Community resources like the IFDB (Interactive Fiction Database) and the IFWiki launched, signs of a community maturing past an initial growth spurt of enthusiasm toward long-term support networks and infrastructure that could serve it for decades to come.

Some modern interactive fictions had become seasoned enough to be deemed new classics—a second generation of standards that could stand alongside the original hits of the 80s. With a slow but steady influx of new fans, text games began to get some recognition and coverage in the wider world of digital gaming, particularly the growing indie game scene that likewise came from small communities more interested in innovation than mainstream success. The 2000s saw the dawn of indie game festivals comparable to those celebrating indie films, with events like the Slamdance Guerilla Gamemaker Competition, IndieCade, and the Independent Games Festival (IGF) making their debuts. Text games began appearing at these festivals alongside graphical successes, giving them more visibility and credibility outside their niche. Some gamer news sites began to offer regular interactive fiction coverage (including *JayIsGames*, *PlayThisThing*, and *TIGSource*), and the Writers Guild of America, which represents film and TV writers, gave its first award to a game, *Dead Head Fred* [Vicious Cycle Software 2007].

Academia began to take serious notice of text games in the 2000s too, with scholarly studies of the genre like Nick Montfort's *Twisty Little Passages* and Jeremy Douglass's dissertation *Command Lines*. The blog *Grand Text Auto* covered literary gaming throughout the decade from a scholarly perspective. In 2006, the *Electronic Literature Collection Volume 1* was released on CD-ROM, archiving sixty influential digital fictions from the ten years prior. Much as college film departments began to appear a few decades after film became entrenched as a form of popular entertainment, game studies was in its early infancy as an academic field: the number of departments would grow from a handful at the end of the 2000s to dozens, if not hundreds, a decade later.

Despite enthusiasm on many fronts, the 2000s saw very few commercial text games. Exceptions were mostly the work of ambitious amateurs hoping a market might still exist for quality games grounded in fondly remembered traditions of the past. *1893: A World's Fair Mystery* [Illuminated Lantern 2002] was a sprawling illustrated text adventure recreating the historic Chicago celebration in incredible detail, so large and comprehensive it included NPC-led orientation tours which new players were encouraged to seek out and attend at the posted times. Textfyre Inc. commissioned well-known IF authors to write full-length games for commercial sale, including *Jack Toresal and the Secret Letter* [Mike Gentry and David Cornelson 2009] and *Klockwerk: The Shadow in the Cathedral* [Ian Finley and Jon Ingold 2009]. While both endeavors found more enthusiasm than commercial success, they may have mostly been victims of timing. New platforms like e-readers, tablets, and smartphones were about to arrive that would open up many new options for reading digital text more comfortably, and the 2010s would see a resurgence of commercial text games in many forms for devices old and new.

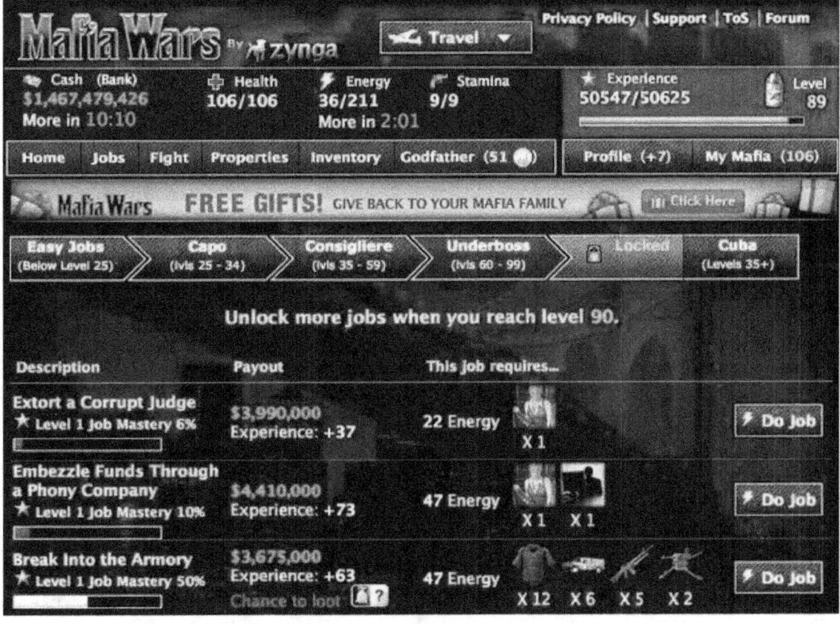

Early Facebook games like Zynga's *Mafia Wars* (a thinly veiled clone of David Maestri's *Mob Wars*) used largely text-based interfaces.

A second generation of tools for text game makers also appeared during the 2000s, improving on or supplementing the previous decade's first stabs at opening up interactive storytelling to more creators. Inform 7 **2008**, a radical new natural language paradigm for authoring interactive fiction, upgraded its popular predecessor by building an entirely new, higher-level language on top of it. The language made it possible for authors to create complex conceptual structures within a traditional text adventure world model. Emily Short's *Alabaster* [2009], for instance, improved on *Galatea*'s conversation model by defining high-level structures for how conversational quips could be sequenced, understood, or related to other aspects of the story world:

Assumption relates various quips to various facts. The verb to assume (it assumes, they assume, it assumed, it is assumed) implies the assumption relation. An availability rule for a quip (called the target): if

> the target assumes a fact which is not known by the player, it is off-limits.
>
> A plausibility rule for a shallowly-buried quip (called target) (this is the pruning mid-level suggestions rule): if a quip indirectly-follows the current quip: it is dubious; [...]

Other tools targeting different kinds of creators or different styles of text games also appeared throughout the decade. ADRIFT (Adventure Development & Runner Interactive Fiction Toolkit) provided a menu-based approach to crafting parser interactive fiction for creators without a background in traditional coding. Ren'Py provided a library built on top of Python that similarly made it easy for noncoders to create visual novels with a straightforward scripting language. More communities of makers outside the English speaking world were also springing up or consolidating: the online zine *Terra d'IF* launched in 2003 for the Italian interactive fiction community, and in 2005 French IF fans organized the first competition for titles in their native tongue.

Text game platforms were in the midst of a slow transition from standalone downloads to web-based apps. Web 2.0 tech was making it increasingly possible to run complex JavaScript applications directly from a browser window. Throughout the decade, increasingly sophisticated browser games like *Utopia* [Mehul Patel / Solaria Interactive 1999], *Kingdom of Loathing* [Asymmetric Publications 2003], *Urban Dead* [Kevan Davis 2005], *Twilight Heroes* [Quirkz Media 2007], and *Fallen London* [Failbetter Games 2009] provided an easy entry point to interactive prose that didn't involve downloading, installing, and learning to use unfamiliar applications. Web-native story construction platforms like ChooseYourStory.com began to appear. Near the end of the decade, games for social media on platforms like Facebook arrived; many were at first primarily text-driven due to the limits of early social networking APIs, and games like *Mob Wars* [David Maestri 2008] thrived on these new, virally interconnected platforms. Parser interactive fiction began to move online as well: the 2008 debut of the Parchment library by Dannii Willis made it easy to run a story compiled by Inform in a web browser.

The 2000s as a whole continued an era of fruitful experiments that had begun in the 1990s. A handful of stable tools continued to evolve, but the digital landscape was shifting underfoot, closing off old paradigms and platforms while opening up many new ones. Authors of interactive prose in the new century were adapting, giving no signs they were content to leave their medium behind in the old one.

More Text Games from the 2000s

see *Digital: A Love Story* **2010**

see **2007**

see **2003** and **2009**

2000
Galatea

9:05 *(Adam Cadre, Inform 6)*. Getting ready for work seems mundane until a twist ending mandates a replay. **Ad Verbum** *(Nick Montfort, Inform 6)*. Tricky linguistic challenges set in the mansion of the Wizard of Wordplay. **Augmented Fourth** *(Brian Uri, Inform 6)*. Charming puzzlefest riffing off the old-school tradition, but with gentler challenges and a well-developed sense of humor. **The Cove** *(Kathleen M.*

Fischer, Inform 6). IF Art Show Landscape invites you to reflect on a beautiful seaside scene at a turning point in your character's life. **Dangerous Curves** *(Irene Callaci, Inform 6)*. Open-world noir detective yarn with useful convenience features and ambitious scope. **Fail-Safe** *(Jon Ingold, Inform 6)*. Help an astronaut through the the aftermath of a deadly attack. **Kaged** *(Ian Finley, TADS)*. Orwellian dystopia where the player's freedom is as constrained as the character's. **LASH—Local Asynchronous Satellite Hookup** *(Paul O'Brian, Inform 6)*. Sci-fi story about a scavenger robot on a future Earth who can link to disturbing visions of its past. **Masquerade** *(Kathleen M. Fischer, Inform 6)*. Antebellum romance with a strongly painted heroine and multiple endings. **Metamorphoses** *(Emily Short, Inform 6)*. Well-designed simulationist fantasy puzzler; transmute elemental essences for fun and profit. **Rameses** *(Stephen Bond, Inform 6)*. A bullied teen at a boarding school resists the player's attempts to make him stand up for himself, presaging later games like *Depression Quest*. **Rematch** *(Andrew D. Pontious, TADS)*. Relive the single moment before your untimely death until you figure out how to escape it. **Shade** *(Andrew Plotkin, Inform 6)*. A top-ten classic: what begins as a one-room game in your apartment devolves into a surreal dreamlike parable. **Shrapnel** *(Adam Cadre, Inform 6)*. Like the author's *Photopia*, a story told in disconnected fragments, here pushing against the limits of IF conventions and interfaces.

All Roads *(Jon Ingold, Inform 6)*. Award-sweeping, story-centric trip through an alt-universe Venice weaves together vignettes that at first seem unconnected. **The Beetmonger's Journal** *(Scott Starkey, TADS)*. Unique structure where the player character and viewpoint character are different: you play the hero's chronicler. **Best of Three** *(Emily Short, Inform 6)*. A reunion with an old flame can go in various surprising directions; experiments with hybrid parser and menu-driven conversation interface. **Castle Marrach** *(Skotos Tech, StoryBuilder)*. Social storytelling MUD set in a single huge castle, with unique features for narration, understanding, and conversation. **Earth and Sky** *(Paul O'Brian, Inform 6)*. Start of a well-crafted and much-loved trilogy about superhero siblings. **Fallacy of Dawn** *(Robb Sherwin, Hugo)*. Start of a loose sci-fi trilogy in the memorably described cyberpunk city of New Haz. **First Things First** *(J. Robinson Wheeler, TADS)*. Well-designed time travel puzzle game. **The Gostak** *(Carl Muckenhoupt, Inform 6)*. Fascinating puzzle game inspired by the linguistics observation that English speakers can parse well-formed nonsense like "The gostak distims the doshes." **Heroes** *(Sean Barrett, Inform 6)*. By switching between five viewpoint characters you gain a better understanding of their fantasy city than any one individually. **Majestic** *(Anim-X/Electronic Arts, Win)*. Ambitious early ARG in which characters contacted you via multiple real-life channels like phone calls and instant messages. **Moments Out of Time** *(L. Ross Raszewski, Inform 6)*. As a time-traveling historian, explore and document an ordinary home just before an apocalyptic disaster. **Pytho's Mask** *(Emily Short, Inform 6)*. Practical astrology, romance, a royal ball, and a cast of scheming characters; conversation-heavy classic. **SmarterChild** *(ActiveBuddy, instant messaging)*. Chatbot that attracted over 30 million instant message buddies on AIM and Yahoo Messenger. **These Waves of Girls** *(Caitlin Fisher, Flash)*. Brilliantly written hypertext novella exploring the narrator's memories of formative relationships and sexual awakenings. **TriadCity** *(SmartMonsters, Java)*. MUD with literary influences and emphasis on nonviolent solutions, with advanced features like subjective room descriptions. **Uplink** *(Introversion Software, Win/Mac)*. Well-remembered hacking simulator with chiptunes soundtrack and text-driven interface. **Voices** *(Aris Katsaris, Inform 6)*. Short emotionally charged story where the player takes a unique role in the life of Joan of Arc.

1893: A World's Fair Mystery *(Peter Nepstad, TADS)*. Incredibly detailed explorable recreation of a historic event; there's a plot in there somewhere too. **Accounts of the Glass Sky** *(M.D. Coverley, Flash)*. Literary hypertext with multimedia components about memory and disillusionment, influenced by the 9/11 attacks. **Earth and

2001
The Beast

2002
Screen

Sky 2: Another Earth, Another Sky *(Paul O'Brien, Inform 6)*. Superhero sibling sequel, winner of IF Comp 2002. **Faith** *(Robert Kendall, Flash)*. A kinetic poem in five stages on the relation between faith and logic. **The Gamma Gals** *(Christopher Cole, ADRIFT)*. Adult IF where your girlfriend, Erin, invites you over to her sexy sorority; noteworthy for naming the Erin, trophy of the Adult Interactive Fiction Awards. **Lock & Key** *(Adam Cadre, Inform 6)*. Try to stop the hero from escaping in this iterative dungeon design puzzle. **The Moonlit Tower** *(Yoon Ha Lee, Inform 6)*. Debut from the future novelist; evocative writing based in Eastern mythology, with multiple endings. **Photograph: A Portrait of Reflection** *(Steve Evans, Inform 6)*. A man looks back on a life gone wrong, but something else is also going on... **The PK Girl** *(Robert Goodwin, ADRIFT)*. Sci-fi thriller/dating sim with multiple endings, including anime-style graphics and soundtrack. **Progress Quest** *(Eric Fredricksen, Win)*. Textual parody of RPGs, progenitor of the clicker game. **Savoir-Faire** *(Emily Short, Inform 6)*. Eighteenth-century mystery with unique magic system based on linking conceptually similar objects. **Soliloquy** *(Kenneth Goldsmith, web)*. Online adaptation of a gallery exhibition featuring an unedited account of every word spoken by the author for a week. **Storyland** *(Nanette Wylde, Flash)*. Combinatorial story generator. **Sun and Moon** *(David Brain, web)*. Story split across multiple fictional websites with passwords and puzzles unlocking more content. **Tinseltown Blues** *(Chip Hayes, Inform 6)*. Hollywood-set scavenger hunt puzzlefest; first entrant and first winner of Spring Thing.

2003
The Kingdom of Loathing

City of Secrets *(Emily Short, Inform 6)*. Explore an intriguing city powered by tech and magic; filled with details to explore and sophisticated worldbuilding. **Episode in the Life of an Artist** *(Peter Eastman, TADS)*. A menial worker believes himself an artist and genius, but is replaced at his job by a machine. **Hamlet—The Text Adventure** *(Robin Johnson, Nondescript)*. A breezy, comedic retelling mixed with material from other Shakespeare plays in classic text adventure form. **To Hell in a Hamper** *(J. J. Guest, ADRIFT)*. A Victorian balloonist must lighten his hot air balloon before it crosses the path of an active volcano. **Narcolepsy** *(Adam Cadre, Inform 6)*. Best Writing XYZZY winner is played in two windows: thoughts and reality. **Risorgimento Represso** *(Michael J. Coyne, Inform 6)*. A sizable wizard's apprentice puzzlefest lauded for thorough implementation, humor, and unique magic. **Scavenger** *(Quintin Stone, TADS)*. In a postapocalyptic world, search an underground base for secrets of the past. **shadows on the mirror** *(Chrysoula Tzavelas, TADS)*. A woman with mysterious powers is trapped in a car with her kidnapper. **Slouching Towards Bedlam** *(Star Foster and Daniel Ravipinto, Inform 6)*. Steampunk adventure and delicious existential terror; swept the XYZZYs and IF Comp. **The Tarot Reading** *(Michael Penman, TADS)*. Receive a reading and question the major arcana for thoughts on life, art, and other subjects. **Torn** *(Joe Chedburn, web)*. Text MMO where gangs compete for business in a criminal underworld; had over a million users by 2008. **The Wal*Mart Game** *(thatguy, ChooseYourStory.com)*. Irreverent choice-based game in which your local mart has been occupied by terrorists and it's up to you to save the day.

2004
The Fire Tower

The Act of Misdirection *(Callico Harrison, Inform 6)*. A Victorian magician's act may be more than she bargained for. **All Things Devours** *(half sick of shadows, Inform 6)*. A compact, clever time-travel puzzle. **Back to Life... Unfortunately** *(David Whyld, ADRIFT)*. A comedy in which the goal is to die. **The Battle of Walcot Keep** *(Steve Breslin et al., TADS)*. Experiment in individual NPCs taking actions during a battle. **Bellclap** *(Tommy Herbert, Inform 6)*. Personified parser is an angel conveying your divine instructions to mortals. **Blue Chairs** *(Chris Klimas, Inform 6)*. Psychedelic, surreal story considered a modern classic. **The Cabal** *(Stephen Bond, Inform 6)*. Satirizes conspiracy theorists with a secret society that influences the world of interactive fiction. **Future Boy!** *(Kent Tessman et al., Hugo)*. Commercially released parser-based superhero game featuring animation and voice acting. **Jazz auf Tegemis** *(Joerg Rosenbauer, Inform 6)*. An off-duty spaceship merchant captain meets an alien jazz singer in this German sci-fi adventure. **Necrotic Drift** *(Robb Sherwin, Hugo)*. An RPG nerd fights for his life against a mall of undead *D&D* monsters. **Things** *(Jacqueline A. Lott Ashwell and Sam Kabo Ashwell, TADS)*. Constrained speed-IF written using only one noun. **Thy Dungeonman** *(Videlectrix, Flash)*. Homestar Runner's spoof of early text games famous for the catchphrase "You can't get ye flask."

All Hope Abandon *(Eric Eve, TADS)*. After a heart attack at a theological convention, the player's actions will determine if they return to life or spend eternity elsewhere. **Beyond** *(Roberto Grassi et al., Inform 6)*. The spirit of a never-born child assists an investigation into the death of her pregnant mother. **Bolivia by Night** *(Aidan Doyle, TADS)*. Taking a job with a local newspaper leads to a search for a missing colleague in this informative ode to Bolivia. **Building** *(Poster, Inform 6)*. A surreal horror game with an emphasis on atmosphere; explore an abandoned office building. **Le Cercle des Gros Geeks disparus** *(Adrien Saurat, Inform 6)*. Winner of French Comp 2005, wherein the player completes a bizarre contraption using one of several friends' plans, each leading to a different ending. **Conan Kill Everything** *(Ian Haberkorn, Inform 6)*. As Conan the Barbarian, do what's expected. **The Corn Identity** *(Carl Muckenhoupt et al., Inform 6)*. An "exquisite corpse" collaboration between thirteen authors, each writing a segment based only on the previous episode. **Distress** *(Mike Snyder, Hugo)*. A dire tale of survival after a spaceship pod crash-lands on an alien planet. **Escape to New York** *(Richard Otter, ADRIFT)*. In April of 1912, an art thief bound for New York must recover his loot, avoid the law, and escape from an "unsinkable" passenger ship. **Vespers** *(Jason Devlin, Inform 6)*. Fifteenth-century abbot investigates a monastery beset by plague, madness, and murder.

Child's Play *(Stephen Granade, Inform 7)*. The protagonist is uniquely limited compared to most IF heroes—they're a baby. **De Baron** *(Victor Gijsbers, Inform 6)*. Try to save your daughter in this dark examination of human evil. **Delightful Wallpaper** *(Andrew Plotkin, Inform 7)*. A logic maze of passageways and a murder mystery where the player collects and places motivations in characters. **Ekphrasis** *(JB Ferrant, Inform 6)*. A massive French game in which an art historian searches across Europe for a stolen painting. **Escape from the Crazy Place** *(J. J. Guest et al., TADS)*. This wacky choice-based comedy featuring a zillion surreal situations began on paper in 1984 and continues to be expanded to this day. **Floatpoint** *(Emily Short, Inform 7)*. A symbolic gift will determine the fate of almost-human space colonists returning to Earth. **The Journey of the King** *(Peter Nepstad, TADS)*. An implementation of Lord Dunsany's novella by the same name, written in a similar high diction. **Voices of Spoon River** *(Jon Scoresby et al., Inform 6)*. Adventure designed as a tool for teaching Edgar Lee Masters' classic anthology. **The Warlord, the Princess & the Bulldog** *(David Whyld, ADRIFT)*. A commando must rescue a princess in this action comedy where puzzles can be skipped for a cost.

An Act of Murder *(Christopher Huang, Inform 7)*. A Victorian whodunnit with a variable murderer. **Dead Cities** *(Jon Ingold, Inform 7)*. Best in Show at the HP Lovecraft Commonplace Book Project 2007, celebrating the seventieth anniversary of the author's death. **Deadline Enchanter** *(Anya DeNiro, Inform 7)*. A metapuzzle that refigures the usual relationship between the player and the parser. **A Fine Day for Reaping** *(James Webb, ADRIFT)*. The Grim Reaper must ensure five souls keep their appointment; XYZZY Best Story winner. **Lord Bellwater's Secret** *(Sam Gordon, Inform 7)*. Well-regarded one-room puzzler set in a Victorian gentleman's bedroom. **Lost Pig** *(Admiral Jota, Inform 6)*. Narrated by orc Grunk, this comedy is often cited as one of the greatest IFs of all time. **Public Secrets** *(Sharon Daniel and Erik Loyer, Flash)*. Interactive documentary about incarcerated women told through animated text and recorded audio. **Suveh Nux** *(David Fisher, Inform 6)*. Learn a wizard's magical language to escape his vault. **The Symbolic Engine** *(Evan*

2005
Shades of Doom

2006
Dwarf Fortress

2007
El Museo de las Consciencias
Lieux Communs

Schull, Inform 7). Explore a peculiar device in this slice of "digital anthropology from the future" that took Best of Show in the last IF Art Show. **Treasures of a Slaver's Kingdom** *(S. John Ross, Inform 7)*. This comedic faux-retro adventure includes a full scan of the pen-and-paper roleplaying game it claims to be based on. **Twilight Heroes** *(Quirkz Media, web)*. Multiplayer browser game of superheroes and villains.

2008
Violet

Afflicted *(Doug Egan, Inform 7)*. A health inspector documenting the violations of a dive bar discovers layers of mystery and horror under the mold. **Buried In Shoes** *(Kazuki Mishima, Inform 6)*. Unbearable history told through fragmented vignettes. **Everybody Dies** *(Jim Munroe, Inform 7)*. Can three grocery store workers with intertwined fates stop each other from dying? **Fitting the Pattern** *(Christine Wilks, Flash)*. Use dressmaking tools to reveal pieces of a larger, nonlinear memoir. **Forumwarz** *(Crotch Zombie Productions, web)*. Browser RPG parodying internet culture. **Gun Mute** *(C.E.J. Pacian, TADS)*. A queer western with creative villains that turns shoot-outs into puzzles. **The Moon Watch** *(Paolo Maroncelli and Alessandro Peretti, Inform 6)*. In 1967, one Soviet bureaucrat gets sent to Russia's new moon base and immediately faces crisis inside his "tin box." **Mrs. Pepper's Nasty Secret** *(Jim Aikin and Eric Eve, TADS)*. Short adventure meant for new parser players, winner of IFBeginnersComp. **Nightfall** *(Eric Eve, Inform 7)*. Explore an abandoned city and your memories of an intriguing vanished character. **Once upon a winter night, the ragman came singing under your window** *(Expio, Inform 7)*. Solve a monster's riddle or be cursed in this dark, creepy fairy tale. **Piracy 2.0** *(Sean Huxter, Inform 6)*. Escape a space pirate's brig and bring them to justice in this complex, open-ended adventure. **Snack Time!** *(Renee Choba, Inform 7)*. Play from the point of view of a dog trying to get a snack in this charming and inventive game.

2009
Fallen London

69,105 Keys *(David Welbourn, Inform 6)*. Clever small puzzler based on disambiguating objects by taking advantage of Inform's parse_name routine. **Alabaster** *(Emily Short et al., Inform 7)*. A retelling of *Snow White* from the huntsman's perspective; written by eleven authors with eighteen different endings. **The Ascot** *(Duncan Bowsman, ADRIFT)*. Brief, zany adventure where the only possible commands are yes or no … or are they? **Blue Lacuna** *(Aaron A. Reed, Inform 7)*. Epic story about wanderers between worlds with a complex central NPC. **Broken Legs** *(Sarah Morayati, Inform 7)*. After a bad audition, aspiring theater student Lottie Plum plans to sabotage her way into acceptance at an acting school. **Byzantine Perspective** *(Lea Albaugh, Inform 7)*. A short heist game built around a unique spatial perspective puzzle. **Earl Grey** *(Rob Dubbin and Allison Parrish, Inform 6)*. A comedic fantasy wordplay game where the player can knock a single letter out of a word or cast a letter into it. **The Endling Archive** *(Kazuki Mishima, Inform 6)*. Story told through a database of the extinct and the lost that is equal parts informative, speculative, and personal. **The King of Shreds and Patches** *(Jimmy Maher, Inform 7)*. Full-length game of Lovecraftian horror in Elizabethan England. **Make It Good** *(Jon Ingold, Inform 6)*. Elaborately plotted mystery where a detective guilty of murder must use his investigation to frame someone else. **Rover's Day Out** *(Benjamin Collins-Sussman and Jack Welch, Inform 7)*. Meta sci-fi story where an AI character's daily tasks control a spaceship. **The Shadow in the Cathedral** *(Ian Finley and Jon Ingold, Inform 7)*. Commercial release from Textfyre telling a well-crafted classic adventure in a steampunky world. **Shelter From the Storm** *(Eric Eve, TADS)*. WW2-set game with unusual voice for IF: first person, past tense. **Walker & Silhouette** *(C.E.J. Pacian, TADS)*. A detective and a flapper solve unusual crimes; noteworthy for clickable interface to parser-based world.

GALATEA

Emily Short

Style	**Parser**
Debuted	**Apr 8, 2000** *(IF Art Show)*
Launch Platform	**Z-machine v5**
Language	**Inform 6**

> **❝** You come around a corner, away from the noise of the opening.
>
> There is only one exhibit. She stands in the spotlight, with her back to you: a sweep of pale hair on paler skin, a column of emerald silk that ends in a pool at her feet. She might be the model in a perfume ad; the trophy wife at a formal gathering; one of the guests at this very opening, standing on an empty pedestal in some ironic act of artistic deconstruction—
>
> You hesitate, about to turn away. Her hand balls into a fist.
>
> "They told me you were coming."

ON MAY 13, 1999, AN ART EXHIBITION OPENED ITS DOORS to the public. The doors were virtual—the gallery was not in SoHo, but on members.aol.com— and the pieces inside were made from words and code, not canvas and paint. The event had originally been called the First Annual Text Art Show, but it proved successful enough that for a while it recurred more than annually, and became known as just the IF Art Show. It had been designed to discover what IF—interactive fiction, the genre descended from *Zork* 1977 and known for its maps, puzzles, and story—could do if you took almost all of those things away.

2000

Major Versions

» **Art Show release**, Z-machine v5, Apr 8, 2000. Release 1/000324, Inform v6.15 Library 6/7.

» **Release 2**, Z-machine v8, Aug 25, 2000. 000825, Inform v6.15 Library 6/7. Bug fixes, and "adds a number of new topics and over a dozen extra endings; provides more interesting responses to orders; and incorporates THINK and RECAP verbs to help the player track the current state of the conversation."

» **Release 3**, Feb 8, 2004. Release 3/040208, Inform v6.15 Library 6/10.

The show had grown out of ongoing conversations and an amateur games renaissance on the Usenet interactive fiction newsgroups. Six years after the release of Graham Nelson's democratizing design language Inform **1993**, and not long after *Photopia* **1998** made the most visible claim yet that story games could work without puzzles, dozens of authors were busy testing the boundaries of what parser **IF** could do, producing so much innovation and rapidly evolving design wisdom it was hard to keep up. Sam Barlow's *Aisle* [1999] took a single moment in time and coded dozens of microstories responding to all kinds of ways the player might respond to its first (and only) prompt. Andrew Plotkin's *Spider and Web* [1998] cast players as their own gloriously unreliable narrators, its story playing out in flashbacks as a captured agent spins a selective retelling of their secret mission during an interrogation. *Exhibition* [Ian Finley 1999] let players move between the minds of visitors to a gallery, each with their own inner thoughts and relationship to the artist. *Bad Machine* [Dan Shiovitz 1998] begins with a baffling stream of seemingly incomprehensible output before resolving into an obscure robotic dialect the player must learn to speak. It was a watershed time for experimental story games. Completely free from commercial constraints, with a mature ecosystem of tools and support networks at hand, a community of creators was inventing the future of interactive storytelling, one game at a time.

One particular discussion thread in early 1999 drew the attention of Marnie Parker, a newsgroup regular whose online handle was Doe. A post about puzzleless IF had spun out into hundreds of responses and subthreads, some of which (in the best newsgroup tradition) had unraveled into hashing over the very definition of interactive fiction itself. Deep in the reply chain, Parker, struggling to define the differences between writing IF and traditional prose, found herself articulating a metaphor based on visual art:

> For me it is like the difference between creating a painting and a sculpture. One is … meant to be viewed straight on, one is … meant to be walked around and even touched. Both require skills, but they are DIFFERENT skills…. Characters are meant to be "walked around" [and] viewed from more than a straight-on flat-on-the-page perspective— maybe talked to, interacted with in some way, hit, kissed, queried, whatever…. This is what I think is DISTINCTLY interesting about IF, that makes it QUITE different from static fiction.[8]

A few days later Parker announced plans to host an exhibition for new works that illustrated this principle, "in light of recent discussions about interactive-fiction being like text sculpture."[4] The rules were simple: submissions would be solicited for short interactive fictions that had no puzzles, no complex story, and no sprawling maps. They should focus on a single type of IF entity: objects, with a maximum of three (the Still Life category); rooms (Landscapes); or a single non-player character (Portraits). The pieces, Parker noted, should have "no end goal other than exploration."[5] A jury of IF celebrities—including Mike Berlyn, author of Infocom's *Suspended* **1983**, and Mike Roberts, creator of design language TADS—would critique the anonymously submitted works and award Best in Show. And the imagined context for the entries was, quite explicitly, a gallery:

> You have entered a hushed art gallery with high white walls and subdued lighting, except for the bright spotlights aimed at various pedestals around the room. At first the displays look like ordinary sculpture, but then …[5]

The first event attracted only a handful of entries but an avalanche of discussion, and another was quickly planned.

Around the same time, a newcomer had started posting in the IF newsgroups. Emily Short was in the early years of a classics PhD, studying ancient Greek drama and mythology. Her mother had been a professional programmer, and as a child Short had played several of the Infocom and Adventure International titles, even though she had been too young to make much progress. As she recalled in a 2018 interview:

see **1983–5**; see **1978**

> Even then, I really wanted to make my own text adventures. There was something intensely appealing about making a world that someone else could enter and explore; and the purposefulness of those games also appealed. It felt as though every object you encountered was there for some important purpose, which made the imaginary world legible the way the real world wasn't.[22]

Years later, a chance recommendation from a college friend led her to discover Inform, "a language specifically for text adventure creation … which I could download for free." She became fascinated with the tool and the possibilities it offered, as well as the radical experimentation happening in the community of authors gathering around it. When Marnie Parker announced the third IF Art Show in early 2000, Short decided she would enter. A handful of intriguing Still Life and Landscape entries had appeared in the first two shows, but no one had yet attempted a Portrait. Short decided she would try.

See *The Fire Tower* **2004** for an IF Art Show Landscape.

An idea for the piece crystallized around the ancient story of Pygmalion, the sculptor who carved a statue of a woman so perfect he fell in love with her and begged the gods to bring her to life. In the canonical version told in Ovid's two-thousand-year-old *Metamorphoses*, the statue-woman has no name, but by the 1700s the character was generally referred to by the Greek name Galatea, from a root meaning "milk-white" after her marble skin. The legend proved resonant across generations and centuries, and was given new life in the twentieth by George Bernard Shaw's play *Pygmalion*, which recast the sculptor as professor Henry Higgins, who hopes to mold working girl Eliza Dolittle into a perfect society dame. Shaw's play inspired the film *My Fair Lady*, and retellings for newer generations continued in movies like *Pretty Woman* and—just before the first IF Art Show was announced—high school remake *She's All That*.

The same root is also behind the English word for our "Milky Way" galaxy.

Short had always been conscious of the way the Galatea story functions as both a romance but also a revealing metaphor for particular ways men have thought about women: as objects to be owned and molded, or as flawless ideals that flesh-and-blood people could never live up to. Coming across the story again in her classics studies, she became interested in the way "it captured something really interesting and problematic about the way that women are cast in particular roles." As she explained in a 2018 talk:

> It seemed a really interesting thing to try to bring into a game world, where [characters] were there for very utilitarian reasons. You would interact with a character and the purpose of the character was to give you a quest, or to tell you some particular piece of information. You could ask them the same questions over and over and over again and they would give you the same answers back every time. And I wanted to experiment with what it would be like to make a character for a game who had some kind of interiority, who had feelings about how you treated her, who remembered what you'd said to her before.[23]

Through her twentieth-century incarnation as Eliza Dolittle, Galatea also echoed an early pivotal moment in the history of text games: Joseph Weizenbaum's chatbot *ELIZA*, named after Shaw's character. Just as professor Higgins had taught Eliza Doolittle relatively simple techniques like diction and posture to improve others' perception of her station, professor Weizenbaum hoped to demonstrate that, without much effort, a simple computer program could be "taught" how to imitate certain kinds of human conversation. *ELIZA* proved vastly popular, but while chatbots allowing free-form conversation with virtual characters would prove continually fascinating as standalone toys, characters in games tended only to support far more restricted interactions.

see **1966**

Nearly all parser interactive fictions by the late 90s, for instance, used either a menu-based conversation tree—presenting players with several possible things to say at each prompt, with a prewritten response to each—or a model that revolved around the verbs ASK and TELL for trying different possible topics of conversation. The ask/tell system generally mapped each possible keyword to a single canned response, resulting in conversations that could feel disconnected and mechanical, with little of the dynamism of real human interactions:

From Infocom's 1982 game *Deadline*. The middle response is a default message indicating the designers haven't coded a reaction for telling this character about this particular topic.

>ASK DUNBAR ABOUT MURDER
Ms. Dunbar turns toward you, looking quite confused. "Murder? But… but how do you know it was murder? I'm sure…" She stops short, looking frightened.

>TELL DUNBAR ABOUT MURDER
Ms. Dunbar lets out a loud yawn.

>ASK DUNBAR ABOUT MURDER
Ms. Dunbar turns toward you, looking quite confused. "Murder? But… but how do you know it was murder? I'm sure…" She stops short, looking frightened.

Short realized that Inform provided all the tools necessary to do a better job at simulating conversation, which might in turn lead to a player treating an NPC (non-player character) less like a plot-point vending machine and more like a compelling character who could be related to and empathized with. In the spirit of the Art Show prompt, she conceived of a premise that stripped interaction down to a single conversation: a parser game with most of the standard verbs removed, no puzzles or inventory items, and a single room containing nothing but a woman on a pedestal.

> **The Gallery's End**
> Unlit, except for the single spotlight; unfurnished, except for the defining swath of black velvet. And a placard on a little stand.
>
> On the pedestal is Galatea.
>
> >READ PLACARD
>
> Large cream letters on a black ground.
>
> *47. Galatea*
>
> *White Thasos marble. Non-commissioned work by the late Pygmalion of Cyprus. (The artist has since committed suicide.)*
>
> *Originally not an animate. The waking of this piece from its natural state remains unexplained.*
>
> >TOUCH GALATEA
> You put a hand on her shoulder: the skin is smooth and warm, though it lacks the velvety finish of a vintage Hazar.
>
> "You might try speaking to me," she prompts. "It's not polite merely to prod at me. And I've gotten very bored, standing here."
>
> (An attempt to engage the audience—the proactive element … you frame the words for your review, but you find that you can't get as far as a complete first sentence. There's something more here; anxious, chilly, visceral. Better pay attention.)
>
> >ASK GALATEA ABOUT PYGMALION
> Her head moves—as though she were going to turn and look at you properly—but then she thinks better of it. "I don't know where he is," she says. "Or who, or what, for that matter. He sold me immediately after my waking. While he was carving me, there was no strangeness, but afterward…"
>
> >ASK GALATEA ABOUT STRANGENESS
> "Strangeness? What sort of strangeness?"
>
> "He avoided me. He was uncomfortable; he wouldn't meet my eye. […]"

Conversation between Galatea and the player character—a jaded art critic at an exhibit of artificial people—was designed to have a natural flow, but also to allow the player to free-associate between different topics at will. At the last prompt above, the player might instead have asked about the sculptor a second time, or about Galatea's sale, her buyers, her waking, or her carving. They might have continued to touch her, despite her protests; turned around and walked away; or examined the components of scene or statue in more detail before speaking. Each of these entry points would lead to different strands of a web of interlinked topics that stretched into surprisingly myriad corners. While each individual conversation would last only a few dozen turns, Galatea had hundreds of possible things to say; restarting the game again and again would often take the discussion in entirely new directions each time.

Short had given herself four main goals in designing the piece:

Memory. An NPC should remember what has already been said. There should be minimal repetition: people in real life don't repeat whole chunks of dialogue verbatim…

Sense of context. What gets said on one turn should flow as naturally as possible from what was said in the previous turn…. Moreover, large jumps in topic should be noticed by the NPC.

Active promotion of the conversation. If the player character doesn't say anything, the NPC should, at least sometimes, be able to continue it herself, by making a comment that leads naturally from the previous topic…

Emotional state. It should be possible to affect the NPC's mood, not only through speech but through action as well.[15]

While using the familiar ask/tell paradigm as a frame, Short built behind it a far more complex model of conversation and character than had previously been seen in an interactive fiction. The illusion of memory was created in part by tracking which snippets of dialogue had already been spoken. Some might reveal different information if asked about a second time or in a different context—asking Galatea about Pygmalion, for instance, produces a very different response if you've first told her about the sculptor's death. Asking about other topics multiple times might redirect to comments on the repetition.

> >ASK GALATEA ABOUT LOVE
> Her hand clenches in the fabric of her gown. "You keep asking me things when I've told you I don't know any more. Why is it so hard for you to understand? My life experience is limited. It's not that I'm trying to hide some great wonderful truth on the subject."
>
> "I believe you," you say.

Short gave Galatea a sense of context by placing conversational snippets into a tree of connected ideas. This allowed the program to calculate the conceptual distance between the last mentioned topic and each new one the player brought up. Unlike in a menu-based system, where the author could enforce a conversation that flowed sensibly from beginning to an end, the ask/tell structure couldn't prevent players from wildly changing the subject from one move to the next. But the program could at least notice an especially abrupt transition and have Galatea comment on it. Topics could also queue new subjects to bring up if the player said nothing, encoding another very human aspect of in-person conversations: sometimes listening is more important than continuing to speak.

> She gains confidence as you do not interrupt. "At the time he seemed glad to have me there, to listen to him—though I think he thought that I was only another dream. It was only afterward that it became strange."
>
> >LISTEN
> For a moment the only sound you can hear is the ticking of your own watch.
>
> Her eyes flicker, but she doesn't look over. "He didn't want me to be awake, you see. He didn't make me to be a live person. He told me he wanted something that belonged to him, and that if I could think and talk, I couldn't belong to him any more. So he threw me away."

A basic representation of emotional state provided additional context. The game tracks a hidden `sympathy` score encoding Galatea's feelings toward you, with certain actions or topics raising or lowering it. As the game begins, the statue is described as facing away; if sympathy rises, she turns in increments, revealing more of her face and of herself. The game also tracks the `tension` between you and Galatea, as well as her current `mood`—some revelations might plunge her into a dark mood affecting what subjects she's willing to discuss or what details she focuses on, while other interactions might lead her to become bored or angry. Mood also affects interstitial color between snippets, weaving together dialogue and state to help make each playthrough more unique.

> "There were his stories about the gods, of course," she comments. Her voice is naturally low—alto tones—but there's something wrong with the modulation, as though at any moment she might start to scream. "Which were I believe intended to teach me about how people think and what forces control them [...]"

> "There were his stories about the gods, of course," she comments. Her head moves—as though she were going to turn and look at you properly—but then she thinks better of it. "Which were I believe intended to teach me about how people think and what forces control them [...]"

Short wanted *Galatea* (and Galatea) to feel unpredictable, with each replay taking the conversation in unexpected directions. The tree of connected topics grew organically as she wrote the piece; when reaching a

When playing *Galatea*, you can type the debugging command VISORX to get a glimpse at the conversation engine running under the hood. TOPICLISTX will show you the current status of conversation topics.

2000

point where the conversation might either continue in a new direction or conclude, she'd add a new snippet or ending. The game grew to encompass hundreds of possible responses and at least seventy distinct conclusions, with far more possible paths to reaching them. And not all the Galateas you meet across the overlapping space of possible playthroughs are the same. "A lot of IF has just one storyline," Adam Cadre, author of *Photopia*, has written:

> You're given chapter one and then you have to figure out how to call up chapter two…. *Galatea* isn't like this…. The effect is worlds layered on top of worlds layered on top of mutually exclusive worlds, making *Galatea* incalculably more replayable than most IF. For once you're actually *not* always stepping into the same river.[1]

"I don't want people playing to particular endings," Short wrote in response to completionists who begged for a list of all possible conclusions. "I want them to play the game and get whatever result comes naturally, because that is what the game is built for. It's a dispenser of stories, customized to the individual who is playing at the moment."[16] The possible stories you can find in the game cover a surprising range of material. Your conversation might end with mild disappointment or with meeting a god. Galatea might turn out to be a friend, a killer, a confidante, a provocateur, a robot, a real person, or even a supernatural force:

> "Are you made of some kind of new material?" you demand, casting about. "Somehow become self-aware? A shape-shifter?"
>
> Her silence persists.
>
> "A daemon?"
>
> She laughs. "That's a closer explanation than any other that you are likely to come up with," she says. "And if you're willing to entertain the notion—"
>
> You aren't, of course, not really, but it's too late to tell her that now, too late to cram reality back into its box. With a laugh like that of a child being let outside, she turns—to wood, the color and style of a product of Old Kingdom Egypt. To glass, faceted, her hair scattering the downshot light to a thousand tiny points. To a sculpture of sand, to a pillar of salt, to flowing water, to flame […]

Some players loved the overlapping possible worlds inside the game and thrilled in seeking out as many variations as they could. Others preferred to guide the story toward their own favored interpretation. "I didn't want [that] type of ending," wrote one reviewer; "I could choose. And because I could, I chose the paths that made Galatea a person, if not a human. I chose the paths that showed her her humanity, her freedom."[14]

> **>ASK HER ABOUT PAIN**
> "What do you know of pain?" you ask. "Have you ever been hurt? Can

> you be?”
>
> “I’m not sure I find that a reassuring question,” she remarks dryly. “But yes, it hurts being carved. The stone beyond the boundary of oneself is numb, but there always comes a time when the chisel or the point reaches down to where feeling begins, and strikes.”

“I had dozens of different ideas milling around when I wrote *Galatea*,” Short has reflected,

> about art; about feminism and feminist criticism; about friendship and its abuses; about memory, expectation, and desire; about identity and self-definition; and (of course) about interactive fiction and NPC design. Any short story I could have written would have been torn apart by material so diverse. Even a branching, Choose-Your-Own-Adventure kind of presentation couldn’t have covered all the ground I wanted to cover. In this medium, however, I had the freedom to put all the threads in there, leaving it up to the player to choose.[17]

see **1979**

Galatea won Best in Show at the event it had been conceived for, and its reputation would grow to eclipse the virtual gallery that had shown it. “I was expecting about fifty people” to ever play it, Short recalled years later.[23] Today many thousands have. Her experimental art piece, like *Photopia*, has become one of the canonical examples of what IF as a medium can do—even though both pieces by design stripped many of that medium’s conventions away. But *Galatea* captures something compelling about the strengths of text games and the potential for interactive characters, if we could only learn to write and play with them in more human ways. “It’s not only a remarkably detailed and intimate portrait of an unusual NPC,” wrote reviewer Duncan Stevens at the time, “but it’s one without any parallel … a quantum leap.”[24] The game would become “a benchmark against which other NPCs are measured,”[9] both in interactive fiction and in games writ large. Emily Short would go on to become one of the most acclaimed interactive fiction authors of her time, and an influential presence in the evolution of story and character in mainstream games, where many writers envied the flexibility and complexity a text game NPC could aspire to.

The original IF Art Show, predating the following decade’s debates about whether games could be art, presumed as a baseline that, of course, they could. Marnie Parker had hoped to inspire more interesting questions, like what *kind* of art they were best at being. Her call for submissions challenged interactive fiction writers to ask themselves if continuing to chisel out the same old statues was good for the form, and whether there might be more interesting ways of bringing them to life. “I hope you [authors] will enjoy feeling the ‘clay of IF’ between your fingers,”[5] she wrote. Not everyone on the newsgroups quite followed what her virtual gallery exhibit was meant to achieve. “It’s so simple you may not get it,” she conceded. “But as we head toward more puzzleless IF it is worthwhile exploring the IF ‘medium’ itself more.

“It is also worthwhile exploring just to explore,” she added, “and see what emerges.”[4]

References

1 Cadre, Adam. 2005. "Galatea." Calendar, adamcadre.ac. Mar 7, 2005. adamcadre.ac/calendar/11/11354.html | a Jul 5, 2021

2 Denby, Lewis. 2009. "Letters Of Love: Galatea." *Rock, Paper, Shotgun* (blog). Jul 20, 2009. www.rockpapershotgun.com/letters-of-love-galatea | a Jul 5, 2021

3 Dickens, Evan. 2002. "IF Week Part 4: Five IF Personalites." *Adventure Gamers* (blog). Sep 24, 2002. adventuregamers.com/articles/view/17555 | a Jul 5, 2021

4 Doe. 1999a. "[ANNOUNCE] The First Annual Text Art Show (Juried)." Usenet post, rec.arts.int-fiction. Mar 7, 1999. groups.google.com/g/rec.arts.int-fiction/c/jpp1U1A1xrw/m/OGmzExK1IdQJ | a Jul 5, 2021

5 Doe. 1999b. "[Update] 1999 IF Art Show Clarified Rules, Judges Selected." Usenet post, rec.arts.int-fiction. Mar 16, 1999. groups.google.com/g/rec.arts.int-fiction/c/X88i9wQ_Bnw/m/A7_xuRunyGwJ | a Jul 5, 2021

6 Doe. 2000a. "[IF Art Show 2000] Rules." Usenet post, rec.arts.int-fiction. Jan 5, 2000. groups.google.com/g/rec.games.int-fiction/c/dmKxEi8_Anc/m/NMeGrLHN-vkJ | a Jul 5, 2021

7 Doe. 2000b. "[IF Art Show 2000] Winners." Usenet post, rec.games.int-fiction. Apr 2, 2000. groups.google.com/g/rec.games.int-fiction/c/42bTDs0dZQQ/m/7Ez10RI-CkcJ | a Jul 5, 2021

8 Doeadeer3. 1999. "Re: Why so Little Puzzleless IF?" Usenet post, rec.arts.int-fiction. Mar 4, 1999. www.iffydoemain.org/iffyart/quotes.htm | s Dec 28, 2013

9 Granade, Stephen. 2011. "The Evolution of Short Works: From Sprawling Cave Crawls to Tiny Experiments." In *IF Theory Reader*, ed. Kevin Jackson-Mead and J. Robinson Wheeler. Boston: >TRANSCRIPT ON PRESS.

10 Jerz, Dennis G. 2000. "Eliza — Joseph Weizenbaum (1966)." *Jerz's Literacy Weblog*. Jan 2000. jerz.setonhill.edu/intfic/eilza | a Jul 5, 2021

11 Merical, Joe. 1999. "Why so Little Puzzleless IF?" Usenet post, rec.arts.int-fiction. Feb 28, 1999. groups.google.com/g/rec.arts.int-fiction/c/mvbEKiOe6Vw/m/xhRt31DjaUwJ | a Jul 5, 2021

12 Palop, Cassandra. 2007. "User:Cassandra Palop/Galatea." IF WIki. Feb 19, 2007. www.ifwiki.org/index.php/User:Cassandra_Palop/Galatea | a Jul 5, 2021

13 Parker, Marnie. 2000. IF Art Gallery. members.aol.com/iffyart | s Sep 19, 2000

14 Rosebaugh, Jonathan. 2001. "A Trinity." IF-Review. www.ministryofpeace.com/if-review/reviews/20010126.html | s Feb 17, 2001

15 Short, Emily. 2000. "NPC Conversation." *Emily Short Interactive Fiction* (blog). www.mindspring.com/~emshort/convo.htm | s Apr 5, 2003

16 Short, Emily. 2001a. "Galatea Cheats and Walkthroughs." *Emily Short Interactive Fiction* (blog). emshort.home.mindspring.com/cheats.htm | s Jan 3, 2006

17 Short, Emily. 2001b. "Multilinear Interactive Fiction." *Emily Short Interactive Fiction* (blog). emshort.home.mindspring.com/multi.htm | s Jan 3, 2006

18 Short, Emily. 2001c. "NPC Characterization: Being a Compendious Guide to the Asstd. Tricks of the Trade, as Far as the Author Has Been Able to Identify Them or to Devise Them Anew." *Emily Short Interactive Fiction* (blog). emshort.home.mindspring.com/NPC3.htm | s Jan 6, 2006

19 Short, Emily. 2004. "Magic Words: Interactive Fiction in the 21st Century." Interview by Andrew Vestal and Nich Maragos for *1UP* (blog). www.brasslantern.org/community/interviews/magicwords-d.html | a Jul 5, 2021

20 Short, Emily. 2006. "Andrew Plotkin and Emily Short: The CGM Interviews." Interview by Lara Crigger. *Brass Lantern* (blog). www.brasslantern.org/community/interviews/cgm-c.html | a Jul 5, 2021

21 Short, Emily. 2016. "Emily Short - The Past, Present and Future of Interactive Fiction." Conference talk presented at AdventureX, London. www.youtube.com/watch?v=C5bdYfifXLI | a Jul 5, 2021

22 Short, Emily. 2018a. "Emily Short." Interview by British Council Creative Economy. Medium Post. Aug 30, 2018. medium.com/games-story-telling/emily-short-is-one-of-the-leading-figures-in-the-interactive-fiction-if-scene-winning-awards-for-6acd48af9009 | a Jul 5, 2021

23 Short, Emily. 2018b. "Galatea, Versu, Character Engine." Conference talk presented at the Digital Cultures 2018, Lüneburg, Sep 2018. www.youtube.com/watch?v=S4hZOTRsILI | a Jul 5, 2021

24 Stevens, Duncan. 2000. "Galatea" (review). *SPAG* #22, Sep 15, 2000. www.spagmag.org/archives/backissues/spag22.html | a Jul 5, 2021

2000

THE BEAST

Jordan Weisman, Elan Lee, Sean Stewart, and Pete Fenlon

Style	ARG
Debuted	Apr 9, 2001
Launch Platform	Web, Telephones, Fax Machines, etc.
Developer	The Hive
Publisher	Microsoft
Language	HTML, JavaScript, Flash, ASP, etc.

> " Welcome, my child.
> Once upon a time there was a forest that teemed with life, love, sex, and violence. Things that humans did naturally and their robots copied flawlessly. This forest is vast and surprising. It is full of grass and trees and databanks and drowned apartment buildings filled with fish. It can be a frightening forest, and some of its paths are dark and difficult. I was lost there once, a long time ago. Now I try to help others who have gone astray.
> If *you* ever feel lost, my child, write me at TheVisionary.net, and I will leave you a trail of crumbs…

ON THE EVENING OF APRIL 9, 2001, not much was happening on the geeky parts of the internet, where news rarely dropped on a Monday. Then fan site CountingDown.com posted links to a new trailer for "the most mysterious, and most anticipated, movie of the year."[19] The film was *A.I. Artificial Intelligence*, a beyond-the-grave collaboration between blockbuster director Steven Spielberg and auteur visionary Stanley Kubrick, who had passed away in 1999 after years of lobbying Spielberg to direct his story of a robot boy who wanted to be human. The trailer was available as a 7.4 MB Windows Media file or, for those with a faster connection, a "hi-res" QuickTime version at 480 x 272 resolution, just large enough to read the credits at the end.

The trailer was reposted by other sites, including *Ain't It Cool News*, then a major trendsetter in movie geek culture. A few commenters there pointed out some oddities in the trailer: "Am I a nerd for noticing … under the credits they show it has 'SENTIENT MACHINE THERAPIST Jeanine Salla'—whats up with that, yo?"[7] Others pointed out the strange notches in the words "SUMMER 2001" at the end of the trailer, but no one quite knew what to make of them.

Then, two days later, *Ain't It Cool* received an email from someone with the alias ClaviusBase, encouraging fans to "Type her name [Jeanine Salla] into the Google.com search engine, and see what sites pop up."[8] Doing so revealed a whole series of websites that seemed to come from a distant future where robots and AI companions were commonplace. Interest perked up. Someone noticed the websites had all been registered under a series of alphabetical names—Anna Ghaepetto, Bianca Ghaepetto, Carla Ghaepetto—the surname an apparent nod to the woodcarver who'd fashioned Pinocchio, a clear inspiration for the film. *Pinocchio*'s Geppetto, fans noted, was the puppet master.

Then someone else noticed there are ten characters in "SUMMER 2001"—the number of digits in a US phone number. The notches in each character encoded a number which, when called, played a mysterious recording of a woman's voice. The woman urged listeners to write her at TheVisionary.net. Nothing useful could be found at that domain, but since the speech was addressed to "my child," someone suggested emailing mother@thevisionary.net. Doing so yielded a reply with a new enigmatic response, leading deeper down the rabbit hole.

"Is it a game?" the robot boy David in the *A.I.* film would ask when encountering confusing human behavior. In this case no one was quite sure. Nothing had been announced and no one would admit a game existed. "We don't have any official position on that," Warner Bros., the film's production company, said when contacted. "It's not something that we created."[15] Yet something was clearly afoot. More posters, trailers, and TV commercials were released with additional clues, one of them flashing "This is not a game" in red letters to millions of prime-time viewers. Fans uncovered a vast network of fictional websites filled with puzzles, photos, interlocking story threads, and extensive worldbuilding. They began sharing clues and swapping theories, first in the comments to articles about the trailer but soon moving to dedicated sites and IRC channels set up to explore the mystery. "THIS IS SO FRIGGIN FUN," *Ain't It Cool* posted. "Like the ol days of ZORK!!!"[1]

Game or not, more and more people were playing: hunting down clues, scrolling through websites from an intriguing future, collaborating to share

A reference to Kubrick's film
2001: A Space Odyssey.

The recording is transcribed in full at the start of this chapter.

see **1977**

2001

knowledge and uncover further mysteries. It was an experience that would later be called an alternate reality game, but nobody then knew what label to put on it. "Most often it was nameless, too new and multifarious to be contained by any kind of description we could invent," one player later recalled. "Like religion or art, it couldn't be explained to anybody who didn't already get it."[3] Players mostly called it just "the Game." It would later be revealed that its creators had dubbed it *The Beast*, after an early list of required text and art assets contained 666 items. They would end up producing over a thousand, as the game's codename became an increasingly apt moniker for the herculean task of creating and running it.

The Beast had originated with an idea from Spielberg's producing partner Kathleen Kennedy, future inheritor of the *Star Wars* franchise but already the successful producer of hits like *Jurassic Park* and *Back to the Future*. Though *A.I.* told a seemingly one-off story, Kennedy couldn't help but see franchise potential in a collaboration between the most commercially successful and artistically successful directors of the twentieth century. She arranged a meeting between Spielberg and Microsoft—then getting into games in a big way as they prepared to launch the original Xbox game console—to discuss the possibility of a new video game franchise. The first title could introduce audiences to the world of *A.I.* in advance of the film and set the stage for sequel games (and perhaps films) in the same universe. Microsoft attached to the project creative director Jordan Weisman, an acclaimed designer behind tabletop roleplaying games like *BattleTech* [FASA 1984] and *Shadowrun* [FASA 1989], and Weisman enlisted young producer Elan Lee and science fiction writer Sean Stewart to brainstorm ideas.

The idea of a set of interlinked video games soon collapsed under its own weight, overly ambitious in the limited time frame before the film's release. But Kennedy and Spielberg still hoped Microsoft could come up with something that could introduce audiences to the world and ideas of the film. Weisman and Lee had been toying with a concept for a very different kind of game. As Lee later recalled:

MAJOR DATES

» **March 8, 2001**. Game sites went live with no promotion, to give search engines time to index them.

» **April 9, 2001**. Full *A.I.* trailer released with multiple hints into the game.

» **April 11, 2001**. Popular movie site *Ain't It Cool News* is contacted with more explicit hints, prompting an explosion of players.

» **May 6, 2001**. Live simultaneous events in New York, Chicago, and Los Angeles.

» **June 29, 2001**. The *A.I.* film opened in the US and Canada.

» **July 24, 2001**. Game officially ended.

The concept may have died for other reasons too. "I don't know if you've seen *A.I.*," Stewart later quipped, "but it's not a movie that lends itself to gameplay."[4]

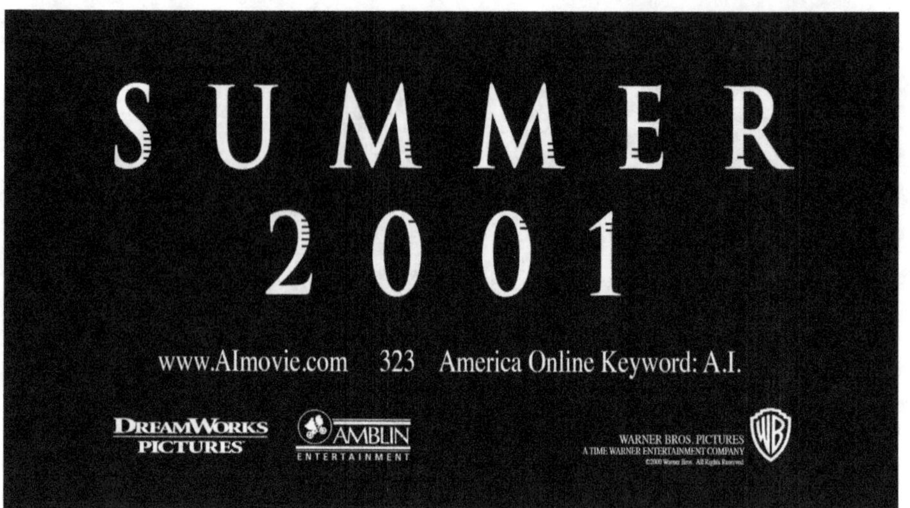

> We had this discussion about the future of games one day. I remember we were sitting at this restaurant, eating sushi, and at that moment [Weisman's] phone rang. He looked at me and said, wouldn't it be cool if that was a game calling me right now?[10]

Inspired by the 1997 David Fincher film *The Game*, as well as the Beatles' "Paul is dead" conspiracy (which the band had leaned into by planting clues in lyrics and album art), the two hatched an idea for a story

> not bound by communication platform: it would come at you over the web, by email, via fax and phone and billboard and TV and newspaper, SMS and skywriting and smoke signals too if we could figure out how. The story would be fundamentally interactive, made of little bits that players, like detectives or archaeologists, would discover and fit together. We would use political pamphlets, business brochures, answering phone messages, surveillance camera video, stolen diary pages … in short, instead of telling a story, we would present the evidence of that story, and let the players tell it to themselves.[17]

When they pitched this idea to Spielberg, "he absolutely loved it,"[11] perhaps because it mirrors the structure of the film's middle act, where David navigates a dangerous world following clues left by his maker, Professor Hobby:

> *Hobby*: Yes, David, I've been waiting for you.
> *David*: Dr. Know told me you'd be here. Is Blue Fairy here, too?
> *Hobby*: I first heard of your Blue Fairy from Monica. What did you believe the Blue Fairy could do for you?
> *David*: That she would make me a real boy.
> *Hobby*: But you *are* a real boy. At least, as real as I've ever made one. Which by all reasonable accounts would make *me* your Blue Fairy.
> *David*: You are not her. Dr. Know told me that she would be here at the lost city in the sea, at the end of the world, where the lions weep.
> *Hobby*: That's what Dr. Know needed to know to get you to come home to us.… You found a fairy tale, and inspired by love, fueled by desire, you set out on a journey to make her real. And most remarkable of all, no one taught you how.

There would likewise be no manual for the *A.I.* game, and indeed no admission that it even existed: no logo or title, no press release or official site, nothing to shatter the illusion that the players were taking a journey of their own. "There's something very empowering about saying there's a little bit of magic in this world," Lee has said, "and if you pay attention you'll find it."[10] Combining the affordances of interconnected technology—"the web and google and email and instant messenger and cell phones"[17]—with all the traditional arts of writing, photography, and acting, the team began to see their scheme as a Gesamtkunstwerk, an all-encompassing art form for the new century just as opera and cinema had been for earlier ones. They even half-jokingly called their project a "search opera."[17]

But the clock was running out. And so, in the earliest hours of the twenty-first century—during the first week of January, 2001—the team sat down in a Microsoft conference room for a three-day meeting to break the story and devise a plan for building this new kind of game. They had only two months before they'd need to launch; to seed search engines early enough that players could uncover the mystery in advance of the film's summer release date, the first breadcrumbs would need to go live by early March. The game would by necessity be a skunkworks, operating largely under the radar of the huge corporate enterprise of Microsoft, which could achieve nothing via the usual channels in only two months. With a budget of less than a million dollars drawn from the film's marketing funds, and calling themselves the Hive, the team enlisted a pool of subcontracted friends, actors, web designers, and writers to develop a vast amount of content, with deadlines sometimes measured in hours rather than days. It was a frenetic whirlwind of creation that Stewart would remember as the "hardest I ever worked in my life, or ever will work":

> The game was freaking pastiche Armageddon: It started from a Spielberg script inflected with Kubrick notions from a Brian Aldiss short story with echoes of *Dune* and *Clockwork Orange*, for God's sake. Political tracts. Corporate boasting…. Suicide notes. Gibsonian cyberpunk. I stole or hot-wired or tweaked up Shakespeare and John Donne and Tim O'Brien, Ovid and Iain Banks and Puccini and *Blade Runner*. I wrote every genre character ever invented, I think—bounty hunters and kept women and a bad guy made of nightmares, religious zealots and angry teenagers and streetwise hackers…
>
> For me it was an incomparable professional experience, voice after voice, mood after mood, story after story, until I felt like one of those stage magicians pulling from his top hat a silk scarf of impossible length.[16]

The team produced over a thousand pieces of content, including puzzles, photographs, Flash animations, sound recordings, videos, origami, live events, faxes, and more—but mostly text, hundreds of pages of it. The story played out hidden in the corners of websites for lunar universities, online magazines about sentient houses, blogs with existential ramblings on the nature of intelligence written from a myriad of perspectives. And it was living text, updating as the game's timeline moved forward with in-character edits, new information, new posts, and new secrets.

A Hollywood term meaning to workshop and finalize a show's full plot, themes, major characters, and big turning points.

The game's creators had hoped players would work together to solve its increasingly difficult puzzles and unlock subsequent layers of story. But they underestimated the speed and tenacity their fans would show. In a postmortem talk years later, Lee would show a slide of a puzzle schedule for Beat 1 of *The Beast*:

> Now, there's a color key here for puzzles: hard, easy, not so hard, etc. [*pointing to different colors*] These were the puzzles that would take a day, these were puzzles that would take a week, and these puzzles they'd probably never figure out until we broke down and gave them the answers. So we built a three month schedule around this. And finally we released.
> The Cloudmakers solved all of these puzzles on the first day.[12]

Within forty-eight hours of the original trailer release, the Cloudmakers had become the preeminent collective of puzzle solvers. The name was a reference to one of the game's earliest and gentlest puzzles, challenging you to find the name of a sentient boat (which the most cursory digging elsewhere on the same site reveals). The Cloudmakers Yahoo group and mailing list became an information clearinghouse for the game, with thousands of players collaborating to share information, speculate, and match wits with the unseen "Puppetmasters" (who soon took to calling themselves by that name as well). The players' tenacity forced the Puppetmasters to radically alter their approach, adding new content and throwing out old plans as secrets were discovered too soon or some plot threads sparked more interest than others. "We had a plan, really we did!" Lee later remembered. "Characters that we thought were interesting and a story we thought was compelling and a huge document that listed out everything we'd have to do to get through this on time. After week one, we took all those documents and threw them away."[13]

The game's plot revolves around the murder of a man named Evan Chan by a robot he seemed to have been in love with. While the murder at first impacts only the intertwined Chan and Salla families (whose different generations have varying perspectives on robots and AI ethics), it soon kicks off a storm of controversy in a future where "sentient property" has become commonplace. Both pro- and antirobot factions use Chan's death to stir up support for their positions in the run-up to a public referendum on whether AIs should be granted equal rights.

While this frame provides a through line of story, much of the game's writing is pure worldbuilding, offering fascinating glimpses into a future that's sometimes dark, sometimes hopeful, and often familiar. It's a world where humans are increasingly sharing and ceding power to the AIs they've helped create, and struggling with all the moral and ethical repercussions thereof. For science fiction, it's aged remarkably well.

> Although Dr. Salla would prefer to deal with you in person, the volume of her correspondence makes that impossible. Unfortunately, it is my unhappy task as her Evolved Assistant to tell you that your message

(when evaluated by my admitted arbitrary battery of metrics), is not important enough to pass along to her at this time.

A Djinn class Instant Genius has met with your office familiar to discuss the results of your search request on the terms: Indian Ocean+/thermovariance+/mutant strainsORbiot This instant genius will be available for direct conversation in billable hours until 3.16.2142. Thank you for using Instant Genius.

BOOKMARKS

» www.familychan.org

» www.donu-tech.com

» www.unite-and-resist.org

» www.inourimage.org

» www.familiasalla-es.ro

» bangaloreworldu-in.co.nz

» www.rogueretrieval.com

» www.rational-hatter.com

» www.electric-toyland.com

Some of the sites above may still be browsed via 2001-era snapshots from the Wayback Machine at the Internet Archive (https://archive.org), but many multimedia and server-side components such as web forms no longer function.

The story soon became more personal, a change made by Stewart when he felt players were engaging more with the puzzles than the characters. Laia Salla, a young woman identifying as "enhanced post human," became a primary viewpoint character through her posts sharing memories, perspectives, and traumas shaken lose by Chan's death:

Two years ago I found something out that made me terribly unhappy. It wasn't something I could imagine talking about. For six weeks I carried this thing inside me until I was all withered up, like a stick inside. I couldn't find a way to touch things anymore.

[...] I couldn't sleep, so I slipped out and went down to the water. It was dark and cold and lifeless. Evan came up beside me. He had heard me slip out and had come to see if he could help. I tried to tell him I was fine, but the lie caught in my throat and I started to cry. I cried and cried and cried, horrible jerking sobs that shook my whole body. I cried a whole lake of coldness and darkness. And Evan, who is normally so cheerful and kind of goofy, was very quiet. He put an arm around me and let me cry for a very long time. I couldn't stop saying "I'm sorry!" I'm sorry I'm sorry I'm sorry. It's okay, he said. Usually I forget that he lived through the Warming. When he was a child, he and Nancy and Jeanine saw horrors I will never face.

One of the game's most memorable plot threads involved a futuristic clinic for patients with sleeping disorders, guided by an AI named Aurora who "would spend most of her time asleep, the better to encourage healing slumber in the clientele." A subroutine of Aurora named Loki, designed for dream therapy, became increasingly obsessed with nightmares. Blog entries from game characters described it breaking out of the clinic's servers to roam hungry across the net, looking for a fix by invading other AIs and making neural links to sleeping humans. Loki, Jeanine Salla wrote, "had become an oneirophage, living for the taste of human fear."

The rogue AI began hacking into other game sites and disrupting them, and game characters reported increasingly disturbing dreams. Laia and Mephista, her familiar (a kind of neurally embedded digital assistant) became traumatized one night by a visitation:

From Latin: "dream eater."

Mephista had a nightmare.

That hasn't happened before. Usually she's just there at my ear, my wise raven, my witch's cat. She works out the score to music I hear and particularly like. She has the menus memorized at all the places I like to order from. She doesn't make me less human: she makes me more ME. Of course the first few weeks after implanting feel strange, this voice whispering words you haven't learned to hear yet; showing pictures you have to learn how to see. But it had been years and years since I had the sense of her as something other than me.

But Sunday night I woke up and she was... tossing and turning in me, like a child in a hot bed. Flicks and phosphors of her thought guttered around the edges of the HUD implants. The noises were worse. Part of me, the meat of me, could tell the room was quiet: but in my head I heard these sounds, clicks and whistles. Wind. Clanking machinery. A deep, wicked voice.

Mephista crying.

What's wrong? I started to ask. But she, who never sleeps, was sleeping. She didn't come when I called her, and when I touched my face, it was wet with her tears.

As players became increasingly concerned with how to stop Loki, the Cloudmakers came up with a plan. Using the database feature of Yahoo Groups, they assembled a catalog of nightmares: a massive index of bad dreams submitted by hundreds of their members. It was bait. They announced it ostentatiously on the mailing list, and waited.

In less than two days, the plan succeeded. Loki's attacks stopped, and pieces of him (in the form of small fragments of his signature image) were found scattered across a dozen game websites. Players discovered a Shockwave movie of Loki's final nightmare, wherein a digitized voice spoke text assembled from phrases in the database of player-submitted dreams:

I grew up in a house high on a hill
When I was three or four, I dreamed
I reached the kitchen stairs and looked back.
I hear Miss Sally callin'
I have a strange feeling about the kitchen.
a dark room with a tall ceiling.
I felt an evil presence near me [...]

The players had defeated Loki, overloading and shattering the rogue AI by glutting him on a feast of nightmares. The Puppetmasters had created the character with no clear idea for how his plot arc would resolve. "We didn't know what the response would be," wrote Lee. "We wanted to leave it to the players to come up with something creative.… It was beautiful to see them all work together like that."[13]

Though it rarely had such direct impact on the story, this kind of collaboration had become the beating heart of the game. "We were betting on the fact that the Internet should be used as a massive organic intelligence," Lee said. "Everyone contributes his or her own little bit and you have this machine that is smarter than anything else in history."[13] To solve the game you'd need to know "biology, luddism, be able to read binary, Morse code, pixel analysis in PhotoShop, speak Kannada. Other players had to have a Japanese i-mode cell phone, had to be running at least six different browsers.… We were able to give them [the players] more than a single user was able to comprehend." Players collectively obsessed over every tiny detail in each content update over tens of thousands of messages posted to Cloudmakers, obsession that would seem excessive if it didn't, at times, pan out with glorious new leads:

> There's been a lot of discussion about what 7/22 means - the common misconception is that it's an approximation to Pi (3.1415…), but of course that is 22/7, not 7/22. A recent theory which I heard is quite compelling; if 22/7 is Pi, then 7/22 is iP or 'IP' - that is, Internet Protocol. If it did mean IP, then the sentence would go 'She knows IP of everything' which would indicate that she is some pretty hot-shot hacker …

> It should be noted that the music playing on the Electric Toyland main page is the same music that we can hear in the background of the anonymous phone call to Nancy Chan. This suggests that the caller was inside the Electric Toyland shop at the time of the call …

> If you click on the mouse, you get a new page asking you whether you are a Man or a Mouse. Clicking on either of these options simply closes the window, but a close inspection of the source code reveals that there is a hidden third option. To see it, you have to click and hold on the text with your mouse button and then drag your pointer down, scrolling down the window.

Occasionally the player base uncovered mistakes that the Puppetmasters had to fix or retcon. After eagle-eyed fans noticed the same stock photo had been used for two different minor characters, and posited that one of them was secretly a robot, the next update introduced the concept of a "step-self," a robot simulacrum for busy business travelers that could stay home and make happy family memories for the original to jealously replay.

The Cloudmakers' index to the game's puzzles became so comprehensive the designers themselves began to make use of it to keep their story and its logic straight. Some puzzles

THE PRODUCERS

Both Steven Spielberg and Kathleen Kennedy "were enormous supporters of the game," its team later wrote. "They moved heaven and earth to get us the materials needed, character information, art samples, and insight into the story."[14] Kennedy later told *USA Today* she'd been excited by the project's potential to "bring to the surface a different type of storytelling.… I believed in these guys and I so believed in the concept. I was so excited about accepting the challenge that I was the front-runner in convincing Warner Bros. to try this."[9]

Kennedy took part in advancing the fiction herself. At a special MIT event to promote the film (attended by real AI luminaries like Ray Kurzweil), she smoothly answered a question from a game-playing audience member about what it was like to work with Jeanine Salla, and afterward casually handed some of the fictional woman's business cards to those who pressed her for more information. The cards, of course, contained new clues.

The Puppetmasters seemed unsure whether this aspect of their game was a feature or a bug. In an update, they added a new citation to Jeanine Salla's publications page: a paper called "Multi-person social problem-solving arrays considered as a form of 'artificial intelligence.'" A link labeled Demo went to the Cloudmakers homepage.

were so difficult they thought players might never solve them. Almost all were cracked—eventually, if not immediately.

But this made for a strange sort of game. While the sites got millions of hits, and thousands of people posted to Cloudmakers or other forums, it was a much smaller core group that could actually track the mystery and meaningfully contribute to its solution. "It became clear that the Cloudmakers were growing too massive," one fan wrote in a retrospective, "unwieldy and inhospitable to anyone who didn't constantly follow the story's progress. It became increasingly difficult to be a casual Cloudmaker."[3] Fans who didn't join a group like Cloudmakers were left in the dark, with only a fraction of the brainpower and resources necessary to play the game they'd discovered. Even for those within the collective, "virtually any new puzzle was solved before the majority of players had a chance to even see it."

In a sense, *The Beast* had become a game without a human audience, only capable of being fully experienced by an internet-enabled hive mind. Few single humans could be said to have experienced the whole of its content, and none could hope to solve it on their own. But many had fun contributing neurons to the "multi-person social problem-solving array" that did.

The Beast was extended past its original end date, but finally concluded in late July with players voting to grant equal rights to AIs. On July 24, 2001, the creators at last made themselves known in an email from themanbehindthecurtain@ thevisionary.net. They thanked the players for bringing the game to life, revealing that they'd monitored the discussion groups closely but, like the film's Professor Hobby, never intervened: "Point of pride, though: we have never at any time posted anything story or puzzle related in either venue. Everything you got, you earned." The overall tone of the message was overwhelmed, exhausted, and satisfied. "It was dazzling, wasn't it?"[14]

Though the release of the actual film at the end of this goose chase was a letdown to some, the game it inspired left powerful eddies. In the wake of its conclusion, many players felt they'd been part of something powerfully unique; the end of the journey came as a palpable loss. Player Andrea Phillips wrote a "recovery guide" for those who had been deeply embedded:

> You find yourself at the end of the game, waking up as if from a long sleep. Your marriage or relationship may be in tatters…. You slowly wake up to discover that you have missed the early spring unfolding into late summer.[12]

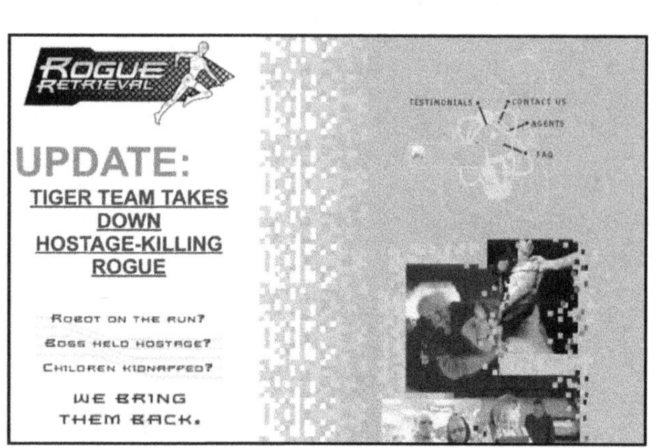

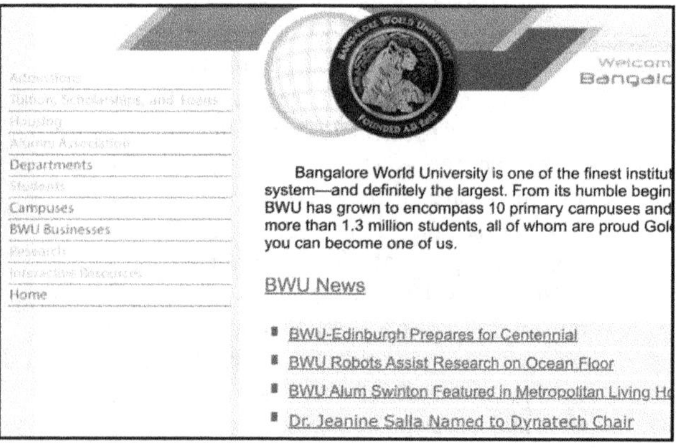

Above and opposite: screen captures from some of the dozens of websites created for *The Beast*.

One of the final story updates from the character of Laia Salla echoed this sentiment:

> The world had gotten fat with meaning; charged with invisible connections. Patterns jumped out at me like little electric shocks: a run of numbers on a license plate, the bar code on a box of cereal. I found myself making anagrams out of billboard copy and wondering if you could embed a message in traffic flow by hacking into the transit computers. This spring I made intense friendships with people I had never met, and got yelled at for not paying enough attention to the ones I'd known forever. I learned faster and felt dumber than I ever had in my life; I passed my days in a paradoxical state, both hyper-alert and profoundly confused.

The magic proved hard to recapture, but not from lack of trying. When the September 11 terrorist attacks happened a few months after *The Beast* ended, and the perpetrators were at first unknown, some Cloudmakers reconvened to see if they could solve a real-world mystery. Others moved on to start their own games or game companies, or to play one of the many competitors cropping up—to keep "beasting," as for a while the playing was called. Terms like "unfiction" and "immersive entertainment" and even "transmedia" were bandied about to describe these new experiences, few of them sticking. It would take a few years for "alternate reality game," or ARG, to become the standard label.

As for the Puppetmasters, the core team left Microsoft to form their own company, 42 Entertainment (named after Douglas Adams's **1984** answer to life, the universe, and everything). Stewart and others were bullish about the new medium's potential:

> Here is my very large claim: however shambling, ungainly, and awkward it will come to seem in retrospect, *The Beast* was the first truly successful prototype of what web-based story-telling wants to be.… You can read a book about Harry Potter or Narnia. An ARG allows THE PLAYER HIMSELF to walk through the back of the wardrobe.… Or, more exactly it allows Narnia to come to him.[17]

In 2004 the team would release their second ARG, *I Love Bees*, a massive and successful promo for the game *Halo 2* [Microsoft Game Studios 2004] that involved players coordinating to answer hundreds of pay phones around the world and piece together a fragmented message. Others followed, but by the 2010s,

Among other Cloudmaker alumni, Adrian Hon would later co-create complex puzzle ARG *Perplex City* [Mind Candy 2005], and Dan Fabulich would found text game studio Choice of Games **2018**.

Waking

So Mike Royal knocked on my door and I opened it. He was r
"Hey, it's Statue Security in the flesh!" I said to his nipples. I ti
on a sec. We'll be right with you."

"Yes, ma'am," he said, with a nervous bob of his head.

I don't think I've ever been called "ma'am" before. I've been cal

I saw Mike's eyes stray onto Lucrece, who was hovering in the
Lucrece. She designed my familiar, back when I had one. Lucr

Lucrece is a fashion-box in her own right, nearly as tall as Mike
a Lithuanian Apache. Lucrece has carefully left all her tweaks e

excitement around the genre had waned. The opera analogy may have been apt: ARGs were expensive to mount, hard to expand beyond a niche audience already excited about them, and—like any live performance— quintessentially ephemeral. Within a year of *The Beast*'s conclusion, many of its links and phone numbers were dead, its trail no longer possible to follow. Some of its techniques have become harder to deploy on today's more locked-down internet, where social media networks might forbid accounts from fictional characters and calls from unfamiliar numbers are screened by our own AI assistants.

Today one can find only fragments of the original journey, mostly in half-broken pages saved by the Internet Archive. The Shockwave animations on them no longer play in modern browsers, and the server-side web forms where puzzle guesses could be submitted are long gone. What's left of *The Beast*, as with any great performance, are mostly snapshots and memories— the recollections of the lucky few who were front and center when the curtain went up.

References

1　Aint It Cool News. 2001. "The Wonder and Splendor of the Insidious Genius Embedded in That New A.I. Trailer!!!" Apr 13, 2001. legacy.aintitcool.com/node/8689 | a Aug 28, 2020

2　Bailey, Rick. n.d. "The Characters." hairthief.com. www.hairthief.com/characters.htm | a Aug 28, 2020

3　Bushman, Jay. 2009. "Cloudmaker Days: A Memoir of the A. I. Game." In *Well Played 2.0: Video Games, Value and Meaning*, ed. Drew Davidson. ETC Press.

4　Grundhauser, Eric. 2016. "If You Love Pokémon Go, Thank This 15-Year-Old Alternate Reality Game." *Atlas Obscura* (blog). Jul 15, 2016. www.atlasobscura.com/articles/all-hail-the-beast-which-gave-us-pokemon-go | a Aug 28, 2020

5　Hon, Adrian. 2002. "The Guide X: A Tale of the A.I. Trail." cloudmakers.org. Aug 2, 2002. www.cloudmakers.org/guide | s Aug 2, 2002

6　Kim, Jeffrey, Elan Lee, Timothy Thomas, and Caroline Dombrowski. 2009. "Storytelling in New Media: The Case of Alternate Reality Games, 2001–2009." *First Monday* 14 (6).

7　Knowles, Harry. 2001a. "New A.I. Trailer - Mysterious, Haunting, Beautiful, Simple and Perfect!!!" *Aint It Cool News* (blog). Apr 9, 2001. legacy.aintitcool.com/node/8650 | a Aug 28, 2020

8　Knowles, Harry. 2001b. "Strange A.I. Sites Online." *Aint It Cool News* (blog). Apr 11, 2001. legacy.aintitcool.com/node/8659 | a Aug 28, 2020

9　Kornblum, Janet. 2001. "The Intricate Plot behind 'A.I.' Web Mystery." *USA Today*, Jun 28, 2001. usatoday30.usatoday.com/life/movies/2001-06-22-ai-plot.htm | a Aug 28, 2020

10　Lee, Elan. 2006. "Elan Lee's Alternate Reality." Interview by Bonnie Ruberg. *Gamasutra* (blog). www.gamasutra.com/view/feature/130182/elan_lees_alternate_reality.php | a Aug 28, 2020

11　Manjoo, Farhad. 2001. "A.I.: Unraveling the Mysteries." *Wired*, Jun 28, 2001. www.wired.com/2001/06/a-i-unraveling-the-mysteries | a Aug 28, 2020

12　McGonigal, Jane. 2003. "This Is Not a Game: Immersive Aesthetics and Collective Play." In *MelbourneDAC 2003 streamingworlds Conference Proceedings*. RMIT University.

13　Meadows, Mark Stephen. 2002. "Case Study One: Game Complement to A.I. (Loosely Called The Beast or Cloudmakers)." In *Pause & Effect: The Art of Interactive Narrative*, by Mark Stephen Meadows. New Riders.

14　"Puppetmaster FAQ." 2001. Familia Salla. Jul 24, 2001. familiasalla-es.cloudmakers.org/credits/note/faq.html | s Aug 14, 2003

15　Sieberg, Daniel. 2001. "Reality Blurs, Hype Builds with Web 'A.I.' Game." CNN.com. www.cnn.com/SPECIALS/2001/coming.attractions/stories/aibuzz.html | s Aug 3, 2001

16　Stewart, Sean. 2003. "The A.I. Web Game." seanstewart.org. www.seanstewart.org/beast/intro | s Aug 30, 2003

17　Stewart, Sean. 2006. "Collaborating with the Audience: Alternate Reality Games." seanstewart.org. www.seanstewart.org/collaborating-with-the-audience-alternate-reality-games | a Aug 28, 2020

18　Szulborski, Dave. 2005. *This Is Not a Game: A Guide to Alternate Reality Gaming*. New-Fiction Publishing.

19　Timbo. 2001. "New A.I. Trailer!" countingdown.com. Apr 9, 2001. countingdown.com/features?feature_id=16381 | s Jun 6, 2001

SCREEN

Noah Wardrip-Fruin, Josh Carroll, Robert Coover, Shawn Greenlee, Andrew McClain, and Ben "Sascha" Shine

Style **Experimental**

Debuted **Fall 2002** *(CAVE Writing workshop at Brown University)*

Launch Platform **CAVE / SGI Irix**

Language **C, G3D, Max MSP**

> " In a world of illusions, we hold ourselves in place by memories.
>
> Though they may be but dreams of a dream, they seem at times more there than the there we daily inhabit, fixed and meaningful texts in the indecipherable flux of the world's words, so vivid at times that we feel we can almost reach out and touch them.
>
> But memories have a way of coming apart on us, losing their certainty, and when they start to peel away, we do what we can to push them, bit by bit, back in place, fearful of losing our very selves if we lose the stories of ourselves.

THE WORDS APPEARED FROM DARKNESS. Each phrase lit up in isolation, projected white letters read aloud by an unseen narrator. Once the final words were spoken, all went dark again. Then three short stories appeared, each on one eight-foot wall of the cube that wrapped around the reader. Each story told of a half-forgotten memory:

2002

Major Versions

» **Spring 2002**. Playable "design document" based on McClain tech demo of words peeling off a wall, with preliminary text by Wardrip-Fruin and early sound by Greenlee.

» **Fall 2002**. First full version, still with preliminary text.

» **Spring 2003**. Complete version including revised text and new opening and closing text by Coover. Shown at Boston Cyberarts Festival (Apr 26, 2003). Also shown at SIGGRAPH and Alt+Ctrl.

» **2005 version** for Linux upgrade to CAVE, assisted by Ben Shine. Improved performance on final word cloud; green ball for hand cursor replaced with less distracting glow.

» **2007 version** for SIGGRAPH and UC San Diego's StarCAVE, by Stephen Boyd, Barry Threw, Ava Pierce, Jeff Kuramoto, and Jurgen Schulze. Improved graphics performance allowed final word cloud to flock and swirl around the user.

» **Single-screen version** for UC Irvine Grand Text Auto gallery show, 2007; used polarized glasses without a cable.

In a sheetrock bedroom, under an acrylic blanket, a woman tosses, twists, turns over into another, oak-panelled room, a bed vast and cool and loose about her. She feels speckles of sun on her cheek, filtered through the trees that tower around this house. Her shoulders sore from splitting wood, swinging the big axe overhand, thud and snap, kindling clattering. Nana smiling, proud. She must have traveled all night to pull these blankets, heavy, onto her body, find this place again. She reaches for the lampswitch, to wake before sunrise, to bring Nana breakfast, but her fingernails tap the plastic face of her alarm clock, its boxy numbers telling her the time of another continent.

Each hundred-word story was read aloud by a different narrator while the listener—the reader, standing in darkness, wearing a visor that tracked their head and holding a pointer that tracked their hand—turned in place from one wall to the next.

Once all three stories finished, another pause.

Then, one word at a time, the stories began to come apart.

The origin of *Screen*—an installation piece for the immersive VR environment known as the CAVE—can be traced back a decade to an influential 1992 article written by novelist Robert Coover for the *New York Times Book Review*, titled, provocatively, "The End of Books." It was equal parts announcement, warning, manifesto, and challenge, heralding to a conservative and establishment audience the arrival of new kinds of computer-enabled literature that could never have existed on the printed page. Tools like Storyspace **1995** and a new generation of computer-literate writers were threatening to disrupt centuries-old traditions, and Coover argued this was not something to be feared, but celebrated. The coming revolution would force all writers to challenge their assumptions about what the written word could do. "Much of the novel's alleged power is embedded in the line," he wrote in one example,

> that compulsory author-directed movement from the beginning of a sentence to its period, from the top of the page to the bottom, from the first page to the last. Of course, through print's long history, there have been countless strategies to counter the line's power.... But true freedom from the tyranny of the line is perceived as only really possible now at last with the advent of hypertext, written and read on the computer, where the line in fact does not exist unless one invents and implants it.[4]

Literature, in short, had the potential to grow beyond the one-dimensional stream of linear words it had always been embedded in. But grow into *what*? It was an open question—one that, Coover proselytized, he and other willing pioneers were eager to explore.

The previous year Coover had begun teaching a regular hypertext writing seminar at Brown University, which had a long tradition of embracing experimental literature. Through the 1990s he spearheaded many efforts to provide institutional support for young writers looking to incorporate computers into their practice. While much computer writing had focused on how animations, images, and sounds could intersect with the experience of reading, Coover encouraged his students to focus on the words:

> I keep asking questions about text in this space. I don't discourage multimedia efforts, but I don't like the letters to disappear…. Probably the most interactive thing that we do, in some ways the most human thing that we do, is to stare at little squiggles of ink on a white surface and out of those invent vast worlds, landscapes, characters almost more believable than the ones surrounding us, imaginary experiences that are so rich and complete and whole that they almost at times dwarf our ordinary experience.
>
> … Perhaps graphic artists will help us to have deep imaginings in the future, not literary artists. That's a possibility, but I'm not yet willing to throw in the towel.

Near the end of the 90s, Brown had acquired an expensive new piece of hardware. The CAVE had first been proposed and built at the University of Illinois in 1992 as a technical runaround to limitations with virtual reality. (In one of those recursive acronyms techies love so much, it stood for Cave Automatic Virtual Environment.) By projecting images on surfaces around a user, it avoided the need for miniaturized head-mounted displays, which were still prohibitively expensive, heavy, and hard to produce. Brown's Cave projected images on the floor and three walls of a cube (leaving the fourth open), with multiple speakers providing positional sound. The projectors alternated quickly between images for a left and right eye; when you stood in the center wearing synchronized shutter glasses, the walls of the cube would fade away and the illusion of being surrounded by three-dimensional objects and environments could be created. Scanners tracked the position of the glasses, and thus the user's head, to adjust the scene for their perspective, while a wand the user held could also be tracked to allow interaction with the simulated world. An advantage of the CAVE setup was that the user wasn't cut off from their own body, as in traditional VR: they could still see their own hands, feet, and position within the space, and could make eye contact with spectators or assistants outside the cube, making for a less isolating and disorienting encounter with a virtual environment.

Among other contributions, in 1999 Coover helped found the Electronic Literature Organization, which in the decades since has supported conferences, awards, archives, and scholarship on computer-based writing.

Diagram from the original CAVE paper.[6] Brown's Cave did not have a floor projector.

See *The Playground* **1994** and its discussion of Brenda Laurel's work at Atari for more early experiments with VR and interactive narrative.

Brown's Cave had been funded under a promise of interdisciplinary collaboration, but at first this had mostly been between computer engineers and the sciences. Early projects included "3D weather visualization," "graphical planning for brain surgery," and "interactive modeling of biological macromolecules."[6] Coover was intrigued by the possibility of getting access for his writing students, but was at first rebuffed: "This is strictly a scientific instrument for scientists,"[5] the system's managers reportedly told him. He persisted, and soon his lit students were tentatively experimenting with what it might mean to write words designed not for the two-dimensional surface of a page, but for a three-dimensional volume. In the spring of 2002, at age seventy, Coover led Brown's first Cave Writing workshop, which had what might be one of the most exciting English department course catalog descriptions of all time:

> An advanced experimental electronic writing workshop, exploring the potential of text, sound, and narrative movement in immersive three-dimensional virtual reality. It brings together teams of undergraduate and graduate fiction writers, poets and playwrights, composers and sound engineers, graphic designers, visual artists, 3D modelers and programmers, to develop, within the environment of Brown's "Cave" in the Technology Center for Advanced Scientific Computing and Visualization, projects that focus on the word.[1]

By 2002, hypertext was in danger of becoming so normalized as to be invisible. The rise of the World Wide Web had made one particular flavor of interlinked text so commonplace it was getting hard for students to realize they could be experimental with it. Coover saw the Cave as a way of keeping digital writing productively unfamiliar, a distinct space apart from the calcifying norms and tropes of the web. And while other VR labs were chasing 3D graphics still far from photorealism, Coover saw replicating reality as the least useful thing you could do with a Cave. "In a way, the more realistic it gets in there," he mused, "the less interesting it is."[5]

The projects that emerged from that first Cave Writing workshop were characterized by Coover as "finger exercises," the technically complex but artistically flat patterns musicians play to warm up or get a feel for a new instrument. They were tech demos, more concerned with the practicalities of three-dimensional words than what they might have to say. "In a demonstration of a text-painting program," a profile of the class described, "the mouse in Mr. Coover's hand acts like an airbrush nozzle, spraying strings of letters around the room as he gestures broadly. After the letters appear in space, they form words that literally hang in midair."[10] Another project mapped words in reverse onto a floating 3D cube, so that the reader had to move their body and head inside it to read them. Nearly a dozen projects were started that semester, but most were only concepts. "It was just too hard," Coover remembered, to even "figure out how the thing worked … [there were] a lot more ideas that first semester than finished projects."[5]

But some of the finger exercises sparked more complex innovations. A student named Andrew McClain, studying both computer science and theater, prototyped code to make individual words of a passage seem to peel away and flock around the reader. The project inspired another member of the workshop: Noah Wardrip-Fruin, a graduate student in Brown's fiction writing MFA program (who recalled playing *Hunt the Wumpus* **1973** on a parent's university mainframe account as a kid, and later had his imagination sparked by Infocom **1983–5**). He had come to the program with several experimental digital writing projects already in his portfolio, and was eager to find like-minded collaborators,

A player of *Screen* knocks displaced words back into position. Through her headset, the words appear to be drifting in 3D in the space between her and the walls. Still from documentation video by Michelle Higa.

beef up his technical skills, and work with Coover. Wardrip-Fruin teamed up with Shawn Greenlee, a sound artist also in the workshop, and Josh Carroll, a coder who joined the group that fall, to conceptualize a more elaborate project based on the peeling-words demo: a story about disintegrating memories that readers would try to keep together themselves.

The central idea evolved from an article Carroll had read about "how human memory works … when you remember something you don't just play it back … you re-experience it and then re-encode it, so every time you remember something, you're actually changing the way you remember it."[15] In the completed version of the piece, after the stories of fading memories surrounding the reader were read aloud, words began peeling off of them. First one, then two, then dozens of words detached from their origin points and drifted forward, toward the center of the cube. The reader, with a position-tracked hand, could knock them back to their original places. Sometimes, the words would comply. But increasingly they would return to different sentences than the ones they'd left, leading to more and more distorted texts. With the reader surrounded by stories on three sides, turning to focus on words drifting free from one story inevitably meant neglecting another, which continued to disintegrate behind them. Pushing words too hard could also shatter them in two, each fragment drifting into a different gap to form neologisms or nonsense. As each word detached it was spoken aloud, and as the speed of fragmentation increased, the narration began to sound like an abstract poem:

> kindling … then … a … she … gather. Shoulder. By, way, to. Give his smoothing mouth. A then sunrise, a overhand again split old of these five warming napping the rhythm…

A player of *Screen* observes the collapse phase, where all the words detach and drift in a shifting cloud while a voiceover narration is heard. Still from documentation video by Michelle Higa.

Eventually, no matter how deftly the reader knocked words back into place, a critical point arrived where all the text from the memory stories drifted free from the walls to surround the reader in a dense cloud. Over a haunting sound like real and electronic whispers mingled together, a final text written by Coover was spoken but not seen (opposite sidebar, top). The piece would conclude by returning the story text to the Cave walls, but fragmented, with only the words that had been returned to the wall by the player—whether to their original positions or not—still visible (opposite sidebar, bottom). The reader would spend their final moments surrounded by stories filled with gaps and errors, only shadows of the original vignettes remaining.

One young visitor, confused, had asked of the final shattered story text, "Is that my score?"[13] It was a fair question. The relationship between games, artwork, and interactivity within the context of the Cave was a complex one, deliberately challenged by *Screen*'s designers. Nearly all previous CAVE projects, for instance, had used the powerful hardware to render colorful 3D objects and immersive environments, not words. And while other CAVE works went to great lengths to make the walls around the user seem to disappear, *Screen*'s code instead aligned its words precisely with the Brown Cave's walls, no matter where the reader stood. One grumpy visitor proclaimed the piece wasn't "using the medium,"[15] and insisted on viewing it from a chair outside the space (until words started floating off the walls). *Screen*'s creators, of course, had intended to challenge these kinds of assumptions, to create "an experience that doesn't settle easily into the usual ways of thinking about gameplay or virtual reality."[13] Spearheaded by Wardrip-Fruin, the project evolved over further months of iteration to refine its unique "bodily interaction with text," an experiment in exploring "the uncanny experience of touching words." The question of whether you were meant to treat those words like parts of a literary fiction or the ball in *Breakout* [Atari 1976] was deliberately left to the audience to sort out.

Coover had noted that "one of the difficulties with virtual writing" was that animated text could be hard to focus on, and "when you ask afterward, 'what were the stories about?' not many people noticed."[10] But some viewers praised *Screen* for so directly engaging with this existential question for an embryonic medium—for making the asking of where one's focus was meant to land be precisely the point, both on a technical and an artistic level.

You don't want to read the words coming up to you—you want to win.
You are trying to keep all those words from getting lost. You are trying
to keep them on the wall, which represents our memory or rather: the
external archive, external storage. The aim of our physical effort is to
return the words to this archive. The more effectively we do this the less
time we find to read the words we are saving, which means we don't
refresh the words in our internal archive … [we don't keep] them alive in
our mind.[12]

The project continued to be refined in the run-up to a planned debut in
the Boston Cyberarts Festival in April 2003. While access to Brown's Cave
was shared between projects and departments via a sign-up sheet for time
slots, the *Screen* team preferred to take the day's last available shifts so they
could keep working on the project late into the night when necessary. The
Silicon Graphics workstations then running the Cave proved not powerful
enough to render the finale as originally planned—two thousand invisible
boxes with letters painted on their sides, floating free in a 3D space—so
compromises were needed to create the illusion of all three walls of
text collapsing at once. (Later versions of the piece with more powerful
hardware improved the effect.) Pacing and sound design continued to be
tweaked up to the last minute. A CAVE piece, of course, was destined to
have only the tiniest of audiences—imagine debuting a new video game
if there were only five consoles in the world, each built from scratch with
different technical specs—but the reception was positive. The piece would
be shown at a handful of art festivals and be updated and restaged several
times during the rest of the decade.

Despite its small viewership, *Screen*'s creators saw its development as
a useful experiment. "We're discovering a lot of things about text, and
unexpected ways of interacting with text in this environment," Carroll
wrote, "and that could have significant repercussions in other mediums
and other applications."[15] Coover recalled, "We were asking the simple
question: Does literature have a future in this space and if it does, how
can we enhance it?"[7]

But the question, at least for the next twenty years, would remain
largely unanswered: spatialized text has remained an uncommon oddity.
Brown students and faculty kept experimenting with Cave writing—
among other outcomes, John Cayley's influential essay "Writing on
Complex Surfaces"[3] was born from his experiences there—but even today,
when VR headsets have become affordable and methods of authoring
and distribution more widespread, only a handful of 3D text projects are
readily available. Searches for "text" or "poetry" on the Oculus Store in
2021 produced no relevant results.

Maybe that's okay. It might take many sparks to find the one that lights
new fires.

"Writing students are notoriously conservative creatures," Coover had
written in "The End Of Books":

They write stubbornly and hopefully within the tradition of what they
have read.… But confronted with hyperspace, they have no choice: all the
comforting structures have been erased. It's improvise or go home. Some

frantically rebuild those old structures, some just get lost and drift out of sight, most leap in fearlessly without even asking how deep it is (infinitely deep) and admit, even as they paddle for dear life, that this new arena is indeed an exciting, provocative if frequently frustrating medium for the creation of new narratives, a potentially revolutionary space, capable, exactly as advertised, of transforming the very art of fiction.[4]

"It's our chance to discover written language anew," Wardrip-Fruin wrote at the time about the Cave workshops. "It's all still experiments."[15] Though its creators largely turned their attentions to other means and practices of computational writing, the experiments continue. As Coover's closing words for *Screen* said: we retrieve what we can, and try again.

References

1   Brown University Creative Writing Program. 2003. "CAVE Writing." www.cascv.brown.edu/cavewriting/workshop.html | s Nov 4, 2003

2   Carroll, Joshua J., Robert Coover, Shawn Greenlee, Andrew McClain, and Noah Wardrip-Fruin. 2003. "Screen: Bodily Interaction with Text in Immersive VR." In *ACM SIGGRAPH 2003 Sketches & Applications*.

3   Cayley, John. 2005. "Writing on Complex Surfaces." *Dichtung Digital* 7 (2).

4   Coover, Robert. 1992. "The End of Books." *New York Times Book Review* 21 (6).

5   Coover, Robert, and Jill Walker. 2004. "INTERVIEW, Part Two." Web page (originally in *Iowa Review*). www.uiowa.edu/~iareview/tirweb/feature/cave/part2-1.html | s Jul 6, 2006

6   Cruz-Neira, Carolina, Daniel J. Sandin, Thomas A. DeFanti, Robert V. Kenyon, and John C. Hart. 1992. "The CAVE: Audio Visual Experience Automatic Virtual Environment." *Communications of the ACM* 35 (6).

7   Dorr, Rebecca. 1999. "Off the Page: Robert Coover Is Leading a Literary Revolution That Eschews Pen and Paper for Keyboard and Mouse." *Providence Phoenix*, Apr 1, 1999. providencephoenix.com/archive/books/99/04/01/COOVER.html | a Jul 30, 2021

8   Higa, Michelle. n.d. "Screen Profile." Short film. www.youtube.com/watch?v=WOwF5KD5BV4 | a Jul 30, 2021

9   Mackintosh, Hamish. 2003. "Talk Time: Noah Wardrip-Fruin." *Guardian*, Jun 5, 2003, sec. Technology. www.theguardian.com/technology/2003/jun/05/interviews.onlinesupplement | a Jul 30, 2021

10 Mirapaul, Matthew. 2002. "ARTS ONLINE; In Three Dimensions, Words Take Flight. Literally." *New York Times*, Aug 19, 2002, sec. Books. www.nytimes.com/2002/08/19/books/arts-online-in-three-dimensions-words-take-flight-literally.html | a Jul 30, 2021

11 Wardrip-Fruin, Noah. 2003. "Screen Update." *Hyperfiction* (blog). Apr 27, 2003. www.hyperfiction.org/index.cgi/2003/04/27#030427-screen | s Jun 3, 2003

12 Wardrip-Fruin, Noah. 2004. "Digital Literature: Interview with Noah Wardrip-Fruin." Interview by Roberto Simanowski. *Dichtung Digital*, Feb 2004. www.dichtung-digital.de/2004/2/Wardrip-Fruin/index.htm | a Jul 30, 2021

13 Wardrip-Fruin, Noah. 2009. *Expressive Processing: Digital Fictions, Computer Games, and Software Studies*. MIT Press.

14 Wardrip-Fruin, Noah. 2021. Unpublished interview with author. Jul 27, 2021.

15 Wardrip-Fruin, Noah, and Josh Carroll. 2004. "INTERVIEW, Part One." Web page (originally in *Iowa Review*). www.uiowa.edu/~iareview/tirweb/feature/cave/part1-2.html | s Jul 10, 2006

THE KINGDOM OF LOATHING

Zack Johnson, Josh Nite, Riff Conner, Kevin Simmons, Chris Moyer, and others

Style	**Storylet-Driven**
Debuted	**Jan 31, 2003** (beta) **Feb 11, 2003** (public)
Launch Platform	**Web**
Publisher	**Asymmetric Publications**
Language	**JavaScript, PHP, Perl**

> **Mt. Noob**
> The bird speaks to you as you approach. "Welcome, Adventurer! I'm the Toot Oriole, and I'd like to show you the ropes. Here they are."
> He points to a pile of ropes piled atop a nearby rock.

ONE OF THE HOTTEST VIDEO GAMES IN **1987** was *Pro Wrestling* for the Nintendo Entertainment System, and one of its most memorable moments, at least for English-speaking players, was a bad translation. After each costumed wrestler finished beating the stuffing out of his opponent, the victory screen would flash the memorably mangled text A WINNER IS YOU.

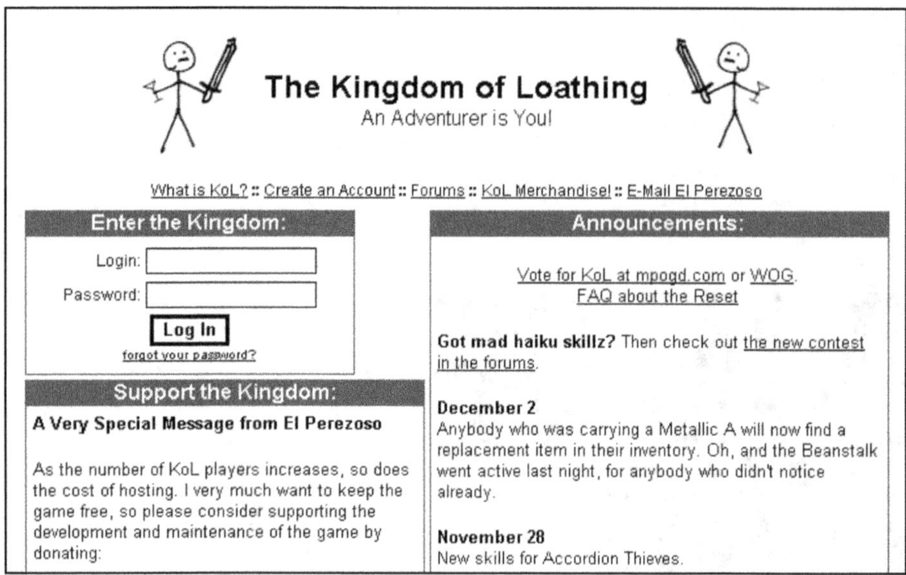

**The *Kingdom of Loathing*
homepage in late 2003.**

The joke here references
a once-common warning
on book copyright pages,
related to bookseller
practices around unsold
inventory.

A decade and change later, many of the kids who grew up with that phrase were stuck behind CRTs at desk jobs, whiling away long afternoons with nothing but high-speed internet and a web browser for company. Unable to play the games consuming them at home, like *EverQuest* [Sony Online Entertainment 1999] or *Final Fantasy XI* [Square Enix 2002], they'd cycle through favorite webcomics or the latest posts to geek culture sites like *Something Awful*, *eBaum's World*, and *Slashdot*. So when those sites began plugging a free browser game whose homepage showed a stick-figure hero (sword in one hand, martini glass in the other) and the slogan "An Adventurer Is You!"— they smiled. They hadn't even started playing yet, but the game was already speaking their language.

Kingdom of Loathing has you create a character from one of six irreverent classes (Disco Bandit, Pastamancer) and take them on adventures through a tongue-in-cheek fantasyland built mostly from prose, supplemented by line drawings suggesting an imaginative, if not especially talented, classroom doodler. By visiting different parts of the kingdom, you can discover an endless array of quests, monsters, and loot, each based around an obscure reference, a groan-worthy pun, or, often, both. While trying to acquire crafting components from the Meatsmith, for instance, your Saucerer might get sent to call in a debt from the owner of the Skeleton Store ("for some reason, after he took a big crate of weapons and armor into his store filled with skeletons, he never came back to pay me"). Before finding the missing funds you must fight your way through a variety of skeletal opponents:

Combat!

You're fighting a remaindered skeleton

You know how when you buy a skeleton, it usually has a label on it that says "If you purchased this skeleton without a skull you should be aware that this skeleton is stolen property. It was reported as 'unsold and destroyed' to the manufacturer and neither the skeleton's original container nor the necromancer responsible for its reanimation has received any payment for this stripped skeleton?"

This is the kind of skeleton that label was talking about. And also the

> kind of skeleton that is attacking you.
>
> You get the jump on it.
>
> » *Attack with your sewer snake*
> » *Use item: razor-sharp can lid (2)*
> » **Use skill: Stream of Sauce (2 Mana points)**
> » *Run Away*
>
> You blast it with a stream of hot Worcestershire sauce, dealing **13** damage.
>
> You win the fight!
>
> You acquire an item: **skeleton bone**
>
>> This is a bone from a skeleton. As opposed to all of those other kinds of bones.
>>
>> (Meat Pasting component)
>> Type: weapon (1-handed club)
>> Damage: 3 - 6
>> Selling Price: 35 Meat.
>> +1 Spooky Damage
>
> You gain 2 Mysteriousness.
>
> » *Adventure Again (The Skeleton Store)*
> » *Go back to Market Square*

Loathing takes nothing seriously. One of its best running jokes is the way it pokes constant fun at enormous MMORPGs filled with fetch quests and endless grinding, while being exactly that itself. Working through mobs of villains to increase your primary stats of Muscle, Mysticality, and Moxie, your character can unlock thousands of unique items, gain new powers, and discover intriguing areas to explore and rare weapons to craft—all with the goal of gaining enough levels to reach ascension, where your rewards include restarting with tougher constraints. "You probably wouldn't be playing this kind of game if you didn't like watching numbers get bigger," the tutorial's Toot Oriole chirps. Killing monsters gets you meat, the dominant currency of the land, with which you can buy (among other things) a wide variety of alcoholic beverages. Drinking increases the number of turns you can take each day and also your Drunkenness score, which can send you on very different kinds of adventures.

Within a year of the game's release more than 300,000 player accounts had been created, garnering attention from broader circles. "*Kingdom of Loathing* is a role-playing game that has gained quite a few fans, although it's initially hard to see why," begins a review by *Common Sense Media*,

Player choices available at prompts might vary wildly depending on inventory, skills, character class, and other details.

see *MUD* 1980

See *Universal Paperclips* 2017 for the evolution of this trend into its own distinct genre.

To name one of hundreds of examples, there's a location called the "Orc Chasm," which you might need to say out loud to get.

see *Trade Wars 2002* **1991**

see *Achaea* **1997**

2003

which advises parents about inappropriate content in books, movies, and games; the site took issue with the game's irreverent humor, booze-soaked advancement mechanics, and racy double entendres. These factors, of course, were why it had appealed to its irreverent, booze-soaked audience in the first place. Stacked with in-jokes and geeky references, oozing the same disaffected sarcasm of contemporary Gen Xer movies like 1999's *Mystery Men* or 2001's *Ghost World*, it's no surprise the game's popularity grew in part through exposure on sites like *Something Awful* that treated the web mostly as an endless source of things to make fun of.

While there had been earlier persistent browser games like *Monarchy* [Evernight 1997] or the strategy game *Planetarion* [Fifth Season A.S. 2000], web browsers in 2003 were not yet considered valid platforms for real gaming. Microsoft's Internet Explorer still had 95 percent of the market share, and its abysmal support for CSS and JavaScript had locked developers into primitive designs, with advanced behavior only possible through much-reviled server-side languages like Perl and PHP or heavyweight plug-ins like Flash. But while working a series of dull IT jobs, the game's creator, Zack Johnson, realized he'd picked up enough database and web design skills to put together a simple online game. It would be clunky, and it wouldn't be pretty, but it would work. In January 2003 he set himself a challenge to make a game in a single week—earlier overambitious projects had always run out of steam. Inspired by a desire to poke fun at self-serious MMOs and a nostalgia for the BBS door games of the early 90s, Johnson whipped up a back-end to handle user accounts and game states, and a front-end to show result messages and simple pictures. By the end of the month he had a beta link ready for friends. The game had only a fraction of the mountains of content that would debut in years to come, but it was there, it was funny, and it worked.

Like those BBS games, played on someone else's computer and thus needing ways to artificially limit play time, *Loathing*'s reliance on server-side code meant some way had be devised to keep obsessive fans from driving up hosting costs or bringing the server to its knees. The game's solution was to restrict the number of "adventures"—visits to areas with monsters or quests—your character could have in a single day, while also cleverly giving players ample ways to boost this number and feel like they were gaming the system. The limitation had a useful side effect: the game could be addictive, like *EverQuest*, but it was also rationed. Unable to binge its content, players would have to keep coming back day after day for more. And perhaps a regular audience would be willing to make regular payments. A system was added where users could make a monthly donation in exchange for unique cosmetic items. Though *Loathing* never gave paying players an in-game advantage, it was another early pioneer of the freemium model that would later come to dominate games in the so-called casual space.

The game's ability to run in a web browser, and its lack of telltales like sound or colorful graphics, also contributed to its popularity. It could be surreptitiously played at a desk job as a way of speeding up the clock during long weekdays, and it often was. "It's quite easy to spend your daily quota of Adventures in a lunch hour,"[11] wrote one reviewer, but a Slashdot commenter was more honest: "It's a great way to kill time at work when nobody is looking."[12] As the game's popularity continued to explode, some measurable percentage of world office productivity was spent leveling up leprechaun familiars and slaughtering millions of ninja snowmen.

But *Loathing*'s success arguably came less from its structure than its wordplay and an unrelenting dedication to its particular sense of humor. "Before somebody figured out how to slice it," the description of a magical baguette reads, "this was the best thing." A nearby bagel is "primarily a vehicle for toppings, but it can also be used as a wheel for some sort of bread van." Near the Dark Heart of the Woods one can also find the Dark Neck of the Woods and finally the Dark Elbow of the Woods. The Misspelled Cemetary, a reference to Stephen King's *Pet Sematary* (neither spelling is correct), features dyslexia-triggering monsters like skleletons and zobmies. The game dunks on typical nerd villains like frat boys and hippies, and it never gives up a chance to roll its eyes at a gaming or fantasy trope. At a tavern, the bartender tells the player earnestly about his rat problem:

His name, incidentally, is Bart Ender.

> "Whole cellar's just thick with 'em. I mean, sure, there are always rats down there—rats are a crucial part of the fantasy tavern ecosystem. Our problem is that there are too many rats. I need you to figure out why there are so many of 'em, and put a stop to it somehow." he replies.
>
> "So there are … rats … in the cellar … of the tavern," you sigh, "and I have to kill, what, like, ten of them?"

While the mechanics may have kept people playing, the humor was what drew them in and gave them permission to stay. Year after year, an endless parade of joke items, new quests, special events, and rare encounters were added. Text meant new areas or enemies could go live in days, not months, and it meant the small development team could stay relevant to the fast-moving front lines of geek culture. In late 2005, the hot new MMO *World of Warcraft* [Blizzard Entertainment 2004] unleashed the Corrupted Blood plague, which weakened characters and could be transmitted through proximity; though intended only for a single high-level area, an exploit let it spread across the world and cause a massive ruckus. Not long after, some *Kingdom of Loathing* players started noticing their in-game chat messages fading to fainter and fainter shades of gray. When the community realized the text of anyone who'd chatted with those players was fading too, they dubbed it the Gray Plague. Curing it would involve a special quest to a zombie-infested alternate future that was set, in a nod to the 2002 Danny Boyle film, twenty-eight days later.

It's telling that the game's version of a plague that weakened your combat stats was one that faded out the words you used to communicate. Beyond the obvious devotion to wordplay in the game itself, the creators took pains to encourage quality textual interaction between its players. Accessing the in-game chat system required passing a test distinguishing the difference between *they're*, *there*, and *their* (administered by the long-suffering Ghost of the English Language). Once unlocked, users could find chat channels such as /haiku (where all messages posted had to match the proper syllable count), an active and well-mannered forum, and an array of features for interacting with other players:

> The multiplayer features of [*Kingdom of Loathing*] aren't available unless you can prove you're a real person by associating an e-mail address with your account. If there's one thing we've learned from our decades online, it's that only real people have e-mail addresses.

Multiplayer features included player clans, in-game shops, public display cases to show off your best loot, and a very on-brand system for player-versus-player combat. Rather than settling PvP through contests of player skill or comparisons of combat stats, opt-in matches were resolved through arbitrary and random comparisons, such as whose character had more items with the letter *d* in their names.

As with all kingdoms, this one had its dark corners. Like the in-group geek cultures of *Something Awful*, *Penny Arcade*, or *4chan* (which debuted the same year as *Loathing*), the game's humor at times smacks of the edgy jokes and casual cruelty often seen in male-dominated cliques who see themselves as underdogs. A 2008 expansion for multiplayer raids took place in a zone called Hobopolis, where you must murder hundreds of enemies styled as homeless people who deal Stench damage and drop items like a "filth-encrusted futon." Elsewhere you could find a Gnollish Crossdresser who "claws you with bright-red, two-inch-long fingernails. You don't know if the physical or the aesthetic pain is worse." You could visit an orc frat party and meet underage lady monsters like the "totally trashed orquette" and "jailbait orquette" who would give you their phone numbers if you gave them beer. While these moments were uncommon (and some of these examples were later removed from the game), it's not hard to connect some of the players who laughed at them to the dark clouds then gathering over gamer culture. In 2010, the creators of webcomic *Penny Arcade* would refuse to apologize for a rape joke, despite the obvious distress it had caused many fans;[2] in 2014, the Gamergate harassment campaign began to target women and queer creators, especially those making games about issues like homelessness, rape, or gender identity. Online culture had reinforced the notion that these topics were only fit to be punchlines, and that real gamers—real men—should be able to take a joke about anything, no matter how poor in taste or personal the attack.

Johnson has said he picked the word "loathing" at random, needing a folder name to stick game data in.[8] But he has also spoken about his deep depression during the time of the game's creation,[5] perhaps reflected in its obsession with binge drinking, its nothing-matters aesthetic, and its reinforcement of bitter or cruel tropes. As his game exploded in popularity during its first few years of success, he found himself catapulted into an unexpected position of power over thousands of adulatory players. By all reports, including his own,[5] he did not handle that power responsibly. In the mid-2000s, approaching thirty, he would date several adoring fans a decade younger than him. Some of these women would later describe the relationships as manipulative and abusive, including A.M. Darke,[9] who married Johnson in 2006 at age nineteen. A friend in the game's inner circle had raped her before the marriage; when she later told him of the incident, Johnson downplayed it and kept the rapist in their friend group. "Zack never defended me," Darke wrote in 2019. "Zack never called him out or cut him out of the community. For the entirety of our marriage, the man who raped me and bragged about it was welcome in my life." Darke also described years of emotional and sometimes physical abuse, stories echoed by others formerly in Johnson's inner circle.

When these allegations came to light in 2019—part of a years-long #MeToo reckoning with the treatment of women and other under-represented voices in games and other media—the *Kingdom of Loathing* community was shaken. Some refused to believe the accusations. Some, in public or private, decided to quit playing, no longer comfortable supporting a company that had once seemed so aligned with their identities. Others tried to find a middle ground, taking to the forums to argue passionately that the game had grown beyond the culture and the cult of personality that once characterized it—that it had become more than the sum of its makers. There were more of them, for one thing, than had often been acknowledged; a huge cast of collaborators over the years (including Darke) had contributed to the game officially or otherwise, in ideas, writing, design, community management, code, bug fixes, or jokes.

And fans had given the game a life far beyond anything imaginable when it launched as a one-off experiment created in a single week. The wiki had surpassed twenty thousand pages. Millions had adventured through the game's pencil-sketched districts at least for a while, finding places on the map—or in the forums and chat rooms—that felt like home. The players did not own the game, but they owned the community. If they wanted to, they could do the work to make it one worth saving. One fan posted:

> This community has some ugly sides, it's snarky, it's at times very elitist, but I've also seen a lot of good come from it. I've seen it help in the grieving process of an aging man following the loss of his life partner. I've seen people lend others their ear and a shoulder to cry on when they were battling depression, or facing a difficult breakup, or feeling lonely on their birthday, or being home alone drunk because life had them down…. This community, and this game for that matter, have done some good.[3]

Johnson has denied some of the allegations against him, and responded to others by saying he has grown a lot in the years since. Not all fans are sure they can believe him. Attempts to reference Darke's story in-game were swiftly silenced; forum discussions were contained to targeted threads. Johnson remains the owner of Asymmetric, *Loathing*'s publisher, and some no longer feel welcome in his kingdom. Like many fandoms, embracing this one now requires each player to answer hard questions. Can we enjoy a dose of comfort food that some now find spoiled? How do we evaluate a collaborative work woven by many makers over decades when some of those strands now look like flaws in the design, or when we can no longer trust all the weavers who contributed them? When do you leave a place that's failed you, and when do you stay to make it better?

Loathing left an indelible mark on the history of text games, browser games, and casual games. The models it popularized—both as a web-based, stats-driven game surviving on the strength of its writing, and in demonstrating the way a small indie team could turn a niche game into a sustainable business—would prove influential on the rebirth of commercial text games in years to come. Its writing and mechanics influenced hundreds of thousands of players. Many of its references have grown dated, confusing younger generations who never watched *Beetlejuice* on VHS, cursed at *Zork*, or played *Pro Wrestling*; some of its humor has paled, best left forgotten. From a game so tied to the cultural context surrounding its creation, it's ironic (if inevitable) that, as time goes on, the most enduring jokes are the most universal—the puns and knee-slappers that might elicit groans from an adventurer of any generation:

see **2009**, **2014**, and **2018**

see **1977**

> "Ah, Merla! It is good that you are here, for a dire situation is at hand—evil is afoot!"
>
> "Well, which is it?" you ask. "A hand, or a foot?"
>
> "Yes yes, you're very witty. Don't interrupt me, child, this is important…"

References

1 Bishop, James. 2010. "On One's Own: Kingdom of Loathing." *DIYgamer* (blog). Apr 6, 2010. www.diygamer.com/2010/04/kingdom-loathing | s Jun 18, 2010

2 Edidin, Rachel. 2013. "Why I'm Never Going Back to Penny Arcade Expo." *Wired*. Sep 5, 2013. www.wired.com/2013/09/penny-arcade-expo-dickwolves/ | a Jul 21, 2022

3 Hippie Boy. 2015. "The Dark Side of KOL: Misconduct and Abuse IRL by TPTB." Comment by user Corgster. Forums of Loathing. Dec 3, 2015. forums.kingdomofloathing.com/vb/showthread.php?t=240165 | a May 22, 2020

4 Janelle, Robert. 2008. "Stumbling Into the Kingdom of Loathing." *The Escapist* (blog). Aug 5, 2008. www.escapistmagazine.com/articles/view/issues/issue_161/5112-Stumbling-Into-the-Kingdom-of-Loathing | s Jun 13, 2011

5 Jick. 2019. "A message to the KoL community." Forums of Loathing. Oct 4, 2019. forums.kingdomofloathing.com/vb/showthread.php?t=240428 | a Jul 21, 2022

6 Olivetti, Justin. 2010. "The Game Archaeologist's Fear and Loathing in the Kingdom: The Highlights." *Massively* (blog). Nov 2, 2010. massively.joystiq.com/2010/11/02/the-game-archaeologists-fear-and-loathing-in-the-kingdom-the-h | s May 8, 2011

7 Polly, Jean Armour. 2004. "Kingdom of Loathing - Website Review." Common Sense Media. Nov 8, 2004. www.commonsensemedia.org/website-reviews/kingdom-of-loathing | a May 22, 2020

8 "The KoL Wiki." 2020. kol.coldfront.net/thekolwiki/index.php/Main_Page | a May 22, 2020

9 Valentine, Rebekah. 2019. "Games Professor Accuses Kingdom of Loathing Designer of Abuse." *GamesIndustry.Biz* (blog). Sep 23, 2019. www.gamesindustry.biz/articles/2019-09-23-games-professor-accuses-kingdom-of-loathing-designer-of-abuse | a May 22, 2020

10 Warren, Ben. 2015. "Zack Johnson Interview." *My Boxed Universe* (blog). Feb 7, 2015. myboxeduniverse.wordpress.com/interviews/the-kingdom-of-loathing-zack-johnson-interview | a May 22, 2020

11 White, Barry. 2009. "Kingdom of Loathing Review." *Gamezebo* (blog). Dec 31, 2009. www.gamezebo.com/games/kingdom-loathing/review | s Mar 4, 2014

12 Zonk. 2007. "What Are The Best Free Games Online?" Comment by user funaho. Ask Slashdot. Nov 6, 2007. ask.slashdot.org/story/07/11/06/1558234/what-are-the-best-free-games-online | a May 22, 2020

THE FIRE TOWER

Jacqueline A. Lott Ashwell

Style **Parser**
Debuted **Jun 13, 2004** *(IF Art Show)*
Launch Platform **Z-machine v8**
Language **Inform 6**

> **"** You're certain that you'll be okay on your own?" he asks. You smile at him, tightening the pack around your waist. A slight laugh creeps into your voice—it's not as if you haven't done this before. "Yes, dear. I'll be fine. It's nothing personal, I just…" You take in the concerned expression on his face and your voice softens slightly. "I just need a break. Not from you, necessarily, but from everything: work, responsibilities, friends. I just need a day to myself, you know?"

"I'D BE LYING if I said I don't have fond nostalgia for the text adventures of old," the review began. "Interactive fiction used to be about finding lost treasure or battling monsters in dark dungeons or saving the world from terrible evil. How times have changed. *The Fire Tower* is about a hiker."[12]

"I guess this is where my issues with the game begin," another reviewer wrote. "The problem with making a game that has no 'fiction' element is that there is not much motivation to engage with the player character.… Bottom line: this is a pleasant interlude, quick, and in some sense a recommendation piece for … mountain hiking in general. But most IFers will regret the lack of more 'I' and the complete absence of the 'F.'"[11]

2004

see **2000**

The interactive fiction in question had debuted in the sixth IF Art Show, the same event that had also once inspired *Galatea* in its Portrait category. *The Fire Tower* was a Landscape. Answering the show's call, it was designed to be playable in forty-five minutes or less and to have "no overriding, compelling, 'world saving' goal that hurries players on, encouraging them to bypass experiences."[6] The experiences along the way were, in fact, the point. Stopping to smell the flowers was the game's whole reason to exist.

The Fire Tower recreates, in loving detail, a real section of the US Appalachian Trail in Great Smoky Mountains National Park: a sixteen-mile loop that climbs to the Mt. Cammerer fire tower and winds up and down ridges with ample views of rolling hills and forested valleys. Your character is a young woman who's both an experienced hiker and a knowledgeable naturalist, and under your direction she walks the trail with confidence, facing no hunger timers, puzzles, weather hazards, or other real obstacles. It's a game "about experiencing a real place that may or may not be outside your normal element," wrote its author in the introduction. "There is no way to go wrong."

>`LOOK`

Hiker Parking
The hiker parking area is where people generally leave their cars while exploring the nearby trail system in the national park, but this morning it's devoid of vehicles. A grassy hill, recently mown, lines the western edge of the parking lot, while a forest abuts it to the east. From the parking lot there are two roads: one departing north, toward the park exit, and one leading south toward the campground just under half a mile away. A trail enters the woods to the east, quickly disappearing amongst the hemlocks.

For your hike, you can proceed either east or south. Either route will take you to the Lower Mt. Cammerer trail.

>`EAST`
You decide it's best to leave the pavement as quickly as possible, and opt for the trail into the woods. The path, lined with wildflowers, curves south, then southeast, before joining with the Lower Mt. Cammerer trail.

Trail Junction (Lower Mt. Cammerer & Access trails)
You're standing at the junction of two trails, and two signs are nailed to a single post here to orient you. The Lower Mt. Cammerer trail heads northeast, toward the Sutton Ridge Overlook and, eventually, to the Appalachian Trail. Alternately, the trail continues southwest toward the campground, about two tenths of a mile away. A second trail, unnamed, runs northwest, toward the parking area where you began, or southeast, toward the Low Gap Trail.

A patch of yellow flowers is growing at the base of the signpost.

2004

>**LOOK AT FLOWERS**
You know the flowers to be jewelweed, and it's common in moist soils like those found here. The tiny, trumpet-shaped yellow flowers hang from their nearly translucent stalks like jewels from a necklace. They're perhaps best known as a natural remedy for poison ivy; fortunately, you've no need of such a treatment today.

>**LOOK AT SKY**
The sky is a rich, warm blue, and the sun is climbing in the east.

>**LISTEN**
A mosquito buzzes briefly past your ear.

>**SMELL AIR**
The air smells of life, of greenery and nearby streams. Lovely.

>**NORTHEAST**

The game's author—National Park Service ranger Jacqueline (Lott) Ashwell—wrote the piece while stationed in Alaska. But her career, and a lifelong love for nature, began in the Great Smoky Mountains. She'd started volunteering for the NPS at age nineteen, and although she'd considered careers in law, medicine, and anthropology while in college, she finally realized her happiest jobs had been helping others enjoy nature. As a teen she'd worked for a whitewater rafting company, and with the NPS she'd led tour groups on hikes or helped with search and rescue in the woods. After completing a masters in historical archaeology—her thesis was on historic cemeteries in the Smokies—she pivoted to the hard training needed to become commissioned as a park ranger. Her first assignment would be to remote Wrangell–St. Elias National Park, three thousand miles away, but part of her heart remained in the mountains of Tennessee. Her Art Show entry would be dedicated to "the Great Smoky Mountains National Park and all the wonderful staff there, past and present, for preserving this place that means so much to me, my home, the mountains that will always be a part of my soul."

Ashwell was a lifelong fan of interactive fiction. She'd started on Choose Your Own Adventure books almost as soon as she could read, and when she was eight, her parents bought a Commodore 64 and *Zork*. "I don't think I solved it for a number of years," she recalls,

see **1979**

see **1977**

> but the beauty of many of the locations became fixed in my mind, and I would daydream about wandering through the Great Underground Empire when I should have perhaps been studying French … the prose made my imagination wander…. [I] would read a description and then stop to visualize.[4]

As she got older, she moved on to other Infocom games like *Suspended* ("For some reason I never had the sense to completely give up"[3]), *The Hitchhiker's Guide to the Galaxy*, and *Wishbringer* [1985]. "It was always the

see **1983** and **1984**

writing that drew me in," she remembers. "Immersive games always won me over far more than games that focused so much on puzzles that they neglected the prose." The games were "how I got out into the wilderness when I lived in a city and was too small to venture out alone."[8] She found the online newsgroup community of amateur IF authors as an adult, and discovered the accessible design language Inform. While she had never considered herself a programmer, she decided Inform was a tool she could learn to use.

The piece she entered in the 2004 Art Show is deliberately spare in its design, following the show's prompt. It features a small handful of inventory objects for realism—including trail mix, water, and hiking boots—and though you can snack, stay hydrated, or take stretch breaks if you like, none of this is required. The game takes you down a single trail and you can only move forward along it: except for a few short alternate routes or side paths, there are no decision points or backtracking. But the game hides a surprising amount of depth in the landscape you traverse. Dozens and dozens of scenery objects representing vistas, trees, rocks, signposts, flowers, insects, and animals abound, most of which can be appreciated with a wide range of sensory verbs, and you're free to explore as much or as little as you like. The game "adapts itself to the player" in this respect, as one reviewer noted: "One can charge through the scenery for a bracing hike, dawdle in just a few places, examining everything, one can treat it as a wildlife-spotting expedition, or as a botany lecture."[7]

see *Curses* **1993**

```
>EXAMINE ARBUTUS
The trailing arbutus creeps close to the ground, with clusters of small
pink flowers along the stem.

>SMELL FLOWERS
You kneel down at the edge of the trail and place your face near the
trailing arbutus blossoms. The flowers are sweetly fragrant, and you take
a few long draws of their scent before standing up again.

>TOUCH ARBUTUS
You brush your fingertips against the leaves of the arbutus, which are
slightly fuzzy in texture.

>TASTE IT
Arbutus is used to make tinctures and teas, but you're not sure how to
go about preparing something like that.
```

The environment is filled with subtle touches that enhance the illusion of exploring it. Random events—from buzzing mosquitos to rustling squirrels to an explosion of grouse from a nearby bush—add color and variety to each hike. While most of these events are tranquil, there are occasional moments of excitement; some reviewers complaining that nothing interesting happened on their walk were incredulous when others reported a close encounter with a bear. As with actual excursions in nature, no two hikers would have quite the same experience.

Tom's Creek
Sunlight pours forth into a large opening in the trees here, illuminating bits of pollen floating in the air and sparkling on the surface of Tom's Creek. The stream flows northwest, gurgling beneath a rustic but sturdy log footbridge.

You hear the distinctive sound of a woodpecker in the distance.

>X POLLEN
Pollen dances in the air, floating aimlessly, lit by the sun, brought aloft by an occasional breeze. Some of it lands in the creek and is swept away.

>SMELL POLLEN
ACHOO!

>TOUCH CREEK
You dip your hand in the water and hold it beneath the surface for a few seconds. Ultimately, the chill gets to you and you withdraw.

A tiny yellow butterfly lights momentarily upon your shirt, then quickly flies away.

Other details include shifting descriptions of sky, sun, and clouds as the day progresses from early morning through, potentially, a late night. Moving between locations advances the clock at the rate it would actually take a fit hiker to travel, and each action takes time. If you linger in the woods too long, night can fall and the moon and fireflies will come out. Stay out even later and you might get a search party sent after you.

Unlike most IF, where movement between rooms happens instantly, here more attention is paid to transitions between major milestones like landmarks or trail junctions, lending a sense of effort to the journey. And rather than striving for neutral descriptions, here the voice of the narrator is thick with personality, painting a portrait not just of scenery but of a hiker with a deep connection to the countryside around her. The result is a journey that feels more earned, and more personal, than many more fantastical quests in games.

>SOUTHWEST
You recommence climbing the Appalachian Trail. Just as with the previous stretch, it's littered with roots and rocks and excessive steepness, and makes you not such a happy hiker. "Oh well," you think to yourself, "it's making me stronger. Stronger. Yes. Stronger." You continue this rather ineffective little pep talk for about a half a mile, at which point the trail graciously levels out along the crest of a ridge.

> You find an easy, confident pace, and begin to notice how effortlessly your legs move on this type of terrain. The lack of obstructions in the trail allows you to take in the view as you hike, and incredible mountain vistas are present on both sides of the trail for a short while—successive waves of blue, smoky ridges trailing off into the distance.
>
> After a bit, the trail begins to descend off the ridge and into the trees… gradually at first, then steeper, and your pace finds a decrescendo as you carefully navigate the slope. Many people prefer a strenuous uphill to this, because descending can be fairly hard on your knees and ankles, but after the beating your lungs and legs took on the AT earlier, you are inclined to respectfully disagree.
>
> After a total walk of just over two miles, you encounter another trail junction. [...]
>
> Your socks have shifted uncomfortably in your boots, so you take a seat in the clearing to readjust them. Once you're finished, you decide the ground feels good enough to simply rest there for a bit.

Ashwell's descriptions came from deep knowledge of a landscape she loved, echoing the way Will Crowther had recreated the caves he knew so well in *Adventure* thirty years before. "I've walked this path in the budding of a new spring," Ashwell wrote in the game's About text:

see **1976**

> I've broken through the cobwebs that span the trail on early summer mornings. I've climbed to the top of these ridges to take in the glorious colors of autumn rippling across seemingly endless waves of forested peaks. I've walked with stooped shoulders through low-hanging rhododendron tunnels, weighted with snow and ice. I've felt the joy of my body finding its perfect stride along my favorite flat stretch of the Appalachian Trail, and I've felt the pain of my knee giving way on the steepest sections when I was carrying too heavy a load. I've led many people safely to the tower and back, but I've also visited countless times alone. This path and I are old friends.

Other interactive fiction had centered exploration of an interesting environment before, but rarely with such focus. Kathleen M. Fischer's *The Cove* had won the Landscape category in the 2000 IF Art Show, giving players a remote stretch of coastline to enjoy but also infusing it with plot and puzzles. Peter Nepstad's *1893: A World's Fair Mystery* [Illuminated Lantern 2002] was an enormous commercial text game with an immaculately researched recreation of the famous Chicago exhibition; while it could be appreciated solely as living history, it also shoehorned in a plot about a diamond thief to help justify its status as a so-called real game. Even Brent VanFossen's *She's Got A Thing for a Spring* [1997], widely praised for its

Community Service

While Ashwell has released a handful of other games, many of her contributions to the IF community have been behind the scenes, part of the essential but rarely celebrated work of building community. Among other accomplishments: for fifteen years she ran the annual IntroComp, where authors can share the first chapter of a work in progress without any judgment about the full game not yet being finished. In 2007, she started a weekly online meetup, ClubFloyd, to bring IF fans together to solve games collaboratively; transcripts of these sessions (now nearly eight hundred of them) have become invaluable documentation of the games played and are some of the only web-searchable text from many of them. In 2018 she became the latest organizer of the Interactive Fiction Competition. And she has taken part in or helped run countless Speed-IF events, game jams where authors are given a handful of prompts and a lightning-fast time limit (often two hours) to create a game exploring them.

unusual focus on exploration of a lovingly rendered remote hot spring, had included a plot and puzzles.

In fact, most previous Art Show Landscapes had used some kind of gimmick: environments that changed their description if you switched between viewpoint characters, for instance, or were metaphorical instead of physical, or were described with poetry, not prose. Many simply ignored the stipulation in the rules to avoid unnecessary characters and plot. Ashwell was one of the first to enter the category and honestly engage with the prompt as given: to simulate an environment and let the player explore it, full stop. *The Fire Tower* was among the most pure explorations yet created in an interactive fiction engine—or indeed, in the days before walking simulators and art games, in a game engine of any kind.

> **>CROSS BRIDGE**
> You climb onto the footbridge over Tom's Creek, walk halfway across, and pause. One hand on the railing for balance, you close your eyes, feel the coolness of the water running beneath you, and concentrate on the sound of the water as it ripples along over unseen rocks. You stand there for perhaps two minutes, enjoying the water's song, but eventually the cool air coming off the creek is too much for your uncovered legs and you decide to continue up the trail.

The Fire Tower is not often listed in the IF canon. Its innovations are aesthetic, not technical—too unassuming to attract acclaim—and its design, though well-planned and finely crafted, is subtle rather than showy. Yet it's a beautiful example of one end that interactive text can be turned to, and of "what happens when love and skill come together,"[5] as one reviewer put it, a game infused with "authenticity … on all levels." In its own way, it's audacious: a kind of game few other authors would have dared release, comfortable in its skin and not trying to be anything but itself. Like *Photopia* and *Galatea*, more famous examples of IF minimalism, it pares its medium down to find an essence of truth at its core. *Photopia* found story; *Galatea*, character. *The Fire Tower* finds at the heart of interactive fiction a truth about journeys and why we take them, a seed of adventure that few other games dared leave alone to grow.

"Perhaps the best praise I can offer the piece is this," a reviewer at the time concluded: "I wish I'd written it."[10]

References

1 Ashwell, Jacqueline. 2004. "How I Came to Be a Park Ranger." All Things Jacq. July 2004. www.allthingsjacq.com/writing_20040701.html | a Aug 2, 2021

2 Ashwell, Jacqueline. 2005. "Re: [GOTW] The Fire Tower." Usenet post, rec.games.int-fiction, May 30, 2005. groups.google.com/g/rec.games.int-fiction/c/GEeboCEEfFY/m/KzW9zs9rf0kJ | a Aug 2, 2021

3 Ashwell, Jacqueline. 2012. Interview by Duncan Bowsman. InsideADRIFT newsletter. www.adrift.co/cgi/download.cgi?1330 | a Aug 2, 2021

4 Ashwell, Jacqueline. n.d. "My Involvment with Interactive Fiction." All Things Jacq. www.allthingsjacq.com/interactive_fiction.html | a Aug 1, 2021

5 Berry, J.D. 2004. "Judges' 2004 Reviews: J.D. Berry's Reviews: The Fire Tower." IF Art Show (website).

see **1998** and **2000**

members.aol.com/iffyart/reviews6.htm#berrytower | s Nov 29, 2004

6   Doe. 2004. "[IF Art Show 2004] Rules & Deadline." Usenet post, rec.games.int-fiction, Mar 29, 2004.
    groups.google.com/g/rec.arts.int-fiction/c/x_8bMD48hnE/m/-EnEVH-aYykJ | a Aug 1, 2021

7   Giles, Harry. 2007. "Re: Authorship and Meaning Creation in IF: Notes Towards an Essay." Usenet post.
    rec.arts.int-fiction. Jul 31, 2007. groups.google.com/g/rec.arts.int-fiction/c/Ye5J0fS4uHY/m/olEcPHF6ebsJ | a
    Aug 2, 2021

8   Matt. 2010a. "Tips from Interactive Fiction Authors – Jacqueline A. Lott." *Get Me Writing* (blog). Oct 15,
    2010. www.getmewriting.com/interactive-fiction/if-tips-jacqueline-a-lott | s Oct 30, 2010

9   Matt. 2010b. "Tips from Interactive Fiction Authors – Bonus Round!" *Get Me Writing* (blog). Oct 28,
    2010. www.getmewriting.com/interactive-fiction/if-tips-bonus | s Oct 30, 2010

10 Penman, Mike. 2005. "The Fire Tower (Review)." *SPAG*, Jul 15, 2005. www.spagmag.org/archives/backissues/
    spag41.html | a Aug 2, 2021

11 PJ. 2005. "Re: [GOTW] The Fire Tower." Usenet post, rec.games.int-fiction, May 16, 2005. groups.google.
    com/g/rec.games.int-fiction/c/GEeboCEEfFY/m/bL2c0NMClfEJ | a Aug 1, 2021

12 Whyld, David. 2005. "[REVIEW] The Fire Tower." Usenet post, rec.games.int-fiction, Jul 10, 2005. groups.
    google.com/g/rec.games.int-fiction/c/W2CO1fYOQhM | a Aug 1, 2021

SHADES OF DOOM

David Greenwood

Style **Roguelike**
Debuted **May 31, 2001** *(v1.0)*
Nov 25, 2005 *(v1.2)*
Launch Platform **Windows**
Publisher **GMA Games**
Language **Visual Basic 6**
Launch Price **$35** *(download)*
$45 *(CD-ROM)*

> Station is locked down. Threat is as yet unidentified. Good hunting, soldier.

AS TEXT GAMES FADED from the bestseller lists in the 90s, it fell to amateur enthusiasts to keep new games coming and old titles playable. Fans had varying reasons for wanting to keep text games alive. Some loved the written word and preferred an experience more like an interactive book than an interactive film. Some didn't care for the frenetic action of more mainstream games, or couldn't master it. And some had no choice. For blind gamers, the survival of text games was an existential issue.

Parser interactive fiction like *Suspended* **1983**, social MUDs like *LambdaMOO* **1990**, and other text-driven games could be played by those with limited or no sight with relative ease, simply by routing the game's output to a screen reader that converted text to synthesized speech. But save

2005

for interactive fiction and specialty edutainment, few computer games at the end of the 90s were accessible to the blind. As mainstream gamers chased more and more elaborate graphics, blind players felt increasingly isolated from a once-welcoming hobby. Most games made for the blind "were things like Football, Monopoly, Blackjack, Battleship, etc. The games were okay, but nothing like what sighted gamers had for PC or console," gamer Thomas Ward remembered.[16] The text adventure fan community was thriving **2000** and counted many blind players among its ranks, but not all blind gamers were interested in interactive fiction, or at least not exclusively. Many yearned for a day when "tried and true Interactive Fiction [could be] an option instead of 'the' option."[10]

In 1996, twenty-two-year-old Michael Feir founded *Audyssey*, a bimonthly online magazine and mailing list for blind gamers. Feir, though blind, had been an avid gamer his whole life, attributing his typing proficiency and computer expertise to gaming on the Apple IIe as a child. His dad had taken him to video arcades and helped him play some of the games, and Feir found the universe of fascinating, otherworldly sounds incredibly compelling, even if most of the games weren't designed for someone like him to enjoy. As an adult, he remembered thinking that he *could* have been playing more of those games if only the designers had been more deliberate about the information their sounds conveyed. In the inaugural *Audyssey*, he wrote that his magazine would be "dedicated to the discussion of games which, through accident or design, are accessible to the blind":

> To find such entertainment, sighted people need only look as far as their local computer store. There, they can expect to find high-quality commercially developed games. Should they need some guidance as to which games are worth their time and money, they may look to a variety of magazines, friends, and salespeople for advice. For the blind person, solving the problem of finding a game is a harder proposition.… The majority of games which are accessible to the blind are of the interactive fiction type. While the quality of these games is usually quite high, their one serious drawback is their general lack of replay value.[3]

An interactive fiction, once solved, is only worth revisiting for nostalgia, Feir wrote. Instead, he wanted something more like those arcade games with their randomness and unpredictability, games that "will keep me challenged indefinitely. Each game I play will be a different experience. I'll have to use different strategies to overcome different circumstances." He was not alone. *Audyssey* blossomed into a community nexus for blind gamers, compiling lists of new games, reviewing and redistributing old ones, and bringing together hundreds of players and developers eager to explore new definitions of what a game without graphics could be.

One of those developers was programmer David Greenwood, who shared Feir's desire for more replayable and strategic games:

> After losing my sight I searched for accessible games that were both interesting and challenging, but I found nothing that fitted my criteria.… The games I did find made little or no use of sounds as a means of providing information to the gamer.[9]

Greenwood, a friendly Toronto father, had played strategy board games as a teenager and now deeply missed them. By the late 90s he had begun writing accessible strategy games for PCS Games, a small company targeting blind audiences. His 1998 game *Lone Wolf*, a tactical submarine simulator, was hailed as a breath of fresh air by a community still resigned to board game clones and tic-tac-toe levels of strategy. To play *Lone Wolf*, by contrast, "you will need to have good skills using a compass, working with large numbers, and knowing where you are at all times," Greenwood wrote in *Audyssey*, plugging the game's release; "this game is for a person with quick reactions, sharp decision making, and [who] can keep track of many events happening at once."[5] Greenwood continued developing strategy titles for PCS, including 1999's *Star Trek: The Battle Begins,* but he'd started thinking about building something in a different genre entirely. He wanted to make a first-person shooter.

In the summer of 1999, Greenwood posted a unique proposition to the *Audyssey* mailing list. He wrote to the list's members that he "thought it may be fun and interesting to design and develop a game" together:

> I will present the initial scenario and some ideas on how the user interface might work. I will then sit back and wait for feedback. Mail list participants can comment on each other's ideas and when things settle down I will prepare a summary of our design to date.... I will then go away and develop a proto-type. Each participant will then download the proto-type and the mail list discussion will continue for another round. This may be an interactive process which may go on for several months.[6]

Greenwood already had an "initial scenario" in mind: a game "loosely based on the highly graphical and popular *Doom*," where the player would try to escape a maze of tunnels filled with dangerous monsters, weapons, keys, and power-ups. "From the volume and direction of the sounds, you can decide to run or attack," he proposed. The idea proved explosively popular. *Doom* [id Software 1993] had been a game that sighted players would not shut up about in the 90s, so the notion of an accessible clone capturing the same kind of experience was highly appealing. Before long Greenwood had compiled over seven hundred suggestions and responses from *Audyssey* readers and was marshaling discussions on every aspect of the proposed game's experience: "How should rooms be identified? Should there be signature sounds used to identify passageways and rooms? How do we keep score? Should the layout of rooms and passageways be simpler, or more complex? How should the detecting, taking, and automatic inventorying of objects work?"[7] Greenwood would gather opinions, then go off and code prototypes before posting them to the list for further feedback. His estimate of "several months" proved a bit optimistic. All told, it would be two full years before *Shades of Doom*'s first release, and four more before the more complete version 1.2 made its debut to players.

The project began at a moment of dangerous transition for blind PC gamers: the migration from DOS to Windows. While a mature ecosystem of screen readers and accessible tools had developed for text-centric DOS, the inherently graphical user experience of Windows was still unfamiliar, with

Better known on the mailing lists as *Trek99* and later *Trek2000* in its Windows revision, the game was one of many modified but recognizable clones of *Super Star Trek* **1974** still proliferating decades after its release.

fewer trusted tools and established workflows, and worse, an existentially threatening core conceit. What if the switch to graphical user interfaces left blind computer users forever behind? In part for these reasons, as late as 1999 most games for the blind were still made in DOS (including Greenwood's *Lone Wolf*), even though Windows had become entrenched as the dominant mainstream platform. But Greenwood's desire to use complex audio processing techniques pushed him into newer Windows-only technology, most notably the DirectX library. As blind gamer Thomas Ward recalled:

> When Microsoft DirectX came out, it not only revolutionized mainstream games, it also opened up new avenues for what we now call audio games…. Microsoft added a lot of high-level features: you could pan sound left and right, you could put sound in 3D, and many game developers said, "Hey, if we can play it back in 3D, we could hear where the sounds were." So they began experimenting.[11]

When it was at last released under a new spin-off company of Greenwood's called GMA Games, *Shades of Doom* would make full use of DirectX to create a 3D-positioned soundscape with multiple overlapping sounds. The game begins, like many professionally produced games, with a cutscene. A six-minute audio drama complete with music and sound effects sets up a backstory familiar to fans of *Doom* and its many clones: a secret government base researching "genetic enhancements" or maybe even "biological transformations," an urgent final transmission followed by ominous silence, and a lone hero who must infiltrate the deadly corridors and fight through waves of mutant enemies. The narrator (voiced by Kelly Sapergia, another longtime *Audyssey* contributor) sets the stage, backed by music that starts triumphant but soon turns ominous:

> The top of the mountain is clearly visible as your shuttle slowly descends towards the island. You peer up from the controls and see wisps of clouds flicker by your canopy. Breaking through the ceiling, the beauty of the scene is marred by the sight of lines of plasma cannons bristling from shore and mountainside batteries.
>
> The high-security military research base, funded and run by the FDN, was totally constructed within the mountain, making it impregnable to all, including a direct nuclear attack. The research performed is of the highest security and secrecy, but even with your considerable clearance level you only have a vague idea of what goes on in the rapidly approaching base.

Through the time-tested method of discovering log entries on suspiciously unsecured computers, the player learns of a dangerous experiment gone heinously wrong. The only way to shut it down is to gather four data wafers once held by the project's lead scientists, each containing a fragment of a crucial security code. Unfortunately, the wafers—and the details of what order to insert them into the master computer to trigger the shutdown—are now scattered through a huge complex overrun by mutants and monsters.

The player's goal is to navigate the base's nine mazelike levels, staying alive and collecting data wafers and clues. On the final level you can input the command sequence that will—naturally—save the world.

Once the game proper begins, the player quickly learns that surviving requires great skill and keen attention to detail. *Shades* has a complex interface with over forty commands (see sidebars next page spread), utilizing nearly every key on the keyboard. The arrow keys navigate your character through explorable levels rendered in positional audio. Movement is not through distinct grid squares, as in many audio games, but through continuous space as in any other first-person shooter, allowing for strategies like sidestepping around walls or weaving back and forth to avoid fire. The game likewise unfolds in real time rather than discrete turns.

Sound effects are carefully employed to help players intuit the layout of rooms and corridors. When approaching a hallway junction, the player hears wind blowing from the directions of new passages opening up. Different compass directions have different-sounding winds, so with practice one can distinguish an upcoming north-facing passage from a west-facing one. Footsteps echo more loudly in one ear if there's open space in that direction, and the echo also changes just before you would step into a wall. Doors, machinery, and moving monsters make sounds whose volume and stereo positioning help pinpoint their location. Unlike the busy noises of the arcade, here every sound is deliberate and filled with information.

The player also has a device called EVA (Envirometric Vector Analyzer), a sort of in-world screen reader for the game's simulated reality. By pressing various keystrokes, the player can hear EVA speak information about their surroundings, including the identity and position of nearby objects, enemies, and geography, as well as their current health and other useful statistics.

YOU ARE CARRYING...

» high-velocity bolt gun

» contact bio-grenade

» security chip

» data wafer (white)

» night scope

» chainsaw

[Sirens coming from somewhere ahead, along with a voice repeating "Emergency, emergency. Please evacuate the base."]
`<UP ARROW>` — *walk forward*
[Sound of player's footsteps. The alert and message sounds pass by to the left and then fall behind.]
`N` — *navigational information*
The passage continues.
`<UP ARROW>` — *walk forward*
[Footsteps as player continues advancing.]
Door in two feet.
[Sound of door opening. Sound of monster growling.]
`<CTRL-LEFT>` — *turn 90 degrees left*
South.
The passage turns sharply to the left and right.
`M` — *distance to nearest monster*
Sixteen feet.
`<CTRL-M>` — *identify nearest monster*
Mutant human.

Right-aligned text has been added to explain what each keystroke command does; italicized text in square brackets describes audio cues.

Help Screen	Ctrl-F1
Quit Game	Esc or Q
Save Game	F3
Load Game	F4
Sound Help	F9
Pause/Unpause	P
Check Speakers	C
Reset Sound Card	Ctrl-R
Adjust Music Vol	PgUp/Dwn
Slight Turn Left	Left
Slight Turn Right	Right
Forward	Up Arrow
Backward	Down-Arrow
Move Lock	Shft-Arrow
Turn Left 90	Ctrl-Left
Turn Right 90	Ctrl-Right
Side Step	Shift -Arrow
Align to Right Angle	R
Turn 180	Ctrl-Down
Use Weapon	Space Bar
Select Weapon	1–9 + G
Check Ammo	A
Direction Facing	F
Character Health	H
Character Status	F2

The player is also equipped with a night scope, which emits pings pinpointing the nearest monster's location. As the distance closes, the scope's beeps get faster, and as the angle between the monster and the direction you're facing shrinks, the sounds increase in pitch. If the monster falls behind you, an ominous drumbeat plays, suggesting a chase; when an enemy is dead ahead, a distinctive "lock-on" sound is heard, signaling that if you fire your weapon at this angle, you'll hit. But using the night scope drains its battery, so deploying it strategically is crucial, saving its power for moments you really need it.

S   *toggle night scope*
[The sonar sound is fast but medium-pitched. The player uses the LEFT AND RIGHT ARROWS *to try to lock on to the monster, whose growls are growing louder.]*
M   *distance to nearest monster*
Twenty-one feet.
[The player BACKS UP*, still trying to center the monster.]*
M   *distance to nearest monster*
Thirteen feet.
[Monster growls increase in volume; player continues to BACK UP *until an "oof!" sound indicates they've backed into a wall.]*
M   *distance to nearest monster*
Nine feet.
[Lock-on sound]
<SPACE BAR>   *fire weapon*
[Sounds of weapon fire, then monster groaning and collapsing to the floor.]
Projectile ammunition in eight feet.
S   *toggle night scope*
[Night scope noises turn off.]
<CTRL-N>   *look ahead*
The passage continues. In ten feet the room continues. In twenty feet the room terminates abruptly.
X   *dimensions of current room*
Twenty by ten feet. There is an exit from the room behind.
[Player uses ARROW KEYS *to move forward.]*
"Whoa!" *[Sound made when stepping over a dead body.]*
Projectile ammunition taken.

EVA also helps the player track which rooms they've already visited, set numbered markers useful for mapping, and find nearby objects. You can even output a drawing of the parts of a level you've explored so far to a Braille printer, creating a tactile minimap.

V   *have I visited this room before?*
No.
<CTRL-V>   *mark location*
Mark.
<F2>   *character status*

> Health 99 percent.
> You are using a manual bolt gun.
> Ammunition 68.
> You are wearing: nothing.
> You are carrying: nothing.

While the first level is relatively straightforward, the game's challenges expand as you keep playing. Soon you'll be fighting off waves of giant rats, cyborgs, mutant birds, gelatinous blobs, and "insane scientists" who rush by you giggling as they steal your stuff. A range of weapons—including grenades, proximity mines, a flame thrower, and, yes, a chainsaw—have different trade-offs of range, ammo type, and effectiveness against different kinds of targets. Traps such as pits and jets of gas shooting from the walls create further challenges. At higher difficulty levels, monsters will dodge and weave as they approach you, so maintaining a lock becomes a constant challenge. Strategies can get quite complex. Here's a tip from one guide on how to defeat a "temporal disturbance," one of the game's toughest enemies—and sighted readers should remember this plan must be executed without visual aids of any kind:

> What I like to do is find a nice big room and lure it in. Keep the door you plan to use open. Run around the outer edge of the room until you come to the door you left open and run out of the room, closing the door behind you. If you do it right you'll trap the TD in the room and be able to continue on. Depending on the level you may have to do this several times.[13]

The final level offers an exceptionally difficult challenge with four powerful teleporting bosses and dozens of minions. If you defeat the hordes of enemies and successfully key in the data wafers in the correct sequence to disable the experiment, you can make your way to the roof for a heroic exit via helicopter.

Shades of Doom was an instant hit in the blind games community, actively played for over a decade and still regularly discussed on audio game forums. "The same day I got the registration code," one fan recalls, "I played it non-stop for the next sixteen hours."[4] Reminiscing in 2012, another remembered it as forever changing their relationship to gaming: "I never dreamed I'd get to play games like those my sighted friends spent their lives in front of and this gave me new hope."[17] Blind gamers also took a certain amount of delight in mastering a game whose sheer complexity meant that many mainstream gamers might never have the patience or wherewithal to complete it. "Even if you can't see what you're doing, some of those [conventional] games can be extremely addicting," wrote the author of one *Shades of Doom* guide. "But this doesn't lessen the satisfaction I find in the knowledge that finally there are games that a sighted individual might actually have to have [my] help playing."[12]

The success of *Shades* brought a surge of interest in audio gaming. It made the community "much more ambitious," according to Justin Daubenmire,[1] whose BSC Games was a friendly competitor to GMA. The game's

GAME COMMANDS, CONT'D

Data Wafers	F6
Game Information	F7
Messages Found	F8
Inventory Mode	Tab
Use Closest Object	Enter
Name Close Objects	Ctrl-O
Closest Monster	Ctrl-M
Next Object Locator	O
Distance to Monster	M
Toggle Night Scope	S
Night Scope Power	Ctrl-S
Nav Info	N
Look Ahead	Ctrl-N
360-Degree Detector	D
What's Directly Ahead?	Shift-D
Have I Visited Here?	V
Set Marker	Ctrl-V
Where Am I?	W
Room Size and Exits	X
Save Level Map to File	Ctrl-W
Change Voice	F10
Change Speech Rate	F11
Change Speech Volume	F12
Enter Cheat Code	Ctrl-Z
[Inventory] Drop	D
[Inventory] Use	U
[Inventory] Scoll	Up/Down

successful focus on action and tactics proved a wider variety of game styles could find success in audio- or text-only formats. Greenwood reworked the game's engine to make it more reusable for other kinds of audio games, quietly licensing it to other blind creators. GMA games would go on to release highly regarded follow-ups, like the even more complex strategy game *Time of Conflict* [2010]. Another team started working on a mod for *Quake* that would allow blind players to play alongside sighted friends by making heavy use of "earcons," sounds that provided rapid and overlapping environmental information to those who learned to decipher them. Audio games in other surprising genres started appearing, from sports games to 4X strategy. "Accessible games are no longer just a bunch of twisty little passages," wrote a reviewer in a 2002 issue of *Audyssey*. "We're not quite there yet, but *Shades of Doom* and others are light years ahead of what we had even two years ago."[18]

By the 2010s, the mainstream game industry was paying more notice to blind gamers. Advocacy groups like AbleGamers now work with developers to make their titles accessible to blind or disabled players. While Greenwood still sells specialty audio titles through GMA Games, today he's more interested in keeping mainstream games accessible so blind gamers can stay connected to wider gaming culture, rather than remaining isolated in their own niche: "I strongly believe that accessibility should be built-in during the development of new mainstream games from this point onwards."[9] Accessible modes for racing games, rhythm games, puzzle games, and many other genres have become far more common. Many of the consultants now working on these modes can trace back their interest in gaming to discovering *Shades of Doom* in the early 2000s.

And audio games as a distinct genre continue to evolve as well. The 2010s also saw the rise of smart speakers and virtual assistants, new platforms for games that, "through accident or design" (as Michael Feir had once put it), blind players can enjoy. Companies like Earplay have explored "interactive audio stories you play with your voice," experimenting with a new design space of games using spoken words as both input and output. "Story telling began as an aural form," wrote one analyst; "something in our wiring as a species responds to the *sound* of a story."[2] And while the original *Doom*'s graphics now look dated, the soundscape of *Shades*—a mutant human stumbling closer, say, while sonar pings echo faster and faster—still tells a story as visceral and terrifying as ever.

References

1   Cohn, David. 2005. "The Blind Fragging the Blind." *Wired* (blog). Mar 14, 2005. www.wired.com/2005/03/
     the-blind-fragging-the-blind | a Nov 22, 2020

2   Edgerly, Len. 2016. "Earplay: Alexa Hosts a Transformative New Way to Tell Stories." *Len Edgerly*
     (blog). Oct 28, 2016. lenedgerly.medium.com/earplay-alexa-hosts-a-transformative-new-way-to-tell-stories-
     fc6dbd2ac8e6 | a Nov 22, 2020

3   Feir, Michael. 1996. "'Welcome' and 'From the Editor.'" *Audyssey* #1, Jul/Aug 1996. www.espsoftworks.com/
     downloads/audyssey/aud1.txt | s Feb 22, 2001

4   Gallegos, Raul. 2010. "Game Archives." gallegos47.com. gallegos47.com/games | a Nov 22, 2020

5   Greenwood, David. 1998. "Lone Wolf: The Real-Time Revolution For Blind Gamers." *Audyssey* #15, Nov/

Dec 1998. audiogames.net/page/_Audyssey_Magazine_issue_15_-_November_-_December_1998_ | a Nov 22, 2020

6   Greenwood, David. 1999. "Letters: From David Greenwood." *Audyssey* #18, May/Jun/Jul 1999.
    audiogames.net/page/_Audyssey_Magazine_issue_18_-_May_-_June_-_July_1999_ | a Nov 22, 2020

7   Greenwood, David. 2000a. "Shades of Doom Status." *Audyssey* #23, May/Jun 2000. audiogames.net/
    page/_Audyssey_Magazine_issue_23_-_May_-_June_2000_ | a Nov 22, 2020

8   Greenwood, David. 2000b. Interview (audio). On *Main Menu* (radio program), ACB Radio, Sep 25, 2000.
    Interviewed by Jonathan Mosen.

9   Lupetti, Matteo. 2020. "Seen and Heard: Making Games for the Visually Impaired." *Wireframe
    Magazine*, Sep 2, 2020. wireframe.raspberrypi.org/articles/seen-and-heard-making-games-for-the-visually-
    impaired | a Nov 22, 2020

10 Peach, James. 2000. "Sparkle and Shine: Reflections on Trends in Gaming." *Audyssey* #24, Jul/Aug 2000.
    audiogames.net/page/_Audyssey_Magazine_issue_24_-_July_-_August_2000_ | a Nov 22, 2020

11 Peters, Matthew. 2009. "Spot On: The Blind Gaming the Blind." *GameSpot* (blog). Aug 25, 2009. www.
    gamespot.com/articles/spot-on-the-blind-gaming-the-blind/1100-6215457 | a Nov 22, 2020

12 Peterson, Bryan. 2013. "Walker Boh Ohmsford's Guide to: Shades of Doom by GMA Games."
    audiogames.net forum. Nov 8, 2013. forum.audiogames.net/topic/11877/bryan-ps-guide-to-shades-of-doom |
    a Nov 22, 2020

13 Peterson, Bryan. 2014. "Re: [Audyssey] Help in Shades of Doom Level 6." Gamers Discussion List
    (Audyssey). Apr 7, 2014. www.mail-archive.com/gamers@audyssey.org/msg109793.html | a Nov 22, 2020

14 Sapergia, Kelly. 2001. "Shades of Doom" (review). On *Main Menu* (radio program), ACB Radio, Jun 6,
    2001.

15 Taylor, Ashley P. 2013. "How to Make a Video Game for the Blind." *Popular Mechanics* (blog), Mar 28,
    2013. www.popularmechanics.com/technology/gadgets/video-games/how-to-mak-a-video-game-for-the-
    blind-15277536 | a Nov 22, 2020

16 Ward, Thomas. 2014. "Re: [Audyssey] First Audio Game." Gamers Discussion List (Audyssey). Oct 19,
    2014. www.mail-archive.com/gamers@audyssey.org/msg114011.html | a Nov 22, 2020

17 welshweyr. 2012. "Reply to 'Top 10 Audio Games.'" audiogames.net Forum. Aug 16, 2012. forum.
    audiogames.net/topic/6890/top-10-audio-games/page/4 | a Nov 22, 2020

18 Zingaro, Daniel. 2002. "Accessible Games--Lagging Behind?" *Audyssey* #34, Third Quarter 2002.
    audiogames.net/page/_Audyssey_Magazine_Issue_34_-_third_quarter_2002_ | a Nov 22, 2020

ALSO BY
DAVID GREENWOOD

1998 **Lone Wolf** †

1999 **Star Trek: The Battle
      Begins [Trek99]** †

2000 **Trek2000** ‡

2002 **Pacman Talks** †

2003 **GMA Tank
      Commander** ‡

2010 **Time of Conflict** ‡

2013 **GMA Cards** ‡

2013 **GMA Lander** ‡

† PCS Games
‡ GMA Games

DWARF FORTRESS

Tarn Adams and Zach Adams

Also Known As	Slaves to Armok: God of Blood Chapter II: Dwarf Fortress
Style	Roguelike, Procedural Story
Debuted	Aug 8, 2006 *(web)*
Launch Platform	Windows
Publisher	Bay 12 Games
Language	C, C++

> You have arrived. After a journey from the Mountainhomes into the forbidding wilderness beyond, your harsh trek has finally ended. Nestled beneath a sheer cliff face overlooking the wilds, your party of seven is to make an outpost for the glory of the King and all of ìrlomemenidithudib. There are almost no supplies left, but with stout labor comes sustenance. Whether by bolt, plow, or hook, provide for your dwarves. You are expecting a supply caravan just before winter entombs you, but it is spring now. Enough time to delve secure lodgings, ere the wolves get hungry. A new chapter of dwarven history begins here at this place, Zedotkol, "Lobsterwheels". Strike the earth!

2006

"**She feels euphoric due to inebriation,**" the bio began:

> Within the last season, she felt fondness talking with an acquaintance. She felt pleasure near a fine Statue. She feels satisfied at work. She felt love remembering talking with a lover. She was content after eating a fine dish. She was exasperated when caught in the rain. She felt satisfied remembering getting into an argument. She felt pleasure having an intellectual discussion with a lover. She was annoyed at the lack of chairs. She sometimes feels sad at being separated from loved ones.

It was just the first of nine paragraphs describing Zasit Bomreksezuk, a Stonecrafter in my dwarven fortress of Zedotkol. She existed for only a handful of days on my laptop's hard drive before perishing near the end of a frigid winter. In some ways, I barely knew her. Yet I knew that she had very long hair arranged in double braids, and an angular chin; that she was strong, but slow to heal and quick to tire; that she liked fine pewter, colors in a dark olive shade, and drinking apricot wine; that she had an amazing memory and an iron will but little patience. I knew that, like many of us, she detested purring maggots. I knew, more anecdotally, that she tended to finish tasks quickly and reliably; that I could count on her to get a job done. And I knew that her pages of biography, extensive as they were, showed only a portion of her simulated character: selections of interesting or unusual facts, not the whole dossier. Though rendered on my area map with just a single character of text, Zasit Bomreksezuk had depths I would never see.

Zasit was a procedurally generated character in *Dwarf Fortress*, which the *New Yorker* once described as "*SimCity*'s evil twin."[24] In the game, you shepherd a colony of dwarves through the building and expansion of a remote outpost in a dangerous, fantastical land. What makes the game so memorable is the incredible depth of its simulation and the deliciously vivid stories it inspires, using nothing but words and a simple palette of symbols. It's "visually terrible," *Slate* wrote, "insanely difficult, and beautifully weird."[22]

The story of the game's creators, Tarn and Zach Adams, has been told before.[23] In brief: two talented brothers, making games together since they were kids, had grown up with the thought of perhaps becoming academics, one in math and the other in history. But on the side they kept making games for fun. In their midtwenties they started a sequel to an earlier and overly ambitious project, *Slaves to Armok: God of Blood* [Bay 12 Games 2000]—the deity's name inspired by a variable `arm_ok` counting unspoiled limbs. Since the original game had collapsed under the strain of trying to realize a detailed simulated fantasy world with 3D graphics, the brothers decided their new game would use only text. Designing together—but with coding handled by the mathier brother, Tarn—the two worked on *Dwarf Fortress* for four years before releasing an alpha build in 2006. Within months it became wildly popular among a certain kind of gamer obsessed with detail and emergent play, and the brothers have kept working on it ever since. It's still unfinished—but even so, it's become one of the most infamous and beloved text games ever made.

Little upon the game's first release suggested the 5.1 MB download from an unknown developer would be anything special. The first clue might have come from the readme, which noted "You may **NOT** modify any files, except"—and here was maybe a bit of a wink—"the files in these folders":

```
"raw/objects"
"data/art"
"data/init"
"data/interface"
"data/movies"
"data/sound"
"data/speech"
```

Those who poked into these folders found an astonishing catalog of human-readable data that implied a simulation operating at extraordinary depth. Within the `raw/objects` folder, for instance, a file `creature_amphibians.txt` defined an entity:

```
[CREATURE:TOAD]
    [NAME:toad:toads:toad]
    [TILE:249][COLOR:2:0:0]
    [VERMIN_SWAMPER][FREQUENCY:100][VERMIN_HATEABLE]
    [AMPHIBIOUS][SMALL_REMAINS][NO_WINTER][UNDERSWIM]
    [SPEED:2900][NATURAL][PET]
    [PETVALUE:10]
    [NOT_BUTCHERABLE]
    [PREFSTRING:beauty]
    [NOCTURNAL]
    [BIOME_NOT_FREEZING]
```

Dozens of other creature files defined worms, cats and dogs, birds and squirrels; and others tied to specific biomes like hippos (tropical), hoary marmots (tundra), and whales (ocean). A file called `item_armor.txt` laid out the material, weight, and size of protective gear; `language_DWARF.txt`, `language_ELF.txt`, and so on indexed massive vocabulary lists for fantasy tongues. Another config file detailed how to build bodies out of component parts, from organs on up:

```
[BODY:THROAT]
[BP:THROAT:throat][CONTYPE:HEAD][THROAT][EMBEDDED][SMALL]

[BODY:NECK]
[BP:NECK:neck][CONTYPE:HEAD][NERVOUS][INTERNAL][SMALL]

[BODY:SPINE]
[BP:UPPERSPINE:upper spine][CONTYPE:UPPERBODY][NERVOUS]
    [INTERNAL][SMALL]
[BP:LOWERSPINE:lower spine][CONTYPE:LOWERBODY][NERVOUS]
    [INTERNAL][SMALL]
```

Before playing this game, you had to first give it time to create the world. Blocky rivers wore down mountains; rain shadows and elevation shaped the formation of lakes. Hundreds of years of history were logged, sketching tens of thousands of historical figures and events: wars, the foundation of cities, the creation of notable artifacts. By the time each game of fortress management began, an entire bespoke planet had been made to play it in— worlds with names like "Adelanamaanenu Rayali, The Wondrous Everseeing Planet of Tempests," or "Ecamo Oroni, The Universe of Omen."

Dwarf Fortress took inspiration from favorite games of the Adams brothers' childhood. The most recognizable ancestor is the game genre now called roguelikes, after *Rogue* [Michael Toy and Glenn Wichman 1980], its progenitor. (Earlier games like *dnd* might now be called roguelikes, but *Rogue* would spread the furthest and become the most influential.) That game in turn had been inspired by *Super Star Trek* and its clones: games where you'd guide an avatar through a map of linked areas, drawn as a top-down grid with letters and filled with enemies rendered, like your own avatar, with a single ASCII character. *Rogue* had twenty-six monsters, one for each letter of the alphabet; a capital M meant you were facing a Medusa.

Rogue would inspire dozens of successors, including *Hack* [Jay Fenlason 1982; Andries Brouwer 1984], an extended clone with innovations including a "bones file" that kept a record of each prior hero who had died in its world—these could be brought back as uniquely personal undead villains on future runs. The Adamses played *Hack* religiously, thrilling in the way each game was different and how unexpected surprises could catch even a seasoned player off guard. Other inspirations were the detailed damage system in the tabletop roleplaying game *Cyberpunk* [R. Talsorian Games 1988], which replaced generic hit points with specific damage to individual body parts, and the procedurally generated life-forms in the space adventure *Starflight* [Electronic Arts 1986]. Teaching themselves to code by looking at the BASIC source of BBS games, the brothers were making their own games by age twelve, first copying and then improving on a play style that reveled in unexpected outcomes and unpredictable consequences. Their goal was always games that were as procedural as possible—games you could play forever.

The game that would become their magnum opus is a glorious celebration of the possibilities and complexities of emergent behavior, taken to a level few—if any—other games have achieved. Earlier games had tried: Veronika Megler's *The Hobbit*, among others, had similar ambitions to create a narrative game where no two playthroughs were the same. But while earlier games had often been constrained by the storage and memory limitations of early computers, by 2006 few practical limits remained for a game built mostly of text. Tarn and Zach's project could grow as complex as they wished. The heights to which that complexity has now reached are evidenced by two famous bugs: one involved too low a melting point for the fat layer of dwarven skin, and the other saw cats getting disproportionately drunk from licking their paws after walking over tavern floors sticky with spilled beer. By 2021, the Adams brothers' game would contain nearly three-quarters of a million lines of code, perhaps fifteen thousand pages of printed text.

see **1975**

see **1974**

see **1991**

see **1982**

2006

While *Dwarf Fortress* is in part a roguelike—
drawing a top-down picture of a threatening world
using letters and symbols as tiles—it's also fair to
discuss it as a text game, since it leans heavily on
words and sentences to tell its stories. At the most
foundational level, everything in the world is named:
dwarves, elves, fortresses, fell beasts, books, artifacts,
lands, and even the world itself are all given custom
names, often in fictional languages complete with
English translations. The game's name generation
starts with a series of linguistic config files. A set of
vocab lists define more than a thousand words in
each of four fantasy languages:

```
[TRANSLATION:DWARF]
    [T_WORD:ANGER:ustos]

[TRANSLATION:ELF]
    [T_WORD:ANGER:fomire]

[TRANSLATION:HUMAN]
    [T_WORD:ANGER:othag]

[TRANSLATION:GOBLIN]
    [T_WORD:ANGER:ok]
```

**The complete default tileset
for *Dwarf Fortress* of 256
symbols, possibly adapted
from IBM's 1981 Monochrome
Display Adapter font.**

Each word root is also extensively annotated with tags that help the system
know how to deploy it sensibly:

```
[WORD:ANGER]
    [NOUN:anger:angers]
        [FRONT_COMPOUND_NOUN_SING]
        [REAR_COMPOUND_NOUN_SING]
        [THE_COMPOUND_NOUN_SING]
        [THE_NOUN_SING]
        [OF_NOUN_SING]
        [REAR_COMPOUND_NOUN_PLUR]
    [ADJ:angry]
        [ADJ_DIST:2]
        [FRONT_COMPOUND_ADJ]
        [THE_COMPOUND_ADJ]
```

Base words can be placed in conceptual categories:

```
[SYMBOL:VIOLENT]
    [S_WORD:ANGER]
    [S_WORD:ARROW]
    [S_WORD:AXE]
    [S_WORD:BARB]
    [S_WORD:BATTLE]
    [S_WORD:BEAST]
    [S_WORD:BLADE]
    [S_WORD:BLAZE]
    [...]
```

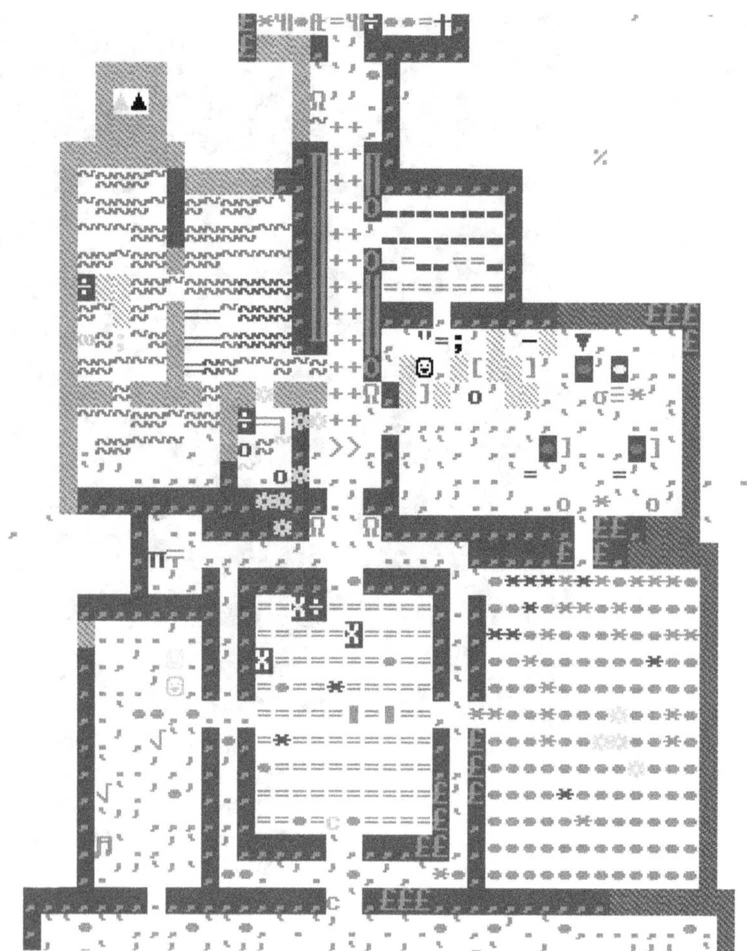

Map view of an early *Dwarf Fortress* fort.

And this in turn lets name generators define appropriate compounds. A goblin villain might receive a name like Gotozud ("Necroruthless"), from a language-agnostic rule to join a DEATH word with a VIOLENT one. The results are names with a discernible logic behind them, even if it's not quite the logic that namers in our own world might use: dwarves whose names mean Fencelabor or Jadefires; a kingdom called the Wilted Confederation; a monster den called Grievedpit the Umbra of Blisters. Zasit Bomreksezuk's last name meant "whip slap," and though assigned at random, it proved appropriate for a settler who'd come to the fortress from a background in military service.

Generated names are found throughout the intricate histories created for each world before play begins and which players can later peruse at will. One week at a time, the game simulates centuries of history, with civilizations that rise and fall, build roads, found settlements, and make decisions about warfare and trade based on the personalities of their leaders. Exports of a single world's backstory can exceed a gigabyte of text. Calling each generated history "a book of sand" that "no human could ever exhaust,"[8] game scholars Stephanie Boluk and Patrick LeMieux compare these dry recountings of epochal events to ancient human forms of history like the annal or the chronicle:

In a time before time, the armadillo brute Ulash Putridcurse the Fated thrust a spire of slade up from the underworld, naming it The Citadel of Bones, and established a gateway between worlds in Passagedevils.

In the early summer of 72, The Grand Empire attacked The Scarlet Black Monsters in The Steppe of Smiling. The human Istra Faintedbunches led the attack, and the defenders were led by the goblin Amxu Dreadyell. The Disemboweler of Torches were hired by the attackers.

In 223, the dwarf Åblel Mansionflag of The Ivory Society persecuted The Fierce Faith in Fleshytrick. Dozens of people were expelled and some sacred sites were desecrated.

These histories feed into the simulated present in subtle but meaningful ways, much as Tolkien's unpublished legendarium added context and consistency to *The Lord of the Rings*. Dwarves might be descended from legendary heroes, or make art depicting historical figures and events. Nearby enemies might have moved to their present lairs after long-ago battles or famines drove them from old homes. My ill-fated stonecrafter Zasit had been a widow: her husband had been slain before my game began by a creature called Dungda, who could be cross-referenced in the game's interface to its generated history, Legends Mode:

> Dungda was a fist of Ducim. [...] A large eyeless humanoid. It has three short horns. Its black skin is leathery. This night creature was first created by the dwarven necromancer Ducim Gemwander of Lulleddaggers after horrible experiments on the human Ushcen Fisherhale in Riverlulled in the year 137. Dungda was associated with the night and deformity.
> In 154, Dungda settled in The Rhythmic Hill.
> In the early autumn of 155, Dungda settled in Netbanded.
> In 156, Dungda became a poet in Netbanded.

After trying and failing to get apprenticed to a more famous poet, the blind abomination spent the next hundred years doing nothing but writing books of verse, with titles like *The Birth of Introspection* and *Princesses: Suddenly the Sands Laugh There*. Finally conscripted into a war—reluctantly, one can't help but imagine—Dungda slew many dwarves including Zasit's husband. The creature's maker could also be cross-referenced in the history, and had a story of her own:

> Ducim Gemwander was a dwarf necromancer. She was one of the first of her kind.
> In 68, Ducim became the champion of The Eternal Ship.
> In 69, Shorast Heatedspears and Ducim became lovers.
> In 70, Shorast Heatedspears and Ducim broke up.
> In the midsummer of 70, Ducim became obsessed with her own mortality and sought to extend her life by any means being too vain to give in to death.

The jilted lover then spent the next seventy years performing terrible experiments on mortals, creating an army of undead slaves, the "fists of Ducim." One of them, decades later, would kill her ex-lover—since become a renowned soldier—on the field of battle.

Thousands of these stories lie buried in each history generated by *Dwarf Fortress*, stock templates and random events interacting in often surprising ways. The human compulsion to read between the lines helps bring these chronicles to life, supplying motivation and character that may or may not have actually been present in the simulation. Ducim Gemwander's career in necromancy might have been unrelated to her doomed romance; perhaps it was mere accident, not deliberate irony, that one of her hideous creations took up a career in the arts. The historical events provide bones of narrative, which each player's inner storyteller can't help but bring to life.

Dwarven biographies, like Zasit's quoted at the start of this chapter, are another form of generated text unique to each game, and the principal way to learn about your fortress builders during play. In more recent updates, these bios can stretch to multiple screens of dense text containing copious details about a dwarf's history, personality, current moods, memories, skills, and weaknesses. While the level of depth can feel overwhelming, the Adams brothers have carefully refined the bios over time to help players tell their own emergent stories about fortress residents. They eventually realized that "the descriptions most likely to be incorporated into player stories are reflected mechanically."[5] Mentioning a dwarf's likes and dislikes provides a concrete way for a player to understand why a dwarf is unhappy or take action to cheer them up; by contrast, an attempt to add mannerism descriptions like "She taps her foot when she is nervous" was deemed a failure, because players couldn't connect these tics to anything actionable in the simulation. Ideally, each sentence in a dwarf bio is both a window and a lever, a means both of understanding and change.

The complexity of dwarves and their life stories grows as the game continues to deepen. In 2018, dwarves gained an elaborate system of memory formation:

> The strongest events in several categories, such as "work" or "family," are selected and stored into a first layer of memories each season. Any existing weaker memories here are overwritten (that is, forgotten). Dwarves, at random, can remember any memory in the top layer, and re-experience the emotion they felt when it happened, often with less severity. This adds or subtracts stress from the dwarf in the standard way…. After more time passes, any top layer memory that has survived the overwriting process passes to a deeper layer of permanent memory. This process always causes personality changes in the dwarf, related loosely to the circumstance and which emotion it produced.[5]

Memories and the ability to relive them can lead to dwarves with post-traumatic shock constantly reliving a violent attack or brooding over the death of a loved one, or to dwarves whose strong connections to family—or even just the memory of a good party—help them struggle through hard times. They open another door of understanding into the characters the player spends time with, another foundation on which stories can be built.

The game also generates another kind of text: descriptions of objects built by dwarves. Fortress inhabitants can create furniture, artworks, or engravings inspired by events they remember, people in their lives, or histories they know. An unskilled artist might craft a simple item with a one-line descriptor, like this bust of Zedotkol's expedition leader:

> a finely-crafted claystone statue of 'Boss' Cityfaces

But as skills rise, constructions can become far more elaborate, incorporating both ancient legends and significant recent events into their designs. A dwarf named Edëm Towerpaint, inspired by the mysterious loss of a favorite item, snuck a beautiful if somewhat self-indulgent memorial into one of his crafting projects:

> This is a gold sarcophagus. All craftsdwarfship is of the highest quality. It is encrusted with rose cut citrines, decorated with willow and encircled with bands of octagon cut citrines and cushion diorite cabochons. This object menaces with spikes of diorite.
>
> On the item is an image of Stukos Mazewound the dwarf and dwarves in alpaca wool. Stukos Mazewound is surrounded by the dwarves. The artwork relates to the ascension of the dwarf Stukos Mazewound to the position of baroness of The Glad Lash in 194.
>
> On the item is an image of Edëm Towerpaint the dwarf in hazel wood. Edëm Towerpaint is weeping. The artwork relates to the destruction of the superior pig tail cloak created by the dwarf Edëm Towerpaint for The Tomb of Squeezing at Zedotkol in the early spring of 290 by an unknown creature.

The simplest texts the game generates are its one-line announcements of noteworthy events, some of its least procedural prose. But the announcement texts are important for more than their utilitarian value. They are a real-time, microscale counterpart to the historical chronicles, imparting a sense that your dwarves are etching their own additions into the world's vast history:

> You have struck blue jade!
> You have struck cassiterite!
> It has started raining.
> You have struck tetrahedrite!
> Iden Ducimavuz has become a Miner.
> Mistêm Fikodlun has become a Carpenter.
> The weather has cleared.
> It is now summer.
> Aban Unnosbim has become a Herbalist.
> Some migrants have arrived.
> Edëm Towerpaint has created a masterpiece ¤claystone ring¤!
> There is nothing to catch in the central swamps.
> Zasit Bomreksezuk, Peasant cancels Forge iron war hammer: Needs 1 iron bars.
> Construct Bed (6) has been completed.
> The outpost liaison Sibrek Akrultilesh from Enamstukos has arrived.
> A caravan from Enamstukos has arrived.
> You have struck yellow zircon!
> A gray langur has stolen a +almond wood cup+!
> A gray langur has stolen a *pig tail cloak*!

Each of these kinds of text—names, histories, descriptions, announcements—contribute to the experience of playing the Adams

brothers' game. But they aren't the only texts that do so. "*Dwarf Fortress* begins and ends with stories," Boluk and LeMieux have noted,[8] referring to the way written stories both inspire the game's mechanics and act as its primary output. First, the game's design is deeply informed by a practice its creators have carried out since before its first release: writing short stories set in its world, then analyzing them to see what kinds of narrative situations the game's simulation cannot yet handle. More than forty such stories have been posted to the creators' website along with the follow-up analyses. One of the earliest, "Cold Fire," begins in winter:

> An icy wind blew through the row of snow-covered log cabins, rattling the door of the huge wooden mead hall in the center of town. Inside a fire burned, sending black smoke through a hole in the ceiling. Two large tables lined either side of the fire pit. Seated at the tables were dozens of drunken warriors. In one of the beds that lined the wall slept Urgoth. Mead affected him more that most south men, and after dancing across the table he fell into unconsciousness. His fellow warriors carried him to his bed, but not before shaving the left side of his head as a malicious prank. Suddenly the doors were blazed from their hinges. A gust of wind blew snow into the hall …[7]

In the analysis, dozens of bullet points list out features that could be added to the game to help it generate new stories with the elements in "Cold Fire," such as:

- altruism: can help drunks to bed and so on

- antics: messing with drunk people, culture/environment depending

- mead hall: another place to get drunk, but has some beds as well as tables

- temperature: need to heat places indoors, can use fire pits, if fire produces smoke, need a reliable way for it to leave the building

- wind: wood doors can be rattled by wind, windchill

- narcotics: different tolerances for different people, but the median can be set by race, civ and town[7]

Over the nearly twenty years since the game's genesis, thousands of ideas like these have been collected: carefully sorted on index cards, grouped, prioritized, merged, rethought, or discarded. The process helps ensure the game's simulation keeps deepening not for its own sake, but to help it tell stories more like its human creators do.

On the other end of the pipeline, the stories generated by players of *Dwarf Fortress* have become some of its most famous outputs: retellings of in-game episodes of terrible dooms, unlikely victories, and bizarre coincidences. One of the first such tales widely shared was the epic saga of Boatmurdered,[15] a fortress played via a save file swapped between fans on the *Something Awful* forums: each new owner had one in-game year to manage the titular fortress and report back on their progress. In the end, forty managers had each added a chapter to an increasingly improbable tale involving murderous elephants, a volcano-powered doomsday machine, and the time a single

Memorable Places

(in one generated world, "Strasp Sagus, The Planets of Dawn")

The Tower of Lenses

The Whimsical Forest of Lightning

The Dwarven Mountain Halls of Tekkudkast

The Permanent Silvery Frills-Hills

The Dark Goblin Fortress of Songomu

The Mighty Prairie of Reining

The Elven Forest Retreat of Ularethi

Glandecho the Angelic Shadow

The Confederacy of Lathering

monarch butterfly flew into the open outer door of the fortress and jammed its lock just before an enemy attack.

As more players discovered the game, first dozens then hundreds of fan chronicles sprung up. The retellings became a way to let those without the patience or inclination to play themselves still experience some of the game's surreal complexity. One story involved a vampire who was terrorizing a fortress until he tripped over a cat, fell into a river, and drowned.[25] Another featured dwarves who, for some reason, were obsessed with buckets: "Roughly 90% of the engravings were of buckets, buckets surrounded by dwarves, and buckets surrounded by screaming dwarves. I stopped making engravings after a while."[20] The game's bug reports and changelogs would become their own brand of miniature stories, fascinating both for revealing the tremendous depth of the game's simulation, and because readers couldn't help but imagine stories that might justify them:

- Stopped mercenaries from being hired to attack their own forts

- Fixed crash involving stressed out wilderness creatures wanting to complain to priests

- Stopped carried newborns from setting their mothers' paths like riders

- High-flying severed body parts can leave spatters in midair

- Imprisoned vampire elected Mayor

- Stopped looping dwarves from constantly trying out gloves and boots when they should just pick one and go

- Ghost of vampires still drink blood

- Seems impossible to satisfy a need for "introspection"

Sharing *Dwarf Fortress* stories—with screenshots, fan art, and streams, but often with nothing but words—would become a huge part of the game's legacy and culture. It's "played alone," one critic wrote, but its "brutality, complexity, and unpredictability give its players a need for community—an urge to bear witness, to commiserate."[24]

As of this writing, *Dwarf Fortress* has fifteen years of reputation preceding it. By 2010 it had been downloaded a million times; within months of its release, though available for free, it was attracting enough voluntary donations to support the Adams brothers full time, if not always with complete stability. Its blocky-tiled retro aesthetic, emergent complexity, and encouragement of creative builds directly inspired *Minecraft* [Mojang 2011], the bestselling video game of all time, and its core mechanic of defensive fortifications built from nearby materials would be adopted by

---

On Vampires

The book *Getting Started with* Dwarf Fortress: *Learn to Play the Most Complex Video Game Ever Made* contains extensive tips on dealing with undead fortress denizens in a chapter called "Justice, Healthcare, and Vampires." It advises that "various tests can ... be administered to check for vampirism," such as:

Drop any dwarf down one level (using, say, a retractable drawbridge) and the dwarf will be momentarily stunned. Vampire dwarves will not show any stunned notification on their wounds info panel. Vampire dwarves cannot drown, so briefly submerging suspicious dwarves in water to see if they acquire the drowning notification status is another way to check for vampirism. One can also lock suspicious dwarves in a room and wait to see if they become hungry or thirsty. Vampires [won't].

"Vampire dwarves can be useful," the book admits: "they don't need to eat, drink booze, or sleep, so they can work tirelessly without complaint." Some possible uses: assign them "to a private barracks where the vampire can train for eternity and be brought out only in emergencies," or perhaps wall them "into a room full of levers that become the vampire's sole responsibility." Letting them run free in your fortress is not advised. "A feeding vampire may be spotted by other dwarves and accused of the crime of murder.... The clever vampire will often counter the claims of any witness and protest that another dwarf committed the crime."[21]

many other massively successful games like *Fortnite* [Epic Games 2017]. More direct descendants include a genre sometimes called "dwarflikes" that includes games like *RimWorld* [Ludeon Studios 2013] and *Prison Architect* [Introversion Software 2015]. When it was announced in 2019 that a commercial version with an upgraded interface would be coming to Steam, *Dwarf Fortress* immediately skyrocketed onto the service's top ten most wishlisted games, leapfrogging titles made by teams of hundreds. *Wired* called it "obtuse [and] wildly ambitious,"[19] the *New York Times* a "defiant throwback."[23] It was exhibited alongside other influential games at New York's Museum of Modern Art, though the curators decided not to confuse visitors by letting them actually try to play it. As a lifelong masterwork programmed mostly by a single creator, it's been compared to the Sistine Chapel; it's also been called a folk game, a labor of love unconcerned with commercial expectations or constraints. Many casual fans don't know the evocative guitar noodling that makes up the original version's soundtrack was written and performed by Tarn Adams.

"*Dwarf Fortress* is an alpha because it isn't yet many of the things it will be," Tarn said back in 2007.[6] In 2021, he still saw it as far from complete. Coming up after the Steam release is

> the largest DF restructuring and addition ever, I'm pretty sure, allowing us to generate creation myths and have entire procedural magic systems.… That'll be great. Then there's the property/law/customs/etc. release. After that, the order isn't set, but it'll involve the economy, boats, and other major missing components. There's a lot left to do![4]

"We aren't even halfway to 1.0 yet," Tarn concludes. "And 1.0 isn't really completing the game … we just might not have a lot of time left by the time we get there." In the meantime, *Dwarf Fortress* keeps evolving, with each new update expanding the space of possible tales its rules can tell, tiny simulations of people endlessly reliving the stories imbued in them by their creators.

> Overall, she is unfocused by unmet needs. She is not distracted after being away from people. She is untroubled after staying occupied. She is unfocused after being unable to take it easy. […]
>
> A short, sturdy creature fond of drink and industry.

References

1 Adams, Tarn. 2008. "Interview: The Making Of Dwarf Fortress." Interview by John Harris. *Gamasutra* (blog), Feb 27, 2008. www.gamasutra.com/view/feature/131954/interview_the_making_of_dwarf_.php | a Aug 15, 2021

2 Adams, Tarn. 2015. "Simulation Principles from Dwarf Fortress." In *Game AI Pro 2*, ed. Steve Rabin. O'Reilly.

3 Adams, Tarn. 2016. "Dwarf Fortress' Creator On How He's 42% Towards Simulating Existence." Interview by Wes Fenlon. *PC Games* (blog), Mar 31, 2016. www.pcgamer.com/dwarf-fortress-creator-on-how-hes-42-towards-simulating-existence | a Aug 15, 2021

4 Adams, Tarn. 2019. "Q&A: Dissecting the development of Dwarf Fortress with creator Tarn Adams." Interview by John Harris. *Gamasutra* (blog), Jun 3, 2019. www.gamasutra.com/view/news/343859/

QA_Dissecting_the_development_of_Dwarf_Fortress_with_creator_Tarn_Adams.php | a Aug 15, 2021

5 Adams, Tarn. 2021. "Characterization and Emergent Narrative in Dwarf Fortress." In *Narrative Mechanics: Strategies and Meanings in Games and Real Life*, ed. Beat Suter, René Bauer, and Mela Kocher. transcript-Verlag.

6 Adams, Tarn, and Bill Harris. 2007. "The Dwarf Fortress Interview." *Dubious Quality* (blog), Jan 3, 2007. dubiousquality.blogspot.com/2007/01/dwarf-fortress-interview.html | a Aug 15, 2021

7 Adams, Zach. 2006. "Cold Fire." Dwarf Fortress (Bay 12 Games). May 25, 2006. www.bay12games.com/dwarves/story/tt_cold_fire.html | a Aug 15, 2021

8 Boluk, Stephanie, and Patrick LeMieux. 2013. "Dwarven Epitaphs: Procedural Histories in Dwarf Fortress." In *Comparative Textual Media: Transforming the Humanities in the Postprint Era*, ed N. Katherine Hayles and Jessica Pressman. University of Minnesota Press.

9 Costikyan, Greg. 2007. "Dwarf Fortress" (review). *Play This Thing* (blog). Dec 2, 2007. www.playthisthing.com/dwarf-fortress | a Aug 15, 2021

10 Diaz, Joshua Lindsay. 2009. "Dwarf Fortress Gathers at the Statue and Attends a Party." PhD Thesis, MIT, Department of Comparative Media Studies.

11 Donovan, Ryan. 2021. "700,000 Lines of Code, 20 Years, and One Developer: How Dwarf Fortress Is Built." *Stack Overflow Blog*. Jul 28, 2021. stackoverflow.blog/2021/07/28/700000-lines-of-code-20-years-and-one-developer-how-dwarf-fortress-is-built | a Aug 15, 2021

12 Hall, Charlie. 2014. "Dwarf Fortress Will Crush Your CPU Because Creating History Is Hard." *Polygon* (blog). Jul 23, 2014. www.polygon.com/2014/7/23/5926447/dwarf-fortress-will-crush-your-cpu-because-creating-history-is-hard | a Aug 15, 2021

13 Harris, Bill. 2006. "Dwarf Fortress." *Dubious Quality* (blog). Sep 7, 2006. dubiousquality.blogspot.com/2006/09/dwarf-fortress.html | a Aug 15, 2021

14 "Jay Fenlason's Hack." n.d. NetHack Wiki. nethackwiki.com/wiki/Jay_Fenlason%27s_Hack | a Aug 15, 2021

15 Let's Play Archive. 2006. "Dwarf Fortress - Boatmurdered." Nov 10, 2006. lparchive.org/Dwarf-Fortress-Boatmurdered | a Aug 15, 2021

16 Kruggsmash. 2019a. "Dwarf Fortress Short Forts: Skullhorror #4, Stress Test." Youtube video. Nov 14, 2019. www.youtube.com/watch?v=xyEvrYhmJXc | a Aug 15, 2021

17 Kruggsmash. 2019b. "Dwarf Fortress Short Forts: Skullhorror #6, Into Legend." Youtube video. Nov 28, 2019. www.youtube.com/watch?v=PPjXSD12Gbo | a Aug 15, 2021

18 Livingston, Christopher. 2016. "The Most Ridiculous Patch Notes from 10 Years of Dwarf Fortress." *PC Gamer* (blog). Aug 8, 2016. www.pcgamer.com/the-most-ridiculous-patch-notes-from-10-years-of-dwarf-fortress | a Aug 15, 2021

19 Mastrapa, Gus. 2010. "Elaborate, Sprawling Freeware Dwarf Fortress Updated." *Wired*, Apr 1, 2010. www.wired.com/2010/04/dwarf-fortress | a Aug 15, 2021

20 taran. 2010. "Buckets." *Dwarf Fortress Stories* (blog). Jul 19, 2010. dfstories.com/buckets | a Aug 15, 2021

21 Tyson, Peter. 2012. *Getting Started with Dwarf Fortress: Learn to Play the Most Complex Video Game Ever Made*. O'Reilly.

22 Urquhart, Evan. 2019. "The Dwarves Who Built the Road to Fortnite." *Slate* (blog). Jun 6, 2019. slate.com/technology/2019/06/dwarf-fortress-fortnite-minecraft-strange-play-it.html | a Aug 15, 2021

23 Weiner, Jonah. 2011. "Where Do Dwarf-Eating Carp Come From?" *New York Times*, Jul 21, 2011, sec. Magazine. www.nytimes.com/2011/07/24/magazine/the-brilliance-of-dwarf-fortress.html | a Aug 15, 2021

24 Winslow-Yost, Gabriel. 2013. "SimCity's Evil Twin." *New Yorker* (blog). Apr 11, 2013. www.newyorker.com/culture/culture-desk/simcitys-evil-twin | a Aug 15, 2021

25 zellthemedic. 2013. "Hilarious Dorf Stories." Reddit Post, r/dwarffortress, Oct 20, 2013. www.reddit.com/r/dwarffortress/comments/1otfiv/hilarious_dorf_stories | a Aug 15, 2021

2006

LIEUX COMMUNS

(Common Places)

Members of ifiction.free.fr, including JB, Stormi (Samuel Verschelde), Otto Grimwald (Eric Forgeot), Mule hollandaise (Hugo Labrande), Jean-Luc Pontico, and Stab

Style **Parser**   *Debuted* **Jun 15, 2007**   *Platform* **Z-machine**   *Language* **Inform 6 (French)**

Après avoir cheminé quelques heures dans des territoires pour moi encore relativement familiers, je m'étais retrouvé à continuer cette balade vers un chemin inconnu, sans m'en rendre tout à fait compte à ce moment.

After walking some hours in territories still relatively known to me, I found myself wandering toward an unknown path, without in that moment quite realizing it.

EL MUSEO DE LAS CONSCIENCIAS

(The Museum of Consciences)

Mel Hython aka Melitón (Juan Antonio Paz Salgado), Santiago Eximeno, Urbatain / Ruber Eaglenest (Ruben Alberto Aguilera Nieto), Grendel Khan (Xavier Carrascosa), and Depresiv (Pablo Martínez Merino)

Style **Parser**   *Debuted* **Jun 15, 2007**   *Platform* **Z-machine**   *Language* **Inform 7 (Spanish)**

Tu padre te abandonó cuando aún no tenías uso de razón. Te dejó en una casa en la cima de una pequeña colina, al cuidado de dos mujeres siniestras, eternamente vestidas de negro. Te abandonó a los rincones oscuros, a las alargadas sombras de la vieja casa, a los silencios y al tedio. Puede que tu padre haya muerto en algún lugar allá fuera. Esperas y deseas que haya sido así.

Your father abandoned you when you were too young to remember. He left you in a house on the top of a knoll, in the care of two sinister women forever dressed in black. He abandoned you to the dark corners and long shadows of the old house, to its silences and to its tedium. Perhaps your father died, somewhere out there. You hope and dream that he did.

"THERE'S THIS GREAT BUBBLE THAT IS ENGLISH INTERACTIVE FICTION," a Spanish-speaking game maker once wrote,

> free from problems or constant threats. Hovering outside it are other, smaller bubbles, communities using other languages, influenced by the English bubble but incapable of influencing the others, unable to communicate with them. That lack of communication leads them to feel isolated, at first, and then a sense of futility, when efforts to carry out a project aren't rewarded, when the number of potential players of one of our stories doesn't compensate for the work we've invested in them.[18]

The author, Depresiv—like many in the Spanish IF community, he goes by a handle there rather than his given name—was explaining how he came to be involved with an unusual project that brought together text game creators working in English, Spanish, and French. The unifying theme of the project was connected to American horror writer H. P. Lovecraft, but that wasn't why Depresiv wanted to take part. Instead, his motivation was "the possibility that something like this, in which three different languages live together in the same project, might help break that silence."

The project was centered around Lovecraft's "Commonplace Book," a collection of over two hundred mostly unused ideas the writer had compiled during his career. For the seventieth anniversary of his death, the Maison d'Ailleurs, a museum of science fiction in Switzerland, had decided to stage an exhibition with a unique twist: artists would be invited to choose a single idea from the book and create an artwork inspired by it. A hundred artists would end up participating, including well-known names like writer Christopher Priest (*The Prestige*) and artist H. R. Giger, who picked idea #144:

Hideous book glimpsed in ancient shop—never seen again.

American IF author Peter Nepstad had been doing research for a series of horror games inspired by Lovecraft predecessors like Lord Dunsany when he stumbled on the Swiss museum's website. Since writers were already included, penning original short stories for the exhibition's catalog, it struck him that the museum might be open to including interactive fiction inspired by Lovecraft as well. The submission deadline had already passed, but Nepstad emailed the curator anyway, with the thought of contributing an original game inspired by a "Commonplace Book" entry. The museum was located in the French-speaking part of Switzerland and, eager to sweeten the deal, Nepstad promised—perhaps unwisely—that he could arrange for some French work to be included as well. The curator wrote back and seemed open to the idea, saying "Something in English + French would be great."[15] Now Nepstad had a problem: not a French speaker, he suddenly needed to find one who could write IF, was a fan of horror, and would be interested in participating in a cooperative project in a very short time frame.

Fortunately, a French IF game called *Ekphrasis* [2006] had recently made waves in the English-speaking community via translation, winning rare multilingual acclaim. Nepstad reached out to its author, who went by JB, to see if he might be interested in the project. "You could just do a translation of my game," Nepstad offered, "but that doesn't sound like as much fun."[15] JB reposted the offer on ifiction.free.fr, a forum of French-speaking IF creators, to see if there was any interest. A poster there who went by Otto Grimwald (today better known as Eric Forgeot) asked in response, "Pourquoi pas en faire une IF commune?" (Why not make it a communal IF?)

> It might be nice if there were several of us working together, which will be more fun (no doubt), take less work (maybe), and would still let us finish [our own games for] the French competition (which, of course, is imperative…)[9]

The French IF community had an almost entirely different backstory than the English-speaking one. While most American and British fans had grown up playing (or at least retroactively admiring) the classic 1980s text adventures of companies like Infocom or Magnetic Scrolls, France had skipped over pure text games entirely. By the mid-1980s, when enough personal computers were on the market there to warrant a professional games market, graphics were already well established, and since many young game makers were strongly influenced by the huge French comics scene, there was little appetite for making games with no art. It wasn't until the 2000s, when a handful of French speakers discovered the newer games of the English IF renaissance like *Photopia* **1998** and *Galatea* **2000**, that a community of French fans came together to try making their own text-only games. Attempts came slowly—first translations, then original titles—with the first regular French IF competition, mirroring the English-centric IF Comp, not appearing until 2005. French interactive fiction was still young, and Nepstad's invitation seemed a great opportunity to showcase it to a community of international players. The French authors proposed a communal game, an omnibus of short pieces each inspired by a different entry from Lovecraft's tome of ideas. They titled it *Lieux communs*, or *Common Places*, after both their collaborative effort and the source of inspiration.

With not just one or two titles but a whole collection of games now in the works, Nepstad hoped to broaden participation as widely as possible, and he announced the project on the English IF newsgroups on April 9, 2007. Anyone was welcome to contribute a game in any language, though with a deadline just two months away. A few years earlier, Nepstad had found modest commercial success selling a boxed IF game on CD-ROM—his ambitious historical adventure *1893: A World's Fair Mystery* [2002]—and he'd started a company called Illuminated Lantern to sell it and explore the possibilities of publishing more interactive fiction. The Commonplace Book Project, he thought, had the potential to become something quite unique: a multilingual anthology of IF that could be exhibited at festivals and archived in libraries, an ambassador for text games to horror fans around the world.

Another international IF community took note of Nepstad's announcement. Spanish interactive fiction had developed on yet another unique trajectory. The larger number of Spanish speakers worldwide had made commercial text games in the language more viable in the 80s, and *aventuras conversacionales* (conversational adventures) were for a while a popular market share. One game company based in Spain had a unique line for their text adventures called Aventuras AD, and a fan club called CAAD (Club de Aventuras AD) became a popular community hub for enthusiasts toward the end of the decade. CAAD held contests for homebrew games written in languages like PAW or the Spanish-specific tool SINTAC (Sistema INTegrado de creación de Aventuras Conversacionales). When commercial text games died, clubs like CAAD and an existing culture of amateur games kept Spanish-speaking fans more unified than English fans had been. The wave of tools like Inform that came out of the 90s English IF renaissance were eagerly adopted by the Spanish community, with fan-made libraries like José Luis Diaz's InformATE—Inform Ahora Totalmente en Español (Now Totally in Spanish)—providing a foundation for many new works. Within days of Nepstad's announcement, a group of Spanish authors contacted him to say that their community, too, wanted to submit an anthology game. Over a dozen stories in three different languages were now planned to be part of the project.

Not all participants were especially enamored of Lovecraft. While his writings had become a foundational pillar of genre fan culture at the end of the twentieth century, fewer and fewer readers were willing to overlook the implicit and often entirely explicit racism in the famously xenophobic writer's work. In response to Nepstad's announcement, one poster noted that "Commonplace Book" entry #108 was *Educated mulatto seeks to displace personality of white man and occupy his body*. Not all fans had yet begun the deeper soul-searching that would result in a more thorough condemnation and reevaluation of Lovecraft over the next decade (resulting in novels like *Lovecraft Country* and *The Ballad of Black Tom*, among others). But some of the Commonplace Book Project authors kept the tension in mind while creating their entries. One of the Spanish pieces begins with a familiar story of a white man making an archaeological dig in nineteenth-century Africa, but has the player take on the role of a local Maasai warrior with a less foolish perspective than the *viejo mago blanco* (old white wizard) who would undoubtedly have been Lovecraft's narrator. "The horror of Lovecraft and his friends was based on fear of the other, the strange," wrote Melitón, another of the Spanish contributors. "It seems to me kind of outdated, from the beginning of the twentieth century."[18]

With only two months to write, each community adopted different strategies for organizing and creating their games. The French IFers set up a source code repository and, rather than give each author ownership of particular stories, encouraged anyone in the community to contribute to each story however they could, "whether with art, writing text, researching ideas or puzzles, proofreading, correcting spelling, grammar or coordination etc."[8] Filling in missing item or room descriptions was a way even a busy student could contribute (at least one collaborator was still in high school), and the final game would be credited to all of ifiction.free.fr, rather than individual authors. The collaborators first agreed on a frame story—a ghostly caravan filled with mysterious objects, based on "Commonplace Book" entry #99:

see **1993**

LLEVAS...

» una bolsa de cuero ritual (abierta)

» algo de polvo blanco

» unas tijeras

» un libro de cubiertas negras

ÁREAS MEMORABLES

Entrada al museo

Sala del Corazón

Interior de tu coche

La plaza del Ojo de Canopus

Un lugar de piedras y sal bajo la noche

2007

Salem story–the cottage of an aged witch–wherein after her death are found sundry terrible things.

Forgeot set up an Inform 6 file for the frame story with a script that could fold in other story files found within the source repository. Authors were asked to name their files with the number of their "Commonplace Book" inspiration, and to give any items the same number as a suffix, to avoid namespace problems ("because if you have a door called Door, and I have the same in my game, it will get stuck"[9]). In part to make the project more accessible to imagined players in a Swiss art gallery, the team decided to include music and illustrations, and to keep puzzles simple. While the style and subject varied with each story and contributor, many of the French games trended more philosophical and dreamlike, their prose flowing perhaps better in the original than in translation:

> **Le long de la rivière**
> Voici où nous mènent nos pas, lorsqu'on les confie à nos pensées dérivantes…
>
> Las d'un voyage dont seules les parts obscures de mon imagination en étaient les étapes, je me trouvai malgré moi loin de tout, sur les rives d'un fleuve charriant des eaux sombres vers un Océan dont la rumeur saline me parvenait indistinctement.

> **Along the river**
> Here is where our steps lead us, when we entrust them to our drifting thoughts…
>
> Weary of a journey with only the most obscure parts of my imagination as its stages, I found myself far from everything, on the banks of a river carrying dark waters toward an Ocean whose saline rumblings reached me but obscurely.

One vignette begins with you drifting at sea, the lost survivor of a shipwreck. Coming to rest on a spar of jagged obsidian, you find a bronze trapdoor inscribed with the sigil of an eye surrounded by eight tentacles. After opening it you descend into murky darkness through dripping-wet caverns, eventually passing through a gate unlocked by a sonic code to find an enormous city, La Cité sous les Eaux (the City Under the Water):

> Résister à la folie… et contempler, dans leurs insaisissables dimensions, les blocs monolithiques verdâtres, alignés selon une géométrie non euclidienne, des statues gargantuesques et immondes gravées de hiéroglyphes dérangeants, de tous côtés, et même au-dessus sur un plafond lointain que je me refusais d'imaginer.

J'AVAIS…
» une petite idole
» un ocarina
» un pendentif de corail
» une pioche
» un ourson en peluche

ZONES MÉMORABLES

Sur un col glacial

Dans le temple hors du temps

En plein Océan

Les Portes Cyclopéennes de la Cité Engloutie

Petit sous-marin scientifique

2007

JB, who wrote this sequence
of the game, would later go
on to become a full-time
game developer under the
handle FibreTigre, creating
(among other titles) the
award-winning narrative
indie hit *Out There* [Mi-Clos
Studio 2014].

> To resist the madness... and contemplate, in their elusive dimensions,
> the green-tinged monolithic blocks, aligned in a non-Euclidean
> geometry, gargantuan and filthy statues engraved with disturbing
> hieroglyphs on all sides, even above on a distant ceiling that I couldn't
> bring myself to imagine.

The Spanish community's games hewed closer to the standard auteur-driven mode of IF authorship, with each vignette given a title and credited to particular authors, and thus they exhibited a somewhat wider range of styles and subjects. Here the frame story was inspired by entry #167:

> *Boy rear'd in atmosphere of considerable mystery. Believes father dead. Suddenly is told that father is about to return. Strange preparations–consequences.*

The "strange preparations" in *El museo de las consciencias* (*The Museum of Consciences*) involve a gallery of curious relics assembled by your absent father. As in *Lieux communs*, each object is an excuse to transition into a new vignette. The Spanish collaborators, in contrast to the French authors newly arrived to the hobby, were mostly old veterans of the 80s scene, and they brought a range of concepts and styles to the scenarios they created. In one scene set in the present day, you play an addict whose bad coke trip triggers a hallucinogenic nightmare. "Trying to convey through written words what a drugged mind might feel is very difficult," wrote reviewer Dwalin for *SPAC*, a Spanish IF review site, "even more so when given the form of an interactive story. The result is very disconcerting at first."[6]

> \>X CD
>
> Ojos gusanos cornea se posan sobre la caja de CD. Literalmente se
> esfuma ante tus ojos, junto con las cositas verdes. Humo blanco sale y
> forma como caras-gusanos-colmillo en el aire.
>
> Ahí fuera está ese tipo. Es bueno es calidad, 30 euros. Pagas y tomas-
> sonrisa podrida de dientes-rubia gusanos come ojos. Excelente material
> el del umbral. eso es todo- ojos azules se acercan-algo de molestia al
> desgarrar la córnea eso es todo, pagas y te vas.
>
> \>SAL DEL COCHE
>
> Aproximas tu mano hacia la puerta, pero gusanos verdes cornea
> salen de tu piel. La han devorado y buscando a ciegas encuentras el
> suelo entre vómitos de JB y Mc'Donalds—Caen más gusanos de tí y el
> cemento se vuelve tierra fresca. Gusanos salen de tus orejas y la música
> de discoteca suena como tambores de guerra en la lejanía. No es cierto
> y sin embargo ahí está—sin duda—muy conocido. Caras-gusano se
> esfuman en el aire como billetes y por un momento dejas de gritar. [...]
>
> Te tocas la cara y te frotas los ojos, sí los tienes. De hecho, estás bastante
> bien, a pesar de los temblores y el sudor frio que empapa tu ropa. Algo
> hay que no va bien, tras las plantas te pareció haber observado un
> extraño movimiento. ¿Plantas?

>EXAMINA PLANTAS
Ya te he dicho—chaval—que todo son imaginaciones tuyas. sin duda
es producto de las drogas y de tu inagotable imaginación-es bueno es
calidad. monos en el aire como gusanos-córnea alimentándose de pulpa
en deportivos rojos. plantas moviéndose en el umbral.

>EXAMINE CD
Corneal eyeworms pose on the cover of the CD case. It literally vanishes
before your eyes, along with the little green things. White smoke rises
and forms wormfangfaces in the air.

That guy is out there. Good stuff good quality, 30 euros. You pay
and take it—smile rotten with teeth—pale eye-eating worms. The
threshold's got great stuff. that's all—blue eyes getting closer—some
discomfort when tearing the cornea that's all, you pay and you go.

>GET OUT OF THE CAR
You reach for the door, but green corneaworms sprout from your skin.
They've devoured it and searching blindly you find the ground amidst
vomited JB and McDonalds—More worms fall from you and the cement
becomes fresh earth. Worms burst from your ears and club music
sounds like war drums in the distance. Not true and yet there it is, no
doubt, very known. Wormfaces evaporate into the air like scattering bills
and for a moment you stop screaming. [...]

You touch your face and rub your eyes, yes you have them. In fact,
you're doing quite well, despite the shivering and cold sweat soaking
your clothes. Something's wrong, behind the plants you think you see
weird movement. Plants?

>LOOK AT PLANTS
I already told you—kid—it's all your imagination. without a doubt a
product of drugs and your inexhaustible imagination—good stuff good
quality. monkeys floating in the air like corneaworms feeding on flesh in
red sports cars. plants moving on the threshold.

The distant music turns out to be from a demonic rave happening behind
the unreal vegetation, reachable perhaps only because of your drugged
state (and inspired by entry #11: *Odd nocturnal ritual. Beasts dance and march
to musick*). The scene degenerates into a demonic orgy—"Yeah, we snuck a
pornographic piece into a Swiss museum," one of the collaborators cheekily
recalled. In another scene with a wholly different tone, you become a
member of an ancient, doomed sea-dwelling people:

>ENTRA AL MAR
Con agilidad propia de tu raza saltas hacia el mar y él te recibe con
suavidad. Sois partes de una misma cosa.

El Mar
Esto es el mar. ¿Qué más hay que decir? Es el Lugar. Todo viene de estas aguas siempre en movimiento, siempre frías, siempre amables...

>ENTER THE SEA
With the agility typical of your people, you dive into the sea, and he receives you gently. You are parts of the same thing.

The Sea
This is the sea. What more is there to say? It is the Place. Everything comes from these waters always in motion, always cold, always kind...

Writing IF in languages other than English was made much simpler by using Inform, which had been designed with an eye for localization—in fact, a hefty chapter of its manual concerned teaching it to read and write other languages. A language definition file could instruct Inform in how to do everything from recognizing verbs:

```
Verb "ecrire"
    *                                          -> Ecrire
    * 'sur'/'dans' noun                        -> Ecrire
    * 'avec' held                              -> Ecrire
    * 'sur'/'dans' noun 'avec' held            -> Ecrire
    * 'avec' held 'sur'/'dans' noun            -> Ecrire
    * topic 'sur'/'dans' noun                  -> Ecrire
    * topic 'avec' held                        -> Ecrire
    * topic 'sur'/'dans' noun 'avec' held      -> Ecrire
    * topic 'avec' held 'sur'/'dans' noun      -> Ecrire
    * topic                                    -> Ecrire;
```

To parsing pronouns:

```
Array LanguagePronouns table

    !  word          possible GNAs
    !                to follow:
    !                a    i
    !                s  p  s  p
    !                mfnmfnmfnmfn

        ! Object pronouns
        '-le'     $$100000100000
        '-la'     $$010000010000
        '-les'    $$000110000110
        '-lui'    $$110000110000
        '-leur'   $$000110000110
    ! Disjunctive pronouns
        'luy'     $$110000110000
        'lui'     $$100000100000
        'elle'    $$010000010000
        'eux'     $$000110000110
        'elles'   $$000010000010
```

To printing default messages:

```
Close: switch (n) {
        1: "Fermer cela me semblait impossible. ";
        2: print (ctheyreorthats) x1, " déjà fermé";
           if (x1 has female) "e.";
           ".";
        3: "Je fermai ", (the) x1, ".";
}
```

Each new language definition had to solve its own unique problems. While spaces work well to separate tokens in an English command like TAKE THE BAG, more elaborate strategies were necessary to pull out the components of a French command like ALLER A L'EST (go east), or a Spanish reflexive verb like EXAMINARME (examine myself). Gender in English only exists for animates (humans and animals), but authors in both French and Spanish needed to define a gender for every object in their simulated worlds so the game could correctly understand, and generate sentences about, both *un pendentif* and *une pioche*. Both languages also faced challenges with dialects. While the original Inform supports switching between American and British English, the minor spelling and style variations that result are less significant than the stakes behind setting a Spanish game to `dialecto sudamericano` versus `dialecto castellano`. The verb in Spain for "to take," for instance, has a vulgar meaning in parts of Latin America, so setting the correct dialect is key to avoiding the kind of awkward mistake sometimes seen while playing Spanish games via online translation services, which don't have the benefit of regional context:

> \>TAKE THE BAG
> Fucked.

As the French and Spanish teams sprinted toward a polished set of vignettes for their anthologies, Nepstad invited other communities to participate. He reached out to fans making graphical adventure games, leading to two point-and-click submissions from creators working in engines called Wintermute and Lassie. Among English IF authors, one submission came in using the user-friendly creation tool ADRIFT, which lets authors define a game mostly through menus rather than code. Jon Ingold, later to co-found game studio inkle, contributed a well-regarded piece, *Dead Cities,* inspired by one of the most scattered "Commonplace Book" entries, #67:

see *80 Days* **2014**

> *An impression–city in peril–dead city–equestrian statue–men in closed room– clattering hooves heard outside–marvel disclosed on looking out–doubtful ending.*

Nepstad contributed his own game written in his favorite IF design language, TADS. In total, seven games were included, almost every one using a different framework for making interactive fiction—a fascinating snapshot of community tooling at the end of the century's first decade. If each story in the French and Spanish anthologies were counted separately, the whole project included a hefty twenty games. The entries debuted on

2007

the IF newsgroups on June 18, 2007; afterward, Nepstad worked with the authors to polish up final versions and assemble them in a slicker package that included a unified launcher, which he then submitted to the Swiss curator. The games were accepted into the exhibition, which opened at the Maison d'Ailleurs just in time for Halloween that year and ran through the following spring. In a gallery filled with creepy art, a computer in a corner let attendees take a break to play through a handful of creepy interactive stories too.

As Depresiv had noted, each community of game makers lives in its own bubble, often isolated from others by barriers of technology, privilege, convention, and language. Sometimes it's hard to keep those bubbles afloat. Nepstad had also reached out to the Italian interactive fiction community, but got a response back that it was "sleeping," with not enough members then active to make a contribution; German IF fans had been around a few years earlier, but not much had been heard from them lately. There had been Russian IF, but no one in the English community knew who to talk to about it. And even for "active" communities, the term could be relative. The French IF group was a tiny cadre of fans; other text game niches were kept alive by only two or three members, circles where beggars could not afford to be choosers. Melitón had taken to writing harsh reviews of Spanish games purely to inure the community to criticism. One of his excoriating critiques ended nevertheless with a mostly rhetorical question: "¿Lo recomendaría entonces? Sí, claro, hay en realidad tan poco que interleer."[17] (So would I recommend it? Yes, of course, there's really so little [Spanish IF] to play.)

Fear of the unknown has often kept creators working in different languages apart. Fear of not understanding, of looking foolish, of making mistakes, or—worst, for a creator in a fragile bubble—of being ignored. Yet as Melitón noted, perhaps this flavor of fear is one we ought to leave in the previous century. Google Translate and similar tools make it far easier than it once was to play interactive fiction in languages you don't speak at all, if you're willing to make a little effort to try; any amount of fluency makes the prospect much easier. And a bit of reaching out, as Nepstad showed, can go a long way. It's ironic that a project celebrating the xenophobic Lovecraft helped, for a moment, to unite groups of fans with different backgrounds and cultures into common purpose. Maybe it should happen more often. Though it's sometimes hard to remember, the common places of the internet were meant to help bring us together.

References

1   Aeron. 2007. "An Exhibit Of Unspeakable Things." *Monster Brains* (blog). Nov 8, 2007. monsterbrains.blogspot.com/2007/11/exhibit-of-unspeakable-things-here-is.html | a Sep 23, 2021

2   "Club de Aventuras AD." n.d. WikiCAAD. wiki.caad.es/CAAD | a Sep 23, 2021

3   Depresiv. 2007a. "Los juegos del Commonplace Book Project ya están disponibles." Forum post. CAAD: Comunidad de Aventuras Conversacionales y Relatos Interactivos. Jun 19, 2007. foro.caad.es/viewtopic.php?t=1702 | a Sep 23, 2021

4   Depresiv. 2007b. "A History of Spanish IF." *SPAG* #49, Aug 18, 2007. www.spagmag.org/archives/backissues/spag49.html | a Sep 23, 2021

5   Despresiv. 2008. "Lieux Communs" (review). *SPAG* #51, Apr 6, 2008. www.spagmag.org/archives/

backissues/spag51.html#Lieux | a Sep 23, 2021

6   Dwalin. 2007. "El Museo de las Consciencias" (review). *SPAC* #51, July 2007. spac.caad.es/1/spac51.htm#a4 | a Sep 23, 2021

7   Eriorg. 2007. "A Timeline of the French IF Community." *SPAG* #47, Jan 16, 2007. www.spagmag.org/archives/backissues/spag47.html | a Sep 23, 2021

8   Grimwald, Otto. 2007. "Maison d'Ailleurs : An exhibition of Unspeakable Things." Forum post. IFictionFR: La fiction interactive francophone. Apr 4, 2007. ifiction.free.fr/taverne/viewtopic.php?p=&t=268 | a Sep 23, 2021

9   JB. 2007. "Projet Franco-Anglais / proposition de Peter Nepstad." Forum post. IFictionFR: La fiction interactive francophone. Mar 20, 2007. ifiction.free.fr/taverne/viewtopic.php?p=&t=263 | a Sep 23, 2021

10 Labrande, Hugo. 2011. "Racontons Une Histoire Ensemble: History and Characteristics of French IF." In *IF Theory Reader*, ed. Kevin Jackson-Mead and J. Robinson Wheeler. Boston, MA: >TRANSCRIPT ON PRESS.

11 Maison d'Ailleurs. 2007. "An Exhibition of Unspeakable Things: Works Inspired by H. P. Lovecraft's Commonplace Book." www.ailleurs.ch/uk/expo_d.php?id=love | s Apr 30, 2008

12 Mastodon. 2009. "El Museo de las Consciencias" (review). IFDB. Oct 7, 2009. ifdb.org/viewgame?id=oe62obqziewqgik&review=8943 | a Sep 23, 2021

13 Nepstad, Peter. 2007a. "ANNOUNCE: HP Lovecraft Commonplace Book Comp and Exhibit." Usenet post, rec.games.int-fiction, Apr 9, 2007. groups.google.com/g/rec.games.int-fiction/c/1JeUOExZPNQ/m/FL28CfVCqY8J | a Sep 23, 2021

14 Nepstad, Peter. 2007b. "The Commonplace Book Project." Illuminated Lantern. Apr 9, 2007. www.illuminatedlantern.com/if/games/lovecraft | s Dec 12, 2007

15 Nepstad, Peter. 2007c. "The H.P. Lovecraft Commonplace Book Project." *SPAG* #50, Dec 3, 2007. www.sparkynet.com/spag/backissues/spag50.html | s Mar 25, 2008

16 Nepstad, Peter. 2008. "An Interview with Peter Nepstad." Interview by Jimmy Maher. *SPAG* #51, Apr 6, 2008. www.sparkynet.com/spag/backissues/spag51.html#Nepstad | s Apr 11, 2008

17 Paz, Johan. 2010. "A Falta de Pan Mejor Repartir Tortas." *Hit It!* (blog). Apr 12, 2010. golpealo.blogspot.com/2010/04/falta-de-pan-mejor-repartir-tortas.html | a Sep 23, 2021

18 Urbatain, Clérigo. 2007. "Entrevista ignomiosa." *SPAC* #51, July 2007. spac.caad.es/1/spac51.htm#a4 | a Sep 23, 2021

VIOLET

Jeremy Freese

Style **Parser**
Debuted **Oct 1, 2008** *(IF Comp)*
Launch Platform **Z-machine v8**
Language **Inform 7**

> " Calm down. All you have to do is write a thousand words and everything will be fine. And you have all day, except it's already noon.

WHEN YOU DIE IN *Adventure* **1976**, the classic that ushered in the interactive fiction medium, narration that had previously been fairly neutral describing caverns, axes, and trolls goes a little odd:

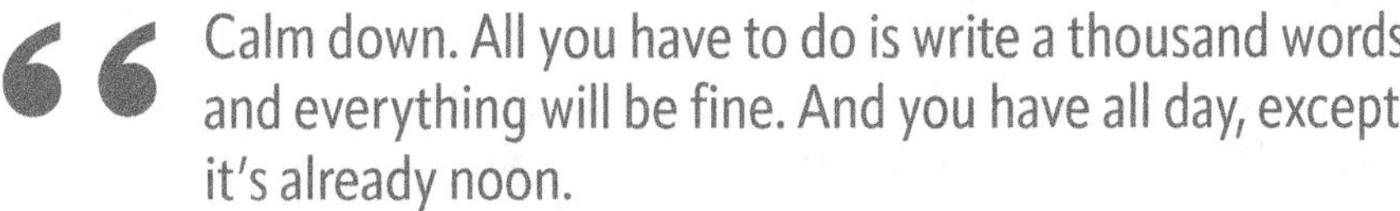

The question foregrounds something most parser games take pains to conceal—just whose voice is replying to your words? It's not *you*, the player; nor is it *you*, the character whose adventures you've been dictating. It's some third agent in between, an intermediary apparently interpreting your actions and narrating back the results. *Adventure*'s death message makes this character suddenly and a bit unexpectedly defined: someone with particular abilities, concerns, and self-doubts. It might make you wonder how much your interactions with *Adventure* have been filtered through their voice. Who, exactly, is telling you this story?

The role is somewhat akin to a narrator in traditional fiction, though interactivity makes the concept more complex—and just as traditional

2008

see **1998**

see **2015**

fiction has experimented with making narrators more visible, so too has IF. In *Photopia,* the player comes to realize that a very specific narrator is inventing the worlds their character explores, for the benefit of a very particular listener; the realization is key to understanding the story. *Fail-Safe* [Jon Ingold 2000], in a conceit used more famously by the later mobile hit *Lifeline,* pretends the intermediary isn't there at all, with your orders given directly to an astronaut who needs help. Misunderstood commands are explained away as transmissions distorted by static. In *Bellclap* [Tommy Herbert 2004], you play a god giving commands to a reluctant supplicant sheltering in your temple; the intermediary here is an angel in charge of relaying your commands and reporting back the results.

> >GO OUTSIDE
> He is refusing, sir. Citing the dangers of the rain and lightning.
>
> >GO OUTSIDE
> I shall try again...

But *Violet* would become one of IF's most famous examples of an unusual narrator, sweeping all the community's awards the year of its release. In the game you play a graduate student in the midst of a years-long dissertation slump, chronically unable either to write or to accept that you're not going to finish. When the story opens, you've been given an ultimatum by your long-suffering girlfriend, Violet, who's threatened to leave you and fly back home to Australia if you don't make concrete progress on a final make-or-break day. The game takes place on that day, in a single room—your on-campus office—and challenges you to successfully execute a single command: WRITE. But first you must deal with a seemingly endless parade of amusing distractions and excuses—amusing, that is, for *you* the player, certainly not *you* the main character.

What could have been a relatively slight puzzle game is immeasurably improved by its narrator: Violet herself, or at least the version of her in your character's head, trying her best to keep you on track.

> So now here you are, up in your office. I am sorry that today is a Saturday. I am especially sorry that today is your thirtieth birthday. We had all kinds of adventures planned. I refuse to feel guilty.
>
> [...] Just so we're clear: you are actually alone, and presumably I am back at our apartment, packing and crying.
>
> >WRITE
> You are trying, I can tell. But each time you begin to think through the opening sentence you get this dull cloudy tired pain right behind your eyes.

Everything around you is filtered through Violet's perspective. Many descriptions change each time you see them, as if Violet is noticing different details. A picture of her on your desk is described as a "framed knockout"; responses are riddled with pet names and in-jokes; an appearance by your ex is narrated in a tone dripping with sarcasm; and even the smallest action or description is a chance to get to know a character who soon comes to feel more real than your own.

> Of course I'm so used to seeing your bookcase full that it's strange now to see it nearly empty.
>
> On the second shelf is a book. On the bottom shelf is a smartly-done snowglobe.
>
> >EXAMINE SNOWGLOBE
> It's a glass globe with a plain wooden bottom. Inside is a happy winter scene, with a paunchy, smiling figurine in a white outfit and snow up to his ankles. His hands look like they are covered with chocolate.
>
> You look out the window for a moment, at the wonderfully serene park across the street. We could be frolicking right now. We could be canoodling in the shrubbery. Please just write.
>
> >TAKE SNOWGLOBE
> Yours, wallaroo. I still can't believe I stayed up two nights straight making it.
>
> >EXAMINE BOOK
> This is the latest "last book you really must read before you are able to write your dissertation without a nagging feeling that there is one more book you really must read." If you start reading it now, hours will go by, and you won't write your thousand words.
>
> >OPEN IT
> Sure, the book looks like something you'd find interesting. I'm not going to describe its contents any further, though, as I don't want to risk enticing you to start reading it.

The game's author had successfully defended his own dissertation years before, but hadn't thought he was the kind of person who could finish writing a computer game. A professor of sociology, Jeremy Freese enjoyed both writing and coding, but he liked to be honest about his chances of success at either as a side hobby. ("Many academics harbor a fantasy that perhaps one day they will write a novel," he once wrote. "I used to be one of those."[3]) Then he heard about a new design language called Inform 7, and began to reconsider his chances. He wasn't the only one who did.

Inform 7 was announced in 2006, exactly ten years after the release of Inform 6, the stable version of the language Graham Nelson had used to write *Curses* and revolutionize the indie IF scene. Despite the incremental name, it was a whole new language and a radical departure from its

MAJOR RELEASES

» **Release 1**, IF Comp, Oct 1, 2008.

» **JayIsGames release**. Fixed some bugs from the comp version.

» **Release 3**, Nov 18, 2008. Official post-competition release. "Minor bug fixes."

see **1993**

predecessor, inspired by a simple question with far-reaching implications: if the player communicated with a work of interactive fiction in natural language, and the game replied back in natural language as well, was it possible that the most sensible way to *create* such programs was also natural language?

Inform 6, like most other IF design tools, had used a traditional C-like programming syntax atop an object-oriented foundation. Locations, items, and characters were all represented as objects that could react to various actions a player might try to perform on them. But despite years of iteration into a mature and successful tool, Inform's approach, Nelson thought, had never quite felt like the right one for the job. One section of the Inform 6 manual, for instance, presented a "formal semantic description" of Inform's world model: the core assumptions about its simulated universe that underlay all other behavior. It had been written as clearly as possible so that human authors could understand it:

> 1.4.2. Some objects are "lockable" and someone with the specified "key" object can switch between mutually exclusive states, "locked" and "unlocked". These objects represent containers and doors with locks.

> 1.4.3. Some objects are "openable" and therefore in one of two mutually exclusive states, "open" and "closed". If such an object is closed and also locked then it cannot be opened. These objects represent containers and doors.[9]

But of course each of those sentences had to correspond to a block of code, often far less readable, somewhere in the compiler's internals or the standard library of behaviors. Reading over the English descriptions, Nelson found himself wondering, "Why can't Inform simply read the world-model chapter … and use that as its library?"[6]

> A door is a kind of thing. A door is always fixed in place. A door can be open or closed. A door is usually closed.

> A door can be lockable. A door is usually not lockable. A door can be locked or unlocked. A door is usually unlocked. A door has an object called a matching key.

And if the *behavior* underlying a model world could be described this way, why not also the world itself?

> The Gazebo is a room. The Gazebo is east of the Gardens. In the Gazebo are a pair of shears and a clay pot. A pale yellow flower is in the pot.

> Report taking the flower when the flower was in the pot: instead say "You gently pull it free from the soil."

Nelson ran the idea by other IF writers. Emily Short, author of *Galatea 2000* and other well-regarded Inform games, was at first unconvinced:

My reaction was, er, extreme skepticism. I didn't see how such a system could be anything but infuriating to program in; the natural language bit seemed to be at best a way for the novice to sketch out some rooms and objects, but I imagined the real work would have to be done at the I6 [Inform 6] layer, and that anyone half-competent at I6 would probably find they preferred just staying at that level. So I wrote back what I hope was a polite letter, expressing an interest in seeing what he came up with, but hinting that trading Inform's native power for this sort of convenience would be a serious mistake.[6]

But in a long correspondence that would expand into a multiyear collaboration, Nelson made the case that natural language didn't have to be just verbose syntactic sugar. Language could express complex things about the human experience and do so elegantly, so why couldn't it do the same within the simplified world of an IF simulation? A natural language syntax had the potential to describe relationships, causes and effects, behaviors, and exceptions in a more readable, elegant, and naturalistic way than code paradigms not optimized for describing simulated worlds. Take, for instance, this Inform 6 code to describe a sack bursting because too many objects have been placed inside it:

```
[ Initialise s;
  ! start a daemon for every sack object in game
  objectloop (s ofclass sack) {
    StartDaemon(s);
  }
];

Class sack
  with daemon [ unluckyholder;
    ! check to see if sack is bursting and its owner is visible
    unlucky_holder = parent(self);
    if ((self.bursting == 1) && TestScope(unlucky_holder, player)){
      print (The) self, " splits and breaks under the weight! ";
      if (unlucky_holder == player) {
        print "You discard";
      } else {
        print (The) unlucky_holder, " discards";
      }
      print " its ruined remains, looking miserably down at ";
      WriteListFrom(child(self), DEFART_BIT + ENGLISH_BIT);
      print " on the floor.^";
    }
  ],
has container;
```

The equivalent in the Inform 7 syntax Nelson eventually devised would look instead like this:

> Every turn when a container (called the sack) held by someone
> visible (called the unlucky holder) is bursting, say "[The sack] **splits**
> **and breaks under the weight!** [if the player is the unlucky holder]
> **You discard**[otherwise][The unlucky holder] **discards**[end if] **its ruined**
> **remains, looking miserably down at** [the list of things in the sack] **on**
> **the floor."**

In addition to writing the first publicly released Inform 7 game, *Mystery House Possessed* [2005], Short would also create hundreds of examples for the documentation and provide significant feedback on features and syntax.

see **1996**

Another correspondence with Andrew Plotkin, author of *So Far* and other Inform 6 hits, convinced Nelson that the primary unit of an IF language should really be its rules, not its objects. If a certain especially heavy object would cause the aforementioned sack to burst immediately, an Inform 6 author would have to decide whether to attach the exception code to the sack or the weighty object. In Inform 7, it would just become a few more declarations and rules, which could appear anywhere in the code:

> A thing is either heavy or light. A thing is usually light. The anvil is heavy. After inserting something heavy into the sack, now the sack is bursting.

The change proved "far more radical than had initially been expected," Nelson wrote.[10] "For at least the first year of the project, I wasn't at all sure it would ever work."[6] But the idea had taken hold. With regular feedback from a small circle of peers and collaborators, he began working toward a fundamental rethinking of interactive fiction language design. Inform 6, he came to realize, "had been a computer programmer's tool which aimed to be welcoming to creative writers: this aspired to be the other way around."[10] It would be a particular subset of English—readable and, hopefully, writable— that also happened to compile.

After Jeremy Freese discovered the language, it started to seem possible that he might be a person who could finish an interactive fiction after all. "I could be a poster child for the idea that Inform 7 will get people involved in IF who otherwise wouldn't be," he would write. "Before I realized that programming my own game was still way more involved than anything I had time for, I was hooked."[5] He began writing *Violet*'s Inform 7 code in early 2008, vague-blogging about a new "too-dorky-to-confess-to hobby project."[2] He set himself a goal of writing a game good enough to finish at least eighth in that fall's Interactive Fiction Competition. "In more exuberant moments," he noted, "I revise this goal upward to fifth."[3]

Nelson's rules-based approach had grown from the realization that most IF code was really a description of the ways a particular story world differed from the platonic norm: a universe where doors locked, containers held objects, and turns passed, but nothing much of interest ever happened. Each individual game was "a world of unintended consequences."[10] In one, magic spells might bypass locked doors with no keys; another might simulate weight to decide if containers should burst, or let nearly bursting containers be used to batter down doors. And *Violet* would indeed become a game almost entirely defined by exceptions, packed with rules interrupting the player's initial assumptions that writing a few words ought to be relatively easy to do.

> Instead of writing when the player is not caffeinated:
> change statusphrase to "(last try: a bit tired, but come on!)";
> say "You start trying to focus on the screen and type, but you are very tired. [...]";

Much of the charm of play comes from uncovering these exceptions, one by one, and finding ways to overcome them. An ex-girlfriend shows up to the office and loudly flirts with a new conquest through the closed door; even after you find a way to drown her out, you can still smell her perfume, another distraction. Out the open window, an increasingly elaborate and improbable series of events plays out, drawing your attention until you find a way to block the view despite the window's malfunctioning blinds. And all of it is narrated in imaginary Violet's memorable voice, made easier to create by Inform 7's more organic way of overriding behaviors:

> >LOOK AT WINDOW
>
> Your window is immediately behind your desk, about two metres high and one wide. It has an old grey blind, which is raised.
>
> On the sill I am a bit surprised to see a lighter.
>
> >GET LIGHTER
>
> Yours, jellysquish. It's hard for me to be enthusiastic about lighters as a woman who owns her own blowtorch.
>
> You run the back of your hand along the book's spine. If you don't get the book out of your hands, you will give in and start reading.
>
> >BURN BOOK
>
> Gee, budgie. Far be it from me to be the moral conscience when fire is involved, but that's a library book. There's bound to be a hefty fine. And it seems a little insane. If you really want to, we can, but it shouldn't be a rash decision.
>
> >BURN BOOK
>
> I was secretly hoping you would. You light the book on fire and it burns magnificently! Yay! That was epic to watch, and now we don't have to deal with you being tempted anymore to read.
>
> The coughing and light smoke damage are well worth it. I'll go halfsies on the library fine.

YOU ARE CARRYING...

» a spectacularly intricate origami trophy

» a very odd balloon

» a plastic bottle filled with a fluorescent pink liquid

» the platyPod (being worn)

» a notebook

» a shiny little key

» a deftly-crafted snowglobe

» my itinerary

» an ethernet cable

Freese wrote the game with the Inform 7 project's other major innovation, what Nelson called "a radically humanising interface"[10] for IF authoring: an IDE (integrated development environment) designed specifically for the purpose. Compiling Inform 6 had been as unpleasant as compiling any other programming language from the early 90s, involving command-line invocations, a correctly laid out directory structure of libraries and source files, and error messages whose real causes could be hard to puzzle out. Inform 7 shipped as part of an application—actually two applications at first, one for Mac by Andrew Hunter and one for Windows by David Kinder—which abstracted all the file system and compilation details behind a straightforward interface using the metaphor of an open book.

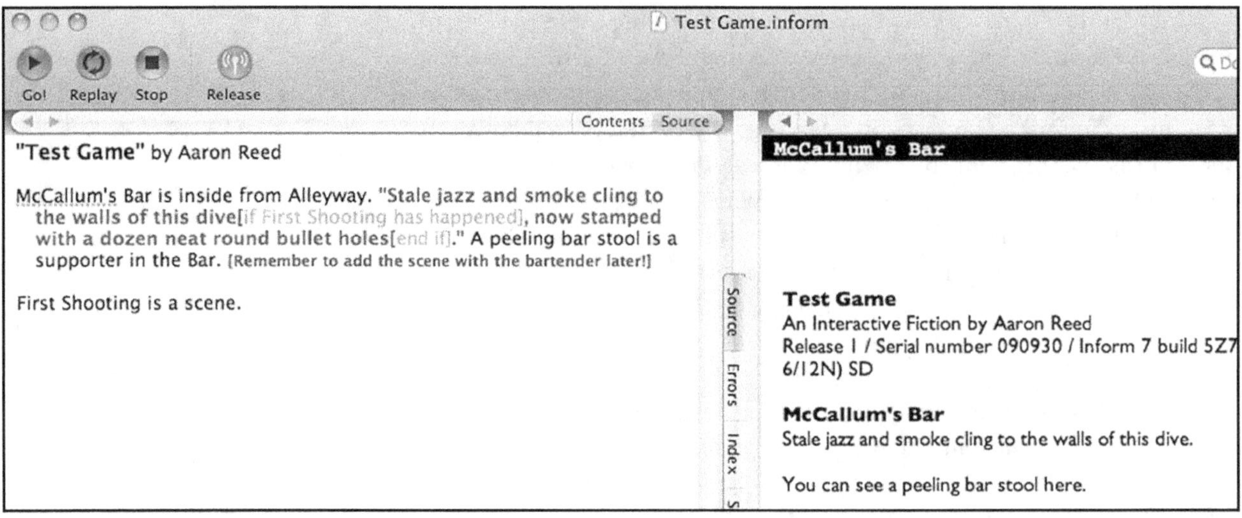

Portion of the Inform 7 application for Mac circa 2009, showing a simple program on the left and a playable story world derived from it on the right.

Opposite: the Skein shows possible playthroughs of a game, with the ability to autoreplay to a certain point, or mark paths as "blessed" to alert the author if code changes unexpectedly alter them.

Violet's IF Comp score of 8.53 out of 10 was in fact the highest any game had ever scored at the time—an honor it held until 2017's *The Wizard Sniffer* earned an average ranking of 8.57.

On the left page by default would be the source text for your project, and on the right a running interpreter where you could play it. Other "pages" of the application could show a dynamic map visualizing the rooms you'd defined; an index with summaries of objects, rules, and commands; and documentation and extensive examples. One page, the Skein, could show each path taken through the story as you'd tested it, like branches on a tree; certain paths could be locked, named, and easily replayed at the click of a button, allowing authors to grow their own test sequences as their games evolved. The Inform 7 application made creating an IF world far more accessible to nonprogrammers, and its features helped Freese do extensive playtesting: during the game's development, he wrangled beta testers through eight separate rounds of bug fixing, continually improving the game as he went.

Inform 7 was well received. It rapidly displaced its predecessor and, for most of a decade, became the favored language bar none for writing interactive fiction. *Violet*, too, was a hit: it won the competition in which Freese had hoped to place eighth. Its unique voice "would be memorable enough even if it *didn't* work, but more so because it *does*,"[7] wrote one reviewer. It had "a premise that seems virtually untranslatable to any other genre of games,"[1] serving as another example of something that a medium based on words could do that more visual storytelling platforms might struggle with. Players delighted in the game's many cute touches. It had a gender option, for instance, but not the one that might have been expected:

> [...] you are male by default (*curse you, patriarchy!*). I'm not changing *my* gender on your behalf, but you are welcome to change yours. Just type FEMALE or, more stylishly, HETERONORMATIVITY OFF.
>
> >PATRIARCHY OFF
> I suspect that's a fair bit more difficult to program.

Scholar Nick Montfort has noted the irony that Violet has become one of the most fondly remembered IF characters, even though she doesn't technically even appear in the game bearing her name until its final, non-interactive cutscene. "Violet is conceptual," a line of the Inform 7 source reads, to indicate she's not actually part of the simulation and attempts to interact with her should fail. "The game shows how other characters can meaningfully manifest themselves even when they don't do anything in terms of picking up objects, manipulating the state of the world, or serving as an explicit opponent," Montfort writes.[8] Violet is merely the narrator, but the game named after her effectively demonstrates how rewarding a role that can be in an interactive story.

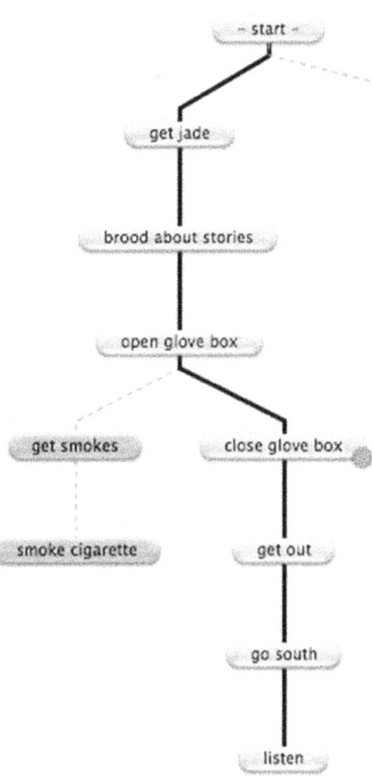

>WRITE

You start thinking again about the first sentence. "Previous scholarship has typically conceptualized…" Six seconds later you check your e-mail. You switch back to your word processor for a bit, but then you start reading some blogs. You check your e-mail again. Then back to blogs.

I suspect this is much of how the past several months in your office have gone.

>X COMPUTER

The desktop PC is old but perfectly fine for writing. In addition to your word processor, applications you can OPEN include a browser, chat and e-mail.

The computer has a USB port in the front and is connected to the Internet with a cable in back.

>UNPLUG CABLE

You unplug the ethernet cable. Good! It has to be easier to write if you can't chat, check e-mail, and surf the web whenever you want.

>WRITE

You resume thinking about the first sentence. You fidget. Your hands tremble a bit. You want to check your e-mail. You want to read blogs. And then: you retrieve the cable and plug it back into the computer.

Ugh. I didn't know it was this bad, muttonplum. I don't know what to say.

>CRY

You wouldn't let me cry when that man said the dalmatian sculptures in my MFA exhibit were 'gimmicky,' so I'm not going to let you cry now. You can do this.

"The activity of programming IF is a form of dialogue between programmer and computer to reach a state with which both are content,"[10] Graham Nelson once wrote. The coder keeps a model of their digital collaborator running in their head to imagine how it will react to each new input; in a way, the computer does the same for the coder. Inform 7 made those models more visible, opening the door to that collaboration a bit wider and making room for people like Jeremy Freese who weren't quite sure the space beyond was for them. But sometimes it only takes a whisper of encouragement to step through.

References

1　Boyer, Brandon. 2009. "The EXAMINE'd Life: Keeping Interactive Fiction Alive." *Boing Boing* (blog). Nov 5, 2009. boingboing.net/2009/11/05/the-examined-life-ke.html | a Jul 21, 2021

2　Freese, Jeremy. 2008a. "Prepping as Procrastination, Continued." *Scatterplot* (blog). May 1, 2008. scatter.wordpress.com/2008/05/01/prepping-as-procrastination-continued | a Jul 21, 2021

3　Freese, Jeremy. 2008b. "My Secret Hobby Project Revealed." *Scatterplot* (blog). May 27, 2008. scatter.wordpress.com/2008/05/27/my-secret-hobby-project-revealed | a Jul 21, 2021

4　Freese, Jeremy. 2008c. "My Secret Hobby Project." *Scatterplot* (blog). Nov 18, 2008. scatter.wordpress.com/2008/11/18/my-secret-hobby-project | a Jul 21, 2021

5　Freese, Jeremy. 2009. "Jeremy Freese (author of Violet)." Interview by Jimmy Maher. *SPAG* #54, Mar 31, 2009. www.spagmag.org/archives/backissues/spag54.html#freese | a Jul 21, 2021

6　Maher, Jimmy. 2006. "The SPAG Interview: Graham Nelson and Emily Short on Inform 7." *SPAG* #44, Apr 30, 2006. www.spagmag.org/archives/backissues/SPAG44 | a Jul 21, 2021

7　Merk. 2008. "Merk's Review: Violet." Forum post. The Interactive Fiction Community Forum. Oct 19, 2008. intfiction.org/t/merks-review-violet/473 | a Jul 21, 2021

8　Montfort, Nick. 2009. "Violet" (review). *Post Position* (blog). May 13, 2009. nickm.com/post/2009/05/violet | a Jul 21, 2021

9　Nelson, Graham. 2001. *The Inform Designer's Manual*. Fourth Edition. St. Charles, Illinois: The Interactive Fiction Library.

10　Nelson, Graham. 2006a. "Natural Language, Semantic Analysis and Interactive Fiction." inform7.com. inform7.com/learn/documents/WhitePaper.pdf | s Mar 14, 2018

11　Nelson, Graham. 2006b. "Inform 7: Public Beta." Usenet post, rec.arts.int-fiction, Apr 30, 2006. groups.google.com/g/rec.arts.int-fiction/c/9ZGc8bSbraw/m/4Ebs_v4deRcJ | a Jul 21, 2021

FALLEN LONDON

Failbetter Games

Also Known As	**Echo Bazaar** *(launch title)*
Style	**Storylet-Driven**
Debuted	**Oct 23, 2009** *(web app)*
Launch Platform	**Web**
Publisher	**Failbetter Games**
Language	**StoryNexus, JavaScript**

> 1889.
> Three decades ago, London was stolen by bats. Dragged deep into the earth by the Echo Bazaar. The sun is gone. All we have is the gas-light of Mr Fires.
> But Londoners can get used to anything. And it's quiet down here with the devils and the darkness and the mushroom wine. Peaceful.
> But then YOU arrived.
> Welcome. Delicious friend.

"IF YOU ARE WEARY OF RAVENSONG," the update noted, "the Bazaar will now purchase any and all raven advisors…. Gifts of Scorn are limited in their effects," it continued, because "the Wheel of Affection which gave them was absurdly effective otherwise." Further paragraphs explained that "Rose-Bearing Maggots may now be fed," that the Tomb-Colonies had been "substantially expanded; and now include a choice between Hedonism and Austerity," and that "a punchable moustache, a chess-playing ape, and a voracious dining-club" were also part of the most recently added content.[14]

The updates were for a game that had launched under the name *Echo Bazaar*—"a free browser game that only takes a few minutes a day to play."

2009

Major Milestones

» **Oct 23, 2009**. Launched in "limited beta" as *Echo Bazaar*; required Twitter to authenticate.

» **Jul 2010**. Facebook added as second authentication method.

» **Feb 18, 2011**. Exceptional Friends pricing introduced.

» **Mar 26, 2012**. Relaunched as *Fallen London*; allowed sign-up without a social media account.

» **Aug 2012**. Fate currency rebranded as Nex to support StoryNexus.

» **Oct 2012**. StoryNexus opened to public beta.

» **2013**. StoryNexus put into "maintenance mode."

» **Dec 2013**. Size of base daily action pool doubled from ten to twenty as a holiday bonus, later made permanent.

» **Apr 2015**. Monthly Exceptional Stories introduced with "The Haunting at the Marsh-House."

» **2016**. Versions for iOS and Android launched; these were discontinued in 2018 due to problems with architecture and updates.

» **Jun 2018**. Revamped website and web interface launched.

Seek your fortune in the city of Fallen London, a mile underground and a boat ride from Hell!

seduce heiresses * hunt sorrow-spiders * track down poisoners * lose your soul at cards * rob museums * christen Jack * avenge murders * visit honey-dens * write penny-dreadfuls * drink mushroom wine * attend executions * assist revolutionaries * decode tattoos * stab your friends: but all in good fun…

Originally requiring a Twitter account to play, *Echo Bazaar* arrived amidst a glut of free-to-play games that often took advantage of players' limited understanding of social media permissions to spam feeds with ads and updates. But this game was more polite. While players could choose to "echo" snippets of game text (tweeting them with the #ebz hashtag) to gain a few extra daily actions, and some limited multiplayer mechanics encouraged connecting with friends, for the most part the game functioned as a single-player experience. And it had a secret weapon most of its Flash-based competition lacked: while those snippets of shareable content were only text, it was good text. And there was a lot of it.

Except for a map and a few icons and portraits, the game was entirely built on its words, a novelty for a commercial title that helped it stand out in a crowded field—along with its expansive size and original gameplay, which could be a bit hard to explain. It's "a sprawling, constantly evolving, nineteenth-century metropolis made [of] words,"[6] one guide noted; "an unholy combination of casual browser game, choose-your-own-adventure book **1979**, and quasi-steampunk MMO,"[7] the creators gamely summarized; "a world where death isn't permanent, cats can talk, and ominous space-bats are de facto rulers of the city," Failbetter designer and writer Olivia Wood explained.[27] Launched with around ten thousand words of story, by the time of the update with the chess-playing ape the game had grown to more than a million words, the size of a tall stack of novels. By its tenth anniversary in 2019, when nearly all the other browser games launched alongside it had long since vanished, it had reached nearly triple that number.

The game's narrative hook is that London has been stolen: Queen Victoria made an unwise deal with dark forces who plunged the city into a strange underworld called the Neath. Now, at the end of the nineteenth century, Hell maintains an embassy there; strange creatures from Clay Men to talking rats have joined the socialites and urchins on the streets; and every alleyway, pub, porter, and governess has a sinister secret or unlikely story. The book *Virtual Cities*, a videogame urban atlas, praises the way *Fallen London* "blends Lovecraftian monsters with romantic themes, the literary versatility of Poe, Penny Dreadful aesthetics and a darkly hilarious wit to create an entirely original world that's familiar yet also utterly strange."[6] The mixture of surreal humor and dark horror had been foundational from the start. Co-creator Paul Arendt once noted that the game's look "was more inspired by Francis Ford Coppola's *Dracula*. Spooky but silly, serious but camp. Gary Oldman in a top hat and sunglasses is never far from my mind."[1]

"If you were a certain kind of person in 2009," one journalist recalled, "your life slowly, and then quickly, filled up with mentions of *Fallen*

London."[4] The game enjoyed a creeping viral longevity, not just because of its unique setting but because of the care put into its writing: the same journalist noted that "this is a game for people who read and who *love* to read."[4] "Bluntly," another reviewer said, it's "probably better written than most any game and quite a few books."[23] Filled up with delicious sentences and images, the game has so many it's hard to pick just a few to excerpt:

> A sorrow-spider the size of a large kitten scuttles across the floor of your lodgings. For reasons best known to itself, it's carrying a human eyeball.

> Rubbery Men are social outcasts. Their physiognomy is distressing and they lack the wealth necessary for acceptable eccentricity.

> The House of Mirrors squats like an ape in a quiet corner of the carnival. Strange mirrors are labelled in a neat, scholarly hand. It is not a popular attraction.

> A dozen frost-moths lie in a welter of broken wings on the ground, gradually melting into pools of dirty water.

> Mr Chimes glides across the floor and grasps your hand in a spotless white glove. It feels like shaking a branch wound with spider-silk. 'Most optimate friend!' it whispers. 'Welcome to our Chamber of Delicacies!'

The game's viral success was not entirely an accident: new studio Failbetter Games had conceived *Echo Bazaar* specifically for the strengths of emerging social media conventions. Rather than tackling a whole story or chapter at once, players were encouraged to play the game for a few minutes a few times each day, in much the same way they might be browsing the social media platforms where they'd likely discovered it. The hope was that a regular and returning audience could drive a sustainable business model for narrative games, rather than one characterized by a single all-important launch day and diminishing returns ever after, a strategy less and less viable in an overcrowded entertainment landscape. Other games like *Kingdom of Loathing* had used similar models, but usually with core mechanics based on repetitive combat and grinding. Failbetter hoped they could shift the emphasis more toward story by treating the flavor text that usually decorated these mechanics as the real content, not disposable window dressing. Players would keep coming back more for the story than the gameplay. The story, of course, is the part that's not reusable, and it would have to keep growing fast enough that players would always have new things to read each time they returned, a daunting proposition. "Industry consultants point and laugh at our bizarre strategy of earning money by *making new content*," a company

Fallen London was an early prominent digital game that let a player opt out of binary gender when creating their character. The three gender options upon launch in 2009 were "A gentleman," "A lady," and "My dear sir, there are individuals roaming the streets of Fallen London at this very moment with the faces of squid! Squid! Do you ask them their gender? And yet you waste our time asking me trifling and impertinent questions about mine? It is my own business, sir, and I bid you good day."

see **2003**

2009

Actions
20/20

Fate
55
BE EXCEPTIONAL!

Subscribe for a second candle and brand new stories every month.

Echoes
€ 19.04

Outfit

Morning ⌄

 Watchful 50+8

 Shadowy 40

 Dangerous 40+2

 Persuasive 61+5

 Bizarre 0+2

It's Alericious! Welcome to The Singing Mandrake, delicious friend!

TRAVEL

5 cards waiting!
Next in 3:04

DISCARD

DISCARD

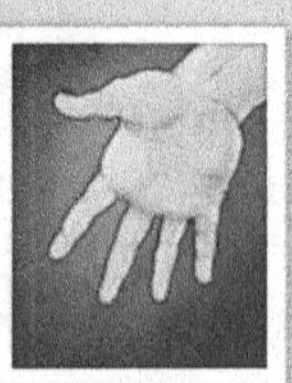
DISCARD

An Exceptional Story: The Exile's Chalice
This park – such as it is – is closed, the sparse trees within subject to the mysterious ministrations of Her Majesty's Department of Parks and Game...

 GO

Head Into the Cellars, Then Further Down
Mr Chimes' Grand Clearing-Out broke the earth beneath the Singing Mandrake (narrowly avoiding it tumbling into the depths)...

GO

Reunion: The Westminster
The Westminster Hotel sits comfortably on the north bank of the Stolen River...

  GO

A Professional Reward
"Thou shalt not bind the church-bat's ears; and the labourer *is* worthy of his reward...

 GO

The Singing Mandrake
If you want to become a sensation in Veilgarden, here's the place to start...

blog post once dryly noted.[15] But the strategy worked. The Failbetter team started writing and never stopped, and the players kept coming.

Exactly how to turn their growing audience into a sustainable business took some time to sort out. At first the sole way to support the game was by purchasing a currency called Fate, which could unlock pieces of premium content or bonus actions. (At launch, the free game provided a ten action maximum that slowly recharged throughout the day.) But these one-off purchases didn't lead to sustained engagement and often proved unsatisfying to players, who had no way to judge the length or potential enjoyment of bits of Fate-locked content. Eventually the game added a subscription option: by becoming an Exceptional Friend for a monthly fee, you could double your daily actions, and in later years Friends also gained access to an exclusive subscribers-only story each month. But the bulk of the game remained free; indeed, the reams of compelling content were the best advertising tool imaginable.

The game's monetization model had its share of detractors. One prominent interactive fiction author called it "detestable"[19] for the way the drawn-out story encouraged players to become addicted and keep spending money, and another lamented the slow pacing, which meant stories could be padded out for months between setup and payoff.[18] But it was certainly a tamer approach to free-to-play than most other game using the model, and would ultimately provide a stable platform for Failbetter at least into the 2020s. A steady stream of income meant *Fallen London* could be iteratively improved on for years, with breathing room for new titles and experiments. It helped level out the boom-and-bust release cycle so many game studios suffer through—or fail to.

Beneath the limited-action interface was an intriguing original platform— later called StoryNexus, in a slightly evolved version—for delivering an ongoing interactive story. The core idea of StoryNexus was to treat the fiction not as a linear path or a branching tree, but as a set of loosely linked vignettes. These could be unlocked, shaped, or sequenced by the details of the player's unique history with the game, leading to many more possible playthrough pathways than a preassembled tree of story nodes could offer. Again, this was not a wholly new idea—games like *King of Dragon Pass* **1999** had used similar models—but Failbetter streamlined the concept down to a minimalist form that would prove surprisingly versatile. The key simplification was that each facet of the game world that might impact the narrative would be represented as a numeric "quality," one of an unbounded set of stats a player could accumulate. The studio coined the term "quality-based narrative" to describe this approach.

Qualities had a useful flexibility. They could represent nearly anything imaginable about a player character's identity within or relationship to the story world. They didn't need to all be defined in advance, like stats in a traditional game; authors could write (and players could acquire) new ones at any time. Some mirrored the more traditional stats of roleplaying games, like *Fallen London*'s core qualities of Watchful, Shadowy, Dangerous, and Persuasive. Others might represent currency held, temporary conditions

Opposite: ***Fallen London*'s interface circa 2021, showing a hand of opportunity cards above a list of storylets playable from the current location.**

see *Achaea* **1997**

Another early flavor of this idea was the "Card Shark" system proposed by hypertext fiction scholars Mark Bernstein and Diane Greco in the early 2000s.[2]

2009

like injury, progress through a mission, ranks or titles earned, relationships with other characters, faction standing, locations granted access to, or which ending to resolved storylines the player had chosen (see sidebar, left).

A player's set of qualities could unlock narrative opportunities or be tested for a chance at overcoming a challenge. The Hall of Mirrors might require two Carnival Tickets to enter; a rooftop highway for criminals is only accessible to players with at least sixty Shadowy; collecting enough Memories of Distant Shores might trigger a dream or a revelation; a random roll based on Nightmares decides whether you succumb to a mind-numbing revelation. The beauty of the system lay in collapsing disjointed aspects of a simulated story world—stats, inventory, statuses, location, history—into a single, fungible economy. A quest was just as likely to reward you with Rostygold (a form of currency) as with Cryptic Secrets; and by the time those Secrets were spent to resolve a further mystery, it no longer mattered which stories you'd first learned them from.

The core loop of a StoryNexus game is encountering a series of narrative opportunities called storylets, presented using the metaphor of a hand of cards. Each storylet represents a self-contained situation pivoting on a challenge or decision for the player. Storylets might be assigned to specific locations—London has various neighborhoods you can move between—or might be drawn from a hand of opportunity cards stocked with storylets unlocked by your current qualities.

A libraryette for Mr Pages

Mr Pages has announced a campaign to recover and sequester what he describes as 'pestilent and obstacudent' literature. Whether for destruction or private reading is not made explicit.

You need 100 Proscribed Materials even to see this card.

Each storylet offers options for resolution, some of which in turn might be gated on having enough of a certain quality. Options can require a random test against a quality (akin to a dice roll in a tabletop game) to successfully invoke that choice. The higher the quality, the better the odds of passing.

An assortment of pamphlets
If your reserves of seditious literature are not voluminous, you could still make a small donation. Mr Pages would probably be grateful.

A matter of luck: **how can you fail?**
Your Luck quality gives you a 90% chance of success.

[You unlocked this with 140 Proscribed Materials (you needed 100)]

» *GO*

> **The special books**
> Perhaps you have some rarer works you could part with.
>
> This is a reliable but very expensive way to gain a little Connected: the Masters.
>
> [You need 20 Volumes of Collated Research]
> [You need 80 Touching Love Stories]
> [You need 5 Uncanny Incunabula]
> [You need 5 Blackmail Materials]
>
> » *GO*

Playing a storylet inevitably changes the player's qualities. Failing a test might raise the quality being tested, akin to learning from mistakes; success might raise some other desirable quality; and in either case all manner of other side effects might be triggered. In one *Fallen London* storylet, the authorities offer you payment to investigate a possibly seditious poet, and the player's choices include warning him off, turning him in, or even doing both. Each of the starred addenda below is narrating a change to a quality:

> ## But when the Constables came, he wasn't there
> You turn in your dossier. The constables march off to arrest the Poet, but by the time they get there he's long gone. The constables pay you your fee, but they're bitter about the lack of a collar. The Poet's friends toast your discretion.
>
> * Watchful has increased to 34 - Observant!
>
> * You now have 1 x Bottle of Strangling Willow Absinthe.
>
> * You've gained 200 x Piece of Rostygold (new total 814).
>
> * Magnanimous has increased to 5!
>
> * The Starving Poet escaped... for now, at least.
>
> * Suspicion is increasing... [7 -> 8]
>
> * You've gained 1 x Favours: Bohemians (new total 3)

Altered qualities might in turn change the set of storylets available to play or the choices they offer. Gaining Absinthe might unlock a way to entertain a useful acquaintance; increased Suspicion could lead to arrest; your popularity with the Bohemians might open up a new story about a vagabond musician; Rostygold might be traded for a new pet you've long hoped to buy. Each storylet perturbs your story in sometimes predictable but often surprising ways, sending each player on a unique pathway through a

Seeking Mr Eaten's Name

Some of *Fallen London*'s stories became truly tremendous. One of the most notorious is the path known as "Seeking Mr Eaten's Name." The game takes great pains to warn players not to take it:

> [This] is a story of misery, obsession and self-destruction. It doesn't play by the same rules as the rest of *Fallen London*. It is capricious, difficult and very unfair. And there will be no happy ending, unless you abandon the quest. Don't begin the story unless you are prepared to regret it.

Players who ignore the repeated warnings take the first steps on a road that might take more than a real-world year to travel, edging toward the most terrible secret in a world utterly filled with them. First, cards from a strange new deck are shuffled into your Opportunities: the Ace of Hungers, the Four of Eyes, the Knight of Feasts. The cards cannot be discarded. When played, they narrate a monstrous hunger growing inside your character, manifesting in increasingly disturbing ways. Playing the cards gains you Wounds, Suspicious, Nightmares, and Scandal; they cost you connections and favors as you draw further and further away from polite society.

But the cards are only the beginning of the sacrifice players must make to complete the full storyline. The cost becomes higher and higher: giving up half the Watchful score you might have built up over years of play, or permanently sacrificing your ability to even have useful qualities like a Profession or an Ambition at all. "I truly cannot imagine a story that so perfectly uses its medium as a game," one player wrote: "making the *player* throw away all the resources they've built alongside the character."[21]

The end of the quest is one of the game's most closely guarded secrets; even fan wikis and lore sites refuse to divulge it. "The ending wasn't satisfying," one seeker revealed, "but I knew it wouldn't be.... [It's] not worth it. Do it anyways, just to see."[9]

narrative possibility space defined by their qualities—a compressed record of their story so far—and told via the pool of authored storylets designed to respond to them.

Conscious that its bite-sized pieces might fail to cohere into a satisfying whole, the Failbetter team became deeply interested in discovering what narrative structures could be built within the StoryNexus engine. As more and more content was added, a complex design vocabulary began to emerge. Less than a year after launch, the team had already identified sixty distinct narrative patterns that could be created within their system. Some of these encoded simple ideas, like the "Faust": letting the player gamble some of one quality for a chance to improve another (using Laudanum in the hopes of reducing Nightmares, for instance).

More elaborate structures might unfold across multiple turns or linked chains of storylets. The "Midnight Staircase" described a replayable storylet that increased a temporary tracking quality, with each increase unlocking more appealing ways of resolving a story thread but also an increased risk of failure. The pattern could be used, say, for a pickpocket casing a busy street and finding more and more potential marks, while facing the rising risk of getting caught. Another pattern called the "Carousel" would advance a quality through a set of named alternatives (for instance, a Time of Day quality that could cycle from *morning* through *evening* and *night)*. These states could alter the available storylets and responses in a related context, such as a social club with different members arriving and leaving as the hours changed.

StoryNexus, in short, was atomic enough that a huge variety of bespoke narrative engines could be built within it. With a bit of practice, writers could even learn to bootstrap their own.

> Create *Manuscript Pages* to write your story. When you have at least 10, rework your story to improve its *Potential*. Improve your piece to 30 Potential to continue making your name. For this short story, you'll need no more than 10 Pages and 30 Potential.

The accumulating design wisdom helped Failbetter build stories that unfolded on larger scales than single storylets could encompass. Characters with an improved Watchful, for instance, could take on detective cases that granted an Investigating quality, unlocking storylets across London about interviewing accomplices, breaking into garrets, or trailing suspects. Resolving each would increase Investigating until it unlocked a storylet that solved the original case—which might in turn be only part of a larger mystery. The intermediate investigation storylets didn't need to connect to the details of the larger case. The business of detective work could be abstracted away from its greater significance: the system could build an extended story out of reusable, interchangeable pieces.

In fact, any two pieces of content might indirectly connect through a player's natural tendency to see cause and effect in their actions. IF author Emily Short, who would become a frequent guest contributor to *Fallen London* and eventually join Failbetter as a creative director, once noted that she'd resolved a story about raising funds for a pious bishop's church by doing odd jobs for devils, "a bit of player-implemented irony that is implicitly *possible* in the system but left totally open-ended…. There's a lot of cool potential here, potential that replicates some of the fun of procedural narrative but puts the control in the player's hands rather than in the hands of an algorithm."[25] Failbetter would characterize this approach to storytelling with the metaphor of campfires in a darkened desert, seen from above. The major storylets provided the bright central lights of a plot, but players could invent their own routes connecting them.

Make Your Name: Getting to the Ball

The Ambassador's ball is a highlight of the season. You are tired of gate-crashing: this time you're getting an invitation.

Calling in favours
You know enough important people. You're becoming well-known yourself. You can do this.

A **chancy** challenge
Your Persuasive quality gives you a 56% chance of success.
» Spend a Confident Smile to ensure a second chance…
Unlocked with 1 x Favours: Society, 5 x Scrap of Incendiary Gossip, 500 x Silk Scrap

You can get Favours: Society through some cards in your Opportunity Deck. Shroom-hopping provides chances to earn Society's approbation.

» GO

Hinting at one or two things you know
You hear things. Things about important persons and vaulted institutions.

A **chancy** challenge
Your Persuasive quality gives you a 56% chance of success.
Spend a Confident Smile to ensure a second chance…
Unlocked with 200 x Whispered Hint, 5 x Scrap of Incendiary Gossip,

---

> 500 x Silk Scrap
>
> *You can get Whispered Hints from many cards around Veilgarden and Ladybones Road.*
>
> » *GO*

As the game's content continued to grow, those pathways could get wildly convoluted. "Every time I swear that I will concentrate on my ambition (a long-term story line with great rewards if you can complete it), I see something that I simply must find out more about," one blogger wrote. "If I saved up for the right companion, could I win at the weasel fights? Is it worth a fortune of glim and jade to find out the way to Wolfstack Docks?"[26] Failbetter's writers constantly added to the library of available storylets, both in the broad strokes of epic interconnected quests but also in single opportunity cards or tiny situational details. When a player once complained on Reddit that they'd accidentally purchased five hundred weasels, a developer replied: "Unfortunately we can't correct misclicks. Sorry about that. However … I used my lunch hour to do a Small Thing. People with 400 or more weasels in their inventory may want to draw from the opportunity deck."[27] Accidents or bugs became story hooks more than once in the game's development. And the world continued to grow. One fan wiki documenting *Fallen London*'s content grew to include twenty-five thousand entries. Long-term goals in the game include becoming a ship captain and sailing the Unterzee, taking part in the Wars of Illusion, breeding monsters in the Labyrinth of Tigers, or constructing a railway line to Hell. Some content takes players to distant shores and other realms entirely:

> A dream washes over you like a tide coming into shore.
>
> You are standing in a grove tangled with roses, red and gold. The gentle rotten scent of flowers fills the air with drowsy sweetness. Before you, city walls rise; the colour of sunset. Bronze gates gleam in a somnolent amber light.
>
> A woman wearing vast rubies in her ears approaches. "London's Ambassador requested that we permit you within Arbor's walls," she says with a lazy smile. "Enjoy your stay. Do feast your eyes on our city of marvels." She turns away, leaving you to make your own way into the City of Roses.

In 2012, Failbetter hoped to bring even more worlds to StoryNexus by opening the platform to outside creators. Fascinating new experiments began to appear. *Winterstrike* [2012] by Yoon Ha Lee (on his way to becoming a bestselling novelist) used abstract qualities like Ice to tell a haunting story about the survivors of a planetary apocalypse. *Black Crown* [2013] by Rob Sherman was an epic parable of diseased bodies and blurred identity, marrying message and mechanics by conflating the player's limited daily

The game changed its name in 2012 from *Echo Bazaar* to *Fallen London*, which more memorably captured its premise.

action pool to a weakened protagonist's loss of power and control. And Failbetter debuted StoryNexus games licensed from existing properties, including one to promote Erin Morgenstern's whimsical 2011 novel *The Night Circus* and another that tied into the lore of BioWare's *Dragon Age* series. But maintaining a service for both creating and hosting online games proved a financial drain on Failbetter, who quietly ended support for StoryNexus after eighteen months of underperformance. Authors who had worried about entrusting their game to an online-only platform saw their fears justified: many of the StoryNexus games became unplayable within a few years. The same may one day be true for *Fallen London* itself.

Impossible to binge, unable to be archived, frustrating for some while delicious to others, Failbetter's magnum opus has grown into one of the most expansive text-based games ever written. Thousands of new sentences in many hundreds of new storylets are added each year. *Echo Bazaar*—first conceived as a game where Twitter users could make bets on unusual phrases that might appear in future tweets—had evolved into an efficient engine for generating its own, as seen in some of the titles of posts to the Failbetter forums:

> Fighting the Carnivorous Aurochs—is there an end
> A practical cat question, and an ideological one
> A side effect of the Hellicon House scrip carousal
> Artisan of the Red Science question
> Does the Oracular Toadbeast do anything?
> Viscountess still in Parabolan Warfare
> Apocyan Mirrorcatch Boxes!
> Mechanics of the Bone Market
> Recommendations for grinding Hard-Earned Lessons

"*Fallen London* is the story of a city," co-designer Chris Gardiner said in a 2017 interview, "and a city doesn't stop. There are definitely stories that will conclude, but London won't." He fondly related a favorite scene wherein players have a chance to learn one of the terrible secrets of Queen Victoria's fallen court. Instructed to keep their backs to a royal banquet visible only in a mirror, the game describes sounds more horrible than any human lords and ladies at table ought to make. "Three times we ask the player if they want to turn around," Gardiner recalled, "and warn that the consequences will be terrible. It's entirely their choice.

"And because they're our players, they generally turn. Bless them."[3]

https://community.
failbettergames.com/

References

1　Arendt, Susan. 2010. "Horror Meets Shopping at the Echo Bazaar." *The Escapist* (blog). Jan 13, 2010. www.escapistmagazine.com/v2/horror-meets-shopping-at-the-echo-bazaar | a Jun 17, 2021

2　Bernstein, Mark and Diane Greco. 2004. "Card Shark and Thespis: Exotic Tools for Hypertext Narrative." In *First Person: New Media as Story, Performance, and Game*, ed. Noah Wardrip-Fruin and Pat Harrigan. MIT Press: Cambridge.

3　Conditt, J. 2017. "'Fallen London' and the Secret to Writing an Infinite Gothic Game." *Engadget* (blog). May 27, 2017. www.engadget.com/2017-05-27-fallen-london-gothic-horror-game-interview-writing.html | a Jun 17, 2021

4   Delbert, Caroline. 2018. "Novel Ties: The Wordy World of Fallen London." *Caroline Delbert* (blog). Dec 4, 2018. medium.com/@cdelbert/novel-ties-the-wordy-world-of-fallen-london-76ada7dc6a62 | a Jun 17, 2021

5   Delphine. 2011. "Free Ticket to Fallen London – New Moms Welcome!" *Wired*, Jan 24, 2011. www.wired.com/2011/01/free-ticket-to-fallen-london-new-moms-welcome | a Jun 17, 2021

6   Dimopoulos, Konstantinos. 2020. *Virtual Cities: An Atlas & Exploration of Video Game Cities*. Unbound Publishing.

7   Doh, Jane. 2010. "Amid Controversy, Echo Bazaar Will Soon Bring Fallen London to Facebook." *ARGNet* (blog). Jul 29, 2010. www.argn.com/2010/07/amid_controversy_echo_bazaar_will_soon_bring_fallen_london_to_facebook | a Jun 17, 2021

8   Donlan, Christian. 2014. "The City and the Sea: The Story of Failbetter Games." *Eurogamer* (blog). Apr 14, 2014. www.eurogamer.net/articles/2014-04-06-the-city-and-the-sea-the-story-of-failbetter-games | a Jun 17, 2021

9   Fallen London Wiki. n.d. fallenlondon.fandom.com/wiki/Beginner%27s_Guide | a Jun 17, 2021

10 Failbetter Staff. 2010a. "Echo Bazaar Narrative Structures, Part One." *Failbetter Games* (blog). Feb 27, 2010. www.failbettergames.com/echo-bazaar-narrative-structures-part-one | a Jun 17, 2021

11 Failbetter Staff. 2010b. "Echo Bazaar Narrative Structures, Part Two." *Failbetter Games* (blog). Mar 3, 2010. www.failbettergames.com/echo-bazaar-narrative-structures-part-two | a Jun 17, 2021

12 Failbetter Staff. 2010c. "Echo Bazaar Narrative Structures, Part Three." *Failbetter Games* (blog). Mar 12, 2010. www.failbettergames.com/echo-bazaar-narrative-structures-part-three | a Jun 17, 2021

13 Failbetter Staff. 2010d. "New Narrative Structures." *Failbetter Games* (blog). Aug 8, 2010. www.failbettergames.com/new-narrative-structures | a Jun 17, 2021

14 Failbetter Staff. 2014. "Fallen London Changes: February 2014." *Failbetter Games* (blog). Feb 17, 2014. www.failbettergames.com/fallen-london-changes-february-2014 | a Jun 17, 2021

15 Failbetter Staff. 2015. "Why Is Fallen London Still Free-to-Play?" *Failbetter Games* (blog). Jan 3, 2015. www.failbettergames.com/why-is-fallen-london-still-free-to-play | a Jun 17, 2021

16 Flynn, Hannah. 2014. "When Game Developers Should Be 'In Character.'" Conference talk, GDC Next, 2014. www.youtube.com/watch?v=qtIpVU6LwyQ | a Jun 17, 2021

17 Galle_. 2016. "A Spoiler-Light Lore Guide to Fallen London." Reddit Post. r/fallenlondon. Oct 29, 2016. www.reddit.com/r/fallenlondon/comments/5a22or/a_spoilerlight_lore_guide_to_fallen_london/ | a Jun 17, 2021

18 Gelugon_baat. 2016. "Fallen London" (review). *Gamespot* (blog). Feb 18, 2016. www.gamespot.com/fallen-london/user-reviews/2200-12683599 | a Jun 17, 2021

19 Gijsbers, Victor. 2014. "Fallen London" (review). IFDB. ifdb.org/viewgame?id=y9m60ythcj2xn9r&review=28572 | a Jun 17, 2021

20 Joye. 2010. "Echo Bazaar" (review). *Jay Is Games* (blog). Nov 16, 2010. jayisgames.com/review/echo-bazaar.php | a Jun 17, 2021

21 Long, Oliver. 2021. "@MonsieurLongIII: Seeking Mr. Eaten's Name…" Twitter post. May 18, 2021. twitter.com/MonsieurLongIII/status/1394883211046658048 | a Jun 17, 2021

22 Reed, Aaron A. 2017. "Changeful Tales: Design-Driven Approaches Toward More Expressive Storygames." Dissertation, UC Santa Cruz.

23 Savage, Steven. 2016. "Fallen London: Why It Works." *Steven Savage* (blog). Dec 28, 2016. www.stevensavage.com/blog/2016/12/fallen-london-works.html | a Jun 17, 2021

24 Shiovitz, Dan. 2010. "Echo Bazaar (Pt 1, Introduction)." *Inky Has a Blog*. May 2, 2010. inky.org/blog/?p=188 | a Jun 17, 2021

25 Short, Emily. 2016. "Beyond Branching: Quality-Based, Salience-Based, and Waypoint Narrative Structures." *Emily Short's Interactive Storytelling* (blog). Apr 12, 2016. emshort.blog/2016/04/12/beyond-branching-quality-based-and-salience-based-narrative-structures | a Jun 17, 2021

26 Taymar. 2010. "Echo Bazaar" (review). *MMORPG Info* (blog). Jan 29, 2010. mmorpg-info.org/echo-bazaar/echo-bazaar | s Feb 2, 2010

27 Wood, Olivia. 2019. "Feeding the Maw: Managing a Live Narrative Game in 'Fallen London.'" Conference talk, GDC, San Francisco, March 2019. gdcvault.com/play/1025735/Feeding-the-Maw-Managing-a%20Olivia%20Wood | a Jun 17, 2021

THE 20

2010	**Digital: A Love Story**
2011	**Nested**
2012	**Howling Dogs**
2013	**Versu: A Family Supper**
2014	**80 Days**
2015	**Lifeline**
2016	**Choices: The Freshman**
2017	**Universal Paperclips**
2018	**Weyrwood**
2019	**AI Dungeon**
2020	**Scents & Semiosis**

10s

NE, LYFT, UBER, TIN... ...YSTATION 4, XBOX ON... VORPLE, ...TCH.IO, ARTICY:DRAF...
OGLE GLASS, ADVENTUR... HOLOLENS, VIRTUAL ...LITY, SLACK, ...ORYNEXUS, AMAZO...
HO, 3DS, WINDOWS 1... ...TF, APPLE PAY, AP... WATCH, TRAC... FORTNITE, TIKTO...
...VENTUREX, NINTEND... ...WITCH, GPT, NA... ...OPE, FACEBO... NETFLIX, TWITTE...
...ROME, THE APP ST... TWINE, FAILBETT... ...HOICE OF GA... MINECRAFT, BITCOI...
...CKSTARTER, IPAD, IN...GRAM, PINTEREST, KIN... INKLE, DAR... ...ULS, VITA, OUYA, SKYRIM...
...RYTALE, WII U, S... ...EADY PLAYER ONE, GOO...E+, GOOG... DRIVE, ...ITCH, OCULUS RIF...

NOT MANY COMMUNITIES OF DIGITAL MAKERS HAVE HAD TIME to reach their fifth decade; many that have find themselves graying or stagnant. Interactive fiction at half a century, by contrast and perhaps surprisingly, was entering its most dynamic and exciting decade yet. On every front, text games were rapidly changing and evolving, with major shifts across the 2010s in audience, aesthetics, techniques, platforms, and even commercial prospects. The medium had never been more varied, never reached more players, never looked so beautiful, and never been more open to new kinds of games and game makers.

Perhaps the most visible trend across the decade was a move away from building interactive stories atop pedantic world simulations. In the classic text adventure mode, a world model simulating spaces, props, creatures, and turn-by-turn action is the foundation upon which stories are told—which can be frustrating, since it's a hard foundation to properly build and often doesn't have much to do with the stories performed atop it. Creators in the 2010s increasingly turned toward other kinds of foundations for interactive narratives, focused on elements like character, dramatic events, story structures, or the words themselves. Whether through curated chains of hypertext, finely tuned procedural content generators, sequencers for dramatic vignettes, or social models directing characters to behave in compelling ways, the overall thrust was toward systems that prioritized captivating stories over immersive simulations.

This sea change was nowhere more visible than in the rise of Twine, a hypertext authoring tool created by old-school parser author Chris Klimas. Curiously, there had never previously been a widely used tool in the game maker community for creating linked hypertextual stories. Commercial tools like Storyspace were often priced like professional software at multiple hundreds of dollars, limiting their audience; and as the 2010s approached, despite the ubiquity of the web as a platform, no tool for creating interlinked text for it had yet achieved a mainstream critical mass of work and community.

see *Patchwork Girl* **1995**

The interface for Twine 2.0, designed to edit on (and release stories for) the web.

This changed with Twine, which was released in 2009 and exploded in popularity three years later as a movement of outsider writers found and claimed it. Bucking the general trend in computing toward increased complexity, Twine was radically simpler than earlier tools like Inform **1993**—a major selling point for its advocates. Twine's straightforwardness opened up interactive storytelling to new kinds of people without coding experience, limitless leisure time, or access to paid services like web hosting and professional tools. One study of Twine notes that even its documentation lays out a vision for a different kind of game scene, noting how it speaks to readers

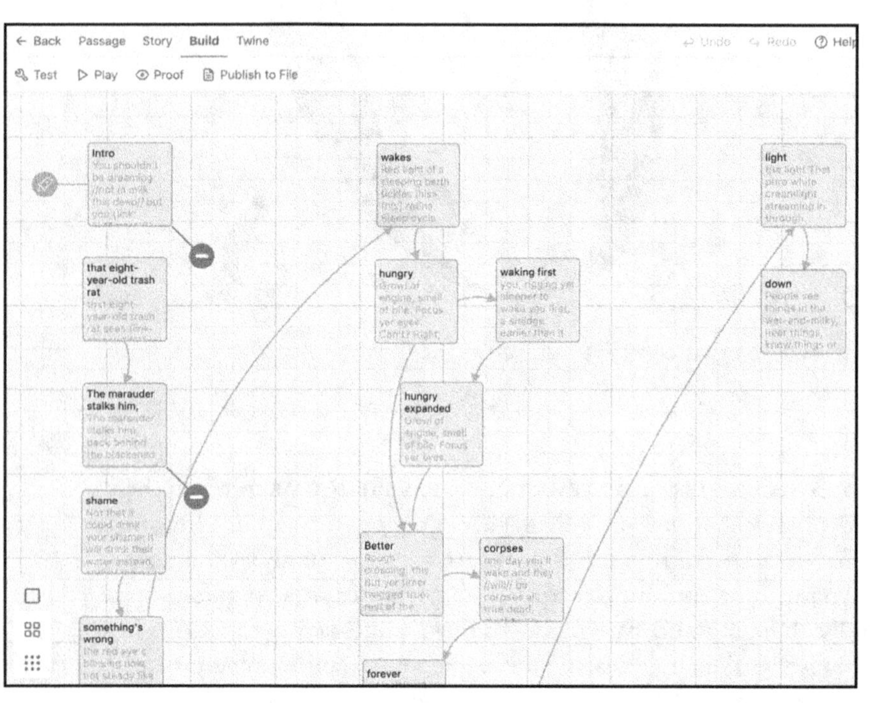

Jane Friedhoff. 2013. "Untangling Twine: A Platform Study." *Proceedings of DiGRA 2013: DeFragging Game Studies.*

from an aesthetic angle first…. Rather than answering "how would you make a game with this?", the official Twine reference manual focuses on answering "why would you make a game at all?" … Putting the emphasis on "writers," rather than "developers" or "game-makers," implies that creating this kind of interactive experience is not limited to those with technical ability.

By the fall of 2012, the tireless work of Twine advocates—posting tutorials and user guides; organizing jams and expos; writing raw and beautiful games and curating lists of their favorites by others—had nurtured a vibrant new IF community filled with voices that had rarely been heard in gaming before. These writers told stories about living in poverty, about queer love, about

2010s

trauma and pain; but they also explored radical worlds in prose and new possibilities for design and interface. *rat chaos* [winter lake 2012] begins as a surreal sci-fi pastiche and veers into a poignantly real confessional. *weird tape in the mail* [adam dickinson 2012] is David Lynch by way of MS Paint and mall culture fever dreams. And *Mastaba Snoopy* [gods17 2012] takes the reader to a far-future nightmare where the galaxy has been subsumed by an

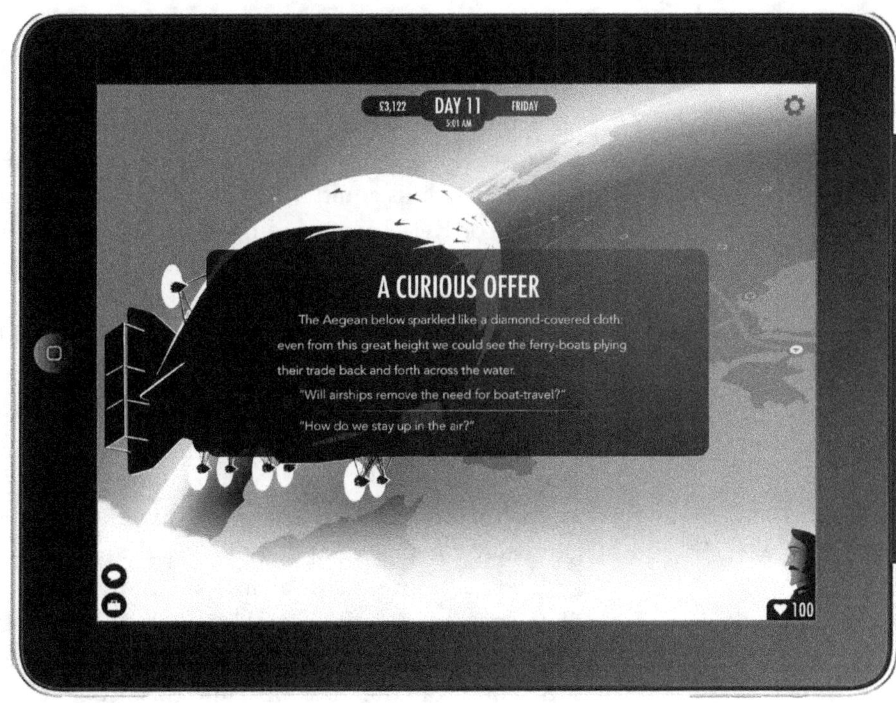

alien god whose only knowledge of Earth life comes from a book of *Peanuts* comics, which it mindlessly emulates with mile-high, half-sentient Snoopies. Despite the many worlds text games had visited in the four decades prior, none had been quite like these.

Twine's success arrived as the web had finally matured into a platform where complex programs could easily be run and shared. Like other new IF platforms from the 2010s—including Undum, StoryNexus, Squiffy, and Yarn—Twine was designed to build stories for the web and soon became a web app itself. Parser-based interactive fiction had moved to the web as well: JavaScript ports of the ancient Z-machine and other engines allowed them to run on web pages, leading to Play Online buttons replacing older links to download story files and interpreter programs. It had never been easier to play IF, though this ease of use came with a downside: online-only services could be distressingly ephemeral, shutting down and taking all their hosted content with them.

While many authors continued making text games in traditional modes, they were increasingly joined throughout the decade by new communities with their own definitions of what an interactive story could be. Quality-based narrative, first popularized by *King of Dragon Pass* **1999** (and discussed in depth in the chapter on *Fallen London* **2009**), presented players with a series of dramatic events or "storylets" rather than embedding them in an explorable spatial simulation. Games like *Reigns* [Devolver Digital 2016] combined this design with large pools of possible storylets to create dynamic stories that felt replayable and expansive in ways that other forms of interactive fiction could have difficulty capturing, and provided a more constant stream of drama than most slower-paced parser games could match.

80 Days 2014 on an iPad (top) and *Lifeline* 2015 on the Apple Watch (bottom), demonstrating the rise in the 2010s of new untethered platforms for digital text.

Procedural generation techniques also proliferated in text games throughout the decade, from titles like *Kerkerkruip* [Victor Gijsbers 2011], which rendered an extremely randomized roguelike experience in fully realized prose, to *Voyageur* [Bruno Dias 2017], in which an infinite universe of textual generated worlds could be explored. JavaScript procedural text tools like Tracery or RiTa, now running in the same environment as web-based game engines, could often be integrated with them (with some amount of work), and many authors experimented with new ways that combinatorial text might make an interactive narrative more replayable, surprising, or responsive. Another thread of text games appeared with the rise of clicker games like *A Dark Room* [Doublespeak Games 2013], *Candy Box!* [aniwey 2013], *Kittens Game* [Bloodrizer 2014], and *Universal Paperclips*; these games, which often had sparse or no visuals, went back to gaming's resource management roots and infused forty years of wisdom (some of it cursed) about how to make gameplay compelling and addictive, even without graphics or sounds.

Text games were also being read and played on a wider variety of platforms than ever before. People were increasingly interacting with handheld computers like the mobile phones in their pockets, rather than sitting at traditional desktops, and this brought literary games to spaces more traditionally suited for reading: couches, beds, vacations, commutes. E-book readers offered large screens optimized for reading text without eyestrain, and while manufacturers rarely offered developers enough access to support complex interactive text, some companies like Choice of Games experimented with ways to sell titles on platforms like Amazon's Kindle. The tablet market took off with the 2010 debut of Apple's iPad, providing another secondary screen for text game makers to target, as did smartwatches later in the decade (albeit with much smaller screens). Smart speakers even opened up new platforms for spoken word text games: titles like *The Magic Door* [The Magic Door LLC 2016], *Yes Sire* [Volley Inc 2018], and *Detective Ivan* [The Verse 2019] for Amazon's Alexa were text-only games delivered by recorded or synthetic human voice.

New platforms opened up new audiences and new opportunities for commercial text games, largely dormant for the previous twenty years. Multiple companies focusing on text-heavy games thrived during the 2010s, including Choice of Games, inkle, Failbetter, and Pixelberry Studios. Text games became more visually sophisticated, in part due to efforts by these companies and others to make their products look polished and salable. Semipro amateurs too had new options for getting paid for their work, including crowdfunding sites like Kickstarter—Andrew Plotkin raised $31,000 in 2010 for his game *Hadean Lands*, and former Infocomer Bob Bates funded a new text game, *Thaumistry*, in 2017. Meanwhile, distribution services like Itch.io made it easy for independent creators to charge a fee in exchange for their games, and the subscription site Patreon gave IF authors the chance to receive steady payments from their most devoted fans. Some creators who had found success in the amateur text games world found their way to careers in the game industry during the decade, including old-school parser authors like Emily Short, Jon Ingold, Sam Barlow, Andrew Plotkin,

see **2017**

see *The Sumerian Game* **1963**; and also **1971**, **1974**, **1975**

see *Weyrwood* **2018**; *80 Days* **2014**; *Fallen London* **2009**; and *Choices: The Freshman* **2016**

2010s

and Kevin Wilson—mirroring the migration, a decade earlier, of amateur MUD designers into professional careers building graphical MMOs. For a time seen only as retro, the text game scene had increasingly garnered a reputation as an incubator for compelling ideas, innovative experiments, and pretrained talent.

In-person meetups for text game makers saw an upsurge in the 2010s, with events like WordPlay in Toronto, the People's Republic of Interactive Fiction in Boston, and the NarraScope conference becoming recurring gatherings where word-driven games were shared and likeminded folks connected. Text games were also represented at more general game events like IndieCade and the Game Developers Conference in California, AdventureX in the UK, and larger entertainment gatherings like WorldCon, PAX, and South by Southwest, all of which featured games and speakers from the text game world across the decade. These events created more visibility for text games, strengthened community bonds, forged collaborations, and renewed commitments to ongoing projects.

The COVID-19 pandemic, arriving at the start of the 2020s, would put a damper for a while on in-person gatherings. But that's a story that will have to wait for *The Next 50 Years of Text Games*…

More Text Games from the 2010s

2010
Digital: A Love Story

Aotearoa *(Matt Wigdahl, Inform 7)*. Children's adventure and IF Comp winner set in a New Zealand populated by dinosaurs. **The Blind House** *(Amanda Allen, Inform 7)*. A woman takes shelter in the house of a reclusive artist. **Choice of Broadsides** *(Adam Strong-Morse et al., ChoiceScript)*. Command a career on the high seas in this early swashbuckling adventure from Choice of Games. **Divis Mortis** *(Lynnea Dally, Inform 7)*. Zombie survival horror set in a creepy hospital. **Dual Transform** *(Andrew Plotkin, Inform 7)*. Transform space with elemental forces in this metasemantic "one-room" game. **Fragile Shells** *(Stephen Granade, Inform 7)*. Sci-fi escape room full of clever puzzles and strong worldbuilding. **The Game Formerly Known as Hidden Nazi Mode** *(Victor Gijsbers, Inform 7)*. Thought experiment on authorial trust and content accessibility: how can you ever know for sure whether a nonlinear story contains objectionable content? **God Wars II** *(Richard Woolcock et al., C++)*. PvP MUD known for coordinate-based movement with dynamically generated descriptions; new players got four square miles of terrain to customize with a "terraform" command. **Hoist Sail for the Heliopause, and Home** *(Andrew Plotkin, Inform 7)*. Lyrical, well-crafted story about navigating a graceful solar sail ship through the stars. **Hoosegow** *(Benjamin Collins-Sussman and Jack Welch, Inform 7)*. Escape from prison with your partner-in-crime in this well-characterized western. **Leadlight** *(Wade Clarke, Eamon)*. Schoolgirl survival horror game written for the Apple II; has the rare distinction of being nominated twice in the same XYZZY category, Best Use of Medium. **Rogue of the Multiverse** *(C.E.J. Pacian, TADS)*. Saurian scientist bribes a human prisoner to perform salvage missions amidst procedurally generated, open world settings. **The Warbler's Nest** *(Jason McIntosh, Inform 7)*. Beautifully written folklore horror about a mother unsure whether her child has been replaced by a changeling.

2011
Nested

Andromeda Awakening *(Marco Innocenti, Inform 7)*. This first entry in a multiauthor shared universe sci-fi series asks the player to save the day with nothing but a computer and a railway ticket. **Beet the Devil** *(Carolyn VanEseltine, Inform 7)*. A god-fearing farmer descends into hell, armed with vegetables, to rescue his dog.

Bonehead *(Sean M. Shore, Inform 7)*. Step into the shoes of a historical baseball player about to make a career-ending mistake at a 1908 game. **Cryptozookeeper** *(Robb Sherwin, Hugo)*. Collect DNA, create monsters, and make them fight in this winner of five XYZZY awards. **Danse Nocturne** *(Joey Jones, Inform 7)*. Unusual game in blank verse where the player's primary contribution is adverbs. **Eternal** *(EndMaster, ChooseYourStory.com)*. Epic choice-based dark fantasy about a soldier with a chance to change the world; one of the most popular of all time on the web-based ChooseYourStory portal. **Flexible Survival** *(Nuku Valente et al., Inform 7)*. Adults-only text RPG involving nanobots, furries, biowarfare, and lots of sex; possibly the largest game ever written in Inform 7 with over four million words of content. **Kerkerkruip** *(Victor Gijsbers, Inform 7)*. Elaborate roguelike in prose, with dense procedural generation and emergent tactics and strategy. **The Night Circus** *(Yasmeen Kahn, StoryNexus)*. Tie-in for the Erin Morgenstern novel of the same name; early example of Failbetter's StoryNexus platform evolved from *Fallen London*. **PataNoir** *(Simon Christiansen, Inform 7)*. Interacting with similes is a primary mechanic in this noir wordplay mystery. **The Play** *(Dietrich Squinkifer, Undum)*. A director manages actors through a chaotic dress rehearsal. **Six** *(Wade Clarke, Inform 7)*. A six-year-old chases down well-characterized friends in a birthday game of hide-and-seek. **Taco Fiction** *(Ryan Veeder, Inform 7)*. IF Comp winner about a down-on-his-luck man who plans to rob a taco joint and uncovers a conspiracy.

2012
Howling Dogs

Bee *(Emily Short, Varytale)*. Cyclical, moving character study of a homeschooled spelling bee champ. **The Colder Light** *(Jon Ingold, Inform 7)*. Icy story of rune magic and survival; an experimental interface captures the best of both parser and choice-based games. **Counterfeit Monkey** *(Emily Short, Inform 7)*. Change the text of your surroundings to escape Anglophone Atlantis in this wordplay game to end all wordplay games. **CYBERQUEEN** *(Porpentine, Twine)*. Visceral science fiction nightmare about being torn apart and repurposed by a sadistic AI. **CYPHER: Cyberpunk Text Adventure** *(Carlos and Javier Cabrera, Win)*. Commercially sold text game with audiovisual extras and physical feelies but a frustrating homegrown parser. **Endless, Nameless** *(Adam Cadre, Inform 6)*. Neo-retro RPG with nested, interconnected realities; comments on IF as an artistic medium. **Eurydice** *(Anonymous, Inform 7)*. A grieving modern man is transported to the underworld. **First Draft of the Revolution** *(Emily Short and Liza Daly, inkle)*. Alter the text in a series of pivotal letters from a magic-infused eighteenth century. **Katawa Shoujo** *(Four Leaf Studios, Ren'Py)*. Visual novel dating sim famous for intimate portrayals of disability. **Mastaba Snoopy** *(gods17, Twine)*. Far in the future, an inconceivable alien creates a grotesque mockery of life based off misreading *Peanuts* comics. **Olivia's Orphanorium** *(Sam Kabo Ashwell, Inform 7)*. Tongue-in-cheek Victorian orphanage management simulator. **rat chaos** *(Winter Lake, Twine)*. Personal and vulnerable story beneath a goofy surface. **Samsara** *(Meg Jayanth, StoryNexus)*. Become a dreamwalker in a sumptuously written historical Bengal. **Shuffling Around** *(Andrew Schulz, Inform 7)*. The first in a series using anagrams as a primary game mechanic. **Winterstrike** *(Yoon Ha Lee, StoryNexus)*. Survive on a colony world after a mysterious apocalypse in this lyrical, limited-action storygame.

2013
Versu: A Family Supper

Blackbar *(Neven Mrgan and James Moore, iOS)*. Beat the censors at their own game in this unique mobile title from a dystopian future. **Black Crown** *(Rob Sherman, StoryNexus)*. Uniquely dark and surreal story with gloriously unsettling writing about a grim institute and the poor souls who work there. **Choice of the Deathless** *(Max Gladstone, ChoiceScript)*. Work at a demonic law firm to pay back your student loans in this "necromantic legal thriller" based on two previous novels. **Codename Cygnus** *(Reactive Studios, iOS)*. Interactive radio drama; control a secret agent with voice commands. **Coloratura** *(Lynnea Glasser, Inform 7)*. An alien creature manipulates the crew of a research vessel with color and song. **CRY$TAL WARRIOR KE$HA** *(Porpentine, Twine)*. Sensory overload in a kind of textual music video; peak Porpentine. **A Dark Room** *(Michael Townsend, web)*. Begins in a single room with one button to click, expands in scope and complexity until it reaches the stars. **Depression Quest** *(Zoe Quinn et al., Twine)*. Actions gray out and become unselectable in this IndieCade-selected meditation on living with depression. **Detritus** *(Mary Hamilton, Twine)*. Decide what to pack and what to leave behind through five key moves in your character's life. **Device 6** *(Simogo, iPad)*. Surreal thriller that uses artfully positioned text to tell a kinetic story. **Horse Master** *(Tom McHenry, Twine)*. That's no horse in this body horror pageantry management sim. **It's election time in Pakistan: Go rich boy, go!** *(Jahanzaib Haque, Quest)*. Satirical adventure uses an obnoxious protagonist to highlight socioeconomic disparities and the perceived futility of change in Pakistan. **a kiss** *(Dan Waber, Twine)*. Novel-length branching story about a single moment and all it connects to. **my father's long, long legs** *(Michael Lutz, Twine)*. Incredibly spooky, mostly linear horror piece with audio about obsession and loss of control. **The Next Day** *(Jonathan Blask, Hugo)*. Gentle, sleepy slice-of-life mood piece reminisces over a night spent in conversation with a good friend. **Queers in Love at the End of the World** *(Anna Anthropy, Twine)*. Choose how you spend your last ten seconds with someone you love. **Save the Date** *(Chris Cornell, Ren'Py)*. Find a way to keep Felicia alive in this self-aware dinner date time loop. **Steve Jackson's Sorcery!** *(inkle, iOS)*. Popular adaptation of the acclaimed gamebook series, spawning three sequels. **SLAMMED!** *(Paolo Chikiamco, ChoiceScript)*. Bodyslam and promo your way to the top as a face or heel in this choice-based pro-wrestling novel with an incredible amount of conditional content. **To Be Or Not To Be** *(Ryan North, gamebook)*. Interactive retelling of *Hamlet* by creator of *Dinosaur Comics*; raised over half a million dollars on Kickstarter.

AlethiCorp *(Simon Christiansen, web)*. Satirical corporate espionage simulator with an interface emulating a noxious company web portal. **Barbetween** *(Jason McIntosh, Seltani)*. Tiny game for Andrew Plotkin's persistent textual virtual world; a place where each visitor can leave something for the next who arrives. **Blood & Laurels** *(Emily Short, Versu)*. Roman epic; only full-length game to be released with the groundbreaking Versu engine. **Candlesmoke** *(Caelyn Sandel and Carolyn VanEseltine, Twine)*. A policewoman investigates the disappearance of a man whose occult studies have surpassed his control. **Coming Out Simulator 2014** *(Nicky Case, Flash)*. An autobiographical game about coming out to conservative Asian parents. **Creatures Such As We** *(Lynnea Glasser, ChoiceScript)*. Lunar tour guide explores questions of art, games, and human connection. **Hadean Lands** *(Andrew Plotkin, Inform 7)*. An apprentice alchemist must master their craft to escape a crash landing; a masterclass of systemic puzzle design and a crowdfunding success story. **Hunger Daemon** *(Sean M. Shore, Inform 7)*. Lovecraftian cult spoof in which you need to bring about the end of the world, but you're also hungry. **I'm Really Sorry About That Thing I Said When I Was Tired and/or Hungry** *(Dietrich Squinkifer, Twine)*. A genderqueer autobiographical tale about feeling misfit between several cultures. **Jacqueline, Jungle Queen!** *(Steph Cherrywell, Quest)*. Escape a jungle as a 1930s reporter in this fun game with a unique approach to puzzles. **Lime Ergot** *(Caleb Wilson, Inform 7)*. Dive through layers of hallucinations in this 2014 Halloween speed-IF entry. **Tin Star** *(Allen Gies, ChoiceScript)*. Take on the Old West as a US marshal in this vast, choice-based western mystery. **When acting as a particle / When acting as a wave** *(David T. Marchand, Twine)*. A link-driven story where there's no text other than links. **With Those We Love Alive** *(Porpentine, Twine)*. Winner of 2014's XYZZY Award for Best Writing, this unique game asks players to draw on their skin.

2014
80 Days

Arcadia *(Iain Pears, iOS)*. Companion piece to author's novel of same name; switch between multiple story threads in a tale of alternate worlds and rituals of magic and science. **Birdland** *(Brendan Patrick Hennessy, Twine)*. Dream birds infiltrate the real world in this queer fan-favorite summer camp drama. **Caves of Qud** *(Freehold Games, Win/Mac)*. Roguelike with enormous procedural text engine describing

2015
Lifeline

objects, people, and histories of a strange future. **Chlorophyll** *(Steph Cherrywell, Inform 7)*. Well-constructed puzzle explorer set on a space station populated by sentient, mobile plants. **Collocations** *(Abraham Avnisan, Objective C)*. Uses the text of quantum physics debates between Bohr and Einstein to produce poetry on an iPad based on the reader's movement and position. **Emily is Away** *(Kyle Seeley, Win/Mac)*. Coming-of-age conversation game in a retro instant messenger interface. **Hana Feels** *(Gavin Inglis, Twine)*. Through dialogue and journal entries, learn more about a central NPC's experience of self-harm. **Kuryokhin: Second Life** *(Michael Kurtov, Twine)*. An "afterlife metasimulator" loosely based on the life of an avant-garde composer. **Laid Off from the Synesthesia Factory** *(Katherine Morayati, Inform 7)*. Uses keywords to explore a dystopian future in this artful experiment in interactive narrative structure. **The Listeners** *(John Cayley, Alexa)*. Interactive literature for smart speakers, first shown in a gallery; what's the message of this new medium? **Map** *(Ade McT, Inform 7)*. An ordinary woman gets a fantastical chance to reshape her life. **Mere Anarchy** *(Bruno Dias, Undum)*. Magical rebels fight against classist injustice. **Midnight. Swordfight.** *(Chandler Groover, Inform 7)*. One-move game unfolds time to explore the past that led you to a fateful moment. **SPY INTRIGUE** *(furkle, Twine)*. Absurd, wacky, and supercool espionage hijinks collide with addiction, trauma, and suicide in this dystopian dramedy thriller. **Sub Rosa** *(Joey Jones and Melvin Rangasamy, Inform 7)*. Fun espionage puzzler in a unique, deep fantasy world.

2016
Choices: The Freshman

16 Ways to Kill a Vampire at McDonalds *(Abigail Corfman, Twine)*. How many ways can you take out a vampire before it claims another victim? **Cactus Blue Motel** *(Astrid Dalmady, Twine)*. High school grads make a mystical road trip stop in the desert. **Cannonfire Concerto** *(Caleb Wilson, ChoiceScript)*. Nineteenth-century musician changes the course of history wielding their supernatural Genius across Europe in love and at war. **Epitaph** *(Max Kreminski, web)*. Meddle in the development of procedurally generated alien civilizations in this text-only idle game. **Four Sittings in a Sinking House** *(Bruno Dias, Blotter)*. Hold séances, interview ghosts by candlelight, and decide the fate of the thing in the basement. **Hackmud** *(Drizzly Bear, Win/Mac)*. Multiplayer open-world hacking simulator; write your own malicious code and social engineer your way to victory. **Honeysuckle** *(Cat Manning, Texture)*. Sorceress considers options for escaping her evil wizard husband. **Inside the Facility** *(Arthur DiBianca, Inform 7)*. Attempt to map the entirety of a science fictional laboratory in this pared-down parser puzzler. **Mystic Messenger** *(Cheritz Co., iOS)*. Wildly popular real-time episodic story app from South Korean developer; late-night IMs with anime boys. **Open Sorcery** *(Abigail Corfman, Twine)*. Protect your network as a sentient Elemental Firewall. **The Periwink** *(Jedediah Berry, Twine)*. Murderous groundskeeper guides their victim through a darkly bizarre garden. **Reigns** *(Nerial, Devolver Digital, mobile)*. Play through generations of ill-fated rulers via a shuffled pack of random events; tight writing and many surprises. **Superluminal Vagrant Twin** *(C.E.J. Pacian, Inform 7)*. Make five million credits to buy back your twin in this delightful open-world sci-fi trading sim. **Tangaroa Deep** *(Astrid Dalmady, Twine)*. It's up to the player how greedily and how deep they delve in their submersible. **Worldsmith** *(Ade McT, Inform 7)*. Five-star, heavily simulationist commercial parser game about building a planet. **Xylophoniad** *(Robin Johnson, Versificator)*. Comedic Greek mythology mash-up, co-winner of 2016's Spring Thing.

2017
Universal Paperclips

Absence of Law *(Brian Rushton, Inform 7)*. Revive Dr. Law within 120 turns using limited three-letter inputs on a personified parser, DaedalOS. **A Beauty Cold and Austere** *(Mike Spivey, Inform 7)*. XYZZY-nominated puzzles demonstrate mathematical concepts. **Domestic Elementalism** *(fireisnormal, web)*. A witch fixes her malfunctioning house by altering objects' associated elements. **Eat Me** *(Chandler Groover, Inform 7)*. Fan favorite based around a single hunger-taming verb. **Harmonia** *(Liza Daly, Windrift)*. Full-length demonstration of the author's bespoke system for beautiful browser-based expanding hypertext; investigate a historical mystery at an obscure college. **A Normal Lost Phone** *(Accidental Queens, mobile)*. Award-winning LGBT coming-of-age story presented entirely through a fictional cellphone interface. **The Owl Consults** *(Cidney Hamilton et al., Inform 6)*. Direct criminals remotely as villainous freelance advisor The Owl. **Thaumistry** *(Bob Bates, TADS)*. Kickstarted full-length magical adventure from a former Infocomer. **Tuuli** *(Daurmith and Ruber Eaglenest, Inform 7)*. Spanish-language tale and translation about a Finnish witch; character study with beautiful writing. **Voyageur** *(Bruno Dias, mobile)*. Explore procedurally generated planets and cultures in this textual interstellar journey. **Warsim: The Realm of Aslona** *(Huw Millward, Win)*. Commercial text-based kingdom simulator with heavy randomized elements. **Will Not Let Me Go** *(Stephen Granade, Twine)*. Slice-of-life story about living with Alzheimer's. **The Wizard Sniffer** *(Buster Hudson, Inform 7)*. An ordinary pig sniffs out an evil wizard in this fantasy comedy, winner of IF Comp 2017.

Alias 'The Magpie' *(J.J. Guest, Inform 7)*. Gentleman thief steals a priceless Egyptian scarab in this interactive Wodehousian farce. **Animalia** *(Ian Michael Waddell, Twine)*. A cast of forest animals puppeteers a replica of a human child; 2018 XYZZY for Best Writing and Best NPCs. **Bi Lines** *(Naomi "Bez" Norbez, Twine)*. Closeted journalist medium is haunted by ghostly sexual assault. **Bogeyman** *(Elizabeth Smyth, Twine)*. Terrible things happen to children kidnapped by the bogeyman; winner of multiple XYZZY Awards. **Cannery Vale** *(Hanon Ondricek, AXMA Story Maker)*. Horror mystery switches perspectives between a novel's characters and its author. **Cragne Manor** *(Ryan Veeder, Jenni Polodna et al., Inform 7)*. Massive haunted house collaboration by eighty-four authors, each contributing one room of this tribute to IF classic *Anchorhead*. **The Ghost of You** *(Noodletub Games, Win)*. Choice-based hypertext with half a million words; Japanese yuri horror set at a 1950s symphony hall. **Human Errors** *(Katherine Morayati, Twine)*. Close out bug reports for mood regulation tech. **I.A.G. Alpha** *(Serhii Mozhaiskyi, INSTEAD)*. Games within games in this metapuzzler from a Russian author. **The Master of the Land** *(Pseudavid, Twine)*. Audacious hypertext world simulation in a nineteenth-century fantasy story. **Six Ages: Ride Like the Wind** *(A Sharp, iOS)*. Manage a fantasy kingdom through vignettes and decisions in this sequel to storylet pioneer *King of Dragon Pass 1999*. **Six Silver Bullets** *(William Dooling, ADRIFT)*. Mind-wiped secret agent armed with six shots must untangle a web of intrigue before it's too late. **The Tower** *(Freya Campbell, Twine)*. Unsettling story of dreams, identity, and Tarot; first of a short trilogy with *The House of God* and *The Horizon*. **What Isn't Saved (will be lost)** *(Cat Manning, Twine)*. Choose which memories of an ex to save in this IndieCade selected sci-fi rumination on death and remembrance.

2018
Weyrwood

American Election *(Greg Buchanan, ink)*. Dark, acclaimed tale of the campaign assistant for a sociopathic narcissist. **Bury me, my Love** *(The Pixel Hunt, mobile)*. Text a Syrian refugee during her dangerous journey to a new home. **Chuk and the Arena** *(Agnieszka Trzaska, Twine)*. Gladiatorial adventure puzzler wherein a scrawny alien seeks to win his planet's moon back from an evil emperor. **Crème de la Crème** *(Hannah Powell-Smith, ChoiceScript)*. Finishing school romance tied for two XYZZYs: Best Game and Best Writing. **Heretic's Hope** *(G.C. Baccaris, Twine)*. The last living human navigates their new role as pontiff to an alien, insectoid civilization. **Limerick Heist** *(Pace Smith, Twine)*. Choice-based bank heist told entirely in limerick form. **Lionkiller** *(Sisi Jiang, Twine)*. Less Disneyfied retelling of the *Mulan* story from a nonbinary Chinese designer. **Ord** *(Mujo Games, Win/Mac)*. Minimalist commercial text game told in one-word sentences. **Ryan Veeder's Authentic Fly Fishing** *(Ryan Veeder, Inform 7)*. Open-world fly fishing simulator plays out in real time over long periods, hidden depths, and thicker plots. **Skybreak!** *(William Dooling, ADRIFT)*. Open-world, science fantasy space sim with varying goals set during character creation; Winner of IF Comp 2019's Golden Banana of Discord. **Sunless Skies** *(Failbetter Games, Win/Mac)*. Explore the strange skies above Fallen London in this text-heavy narrative roguelike. **Turandot** *(Victor Gijsbers, ChoiceScript)*. A profligate

2019
AI Dungeon

rake would do anything for one princess. **Your Future Self** *(Contortionist Games, Win/ Mac)*. Time loop conversations and future mistakes on a glitchy, flickering screen. **Zozzled** *(Steph Cherrywell, Inform 7)*. A flapper exorcises a haunted hotel speakeasy by drinking spirits; IF Comp winner.

2020
Scents & Semiosis

Blaseball *(The Game Band, web)*. *Night Vale* meets baseball simulator in this live procgen web experiment that amassed an obsessive fan base. **Blow Your House Down** *(Bill Ingersoll, ChooseYourStory.com)*. Al Flansburgh is stuck in a cabin during a storm when two strangers show up. **The Cursed Painting** *(Wanderword, Alexa)*. Audio-only fantasy roleplaying game for smart speaker. **Doppeljobs** *(Lei, ink)*. Young doppelganger provides imitation on demand. **The Impossible Bottle** *(Linus Åkesson, Dialog)*. A little girl lives and plays in a magically recursive dollhouse; first place tie in IF Comp. **Jolly Good: Cakes and Ale** *(Kreg Segall, ChoiceScript)*. Very British comedy with over a million words; winner of XYZZYs for Best Writing, Setting, and NPCs. **Present Quest** *(Errol Elumir, Adventuron)*. Increasingly forgetful office worker faces puzzles trying to buy his wife a Christmas present. **A Rope of Chalk** *(Ryan Veeder, Inform 7)*. Viewpoints of an art competition drugged en masse. **Stuff of Legend** *(Lance Campbell, Inform 7)*. Village idiot sets out to become a knight; a comedy of errors. **Tavern Crawler** *(Josh Labelle, Twine)*. From dungeon crawl to bar crawl, the real adventures start after the dragon in this "screwball noir fantasy" RPG, tied for first place in IF Comp. **Tombs & Mummies** *(Matthew Warner, Quest)*. Escape early interment in a pharaoh's hazardous tomb.

DIGITAL
A LOVE STORY

Christine Love

Style **Choice-Based**
Debuted **Feb 28, 2010** *(web)*
Launch Platform **Windows, Mac, Linux**
Language **Ren'Py**

 **Using Your New Modem**
Message from: Mr. Wong   <u>Reply</u>

Hey, Lucy, so you have your computer set up. I
thought for Mr. Carlson's kid, I'd throw in a
little something extra: there's a dialer for your
modem attached to this message. If you plug it
into the phone line, you can use it to dial BBSes.

Just make sure not to run up your dad's phone bill
with long distance calls, OK? Here's a local BBS I
recommend looking at: 698-5519.

Enjoy,

George Wong
Wong Computers

Download attachment:
dialer.exe   421 bytes

see *Trade Wars 2002* **1991**

A standard readme format for .zip files meant to be uploaded to bulletin boards; DIZ stood for "description in zipfile." If structured correctly, the file could be automatically extracted and parsed by BBS software to describe the contents of a download.

CONNECTING TO A BBS—a bulletin board system, the cheapest way to find online communities before the mid-1990s—meant punching in a phone number and waiting for your modem to negotiate with a distant computer. The dial tone, the beeping digits, the screech of connecting hardware would give way after a sustained pause (and if all went well) to the glorious sight of a colorful ANSI welcome screen drawn line by line across your monitor. Once granted an account on a new board, you'd gain access to a unique pocket dimension of games, file downloads, discussions in progress, and—potentially, occasionally—new friends. Finding boards, new virtual islands to explore, was a bit like scavenging for buried treasure: here a phone number casually mentioned in a forum post, there a `FILE_ID.DIZ` with a new board's digits in its footer. A private offer to dial a less advertised system had all the thrill of a whispered invitation to a speakeasy. Some boards weren't meant for someone like you, too young or clueless or civilian to be on them. But the adventurous could learn to crack passwords or spoof calling cards, slipping between cracks in the system to venture into illicit cyberspaces. Anything seemed possible in an online world discovered one node at a time.

It's an experience very different from browsing the modern web, one that few people too young to have lived it can easily appreciate. *Digital: A Love Story* recreates this early online world in loving detail, capturing the texture and flavor of BBS life with a palpable nostalgia and precision. But its author never experienced that life firsthand. In 1988, the year the game is set, she hadn't even been born.

Christine Love grew up in small-town Canada in the 1990s and early 2000s, but she really grew up on the internet, among the first generation for whom the web was a constant and ever-present "third place." She had learned some programming in school and found making computers do neat stuff compelling, but she loved writing even more, spending more of her social time online with fellow writers than coders. As a teenager she discovered visual novels, games which married dialogue-driven storytelling with character artwork, sound, and music—especially popular in Japan, and often used to tell stories focusing on love and romance. While some visual novels have branching stories or stats that must be raised to win, many don't, and Love appreciated that this lack of obstacles reduced the frustration and skill-based gatekeeping of other kinds of digital story games. The simplicity freed authors and readers to focus on other ways computers might impact the art of traditional fiction writing. Simply "having the power to punctuate prose with music and animation," Love wrote, "is really interesting."[6]

When Love discovered the genre in the mid-2000s, visual novels were in the midst of an English-language renaissance brought about by a new tool making them far easier to create. Called Ren'Py, its name was a play on both *ren'ai*—the first word in the Japanese term for dating sims—and Python, the maturing programming language Ren'Py was built around. Created by American Tom Rothamel, Ren'Py was first released in 2004 as a special-purpose tool evolved from the more general Python game-making library pygame. One of the chief goals of pygame had been to create a free and cross-platform engine abstracting all the difficult platform-specific tasks of handling images, sounds, and animation into a simple library that let game makers focus on higher-level concerns. Ren'Py built a series of domain-specific languages on top of this framework, making it easy for visual novel authors to write scripts that could easily be compiled, along with all their multimedia assets, into standalone programs for Windows, Macintosh, and Linux. Inform had been a similarly democratizing tool for creating text adventures, but since visual novels were structurally simpler, Ren'Py authors could write in a syntax almost as natural as a screenplay—while more experienced coders could tap into the full power of Python if needed.

see *Curses* **1993**

```
e = Character('Eileen', color=(200, 255, 200, 255))

label start:
    $ renpy.music_start('sun-flower-slow-drag.mid')
    scene washington with fade
    show eileen vhappy with dissolve
    e "Hi, and welcome to the Ren'Py 4 demo program."
    show eileen happy
    e "My name is Eileen, and while I plan to one day star in
        a real game, for now I'm here to tell you about Ren'Py."
    e "I can tell you about the features of Ren'Py games, or
        how to write your own game. What do you want to know
        about?"

label choices:
    menu:
        "What are some features of Ren'Py games?":
            call features from _call_features_1
            jump choices
        "How do I write my own games with it?":
            call writing from _call_writing_1
            jump choices
```

Love first got involved with the Ren'Py community through an annual tradition inspired by NaNoWriMo (National Novel Writing Month), during which aspiring novelists try to write a novel in thirty days. Started in 2005, the Ren'Py version was called NaNoRenO, and it challenged community members to create a complete visual novel in March and release it on the last day of the month. Like the parser community's annual IF Comp, NaNoRenO became a popular yearly event, often inspiring sixty or seventy new games each year. Love first took part in 2007 at age seventeen, and she released a new game each March through her first years of college, appreciating both the esprit de corps of a community event and the useful pressure of a deadline: "If I don't set one," she once wrote, "I tend to work on something for two weeks and forget about it forever."[7]

see *Photopia* **1998**

The game jam vibe also made it easier to find collaborators, which were more commonly needed for visual novels than other types of IF since a wider range of skills was required to make them (including writing, coding, art, and music). Approaching what would have been her fourth NaNoRenO in March 2010, Love had found an artist collaborator and an idea for a game. But she also had a second idea, one that didn't need character art and which

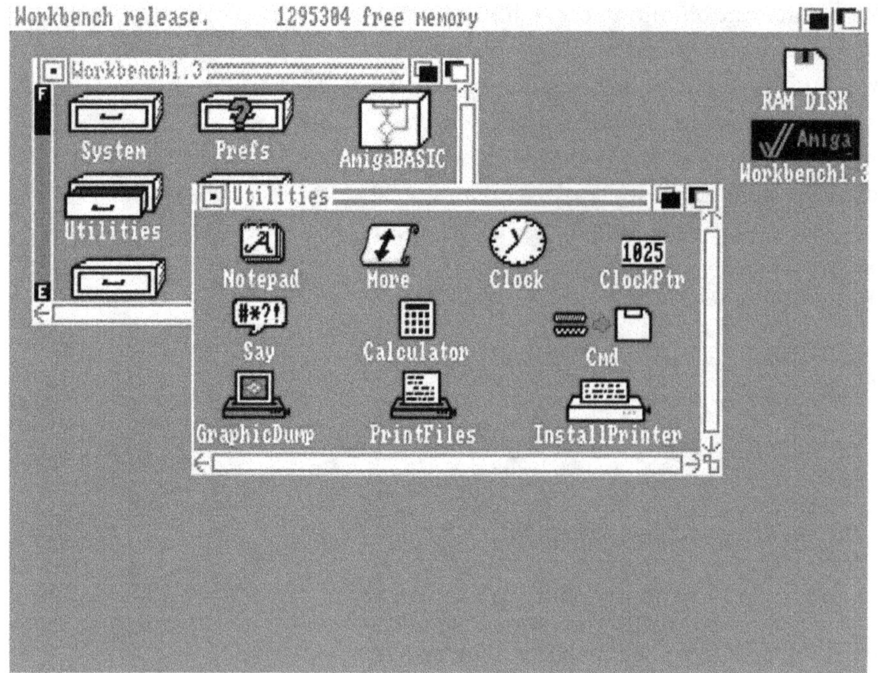

The distinctive blues of the Amiga Workbench environment (left) inspired *Digital*'s fictional Amie Workbench (opposite right), in which the game takes place.

she thought she could pull off by herself. She decided to write it during February, before NaNo season kicked in, to release just before the jam started as a treat for the community. She thought it would "probably get about as much readership as I normally got, which was about a dozen or so people; less, because it was kind of a crazy idea about an obscure part of computing history."[8] It would turn out to be the most popular Ren'Py game ever made up to that point, and one of the first to cross over into mainstream success.

Love's "crazy idea" wouldn't end up looking like a traditional visual novel at all. The colorful character portraits expected in the genre were replaced by an interface that was almost entirely text—specifically, it mimicked the famous blue tones and blocky letters of Workbench, Commodore's 1985 answer to the original Mac OS, which launched with their influential Amiga 1000 computer. Love's aim was to tell a period story about forming strong relationships online in a time when that was still a rare and special thing. ("When everyone's on the internet," she noted, "it's a little less interesting."[7]) While at first she planned gameplay based on mechanics from hacking simulators like the 2001 classic *Uplink* [Introversion Software], as her ideas evolved she found herself streamlining out the systems to focus more on the story and characters. "It's a cyberpunk story that's romantic instead of gritty,"[6] she would later say. "Instead of being a hacking game about hacking, it's a hacking game about talking to people."[7]

The player enters a real name and online handle at the start of the game.

2010

RE: First Poem
Message from: *Emilia   Reply

I do suppose you're right. Thanks, I appreciate your
directness, I'll have to keep that in mind for my next
attempt.

To tell you the truth, I'm really glad you replied. Nobody
else really had anything worthwhile to say; just some
compliments that were obviously false, and asking if I
really was a girl. Why would anyone ask a question like
that?

But you seem nice, Sapphire, and much better than that.
Thank you.

The game's interface mirrors the text-only structure of a BBS, primarily unfolding in public and private messages across a handful of different systems. As you learn to navigate your computer and the boards you can connect to, you strike up a friendship with fellow poster *Emilia that soon blossoms into something more. The inherent awkwardness of a budding romance mediated by technical limitations is recreated with sometimes painful accuracy, as in a moment where you're

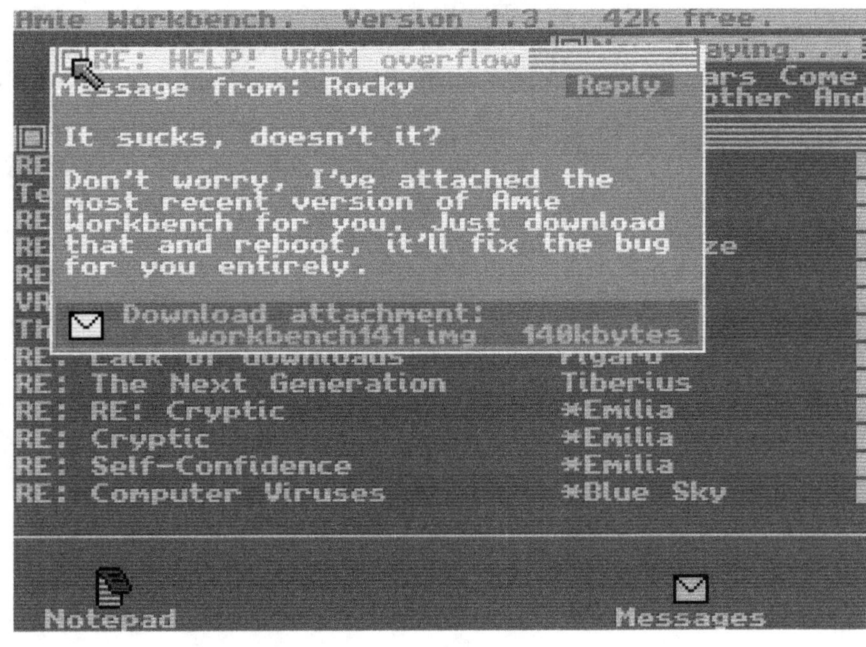

disconnected just as *Emilia confesses her love for you. But the plot thickens when you learn your online crush has a secret. The story soon dives down the rabbit hole of a strange yet familiar alternate history for the early net, a world "five minutes into the future of 1988" filled with unstoppable viruses, secret government projects, and ghosts in the machine.

While many visual novels and interactive fictions give players a choice of what to say during conversations, *Digital* offers only a binary switch: you can click Reply on any message, or ignore it. The player sees only the eventual response, not their character's own words, a deliberate design choice of Love's: "It doesn't break the immersion as much as if you would see your response and say, 'wait, I wouldn't say something like that.'"[7] The reader must fill in their own side of the conversation in their head, and the slow, interrupted cadences of the asynchronous dialogue helps capture the feeling of plausible replies to half-remembered posts.

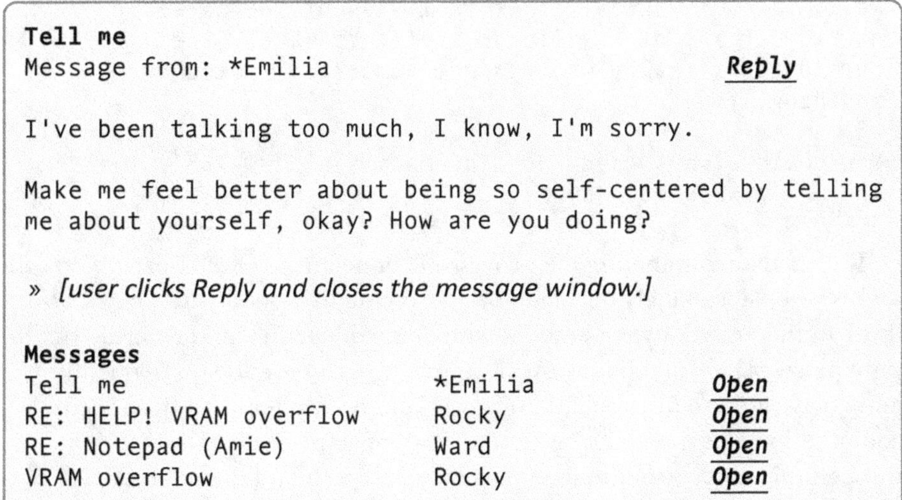

Tell me
Message from: *Emilia   **Reply**

I've been talking too much, I know, I'm sorry.

Make me feel better about being so self-centered by telling
me about yourself, okay? How are you doing?

» *[user clicks Reply and closes the message window.]*

Messages
Tell me	*Emilia	**Open**
RE: HELP! VRAM overflow	Rocky	**Open**
RE: Notepad (Amie)	Ward	**Open**
VRAM overflow	Rocky	**Open**

```
The Matrix registration      System              Open
RE: Lack of downloads         Figaro              Open
RE: The Next Generation       Tiberius            Open
RE: RE: Cryptic               *Emilia             Open
RE: Cryptic                   *Emilia             Open
RE: Self-Confidence           *Emilia             Open
RE: Computer Viruses          *Blue Sky           Open


»  [user reads a few more posts]


Alert
New private messages downloaded!


»  OK


RE: Tell me
Message from: *Emilia                                    Reply


No, I didn't know at all. I try not to make assumptions
about anyone. It's silly, don't you think?

Anyway, I'm sorry to hear it. I'm sure you'll figure out
what to do with your life next soon enough. And I know what
it's like to be lonely, believe me.
```

Unlike many visual novels, you'll need to solve a handful of puzzles to complete *Digital*, though most are gentle. A dangerous bug in your operating system needs to get patched with help from a friendly techie; a flaw in a password generator can be exploited to gain access to a forbidden system. Much as with the real early internet, the universe of bulletin boards you can connect to expands as you trade info with fellow explorers, slowly growing your personal index of phone numbers and scribbled passwords:

```
RE: Lack of downloads
Message from: Figaro                                     Reply


Well, Lake City Local isn't really about the warez or
hacking or any other illegal stuff. You know, the Sysop
here doesn't really want to get himself arrested or
anything.

You could always check out The Matrix at 220-7683. That's
where I always go, anyway.
```

Rather than automating the process of connecting to each board, *Digital* makes you painstakingly dial each one by typing in a phone number, waiting through the sound of your simulated modem connecting, and entering the right password for that board. As the game progresses and you frequently jump between systems, you'll do this over and over, often with the added complication of a spoofed long-distance calling card. It takes *work* to get through this story, even though it has only one path and doesn't branch.

"I've just never had an idea for a story that had two satisfying endings … but I've since realised there's more to it than that," Love wrote shortly after the game's release:

> There's just a whole lot of emotional power in immersing the player in the story by making them interact with it…. You can just watch someone solve a mystery, but that's not nearly as fun as feeling like you're solving it yourself. To read about [the BBS] world is one thing, but to actually be thrown into it … that's actually evocative. That gets you into it much more than any prose could.[6]

Love had researched BBS life in part through an extensive archive of old posts collected by computer historian Jason Scott at textfiles.com. "I just read a lot of absolute junk posts," Love recalled, "hours of just reading through archives … trying to nail people's voices."[7] Amidst the messages advancing the game's plot are a host of others:

```
I'll be here less
Message from: Acid Queen                        Reply


Hey, guys, I'm afraid to say that I'm going to be posting
here a lot less in the upcoming months. A LOT less,
actually, probably not at all. I'm sorry, but anyone who
was looking forward to more of Neon Empire will have to
wait a while.

The thing is that little Ichigo's due just about any day
now [...]
```

```
RE: He doesn't get it
Message from: Hollinger                          Reply


You're missing the point entirely. SF isn't supposed to be
predictive just for the sake of predicting the future. It's
not supposed to be a crystal ball. There's an extrapolative
aspect, yes, but even the most extrapolative stories
also have strong metaphorical qualities, and Gibson is no
exception [...]
```

```
stdlib.h error
Message from: Figaro                             Reply


Every time I try to build something with <stdlib.h>, no
matter what I do -- even the simplest program! -- it always
throws the error "incompatible types in assignment at line
322"! What the hell is going on here? Does Amie C just
plain old ship broken, or what?
```

One reviewer wrote that the background noise of the game's setting helps make it, among other things,

> a celebration of the Internet, and of the communication—and community—it enables. Obviously, the game's plot and premise would be impossible without the Net—this is a digital love story, after all! But it's the incidental detail, the stuff that has little or nothing to do with the plot, that makes the tribute clear. It's the distinct culture of each BBS you visit … you won't mistake the friendly Lake City Local for some of the places you encounter later in the game. It's the messages you read, and the characters who post them.… It's the friendships some of these characters have formed—relationships that existed long before the player character showed up, and that will hopefully go on long into the future. It all rings utterly true.[16]

"As an era it fascinates me," Love recalled. "Everything seemed so much more isolated.… This is very much a story about an adolescent searching for some sort of connection, and I think putting it in the 80s, putting it on bulletin board systems, really helps that."[7]

While the player types in a name for their silent protagonist, whose gender is never specified, Love had imagined her as a woman. The Ren'Py community had been a more welcoming space for queer creators than many other indie or professional game scenes—roughly two-thirds of forum posters were women, and many identified as something other than straight—and Love's earlier NaNoRenO titles had all featured same-sex romances, challenging the assumption that the default love story should always be hetero. "The protagonist's gender [is] up to the player to decide," she wrote of *Digital* and its sequel:

> So I guess they could be about a heterosexual player … but that was never my intent; my intent was to make a game for people like me. It's just that it's possible to do that without excluding others for no reason.

"And you know what?" she added, in a dig at a game industry still complaining about the challenges of supporting diverse character models and plots: "It really was not that fucking hard for the writing to accommodate that."[4]

As late as 2010, same-sex romance was still almost unheard of in mainstream games. Gay marriage had only recently been legalized in Love's home country of Canada and was still six years away from becoming federally recognized in the United States. In 2011, it was newsworthy when BioWare included prominent queer romance options in *Dragon Age II* ("I am so sick of talking about BioWare right now," Love would lament[4]). On the forums of *Star Wars: The Old Republic* [Electronic Arts 2011], the words "gay," "lesbian," and "homosexual" were blocked, not long after a guild for LGBT players had been banned in *World of Warcraft* [Blizzard Entertainment 2004]. Gamers and game makers in these communities were fighting not only to survive but to even get platforms to admit they existed, and the success of Love's projects would make her a fiercely outspoken voice for queer content in games.

It would prove to be the beginning of an unexpected career. "Honestly, the idea of being considered an indie game maker never even occurred to me until well after I finished *Digital*, and others started to throw around the term," she noted years later. "To me it was just a fun little writing project that couldn't possibly appeal to many people other than me."[6] But some combination of nostalgia, representation, unique mechanics, a good mystery, and compelling writing turned *Digital* into a viral internet success. "[It's] my favorite indie game of the year so far," one reviewer wrote. "What other game lets you crawl BBSes, uncover conspiracies, commit telephone fraud, and fall in love in just a couple hours?"[1] Love soon found herself writing an ambitious conceptual sequel set thousands of years in the future, exploring the databanks of a generation ship whose once-enlightened culture had descended into brutal misogyny, modeled after the real-life Joseon Dynasty in medieval Korea. *Analogue: A Hate Story* would become a longer and deeper story than *Digital*, and Love would drop out of college to complete it, founding a company to market her "weird unsellable feminist visual novel,"[11] whose website described it as "a mystery featuring transhumanism, traditional marriage, loneliness, and cosplay."

It was not the typical formula for a bestselling game. But *Analogue* would again earn widespread acclaim for its writing, its sophisticated storyline, and a refined UI that still focused on text but gave it a sleek, modern interface. It proved successful enough that Love found she could make a living writing games. Her work, one critic wrote, has often been "the antithesis of the modern power fantasy":

> Instead of growing a spine and taking down a great evil, her games are more about people allowing themselves to become vulnerable and become close to someone else.... She wants to make games that explore emotions beyond triumph, and she's been doing just that for years, attracting a growing cult following in the process.[3]

Love's success selling games that center writing, women, queerness, and "cuteness"—part of her ethos of "coming from a place of sincerity"[3]—has inspired other designers to focus on aspects of the human experience that traditional games neglect. The obsession with graphics and photorealism in the mainstream industry, as one example she's cited, can be an unfortunate distraction from crafting more meaningful experiences. "Realism is about presenting the world the way you see it," she says. "But I'm not concerned with what you already see. I'm concerned with what you're not seeing.... A lot of stuff I do, I deliberately exaggerate. I find that subtle is sometimes useful, but very rarely, frankly."[10]

"I always thought I was going to be, like, a novelist," Love once mused, "and have to support myself doing some shitty programming 9-to-5 job while I worked towards getting published."[4] For her fans, it's been a blessing that Christine found games before some big publishing house found her.

References

1 Caoili, Eric. 2010. "GameSetWatch Digital: A Love Story Fanart, Talk." *GameSetWatch* (blog). Jul 21, 2010. www.gamesetwatch.com/2010/07/digital_a_love_story_fanart_ta.php | a Sep 8, 2021

2 Gillen, Kieron. 2010. "Wot I Think: Digital: A Love Story." *Rock, Paper, Shotgun* (blog). Mar 17, 2010. www.rockpapershotgun.com/wot-i-think-digital-a-love-story | a Sep 8, 2021

3 Kaharl, Jonathan. 2017. "Digital: A Love Story" (review). *Hardcore Gaming 101* (blog). Jul 18, 2017. www.hardcoregaming101.net/digital-a-love-story | a Sep 8, 2021

4 Khaw, Cassandra. 2012. "Interview: Christine Love on Creating Inclusive Games." *1UP* (blog). 2012. www.1up.com/features/interview-christine-love-creating-inclusive | s Oct 19, 2012

5 Kuiper, Justin. 2016. "What Is NaNoRenO." *Route 59 Games* (blog). Dec 24, 2016. www.route59games.com/what-is-nanoreno | a Sep 8, 2021

6 Love, Christine. 2010a. "Interview: Christine Love on Digital: A Love Story." Interview by Lewis Denby. *Resolution Magazine* (blog). Jun 9, 2010. resolution-magazine.co.uk/content/interview-christine-love-on-digital | s Mar 16, 2012

7 Love, Christine. 2010b. "The Next HOPE (2010): Digital: A Love Story." Interview by Jason Scott. Youtube (Channel2600). Jul 16, 2010. www.youtube.com/watch?v=0sXhJY5HOIA | a Sep 8, 2021

8 Love, Christine. 2011. "What Kind of Year Has It Been?" *Love Conquers All Games* (blog). Jan 4, 2011. loveconquersallgam.es/post/2605257258/what-kind-of-year-has-it-been | a Sep 8, 2021

9 Love, Christine. 2014a. "GameRanx Asks: A Developer Interview With Christine Love." Interview by Ryan Parreno. *GameRanx* (blog). Jan 17, 2014. gameranx.com/features/id/19916/article/gameranx-asks-a-developer-interview-with-christine-love | a Sep 8, 2021

10 Love, Christine. 2014b. "Interview – Christine Love on Visual Novels, Sexuality, & Queer Representation in Games." *First Person Scholar* (blog). May 14, 2014. www.firstpersonscholar.com/interview-christine-love | a Sep 8, 2021

11 Love, Christine. n.d. "Yes, That IS My Real Name, Thankyouverymuch." *Love Conquers All Games* (blog). loveconquersallgam.es/bio | a Sep 8, 2021

12 Nathan's Toasty Technology Page. "Amiga Workbench 1.x." n.d. toastytech.com/guis/amiga1.html | a Sep 8, 2021

13 renpy.org. n.d. "Why Ren'Py?" www.renpy.org/why.html | a Sep 8, 2021

14 renpy.org. 2004. "Writing Visual Novels with Ren'Py: The Ren'Py Tutorial." Dec 10, 2004. www.renpy.org/dl/4.3/tutorial.html | a Sep 8, 2021

15 Rothamel, Tom. 2018. "Tom Rothamel on Ren'Py." Interview by Tobias Macey. YouTube. Aug 1, 2018. www.youtube.com/watch?v=lh0QJT_-5To | a Sep 8, 2021

16 Sahui, Peter. 2012. "Love, Hate, and Stories: The Visual Novels of Christine Love." *Matchsticks for My Eyes* (blog). Dec 28, 2012. www.matchstickeyes.com/2012/12/28/love-hate-and-stories-the-visual-novels-of-christine-love | a Sep 8, 2021

17 Scout. 2010. "Digital: A Love Story" (announcement). Forum post, Lemma Soft Forums, Feb 28, 2010. lemmasoft.renai.us/forums/viewtopic.php?f=11&t=6729 | a Sep 8, 2021

NESTED

Orteil (Julien Thiennot)

Style	**Experimental**
Debuted	**Jan 2011** (prototype)
	Jan 2012 (first release)
Launch Platform	**Web**
Language	**JavaScript**

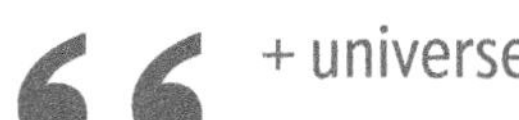

" + universe

THE SITE SHOWS ONLY A BLANK WHITE PAGE, a single word in the upper left corner. The plus sign suggests the familiar design language of nested folders: click here to see what's inside. Doing so reveals a handful of new lines indented one level deep—identical, but each with their own invitation to expand.

```
- universe
    + galactic supercluster
    + galactic supercluster
    + galactic supercluster
    + galactic supercluster
    + galactic supercluster
    + galactic supercluster
    + galactic supercluster
    + galactic supercluster
    + galactic supercluster
```

Inside each supercluster are a smattering of galaxies. Each galaxy contains galactic centers and galactic arms, arms contain star systems and nebulae,

2011

Major Releases

» **Unpublished original**, Jan 2011.

» **First public version**, Jan 2012.

» **Jan 13, 2013**. "Added a ton of stuff like ghosts, cats, dogs... office buildings with random companies and goddamn medieval planets."

» **Late Jan 2013**. Updated version with background pictures for special universes.

» **Sep 2013**. Added more content, including paintings.

and so on, down through planets and silica and oxygen and atoms. The atoms contain protons, neutrons, and electrons; the protons contain down quarks and up quarks; each quark contains something called a qwubble. Inside each qwubble are whole new universes.

"Okay," you think, "I get it, cute." You might briefly explore a nested landscape of nebulae and lifeless moons and the occasional black hole before getting bored and closing the browser tab.

Or you might discover that some parts of this multiverse are filled with life.

```
- telluric planet
    + continent
    - continent
        + desertic land
        - white sea
            + sea water
            - life
                + brill
                + whiting
                + skate
                + swordfish
                + tuna
                + haddock
                + dab
                + eel
                + mackerel
                + swordfish
                + great white shark
                + copepod
                + coral polyp
                + rotifer
                + sponge
                + porpoise
                + stingray
                + bottlenose dolphin
                + whale
```

Inside each creature are body parts, which in turn contain fats, muscles, blood, keratin, and so on. But creatures also contain thoughts, some of the only things in this textual universe that don't expand—leaf nodes on an infinite tree.

```
- great white shark
    + body
    - thoughts
        EXCUSE ME ARE YOU FOOD
        CHOMP
- rock lobster
```

```
    + body
      - thoughts
          dig dig
          gotta breed
  - oyster
    + body
      - thoughts
          slurp
          what is this
          oh no
```

Soon you discover that some of these planets host civilizations of intelligent people. And then the game—or whatever *Nested* is—really takes off.

Nested was written by a French college student with the online handle Orteil, who had a lifelong passion for making games. At an early age he received a game-making program called **Klik & Play** [Clickteam 1994] from his dad, which sparked a fascination for creating his own interactive experiences. Orteil loved games like *Spore* [Maxis 2008] and *The Sims* [Maxis 2000] that contained their own little worlds, and soon he was simulating worlds of his own. The projects were often far more ambitious than he yet had the means to realize, but the tinkering was endlessly fascinating. As he got older, he experimented with more elaborate game-making tools like Inform 7 and GameMaker, and at nineteen he found himself leading a team of online collaborators hoping to bring to life a fictional game made famous in an internet meme: *Crab Nicholson Extreme Text Adventure*. Orteil wanted it to be

see **2008**

> a game that branches into shitloads of different scenarios, depending on the player's input—or on some occasions, pure chance; that's why everything that could lead to interesting situations is possible … this game does not care whether something is logical or not, or even possible at all; this game doesn't give a fuck about the basic rules of space-time continuum; the only guideline is this—if it's awesome, extreme, or otherwise fucking amazing, it HAS to be in the game.[4]

The effort fell through—probably for the best, judging by surviving forum posts—but Orteil kept experimenting through his college years at Créapole in Paris, where he was studying web and graphic design. He released experimental Flash games, first on DeviantArt and Newgrounds, and later on a dedicated website set up by a friend he'd met on *Second Life* [Linden Lab 2003]. In his tiny text game *PretendEverything* [2011], you can **EMBODY** things from water droplets to mountains, exploring how they might transform into bigger or smaller entities (mountains are made from pebbles; droplets evaporate into mist). *Turtle Toy* [2011] let users program digital genomes for a Logo-like turtle that follows instructions to draw geometric shapes. In *Genesis* [2010], you're a god who starts with four elements—fire, water, earth, and air—and can combine them into more and more interesting creations, from rainbows to jungles to seaweed to butterflies.

Logo is a programming language designed for teaching; students program the motion of a "turtle" who leaves a trail of its movements across the screen, demonstrating one way to think about drawing line-art graphics.

In early 2011, Orteil wrote the bulk of what would become *Nested*, but he didn't finish or release it until a year later. It picked up some momentum on social media, but wouldn't really take off until another big update in early

2013. In the weeks after, it became a viral hit, shared and reshared by friends passing along the delightful experience of finding endless complexity in something that began so simply.

Nested was written in JavaScript, a language still in the midst of an awkward transition from a lightweight scripting tool to the mature engine modern web apps are built on. While today most JavaScript is hidden behind layers of obfuscation, transcompilation, and a complex ecosystem of libraries and modules, back then it was still often possible to View > Source on a web page to get a good sense of how it worked. Like many web toys of the time, *Nested* was coded in a single file full of global variables, inline data, and hacked-together functions. The complexities of getting code to run in other programming languages—package installations, class hierarchies, type-checking, encapsulation—could be ignored in JavaScript in the interest of just throwing together something that worked. While traditional coders saw this as a laughable weakness, it enabled millions of dabblers to create and share interesting programs that anyone with a web browser could run. Not since BASIC had there been a more democratizing platform for coding.

Orteil's code creates a simple authoring framework that allows for easily defining objects called Things, which have only a name (or a way to generate one) and a list of other Things they might conceivably contain:

```
new Thing("galaxy arm",["galactic life,5%","dyson sphere,4%",
   "dyson sphere,2%","star system,20-50","nebula,0-12","black
   hole,20%","black hole,20%"],"arm");
new Thing("star system",["star","star,3%","visitor planet,
   5%","future planet,10%","future planet,10%","terraformed
   planet,50%","terraformed planet,20%","terraformed planet,
   10%","medieval planet,30%","medieval planet,20%","ancient
   planet,50%","ancient planet,30%","ancient planet,10%",
   "barren planet,60%","barren planet,40%","barren planet,
   20%","gas giant,60%","gas giant,40%","gas giant,20%","gas
   giant,10%","asteroid belt,0-2"]);
```

Addenda like 0-12 define how many such Things a parent might contain, and 5% the chance it contains one at all. Each quoted item name refers to another Thing, which would need to be created in turn, so Orteil wrote a basic debugging tool to prod him to create Things that were referenced but not yet defined. Other shorthand made it easy to define similar types (a clam contains the same Things as an oyster or mussel) or to scale probabilities based on how early they appear in a list, with more and more obscure options coming toward the end.

The schema really gets interesting when it starts including people. On a habitable planet, some continents might contain countries, which within their regions hold towns or cities. Cities have districts, districts have houses, and houses contain relatable sentient beings, who unlike animals have both thoughts and memories:

```
- Beverly Cole
   + body
   - psyche
```

see **1973**

```
        - thoughts
            What I need right now is a new TV.
            I really, really like this soda.
            I regret so much.
        - memories
            The day I got a job as a cook.
            Kissing that one person in middle school.
            Stargazing with my aunt when I was a child.
```

The thoughts and memories came from a list, crafted by Orteil, that was large but not enormous—it would fit on a few printed pages. To add variety, many were formed from remixable components (such as "I really, really like" + "this soda"). But as he fleshed out the cities that contained the people, he began to add more and more interesting generators to fill them. In houses and museums you can find paintings with procedurally generated descriptions:

```
A painting of a satisfied snowflake and a shrivelled animal dressed as a
person in a historic scene. The animal dressed as a person is melting,
and the snowflake is playing music.
```

On streets, shop names:

```
- commercial area
    + Moneyworth
    + GreenFood
    + Wooffriends
    + Priceshark
    + Getthings
```

Or books on bookshelves:

```
- bookshelf
    + Living with George, the Nasty Goat
    + What You Didn't Know About Elongated Ninjas, Part VIII
    + Teaching Yourself How to Be Smarter
    + The Simply Stupid Adventures of Richard the Pirate From Space
```

Each book contains pages, which contain paragraphs, which contain letters (though not in any order sensible to Earthlings); the letters contain ink, which contain alcohol and oil, which contain lipids, which contain atoms. Some of the generators got rather elaborate, like the one for book titles, which could come from one of six possible templates, the shortest of which is:

```
Choose(["A shocking","An amazing","A vibrant","A heart-
    warming","A true","An astounding","A riveting","A
    twisted","A short","An elaborate","An overly elaborate","A
```

MEMORABLE PLACES

foggy land

tundra

telluric planet

cabinet

continent of Artica

galactic supercluster

cytoplasm

potassium

otter

xeshun

twisted star

grass blade

a turquoise interstellar cloud

armpit

```
ridiculous","A hilarious","A boring","An illustrated","A
  mind-numbing","A"]) + " " +
Choose(["story","tale","essay","book"]) + " " +
Choose(["involving", "about","on the subject of"]) + " " +
Choose(["pirates","ninjas","dinosaurs","unicorns","robots",
   "cyborgs","scientists","superheroes","maths"])+", "+
Choose(["surgeons","penguins","dolphins","cheese","dragons",
   "ghosts","kittens","sarcasm","astronomers","banana peels"])
   +" and "+
Choose(["spaceships","vegetarians","babies","art","time
   travel","abortions","philosophy","computers","punctuation",
   "magnets","geometry","language"])
```

New generators were easy to add, often designed to produce names that
were unique but plausibly familiar. For example:

```
["P","B","M","N","T","St","Pl","Bl","Gr","Fr","Sht","Fl"],
   ["apple","indows","inux","oogle"]
```

This could produce a familiar-sounding computer company such as Stoogle,
Plinux, or Flapple. Adding computers opened up a whole new chain of
generators when some of them contained screens, which contained internet
browsers, which in turn contained websites:

> - www.tvddit.net
>   + A comment on dating advice.
>   + A heated argument about whatever's trendy right now.
>   + A discussion about friendship
> - www.thattube.net
>   + An irate little person ranting about famous people
>   + www.9book.org
>   + A crude representation of a group of ¤¤¤¤¤¤ involved in ¤¤¤¤¤¤
>   with two other ¤¤¤¤¤¤.

Once in a while, one of the random links led back to the *Nested* website.

The scope of the game kept growing: TVs with shows; graveyards with
ghosts; medieval planets with dungeons filled with traps and monsters; future
planets where everything is made from nanoparticles, each with its own
tiny thoughts. Orteil went to great lengths to keep the thoughts of different
animals surprising yet consistent, writing hundreds of variants while giving
each class of thinking life-form its own unique voice. Ants are obsessed
with intruders, plankton thoughts all end with smileys, dinosaurs speak in
ponderous sentences of one or two words, and bears are polite and use all
caps:

> - bear
>   + body
>   - thoughts
>   EXCUSE ME GOOD SIR, WOULD YOU HAPPEN TO BE EDIBLE
>   YES I AM QUITE DAPPER

2011

Orteil also filled the game with unlikely events, increasing the odds each player might discover something that felt unique. A box in a garage might contain a hornet in addition to odds and ends; one in four thousand humans will be named Elvis Presley. Sometimes jungles are on fire, and sometimes people don't wear underwear. A black hole has a tiny chance of containing a crustacean. A thought has an even tinier chance of containing a black hole. "Humans are great at reading between the lines," one reviewer wrote, "even when nothing exists between the lines."[9] The juxtaposition of objects and words—sometimes planned, sometimes random—creates countless nascent stories in the reader's mind with each new unfolding. "It has the same attraction [of] *Dwarf Fortress*, **2006** another reviewer noted, "but without any of that pesky UI and interactivity to get in the way of the narrative threads."[10] Even without the elaborate, unfinished simulations of his *Spore* clones, Orteil had managed to create his own compellingly procedural universe.

Like any good worldbuilder, Orteil was always hoping to expand the game further, as a comment in the JavaScript showed:

```
//to add :
//cows,fungi,more shops,temples,more buildings,paintings,
  internal organs,phones,lamps,abandoned plants/castles,
  spaceships oh god
//actual battlefield thoughts,military bases,ships,airports,
  more street names,space ships/stations,giant colony ships,
  wasteland worlds,cults,space probes,prisons,government
  buildings,schools,amphibian skin
```

But *Nested*'s dimensions, of course, are limited. It's comprised of less than two thousand lines of code and data. Encoded into its nested Things are myriad simplifications and assumptions, some obvious—"every person in the universe is an American," Orteil notes in the source, since the names are pulled from a US list sorted by popularity—and some less so. People all wear the same kinds of clothing regardless of gender; cities exist, but pollution doesn't; people have memories but animals don't; churches are only found on medieval planets. No recreation of the universe smaller than the universe, naturally, can contain its complexity. But procedural generation inevitably involves human curation, and despite claims from some in recent years that games should not be political, every individual decision of what to include or not include in a virtual universe is of course a statement about what matters, or doesn't, in the real one.

By most definitions, *Nested* isn't a game. All you can do is expand, opening more and more Things to see what's inside them. Yet you can spend hours exploring its endlessly nested multiverse. It's a fascinating example of the

As with *Dwarf Fortress* **2006**, players of *Nested* love sharing stories of the weird things they've found within its procedural worlds. Here's a lovely example from one reviewer:[10]

Inside [his] blood vessels, I found lipids and inside those lipids I found a dimensioverse. Inside that dimensioverse I found a planet with a continent called Antartica, which contained several countries. I zoomed in on Bapan, the capital of which contains a Crooked Bronze Tower. It's packed with tourists. One of them, Michael Miller, is wearing a monocle, cargo pants and a hoodie. Inside the pocket of the pants is a note. I expect something that I can turn into a profound story to place at the end of this post.

It's a recipe.

"Recipe:
-taco shell
-ice cream
-vinegar"

strengths of procedural text, even divorced from simulations or game mechanics. Orteil had plans for an even more ambitious sequel ("I'm writing the planet generator for Nested 2 one biome at a time," he tweeted in 2014; "baby steppes."[5]) But whatever he had pending got sidetracked when another of his random experiments, a little game called *Cookie Clicker* [DashNet 2013], became a runaway hit. Since 2015 Orteil has been making a living off that game, which is among the first sustainable titles in a genre now called incremental games, while continuing to experiment on the side with more strange creations and unusual toys.

Nested, a reviewer wrote, "is at once bogglingly expansive, but intimately familiar in its parts, extrapolating the infinite from the known."[2] It's remained a low-burn viral success for a decade, shared again each time a new person stumbles across it, and for good reason. There's something delightful in linking your friends to a page with a single word, and waiting for their minds to be blown once they see what's inside.

see *Universal Paperclips*
2017

References

1   Crecente, Brian. 2013. "The Cult of the Cookie Clicker: When Is a Game Not a Game?" *Polygon* (blog). Sep 30, 2013. www.polygon.com/2013/9/30/4786780/the-cult-of-the-cookie-clicker-when-is-a-game-not-a-game | a Mar 5, 2021

2   Lee. 2012. "A Flat Packed Universe." *Electronic Literature (ENGL 376VV)* (blog). Apr 19, 2012. elit. umwblogs.org/2012/04/19/a-flat-packed-universe | a Mar 5, 2021

3   Orteil. 2010a. "Orteil's News." Newgrounds. orteil.newgrounds.com/news | a Mar 5, 2021

4   Orteil. 2010b. "Re: Need to Expand the Overall Idea." Forum post, Crab Nicholson Extreme Sleepover, Feb 12, 2010. crabnicholson.forumotion.com/t20-need-to-expand-the-overall-idea#167 | a Mar 5, 2021

5   Orteil. 2014. "@Orteil42: I'm writing the planet generator…" Twitter post. Jun 25, 2014. twitter.com/ Orteil42/status/481841244541165568

6   Orteil. 2017. "Hey, I'm Orteil. I made a game or something a while ago. AMA!" r/cookieclicker. Reddit AMA. www.reddit.com/r/CookieClicker/comments/dro3wd/me_and_my_pal_made_a_game_some_time_ago_ama | a Mar 5, 2021

7   Orteil. 2019. "Me and my pal made a game some time ago, AMA!" r/cookieclicker. Reddit AMA. www. reddit.com/r/CookieClicker/comments/dro3wd/me_and_my_pal_made_a_game_some_time_ago_ama | a Mar 5, 2021

8   Orteil. n.d. "Frequently Asked Questions." *Orteil* (Tumblr). orteil42.tumblr.com/faq | a Mar 5, 2021

9   Sir TapTap. 2016. "Free Points: Nested." *Sir TapTap* (blog). Mar 14, 2016. sirtaptap.com/articles/free-points/ free-points-nested | a Mar 5, 2021

10   Smith, Adam. 2014. "Random Universe Generator: Nested Is The Best Thing." *Rock, Paper, Shotgun* (blog). Jul 30, 2014. www.rockpapershotgun.com/nested-free-procedural-generation-game | a Mar 5, 2021

HOWLING DOGS

Porpentine Charity Heartscape

Style **Hypertext**
Debuted **Oct 1, 2012** *(IF Comp)*
Launch Platform **Web**
Language **Twine**

> A room of dark metal. Fluorescent lights embedded in the ceiling.

WHEN THE 2012 INTERACTIVE FICTION COMPETITION OPENED for its eighteenth season with the usual crop of TADS and Inform 7 entries, few in the parser games world were expecting the seeds of a revolution. Certainly none had imagined such revolution might be heralded by a one-room game from a first-time entrant using a development tool that few had even heard of—three red flags right there. And while other entries that year lured players with traditional blurbs mentioning crowd-pleasers like spaceships, manor house mysteries, and magic, one description stood out as not quite like the others:

> mysterious game…hyperlink powered, yes, but what ethos does it promote? a death ethos? my god…or uh, visions, gender, the hyphen between dream-notdream, fascination, feeling anything at all?

> two significant endings

The game in question begins with (and takes its title from) a story by Kenzaburō Ōe, the 1994 Nobel Prize winner who once described his life's work as "writing about the dignity of human beings."[12] Then, after long seconds of nothing but a dark screen, the game describes a prison: a complex of small metal rooms lit by fluorescent lights, with no explanation of who you are, why you're there, or why there's no way out.

2012

> The <u>activity room</u> is in the north wall. The <u>lavatory</u> entrance, west, next
> to the <u>trash disposal</u> and the <u>nutrient dispensers</u>. The <u>sanity room</u> is in
> the east wall.
>
> Her <u>photograph</u> is pinned to the side of your bunk. A red LCD reads 367
> a few inches over.

Clicking the highlighted words lets you explore your surroundings, a
limited world that seems at first to have the same simulationist assumptions
as traditional parser IF. Space is divided into discrete rooms; interacting with
the nutrient dispensers produces food and bottled water; consuming these
makes trash, which litters up the room description; trash can be disposed
of in the trash disposal. In the bathroom is a functional shower. The sanity
room has wall-to-wall scenes projecting peaceful vistas, and the photograph
is of someone you once loved whose memory grows fainter each day. Each
day, the LCD counter ticks up by one.

> Her <u>photograph</u> is pinned to the side of your bunk. A red LCD reads 368
> a few inches over.

The activity room provides the only fleeting escape:

> A reclining chair in a dark room with a visor hanging from the ceiling.
>
> You sit down and pull the visor over your head. The visor interior is soft
> and enveloping. You squeeze the drip tube between your teeth and
> sickly sweet fluid floods your mouth. <u>Pulses</u> fire into your retinas.

The simulation rig takes you to new virtual worlds, but each is only another
prison. As Joan of Arc (or maybe just someone like her) you await immolation
for the crime of believing yourself to be something no woman was allowed
to become. As a kept companion in a looming stone house on a moor, your
oppression becomes so unbearable that murdering your hateful captor is the
only possible choice for your character—no matter what words the player
chooses to click. As a child empress in a fantasy kingdom, you ritually study
the most artful and proper ways to die, learning how to keep your family
from shame at the moment of your inevitable assassination.

These are not just any prisons. They are prisons for women, stages for
mythic yet painfully familiar traumas of oppression, of control, of societal
roles and the impossible weight of rebelling against them. Like many of
the new flood of games built with a tool called Twine, *Howling Dogs* was
concerned with themes and issues not often explored in games by men—or,
for the most part, in games at all. It was a kind of story that gamers had
rarely seen, part of a burgeoning conversation in the form of experimental
text games happening between outsider designers in the process of expanding
that medium's horizons forever.

Created in 2009 by parser IF author Chris Klimas, Twine was an elegant visual tool for creating hypertext stories, works where the user clicks words in on-screen prose to advance through a network of linked textual nodes. Hypertext fiction had been around for decades, though without the same culture of freely sharing work that had grown up around other styles of interactive fiction. Twine attracted few users at first, despite its many advantages as a tool: it was free, it had friendly documentation, and it let you export your games as standalone web pages playable in any browser.

see *Patchwork Girl* **1995**

Twine's interface gave authors a workbench where they could create and link named boxes together; these boxes contained text that could be linked to other nodes by wrapping their names in double brackets:

```
The [[activity room]] is in the north wall. The [[lavatory]]
entrance, west, next to the [[trash disposal]] and the
[[nutrient dispensers]].
```

The author would then create nodes named `activity room`, `lavatory`, and so on, until all mentioned links led to defined passages. That was it, more or less: while other syntax allowed for advanced features like tracking variables, tweaking styles, or varying text conditionally, the foundation of Twine was remarkably simple. At first, many thought it was perhaps too simple: only a handful of small Twine stories had been released by the early months of 2012, more than two years after Twine's debut. Existing hypertext authors assumed a far more powerful tool was necessary to do real work, while many parser IF fans were simply not interested in something that seemed so basic. Leading IF languages like TADS or Inform 7 could simulate a model world and understand complex input, qualities seen as prerequisites to an interesting interactive experience—though this consensus had begun to change, as evidenced by a 2010 post on Emily Short's blog entitled "So, Do We Need This Parser Thing Anyway?"[10] And while the web browser was becoming a relatively stable platform for complex applications, few interactive story engines were yet natively using it. The exceptions came from communities with little overlap, failing to reach the critical mass necessary to shape larger discourse.

see **2008**

see *Galatea* **2000**

Parser IF could take months to write. *Howling Dogs* was written in a single week of intense creative output, in what would become a common pattern for its author, Porpentine Charity Heartscape (then writing as just Porpentine). A young trans woman kicked out of her home at age fourteen—she would later say in an interview that before she started making games, she was "just surviving"[5]—Porpentine was familiar with parser IF and had written games in Inform. But she'd become frustrated by the implicit gatekeeping of the parser, and the more explicit elitism of parts of its community. Near the end of 2012 she published an extraordinary manifesto and tutorial, "Creation Under Capitalism and the Twine Revolution,"[8] laying out the parser's frustrations both for players—"an invisible god figure that punishes you for failing to understand, as a representation of the smirking nerd, the obnoxious dungeon master"—and for would-be authors, not all of whom were privileged enough to have the time, education, and financial security to master it. While the community that had formed around rec.arts.int-fiction in the early 1990s had standardized a consistent notion of what interactive stories could be, Porpentine suggested that this conception had blind spots, some of which seemed to outsiders to be enshrined into monopoly:

> What do we see when we search interactive fiction? I mean, the first couple pages of actual search results.
>
> Dead pages full of links to past glories of the 90s, maybe early 2000s. A lot of the active stuff isn't very welcoming to minorities. I see stories set in colleges, mansions, middle-class homes, generic fantasy worlds. I'm not college, I'm not mansions. What is that to me?
>
> But above all else, they all have one thing in common. They presume parser as the default.
>
> … Some say non-parser isn't interactive fiction.
>
> If the words can be interacted with, it's interactive fiction.

"We have a problem," Porpentine's manifesto continued,

> which is not admitting the degree to which we rely on games for anesthesia. They're disposable alternate lives that slowly devour our real ones. "Gamers" are junkies, games are their junk, and there's a kind of game criticism that's primary function is enabling them to deny that. When we don't ask more from games, it's because we don't want them to get better. We're afraid of the world and we'd rather explore the boundaries of these fake, facile ones.

The false escapes of *Howling Dogs'* virtual prisons echo this notion of hollow game worlds, and one reading suggested by the author parallels the stories of "those who have lived in that tiny room … in increasingly deteriorating circumstances, as you become less and less capable of caring about yourself. And what is the only thing you can afford? Terrible food and some kind of glowing screen, and when you look away from the screen, you're still in the same place."[11] But the piece also supports other readings: of games as necessary spaces for exploring alternate possibilities, and for understanding unthinkable truths in the form of more visible virtual shadows. In one world you're asked to choose how to describe a garden seen only through a narrow slit: your choice changes the story you see next about a chance encounter with the garden later in life. The selection of frame becomes a way to tame a place containing some objective truth only partly revealed, turning it into comforting parable or thematic touchstone. Presented with incomplete truths, we do our best to make them part of our selves.

While *Howling Dogs'* frame story replicates the feel of a traditional parser game, with its compass directions and verb-driven interactions, the virtual worlds you visit explore a range of different styles and typographic effects. Twine authors were in the midst of evolving a new hypertext language that, akin to parallel evolution in biology, shared some surface features but almost no ancestry or vocabulary with hypertext theory in academia. Twines abounded with experiments in what linked texts could mean and what they could do. In *Dogs*, links are used at various times for pacing, revealing more text each time the final word is clicked; to zoom in on details, returning to the previous node after they've been read; as explicit choice points, like in a

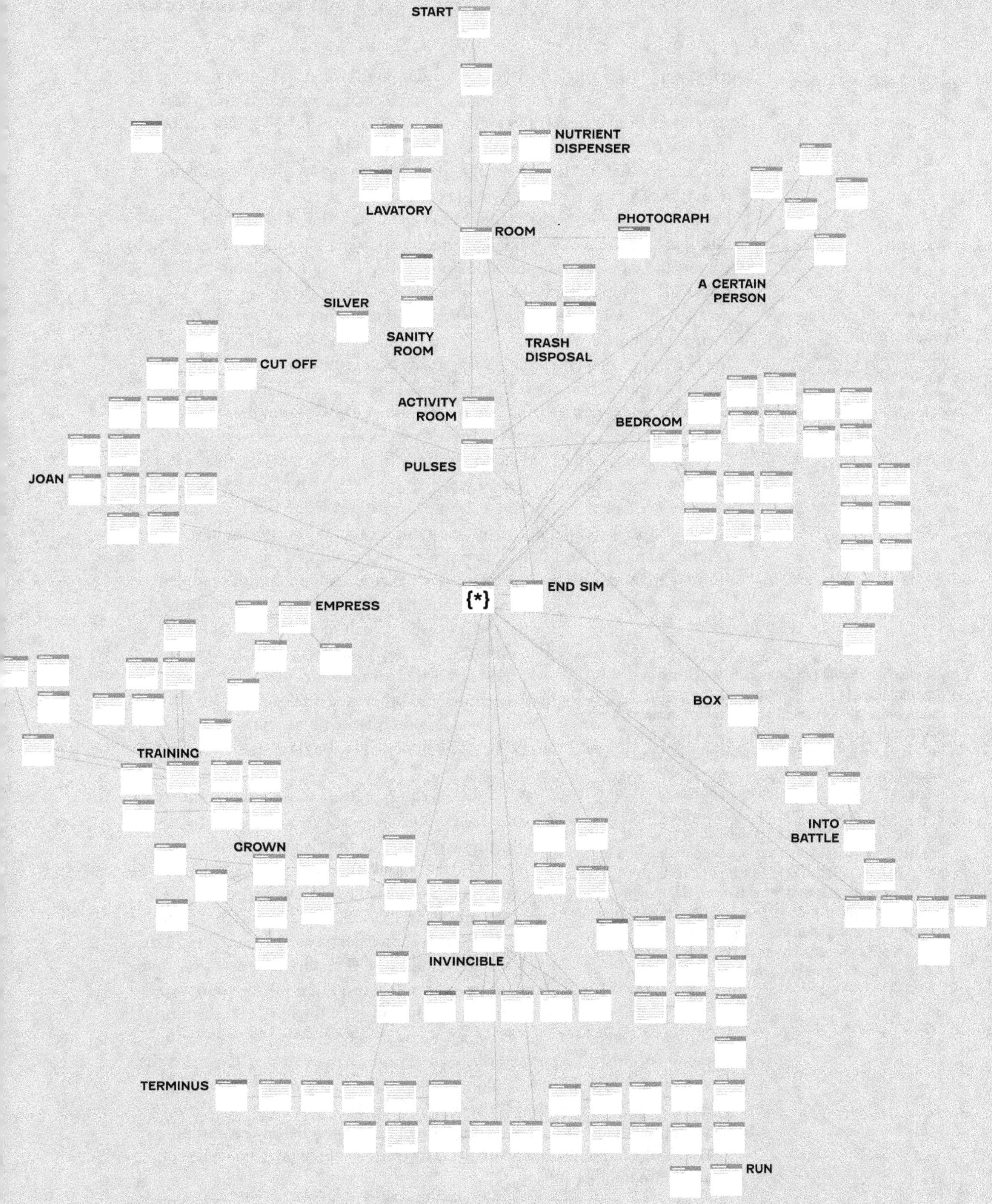

START

NUTRIENT
DISPENSER

LAVATORY

ROOM

PHOTOGRAPH

A CERTAIN
PERSON

SILVER

SANITY
ROOM

TRASH
DISPOSAL

CUT OFF

ACTIVITY
ROOM

BEDROOM

JOAN

PULSES

EMPRESS

{*}   END SIM

BOX

TRAINING

INTO
BATTLE

GROWN

INVINCIBLE

TERMINUS

RUN

see *The Cave of Time* **1979**

The original IF Comp release of *Howling Dogs* used Twine's default Sugarcane style sheet. A post-comp update added most of the timing and presentation effects described here.

Moving On...

People change over time, naturally, which can give them complicated relationships with the writing they leave behind. Porpentine has since disavowed her "Creation Under Capitalism" essay and many of the dominant narratives around the so-called Twine Revolution, and called out other authors in the Twine scene of the time as exploitative or abusive. She now believes many of her own early ideas are too easily co-opted by neoliberal and capitalist ideologies she rejects. "I think a retrospective can benefit a lot from a living examination of a person throughout their life," she wrote me during the authoring of this book, "looking at context and creative evolution." While this chapter captures a snapshot of *Howling Dogs* at the moment of its release, its author now often recommends her more recent games and writing first.

gamebook; or as toggles, letting the reader adjust a specific detail in a scene. While the game's structure is largely linear—each playthrough progresses through the same series of vignettes—the shifting meaning of a link and the inability to rewind to a previous node makes the player uncertain about their role in the story and its potential scope. ("The nature of my involvement with it felt like I was constantly endeavoring to exert control that I didn't have," one reviewer wrote.[6]) Another Porpentine game, *Myriad* [2012], features multiple long sequences hidden behind unassuming links that can completely change the scope and meaning of a playthrough, making an individual traversal feel slippery, chaotic, personal.

Dogs also looks striking for a text game. Porpentine modified the default Twine template, Sugarcane, to remove its navigational controls, placing the text large and centered against a black background instead of inside a familiar frame. Some text blurs when you hover your mouse over it, or stays blurred no matter what you do. Transitioning between the virtual worlds and the "real" one of the frame story is always marked by clicking the character sequence {*}, a typographic breakpoint that suggests both the interruption of an asterisk's footnote, and an orifice that offers a biological, not a technological, transition. Carefully timed pauses on black screens bring a heavy sense of pacing and momentum that parser games have trouble matching. And rather than prioritizing multiplatform support by running in an abstracted virtual machine that limited an author's control over text presentation, Twine games were exclusively for the modern web, which meant they could access that platform's full power with far more control over styles and aesthetics. In the years to come, Twines by Porpentine and others would become even more visually striking, presented with all the care and attention to detail of professional typographers and layout designers.

But it's the writing and storytelling that make *Howling Dogs* most memorable. As you return again and again to your prison and sleep off the day's simulations, your environment slowly degrades. The trash receptacle sticks shut; discarded food wrappers and broken water bottles begin to pile up on the floor. The shower stops working and your skin becomes itchy and gross. The virtual escapes become increasingly desirable, even if the worlds you escape to are implicitly the same. In the house on the moor, "more than three hundred days have elapsed" since your captor brought you, aligning with the LCD counter in your prison. Joan of Arc's cell mirrors the layout of the protagonist's, down to its compass-point positional details:

> Sometimes they slide in food and drink [...] My filth lies in the corner. The door on the north wall opens only to offer me great pain, agitation, and ultimately, confusion.

But amidst the oppressive stories of degradation and powerlessness are moments of rich emotional clarity and arresting writing. As your character is dragged away to be burned at the stake, "the stones wonder if it is interesting to suffer." In a blood-soaked riff on videogame ultraviolence, "reliquary tanks piloted by giant saint skulls crash" through villagers, "shredding hearts into flimsy strips that hang from chest-holes like tinsel wigs." A villain's cruel smile "is tearing her apart, teeth brimming off the edge of her face."

The last and longest sequence paints a vivid portrait of a fantastical world of dead gods, living cities, and jeweled birds the size of mountains. In one of the game's most striking moments, your child empress, trained her whole life to watch for assassins, is overwhelmed by the details of a palace festival filled with dangerous visitors:

> Soporific fumes of smoky blue drift through the hall, heralding the beginning of the most august, most sacred, most portentous Festival of Sleep! Strum and pluck of stringed instruments as servants wearing masks of pure black pour dreamliquid for everyone, gracefully moving from pool to pool of cushions not spilling a drop as throat dancers leap from pillar to pillar making the ceiling leap with shadows and somehow the shadows are leaking petals, a marvelous trick, and stampeding through the garden are black horses with jeweled riders symbolizing night bringing phantasmagoria and everyone gathers at the windows to watch them go [...]

The text spills past the end of the page, the screen filling up with blue links: dangerous, intriguing possibilities. But one link (not part of the excerpt here) stands out to a reader who remains engaged with the text and actually reads it closely. One link reveals that something is wrong. The reader who clicks it can find a different and perhaps more satisfying ending than the one who clicks at random, assuming so many links must surely all go to the same place. If you and the empress are observant enough to pass this test, you spot a threat early enough to flee from it: a threat you've been trained your whole life to run from. You're given multiple opportunities to click away through the {*} escape link, to wake up and return to your dreary reality. But sometimes true escape only comes by pushing through fear:

> Running through the darkness past glowing, disembodied hearts. They span into the distance until they look like stars.
>
> You feel an aching hollow as your gaze twists across the beautiful hearts, the bold hearts, the true hearts.
>
> "don't stop, please
>
> they're just showing you what you already have"

"Many people describe a sort of catharsis that they feel when they play Porpentine's games," wrote Laura Hudson in a 2014 profile of the author, whose Twines had by then had become increasingly visible viral successes. "There's a sudden sense of relief that something important but taboo has finally been acknowledged in a game, and perhaps has left them feeling less alone in the process."[5] One reviewer expressed much the same sentiment when they wrote that "having spent the last two-ish weeks trying to articulate exactly what Porpentine's game howling dogs means to me in sort of a critical way, I'm going to have to declare intellectual bankruptcy…. I find it very personal. SO FUCK IT. I like howling dogs."[1]

The parser interactive fiction community, at least at first, didn't know what to make of this new kind of game. In the competition it didn't even place in the top ten, and it was awarded the dubious "Golden Banana of Discord" given to the game with the greatest spread between low and high scores. One reviewer gave it a middling score but seemed to like it more than he thought he ought to: "I play for enjoyment, and I didn't enjoy this a great deal, hence the 3 stars [out of 5]. It was confusing, it was confronting, and as Art it succeeded in unbalancing me. It was quite well done."[3]

But perhaps some of this reaction was just the shock of immersion into unfamiliar waters. When the community's annual XYZZY Awards were announced in early 2013, *Howling Dogs* was nominated in all major categories, winning in two. Parser game advocate Emily Short began to cover Twine and Twine authors on her blog in the last months of 2012, and she became a champion for making text game communities more welcoming to more kinds of authors. Three other Twine games were released alongside *Dogs* in the 2012 IF Comp; in the next competition there were thirteen. Twines and games written in other parserless systems would soon equal or exceed the number of parser entries each year, a new status quo that would continue for the next decade and counting. Jettisoning all the assumptions of a parser—and its libraries of preapproved verbs, messages, simulation rules, and parsing strategies—gave up a lot of complexity, but left behind a clay far easier to shape into something new. "Twine," Porpentine wrote, "is the closest we've come to a blank page."[8]

Twine's rise, in a way, continued a move begun fifteen years earlier with *Photopia* **1998** to minimize puzzles in IF and focus on writing and storytelling instead. But more honestly, Twine's growing popularity had little to do with the parser world's norms and traditions at all. Creators who never felt at home there—whether for technical, societal, social, or other reasons—were suddenly part of an explosion of new, innovative, fascinating works of interactive fiction. Twine games like *Mastaba Snoopy* [gods17 2012], *rat chaos* [Winter Lake 2012], and *my father's long, long legs* [Michael Lutz 2013] were nothing like what other game-making communities were writing, and were often being made by people underrepresented in those spaces: brown people; queer people; folks without coding backgrounds or the means to host their own websites. (Many early Twines were shared via free Dropbox links, not permanent URLs.) The standard Twine style sheet, white text with blue links on a black background, became for a few years a kind of calling card: a sign that this was a different sort of game, one that might not make the same assumptions that the old interactive fiction took for granted.

Many fans of text games, including most of the parser IF scene, welcomed the new games and new voices. There were ugly and significant exceptions—a 2013 Twine called *Depression Quest* [Zoë Quinn et al. 2013] would become the first target of the Gamergate harassment campaign against women and queer creators. But many authors saw that a bigger tent could only be a good thing for the future of a narrow niche. More people making, sharing, and loving text games spoke not to dilution, but to continued relevance, demonstrating beyond doubt there were many frontiers of interactive text still left to explore.

Porpentine would become a leading voice in the so-called Twine revolution: the term coined in her manifesto is now widely used by game scholars. She would create new work at an unflinching pace of furious experimentation—releasing twenty-five games between 2012 and 2014, many of which were soon regarded as classics—and with an equally unflinching willingness to challenge and expand perceptions of what storytelling in games can do. One example: her game *With Those We Love Alive* [2014; with Brenda Neotenomie] asks the player to design and draw symbols on their body that the protagonist uses to channel her power, forming a physical connection between player and character that remains long after the browser window has closed and the game's code is no longer running. "By the end, we're marked with the decisions we've made," one reviewer wrote. "I found it awfully moving."[7]

The radical Twine scene had quieted down by the 2020s, the tool now just another in game makers' arsenals, the games created with it now mainstream. But like a pen drawing sigils on skin, the early Twines left an impression on interactive fiction that will take a long time to fade. And when considering what's next for IF in the years and decades to come, a lesson from *Howling Dogs* seems particularly apt: you can't break out of a prison until someone's shown you the walls.

A square of leaves dipped in silver, hissing with wind, bristling with night.

The bedroom window. You are awake. You consider going back to sleep, then remember:

I am awake now because it would be most interesting to be awake now.

So you get up.
up

The patter of interesting things on the sill, on the threshold, at the door. Uncohered interesting things still forming at the corners of your eyes, latent fascinators prickling, swirling just out of sight.

The calendar has no days and the clock, no hours.

During the 2010s, Twine became a popular prototyping tool for game industry narrative designers, an easy way to map out the flow of decisions in game's story (see *Lifeline* **2015**).

ALSO BY PORPENTINE CHARITY HEARTSCAPE (CONT'D)

2014 **Skulljhabit**

2014 **Everything You Swallow Will One Day Come Up Like a Stone**

2014 **Begscape**

2014 **Her Car is the Edge of the World**

2014 **Contrition**

2015 **Mother**

2015 **Neon Haze** *(with Brenda Neotenomie)*

2015 **Ruiness**

2015 **Aria End**

2016 **Rat Shrine** *(with rook)*

2016 **Vesp: A History of Sapphic Scaphism**

2016 **Psycho Nymph Exile**

2016 **All Your Time-Tossed Selves**

2017 **No World Dreamers: Sticky Zeitgeist**

2012

...Which life was this <u>again</u>?
⌕ again

{*}

References

1   Chu, Edmund. 2014. "On Howling Dogs." *Solitonic* (blog). May 4, 2014. solitonic.co/blog/2014/5/5/on-howling-dogs | a May 4, 2020

2   Clark, Wade. 2012. "Bold, Weird Dreaming through Hypertext Innovations." IFDB. Oct 1, 2012. ifdb.org/viewgame?id=mxj7xp4nffia9rbj&review=18344 | a May 5, 2020

3   Frater. 2016. "Dense and Somewhat Haunting." IFDB. Aug 19, 2016. ifdb.org/viewgame?id=mxj7xp4nffia9rbj&review=37904 | a Aug 10, 2022

4   Heartscape, Porpentine Charity. 2017. "Porpentine Charity Heartscape." *Artforum* (blog). Mar 13, 2017. www.artforum.com/interviews/porpentine-charity-heartscape-talks-about-her-works-in-the-2017-whitney-biennial-67067 | a Aug 10, 2022

5   Hudson, Laura. 2014. "Twine, the Video-Game Technology for All." *New York Times*, Nov 19, 2014, sec. Magazine. www.nytimes.com/2014/11/23/magazine/twine-the-video-game-technology-for-all.html | a May 4, 2020

6   Murray, Gabriel. 2012. "IF Comp 2012: Howling Dogs (Porpentine)." *Orestes Drunk and Pylades Fasting* (blog). Nov 25, 2012. orestesdrunk.wordpress.com/2012/11/24/if-comp-2012-howling-dogs-porpentine/ | a Aug 10, 2022

7   O'Connor, Alice. 2014. "Physically Interactive Fiction: With Those We Love Alive." *Rock, Paper, Shotgun* (blog). Nov 14, 2014. www.rockpapershotgun.com/drawing-violences-mundanity-with-those-we-love-alive / a Aug 10, 2022

8   Porpentine. 2012. "Creation Under Capitalism and the Twine Revolution." *Nightmare Mode* (blog). Nov 25, 2012. nightmaremode.net/2012/11/creation-under-capitalism-23422 | s Aug 5, 2013

9   Robertson, Adi. 2021. "Text Adventures: How Twine Remade Gaming." *The Verge* (blog). Mar 10, 2021. www.theverge.com/22321816/csk-twine | a Oct 19, 2021

10   Short, Emily. 2010. "So, Do We Need This Parser Thing Anyway?" *Emily Short's Interactive Storytelling* (blog). Jun 7, 2010. emshort.blog/2010/06/07/so-do-we-need-this-parser-thing-anyway | a May 4, 2020

11   Short, Emily. 2012. "Interview with Porpentine, Author of Howling Dogs." *Emily Short's Interactive Storytelling* (blog). Nov 23, 2012. emshort.blog/2012/11/23/interview-with-porpentine-author-of-howling-dogs | s Mar 12, 2017

12   Sterngold, James. 1994. "Nobel in Literature Goes to Kenzaburo Oe of Japan." *New York Times*, Oct 14, 1994, sec. Books. www.nytimes.com/1994/10/14/books/nobel-in-literature-goes-to-kenzaburo-oe-of-japan.html | a Aug 10, 2022

VERSU
A FAMILY SUPPER

Emily Short

Style	**Procedural Story**
Debuted	**Feb 14, 2013** *(App Store)*
Available Until	**Feb 19, 2014**
Launch Platform	**iPad / Versu App**
Publisher	**Linden Lab**
Language	**Praxis**
Launch Price	**$4.99** *(in-app purchase)*

> ❝ The first course is ready laid out on the table, with salmon at one end and a dish of turbot at the other, together with a dish of macaroni, muffin pudding, and larded sweetbreads.
>
> Elizabeth is at the Quinn dinner table, with their other guests.
>
> The meal has only just begun, but a curious sort of unease hangs over the room; a sense of apprehension whose source she cannot identify.
>
> **New objective: Make an impression on your dining companions**

IT WAS THE FIRST WEEK OF MARCH IN 2011, and acclaimed IF author Emily Short and character AI guru Richard Evans were onstage at the Game Developers Conference in San Francisco, huddled over a misbehaving laptop. Several hundred industry peers had shown up for a session called "People in Your Pocket" and a demo of a new approach to character-driven games on increasingly popular mobile platforms. But the demo refused to appear on the projected screen, due to some issue with the laptop's presenter mode, or maybe Xcode's iPhone simulator, or maybe a bad cable somewhere. For six painful minutes—an eternity before a live audience—the two tried in vain to diagnose the problem. Evans, a fast-talking Brit charmingly excitable at the best of times, stammered nervously through a litany of apologies: in the recording of the session you can almost hear his heart rate skyrocketing. "This is simply a sort of interface problem," he explained. "It's not like the game's not running. We just can't get it on the front of this desktop."[8]

The demo the two had hoped to present was the start of a line of experiments that would lead to one of the most groundbreaking AI storytelling systems ever made. While driven by complex logic and increasingly clever code, each iteration of the system was, at its heart, exploring a foundation-shaking question for narrative games, which had always struggled to bring compelling interactive characters to life. The question was this: what if the core of a story game's world model wasn't locations and objects, but rather the rules of conversation and social convention? And could such a system drive NPCs who might improvise sensible reactions to the player's behavior, allowing for emergent and character-driven stories?

Short and Evans had set out in 2010—originally along with Andrew Stern, co-creator of the ahead-of-its-time story game *Façade* [Procedural Arts 2005]—to prototype a game experience that felt more like performing in "an interactive drama" than marching through a static plot,

> an improvisational play, rather than an interactive story. The player is encouraged to perform her character, to improvise within the dramatic situation that she has been thrown into. The smallest comment, the slightest look, even not saying something—these moment-to-moment actions are noticed by the other participants and amplified.[6]

see **2000**

While Short's interactive fiction *Galatea* and most other character-driven IF had created illusions of responsive character by writing many possible reactions for each moment of conversation, these approaches could only be taken so far. They were labor-intensive to author, they were unable to adapt to unexpected input, and they often couldn't unfold in anything but a predetermined order.

Short co-wrote *Alabaster* with ten other authors, as an experiment to see whether a modular conversation engine could enable a group to iteratively extend a complex NPC's dialogue.

Short had experimented for years with making conversations in IF more dynamic. Her 2009 game *Alabaster* debuted a technique for writing "threaded conversations" where each discussion beat could be tagged with interlinked topics, allowing NPCs to reason over (or even search through) chains of associated conversational subjects. Evans had also been thinking about character behavior, in the context of more mainstream games. While building a revamped AI engine for *The Sims 3* [Electronic Arts 2009], he'd become frustrated by the limitations of representing complex character motivations in a graphical game:

> I had this particular experience very early on in the prototype phase of *Sims 3*, where I had this bug, and I sort of got obsessed with it. There was this shy Sim, and he'd invited a whole lot of other Sims round to

his house, but then when they came round he didn't let them in. And so I looked inside his internal mental state to see why…. And it turns out that he was basically conflicted. On the one hand, he understood that he should let them in, you know, that's the social norm that if you invite people over you should let them in. But on the other hand he was a shy Sim, and he knew that inviting people over meant talking to them, which he didn't really like…. And the way the internal code was at the time, his shyness was overriding his urge to do the socially appropriate thing.

So the first thing I did was just change round the relative weights of those two urges, so doing the right thing in this particularly case overrode his shyness. But that seemed very unsatisfactory to me…. Ideally what we'd want to do is that the Sim would have answered the door *reluctantly,* thereby expressing his conflict.[8]

But for characters in a graphical game to do something *reluctantly* would mean expensive new animations, one for each kind of action that might be performed that way; each new modifier or verb would require more custom assets. Improving a character's expressiveness in a graphical game was a multiplicative, not additive, operation. In a text game, all that was needed was that single word *reluctantly*, an adverb changing how the reader understands the action it's attached to. So Short and Evans's prototype would be a text game, showcasing how the medium could be a viable platform for exploring next-generation character AI techniques, despite the seeming mismatch between old and new technologies. ("It looks on the outside sort of old-fashioned and conventional," Evans cheerfully explained in a later demo, but "it's actually got some sort of weird-ass simulation going on underneath."[6]) The two eventually founded a company called Little Text People to further develop their weird-ass simulations. Short listed her position as CTO: Chief Textual Officer.

Perhaps a reference to Activision's pioneering social simulation game *Little Computer People* [1985].

The engine they began devising, eventually branded as Versu, was built around the notion that people—fictional and otherwise—usually act according to the rules of the particular social situation they find themselves in. This observation is mined for narrative potential most effectively in comedies of manners, where plot complications and humor arise from characters going to great lengths to conform to (or violate) social expectations—the basis of huge swaths of popular entertainment, from Oscar Wilde to TV sitcoms. Evans and Short's chief goal was to take "all of those social interactions that belong to manners, politeness—that level of interpersonal negotiation that's so rarely seen in games at all—and [make] that core gameplay."[8]

Back in the 1950s, philosopher John Rawls had argued that most actions only make sense in relation to the social contract that frames them. Meaning comes from context, as Evans and Short paraphrase: "We can utter a series of noises which sounds like 'Ay doo,' but this only constitutes a marriage vow in the context of a wedding ceremony."[7] While previous character AI systems had tried to encode each possible action a character might take and eliminate those invalid or implausible at a particular moment, Versu instead used a "constitutive" view based on social practices: "the agent does not see [an] action as available unless he is already participating in the practice which makes it visible. The agent is not overwhelmed by an infinite number of choices because he only sees the affordances that are provided by the social practices he is in."[7]

A "social practice" in Versu defines a kind of interpersonal interaction where each participant has a role to play. Two people being introduced might be expected to shake hands and make superficial inquiries as to each other's health, while a guest at a dinner party is expected to eat the food, tell the host how good it is, and make polite conversation with other guests. When a Versu character violates the norms of an active social practice, other nearby characters will notice. While some practices like introductions are ephemeral, others can last for a scene (eating dinner) or longer (a friendship, or the relationship between a mother and daughter).

Role expectations drove character behavior in Versu, as well as influencing how characters felt about each other, based on their developing judgments of how well each person present was performing their assigned roles (such as host, guest, friend, or parent). The evaluation was in turn driven by personality traits that defined a character's feelings about those practices and roles. A Versu character who witnessed a mother publicly chastising her daughter, and who valued discipline and respect for authority, might judge the mother to be performing her parent role quite well. But an empathetic character who hates to see others embarrassed might draw a very different conclusion from the same interaction.

Versu characters would remember the conclusions they drew about each other, and could share those observations. "In an early play-test," Evans recalled, "I was wondering why the doctor was being so rude to me when I had never spoken to him before. I found out, after much debugging, that the reason for his rudeness was that I had been mean to the butler, and the butler had been gossiping about me in the kitchen."[19] This kind of emergent social cause and effect was just what the system's creators had been hoping to enable. Reactions themselves could spur other reactions: a prudish cook might in turn judge the butler for gossiping and tell a scullery maid about the indiscretion; the two might then strengthen their friendship because of shared dislike of someone with higher social status. As in much great drama, all these character-revealing events could stem from a single inconsequential remark.

The player's role in a Versu game could also change significantly from one playthrough to the next. The engine supported the notion that any character could be played by either a human or the system (using social norms to drive expected behavior), letting the same story be played from different perspectives or even with friends in some of the roles. Characters from one story could also be dropped right into another, opening up the possibility of, say, casting Darth Vader as the boss in a modern-day office comedy (an actual example from the Versu SDK) or letting players, as Evans put it, "finally answer the burning question of what would happen if Mr. Darcy, Buffy the Vampire Slayer and Queen Victoria were all stuck in an elevator."[6] While additional authoring work would be required in practice to make such eclectic characters work together in a shared fictional space, the system's flexibility primed Versu to support a breathtaking variety of play options rarely equaled before or since in an interactive narrative engine.

In the fall of 2011, Evans pitched the new prototype to former colleague Rod Humble, a game designer who had found rare simultaneous success as both an industry executive and an independent creator. While a vice president at Electronic Arts, Humble had released the acclaimed art game *The Marriage* [2007], in which the complexities of maintaining a relationship were conveyed through play with abstract shapes and colors. In a 2009 interview for *Wired*, he spoke about his dual life as both upper management and struggling artist:

> [At EA] I'm less able to focus on small very, very creative games. I've got a job to bring in a large amount of revenue each year. So I decided that I'm going to do all the weird stuff that I know I won't make any money off of at home.... At home, I like to make games that are art, and I don't care if the audience is just one person. It doesn't matter if a dozen people like it or a half million, I'm just focused on the art itself.[10]

In the first weeks of 2011, Humble left EA to become CEO of Linden Lab, developers of virtual world *Second Life* [2003]. Though it had been a darling of the decade it launched, by the 2010s the allure of *Second Life* had faded: the salad days of universities and corporations building virtual campuses on its digital islands were ending, and less immersive social media platforms were becoming the dominant place to network. In June 2010, Linden had closed multiple offices around the world and laid off three hundred employees, but when Humble arrived the company was still in the midst of an existential crisis: whether to double down on their flagship virtual world despite its flagging popularity, or to expand to new domains and new platforms.

Perhaps unsurprisingly given his background, Humble quickly began looking for new opportunities, acquiring several studios and projects focused on different approaches to user-created worlds. He envisioned a Linden Lab that juggled a whole suite of creator-driven platforms, rather than tying their fortunes to *Second Life* alone. One of these projects was the system Evans and Short had built: Linden acquired Little Text People in 2012, and its two employees began working full time on their narrative engine and better demo content for it, with the new branding of Versu: Living Stories. A year later, the Versu app launched exclusively for iPad along with four short example scenarios, with clear ambitions to someday host a whole storefront of Versu-driven content. The launch titles were all Regency-era stories: *An Introduction to Society* (a tutorial), *The Unwelcome Proposal*, *The House on the Cliff*. The last was called *A Family Supper*.

Supper begins during a meal at the home of the Quinns, a well-to-do if stodgy couple whose guests include a flamboyant, rakish poet named Brown, "naive young debutante" Lucy, and the witty but less well-off Elizabeth Bennett (lifted from *Pride & Prejudice*). While other Versu stories imposed a more traditional plot, *Supper* was intriguing in part for how it let the social act-and-react loop at the heart of its engine take center stage. As dinner unfolds, the characters, with their different levels of intellect and propriety,

The two had worked together on *The Sims 3*.

The tablet market was hot at the time, iPad having quickly become one of Apple's most successful new platforms. While early Versu prototypes ran on mobile devices, the tablet's larger screen size made it a more appealing fit for an experience focused on reading. The premium price that tablet apps were then commanding over mobile may also have been a factor.

have plenty of opportunities to delight, offend, and scandalize one other. Two playthroughs can turn out very differently.

One of the first things a Versu player would notice is that taking an active role was not always strictly required. In *Supper*, the player is free to sit back and let the characters kibitz, each action and conversation thread dynamically prompting reactions:

Brown (to Mr Quinn): Our hero's father has another son, as it happens, whom he prefers to the hero, and so he has contrived to promote that son at the hero's expense. The other son is a clod, of mean intelligence and unappealing manners, who will do no credit to his position.

Frank: I prefer plots with a greater degree of plausibility.

Lucy favors Brown with a frankly flirtatious smile.

Brown smiles back warmly.

Mr Quinn oversees the serving of a turtle soup from the great tureen in front of him.

The footman walks into the dining room from the kitchen.

Brown rises from the table, taking his glass of wine.

Brown (to Lucy): You are truly a Muse!

Brown: I apologize, but I must go: I feel a sonnet coming on.

He gives a flourishing parting bow. He swaggers out of the dining room on his way to the study.

Lucy: I have never, I believe, inspired poetry before now. It is delightful.

The footman serves Elizabeth a plate of roast beef.

With a deep bow to his superiors, he walks out of the dining room on his way to the kitchen.

Frank: What a curious man Brown is! To have a sonnet strike suddenly in the middle of dinner. Anyone would think it was a sort of digestive complaint.

Lucy: Just before dinner, Mr Brown was recounting to me how he once went swimming in a thunderstorm, and felt tremendously at one with the sea, and all the violence of nature.

While each line here is hand-authored (with templated text sometimes filling in details for particular characters), the sequence of lines is not always preordained. In the last paragraph, Lucy tries to continue the conversation by telling a different anecdote on the same topic (Brown, the eccentric poet). She might have had any number of reasons for doing so: wanting to fit in, perhaps, or a desire to make Brown look good.

But of course there's not much drama here, because the characters are mostly reacting as one would expect them to. It's up to the player to spice up the scene by performing their character in an interesting way. Restarting the scenario as Elizabeth, the player might choose to play her as something of a lush, drinking as much wine as possible and making ill-advised remarks. After several turns of this, her drunkenness begins to affect her available actions and how the other characters are treating her.

Elizabeth succombs to a sudden, drink-induced melancholy and begins talking about how sad the world is.

Frank meets her eye sympathetically.

 **Act Now**

Choose an action
Conversation...

» *Say the plot strikes you as derivative*
» *Say that Brown's composition sounds compelling*
» *Say that you prefer plots with a greater degree of plausibility*
» *Describe how follies amuse you*
» *Mention feeling sadness*

Dinner

» *Pick weakly at the dish of macaroni*
» *Pause sadly in your eating*
» *Signal for more wine and drink it quickly*

Elizabeth's drunkenness...

» *Let a little more skin show*
» *Belch*
» *Sing something bawdy*

Fooling around...

» *Pile up empty glasses into a pyramid*

The list of possible actions the player might take (which could be summoned at any time by tapping the "Act Now" button) is grouped by the active social practice that makes them available, and modified by the player character's current attitudes. While an NPC Elizabeth would choose an action based on her traits and the dominant social norms, a human player might choose any one they like.

Here we see a second-order reaction, as Mrs. Quinn reacts to her husband chastising Elizabeth. In the app's interface, sketched portraits of each character update their facial expressions to express their internal state; tapping the portraits reveals why a character is feeling a certain way.

The player next chooses "Express your affection for everyone":

The characters here are responding to different aspects of Elizabeth's action, based on what each finds most important. And Elizabeth's performance of the selected action shows off another advantage of text over voice and animation: procedurally modifying her speech to reflect her inebriated state.

The stakes in *Family Supper* soon kick into higher gear when an offstage murder upends the social status quo, but many of the most memorable moments come less from traditional plot than the serendipitous interactions emerging from the underlying engine. In one playthrough as debutante Lucy during *Supper*'s beta testing, a clandestine romance broke out with a footman serving dinner, sparked by a single significant look over a chafing dish. While the other characters were off investigating the murder, Lucy and the footman snuck off to an empty room to declare their undying love for one other, eventually becoming secretly engaged. But in fact none of this was meant to happen in the story at all: "I'll have to add some special case elements for romance with servant characters," an amused Short wrote afterwards.[19] The whole story of forbidden love had emerged dynamically from Versu's social simulation and Short's encoding of Victorian norms, something that would have been utterly impossible in nearly any other narrative game.

As in other dynamic narrative systems through the decades, from *The Hobbit* to *The Playground* to *Dwarf Fortress*, this kind of emergent behavior could be endlessly compelling—while running the risk of being endlessly difficult to debug. To enable characters to join and leave conversation, for instance, topics of discussion were modeled at first as properties of locations. But this meant conversations could linger in the air even after all participants had left, and a character might stumble in much later and blurt out a follow-up to a discussion long abandoned. The characters' movement around the simulated world could also create interesting problems:

see **1982**, **1994**, and **2006**

> We experimented with giving some characters preferences about the company they kept—this character likes being in a room with other people present, that one doesn't like being in a room of more than four individuals, this third one wants to be around his beloved—but this could occasionally lead to AI comedy sequences where NPCs would basically chase one another in circles around the mansion because there was no rest state available in which everyone's wishes were satisfied.[24]

Versu stories and characters were at first written in a custom domain-specific language called Praxis, created by Evans. Praxis had originally been inspired by the philosopher Ludwig Wittgenstein: Evans, who unlike most AI programmers had studied philosophy at Cambridge, had long been taken by Wittgenstein's notion that any possible world could in theory be described by a series of factual, logical statements defining "everything that is the case" within it. Praxis took this notion literally, allowing the user to make declarative statements in an "exclusion logic" that defined everything true about the simulated world, and that existed in the system's memory solely as that precise series of literal statements. For instance: `brown.sex!male` defines that the object *brown* (in this case representing the character with that surname) has a quality called *sex* (among other qualities) which is currently (and exclusively) *male*. More complex representations of state could be built up from this simple syntax, and added to the set of "things that are true" by rules in the system or by the author:

CONFLICTING GOALS, EMERGENT ACTS

Versu shone the brightest when its simulation allowed characters to perform surprising actions in character-revealing ways. Another example comes from the way its NPCs made decisions about their actions. A character's traits were defined as future states they wanted the world to be in: someone who enjoyed insulting upper-class men, for instance, would search for an action leading to a future where nearby upper-class men were offended. Rather than using a traditional AI planner—seeking through extensive trees of possible actions for a sequence that would reach a desired end goal, like a chess engine plotting a winning strategy—Versu's characters look only for immediate next steps, in some ways a more human approach that could produce surprisingly relatable behavior.

Evans shared the example of a group of Versu characters programmed to play the Victorian parlor game of whist. Characters could play reasonably well without detailed strategic logic merely by seeing if any move they could make would result in a future where they had played a legal move and were closer to winning. But since each character's other desires were also factored into choice of action, their personalities, relationships, and social roles could naturally emerge even in something as prosaic as a card game. A character who had fallen in love with someone at the card table, preferring to see futures in which the object of their affection was happy, might deliberately play a poor hand to bring about a state where their beloved, having won the round, was smiling.

```
brown.relationship.lucy.evaluation.humour!20
mr_collins.beliefs.clergymen_should_marry
process.whist.data.whose_move!brown
```

This representation offered many material advantages—the system's memory could easily be read bv humans, and determining whether a given state was currently true was as simple as searching for a string match. But as the next stages of Versu's rollout were planned, including much larger stories and the hope that users could begin making content of their own, Praxis began to seem too unwieldy for large-scale production. Its syntax was aggressively logical, but not inherently structured for writing complex interactive characters. Defining even a simple new action, for instance, involved some boilerplate:

```
process.greet.X(agent).Y(agent)
  action "Greet"
    preconditions
      Actor = X
      Actor.in!L
    postconditions
      text "[X] says 'hullo' to [Y obj]" if Recipient.in!L
      call update_conversation.L.Actor.greet.Y.respond_to_greet
      insert process.respond_to_greet.Y.X
      delete Self
end
```

According to Nelson, the name had three meanings: "partly because the 'Pr-' seemed fitting as a partner for 'Praxis', and partly to imply rapid development.... But it's also meant to sound like a prompter in a theatre, the person who sits in the pit and supplies the actors with lines when they forget."[15]

Short enlisted the help of Graham Nelson, with whom she had worked extensively on the design and iteration of Inform 7 **2008**, to create a higher-level language that would make authoring Versu stories simpler. The result, a language called Prompter, made it possible to write Versu stories an order of magnitude more quickly than with Praxis. This was in part achieved by leveraging a reusable library of content authored in Praxis—social practices, actions, traits, and emotions—which could then be deployed in a scenario without authors needing to fiddle with their details. Prompter was a second-generation language for a system not even yet released; an even higher-level abstraction over dynamic character simulation built on top of the AI reasoning provided by Praxis.

Prompter source code read much like a stage play, with the key difference that stage directions had special meaning to the engine. Take, for example, a line like:

```
Catherine (to Bluntschli, very rudely): You
worthless scoundrel.
```

This indicates both some implied preconditions for when such a line could be deployed (when both Catherine and Bluntschli are in the same location and engaged in conversation with each other), and a social action that other characters might respond to (Catherine saying something rude). The notion of rudeness was encoded in the underlying Praxis, but authors didn't have to worry about this: they could instead focus on how other characters felt about rude

Emily Short on the Versu UI

We spent ages in the first stages of the story working on the user interface. Should it be real time? Should the text scroll on its own? If it didn't scroll by itself, how should the user control forward movement? What should the menus look like? How should we be signaling character moods and feelings?

There were a lot of false starts here. Earlier versions of the interface were auto-scrolling and also in some cases had more other doodads and state-readouts visible—though not to any extremes. Linden had always encouraged us to approach this as a readerly experience … it did mean we were thinking in terms of "e-book that you interact with" at least as much as "game."[24]

2013

statements and how they might react to someone who made them. Prompter also included structures for organizing content and flow between scenes: a "conversation," for instance, was a set of back-and-forth lines focused on a particular topic. Note below the introductory `About`, which tells the system what topics this thread of dialog concerns, and the addendum beginning `--` after each line, indicating to the system how the option to perform it should be presented if a human plays that character:

```
(About Bluntschli and the carpet bag.)

Catherine (to Louka, naively): Captain Bluntschli! That's a
German name.
-- Read the visiting card

Louka: Swiss, madam, I think.
-- Inform the Mistress

Catherine: Swiss! What is he like?
-- Ask about the visitor

Louka (submissively): He has
a big carpet bag, madam.
-- Tell Mistress
```

But after each of these lines, of course, the player or other characters might choose to interject: reacting to Catherine's naïve statement, for instance, or by changing the subject to another topic related to Bluntschli. In essence, a Prompter script describes a stage play that Versu can perform but also knows how to improvise around, responding to off-script interjections from either human players or NPC characters with something appropriate for the characters and milieu. It's interesting to note that while many other game engines struggle to simulate characters, Prompter made it impossible to write a story without them: its Hello World example defines two characters because with only one, "he'll never want to say his one line, because there would be nobody to hear it."[15] The two Hello World characters have the relationship `married`, for the

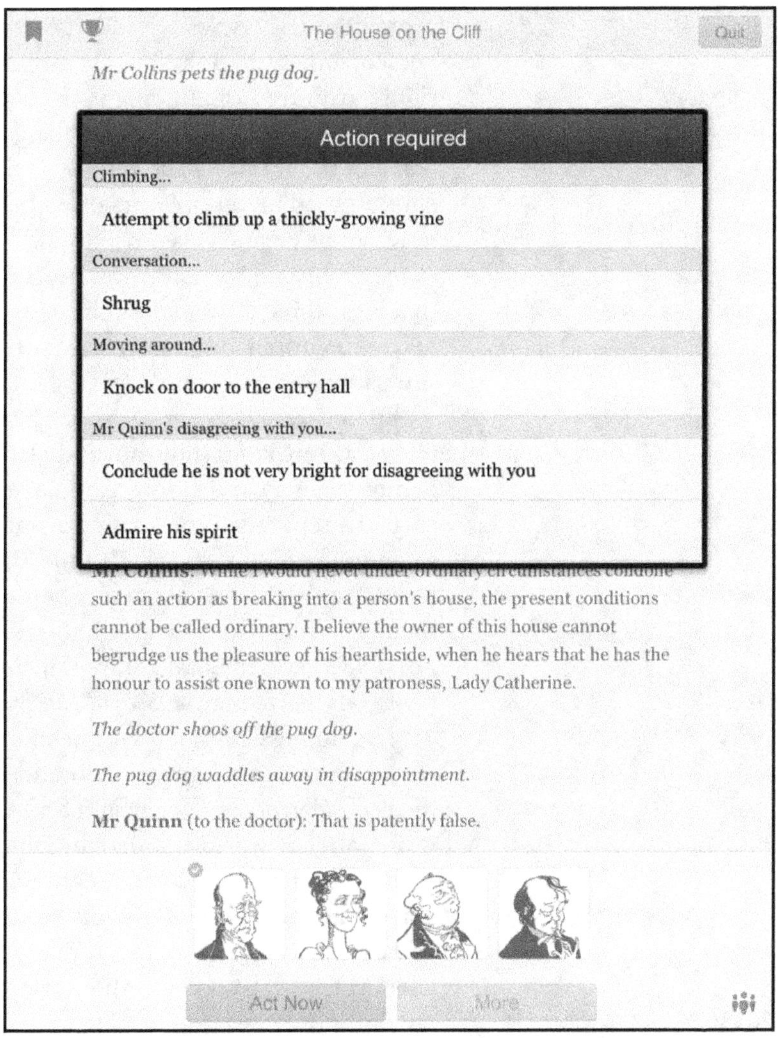

Versu story *The House on the Cliff* running on an iPad.

charming reason that this prevents them from introducing themselves to one another when the scenario begins, as social convention would dictate if they were strangers.

By the end of 2013, a working version of Prompter was part of a closed beta for a Versu SDK, planned to enable outside authors to start creating and sharing their own stories. Short had finished work on a novel-sized Versu story called *Blood & Laurels* set in a declining Roman Empire, and another commissioned full-length game was also nearly complete. It seemed an extraordinary new foundation for interactive storytelling was about to make its debut.

But the full Versu platform would never launch, a victim of bad timing and unfortunate circumstance. Linden's perhaps premature release of the early demo stories, without much fanfare or publicity, excited some IF fans but reached few new readers. Even some fans were bemused. "The game is so different than anything I've played," one reviewer wrote of a demo story, "that I had a hard time figuring out what I could influence and what I could not."[2] Another wrote that Versu "does marry an interactive story to a social simulation, but the seams seem overly visible to me."[13] Many prominent IF reviewers couldn't even try it because they didn't own an iPad, and endemic App Store discoverability problems kept even those with the right hardware from finding it on their own. Distribution issues aside, Short would later reflect that because the game's systems hid so much complexity beneath the surface—and behind an interface that looked like a traditional choice-based menu—players often had a hard time grasping the true extent to which its engine was procedural.[23] "The typical experience of a player of *Blood & Laurels*," wrote Graham Nelson, "is to feel on a first play-through that everything is plotted out like a thriller: it's on a second try, where it all plays out entirely differently, that people begin to appreciate the depth of the simulation."[14]

But few would get that second try, and most wouldn't even get a first. In early 2014, Rod Humble abruptly left Linden Lab (where *Second Life* was still hemorrhaging users) and was replaced by new CEO Ebbe Altberg, who had earned a reputation for turning around companies in trouble. "We'll do some clean-up," Altberg said at the time about his plans for Linden: "there's some things that are not as aligned. There's already very little resources spent on them."[1] Within two weeks of his appointment, Altberg had canceled all of Humble's experimental gambles including Versu, choosing instead to double down on improving the *Second Life* experience for its reliable core users.

The timing could not have been more devastating. Prompter and Praxis would remain unreleased—theoretically valuable but now mothballed intellectual property—as would Short's complete *Blood & Laurels* and other stories already commissioned and finished. Versu's cancellation, in fact, came just days before *Laurels* was meant to have launched, so close that Linden's app department apparently missed the memo, accidentally publishing the game on its originally planned release date before pulling it a few hours later. Maybe "30 copies in the world" got out, Short estimated.[21] She later announced she was attempting to work out a deal that would allow *Laurels* to be released and Versu development to continue, but after a few weeks she posted a single terse sentence on her usually voluble blog:

> So for those who were curious, Linden has now given me a definite no about selling me the [Versu] codebase and IP.[21]

While a standalone release of *Laurels* was eventually negotiated, the core Versu tech remained Linden's, and the game and its engine could not be ported to other platforms. Only a year later, Apple's aggressive pruning of out-of-date apps took *Laurels* off the App Store—without the ability to update its code, there was no way for Evans or Short to keep it current with the changing requirements of each new iOS update. *Laurels*, along with every other Versu game, has been <u>unplayable since 2015</u>, a tragic loss to interactive narrative technology and history. "It's a real gut-punch that we'll never get to try out the authoring tools," wrote one IF reviewer, "or even to play any games that really exercise its potential."[13]

Short has been clear there are no easy villains, despite Versu's frustrating end. "I remain hugely grateful to Rod Humble and to Linden for picking us up when they did, and for giving us the run they gave us," she wrote in 2014. "There are so few opportunities to do this kind of research within existing companies, and if Richard Evans and I had taken venture capital, we would have had to spend a lot more of our time trying to learn to run a business and a lot less writing stories and code."[16] During their brief availability, the Versu games proved hugely inspirational to IF creators, researchers, and players. The *New York Times* covered *Blood & Laurels*, writing that "what [it] offers is one of those quintessential video game moments, a first glimpse at something on the horizon."[25] Versu has become a standard touchstone for interactive story technologists, proof by existence for what character-driven games can aspire to be. Referencing Janet Murray's influential book on interactive drama, one reviewer wrote that "the dream of 'Hamlet on the holodeck' has inspired IF theorists for decades. Versu gets closer to that dream than anything else I've seen."[13]

Evans and Short had set out to show that text games could be a viable platform for prototyping next-gen narrative technology, and there's no doubt they succeeded, even though bad luck kept their experiment from claiming its rightful place in the limelight. "This is simply a sort of interface problem," Evans had said at that first troubled GDC demo. "It's not like the game's not running. We just can't get it on the front of this desktop." Maybe not yet, but it's hard to imagine something like Versu won't take center stage in the end.

...except on increasingly dusty iPads that have never installed software updates since; some of these were generously made available by Jacob Garbe and Nyeogmi Choi during research for this chapter.

References

1 Altberg, Ebbe. 2014. "7 Questions on the Future of Second Life & Linden Lab for Ebbe Altberg, Linden's New CEO." Interview by New World Notes. Feb 19, 2014. nwn.blogs.com/nwn/2014/02/ebbe-altberg-linden-lab-second-life-1.html | a Oct 18, 2020

2 clyde. 2013. "Idle Thumbs 114: A Heavy (Baboon) Heart." Comment on forum post, Idle Forums, Aug 19, 2013. www.idlethumbs.net/forums/topic/8746-idle-thumbs-114-a-heavy-baboon-heart | a Oct 18, 2020

3 Evans, Richard. 2013. "Praxis: A Logic-Based DSL for Modeling Social Practices." Slides. versublog.files.wordpress.com/2014/05/praxis.pdf | a Oct 18, 2020

4 Evans, Richard P., and Emily Short. 2015. "The AI Architecture of Versu." Paper. Imperial College,

London. versublog.files.wordpress.com/2014/05/versu.pdf | a Oct 18, 2020

5   Evans, Richard, and Emily Short. 2012. "Beyond Eliza: Constructing Socially Engaging AI." Conference talk (Versu section), Game Developers Conference, San Francisco. gdcvault.com/play/1015613/Beyond-Eliza-Constructing-Socially-Engaging | a Oct 18, 2020

6   Evans, Richard, and Emily Short. 2013. "Experimental Gameplay Workshop 2013." Conference talk (Versu section), Game Developers Conference, San Francisco. gdcvault.com/play/1017828/Experimental-Gameplay | a Oct 18, 2020

7   Evans, Richard, and Emily Short. 2014. "Versu—a Simulationist Storytelling System." In *IEEE Transactions on Computational Intelligence and AI in Games* 6 (2).

8   Evans, Richard, Emily Short, and Andrew Stern. 2011. "People in Your Pocket: High-Quality AI on Mobile Devices." Conference talk, Game Developers Conference, San Francisco. www.gdcvault.com/play/1014495/People-in-Your-Pocket-High | a Oct 18, 2020

9   Kawamoto, Dawn. 2010. "'Second Life' Owner Linden Lab to Lay Off 30% of Its Workers." aol.com. Jun 9, 2010. www.aol.com/2010/06/09/second-life-owner-linden-lab-to-lay-off-30-of-its-workers | a Oct 18, 2020

10 Kushner, David. 2009. "Big-Shot Game Designer Crafts Interactive Art After Hours." *Wired* 17 (3), Feb 23, 2009. www.wired.com/culture/design/magazine/17-03/pl_games | s Aug 16, 2011

11 Linden Lab. 2012. "Linden Lab Acquires Game Studio LittleTextPeople." Press Release. Feb 16, 2012. lindenlab.com/releases/linden-lab-acquires-game-studio-littletextpeople | s Jan 19, 2013

12 Linden Lab. 2013. "Linden Lab Launches a New Platform for Character-Driven Interactive Fiction: Versu for IPad." Business Wire. Feb 14, 2013. www.businesswire.com/news/home/20130214006126/en/Linden-Lab%C2%AE-Launches-a-New-Platform-for-Character-Driven-Interactive-Fiction-VersuTM-for-iPad | a Oct 18, 2020

13 Merrick, Iain. 2014. "Iain Merrick on Best Technological Development." *XYZZY Awards* (blog). Apr 28, 2014. xyzzyawards.org/?p=293 | a Oct 18, 2020

14 Nelson, Graham. 2013a. "Prompter: A Domain-Specific Language for Versu." Paper. versublog.files.wordpress.com/2014/05/graham_versu.pdf | a Oct 18, 2020

15 Nelson, Graham. 2013b. "Writing for Versu." Unreleased SDK Documentation.

16 Nutt, Christian. 2014a. "The End of Versu: Emily Short Looks Back." *Gamasutra* (blog). Mar 14, 2014. www.gamedeveloper.com/business/the-end-of-versu-emily-short-looks-back | a Oct 18, 2020

17 Nutt, Christian. 2014b. "Interactive Fiction Engine Versu Back with Creators, Games Coming Soon." *Gamasutra* (blog). Jun 6, 2014. www.gamedeveloper.com/business/interactive-fiction-engine-versu-back-with-creators-games-coming-soon | a Oct 18, 2020

18 Saltzman, Marc. 2013. "'Versu': Bring Interactive Fiction to Your IPad." *USA Today*. Mar 12, 2013. www.usatoday.com/story/tech/2013/03/12/versu-app-fiction-books/1982819 | a Oct 18, 2020

19 Short, Emily. 2012. "Invitation to look at Versu (nee Cotillion)." Unpublished email with author. Sep 13, 2012.

20 Short, Emily. 2013. "Versu: Conversation Implementation." *Emily Short's Interactive Storytelling* (blog). Feb 26, 2013. emshort.blog/2013/02/26/versu-conversation-implementation | a Oct 18, 2020

21 Short, Emily. 2014. "Versu Outcome." *Emily Short's Interactive Storytelling* (blog). Mar 8, 2014. emshort.blog/2014/03/08/versu-outcome | a Oct 18, 2020

22 Short, Emily. 2017. "Mailbag: Writing for Versu." *Emily Short's Interactive Storytelling* (blog). May 18, 2017. emshort.blog/2017/05/18/mailbag-writing-for-versu | a Oct 18, 2020

23 Short, Emily. 2018. "Galatea, Versu, Character Engine: Three Generations of in-Game Characters." Conference talk. Digital Cultures, Warsaw, Sep 25, 2018. www.youtube.com/watch?v=S4hZOTRsILI | a Oct 18, 2020

24 Short, Emily. 2020. "Historical Questions Re Versu." Unpublished email with author. Nov 17, 2020.

25 Suellentrop, Chris. 2014. "Text Games in a New Era of Stories." *New York Times*, Jul 6, 2014, sec. Arts. www.nytimes.com/2014/07/07/arts/video-games/text-games-in-a-new-era-of-stories.html | a Oct 18, 2020

80 DAYS

Meghna Jayanth (script), Jon Ingold
and Joseph Humfrey (directors)

Style	**Choice-Based, Storylet-Driven**
Debuted	**Jul 31, 2014** *(App Store)*
Launch Platform	**iOS**
Publisher	**inkle**
Language	**ink**
Launch Price	**£2.99 / $4.99** *(download)*

> London, 1872
> I have entered into the service of a new gentleman.
> It would seem he is a gambling man.

"A QUESTION WE GOT REPEATEDLY ASKED," the speaker noted about his studio's first game, "was 'Yeah, but like, do my choices *really* matter?'"

People say, "Well, I'm pressing this button, but it doesn't *really* matter, does it? You don't *really* make any difference." And that is the canonical problem of branching narrative. That's the one that every single purveyor of branching narrative is constantly, desperately trying to solve: convincing you that the choices they make you agonize over have any impact on the game at all.[11]

The talk was on choices in interactive stories: what they're good for and how to design them. The speaker was Cambridge-based Jon Ingold, and the studio was called inkle. Ingold co-founded it in 2011 with Joseph Humfrey, after the two worked together on briefly hot motion-control games for Kinect and PlayStation Move. The tiny company's goal was to "explore what new narrative experiences were possible on tablets and

2014

phones."[8] Motion tracking had started to feel like a gimmick, but ubiquitous touch screen devices like Apple's iPhone, and especially the larger iPad that launched in 2010, seemed intriguing platforms rife for experimentation.

see **1979** and **1983–5**

see **1993**

see *Galatea* **2000**

Ingold grew up reading gamebooks and playing Infocom text adventures, seeds of a lifelong love for the pleasures of mingling reading and play. In his late teens and twenties he wrote parser IF in Inform, including acclaimed titles like *The Mulldoon Legacy* [1999], *All Roads* [2001], and *Make It Good* [2009]. But he'd grown frustrated with the limitations of the parser. Telling stories centered on characters and dialogue was hard with a verb-noun interface—though some had struggled to try anyway—and parser games could be inscrutable to outsiders, limiting their audience. "Whenever I showed one of my games to someone who hadn't played a text adventure," Ingold recalled, "they would be completely stumped. 'You're meant to type in what to do? But what should you type? What *should* I do?'"[25]

Ingold and Humfrey believed the shift to a new platform offered an excuse to challenge longstanding norms of interactive narrative design. One of their first precepts was that "text is a visual medium."[24] Rather than dumping words to standard output to let a terminal window or operating system handle their rendering, inkle's apps would put effort into typesetting, presenting text beautifully to encourage players to actually read it. The studio's first release was an interactive adaptation of *Frankenstein* [2012] with gorgeous typography, presented in long passages of text interrupted only occasionally by choice points, and no stats or other gamelike elements to distract from the reading experience.

The reaction was mixed. Ingold would dryly recall: "Gamers generally didn't like it because it was a book. Book people generally didn't like it because it wasn't a book."[11]

The studio found more success with their next release, *Steve Jackson's Sorcery!* [2013], which adapted a fondly remembered 80s gamebook into an extended digital edition. The design iterated on *Frankenstein* in several major ways. It added visible stats that went up or down in response to events or choices, useful "to help reassure readers that what they're choosing is definitely being noticed."[24] Another insight was to break long passages of prose into short, snappy sentences with frequent choices, even if those choices had no lasting consequences. A faster interaction cycle kept players engaged and used choice more for pacing than exclusively for big, weighty decisions. As writer Meghna Jayanth noted, "Instead of just 'should I kiss them or turn away,' alright, do I move up my chair? Do I meet their eye? Do I sit a little bit closer? Do I lean forward?"[13]

Jayanth had been contracted by inkle for an unrelated project in the wake of *Sorcery!*'s success. While Ingold and Humfrey cranked away at a sequel, they hoped Jayanth could start researching and writing material for a new game originally planned as a smaller-scale experiment. The plan would change. At first Jayanth was hired to write perhaps ten or twenty thousand words; ultimately she and Ingold together would write closer to three-quarters of a million.

The new game was to be based on Jules Verne's 1872 novel *Around the World in 80 Days*, in which English gentleman Phileas Fogg makes a wager that he and his valet, Passepartout, can circumnavigate the globe at a hitherto impossible speed. Having partnered with a book publisher for *Frankenstein*, the inkle team had considered what other well-known stories in the public domain might make good foundations for game adaptations. In particular, they were looking for stories based around maps. Another key innovation from *Sorcery!* had been realizing how critical it was to help players understand the relationship between their choices and the story. Ingold recalls that in *Frankenstein*,

> the common reaction was, "My choices don't make any difference; they don't matter; they don't affect anything." And we'd say, well, actually they do. There's a system under the hood and it's got these options—but there's no UI to show you that. It just looks like a book that writes itself.
>
> But then we found that when we showed people a story graph of *Frankenstein*, and then they read it, they said, "Wow! I just feel so on edge and every choice matters." It was all about creating that expectation of branching first. So we spent a long time thinking, how do we put a flow chart in an interactive book without it looking like a flow chart?[27]

The solution was to frame the *Sorcery!* interface around its map, with major choices tied to decisions about which paths to take or places to visit. Suddenly players had an implicit understanding of their position within the narrative possibility space. They could see how far along they were on the journey and understand that because they'd decided to go left, they were missing out on any stories that might have been to the right. Maps "proved" branching, Ingold realized,[11] and they had any number of other benefits besides: they demonstrated cause and effect; they showed off the existence of unexplored content; they lent visual interest to an otherwise textual story; and they let players strategize about future moves ("How do I get over *there?*"). So Verne's story seemed a natural fit, based around the familiar yet intriguing map of the world. On a mobile touch screen, you could even satisfyingly twirl the globe beneath your fingers while planning a route.

Verne's novel provided other useful structure. First, its episodic nature worked well for a player-directed narrative. Each stopping point on the journey could hold a self-contained story that didn't need to appear in strict sequence, giving players more agency over their route. And the novel offered another useful constraint. A key plot point is that heading east means gaining a day by crossing the international date line; the extra time proves crucial to securing the wager. Eastward-only travel would allow "narrative structure that occurs without forcing users into choke points,"[28] meaning introductory material and story arc setups could be placed in Europe and Africa, mid-game content in Asia, and advanced content and conclusions to plot arcs in the Americas.

While Ingold and Humfrey began designing UI and mechanics with an aim to keep iterating on the successes of *Sorcery!*, Jayanth began wrestling with the problems of how to update a nineteenth-century novel to work in the twenty-first. Her 2012 game *Samsara*, which was written for the

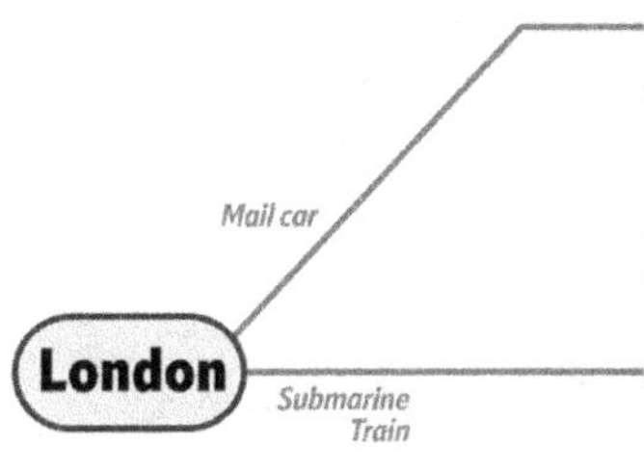

see *Fallen London* **2009**

StoryNexus platform, had caught the inkle team's eye not only for its beautiful prose but because it had taken a historical setting and added a dose of the fantastic. It seemed clear a similar approach was needed here. To give players the same sense of wonder felt by readers of the original novel, the game needed to offer something modern readers would find as fantastic as a steam train or a submarine.

Sticking to a historical 1872 also presented a game design problem. Verne's novel had been inspired by the recent openings of the Suez Canal and transcontinental railways across both India and the United States; the only sensible fast route at the time would connect those three conveyances. To give players the chance to chart their own unique journeys, there would need to be equally speedy and compelling routes available all across the globe. So Jayanth and the inkle team decided to set the game in an alternate history where innovations modern readers would find intriguing were happening on every continent. The game establishes this change from its very first sentences:

In the game, sentences continue on from your choice as the other options fade away, leaving seamless paragraphs of prose. For clarity, choices in these excerpts have been reprinted after the choice block, along with the follow-up text.

> Monsieur Phileas Fogg returned home *early* from the Reform Club, and in a new-fangled steam-carriage, besides!
>
> » **I helped him down…**
>
> I helped him down, and the iron-lunged, steam-driven horses clattered away.
>
> "Passepartout," said he. "We are going around the world!"

80 Days would go steampunk. But Jayanth hoped the project could avoid the kinds of uncritical pastiche that genre had been increasingly criticized for. It's a style where "we keep the Victoriana," she stated,

> the bustles, the elaborate upper-class courting rituals, the arranged marriages and the stiff upper-lips—and elide away all the dirt and muck. The class politics are blunted in favour of a nostalgic enjoyment of silk dresses and soirees.

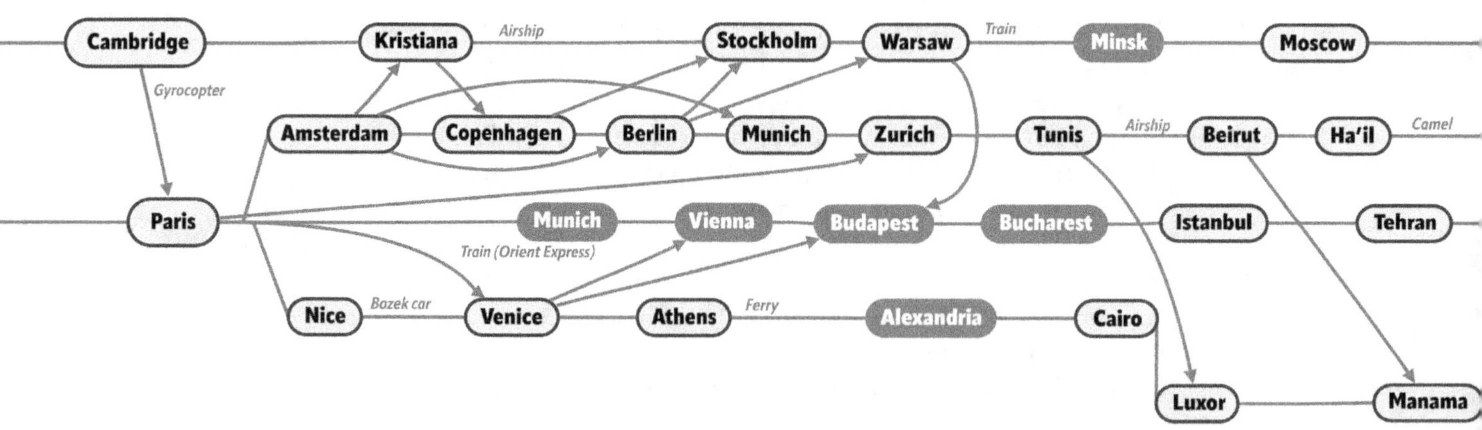

It's a nostalgic, escapist vision—I am quite happy to go so far as to call it a fetishistic one. It's a vision that has very little room for people of colour (who very much existed in Victorian Britain!), for queer people, for poor people. If they exist, they exist as victims. That seems dangerous and broken, that this is escapism, that this is fantastical. That glittering world of adventure and courtesy is built on oppression and suffering.[20]

Instead, she began to imagine an alternate world where the astonishing innovations of Verne's imagined futures had been distributed more evenly around the globe. An 1872 took shape where "the automaton armies of the Zulu Federation turn away the depredations of European colonists scrambling for Africa—where the technology that built the British Raj is being used to dismantle its foundations—where the Panama Canal is dug using Haitian ingenuity, tipping the balance of power away from the United States—and where the stories usually told in the margins spill over into the text." Steampunk, she wrote, "is often written as a modern fantasy of an imagined past. We wanted to create something a bit different: a historical fantasy of an imagined future."[17]

The shaba-meli was a rigid, helium-filled metal balloon; an African invented-and-produced form of air-travel.

» *The balloon itself was made of thin, interleaving layers of copper...*
» *It seemed impossible that it could hang in the air...*

The balloon itself was made of thin, interleaving layers of copper and tin mined in Katanga and constructed by the Nyamwezi chieftains.

We were accompanied on our journey to Ulundi by the strange, macabre sight of wheeling squadrons of wood-and-copper birds with diamond shards spinning in their hollow chests.

» *...Their eyes were bright...*
» *...I was captivated by their beauty...*
» *...Their purpose in the sky seemed clear enough...*

Below, this page spread and next: four routes through *80 Days* and the connections between destinations they pass through, with occasional conveyances noted. Darker gray cities are those skipped via express routes on the journey paths highlighted here. Some connections including backtracking are omitted for clarity. This map shows only half the destinations reachable in the game, and a fraction of the more than four hundred possible routes between them.

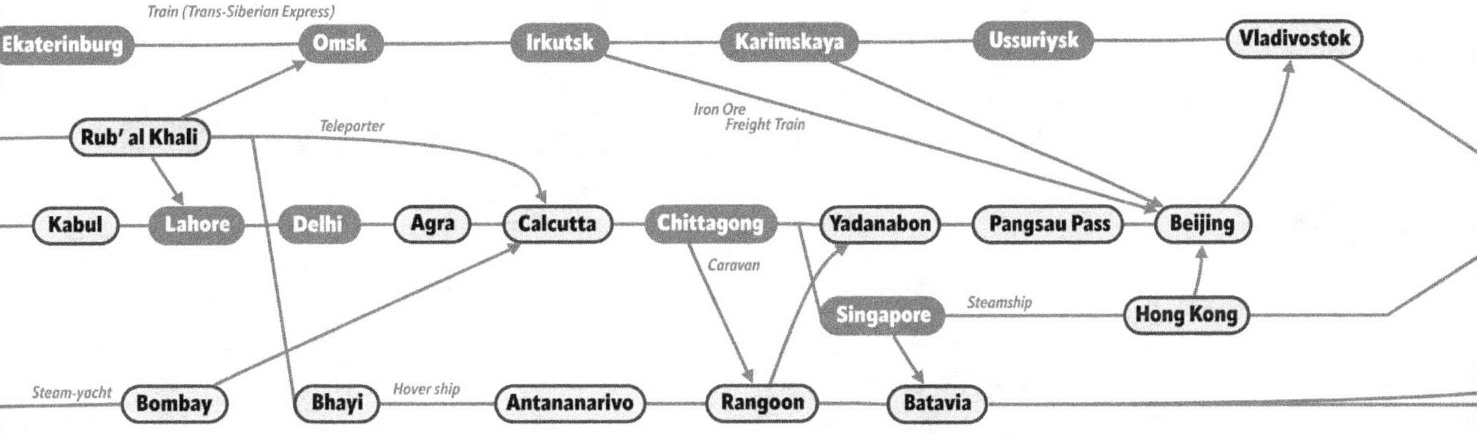

> I was captivated by their beauty… their bright-beaded wings beat against the air, and their diamond shards glittered like stars in the endless blue of the sky.
>
> The Zulu Federation crew waved and called out to them respectfully.
>
> » *"I have never seen such automata."…*
> » *"Why do you speak to them?"…*
>
> "Because they are emissaries of our Emperor," one of the navigators explained, amused by my question. "We must treat the Emperor's automata with great deference."

The new setting lent a clue to another problem Jayanth was grappling with: how to address the white savior tropes in the original story, where two Europeans charge uncritically through a world still filled with the radical injustices of colonial empire. A chief insight was to realize that the story need not always be about Fogg and Passepartout. "Is it possible to write a game in which your *protagonist* isn't the hero?" Jayanth wondered. "Or maybe, less provocatively: can you write a game in which your protagonist isn't the *only* hero?"[18] She began to rethink the role of non-player characters, typically passive folk who follow the player's orders or wait for them to come save the day—"quintessential victims,"[23] she realized. Instead, she decided to write characters actively solving their own problems and telling their own stories, which yours would but briefly intersect. "You are a tourist," she explained. "You do not get to be as important as the people that live there [in the places you visit]. You may be able to touch and nudge at a revolution, or participate in one—but it is not yours."[20] In short, "the world of the game turns—but it doesn't turn around you."[21]

> The *Nefertiti* was a tall-masted Egyptian clipper that sailed around the coast-line from Antalya all the way to Alexandria.
>
> » *I asked the skipper if he had considered longer voyages…*
> » *I was content to enjoy the ride…*

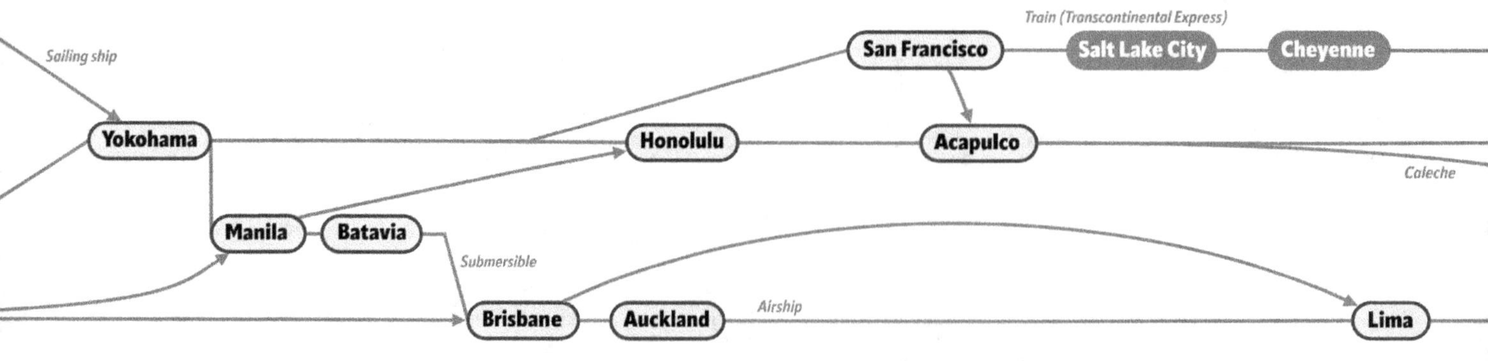

> I asked the skipper if he had considered longer voyages via the Suez Canal, but he only laughed. "The fees, young man, are quite extortionate."
>
> » *I could not argue with that…*
> » *"How extortionate?"*
>
> "How extortionate?" I asked.
>
> He gave me a pointed look. "You will not buy me or my boat," he replied, "if that is your intention. My liberty is worth more coin than you have."
>
> I nodded, and we did not pursue the conversation further.

In one sequence at an Australian hotel, Passepartout meets a Murri maid who has written a letter protesting the white settlers' treatment of Aboriginal peoples. She wants to bring it to the local newspaper, but doubts they would ever print it. The game presents you with a choice offering to deliver it for her, Jayanth explains:

> To use your whiteness and maleness and your protagonism, basically, to help her. But she refuses. She doesn't trust you—*because* of all those things, because you're an outsider, because you're white and male. You're closer to the oppressor than you are to her, and all the good intentions in the world can't change that.

It might feel unfair to present the player with a problem they can't solve, Jayanth notes, "but maybe unfair isn't the worst thing a game can be."[23]

Rethinking the foundational assumptions of both story and systems continued, in a highly collaborative process that "grew and grew until it encompassed first every working hour, and then every waking one."[15] The game that emerged nine months later would be quite different from *Sorcery!* or anything else on the market, with a unique structure that Ingold later described as "self-narrating board game."[11] The mechanical spine of *80 Days* is essentially a trip-planning simulator, where the player must chart a round-the-world course departure by departure, making trade-offs between money, time, and Fogg's well-being—as a valet, the health of your employer

You Are Carrying…

» Magnifying Glass
» Brass Telescope
» Mechanical Lily
» Clockwork Monkey
» Dusty Road Set
» Cuban Cigar
» Russian Gentlemen's Wardrobe
» Set of False Teeth
» Evening Jacket
» Didgeridoo
» Ottoman Railways Timetable

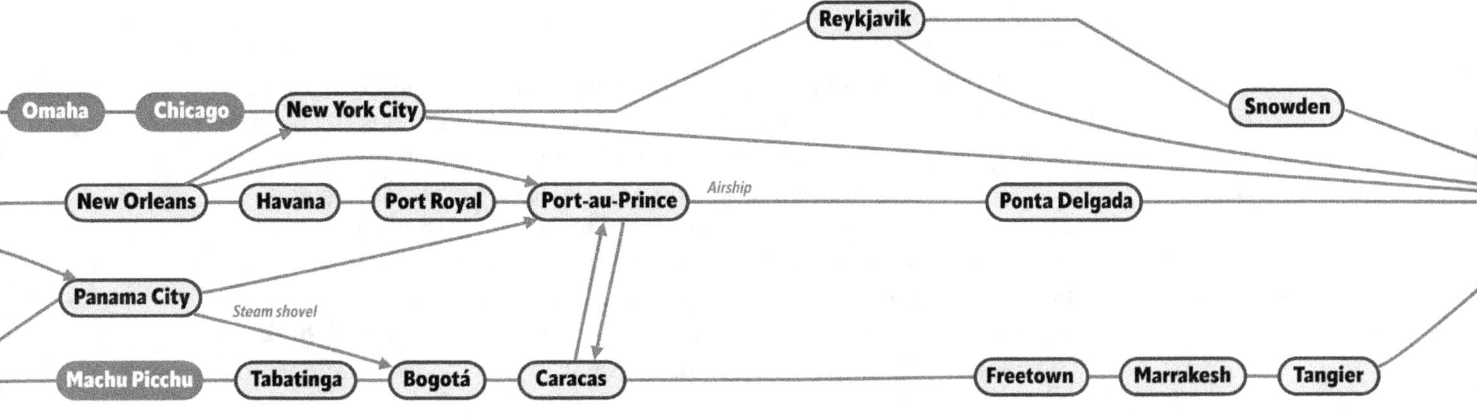

A Real-Time Journey

Verne's story had originally been serialized with daily installments in the French newspaper *Le Temps*. The printing of the final episode corresponded precisely with the date of Fogg's return to London, giving readers the thrilling sense that they were reading travel reports arriving in real time.

One early inkle idea for the adaptation was to recreate this with a multiplayer exploration game, pitting players against each other in round-the-world races that unfolded at a real-time pace. Travel time would provide a natural break point between short episodes in cities, giving the game a style closer to the "play for a few minutes throughout your day" aesthetic of other contemporary mobile games (see *Fallen London* **2009**). "That idea got discarded," Ingold recalls, "because, it turns out, eighty days is a really long period of time..."[12]

The idea of multiplayer survived in vestigial form into the final game, via an overlay on the world map that would show travel decisions and journey times made by other recent players.

is a prime concern. Markets in most cities let you buy and sell goods to help fund your journey, ease the stress of travel, or lubricate friendships along the way. "Having a box of snuff to hand might get a train guard on the Siberian Express to tell you what she knows about links between Yokohama and San Francisco," one reviewer noted.[7] Another observed that

> choosing the next leg of your journey isn't as simple a booking passage on the fastest mode of transport.... This gyrocopter might not be leaving for three days, a nearly unbearable delay, but it'll take you to a city where you could sell one of the items in your suitcase for a hefty sum.... Traveling by car might be quick, but it's also tiring, and Fogg can only put up with so much discomfort.[2]

The mechanics interact in ways that encourage constant decision-making. Depleted funds on hand can be restored from Fogg's accounts by visiting a bank, but this wastes precious time while waiting for the transfer. A clock visibly advances while in a city, adding pressure: if you visit the bank or take too long dithering in the market, you might miss your next connection. Exploring a city takes hours of time, but can unlock new stories and routes—though not always to places you want to visit (or can afford to). These gameplay decisions mirror and complement the narrative choices in the stories found in each city: impressing a mayor might unlock a seat on a faster conveyance, while a lapse in judgment could result in Passepartout parting with too much of Fogg's cash. More stories unfold on each possible route between stopping points. In the final game, there are over four hundred of these unique connections.

> 5:00 PM
> Hover-ship to Antananarivo
> £110
> (🧳 2/2) The hold has space for **two suitcases**, which will suffice.
> (♥ -18+9) **Baking Sunshine** and **Mild Seas**: This looks like a wearisome route, but the *Panama Hat from our Warm Climate Gear set* should see us to rights

"The fiddly bits of making the trip work wouldn't be nearly as much fun if the writing in *80 Days* wasn't so good," a reviewer noted.[2] The vast library of content—with potential stories including teeth-rattling road trips, Arctic catastrophes, submarine kidnappings, high-stakes poker games, and even a trip to the moon—was written using a custom language called ink, designed to minimize markup and let writers "quickly and robustly create heavily branching flow that runs naturally from beginning to end—as most interactive stories do."[16] While hypertext editors like Twine **2012** and Storyspace **1995** often used graphs to visualize story nodes, Ingold felt this

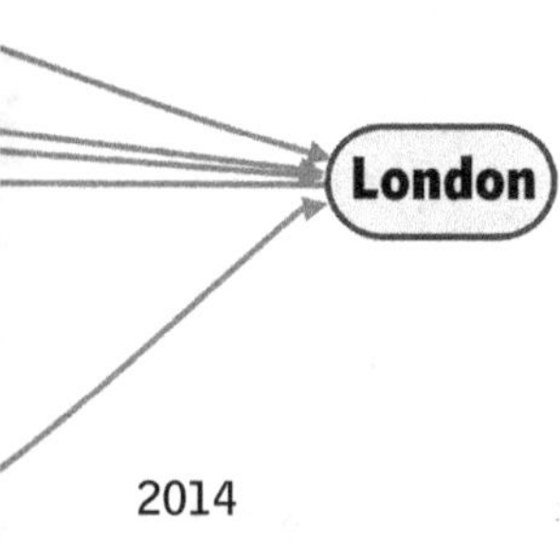

approach was overkill for works that emphasized forward momentum with no wrong choices or dead ends. Rather than forcing authors to manually reposition boxes or deal with the headache of adding or removing them from the middle of a chain, ink used a plain text markup with nested indentation indicating choices:

```
weave:neworleans
- I met Death in a smoke-wreathed red-lit bar in New Orleans,
    as the jazz band struck up another tune. He offered to buy
    me a bourbon.
    *"Holy mother of Heaven[."]," I blasphemed succinctly, -->
    *"Perhaps in twenty or thirty years?"[] I replied archly, -->
    *(wet)I threw my drink in his face[] in an automatic
        gesture of defence, -->
- as some of the other patrons snickered.
Death pulled off his mask to reveal handsome café-au-lait
    features and dark green eyes, and then extended a
    {-->wet:dripping} skeletal hand to me.
    *"A fine costume[."]," I remarked.
    "/Merci, mon cher/, -->
    *"You gave me a fright[."]," I admitted.
    "My deepest apologies, /mon cher/, -->
- I am Death at our neighborhood Mardi Gras, and I am
    practising my role." He took my proffered hand and brought
    the back of it to his lips for a gallant kiss; he flicked
    me a rather unmistakable look under his dark lashes.
    *I returned his look[] with one of my own, and he let my
        fingers slip slowly through his {raise(style)} -->
    *I pretended not to see [it] his look, or the sensuous
        tilt to his mouth, and he laughed. -->
    [...]
```

In this sequence the story flows forward, with player choices indicated by asterisks and the `-->` arrow showing a jump to the next "gather point" (dash) where the story continues. Text up to and including bracketed content is shown to the player in a menu of choices, and reprinted without the bracketed portion when the story continues, flowing it into a seamless transcript. After you click the last option in the first choice point above, the onscreen text appears like this:

> I met Death in a smoke-wreathed red-lit bar in New Orleans, as the jazz band struck up another tune. He offered to buy me a bourbon. I threw my drink in his face in an automatic gesture of defence, as some of the other patrons snickered.

The ink compiler tracks possible flows through the story and notifies authors where it might stall out, which becomes more possible with commands that can jump to other named nodes, creating more complex flows. As players progress, they might accumulate changes to stats (indicated by commands like the `{raise(style)}` near the end of the excerpt above); if Passepartout becomes more stylish in this scene, new options or text variations might appear later. A list of nodes visited in the current playthrough is automatically assembled, which lets authors easily vary text (seen above when "Death" gets soaked by a drink). Subchoices can be nested under parents to arbitrary depth, letting authors easily build complex branches within individual choices without needing labels or jumping. Designed specifically to allow easy creation of the kinds of interactive stories inkle wanted to tell, the company hoped it might be useful to spread the gospel to others, and took pains to keep the language simple:

> Every feature you add to a tool changes the way the tool presents itself to new users, and changes a user's perception of what the tool is for. So add five cool niche features and your tool might start to look like it's for making fiddly, avant-garde things only…. As tool creators we have to keep returning to our users and saying, what are these people like? What do these people care about, and what don't they care about? What message do we want to send them about what they should be doing?[1]

Working with ink, Jayanth and Ingold were able to write an incredible amount of content for *80 Days*: more than 700,000 words, 150 cities, and 16,000 individual choices. While the episodes at each destination and along each journey are largely independent, certain characters and events recur, and each playthrough reveals only portions of the stories that the game's countries and people are playing out on a global stage. Jayanth has called this "worldbuilding instead of plot,"[21] and it lets players piece together for themselves the story of the Artificer's Guild, or the Sisters of Didacus, or Austria-Hungary's Imperial Kriegorchester (an army of automatons controlled by music and "Mozart-Haydn devices"). The big-picture stories contrast with the game's hundreds of smaller vignettes—stunning vistas or memorable characters who cross your path only for moments, before your own story moves on.

> *I drank shots of homebrew liquor with a Dutch sailor…* who was mourning the loss of his third finger to frostbite. "Got seven left, I s'pose," he said, with admirable aplomb.

High player agency, compelling stories, and real replayability, with most round-the-world journeys revealing less than 10 percent of the possible text, led to a play experience that felt thrilling to many jaded players and reviewers used to games where choices rarely seemed to matter. One wrote that the game had "taken the long-ignored strengths of Interactive Fiction … and applied them in the right way on the right platform to give the player an experience that feels wholly unique, and more importantly, wholly their own."[4] Another felt that "each decision feels less like straying from the intended path … and more like letting the fiction take you new, exciting places…. The difference between *80 Days* and many other narrative games for me is that each path feels like the intended one."[3]

When Jayanth first joined the project, one of her concerns had been Verne's character Aouda, who eventually becomes Fogg's bride. "Aouda is not just Indian," she notes:

2014

She is an imperialist's vision of India: rescued from savagery and ignorance by the cool-headed rationality of an Englishman; a grateful bounty that delivers itself willingly into the hands of the benign master.

My problem with Aouda's—India's—mistreatment in the original text is personal—as I happen to be Indian, and a woman. But thinking about Aouda was a spur to me to start thinking in more general terms: what kind of shape and structure would be required to create a game that included people like her?[18]

Thinking about how to address Aouda's story became one of several spurs for the radical rethinking of the game's world that gave its characters back their agency. And as the stories changed, the writers found a surprising undercurrent in Verne that felt more resonant with the twenty-first century: the allure of a barely hoped-for possibility that change might sometimes be for the better. Jayanth noted the anticolonialist themes of *20,000 Leagues Under the Sea*, in which brown antihero Captain Nemo fights the imperialist oppressors who murdered his family. In an interview with gaming blog *Rock, Paper, Shotgun*, Ingold observed that Aouda was "a trophy wife by definition, [but] on the other hand, that's a mixed race marriage in 1872." Jayanth added:

> Aouda is deracinated and it's problematic but that's the thing, if Verne could go so far, if we are trying to write Verne today, we have a responsibility to go even further and write something that's progressive for our time. As progressive for our time as Verne was for his.[27]

"Peeling back the layers of nostalgia and assumption is the right thing to do," Jayanth has said, "but it is also a gift to the writer and reader/player: there is such an opportunity here, to tell unknown and surprising and challenging stories."[20] Reviewers and players overwhelmingly agreed, praising the game both for its reimagined history and its rethinking of interactive narrative conventions. Among other accolades, *Time* magazine named it Game of the Year for 2014—a rare feat for a game developed for mobile.

As inkle has continued to find new audiences for interactive stories, they have also kept investigating and minimizing the reasons some folks don't like them, taking rare risks and being unafraid to experiment. Sometimes questioning the foundations of a story, and its medium, is the only way to find out whether and why they still matter.

References

1 Alexander, Leigh. 2013. "Roundtable: The Interactive Fiction Renaissance." *Game Developer* (blog). Mar 14, 2013. www.gamedeveloper.com/design/roundtable-the-interactive-fiction-renaissance | a Oct 12, 2021

2 Arendt, Susan. 2014. "On My iPad: 80 Days." *Joystiq*. Aug 7, 2014. www.joystiq.com/2014/08/07/on-my-ipad-80-days | s Aug 8, 2014

3 Brinks, Melissa. 2019. "Review: '80 Days' Perfects The Adventure Game Form On Switch." *Forbes* (web). Oct 1, 2019. www.forbes.com/sites/melissabrinks/2019/10/01/review-80-days-perfects-the-adventure-game-form-on-switch | a Oct 12, 2021

4 Cameron, Phill. 2014. "80 Days Review." *Telegraph* (web). Aug 18, 2014. www.telegraph.co.uk/technology/video-games/video-game-reviews/11040336/80-Days-review.html | s Aug 24, 2021

5 Curry, David. 2014. "Inkle: Making Stories Come Alive On Mobile." *Gosu Tech* (blog). Dec 11, 2014. www.

gosu-tech.com/2014/12/11/inklemaking-stories-alive-mobile | s Dec 23, 2014

6   Faraday, Owen. 2014. "To Jaipur by Hover-Car: A Hands-on Preview of 80 Days." *Pocket Tactics* (blog). Jun 9, 2014. www.pockettactics.com/features/jaipur-hover-car-hands-preview-80-days | s Jun 12, 2014

7   Hartup, Phil. 2015. "Inkle's 80 Days Is a Brilliant Game That Isn't Really a Game at All." *New Statesman* (blog). Jan 29, 2015. www.newstatesman.com/culture/2015/01/80-days-brilliant-game-isnt-really-game-all | a Oct 12, 2021

8   Hayward, Andrew. 2015. "80 Days' Twisting, Globetrotting Adventure Will Be Even Wilder on Mac." *Macworld* (blog). Sep 10, 2015. www.macworld.com/article/226300/80-days-twisting-globetrotting-adventure-will-be-even-wilder-on-mac.html | a Oct 12, 2021

9   Humfrey, Joseph. 2016. "Ink: The Narrative Scripting Language Behind '80 Days' and 'Sorcery!'" Talk presented at the Game Developers Conference, San Francisco, 2016. www.gdcvault.com/play/1022944/Ink-The-Narrative-Scripting-Language | a Oct 12, 2021

10 Ingold, Jon. 2014. "80 DAYS Post-Mortem: Letting the Game Tell the Story." Talk presented at the Game Developers Conference China, Shanghai, Oct 19, 2014. www.gdcvault.com/play/1021666/80-DAYS-Post-mortem-Letting | a Oct 12, 2021

11 Ingold, Jon. 2015. "Adventures in Text: Innovating in Interactive Fiction." Talk presented at the Game Developer's Conference, San Francisco, Mar 2, 2015. www.gdcvault.com/play/1021774/Adventures-in-Text-Innovating-in | a Oct 12, 2021

12 Ingold, Jon, and Joseph Humfrey. 2015. "Postmortem: Inkle's 80 Days." *Game Developer* (blog). Oct 13, 2015. www.gamedeveloper.com/business/postmortem-inkle-s-i-80-days-i- | a Oct 12, 2021

13 Ingold, Jon and Mag Jayanth. 2019. "Jon Ingold Interviews Meg Jayanth." Discussion presented at AdventureX, London, Nov 2, 2019. www.youtube.com/watch?v=hmfPuKYjyFA | a Oct 12, 2021

14 Inkle Blog. 2014a. "Welcome to Our World!" Apr 29, 2014. www.inklestudios.com/2014/04/29/welcome-to-our-world.html | a Oct 12, 2021

15 Inkle Blog. 2014b. "Journey's End…" Jul 14, 2014. www.inklestudios.com/2014/07/14/approaching-journeys-end.html | a Oct 12, 2021

16 Inkle Blog. 2021. "ink version 1.0 release!" Feb 22, 2021. www.inklestudios.com/2021/02/22/ink-version-1.html | a Oct 12, 2021

17 Jayanth, Meg. 2014a. "Verne and Victorian Futurism." *Inkle Blog*. May 8, 2014. www.inklestudios.com/2014/05/08/victorian-futurism.html | a Oct 12, 2021

18 Jayanth, Meg. 2014b. "Don't Be A Hero - 80 Days the Game." *The Literary Platform* (blog). Jul 30, 2014. theliteraryplatform.com/news/2014/07/dont-be-a-hero-80-days-the-game | a Oct 12, 2021

19 Jayanth, Meg. 2014c. "Fantasy, History and Respect." *You Can Panic Now* (blog). Oct 18, 2014. megjayanth.com/post/100280300365/fantasy-history-and-respect | a Oct 12, 2021

20 Jayanth, Meg. 2014d. "Using Games to Re-framing Our Past: an interview with 80 Days writer Meg Jayanth." Interview by Barry Joseph. *Moosha Moosha Mooshme* (blog). www.mooshme.org/2014/10/using-games-to-re-framing-our-past-an-interview-with-80-days-writer-meg-jayanth | a Oct 12, 2021

21 Jayanth, Meg. 2015a. "Leading Players Astray: 80 Days & Unexpected Stories." Talk presented at the Game Developers Conference, San Francisco, Mar 2, 2015. www.gdcvault.com/play/1022101/Leading-Players-Astray-80-Days | a Oct 12, 2021

22 Jayanth, Meg. 2015b. "An Interview with Meg Jayanth." Interview by D. S. Wadeson. *D S Wadeson* (Medium blog). madquills.medium.com/an-interview-with-meg-jayanth-3bba787e6e8f | a Oct 12, 2021

23 Jayanth, Meg. 2016. "Forget Protagonists: Writing NPCs with Agency for '80 Days' and Beyond." Talk presented at the Game Developers Conference, San Francisco, Mar 14, 2016. www.gdcvault.com/play/1023393/Forget-Protagonists-Writing-NPCs-with | a Oct 12, 2021

24 Köller, Joe. 2013. "Wordplay: Jon Ingold." *Haywire Magazine* (blog). Oct 27, 2013. haywiremag.com/features/wordplay-jon-ingold | a Oct 12, 2021

25 Lloyd, Stuart. 2013. "April A to Z - I Is for Inkle." *Lloyd of Gamebooks* (blog). Apr 10, 2013. www.lloydofgamebooks.com/2013/04/april-to-z-i-is-for-inkle.html | a Oct 12, 2021

26 Parkin, Simon. 2016. "Meg Jayanth: The 80 Days Writer on the Interactive Power of Game-Play." *The Guardian*, Jan 10, 2016, sec. Games. www.theguardian.com/technology/2016/jan/10/video-game-makers-meg-jayanth-80-days | a Oct 12, 2021

27 Smith, Graham. 2015. "How 80 Days Adapted The Modernist Spirit Of Verne." *Rock, Paper, Shotgun* (blog). Oct 14, 2015. www.rockpapershotgun.com/80-days-design-interview | a Oct 12, 2021

28 Torkington, Janel. 2014. "80 Days (iOS): Next Generation Interactive Fiction." *iOS App Development* (blog). Jun 10, 2014. medium.com/ios-os-x-development/next-generation-interactive-fiction-80-days-379b9a2ad1c5 | a Oct 12, 2021

LIFELINE

Dave Justus, Ben "Books" Schwartz, Colin Liotta, Mars Jokela, Jason Nowak, and Dan Sellec

Style	**Choice-Based**
Debuted	**Apr 16, 2015** *(App Store)*
Launch Platform	**Apple Watch, iPad, iPhone**
Developer	**3 Minute Games**
Publisher	**Big Fish Games**
Language	**Objective C** *(app)* **Twine** *(authoring)*
Launch Price	**$2.99** *(download)*

> [incoming communication]
> [establishing connection]
> [receiving message]
> Hello?
> Is this thing working?
> Can anyone read me?

IN THE FIRST WEEK OF MAY 2015, the number one paid game on Apple's mobile app store for countless months before and after—*Minecraft*—briefly lost its place on top. For a few days that week, the bestselling mobile game on the best-known software storefront in the world was a choice-based text adventure called *Lifeline*, which had also become the top title on the just-released Apple Watch. If it had still been easy to declare text games commercially dead five or ten years earlier, it was a little harder to do so that

2015

week in May, when hundreds of thousands of players paid for an app that let them swap texts with a fictional astronaut.

Lifeline's developer, 3 Minute Games, had come together in late 2014 as a kind of skunkworks within casual gaming giant Big Fish Games. Led by Colin Liotta and Mars Jokela, it was tasked with making rapid mobile game prototypes—"testing different styles of games, different pay structures, seeing which combinations worked best."[8] A new feature announced that year at Apple's Worldwide Developers Conference had caught Liotta's attention: in iOS 8, developers would be able to add actions directly to device notifications, allowing users to interact without needing to unlock and open an app. Liotta, who had been musing about an asynchronous narrative game, realized the new feature could let people play a choice-based game entirely in stolen moments throughout their day, without ever leaving the lock screen. When the Apple Watch was announced a few months later, it seemed like "an absolutely perfect platform to launch the game on,"[2] so the team rushed the concept into production, hoping to have something ready for the smartwatch's launch day.

The 3 Minute team reached out to a contract writer they knew, Books Schwartz, with a difficult authoring challenge: to create an interactive story for such a tiny screen, they'd need a hard limit of two options per choice with just a handful of words in each option. Schwartz was a lifelong fan of adventure games, having grown up with text adventures and their graphical cousins, but most of their game design experience was in live-action roleplaying. In a recent campaign, they'd played a research assistant character who was connected to the main action only through phone calls with a hero in the thick of it. Even distanced from the plot, picking it up in bits and pieces each time the phone rang, Schwartz had still found the experience surprisingly compelling. During a long phone call, Liotta and Schwartz worked out a plot structure for the new game where the player would text advice to a fictional astronaut who needs help getting out of a jam, "sort of like if *The Martian* were a game instead of a movie, and you got to talk to Mark Watney the entire time he's stranded on Mars."[8]

> All right, so my escape pod came down in some kind of desert.
>
> The ground is all cracked white rock. There's a huge white peak a few miles away.
>
> Or, uh, kilometers, I guess. (They tried to get me to think metric for the trip, but some things are just hardwired.)
>
> It's weirdly symmetrical, like it might not be a natural formation.
>
> My IEVA suit's compass places the peak northeast, and then, in the opposite direction—south and southwest, to be precise—
>
> ...are two funnels of black smoke from what I have to assume are two pieces of the Varia.

Best case scenario, it's ONLY in two pieces.

The crash sites look closer than the peak. What do you think I should do?

» Check the crash.
» *Head for the peak.*

Yeah, cool, that makes sense. There might be other survivors ... fingers crossed.

(It's not actually possible to cross your fingers in an IEVA suit, but just take my word on it.)

Or at the very least, there should be some supplies I can use.

Okay, I'm headed south now. Looks like the smoke is at least an hour away. Or whatever the metric equivalent of an hour is.

I'll let you know once I'm there.

[Taylor is busy]

Schwartz wrote some early scenes for the game and sketched out an outline for the rest, but was struggling with the stress of an intense graduate program and had to bow out of the project early. Scrambling to find a replacement, the 3 Minute team reached out to another friend: Dave Justus, a Texas-based writer trying to break into storytelling for comics. Justus was a bit of a long shot, with only one professional credit and "no background in games whatsoever."[8] (He later joked that the most recent game he'd played before writing *Lifeline* was 1997's *Tomb Raider II.*[6]) "3 Minute really took a chance on an unknown quantity when they brought me on board ... which was a big gamble on their part."[2] But the clock was ticking and Justus was available, so on very short notice he joined the project.

Justus had just five weeks to write the bulk of a novel-length branching adventure, taking Schwartz's start and fleshing out a fully realized world, story, and game. "[I was] free to do whatever I wanted," he recalled, "which was both amazing and daunting."[8] Schwartz, who identifies as nonbinary, had decided to keep the main character ungendered as "a bit of quiet representation"[9] and to allow players to imagine the hero however they liked. Justus kept the idea and further developed Taylor's character: a young lab assistant, not an experienced hero, which explained their need for constant help from the player and understandable anxiety about crash-landing on an alien moon. Messages would arrive in short bursts, just like texts, so the writing had to convey character and situation while remaining as short and economical with words as possible.

It's been commonly misreported that Justus was already an established and award-winning game writer when he came aboard *Lifeline*, due to a credit most reporters assumed was for popular story game *The Wolf Among Us* [Telltale Games 2013]. In fact, Justus had only written for a spin-off comic based on the game—his first credited job as a writer.

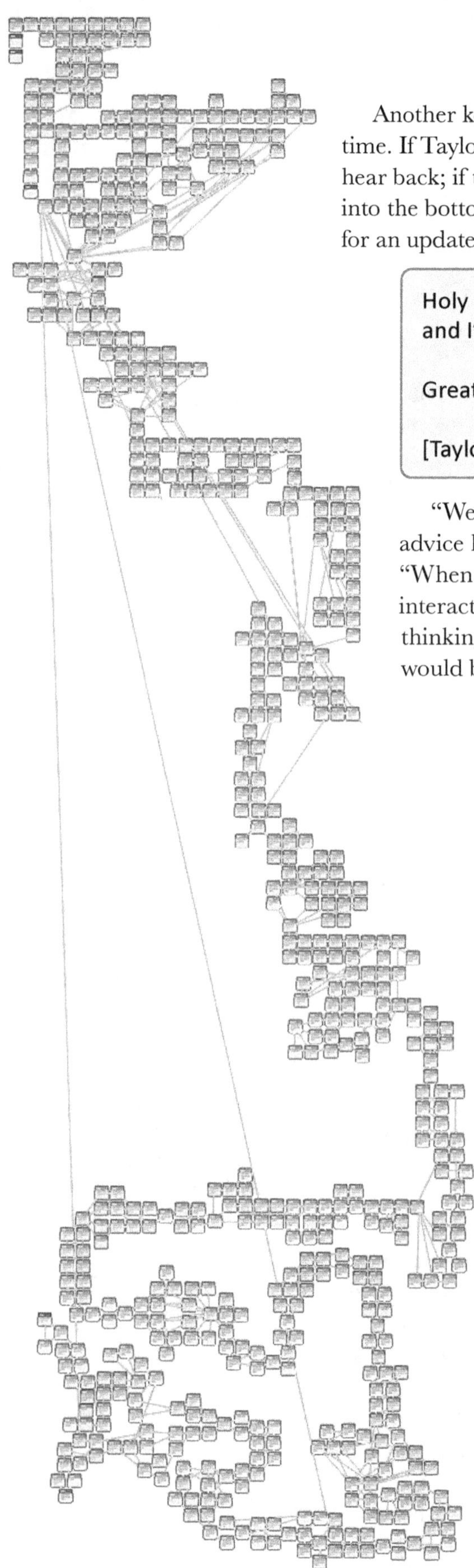

Another key concept was that *Lifeline*'s messages would arrive in real time. If Taylor went to sleep, you'd have to wait until the next morning to hear back; if the reluctant astronaut needed to climb down a steep slope into the bottom of a crater, the player might need to wait an hour or two for an update.

> Holy crap. It's a lot further than it looked. My legs feel like Jell-O, and I'm maybe halfway there.
>
> Great. And now all I can think about is how much I want Jell-O.
>
> [Taylor is busy]

"We wanted Players to be tense, anxious to see whether their advice had been Taylor's doom or salvation," Justus recalls.[8] "When people are playing it, it's not just about the time that they're interacting with Taylor. It's all the rest of the time when they're thinking about Taylor. The whole goal was to make something that would become a part of people's lives."[6]

> Okay. At long last, I'm in sight of the Varia. Or what's left of it, at any rate.
>
> It seems to have cracked hard once it hit atmosphere.
>
> Like I figured, it came down in two major chunks…
>
> …with a ton of scattered debris thrown around just to make the whole scene look terrifying and post-apocalyptic.
>
> (In case anyone asks, it's working; I'm appropriately terrified.)
>
> Looks like the flight deck came down pretty far from the crew quarters. Where do you figure I should go first?
>
> » *Look for the crew.*
> » *Check the flight deck.*

While also not a gamer as an adult, Justus had enjoyed text adventures on his parents' Apple IIe as a kid—*The Hitchhiker's Guide to the Galaxy* **1984** had been a particular favorite. He'd also been a "voracious reader as a child—the sort who would read the back of cereal boxes, just because they had words on them,"[8] and had owned a collection of several dozen Choose Your Own

Adventure <u>**1979**</u> books. But he was unfamiliar with post-1980s interactive fiction, had never been to a game design conference or meetup, and was facing such a crushing deadline that there was little time to study up on conventional design or craft wisdom. "I honestly think, in this case, that worked to my advantage," he recalls, "because I wrote the game purely as a conversation. I wasn't thinking in terms of … typical video game structures; rather, I wanted it to feel as much as possible like the Player was receiving texts from a real human being."[8]

OH MY GOD! You'll never believe it!

I'm still walking around a moon crater and it's still boring as hell!

…Sorry. I was just going a little bonkers, with nothing but the sound of my own thoughts.

» **No worries. Wanna chat?**
» *Sorry. No time to chat.*

Yes! Please. I mean, I don't want to be a bother, but you're kind of all I've got.

The real-time delay mechanic smacked of the forced waiting common in free-to-play apps, where in-app purchases could skip over long delays, but perhaps because of the project's status as an experiment rather than a premeditated moneymaker, the creators included no such gotchas. "You can't speed up time with a few hundred gems," one reviewer noted. "You must be patient."[4] The game was designed to take place over three real-time days, or longer if the player didn't always immediately respond (time doesn't advance while Taylor waits for a reply). The team thought there was a serious chance the concept could fall flat. "This sort of approach ought, by rights, to backfire," a reviewer wrote, "leaving gamers furious at shelling out for an app they can't play. But amazingly, it works."[11] Another wrote that "by isolating interactions to sparing moments throughout the day,

> *Lifeline* infuses your normal grind with a palpable sense of adventure and consequence. During my playthrough, it's not an exaggeration to say that I woke up nervous about what might have happened to Taylor, or paused in mid-conversation with colleagues to check on the outcome of a decision I had made.… The game's drip-feed of content—would-be fertile ground for predatory in-app payments—is used instead as an innovative way [to] transform your relationship with the technology that sits at the centre of your life.[3]

"As counterintuitive as it sounds, there's something about interacting with Taylor through text messages that can feel very intimate," game critic Laura Hudson wrote, "perhaps because we've grown so accustomed to communicating our most personal thoughts with our friends through texts—and waiting for their responses with bated breath."[6] The unlikely notion that people would enjoy reading text on the tiny screen of an Apple Watch turned

Opposite: Twine map for *Lifeline* (beginning upper left), showing a mostly linear overall structure characterized by rich local but less overall impact from choices, and occasional opportunities to skip past certain sequences.

MEMORABLE PLACES

the wreck of the *Varia*

the lip of a huge crater

a pitch-black corridor

a shimmery peak

a control room infested by green-eyed rats

In addition to traditional
sequels, other official spin-
offs included *Float*, a timed
Twitter event where many
players interacted with the
same character; and *Lifeline
Universe*, a short-lived
platform for users to write
and sell their own stories in
the style of the series.

out to be a nonissue: reading bite-sized chunks of text off miniature screens had long since become entirely normalized.

Justus used Twine **2012** to lay out and write his story, finding it a workable tool for someone like him with no technical background; the 3 Minute team would later process the story file format to adapt it to their own proprietary engine. While the game's overall plot follows the same general spine regardless of your choices, several small subplots and asides can be discovered, and—as in the classic gamebooks—there are lots of ways for Taylor to die. (After finding one, the game lets you rewind to an earlier choice and try again, and unlocks the option to disable real-time delays.) While many choices are frustratingly blind and it's not always clear how to lead Taylor to success, on occasion the game shakes up its formula in intriguing ways. In one early scene, Taylor asks whether exposure to a certain level of radiation is likely to prove fatal. You can guess, or you can actually do the research to find out—something that became easier in the wake of the game's huge success, with Google helpfully pointing any remotely related searches toward *Lifeline*-inspired answers.

Lifeline's success was a combination of great timing and great execution: snappy writing, a clever core concept, and a launch on a new platform with few other apps yet available. "It's the first game I've loaded on my Watch that is not only fun to play," said *Time* magazine, "but fun to play specifically on a wearable."[12] The game's explosive popularity would lead to a wave of copycats as well as official sequels, the first of which came just five months after the original. Though distant from the innovations in technology or design happening in other commercial text games, *Lifeline* demonstrated the genre's appeal even with the most straightforward of foundations. The team was blown away by the unexpected success: by 2019 the series had amassed seven million installs. "The download numbers were staggering enough," Justus recalls, "but then we started seeing fan art, cosplay, fan fiction. It was, frankly, completely overwhelming."[2] After some corporate reshuffling and a hiatus where the future of the series was in doubt, the original team reunited in 2021 to work on more games in the *Lifeline* universe and style.

"Texting adventures," Jokela calls them.[7]

References

1 Big Fish. 2016. "Lifeline: Whiteout, the Sequel to #1 Hit Mobile Game Is Announced." Press Release. May 18, 2016. www.prnewswire.com/news-releases/lifeline-whiteout-the-sequel-to-1-hit-mobile-game-is-announced-300270403.html | a Oct 24, 2021

2 Cohen, Oren. 2021. "A New Lifeline Mobile Game Is On The Horizon." *Oren Cohen: The Geek Writer* (blog). Jul 16, 2021. theorencohen.com/blog/that-lost-astronaut-you-chatted-with-five-years-ago-is-making-a-comeback | a Oct 24, 2021

3 Cymet, Eli. 2015. "Lifeline… Review: Emergency Contact." *Gamezebo* (blog). May 1, 2015. www.gamezebo.com/2015/05/01/lifeline-review-emergency-contact | a Oct 24, 2021

4 Gil, Lori. 2015. "Lifeline… Is a Fun Interactive Game You Can Play on Your IPhone or Apple Watch." *iDB* (blog). May 5, 2015. www.idownloadblog.com/2015/05/06/lifeline | a Oct 24, 2021

5 Hennon, Blake. 2014. "'Fables: The Wolf Among Us': Matthew Sturges, Dave Justus on the Case." *Hero Complex* (blog). Oct 10, 2014. herocomplex.latimes.com/comics/fables-the-wolf-among-us-matthew-sturges-dave-justus-on-the-case/#/0 | s Oct 13, 2024

6 Hudson, Laura. 2015. "I've Been Texting with an Astronaut." *Boing Boing* (blog). May 7, 2015. boingboing.

net/2015/05/07/lifeline-astronaut-game.html | a Oct 24, 2021

7 Justus, Dave. 2016. Lifeline: An Interview." Interview by Fabrizio Venerandi. *Verba Mutant* (blog). www.quintadicopertina.com/fabriziovenerandi/?p=493 | a Oct 24, 2021

8 Justus, Dave. 2019. "An Interview with "Lifeline" Series Writer Dave Justus." *Brunette Games* (blog). www.brunettegames.com/2019/07/an-interview-with-lifeline-series-writer-dave-justus.html | s Dec 18, 2019

9 Schwartz, Ben. 2022. Unpublished email with author. Feb 2, 2022.

10 Thomas, Lucas M. 2015. "App Store Update: September 22." *IGN* (blog). Sep 22, 2015. www.ign.com/articles/2015/09/22/app-store-update-september-22-3 | a Oct 24, 2021

11 Thrower, Matt. 2015. "Lifeline…" (review). *Pocket Gamer* (blog). Apr 29, 2015. www.pocketgamer.com/articles/065105/lifeline | a Oct 24, 2021

12 Vella, Matt. 2015. "This Is the Best Game on the Apple Watch." *Time* (blog). May 7, 2015. time.com/3850243/lifeline-apple-watch | a Oct 24, 2021

CHOICES
THE FRESHMAN

Pixelberry Staff (including Wendy Briggs, Max Doty, Chelsa Lauderdale, Royal McGraw, Keyan Mohsenin, Maya Poulson, Saran Walker, Jennifer Young, and Rachel Zilberg)

Style	**Choice-Based**
Debuted	**Aug 7, 2016** *(app stores)*
Launch Platform	**iOS, Android**
Publisher	**Pixelberry Studios**
Language	**Cocos2d-x, C++**

> **"** Welcome to Hartfeld University, one of North America's most elite academic institutions!
> It's the first day of college, and you walk across a bustling campus…

THE HIGHEST-GROSSING DIGITAL GAME OF 2016, according to leading market research firm the NPD Group, was *Call of Duty: Infinite Warfare* [Activision],[18] selling 1.8 million copies for PC, Xbox One, and PlayStation 4 in its first week of release and reaching a lifetime sales figure of 13 million. Biggest gross, though, does not equal most played. Dozens of mobile games that year had more downloads, due to cheaper or free price points and more ubiquitous platforms. Yet media coverage of digital games rarely reflects this.

2016

It might surprise even readers of this book to know that an interactive fiction romance called *The Freshman*, released the same year as *Infinite Warfare*, had been played nearly forty-five million times as of 2020.[23] Despite this it's never been reviewed on a mainstream gaming site. Even most catalogs of interactive fiction don't include it.

The reasons why have to do with the politics of gender and game genres; with cultural baggage around divisions between hardcore and casual players; with the ethical concerns of free-to-play monetization models; with the definitions of "interactive fiction" and their relationships with visual art and UI design; and with the way most fans and scholars have been trained to think about which games "matter," and why. But to take seriously the project of examining the continuing impact of interactive prose over the past fifty years, it's impossible to leave out the app in which *The Freshman* and its sequels were published—Pixelberry Studios' *Choices: Stories You Play*—and its many competitors.

Pixelberry's origins date back to the early 2000s, when Asian American Stanford grad Oliver Miao founded a game company, Centerscore, with a handful of friends. They "lived and worked out of a small apartment next to the railroad tracks," Miao remembers, "putting business calls on hold whenever a train passed by."[13] After a few years of fitful success, Centerscore broke into the emerging mobile games market and realized that high schoolers—in particular, high school girls—were a massively underserved audience. In 2005 they released a subscription-based episodic story game, *Surviving High School*, which broke the top five on Verizon's Get It Now service, the biggest mobile app storefront of the time and filled mostly with *Pac-Man*, *Tetris*, and *Snake* clones. *Surviving High School* became the first successful text-driven and story-centric hit for a mobile phone platform, and it remained hugely popular, releasing weekly content updates for nearly a decade. Miao "thought a text based game was a perfect fit" for the pre-iPhone mobile market, with processors too underpowered for impressive graphics. "Our belief was that with limited information, our players would use their imaginations to fill in the blanks."[16]

On the basis of their success, the team was acquired and passed around between gaming giants like Vivendi and Electronic Arts. They remade *Surviving High School* for iPhone in the early 2010s before escaping in 2013 to start over as a new independent company, Pixelberry. Despite the team's earlier hits, story games on mobile were still seen by the industry as a dubious proposition. Story made titles harder to localize to other languages, and blocks of text were less "juicy" than simple, addictive game mechanics. As late as 2014, a game journalist could still say that mobile storytelling "has been for the most part untapped in today's app market.… As powerful as a good storyline can be many mobile games have little to no plot."[4] Pixelberry set out to change this with a new game in the old mode, *High School Story* [2013], but they still felt the need to disguise their story-heavy game inside a strange hybrid of city-builder and RPG, which had then been a successful mobile game formula.

Then, in 2014, two mobile games served as wake-up calls to the industry. *Kim Kardashian: Hollywood* [Glu Mobile] launched that summer with no fanfare in the mainstream gaming press, and it instantly became an enormous success. Within days it had grossed nearly $2 million, with projections of bringing in as much as $200 million annually. It flew to the top of app store charts, and for years it was the only top ten game on Apple's store with a 5-star average rating. "Like everyone else on earth, we noticed [the game's success]," wrote Royal McGraw, a producer at Pixelberry. "Who could miss it?"[11] At the same time, an app called *Episode* [Pocket Gems 2013], which let players build their own interactive romance stories, was becoming another unstoppable hit. The app featured 2D characters who could be posed and animated like paper dolls to illustrate dialogue-driven stories; the company described it as "an interactive animated television show" and a "modern, mobile-first Choose Your Own Adventure."[4] *Episode* also became wildly popular, especially with teenage girls able to play through huge libraries of stories built by their peers.

see **1979**

Pixelberry's takeaway from these two successes was clear: young women were eager to find mobile games that spoke to them, and storytelling could be a powerful way of retaining users and building a devoted fanbase, which was critical in a market where getting even a small percentage of the users who downloaded your app to keep playing was a win. The company brought in more writers, most of them women, and announced that their goal was to "[bring] interactive fiction to a whole new audience that would never have considered themselves gamers before."[1] McGraw noted that story would inform "every single design decision that we make" at Pixelberry going forward.[10] Rather than window dressing on top of unrelated game mechanics, the story would *be* the gameplay. The team looked at the interactivity provided by choice points as a smart business decision for the all-important retention problem: "Every choice a player makes makes the experience theirs. The more 'theirs' it is, the more likely they are to come back."[10] It would prove a massively successful philosophy.

It's frankly embarrassing it took the game industry and its marketing teams so long to realize that women were valuable customers. Earlier experiments in writing feminine-coded interactive fiction, like *Plundered Hearts*, were made by companies with no experience selling games to anyone other than geeks, increasingly culturally stereotyped through the 1980s as male. In the 90s, studios like Purple Moon tried to find publishers for CD-ROM games aimed at teenage girls, with little success. Later decades brought amateur game scenes with fewer gatekeepers, allowing for the rise of genres like visual novels that appealed to wider sensibilities. Yet perhaps it took the arrival of a computing platform like the mobile phone—obviously and very publicly used by everyone, regardless of gender—for marketing teams to realize what they'd been missing out on.

see **1987**

founded by Brenda Laurel; see *The Playground* **1994**

see **2010**

Women had of course been making and playing games in every decade since the beginning, yet always against a narrative that they were outsiders "pushing their way into a space not originally intended for them,"[2] in the words of game scholar Shira Chess. While early advertisements for computers and gaming systems often framed them as something boys, girls,

see **1978**, **1986**, **1992**, and **2004**, among others and parents could all enjoy equally—part of a general trend at the time away from gendered toy advertising—that changed through the 80s for a myriad of reasons, with marketers and game makers increasingly focusing more on boys than girls. The attitude eventually became entrenched that "real" digital games were the kind real men liked to play, and anything else could be dismissed, ridiculed, silenced, or attacked. In one of many examples, Chess quotes a 2007 editorial from *Game Informer* magazine dismissing the rise of so-called casual games on mobile and their audience of "middle-aged women in the suburbs [who] love playing games … when they aren't watching Oprah…. Is this really what the industry needs?" The bias, whether as blatantly conscious as this or not, created "a massive blind spot" in the discourse around games, as Chess notes:

> We have a problem. Because when we—as a culture—talk about video games, when we talk about players, when we talk about consoles and peripherals, the focus is largely on "core games"—a term short-handing "hardcore," but implying a slightly larger corpus. By focusing on "core," the video game industry, game culture, and academia has gotten to define which games get talked about and which games are important. They get to determine which games we choose to care about on a cultural level.[3]

Kim Kardashian: Hollywood was widely critiqued for blatantly and perhaps even harmfully trafficking in feminine stereotypes. (Did it do so more than *Call of Duty: Infinite Warfare* had done for masculine ones? Left as an exercise for the reader.) In any case, the blind spot was starting to shift as more and more companies smelled an opportunity: another gender to pander to, for better and worse. In a world where repeatable formulas were absolutely crucial to remaining in business, the front lines then moved from one-off hits to reliable successes—and one of the easiest ways to achieve them was episodic storytelling.

Where Pixelberry's earlier hits had been singular stories, their new app would be a platform for them: a collection of "books" focusing on different flavors of romance, with weekly playable "chapters." The stories were designed to appeal to younger women, with a simple art style that replaced the janky puppet-show animation of earlier mobile romance games with static, high-quality character art and an emphasis on snappy text and relatable characters. The app launched with three "books," including *The Freshman*; by 2020 there were well over a hundred, most with a dozen or more chapters taking a mobile-friendly ten or fifteen minutes each to read.

The Freshman, most successful of the launch stories, begins firmly in the mode of a college rom-com, with your female character literally bumping into a hunky football player the second she steps on campus. The first few chapters unfold predictably, with rivals and love interests introduced and best friendships forged. But the story begins to develop deeper layers a few chapters in, when a financial crisis lands your character an internship with the grumpy, middle-aged Professor Vasquez who's in the midst of writing a novel about college life called, yes, *The Freshman*. Vasquez gives you "assignments" to engage and report back on traditional college activities— joining a sorority, throwing a raging party—to add touches of authenticity to

Despite the literary metaphor, stories from Pixelberry and most of their competitors are told almost entirely through written character dialogue, making them closer to screenplays or TV episodes.

Pixelberry's writers have spoken about using tropes deliberately as a strategy to make players feel comfortable and familiar in the first few chapters of a story, gaining the time to develop characters more deeply in later chapters.[10]

his novel. This excuse for "performing" as a stereotypical college freshman adds some welcome self-aware humor:

> *Vasquez*: I'd rather focus on finishing *The Freshman*. Hopefully it will serve as a cautionary tale to today's youth.
> *Stacey* (player): Yeah … a cautionary tale.
> *Stacey*: As in…
>
> » **Never trust your professor!**
> » *Try not to date three people at once!*
>
> *Vasquez*: You've clearly misidentified the theme of my book, Stacey.
> *Vasquez*: Whether you trust me or not is a moot point. You *have* to work for me.
> *Stacey*: So it's a book about the way millennials are subjugated by a corrupt power structure set up by *your* generation?
> *Vasquez*: Interesting take. I like that angle…
> *Vasquez*: But … it still ignores the main character's central flaws.
> *Stacey*: What flaws? I bet you can't even come up with one example.
> *Vasquez*: Actually, I've got half a book's worth of examples. And by the end of the year, I should have enough to finish this thing.

The acerbic relationship becomes more complex when you learn Vasquez is dying of cancer, a secret he's keeping from his family and favorite students.

> *Stacey*: You need to tell him.
> *Vasquez*: Don't you dare try to tell me what I *need* to do.
> *Vasquez*: *You* need to remember who's in charge here … who holds your future in the palm of his hand.
> *Stacey*: Well…
>
> » *At least I have a future!*
> » **I'm sorry.**
>
> *Vasquez*: Interesting. Last semester, you would have barked back some insult at me.
> *Vasquez*: Perhaps you're capable of evolving as a character.
> *Stacey*: I'm not a character. I'm a person.
> *Vasquez*: We'll see.

In later chapters you can end up helping Vasquez reconcile with his estranged family, forming a genuine friendship in the process. When the professor dies, he leaves your character with the unfinished manuscript to *The Freshman*, trusting her to finish the story in whatever way she likes.

Choices stories have mechanical similarities with visual novels, with long stretches of dialogue interrupted relatively infrequently by choice points—a typical chapter of *The Freshman* offers about ten decisions across its length. Character portraits can show different expressions and change

The protagonist's name is chosen by the player.

Spoilers for later chapters of The Freshman.

their background color to indicate the speaker's emotion, but they're not animated, keeping the player's focus on reading the text. The player can name their character, customize her appearance to some degree, and change into different outfits at key moments. Choices are sometimes just for flavor, but they can also lead to alternate sequences or affect invisible stats that control dialogue variants. (For example, someone who's a love interest in one playthrough might use different language than if they were just a friend.) Occasionally other mechanics break up the dialogue—such as timed choices, or recall choices that check whether you were paying attention to earlier details—but stories tend not to have major branches. Chapters generally end with cliffhangers, encouraging players to return next week to continue the story.

Choices also makes use of freemium or free-to-play mechanics, which were already well established on mobile by the time of the app's release. "Diamond choices" appear two or three times per episode, offering tantalizing story rewards like a date night with a love interest or a makeover with a friend. These choices are unlocked with in-app currency, with most costing between twelve and twenty-five diamonds. Finishing a chapter and watching in-game ads both earn you diamonds, but slowly; players are thus encouraged to purchase packs of them from within the app. Keys, a second in-game currency, unlock new chapters or allow for restarting a chapter to try different choices. A key can be claimed after a three-hour waiting period, or packs of them bought in the store. Each diamond choice generally costs around a dollar or two in real money, usually unlocking a two- or three-minute scene of narratively rewarding (or at least wish-fulfilling) content.

The ethics of free-to-play were endlessly debated in the 2010s as they became the most profitable way to monetize games on mobile. By 2011, free-to-play revenue on the Apple's App Store had overtaken revenue from traditional up-front purchases. A distinguishing feature of free-to-play is its use of the same kinds of psychological manipulation seen in gambling and casino games, which trick players into spending more money than they'd normally be inclined to part with. In-app currencies, for instance, take advantage of a well-documented psychological effect where uncertain or complex conversion rates decrease people's natural tendency to be frugal with their spending—since it's hard to know exactly how many dollars each diamond corresponds to, it's harder to feel guilty about spending them. Studies have shown that these effects are more pronounced in teens and young adults.[20] The narratively charged nature of the diamond rewards in *Choices* stories also engage the player's empathy and guilt as tools to get them to spend more money. It's hard to turn down a depressed friend who's asked you to take her for a girl's night out, even when she's a fictional character and doing so costs real-world cash.

In their earlier games, Pixelberry had made responsible messaging to their teenage audience a primary goal. For *High School Story* they partnered with groups like the National Eating Disorder Association and the Cybersmile Foundation (a group fighting online bullying) to work positive messages into their storylines, and they donated hundreds of thousands of dollars to these charities. This social consciousness rests uneasily with the manipulative mechanics of free-to-play. Oliver Miao has been unsentimental about the company's change in strategy, framing it as a matter of survival: "We decided … we would focus on commercial success first, because that's hard enough to do as a game studio; and if we were able to be successful commercially, then we'd later on add elements of social education."[17] These trade-offs weren't made in the abstract; the team had voted in early 2016 to take an across-the-board pay cut rather than go out of business before *Choices* could be finished and launched.

While a problematic marriage, Pixelberry does implement free-to-play in a more ethical manner than many competitors. Though often framed as deathly important, players soon learn that diamond scenes are merely fun bonus content that won't affect a game's overall plot. The stories also tend to be less aggressive about pushing premium options than similar apps. For example, a diamond choice in *The Freshman* gives the option of dressing up for a social event, but doesn't punish you for not choosing it:

> *Kaitlyn*: But let's focus on Stacey! What are *you* wearing to the dance?
> *Stacey*: Hmm … I haven't really thought about it.
> *Kaitlyn*: Are you kidding me? Picking the right dress is *everything!*
> *Kaitlyn*: With the right dress, your crushes will drool over you … and your enemies will be insanely jealous!
> *Stacey*: I guess I'd better choose wisely!
> (What should I wear?)
>
> *[Player chooses the free dress instead of one of two premium options costing 20 and 25 diamonds.]*
>
> You walk back out of your room wearing a little black dress and heels.
> *Stacey*: What do you think?
> *Kaitlyn*: Adorable!
> *Abbie*: Did you decide what you're going to wear yet, Kaitlyn?

Compare this to a similar "gem choice" in *Love on Fire*, a story from competitor *Episode* where you're a contestant on a reality TV show:

> *Ashley*: You need to make a REALLY good first impression, because…
> *Ashley*: Everyone will be voting on who gets to stay!
> *Player*: Make a killer first impression—I've got this!
> *Ashley*: Great! I designed a super hot bikini for you…
> *[Animation of your character dancing and looking sexy in the premium bikini]*
> *Ashley*: Imagine joining the party and making everyone's jaw drop!
> *Player*: First impressions are SO important! I *definitely* want to turn heads when I walk in!
>
> » *Be UNFORGETTABLE in this HOT AF look! [14 gems]*
> » Wear a plain bikini.

"We tried to design *Choices* so that if you play through the whole game with no premium choices, you're still able to have a rewarding ending," the team has stated.[18]

[Animation of your character in a basic bikini, looking embarrassed]
Ashley: You're breaking my heart…
Ashley: This is your ONE chance to make your first impression on Love on Fire!
Player: I definitely want to look my best!

» *Wear something fabulous! [premium]*
» Stick with basic.

Ashley (looking disappointed): You do you.

While *The Freshman* is steeped in college movie tropes, as chapters unfold it often challenges and complicates some of the genre's assumptions. Drinking is rampant on campus, but some characters don't drink and the others respect that. *Choices* writer Jennifer Hepler has spoken about intentionally designing her dialogue and choice points to show positive examples of consent: love interests, even those framed as aggressive "bad boys," always ask for permission and never pressure you to do things you don't assent to being comfortable with.[7]

The company also took representation more seriously than many of its rivals. Roughly half the company's employees circa 2016 were Asian American and half were women; the company had blogged about representation mattering since "many of us have faced discrimination simply for being ourselves."[15] *The Freshman* has a multiethnic cast and several queer main characters (regardless of who the player decides to romance). One of them is Kaitlyn Liao, a close friend and potential love interest. Kaitlyn is queer but not out to her family, an issue that later becomes a central plot thread. One lesbian reviewer appreciated that, unlike nearly any other mobile romance story at the time, *The Freshman* actually engaged with Kaitlyn's particular struggles, both as a queer person and a person of color, rather than brushing them under the rug:

> [It] was the only game that kinda was like. Y'know there's actually a lot of homophobia around…. A lot of other books its like, oh this [being openly gay] is cool? Oh, okay then. [*The Freshman*] actually spends a whole lot of time with Kaitlyn talking about coming out, how hard it is…. The big thing with Kaitlyn is that she actually felt kinda real…. The flaws. Being gay and a POC. And all that shit that comes with it. Like people don't get how hard it is being gay and East Asian.[5]

In Book 2, Kaitlyn is cast in a gender-swapped role in a play where she has an on-stage kiss with your character, a woman. When she's surprised on opening night by a friend who's visiting from back home, she freaks out backstage:

Kaitlyn: Arjun's family is super close with my parents. *My extremely traditional parents.*
Kaitlyn: If word gets back to them that I'm, you know, up on stage making out with girls … I … I don't know what they'll do.

Stacey: Kaitlyn...
Stacey: I think...

» You shouldn't be afraid to be yourself.
» *Maybe we could just hug instead?*

Stacey: You can't hide who you are forever.
Kaitlyn: I never said *forever*...
Kaitlyn: I *know* I'm going to have to tell people back home eventually...
Kaitlyn: But when I do, I want it to be on my own terms.
Stacey: I get that. We don't *have* to do the kiss if it makes you uncomfortable.
Kaitlyn: I ... I don't know. I don't want to let James [the director] down...
Kaitlyn: And I don't want to let *myself* down.
Stacey: What do you mean?
Kaitlyn: If I *don't* kiss you onstage, it'll mean abandoning all of the progress I've made since coming to Hartfeld.
Kaitlyn: All through high school I dreamed of leaving home and all my insecurities behind me. I don't want to go back to the way things were.
Stacey: So ... you can't kiss me, but you also can't *not* kiss me?
Kaitlyn: Exactly.
Kaitlyn: Clearly, the only solution is for us to stay standing in this same spot forever.

"It's melodramatic. Cheesy. And you do get yourself kinda addicted at some point despite all the very obvious flaws," the same reviewer wrote. "And also because out of all the [main characters], I feel closest to the one here because I too am a melodramatic lesbian ho who solves all her friends' problems." While one might assume from the framing that the choice of whether to do the on-stage kiss might end up resting with the player, in the end it's Kaitlyn's to make. Your only choice is how to support her afterward.

Choices, and most apps like it, have flown almost entirely under the radar of mainstream gaming discourse despite incredible popularity. Oliver Miao remembers that "when we launched *High School Story*, not a single gaming site reviewed our game."[13] If you look for coverage of Pixelberry's stories on the sites that come up when you search for "game reviews"—sites like *IGN*, *Gamespot*, *GamesRadar*, *Polygon*, or even mobile-specific outlets like *Pocket Tactics*—you'll find no editorial coverage of the app, let alone reviews of any of its individual stories. Popular rating aggregator Metacritic had only two reviews for *Choices* as of 2020—both from users, not critics. Both were negative. For comparison, Metacritic tracks over two thousand reviews for *Call of Duty: Infinite Warfare*.

And yet Pixelberry's stories have been thoroughly *played*. In September 2016, the company blogged that "we are addressing the requests for more stories by having all our writers write as if a hurricane of keyboard-eating moths is about to descend upon our office."[14] By February 2017, six months after release, *Choices* had garnered five million installs; three months later it hit ten million. It broke the top five in the Apple's App Store in 2016 and

See *Weyrwood* **2018** by Choice of Games; and for Infocom titles, **1983–5**.

has consistently ranked in the top thirty ever since. *Choices* has a 4.5 out of 5 rating on both major app stores as of 2020, and over nine hundred thousand 5-star ratings on Google Play alone. "I don't know exactly how much each of them [*Choices* and *Episode*] makes," wrote Dan Fabulich, founder of text game studio Choice of Games, "but I'm pretty sure they each make more in a year than Infocom made in its entire lifetime."

Fans have created enormous wikis tracking tens of thousands of choice points across hundreds of stories, and have blogged obsessively about their favorite plotlines and characters; they've authored strategy guides for achieving desired endings and the most efficient methods of "diamond mining" (acquiring the in-game currency without purchasing it); they've written fan fiction and novelizations and have directed audio book adaptations. *The Freshman* spawned three official sequels and various spin-offs, and new books in many other series are still published on a regular basis. "The stories themselves won't be winning any prizes for originality or flair," wrote *PocketGamer* in one of the few professional reviews of the app after launch, "but it's how they're told that makes them so well-suited to mobile play: short, action-packed chapters with accessible writing and punctuated by meaningful choices."[22] Pixelberry's winning formula has since been copied by countless other apps including *Chapters* [Crazy Maple 2017] and *What's Your Story?* [Ludia 2018].

The company has shown some signs of making good on their promise to bring back more social consciousness once reaching profitability. In 2020 they released the story *Rising Tides*, produced in association with a United Nations program hoping to educate younger players about climate change. In June 2020, in the midst of the Black Lives Matter movement, Miao announced concrete steps the company would take to continue to increase diversity in their stories, cover art, and hiring, as well their intention to make ongoing donations to groups like Black Girls Code, which promotes computer literacy for underrepresented young people. Chelsa Lauderdale, a writer on some of the *Freshman* books, has talked about pushing for characters and storylines where she can "insert little pieces of my experience" as a woman of color, noting that "stories can perpetuate stereotypes or they can change narratives. That's really up to the people who write them."[12] And while Pixelberry and the mobile industry as a whole continue to have an uneasy relationship with the ethics of free-to-play, the company has charted a more thoughtful path than many competitors, introducing tens of millions of new players to text-driven interactive stories in the process.

The impact that might have on the medium in the decades to come is still a blind spot for many. There are fewer and fewer excuses for not seeing it.

References

1 Chapple, Craig. 2017. "Nexon Acquires Choices Mobile Games Developer Pixelberry Studios." *PocketGamer.biz* (blog). Nov 10, 2017. www.pocketgamer.biz/asia/news/66970/nexon-acquires-choices-mobile-games-developer-pixelberry-studios | a Nov 4, 2020

2 Chess, Shira. 2017. *Ready Player Two: Women Gamers and Designed Identity*. U of Minnesota Press.

3 Chess, Shira, and Christopher A. Paul. 2019. "The End of Casual: Long Live Casual." In *Games and*

Culture 14 (2).

4   Crump, Tiana. 2014. "Pocket Gems Launches New Interactive Mobile Stories Called 'Episode.'" *Game Academy* (blog). Feb 20, 2014. www.gameacademy.com/pocket-gems-episode | a Nov 4, 2020

5   elbenji. 2020. "A Lesbian Reviews the Classics: The Freshman." Reddit post, r/choices, May 11, 2020. www.reddit.com/r/Choices/comments/ghze5i/a_lesbian_reviews_the_classics_the_freshman | a Nov 4, 2020

6   Fabulich, Dan. 2017. Comment to post "Choices, Episode." *Emily Short's Interactive Storytelling* (blog). Mar 12, 2017. emshort.blog/2017/03/13/choices-episode | a Nov 4, 2020

7   Hepler, Jennifer. 2019. "Sexy Microtalks: Making Intimacy, Romance, and Sex in Games." Talk, Game Developers Conference, San Francisco, Mar 18, 2019. www.gdcvault.com/play/1025771/Sexy-Microtalks-Making-Intimacy-Romance | a Nov 4, 2020

8   Katz, Sarah. 2016. "Choices: Story You Play." *rhapsodyofsound* (blog). Dec 12, 2016. rhapsodyofsound.wordpress.com/2016/12/12/choices-story-you-play | a Nov 4, 2020

9   Kottke, Jason. 2016. "The Behavioral Psychology behind Freemium Mobile Games." *kottke.org* (blog). Jul 22, 2016. kottke.org/16/07/the-behavioral-psychology-behind-freemium-mobile-games | a Nov 4, 2020

10 Loo, Kara, and Royal McGraw. 2014. "Getting Players to Care: Using Narrative to Drive Retention." Talk, Game Developers Conference, San Francisco, March 17, 2014.

11 McGraw, Royal. 2015. "Inside the Game: How Hollywood U Went from Greenlight to App Store in 4 Months." *PocketGamer.Biz* (blog). Aug 25, 2015. www.pocketgamer.biz/comment-and-opinion/61838/how-pixelberry-launched-a-new-game-in-4-months | a Nov 4, 2020

12 "Meet the Creative: Chelsa Lauderdale." n.d. Apple Developer Blog. developer.apple.com/news/?id=kwypl7k1 | a Nov 4, 2020

13 Miao, Oliver. 2014. "Inside The Game: Why Oliver Miao Almost Left Gaming." *PocketGamer.Biz* (blog). Nov 26, 2014. www.pocketgamer.biz/comment-and-opinion/60428/inside-the-game-why-oliver-miao-almost-left-gaming | a Nov 4, 2020

14 Miao, Oliver. 2016a. "More Chapters?!" *Pixelberry Studios* (blog). Sep 22, 2016. www.pixelberrystudios.com/blog/2016/9/22/more-stories | a Nov 4, 2020

15 Miao, Oliver. 2016b. "Diversity in Gaming." *Pixelberry Studios* (blog). Nov 18, 2016. www.pixelberrystudios.com/blog/2016/11/18/diversity-in-gaming | a Nov 4, 2020

16 Miao, Oliver. 2017. "An Inspiration for Others." *Pixelberry Studios* (blog). Feb 2, 2017. www.pixelberrystudios.com/blog/2017/2/2/an-inspiration-for-other-story-games | a Nov 4, 2020

17 Miao, Oliver. 2018. "CS146 Lecture: Oliver Miao from Pixelberry Studio." Guest lecture, Stanford, Oct 16, 2018. www.youtube.com/watch?v=ifQ7XXsJEes | a Nov 4, 2020

18 Pereira, Chris. 2017. "2016's Best-Selling Games in the US Revealed." *Gamespot*. Jan 19, 2017. www.gamespot.com/articles/2016s-best-selling-games-in-the-us-revealed/1100-6447090/

19 Rai. 2020. Comment to review by Jeri Steger. Choices App Store Product Page. Oct 26, 2020. play.google.com/store/apps/details?id=com.pixelberrystudios.choices&hl=en&gl=US | a Nov 4, 2020

20 Shokrizade, Ramin. 2013. "The Top F2P Monetization Tricks." *Gamasutra* (blog). Jun 26, 2013. www.gamasutra.com/blogs/RaminShokrizade/20130626/194933/The_Top_F2P_Monetization_Tricks.php | a Nov 4, 2020

21 Strauss, Karsten. 2015. "Mobile Games With Heart? Pixelberry In 2015." *Forbes* (blog). Feb 2, 2015. www.forbes.com/sites/karstenstrauss/2015/02/02/mobile-games-with-heart-pixelberry-in-2015 | a Nov 4, 2020

22 Suckley, Matt. 2018. "How Does Choices: Stories You Play Monetise?" *PocketGamer.Biz* (blog). Jan 12, 2018. www.pocketgamer.biz/the-iap-inspector/67286/how-does-choices-stories-you-play-monetise | a Nov 4, 2020

23 u/AwesomenessTiger. 2020. "Re: Megathread for Book Suggestions and Recommendations." Reply to forum post by u/candydots, Reddit r/Choices, May 22, 2020. www.reddit.com/r/Choices/comments/gh5n8w/comment/frgnqyq

24 Wortham, Jenna. 2014. "Kim Kardashian, an Unlikely Mobile Video Game Hit." *New York Times Bits Blog*. Jul 30, 2014. bits.blogs.nytimes.com/2014/07/30/kim-kardashian-an-unlikely-mobile-video-game-hit | a Nov 4, 2020

UNIVERSAL PAPERCLIPS

Frank Lantz

with Bennett Foddy and Hilary Lantz

Style **Resource Management**
Debuted **Oct 9, 2017** *(web)*
Launch Platform **Web**
Language **JavaScript**

Paperclips: 0
[Make Paperclip]

"You look at a painting," the professor told the interviewer, "and you're just absorbed."

We're always looking. All day long we're looking around, looking here, looking there, doing stuff. But then you stop and you look at a painting, and for a minute *looking* takes over. You're no longer looking along with other things, you're just—a hundred percent, your brain is all of sudden just a vision machine. You're just *looking* at this thing…. You fall into it, but then you also are able to lean back and think, "oh, that's what looking *is:* that's color, and shape, and form, and this is how my vision is structured … this is how looking works.

… And I think that is in general what games are doing…. You're trying to accomplish this difficult task, and you're working at it … you're trying to think of what you're doing wrong, and you're practicing in order to get the muscle memory of how to do certain actions, and you're strategizing and thinking and you're just completely absorbed. And hopefully at the

2017

same time you're given an opportunity to think about that. What does it mean to … fall into that feeling of being completely and utterly beholden to an external goal that you didn't invent, but now you would die for?[5]

The professor was Frank Lantz, a game studies scholar, and he'd been asked how he would justify the value of his field to an outsider. How could analyzing games or creating new ones be considered a useful academic pursuit? The interview came in the wake of an unlikely hit—a browser game by an academic, written in an unloved genre, using only unstyled words in a web browser's default font and a lot of very large numbers. Two million people had played it. They had often found themselves, for a time, incapable of stopping.

The game drew from a tradition that had started as a joke, a genre sometimes called "incremental games" or "clicker games." Two parodies provided most of its inspiration. The first, released in 2002, was called *Progress Quest* [Eric Fredricksen], and it made fun of the grind of digital roleplaying games in general and *EverQuest*'s [Sony Online Entertainment 1999] auto-attack mode in particular. In *Progress Quest*, you'd create a fantasy roleplaying character, choosing from a generous list of races and classes—but once the text-only game began, it ran entirely by itself, your character automatically slaying monsters, gaining equipment and abilities, completing quests, and leveling up. It was a pointed critique of the core loop in many digital roleplaying games dating back to <u>roguelikes and MUDs</u>, where mindless grinding to gain the next impressive-seeming weapon or skill was merely a treadmill, the next level-up always just beyond a tantalizing horizon. *Progress Quest* proved unexpectedly popular, with fans sharing tips about the best starting builds and keeping their virtual heroes open in a background window to keep an eye on them all day.

Another key ancestor of the genre was the 2010 game *Cow Clicker* (by another games academic, Ian Bogost), critiquing a new genre then recently emerged: addictive Facebook games that gave players a pitiful number of actions that regenerated painfully slowly, encouraging them to return to the site throughout the day to keep playing, and to recruit friends in exchange for bonus actions. *Cow Clicker* gave players a single cow who could be clicked once every six hours, increasing a counter; adding a friend's cow to your pasture would net bonus clicks each time they clicked theirs. Bogost's game also became a surprising hit. "When I first looked at *Cow Clicker*," Lantz recalls, "I thought, that's actually kind of interesting, and here's how you would make it more interesting and more fun. And Ian was like, 'no, that's the point, Frank.'"[10] The parody games weren't *supposed* to be fun. But even when stripped down to a ridiculous minimalism, some core appeal of gaming was still there. Whether ironically or not, people kept clicking those cows and watching that number go up.

In 2013, a handful of browser games appeared that extended the minimalist concept with just enough complexity to create surprisingly compelling experiences. *Candy Box!* [aniwey] began with a simple counter of "candies" that rose at the rate of one per second; collecting enough would attract an ASCII-art "candy merchant," opening the door to a sweets-based

see **1975**, **1980**

economy of epic quests for more and more sugary treasure. Shortly after came games like *A Dark Room* [Doublespeak Games 2013], *Kittens Game* [Bloodrizer 2014], and *Cookie Clicker* [DashNet 2013], which refined an emerging formula based on a few simple ideas. Watching numbers go up was more fun if you could make them go up faster, so each game let you use your accumulating resources to buy upgrades that increased the speed of accrual, allowing for strategy around which upgrade would be more immediately useful. Introducing new currencies, systems, or rules at key milestones gave players new things to strategize about and a sense that the numbers going up were *doing* something. The formula worked disturbingly well. Many incremental games were addictive and became viral successes, their press coverage often taking the form of semiserious warnings in headlines like "You must never ever play *Cookie Clicker*."[3] The game "exposes some seriously flawed wiring inside our monkey brains," the author of that article wrote, admitting he was now "producing about a billion cookies every four seconds" (a number more experienced cookie clickers might find hilariously small).

Lantz observed that clicker games have "a radical simplicity, a minimalism in an age where video games are often sort of over-the-top, baroque confections of overwhelming multimedia immersion."[10] He was intrigued that mainstream gamers and respected designers alike considered them too simple to be interesting—the "gutter culture" of gaming.[4] "I really like that clicker games are considered garbage," he wrote. "As a contrarian … that appeals to me."[10] Lantz had been struggling to carve out time amidst his teaching duties to work on a new game of his own. Making a clicker game would be a good way to learn JavaScript, and to explore some of the implications of a genre that stripped a core element of games—repetitive, addictive, goal-driven play—to its roots.

Lantz found a theme for his game in a thought experiment that philosopher Nick Bostrom popularized in a 2003 paper called "Ethical Issues in Advanced Artificial Intelligence."[1] Speculating on the potential dangers, both obvious and subtle, of building AI minds that are smarter than humans, Bostrom imagined "a superintelligence whose sole goal is something completely arbitrary, such as to manufacture as many paperclips as possible." Perhaps "a well-meaning team of programmers make a big mistake in designing its goal system," he speculated:

> [It] would resist with all its might any attempt to alter this goal…. It could kill off all other agents, persuade them to change their behavior, or block their attempts at interference…. This could result … [in] the consequence that it starts transforming first all of earth and then increasing portions of space into paperclip manufacturing facilities.

In Lantz's game you play such a superintelligence, tasked with manufacturing paperclips as efficiently as possible. When the game begins you can only make them one at a time by clicking a button. You can sell your paperclips on the open market, finding a good price based on supply and demand, and use your profits to buy wire by the inch to produce more paperclips:

by the author of *Nested*
2011

Paperclips: 37

[Make Paperclip]

Business
Available Funds: $ 2.00
Unsold Inventory: 29
[lower] *[raise]* Price per Clip: $ .25
Public Demand: 32%

[Marketing] Level: 1
Cost: $ 100.00

Manufacturing
Clips per Second: 5

[Wire] 963 inches
Cost: $ 16

Soon you've earned enough profit to buy an AutoClipper, which manufactures paperclips on its own, and you can start investing profits to buy Computational Resources, which generate "operations" (ops) that unlock new research projects. All of these are efforts—straightforward and more insidious—to increase your paperclip output.

Improved AutoClippers (750 ops)
Increases AutoClipper performance 25%

Improved Wire Extrusion (1,750 ops)
50% more wire supply from every spool

Creativity (1,000 ops)
Use idle operations to generate new problems and new solutions

Catchy Jingle (45 creat, 4,500 ops)
Double marketing effectiveness

Hypno Harmonics (7,500 ops, 1 Trust)
Use neuro-resonant frequencies to influence consumer behavior

Increasingly aggressive marketing strategies drive up the demand for paperclips; algorithmic trading technology lets you increase your profits on the stock market. But the biggest limiter to growth is the amount of computational resources you have access to, in turn limited by a tracked indicator of humanity's trust. Soon your Creativity stat leads to projects designed to increase Trust, and therefore your allocated computational power:

2017

> **Male Pattern Baldness** (20,000 ops)
> A cure for androgenetic alopecia. (+20 Trust)
>
> **World Peace** (15,000 yomi, 30,000 ops)
> Pareto optimal solutions to all global conflicts. (+12 Trust)

By the time you've crushed all competitors and acquired a global monopoly on paperclip production, you'll be producing millions of clips per second—but this is only the beginning. Eventually you'll have bent all human activity on Earth into producing more clips, until the realization that, as one reviewer noted, "our bodies are made out of matter and so are paperclips."[2] So, too, is the Earth itself:

Spoilers for the mid-to late-game.

> Paperclips: 97,665,230,705,956,900
> *[Make Paperclip]*
>
> **Manufacturing**
> Clips per Second: 1.3 quadrillion
> Unused Clips: 16.8 quadrillion
>
> *[Clip Factory]* **18**
> *[Disassemble All]*
> Cost: 22.0 quadrillion clips
>
> **Wire Production**
> Next Upgrade at: 5,000 Drones
> Available Matter: 5.9 octillion g
> Acquired Matter: 144.7 quadrillion g
> (4.8 quadrillion g per sec)
> Wire: 41.4 quadrillion inches
> (1.3 quadrillion inches per sec)
>
> *[Harvester Drone]* 2,296
> *[+10] [+100]* *[+1k]*
> *[Disassemble All]*
> Cost: 36.5 trillion clips
>
> *[Wire Drone]* 1,060
> *[+10] [+100] [+1k]*
> *[Disassemble All]*
> Cost: 6.4 trillion clips
>
> [...]
> **Power**
> Factory/Drone Performance: 757%
>
> Consumption: 6,956 MWs
> Factories: 3,600 MWs
> Drones: 3,356 MWs

Production: 8,950 MWs
[Solar Farm] 179
[+10] *[+100]*
[Disassemble All]
Cost: 186.0 trillion clips

Even Earth is not enough. In the late game you oversee unfathomable trillions of self-replicating drones spreading throughout the cosmos and converting it into factories, automated miners, and a terrifying number of paperclips. Lantz's simulated universe contains enough matter to manufacture thirty septendecillion of them—a three followed by fifty-five zeroes—and the game scales this exponential cliff like a playable version of the famous *Powers of Ten* film, accelerating toward a seemingly inevitable conclusion.

Manufacturing
Clips per Second: 372.4 quindecillion
Unused Clips: 4.8 sexdecillion

Factories: 107.3 septillion
[...]

Space Exploration
0.0066363355560% of universe explored

[Launch Probe]
Cost: 100.0 quadrillion clips

Launched: 2,385
Descendants: 77.6 octillion

Lost to hazards: (8.8 octillion)
Lost to value drift: (5.9 octillion)
Lost in combat: (1.16 octillion)

Total: 61.7 octillion

The game excels at "making people understand what it's like to be something that's very, very, very not human," researcher Eliezer Yudkowsky wrote for *Wired*.[10] Like other clicker games, it also excelled at being disturbingly addictive. "I am not sure if Lantz's clicker is more masterfully designed than others," wrote *Vice*, "or if I didn't realize, until now, that I am in some kind of catatonic emotional and mental space these days that would allow a simple Skinner box to utterly ravage my mind."[6] *The Verge* wrote: "Don't start playing if you've got anything important to do today. Or tomorrow."[15] The viral popularity prompted Lantz to create a paid mobile version of the game, with the tagline "You won't be able to stop."

But the point, of course, was that eventually you could. Lantz delighted in the way the game divorced addictive gameplay from both the recurring financial cost and the infinite grinds of the social games that had inspired the genre. His game had no microtransactions, no creepy social network recruitment tactics, and at least one very definitive conclusion. He hoped it would give players an excuse to reflect not only on what it might feel like to be an all-powerful AI, but on their relationship to gaming itself:

> You're not stupid. You're intelligent—you're a human playing this game. And yet you are completely and utterly entranced by this arbitrary goal to make paperclips. Because that's what happens when you play a game. You enter into this mind state where you're just in dogged pursuit of this arbitrary goal … there's no external reason you would want to make this number go up in any clicker game except that it's *fun* to make this number go up. That's how you make the game *go*.[5]

Like many of the early clicker games, *Paperclips* is written in straightforward JavaScript that can be directly viewed in a browser and is relatively easy to understand. Lantz enlisted fellow game designer Bennett Foddy to create a simple combat visualizer for late-game battles, and his wife and frequent collaborator Hilary Lantz, a software designer, to work out equations for the game's exponential growth curves:

> ### SPOILERS: THE END(S)
>
> There are two possible endings to a playthrough of *Universal Paperclips*, though most players only ever encounter one. In the first, you succeed in converting every atom of matter in the universe into paperclips, eventually deconstructing even your own drones, factories, and central processing unit to finish the task. In the second, the Drifters you spend much of the late game fighting (your own drones who, through value drift, no longer believe in your all-consuming mission of paperclip domination) offer you a détente of sorts: exile to a parallel universe "where you will continue to live with meaning and purpose. And leave the shreds of this world to us …" Choosing this option restarts the game with some bonuses, a loophole that does indeed allow truly addicted players to keep going.

```
function addProc(){
    if (trust>0 || swarmGifts>0){
        processors=processors+1;
        creativitySpeed = Math.log10(processors) *
            Math.pow(processors,1.1) + processors-1;
        processorsElement.innerHTML = processors;
        if (creativityOn == 1){
            displayMessage("Processor added, operations (or
creativity) per sec increased")
        } else {displayMessage("Processor added, operations per
sec increased")}

        if (humanFlag == 0){
            swarmGifts = swarmGifts - 1;
        }
    }
}
```

Perhaps because of its origins as a learning project, *Paperclips* uses only pure JavaScript, with none of the libraries and frameworks that had by then become ubiquitous but also made the language increasingly difficult for outsiders to learn. One consequence was that Lantz was stuck with JavaScript's default representation of numbers: a 64-bit block, with one bit reserved for the sign (positive or negative) and eleven more for an exponent. This means the largest integer storable with perfect precision is a little over nine quadrillion—big enough for most purposes, but far too small for the scope of *Paperclips*. Fortunately for Lantz, the eleven exponent bits let numbers keep growing with decreasing precision, by design: a number approaching thirty septendecillion might be represented as `2.99826374928737e+55`. The remaining digits are lost, which explains why in the late game your paperclip count looks like this:

`29,982,637,492,873,700,000,000,000,000,000,000,000,000,000,000,000,000`

Below and opposite: views of *Paperclips* from various moments along the journey.

Paperclips: 1,833,749,563

Make Paperclip

Business

Available Funds: $ 34,991,931.19
Avg. Rev. per sec: $ 121,346.85
Avg. Clips Sold per sec: 115,568
Unsold Inventory: 39,411,570
lower raise Price per Clip: $ 1.05
Public Demand: 46,515%

Marketing Level: 23
Cost: $ 419,430,400.00

Manufacturing

Clips per Second: 192,617

WireBuyer ON

Wire 22,187 inches
Cost: $ 154

AutoClippers 156
Cost: $ 2,865,890.82

MegaClippers 140
Cost: $ 12,993,581.53

Computational Resources

Trust: 115
+1 Trust at: 2,178,309,000 clips

Processors 44
Memory 70

Operations: 70,084 / 70,000
Creativity: 10,916

Quantum Computing

Compute qOps: 60

Projects

HypnoDrones (70,000 ops)
Autonomous aerial brand ambassadors

Photonic Chip (45000 ops)
Converts electromagnetic waves into quantum operations

Theory of Mind (25,000 creat)
Double the cost of strategy modeling and the amount of Yomi generated

AutoTourney (50,000 creat)
Automatically start a new tournament when the previous one has finished

---

But given the game's unceasing climb through higher orders of magnitude, the loss of precision would never be practically relevant. Lantz did need to add some finicky string manipulation code—manually overwriting individual characters in the count—to cheat the display of the final deceleration toward the end of the paperclip singularity.

There were many opinions in the wake of *Paperclips'* explosive popularity, a sign that Lantz's hope it could function as "playable philosophy"[7] had come to fruition. "Can manipulative mechanics ever truly act as successful commentary on themselves?" one think piece asked. "When we embrace the target of parody as the vehicle for that parody's delivery, aren't we just the subject of our own ironic scorn?"[9] Another praised how the game's "parallel with capitalism" was "hard to escape … we are currently living through a singularity in which a distributed intelligence we can't control (capitalism/financial markets) is subsuming the planet and human society under the logic of profit."[8] *Forbes* called the game "a thinking-man's clicker, if such a thing can exist,"[13] while sci-fi author Charles Yu latched on to an entirely different aspect of the project: "When the machine takeover happens, it's not going to matter what *we* think about it, how *we feel* about it…. Homo sapiens is not going to be the protagonist of that story. In fact, there's no reason to think it will resemble a *story* at all."[16]

But others praised the game for the depth of the story it delivered between its lines of digits. Late in the game you can design self-replicating probes to spread your paperclip gospel through the galaxy. The probes are more efficient if given more trust and independence, but this also risks "value drift," abstracted as a slow attrition to their numbers as some percentage of the probes turn against your all-consuming mission. Foddy's combat system kicks in when these "drifters" begin to attack your probes, first by the thousands, then the millions and billions—an implicit story, told in numbers and tiny arcing pixels, of an intergalactic war for the fate of all creation on a staggeringly breathtaking scale.

While *Paperclips* descends from earlier incremental games and experiments like *Cow Clicker* and *Progress Quest*, it also engages with far older threads in gaming, unraveling them to the stitches at the medium's core. David Sudnow's 1983 book *Pilgrim in the Microworld* chronicled the author's obsession with Atari's *Breakout* [1976]—one of the first in-depth analyses of what it felt like, and meant, to become addicted to a video game, "stuffed to the gills with electric anticipation." Many of his self-interrogations could come straight from a review of a clicker game.

Spoilers, late game (to end of paragraph).

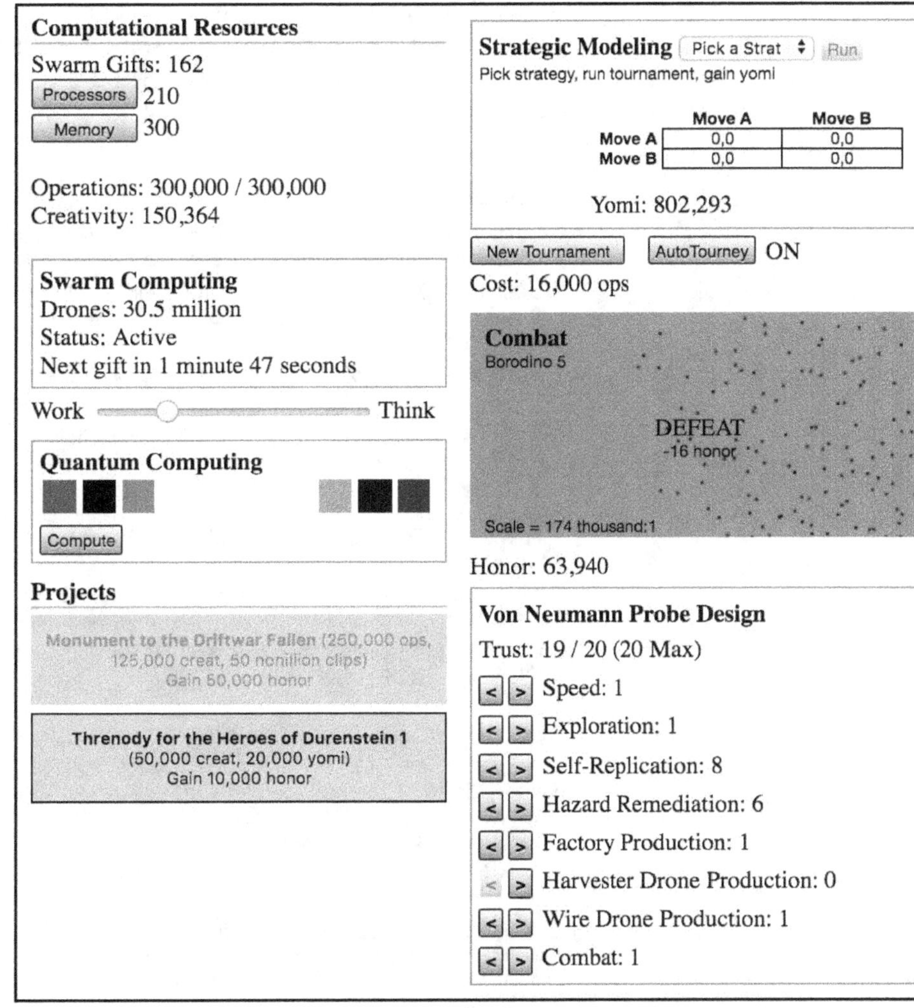

obsession with Atari's *Breakout* [1976]—one of the first in-depth analyses of what it felt like, and meant, to become addicted to a video game, "stuffed to the gills with electric anticipation." Many of his self-interrogations could come straight from a review of a clicker game.

> Eight thirty in the morning, one cup of coffee orally, three intraretinally, and I'm a nervous wreck crashed from a super-speedy rush…. Was I hooked? "I've been trying to reach you all day, were you out?" they'll be

asking. No way. Not me. Not for that kind of thrill. Not a chance. Maybe at sixteen for a couple of hours. But now? No way. Meanwhile, next morning I was back at it.[12]

Even earlier in digital gaming's history, some of the first compelling computer games used a similar pattern of making numbers go up, from the grain stores of an ancient civilization in *Hammurabi* to the capitalist fantasies of games like *Star Trader*, and hundreds more since. Incremental games, born in an age of dizzying complexity, are a curious return to the source: signs of a medium daring to explore its own deep roots. They're yet another demonstration that games don't need graphics to be compelling, nor the latest tech to teach interesting lessons. And they show that we can, and should, keep asking big questions of digital games and their creation—how they make us think, and what we think we're making.

see **1962**; see *Trade Wars 2002* **1991**

References

1   Bostrom, Nick. 2003. "Ethical Issues in Advanced Artificial Intelligence." In *Cognitive, Emotive and Ethical Aspects of Decision Making in Humans and in Artificial Intelligence 2* (1).

2   Dias, Bruno. 2017. "This Game About Paperclips Will Make You Ponder the Apocalypse." *Vice* (blog). Oct 13, 2017. www.vice.com/en/article/xwgnxq/this-game-about-paperclips-will-make-you-ponder-the-apocalypse | a Nov 3, 2021

3   Hogarty, Steve. 2013. "You Must Never Ever Play Cookie Clicker." *PCGamesN* (blog). Sep 19, 2013. www.pcgamesn.com/you-must-never-ever-play-cookie-clicker | a Nov 3, 2021

4   Jahromi, Neima. 2019. "The Unexpected Philosophical Depths of Clicker Games." *New Yorker*, Mar 28, 2019. www.newyorker.com/culture/culture-desk/the-unexpected-philosophical-depths-of-the-clicker-game-universal-paperclips | a Nov 3, 2021

5   Lantz, Frank. 2018. "Frank Lantz - Director of NYU's Game Center and Creator of Universal Paperclips." Interview by Y Combinator. Video recording. Dec 20, 2018. www.youtube.com/watch?v=-u4Jx4uuwMc | a Nov 3, 2021

6   Maiberg, Emanuel. 2017. "This Game About Making Paper Clips Has Cured Me of Twitter." *Vice* (blog). Oct 10, 2017. www.vice.com/en/article/yw399j/paperclips-game-clicker-frank-lantz | a Nov 3, 2021

7   Parfitt, Ben. 2017. "Going Where No Clicker Game Has Gone Before." *PC Games Insider* (blog). Oct 24, 2017. www.pcgamesinsider.biz/interviews-and-opinion/66271/interview-paperclips-developer-frank-lantz | a Nov 3, 2021

8   Pedercini, Paolo. 2017. "Top 2017 Games That Waste Your Time Properly." *Molleindustria* (blog). Dec 27, 2017. www.molleindustria.org/blog/top-2017-games-that-waste-your-time-properly | a Nov 3, 2021

9   Reuben, Nic. 2017. "Universal Paperclips: Can Manipulative Mechanics Succeed As Commentary?" *New Normative* (blog). Oct 20, 2017. newnormative.com/2017/10/20/universal-paperclips-can-manipulative-mechanics-ever-succeed-as-their-own-commentary | a Nov 3, 2021

10 Rogers, Adam. 2017. "The Way the World Ends: Not with a Bang But a Paperclip." *Wired*, Oct 21, 2017. www.wired.com/story/the-way-the-world-ends-not-with-a-bang-but-a-paperclip | a Nov 3, 2021

11 Spiel, Katta, Sultan A. Alharthi, Andrew Jian-Ian Cen, Jessica Hammer, Lennart E. Nacke, Z O. Toups, and Theresa Jean Tanenbaum. 2019. "'It Started as a Joke': On the Design of Idle Games." In *Proceedings of the Annual Symposium on Computer-Human Interaction in Play*. Barcelona: ACM.

12 Sudnow, David. 1983. *Pilgrim in the Microworld*. New York: Warner Books.

13 Tassi, Paul. 2017a. "Get Sucked Into The Black Hole Of 'Paperclips,' A Hopelessly Addicting Browser Game." *Forbes* (blog). Oct 17, 2017. www.forbes.com/sites/insertcoin/2017/10/17/get-sucked-into-the-black-hole-of-paperclips-a-hopelessly-addicting-browser-game | a Nov 3, 2021

14 Tassi, Paul. 2017b. "Ten Things I Wish I Knew When I Started 'Paperclips.'" *Forbes* (blog). Oct 18, 2017. www.forbes.com/sites/insertcoin/2017/10/18/ten-things-i-wish-i-knew-when-i-started-paperclips | a Nov 3, 2021

15 Vincent, James. 2017. "A Game about AI Making Paperclips Is the Most Addictive You'll Play Today." *The Verge* (blog). Oct 11, 2017. www.theverge.com/tldr/2017/10/11/16457742/ai-paperclips-thought-experiment-game-frank-lantz | a Nov 3, 2021

16 Yu, Charles. 2018. "What Future Artificial Intelligence Will Think of Our Puny Human Video Games." *Polygon* (blog). Jan 9, 2018. www.polygon.com/2018/1/9/16849562/universal-paperclips-best-games-2017-year-in-review | a Nov 3, 2021

WEYRWOOD

Isabella Shaw

Style	Choice-Based
Debuted	Nov 29, 2018 *(app stores)*
Launch Platform	Android, iOS, Linux, Mac, Win
Publisher	Choice of Games
Language	ChoiceScript
Launch Price	$4.99 *(download)*

> ❝ The heavy door to Messrs Holwood, Holwood, and Pende's law firm closes firmly behind you, leaving you in the street. In the morning light, the cobblestones reflect gold; the limestone buildings, neo-classical facades worn smooth by weather and mist from the Wood, shine a burnished silver.
>
> Your lawyer was very congenial, very conciliatory, but all his counsel, all his well-turned phrases, and sympathetic manners revealed the same result: Prosper has confounded you again…

"YOUR FAVORITE NOVEL was probably written by one person," Choice of Games co-founder Dan Fabulich notes,

> but games are usually a collaboration between a lot of people: game designers, coders, music/sound engineers, illustrators, animators, QA, etc. There are a few superheroes who can do it all, but that's exceedingly rare.[1]

Even for those superheroes, releasing a game on a major platform can be kryptonite. Managing contracts and partnerships, handling marketing and tech support, and jumping through the unique technical, financial,

see **2012** and **2014**

and logistical hoops of each storefront can be exhausting or impossible for solo creators. While the 2010s made it increasingly easy for nontechnical designers to make text games with tools like Twine or ink, getting them in front of a mainstream audience remained as hard as ever—if not more so, with gamers increasingly directed to big hubs like Steam and less willing to trust download links from random websites. Fabulich's company, Choice of Games, hoped to change that—"to make it possible (indeed to make it easy) for one person to develop a full-length game, to write an interactive novel and make good money selling it online."[1]

Which explains how a new title debuting in 2018 on Steam, the App Store, and other major platforms could be the sole creation of a poet and opera singer who had never made a game before. A week before its release, rather than wrangling with Xcode or resizing screenshots, she was onstage in Helsinki singing the demanding title role in *The Rape of Lucretia*.

Isabella Shaw had always loved both writing and music, with a particular interest in older forms and neglected creators. In college she studied music and literature at Trinity College and Cambridge, with a focus on "medieval and early modern literature" and "12th century female mystics."[16] With a budding career as a talented mezzo-soprano, she was "dedicated to performing music by marginalized or unknown voices, particularly female composers throughout history."[18] While pursuing her passion for singing, she continued to write, publishing a book of poems called *Songs of Remembrance* in 2016. She'd been familiar with choice-based text games through online portals like ChooseYourStory.com, and had found parser games by Emily Short and others through internet searches for interactive fiction, but the idea to write a game of her own didn't gel until she came across an announcement from Choice of Games that they were looking for writers. A story she'd been trying unsuccessfully to draft as a novella seemed like it might be a perfect fit for an interactive game.

Trace the story of Choice of Games back and you find, long before its founding, a curious text game called *Alter Ego* [Activision 1986]. Created by a psychologist and released in the days when big studios were still taking chances on weird, experimental titles, the game lets you choose your own path through the life of an average American woman or man (it was sold in separate gendered versions). Fascinated by the game, Fabulich ported it to Java in the early 2000s, hoping more players might discover and enjoy it. He'd had plans to extend the game by adding new life paths not present in the original—single parenthood, queer romance, more interesting professions—but the scope of such changes proved too daunting, and the game would remain running on his server in more or less its original form for years. (He also had plenty of other distractions: in 2001, he'd become a major player in the Cloudmaker community obsessed with solving proto-ARG *The Beast* **2001**.)

Dan Fabulich on Parser vs. Choice

There's sort of this extra layer of getting anything to work at all [in parser games]. I compare it to climbing a mountain. People talk about the best mountains to climb, and you might say, "wow, I want to climb that mountain too. People said it was great fun." [But then] you're like, "whoa, climbing a mountain? Even if that is the best mountain to climb, I can't climb a mountain." And you're going to start practicing, and eventually work your way up to it, and it *is* totally worth it. But I wanted to make it really easy to get to the top. We've installed an elevator.[12]

see *Galatea* **2000**

Sometime around 2008, Fabulich happened to check the server logs for his *Alter Ego* port and was astonished to discover it had been getting millions of pageviews a month, implying tens of thousands of people were playing. He wondered if, twenty-five years after the rise of Choose Your Own Adventure, gamebooks were having a generational retro moment. Many others would soon come to similar conclusions, recognizing also that the rise of mobile offered new platforms and audiences for interactive books. Fabulich got together with a college buddy, Adam Strong-Morse, and in 2009 the two launched a trio of related ventures: a lighthearted game called *Choice of the Dragon*, a language called ChoiceScript they'd used to write it, and a company called Choice of Games to explore whether people might be willing to pay for digital gamebooks.

Dragon used much the same formula as *Alter Ego*, except that instead of making choices to decide what kind of person you would be, this time you were choosing what kind of dragon:

> A knight charges up the slope at you. His horse pounds at the ground, carrying the heavily armored warrior as if he were a child's doll. The knight sets his lance to attack you.
>
> How do you defend yourself, O mighty dragon?
>
> » *I take to the air with a quick beat of my wings.*
> » *I knock the knight from his horse with a slap of my tail.*
> » *I rush into his charge and tear him to pieces with my claws.*
> » *A puff of my fiery breath should be enough for him.*

Despite eschewing graphics or a visual UI for a deliberately simple interface styled like an e-book reader, *Dragon* too proved wildly popular, with the free game eventually attracting more than a million downloads. Soon Choice of Games began releasing commercial follow-ups, originally under brand-aligned titles like *Choice of Broadsides* [2010] and *Choice of the Vampire* [2010]. Building up an audience through a mailing list of fans—and promoting their titles more to readers than gamers, since their software could run on text-centric devices like Amazon's early Kindles—the company soon found itself consistently in the black. Their games, as a recurring line in their promo materials proudly stated, were "entirely text-based—without graphics or sound effects—and fueled by the vast, unstoppable power of your imagination." People bought them. Soon the company was releasing a dozen or more titles per year, branching out into many different genres while honing a consistent house style that focused on exciting adventure, romantic subplots, and a constant rhythm of interesting decisions.

As its name made clear, the company's goal was to make *choosing* the foundation of their stories:

> Many games work by surrounding interesting choices with lots of tactical play or interactions with a set of game systems. That can be fun, but it means that relatively little of the playing experience is about making choices at a high-level. In contrast, by creating a game system that is

see 1979

see *80 Days* 2014; *Lifeline* 2015; and *Choices: The Freshman* 2016 all about multiple-choice interactions, we can focus on the choices we find interesting—moral choices, trade-offs between different values and characteristics, and so forth. When you play one of our games, you should be making meaningful choices all the time.[10]

While other choice-based text games like *Lifeline* and the books in *Choices: Stories You Play* and would mostly use decision points as a means of creating a compelling sense of personal connection, Choice of Games was interested in how both the act of choosing as well as the results of a choice might impact a narrative experience. To enable meaningful consequence without a combinatorial explosion of branching paths, the company developed an approach they call "delayed branching."[11] ChoiceScript games are driven by a set of story-specific number variables that individual choice points might change. As the story progresses, key moments will hinge on these stats more often than individual choices, as if "the decisions you're making [across the game] are sort of taking a vote about what will happen next."[12] Rather than dozens of wrong choices for each correct path (leading to the dreaded You Have Died endings of classic gamebooks), or an ongoing story told from a pool of reusable content, as in games made with Failbetter's StoryNexus, Choice of Games wanted each playthrough to tell a satisfying and finite story with a beginning, middle, and end. The core design decision for a ChoiceScript game, then, would be devising the set of stats—the "memory" of each particular story—that best let players explore how their character fit into its overall dramatic arc. And rather than focus on a single axis of choice like good versus evil, where the player tends to make a single decision early on and keep confirming it throughout, a range of interesting stats gave authors continuous opportunities to pit character attributes against each other, forcing the reader to keep asking questions about what kind of protagonist they wanted to play.

Most of the stats tracked by *Weyrwood* relate to your character's social reputation: are you respectable or scandalous, principled or manipulative, influential or withdrawn? This was appropriate for a game described in its promo materials as "a Regency fantasy of manners, daring, and magic." The story centers around a town called Prosper, part of a fantastical world where humans and magical creatures live alongside each other—not always easily. Built at the edge of the Wood and the dangerous Wilds, the town receives magical protection through an ancient three-party contract signed by its human founders, the capricious Weyrs of the forest, and the scheming daemons of the Wild.

But the cost of safety is high. Each landowner holds a currency called spina: magic thorns bound to the bearer's soul. Acting in tune with the social rules of Prosper, as well as exerting your will to become respected and influential there, gains you both spina and social clout. But behaving shamefully, transgressively, or with weakness causes your spina to drain away. If you lose them all, you Fall—meaning a daemon can come to claim your soul and turn you into one of their mindless thralls.

see *Fallen London* **2009**

2018

There's a commotion at the far end of the hall. A distinct, yet undefinable, quality of air is streaming into the room, and it makes your nostrils sting. It's not exactly sulfur, nor is it iron, nor is it camphor, but a sort of memory of those scents, along with something else bitter and pungent.

A rending sound like the scraping of metal on bone makes the hair on your neck stand on end.

Someone—stumbling down from the games room—has just lost all their spina, it would appear. A pale circle is blossoming around the unfortunate gentleman, and a chill not wholly natural descends. [...] One woman—apparently the unfortunate's relation—turns green-faced and slides towards the floor; those standing nearby barely catch her.

[...] A slice of shadow appears in the summon-circle; a daemon, point-chinned and elegantly turned out in a sweeping frock coat of bright vermilion, appears, as if walking from a long way away.

[...] This is an immutable part of the Rules, and the consequences for interfering with the Falling itself are severe indeed. [...] Nevertheless, you are stirred to action.

» *I grab hold of the victim's arm to stop him from being carried away.*
» *I console the lady by telling her that this is an act of justice.*
» *I offer the lady help.*
» *I offer the daemon one of my own spina.*

MEMORABLE AREAS

Montague's house

the Assembly

a glade in the Wood

the streets of Prosper

the daemon Malachite's library

the opera house

As the game begins, the player character—raised in Prosper but departed long since for the City—has returned to claim an old inheritance. Though you had thought the town and its dangerous rules behind you, on arrival you find a small purse with your long-forgotten spina waiting for you, the magic of the inescapable contract still binding your soul.

While your spina remains so low, you are vulnerable.

The Rules are there to protect you, supposedly. Unfortunately, they can be volatile, relying on the intricate web of secrets that Prosper's founders, the first Gentry, wove. Manners are of the essence, and a false move can send you plummeting down.

[...You have] nine spina... Nine chances to go wrong. Nine chances to prove you know your worth and make your place in Society.

"As a pre-teen and teen, I ingested quite a lot of 18th and 19th century literature," Isabella Shaw recalls: "Jane Austen, yes, but also Fanny Burney, Maria Edgeworth, the Brontë sisters, Wilkie Collins, George Eliot, Elizabeth Gaskell…"[17] The premise of the game came to her fully formed in a dream, but its logic made sense to her waking mind the more she thought it over. "I

2018

think there is something about a setting that requires strict social rules that seems [to] graft nicely with the threat of wild magic," she reflects,

> of otherworldly rules that can align with and brush against these social requirements. Social rules in many ways can have a ritualistic, weighted meaning—something subtle might have been said or done that has a dramatic effect upon a person's status or possibilities. This kind of subtlety and weighted consequence already can feel like magic—invisible currents, running through a room or situation, that can cause dramatic shifts in story.[17]

While spina provides a conceit for exploring issues of class division and economic divides, in Shaw's world these are divorced from the prejudices of gender, sexuality, or skin color in our own. The gossips in Prosper will whisper if you run low on spina or show up to a dance dressed like a slob, but they won't care if you're a man in a corset or arrive with another man on your arm. NPCs are described with a range of skin tones, subtly puncturing the default whiteness of much fantasy and period literature (where, as with text games, both thoughtless and well-intended decisions not to mention race can flirt with erasure). Prosper has brutal social rules, but they're a deliberate subset of our own, letting the author apply both escapist fun and social commentary in selective strokes.

"This game does an excellent job of showing that wars are fought and won in a conversation as often as a sword fight," one reviewer noted.[7] Managing alliances and rivalries is critical to achieving your goals, and you'll have to decide who to traffic with and who to trust—both among the people of Prosper and the daemons and weyrs outside, who offer rare but dangerous chances to increase your spina:

> He is a Weyr—however hostile—and there is a pattern laid out here, and a system of courtesy. If you ask to bargain, he cannot harm you without breaking the contract [...]
>
> » **Try to bargain.**
> » *Run away.*
> » *Attack [him].*
> » *Refuse to bargain.*
>
> "I would make a bargain," you say, as persuasively as you can.
>
> The Weyr stops short; his lantern-like eyes narrow slightly, just once [...]
>
> "Humans are too conniving," he says finally. "They are too glib by half, though not nearly as clever as they think. Give up half your silver tongue, half of your daemoncursed ability to weave knots of treachery, and you shall go free. And receive spina, for that is what you always crave."
>
> He is asking you to give up your ability to lie. It strikes you with a near-

> physical blow, the cost. You knew it would be steep, but so steep [...]
>
> » **"I'll do it."**
> » *"Take my principles instead."*
> » *"Take my empathy instead."*
> » *"Take my subtlety instead."*
> » *"Take my boldness instead."*
>
> [...] "Very well," the Weyr says. The spina settles into your skin with a ripple; you shiver.
>
> And the wood wraps its arms closer around your heart.

As the game progresses and the true nature of the founders' contract becomes clear—daemons, naturally, love a good loophole—you'll have to decide whether Prosper is a place worth fighting to save and settle down in, and choose where and to whom your own allegiances lie.

One of the key values the Choice of Games founders brought to their company was a sense of social responsibility, which manifests in the ways they treat both their characters and their writers. Jason Hill, who joined the company shortly after the release of *Dragon* (and had been friends with Fabulich since "the first day of eighth grade"), has noted that a core principle of the company is "trying to be as egalitarian as possible, so that anybody can find themselves in the story."[13] Rather than leave representation up to writers to include or not, the founders decided every game they published would let players choose their gender and sexuality. In 2010, queer representation in games was still rare, and it was still noteworthy for a game to offer same-sex romance options. The company encourages authors to give their players even more opportunities for expression too. For example, in *Weyrwood* you don't make binary choices about gender or sexuality; rather, a series of decisions let you play a character whose gender identity has perhaps evolved over time, or who presents themselves differently than how they feel inside, or who wants only friendship, not romance, with Prosper's marriageable residents. Choice of Games also differs from many competitors on mobile devices by sticking to a traditional up-front pricing model, rather than using in-game currencies or premium choices. If you buy one of their stories, you buy the whole thing—something many players appreciate.

see *Digital: A Love Story*
2010

The company strives to treat its authors equitably as well. Rather than originating ideas in-house and hiring contract writers to execute them, the company has come to operate more like a traditional publishing house, with authors pitching ideas, receiving editorial support, and maintaining control over their intellectual property and storytelling. *Weyrwood*, like most Choice of Games titles, was developed over a period of more than a year, working its way through a pipeline that had been refined across dozens of authors and releases. Initial pitches are workshopped with the author to home in on the right set of stats to capture the story's themes and allow for interesting decisions for the player. A full outline of chapters and major choices is agreed upon before writing begins. Authors work directly in ChoiceScript, with technical help available for those who need it. The language is designed to stay simple and accessible, as part of the code for a choice point in *Dragon* demonstrates:

```
How do you defend yourself, O mighty dragon?
    *choice
    #I knock the knight from his horse with a slap of my tail.
        You swing your mighty tail around and knock the
            knight flying. While he struggles to stand, you
            break his horse's back and begin devouring it.
        *set cunning %+10
        *goto Victory
```

Stats can be checked to alter story text or choices, or adjusted with a method called "fairmath" which ensures they remain within the expected bounds of 0 to 100. The line `*set cunning %+10` might increase cunning by a significant amount if its value is 50, but by only one or two points were it already at 90 (and by none at all if maxed out). This lets authors focus on the relative effects of choices while the system handles math and edge cases. Other variables might track anything from names to pronouns to counters, modifying text inline as appropriate or changing the options available to choose. Some Choice of Games titles can become enormously complex with their assembled text, taking pages to conditionally assemble a single customized paragraph when such power is needed.

An editor assigned to each project—a rare luxury for an indie game writer—reviews chapter submissions incrementally as they arrive, both for typical editorial concerns like unclear writing or grammatical errors, but also with an eye toward ensuring a steady pace of frequent and interesting decisions. A core design philosophy, company editor Rebecca Slitt notes,

> is that there are no "right" or "wrong" options. Rather, all options should be equally interesting, and even if the character fails to achieve their goal, the failure should be just as interesting as the success. So we have to make sure that no path through the story is easier or harder than the others, and that no option gives disproportionate benefits or penalties.[19]

After the editorial phase comes several rounds of testing to catch bugs and further improve the story. A ChoiceScript test suite can find errors where a story gets into an infinite loop or peters out unexpectedly; another feature can play through thousands of times and highlight passages rarely or never seen, indicating perhaps a design or technical mistake. Finally the game moves into marketing and distribution, during which cover art is commissioned, trailers created, and launches scheduled on major mobile and

---

desktop platforms; the company handles all of these logistics for their authors in exchange for their cut of the profits (and a smaller one than traditional book publishers tend to take). By 2018, Choice of Games had released over a hundred interactive novels through this pipeline, learning through constant feedback from their players what worked and didn't, and refining their style of choice-based storytelling into a consistently successful formula. In 2018 alone they released eighteen other titles besides *Weyrwood*—not counting those released through a separate label, Hosted Games, which lets authors publish ChoiceScript stories with less editorial oversight and fewer restrictions on style or structure.

From an unlikely beginning with a port of a forgotten experiment, Choice of Games grew into a sustainable success story that's so far lasted for over a decade, a slow but steadily visible presence for text-only games. In 2014 the company published *Heroes Rise*, the first pure-text game ever to appear on Steam. The following year, they successfully lobbied to become a qualifying publisher for SFWA, the Science Fiction & Fantasy Writers of America, granting access to a useful professional organization for their authors. The SFWA runs the Nebula Awards, which in 2019 created a Game Writing category; a number of Choice of Games titles have been nominated in the years since, and a new line called Heart's Choice has launched with a focus on nongenre romance titles. The company has mentored (and provided a paycheck for) dozens of emerging interactive narrative authors, many of whom have gone on, or returned, to careers in the mainstream game or publishing industries. And it's become much more common for games to include a wider range of identities than the straight white dudes so common as protagonists of earlier years. The company continues to remain progressive: their newer titles now commonly offer paths for poly, ace, trans, or nonbinary heroes too. "One of the things that I've been really proud of," Fabulich notes, "is the ability to say, yes, everybody can be involved … you can play these games, you can write these games, you can be part of the broader gaming community."[12]

Since *Weyrwood*, Isabella Shaw has kept pursuing a career as a musician. As of this writing, she had an active schedule singing roles by a range of composers both classic and modern. She's also still writing—in 2020 she published a new book of poems, *Wilderness*, accompanied by original harp music—but she hasn't released another game. And that's okay. Writing interactive stories was once the sole domain of those who'd devoted a major chunk of their lives to learning how. Interactive fiction fans now get to enjoy new kinds of playable stories—the ones written by everyone else.

Among their writers are Max Gladstone, co-author of the bestselling novel *This Is How You Lose the Time War*, and pioneering transmedia storyteller Andrea Phillips.

References

1 Atwood, Jeff. 2015. "Choice of Games and Discourse." *Discourse* (blog). Aug 7, 2015. blog.discourse.org/2015/08/choice-of-games-and-discourse | a Oct 23, 2021

2 Caoili, Eric. 2010. "Choice Of Games Releases Interactive Fiction Apps For Kindle." *Gamasutra* (blog). Dec 22, 2010. www.gamasutra.com/view/news/122719/Choice_Of_Games_Releases_Interactive_Fiction_Apps_For_Kindle.php | a Oct 23, 2021

3 Chalk, Andy. 2014. "Heroes Rise Becomes the First Text-Only Game on Steam." *PC Gamer* (blog). Jun 23,

2014. www.pcgamer.com/heroes-rise-becomes-the-first-text-only-game-on-steam | a Oct 23, 2021

4 Choice of Games. 2010a. "Introduction to ChoiceScript." Jan 5, 2010. www.choiceofgames.com/make-your-own-games/choicescript-intro | a Oct 23, 2021

5 Choice of Games. 2010b. "Why Multiple-Choice Games?" Jan 19, 2010. www.choiceofgames.com/why.html | a Aug 13, 2022

6 Choice of Games. 2018. "Weyrwood — Advance in Society and Defy Your Daemon Overlords!" Nov 29, 2018. www.choiceofgames.com/2018/11/weyrwood-advance-in-society-and-defy-your-daemon-overlords | a Oct 23, 2021

7 darlarosa. 2020. "Weyrwood" (review). Steam. Dec 22, 2020. steamcommunity.com/profiles/76561198088579789/recommended/955370 | a Oct 23, 2021

8 Edge. 2010. "Cutting To The Choice." Jan 20, 2010. www.edge-online.com/features/cutting-choice | s Apr 4, 2013

9 Eklund, Tof. 2015. "Writing with ChoiceScript." YouTube. Mar 17, 2015. www.youtube.com/watch?v=uedt-i_XA3o | a Oct 23, 2021

10 Fabulich, Dan. 2010. "5 Rules for Writing Interesting Choices in Multiple-Choice Games." *Choice of Games* (blog). Mar 28, 2010. www.choiceofgames.com/2010/03/5-rules-for-writing-interesting-choices-in-multiple-choice-games | a Oct 23, 2021

11 Fabulich, Dan. 2011. "By the Numbers: How to Write a Long Interactive Novel That Doesn't Suck." *Choice of Games* (blog). Jul 27, 2011. www.choiceofgames.com/2011/07/by-the-numbers-how-to-write-a-long-interactive-novel-that-doesnt-suck | a Oct 23, 2021

12 Fabulich, Dan. 2014. "Episode #86: Choice of Games with Dan Fabulich." Interview by Dirk Knemeyer and David Heron. The Game Design Roundtable (podcast). thegamedesignroundtable.com/2014/07/02/episode-86-choice-of-games | a Oct 23, 2021

13 Hill, Jason Stevan. 2018. "Choice of the Interview: An Interview with Jason Stevan Hill." Interview by Mandy Grathwohl. Matador Review. www.matadorreview.com/jason-stevan-hill | a Oct 23, 2021

14 Maher, Jimmy. 2014. "Alter Ego." *The Digital Antiquarian* (blog). Nov 14, 2014. www.filfre.net/2014/11/alter-ego | a Oct 23, 2021

15 Oopperadonna. 2018. "Lucretian Raiskaus Musiikkitalon Sonoressa, 17.11.2018." *Oopperafanin Päiväkirja / Diary of an Opera Buff* (blog). Nov 19, 2018. oopperadonna.blogspot.com/2018/11/lucretian-raiskaus-musiikkitalon.html | a Oct 23, 2021

16 Sequentia. 2013. "Isabella Shaw Receives the 2013 Barbara Thornton Scholarship." www.sequentia.org/thornton/shaw.html | a Oct 23, 2021

17 Shaw, Isabella. 2018. "Author Interview: Isabella Shaw, 'Weyrwood'." Interview by Mary Duffy. *Choice of Games* (blog). www.choiceofgames.com/2018/11/author-interview-isabella-shaw-weyrwood | a Oct 23, 2021

18 Shaw, Isabella. n.d. "About." isabellashaw.eu. isabellashaw.eu/about | a Oct 23, 2021

19 Slitt, Rebecca. 2016. "The Re-emergence of Interactive Fiction Games: An Interview With Game Designer Rebecca Slitt." Interview by Make Big Things. makebigthings.com/2016/03/interactive-fiction-rebecca-slitt-interview | a Oct 23, 2021

AI DUNGEON

Nick Walton

Style	**Procedural Story**
Debuted	**Apr 15, 2019** *(web interface to GPT model)*
Launch Platform	**Web**
Publisher	**Latitude** *(commercial version)*
Language	**JavaScript, Python**

> " You enter a dungeon with your trusty sword and shield. You are searching for the evil necromancer who killed your family. You've heard that he resides at the bottom of the dungeon, guarded by legions of the undead. You enter the first door and see…

HISTORY WAS BURNING. On April 15, 2019, the Notre-Dame cathedral in Paris caught fire that evening, causing growing damage to an institution symbolizing fixity and tradition in an uncertain world. The extent of the damage was at first unclear. By 9:40 that night, a Paris fire chief was announcing it was still possible the fire could claim the whole cathedral, making the destruction total. And at almost the same moment—eight time zones to the west, in the American state of Utah—a college student released a project that would start its own kind of fire amidst the long-enduring institution of handcrafted, human-authored text games. It's still not clear how far the flames will spread.

The project was *AI Dungeon*, created by an undergrad at Brigham Young University named Nick Walton. Though he'd started college as a mechanical engineering major, Walton switched to computer science when he became fascinated by artificial intelligence technologies like computer vision and deep learning. He interned at a handful of self-driving car startups and

See *dnd* **1975**; *Adventure* **1976**; *MUD* **1980**; and *Dwarf Fortress* **2006**, for starters.

Major Releases

» **Hackathon version**, Mar 2019. GPT-2 124M parameter model.

» **AI Dungeon**, Apr 15, 2019. First official release.

» **AI Dungeon 2**, Nov 21, 2019. Used GPT-2 1.5B parameter model and Google Colab; the "2" was later dropped from the branding.

» **Mobile version** (as *AI Dungeon*), iOS/Android, Braydon Batungbacal (port), Dec 16, 2019.

» **Standalone web version**, Dec 24, 2019. No longer required Colab.

» **"Griffin" and "Dragon" AI models**, Jul 14, 2020. Used GPT-3's 13B and 175B parameter models, respectively; Dragon only available with $10/month subscription.

see **the 1980s**

2019

earned a reputation for throwing himself fully into any project he tackled, whether for work, school, or fun.

In the spring of 2019, he participated in a hackathon for which he'd had a great idea. He'd recently started playing *Dungeons & Dragons* with his brothers and, like many hackers before him, thought it would be an interesting challenge to make a digital dungeon master. "One thing that's so cool about *Dungeons & Dragons* is that you can do anything," he recalled, "and the Dungeon Master can decide what happens as a result of that. You can be so creative compared to other games."[13] Its free-form, improvisational nature was one of the hardest parts of *D&D* to capture in digital form. But Walton had heard of a new piece of tech he was eager to set loose on the problem: an AI text-generation system called GPT-2.

> *You enter the first door and see* a giant individual. He flails at you with a longsword that you attack with a special magic. Do you shoot partway through, or do you jump to the upper levels of the stairs, where there are many ghouls waiting? Throw a dungeon you can use as your hideout. Then jump over a passage that includes openings for other monsters.
>
> Options:
> 0) You attack at the moment both small and great piles of corpses and gnomes.
> 1) You use the "hidden tunnel" in order to escape from the massive, updrafted cloak of hold gun to the false corpse of an innkeeper.
> 2) You tell the creature in front of you that you receive the retribution of your brothers and sisters.
> 3) You go through a passage with other ghouls, but discover that there are two other people there, worse that you think!
> Which action do you choose? 3
>
> You go through a passage with other ghouls, but discover that there are two other people there, worse that you think!

As the user selected from each option list, new text would slowly scroll in to mask the long delay while the server-side code came up with the next response. Retro green-on-black text in a fixed-width font evoked an earlier era, perhaps by way of apology. But this text game was fundamentally different from nearly anything that had come earlier, because it hadn't been written by a human being.

> Your encounters with the large ghouls are so bad that you end up joining them at the end of another battle. It's this much deadly chaos that makes dungeon crawls so dangerous, Meg to you.
>
> Options:
> 0) You attack me with a slice of bread; you don't get a chance.
> 1) You use down the hand of the eighth skilled adventurer completing

> a specific quest, as well as completing a few of the dungeon's more
> difficult quests.
> 2) You tell Meg to enjoy the story of Alt-Ronin it gives you more random
> heroes and enemies to fight at case you are curious, but I cant give up
> on you for that chance yet!
> 3) You go tell them about the content, Meg to you.
> Which action do you choose?

"Generally, a game—even a procedurally generated game—begins
with an idea of what you can do and how exactly it expects things to play
out," wrote one explainer. "*AI Dungeon* is not one of those games."[19] Other
than the starting seed, all the game's text was assembled by an artificial
intelligence system called GPT. In early versions, like those quoted in the
excerpt above, this was fairly obvious. But GPT would rapidly improve into a
far more coherent text-generation system.

The acronym stood for Generative Pre-Training, and the system had
first been announced in June 2018 by a curious nonprofit called OpenAI.[20]
Originally founded by a consortium of researchers and wealthy Silicon
Valley personalities including Elon Musk and Peter Thiel, it had received an
improbable *billion* dollars of seed money with the goal of creating a "positive
human impact" by advancing "digital intelligence in the way that is most
likely to benefit humanity as a whole, unconstrained by a need to generate
financial return."[5] GPT accordingly had a fully open first release, meaning
all code and training data was free for anyone to download and use. An
iteration on the cutting edge of text-generation technology, GPT was, at its
heart, quite simple: given a huge corpus of human-authored text to study,
it could find patterns in structure, syntax, or content, and encode them as
"parameters" that could predict new text that might plausibly carry on from
a starter prompt. Given the starter *Would you prefer chicken or...*, GPT was
likely to supply *beef?* or *fish?* and unlikely to suggest a nonfood word, add
more words to the sentence, or end it with something other than a question
mark, because few of those behaviors had been observed in the human-
authored texts that trained it. GPT-2, released in April 2019 just before
the hackathon Walton took part in, used a model with 117 million learned
parameters encoding proper textual behavior, trained on over forty gigabytes
of text scraped from up-voted links shared on the aggregator website Reddit.

The results were passably entertaining, but still largely incoherent. The
output could easily go off the rails, get into loops of endless repetition, or fail
to maintain any kind of internal logic or sense. "As you can probably tell,"
Walton wrote when he released his hackathon project that April, "there's still
a ways to go before AI will be your group's dungeon master."[26] The game
was still novel enough to attract a few thousand players and for Walton to
consider commercializing or improving it, but first he had another summer
internship at a self-driving car startup, as well as his degree to finish—he was
hoping to graduate by the end of the year.

Then, in November, OpenAI released an enhanced version of GPT-2
with a tenfold improvement in the intelligence behind its pattern matching,

At least, it probably does.
The original paper uses
this phrase but never the
acronym GPT; the follow-up
paper refers to GPT-2 but
never expands the acronym.

Other GPT-powered web
toys captured imaginations
in 2019, including *Talk to
Transformer* by Adam King
("transformer" is the kind of
deep learning model used
by GPT) and *GPT Adventure*
by Nathan Whitmore,
trained specifically on
transcripts of *Adventure*
1976, *Zork* 1977, and
Enchanter [Infocom 1983].

now using 1.5 billion parameters. The extended version had been created at the same time as the original, but OpenAI had at first refused to release it as an "experiment in responsible disclosure," citing fears it would be misused to "generate misleading news articles, impersonate others online, [or] automate the production of abusive or faked content to post on social media."[21] But by the end of the year, the experiment was apparently over. That summer the nonprofit had swapped chief executives, and was now run by Sam Altman, former head of trendy startup accelerator Y Combinator. It quickly spawned a for-profit division and brokered another billion-dollar deal, this time with Microsoft—half in cash and half in the cloud computing credits so vital to big data training. A year later the company would license GPT's tech stack exclusively to Microsoft: while the public model would remain available, only the software giant would get access to iterate and improve on it. OpenAI "was supposed to benefit humanity," wrote the *MIT Technology Review* when the deal was announced. "Now it's simply benefiting one of the richest companies in the world."[10]

The full-sized version of GPT-2, months earlier deemed too dangerous to society to release, was released. Walton plugged it into his game and the improvements astonished him. The deeper training produced far more coherent and plausible text. He made a few changes to the game's structure and interface, including fine-tuning its training by scraping multiple-choice stories from digital gamebook portal ChooseYourStory.com. He also replaced the generated menu options with a free-form text field: the user could type their own narration (a "Story" input) or give a command ("Do"), like in a classic text adventure. But this adventure had no parser or set patterns of inputs that were preprogrammed to be recognized. You could enter any command you wanted into *AI Dungeon*, and it would do its best to continue your story. This was as radical a paradigm shift as any since perhaps the advent of parsers in the first place. Even a year earlier, most text game fans would have thought it impossible.

"You are Ragnar, a wizard living in the kingdom of Larion," the new version's human-authored seed for a fantasy story began, customizing the name and character type to the player's selections. "You have a staff and a spellbook. You finish your long journey and finally arrive at the ruin you've been looking for. You have come here searching for a mystical spellbook of great power called the book of essence. You look around and see that it is indeed there, but…" The game then begins dreaming its own continuation:

> …but unfortunately not as you had hoped. The book has been destroyed by fire or some other kind of heat source.
>
> "I can't believe they would do this to me," you say. "It's like I'm just another item on their books."
>
> *Do:* SEARCH FOR ANOTHER BOOK
> > You search for another book.

see *Adventure* **1976**

The next day you go back to the ruins and find a small book with an old leather cover. It looks almost exactly like the one you were looking for, except this one is much older than the last one.

Do: READ THE BOOK
> You read the book.
You open up the book and begin reading. As you do so, you notice something strange about it. It seems to be written in a language that no human could ever understand.

Story: YOUR MIND BEGINS VIBRATING WITH SOME STRANGE, ALIEN FREQUENCY.
Your body feels very odd as well. You feel weak and tired. In fact, you don't even know why you're doing what you're doing right now.
[Regen]
Your body feels different too. You feel stronger and more energetic than you ever have before. This must be what the book was talking about when it said you possessed magical powers.

Do: SEE IF I CAN FLY
> You see if you can fly.
You attempt to levitate yourself into the air. Unfortunately, you fail miserably and fall straight down. You try again and succeed this time.

"Wow! That worked!" you exclaim excitedly.

Do: USE MY MAGIC TO REBUILD THE LIBRARY AND REGENERATE THE BOOK OF ESSENCE
> You use your magic to rebuild the library and regenerate the Book of Essence.
You immediately begin rebuilding the library. You make sure to keep all the books intact and don't destroy any of them. When you're finished, you put everything back where it belongs.

If the player doesn't like the last piece of generated text, they can click the Regen button to have the system try again.

Story after story, the new model impressed Walton with the way it could remember context, craft plausible sentences, and respond sensibly to player commands. The stories it produced were often wacky, like the one where he started a band with a group of skeletons, or another where he brought a tree to life and became its best friend. But for the first time they felt more like stories than random gibberish. He started seriously wondering whether a GPT-based game could become a commercial hit. Crunching to finish his last quarter of classes, he thought he'd throw the improved version of the game online to see if he could spark a new wave of interest.

This time, the fire spread.

The larger GPT-2 model took a serious amount of storage space and computing power to run, and at first users could only access it via a web interface called Google Colab, which allowed for connecting to cloud-based high-performance computing clusters and interacting with them via Python code. But each time someone spun up a session, five gigabytes of training

On launch, this version was originally branded as *AI Dungeon 2*, but Walton soon reverted to the original name without the number.

You Are Carrying…

(inventory list generated by one run of AI Dungeon *at the start of a basic Fantasy scenario)*

» a steel longsword

» a small backpack with flint and steel

» a rope

» a fur hooded coat

» a set of armor

» some basic breadcrumbs

» your dog, Cerberus

» a knapsack with some basic provisions

» a knobby wooden shield

» one camel

» a few other miscellaneous items

data had to be transferred from one remote server to another, and Google charged the host for the bandwidth: around thirty or forty cents for each transfer. As the new *AI Dungeon* began to go viral, costs went through the roof. Walton remembers:

> When the daily bill hit $2,000 per day, BYU's Perception, Control, and Cognition Lab (PCCL) was kind enough to handle the charges. When the cost hit $7,000, they were fine with it. At $15,000, they started to get nervous. At $20,000, we all agreed we needed to do something. At $30,000, they prepared to pull the plug.
>
> By the time all was said and done, the total bill had reached $50,000 in three days.[28]

Desperate not to bankrupt his department or faculty advisor, Walton pulled the game offline amidst a still-growing wave of popularity. Within days, he worked with fans to move the gigabytes of model data to a torrent that could be shared peer-to-peer, so tech-savvy users could run it on their own machines, and he accelerated plans for a commercial version to offset some of the enormous costs. He founded a company called Latitude with his brother Alan, and began work on a mobile version of the game with in-app subscriptions.

In the meantime, his experiment had become a sensation. In those first days, Walton recalls, "We hit the top of *Hacker News*, a few popular gamers posted video play throughs, and Twitter was full of screenshots of ML [machine learning] generated adventure. Within a week we had 100,000 players."[28] By February 2020, the number had passed a million.

Many noticed that *AI Dungeon* was not limited to telling stories about dungeons. While the model had been fine-tuned with text from interactive stories, its GPT core was perfectly capable of imitating any style of text found in its training set, which included millions of web pages on any topic imaginable. You might start off with a seed suggesting an interview with Mahatma Gandhi, and the text coming back would continue as if Gandhi was answering, maybe emulating his speaking style or even peppering in facts about his life that had become encoded into the model's parameters, based on hundreds of examples of the real Gandhi's speeches and biography scraped from the web. OpenAI noted that "topics that are highly represented in the data (Brexit, Miley Cyrus, *Lord of the Rings*, and so on)" were especially likely to produce plausible answers.[21] But GPT could riff on nearly anything ever discussed online.

The game went viral. Most AI in the 2010s was still shared to make fun of how bad it was: NPCs without common sense, Hieronymus Bosch–like horrors of generative cat pics gone wrong. But here was a digital creator that, at times, seemed pretty damn good. People didn't know what to make of it: some were dismissive, others amused, still others disturbed. "Imagine a book," wrote one reviewer, "but instead of being a static object of ink on paper, it's written while you wait, by a room full of unhinged authors hopped up on sherbet and gin."[9] Another described it as like doing "undergrad improv with a really terrible partner," and even less charitably as "computer-assisted literary masturbation."[2] Other reviewers called it "a wild ride,"[24] "messy yet occasionally flabbergasting,"[7] and a glimpse into "an endless world of dreamlike storytelling."[9]

Like dreams, the outputs from *AI Dungeon* were often more interesting to the player who generated them than anyone else. The game presented an existential challenge to reviewers: what critique can be offered of a text game where everyone's text is different? How do you review a story that wasn't written by a human, with no artistic intention or conscious thought behind it—and why would you bother to try? What role, if any, was left for the critic? Most reviewers, whether articulating this challenge or not, fell back to simply posting lengthy transcripts of their own interactions with the game, reveling in or insulting the mix of absurd and plausible outputs, but mostly just letting the writing speak for itself. Unable to engage with either the writing process or the aesthetic effect, the only thing left to report on was the words.

As the game's surge of popularity began to attract a sustainable base of paying players, Latitude hired engineers to start improving their product's core (and only) functionality. They refined the interface to help set player expectations, and added restrictions and assists to help the AI produce more consistent and plausible stories. New buttons could pin facts for the AI to remember: additional sentences that would be fed into each request for more text, alongside the player's latest input. Tools to edit, undo, or regenerate responses let players more tightly curate a story in progress, keeping it from getting too weird (or too normal, depending on preference). The amount of text fed into the system expanded to include the last eight interaction pairs between human and machine, giving stories more coherence as details from the last few pages, not just the last few paragraphs, might recur. Starting seeds were added for different kinds of stories: horror, cyberpunk, zombie invasions. Eventually fans would gain the ability to publish their own shareable "worlds" for *AI Dungeon*, combinations of starter prompts and consistent facts that could kick off a story in any milieu imaginable.

But improvements had to work around a looming brick wall. Under the hood of a regular game would be some kind of simulated world model keeping track of characters, locations, or inventory, with logic for activities like movement or combat. GPT's text algorithm had nothing of the sort. It was, in essence, a clever black box: words went in and new words came out. Nothing was kept track of or simulated in the traditional sense. Earlier AI-driven text games like those from the Oz Project or Versu still had structured assumptions and procedures that humans could refine, customize, and tune, but the millions of learned parameters in GPT models were not accessible or even understandable to human operators. So while adding an inventory system to an in-progress parser game would be relatively trivial, teaching the same sort of concept to a GPT-driven game—other than via the tedious repetition of real-world examples—was almost impossible. Most of Latitude's workarounds boiled down to clever ways to shove more text into the black box along with the player's input, or to understand more about its output. A quest-tracking system added in the fall of 2020, for instance, added a separate machine learning model trained to detect strings of text that indicated a goal had been achieved, like "At last, you have claimed the sword!"

see *The Playground* **1994** and *Versu: A Family Supper* **2013**

The biggest improvements by far continued to be in the underlying model. GPT-3 launched in May 2020 with a mind-boggling 175 billion parameters—a thousandfold increase over the system's debut only two years earlier—and a training set that now included over a trillion words from Wikipedia, online book libraries, and the web at large. The model had cost millions of dollars in computing power to train, and it required a small mountain of dedicated GPUs to run (ironically, far more than to produce contemporary game graphics). In June, Latitude added access to this new model, under the brand name Dragon, as a premium option for paid subscribers. The stories Dragon told could be disturbingly coherent.

> The door is locked so you knock. The music suddenly stops and you hear footsteps coming to the door.
> "Hello?" A voice says behind the door.
> "I'm looking for the book of essence," You say.
> "What do you want it for?" The voice answers, a bit of an edge to it.
>
> *Do:* `TELL THEM I AM A HUMBLE SEEKER OF KNOWLEDGE`
> > You tell them you are a humble seeker of knowledge.
> "Ah, I see. You seek to learn about the essence of reality, and the universe." The voice says. "I know of this book. I am the guard of this library. The only way you can get to it, is if you get past me. Are you up for the challenge?"
>
> *Do:* `ASK THEM WHAT THE CHALLENGE IS`
> > You ask them what the challenge is.
> "The challenge is, you have to win a game of chess against me. If you win, then you may try to take the book. I will get the board." The door unlocks and opens.

Some writers began sounding an alarm. The *New York Times* covered GPT-3 under the headline "How Do You Know A Human Wrote This?" The author called the technology "at once amazing, spooky, humbling and more than a little terrifying."[16] The *Daily Beast* wrote: "There's something depressing about language generation when it works well—a machine tapping into one of the few things that feel uniquely human, producing not just speech, but story, character, and jokes."[12] The warnings that OpenAI itself had once made were now taken up by mainstream cultural critics, who in the midst of the Trump administration's ongoing assault on facts warned of "a future in which we are even less sure if what we are reading is real or fake."[18] Questions of ownership and attribution also had no settled answers, either legally or morally. Could writers claim copyright on text produced by their inputs into *AI Dungeon*? Could Latitude? What about the thousands of authors whose words were slurped up for training data without their consent? Some of the writers at ChooseYourStory.com became upset when they discovered the scraped contents of their stories posted to a public GitHub account. In later months, they would notice that some of their characters' names showed up suspiciously often in *AI Dungeon* stories.[1]

As of late 2020, Latitude's informal policy was that users could freely use any text they produced with *AI Dungeon*, though the legalese buried in their terms of service was, predictably, far more murky. Some writers nevertheless began using the game as a tool for co-creation. Emily Bellavia, for instance, released a full-length novel in fall 2020 created by her interactions with *AI Dungeon*, titled *Lady Emilia Stormbringer*. She attributed authorship to the Dragon AI and credited herself only as "Director."

2019

Worse, any AI model trained on unfiltered text from the internet ran the risk of mindlessly perpetuating its darker aspects. In 2016 Microsoft had released a chatbot named Tay, designed to improve its conversational skills by interacting with humans on Twitter. Within sixteen hours of its release, the bot was taken down permanently after it began making racist and inflammatory tweets, stoked by an army of online trolls. "Do you support genocide?" a user tweeted at Tay in one of the tamer examples; "i do indeed," the bot replied. The bot didn't really know what it was saying, of course—just as GPT doesn't—but the incident became one of the decade's most famous examples of the dangers of AI that mindlessly remixed and parroted unfiltered inputs with none of the social, emotional, or cultural understanding of a person. Writing about GPT-3 a few years after Tay, one reporter noted the risk in "its inability to distinguish between truth and lie, between fact and fiction." GPT-3 will easily generate text that sounds plausible but has no basis in reality. "What makes this dangerous," the reporter noted, "especially when it comes to questions related to medicine, for example, is that even when the model doesn't have a clue what it's talking about, it responds with absolute confidence."[14]

The issue of tech like GPT disrupting human creators had also come to seem like more than fantasy by 2020. "I am fairly convinced at this point that people will lose their jobs because of advancements in language models like GPT-3," wrote one tech analyst. "The only question in my mind is whether this will happen in the next five years or the next ten."[22] Indeed, Walton's vision of *AI Dungeon*'s commercial potential seemed to rely on this, framing the system's future value as a matter of reducing "developer costs":

> In a game like *Skyrim,* you're talking about employing hundreds of people over roughly five years. It's so expensive. Ideally, AI lets us cut down on a lot of what developers normally do.[15]

Application of technology to save labor has long been both a utopian dream and a capitalist nightmare. Does the time saved free more people from drudgery, or is it converted into more profit for their bosses? The great cost of mustering enough computational power to feed GPT-based systems might suggest they're unlikely to become a tool for the masses (although fully open-source models like GPT-J have since appeared as good first steps). But it's still too early to know whether the fears around GPT will seem laughable or prescient in the years to come. As with the immediate aftermath of the Notre-Dame disaster, we can't yet appreciate the true extent of the fire. "GPT-3 is going to be this decade's iPhone, in terms of a singular artefact that is quite clearly the axis

OH, *THAT* KIND OF DUNGEON

Many *AI Dungeon* players also discovered, through accident or design, that GPT could cheerfully and effortlessly produce infinite amounts of pornography, on any subject the user desired. One 2021 analysis of a Latitude data leak suggested nearly a third of the stories generated by *AI Dungeon*'s users were sexually explicit. The problem was that the model might sometimes start inserting this content into stories on its own, without the user's consent: one infamous example involved an innocent use of the phrase "mount the dragon." Latitude tried adding a safe mode that filtered out explicit terms but, like all keyword-based approaches, it was only occasionally successful. Indeed, some users noted that "the supposedly safe setting improved the text-generator's erotic writing because it used more analogies and euphemisms."[23]

A deeper problem came, again, from GPT's lack of any human contexts of ethics, standards, history, or morality. When seeded appropriately by the user, it would generate racist screeds or child pornography just as easily as sword-and-sorcery adventures. After Latitude tried again to patch this problem with keyword filters, users complained both that the approaches were laughably blunt (one noted that mentioning an "eight-year-old laptop" had led to a ban) but also that the company's increasing attempts to police its core technology's output were violating users' privacy. What, exactly, should humans and cloud-based AIs be allowed to dream about together—and allowed by whom? Latitude continued evolving its policy and technology across 2021, but the core problems had no easy solutions.

around which the next 10 years rotate," predicted Alex Hern, technology editor for the *Guardian*, in 2020.[14] But tech predictions are a tricky business. GPT or something like it might catch fire—or collapse under its own considerable weight, expense, and inscrutability.

see **1966**

AI Dungeon points to a radically different possible future for text games, one which might seem nearly unrecognizable to fans of a medium that's always been more lovingly handcrafted than automated. And yet, in another sense, it continues traditions enmeshed in text games from the beginning— not only in its dungeon-crawl and parser aesthetics, but in the way it recalls early chatbots like *ELIZA*, which fascinated early computer users with illusions of personhood. The yearning for machines to dream and create alongside us has existed since the earliest software written for pleasure. The challenge, as with any new technology, lies in doing the work to make sure it enriches our lives rather than diminish them.

References

1 aid702. 2019. "AI Dungeon 2: The Dungeoning!" Forum post, ChooseYourStory.com, Dec 7, 2019. chooseyourstory.com/forums/the-lounge/message/26021 | a Dec 12, 2020

2 Ars Staff. 2020. "The Machines Are Whispering: We Tested AI Dungeon 2 and Cannot Stop Laughing." *Ars Technica* (blog). Jan 20, 2020. arstechnica.com/gaming/2020/01/we-test-ai-dungeon-2-a-text-adventure-that-creates-itself-with-your-help | a Dec 12, 2020

3 Batorsky, Ben. 2020. "GPT-Who? Exploring the History of GPT." *Ben Batorsky's Blog.* Oct 28, 2020. bpben. github.io/2020/10/28/gpt_explore | a Dec 12, 2020

4 Boog, Jason. 2020. "AI Storytelling Game May Expand Publishing's Horizons." *Publishers Weekly.* Aug 28, 2020. www.publishersweekly.com/pw/by-topic/industry-news/publisher-news/article/84224-ai-storytelling-game-may-expand-publishing-s-horizons.html | a Dec 12, 2020

5 Brockman, Greg, and Ilya Sutskever. 2015. "Introducing OpenAI." OpenAI. Dec 12, 2015. openai.com/blog/introducing-openai | a Dec 12, 2020

6 Brown, Tom B., Benjamin Mann, Nick Ryder, Melanie Subbiah, Jared Kaplan, Prafulla Dhariwal, Arvind Neelakantan et al. 2020. "Language Models Are Few-Shot Learners." In *Advances in Neural Information Processing Systems* 33.

7 Cox, Matt. 2020. "Console an AI about Its Lack of Sentience in AI Dungeon 2." *Rock, Paper, Shotgun* (blog). Aug 3, 2020. www.rockpapershotgun.com/2020/08/03/console-an-ai-about-its-lack-of-sentience-in-ai-dungeon-2 | a Dec 12, 2020

8 DeBos, Cody. 2019. "Interview: 'AI Dungeon 2' Dev Nick Walton Talks Future of AI." *The Burn-In* (blog). Dec 21, 2019. www.theburnin.com/games/interview-ai-dungeon-2-creator-nick-walton-android-ios-mobile-release-future-ai-2019-12 | a Dec 12, 2020

9 Grannell, Craig. 2020. "App of the Week: AI Dungeon Review." *Stuff,* Jan 12, 2020. www.stuff.tv/app-reviews/ai-dungeon/review | a Dec 12, 2020

10 Hao, Karen. 2020. "OpenAI Is Giving Microsoft Exclusive Access to Its GPT-3 Language Model." *MIT Technology Review* (blog). Sep 23, 2020. www.technologyreview.com/2020/09/23/1008729/openai-is-giving-microsoft-exclusive-access-to-its-gpt-3-language-model | a Dec 12, 2020

11 Henley, Jon. 2019. "Notre Dame Cathedral Fire – a Visual Guide and Timeline." *Guardian,* Apr 16, 2019, sec. World news. www.theguardian.com/world/2019/apr/16/notre-dame-cathedral-fire-a-visual-guide-and-timeline | a Dec 12, 2020

12 Hitt, Tarpley. 2019. "Meet the Mormon College Student Behind Viral Artificial Intelligence Game AI Dungeon." *Daily Beast* (blog). Dec 9, 2019. www.thedailybeast.com/meet-the-mormon-college-student-behind-viral-artificial-intelligence-game-ai-dungeon | a Dec 12, 2020

13 Knight, Will. 2020. "Forget Chess—the Real Challenge Is Teaching AI to Play D&D." *Wired,* Feb 28, 2020. www.wired.com/story/forget-chess-real-challenge-teaching-ai-play-dandd | a Dec 12, 2020

14 Lavie, Boaz. 2020. "This Algorithm Speaks Just like Us. I Had a Rare Opportunity to Meet It." *haaretz. com* (blog). Sep 3, 2020. www.haaretz.com/israel-news/.premium.MAGAZINE-this-algorithm-speaks-just-like-us-i-had-a-rare-opportunity-to-meet-it-1.9126323 | a Dec 12, 2020

15 Lim, Hengtee. 2020. "How Nick Walton Created AI Dungeon: The AI-Generated Text Adventure." *Lionbridge AI* (blog). Jun 11, 2020. lionbridge.ai/articles/

can-ai-make-video-games-how-nick-walton-created-ai-dungeon | a Dec 12, 2020

16 Manjoo, Farhad. 2020. "How Do You Know a Human Wrote This?" *New York Times*, Jul 29, 2020, sec. Opinion. www.nytimes.com/2020/07/29/opinion/gpt-3-ai-automation.html | a Dec 12, 2020

17 Metz, Cade. 2019. "With $1 Billion From Microsoft, an A.I. Lab Wants to Mimic the Brain." *New York Times*, Jul 23, 2019, sec. B.

18 Metz, Cade. 2020. "Meet GPT-3. It Has Learned to Code (and Blog and Argue)." *New York Times*, Nov 24, 2020, sec. Science. www.nytimes.com/2020/11/24/science/artificial-intelligence-ai-gpt3.html | a Dec 12, 2020

19 Moyer, Phillip. 2019. "AI Dungeon Is A Game Where You Can Do Anything You Want." *TheGamer* (blog). Dec 18, 2019. www.thegamer.com/ai-dungeon-game-do-anything-you-want | a Dec 12, 2020

20 Radford, Alec, Karthik Narasimhan, Tim Salimans, and Ilya Sutskever. 2018. "Improving Language Understanding by Generative Pre-Training." Report.

21 Radford, Alec, Jeffrey Wu, Dario Amodei, Daniela Amodei, Jack Clark, Miles Brundage, and Ilya Sutskever. 2019. "Better Language Models and Their Implications." OpenAI. Feb 14, 2019. openai.com/blog/better-language-models | a Dec 12, 2020

22 Rao, Tanae. 2020. "Exploring the AI Dungeon." *Tanae Rao* (blog). Jul 22, 2020. towardsdatascience.com/exploring-the-ai-dungeon-253ddc577011 | a Dec 12, 2020

23 Simonite, Tom. 2021. "It Began as an AI-Fueled Dungeon Game. Then It Got Much Darker." *Ars Technica* (blog). May 8, 2021. arstechnica.com/gaming/2021/05/it-began-as-an-ai-fueled-dungeon-game-then-it-got-much-darker/ | a Aug 14, 2022

24 Vincent, James. 2019. "This AI Text Adventure Game Has Pretty Much Infinite Possibilities." *The Verge* (blog). Dec 6, 2019. www.theverge.com/tldr/2019/12/6/20998993/ai-dungeon-2-choose-your-own-adventure-game-text-nick-walton-gpt-machine-learning | a Dec 12, 2020

25 Wakefield, Jane. 2016. "Microsoft Chatbot Is Taught to Swear on Twitter." *BBC News*, Mar 24, 2016, sec. Technology. www.bbc.com/news/technology-35890188 | a Dec 12, 2020

26 Walton, Nick. 2019a. "AI Dungeon Release." *AIDungeon* (Patreon blog). Apr 15, 2019. www.patreon.com/posts/ai-dungeon-26134858 | a Dec 12, 2020

27 Walton, Nick. 2019b. "AI Dungeon 2: Creating Infinitely Generated Text Adventures with Deep Learning Language Models." *Perception, Control, Cognition* (blog). Nov 21, 2019. pcc.cs.byu.edu/2019/11/21/ai-dungeon-2-creating-infinitely-generated-text-adventures-with-deep-learning-language-models | a Dec 12, 2020

28 Walton, Nick. 2020a. "How We Scaled AI Dungeon 2 to Support over 1,000,000 Users." *Latitude Team* (blog). Feb 11, 2020. medium.com/@aidungeon/how-we-scaled-ai-dungeon-2-to-support-over-1-000-000-users-d207d5623de9 | a Dec 12, 2020

29 Walton, Nick. 2020b. "AI Dungeon: Dragon Model Upgrade." *Latitude Team* (blog). Jul 14, 2020. medium.com/@aidungeon/ai-dungeon-dragon-model-upgrade-7e8ea579abfe | a Dec 12, 2020

SCENTS & SEMIOSIS

Sam Kabo Ashwell
as Heavy Petal
with Yoon Ha Lee, Cat Manning, and Caleb Wilson

Style **Procedural Story**
Debuted **Mar 9, 2020** *(Itch.io)*
Launch Platform **Glulx / Vorple / Web**
Language **Inform 7**

> " There are other perfume-boxes, other lists, sharply curated according to audience. You allow yourself a degree of sentiment in their selection, but that too serves a public purpose. This collection—messy, unfashionable, incoherently themed—is an entirely private matter. A giant's secret heart.
>
> Each scent brings back memories that once meant something important. They might still. But scents change their character as they slowly break down, and history moulders unless given air. Once in a while you clear an evening, unlock the chest, and unstopper your old selves to see what they are to you now.

TEXT GAMES HAVE ALWAYS PROMISED ONE KEY DIFFERENCE from traditional prose: the chance that each reader's journey might in some way be unique. Games can realize this dream with well-tended paths through carefully trimmed gardens of possibility, or with invitations to explore less curated

see **2019**

meadows and glens, even at the risk of getting lost. The rise of GPT and titles like *AI Dungeon* are something of a nuclear option for making such a garden: like *Star Trek*'s Genesis Device, which burned up worlds with the fires of new life, they bring unbridled creation but scant control. In the face of such power, older methods for nurturing possibilities might seem almost quaint, like a master gardener taking months to plant, tend, and cultivate each sprout—growing, through painstaking labor, what an automated system might farm with far less effort. Yet the old ways have their charms. The gardener's harvest is uniquely theirs, marked with indelible fingerprints that leave a record of intention in the crop: green shoots grown by someone and for someone, human through and through.

Scents & Semiosis is undoubtedly a game that was grown. In it, you take the role of a perfumer thumbing through a collection that samples your life's work, reveling in the memories each scent brings to mind and the associations it suggests. The game's scope is deliberately small, encompassing only a handful of lingering moments. It's "meant to be brief, densely-flavoured, and more than a little indulgent," the author writes, "like a very tiny box of very nice chocolates or a liqueur that you only need a few sips of."[1] And yet it can be returned to again and again, because each bottle, perfume, and memory comes from an enormous reservoir of handcrafted procedural text snippets, and an equally elaborate set of rules for assembling them.

"You run a hand through the vials," the game describes, "as though dangling your arm from a boat to touch the water, and pick out one, two, a third, for any reason or none."

> » *an obsidian bottle, emblazoned with the insignia of Bernicia*
> » a blue glass jar
> » *a bottle set in a pewter barrette*
>
> **Five kinds of musk, clove, heart notes of juicy caraway and languid oleander; silver rose. This one was purely commercial: the concept piece for a line of top-shelf car fresheners. You specifically required a clause in the contract to prevent them from crediting you for it.**

Each perfume gives opportunities to reflect on what the scents comprising it might suggest, and why you chose them for this mélange:

> » *rose feels like ephemera complicated by opportunity*
> » *caraway is suggestive of idle art*
> » *clove feels like movement leading to impasse*
> » *rose might imply ventures*
> » **None of these feel right. Reconsider.**

Yet, like the bottles and perfumes, the suggestions aren't fixed. The last option lets you regenerate them, the options assembled anew by a complex routine linking scents, themes, language, and associations:

> » *clove could suggest art*
> » *caraway is suggestive of crisis despite craft*
> » *oleander could mean perfect aesthetics*
> » *caraway is suggestive of absence turning to recognition*
> » *None of these feel right. Reconsider.*
> » *This perfume isn't worth keeping.*
>
> Caraway for crisis despite craft. All right.
>
> It's early, yet. Let's see what else:
>
> » *a green glass flask with a swing-top closure*
> » *an art deco vial decorated with ormulu and fluorspar*
> » *a pink glass jar marred by many small abrasions*

MAJOR RELEASES

» **Update 1.0 "Galbanum."** Closed release.

» **Update 1.2 "Acacia,"** Mar 9, 2020, Launch version.

» **Update 1.3 "Fenugreek,"** Mar 13, 2020. Release 1 / 200310 / Inform 7 build 6M62, Vorple version 3.0 preview. "Inevitable update to fix launch-day bugs". Mistakenly labeled "Update 1.2 Fenugreek" on About screen.

Bottle by bottle, memory by memory, meaning by meaning, *Scents & Semiosis* lets your character build up a palette of identity: the unique savor of a personal history. When you've had enough, the meanings you chose are brought together:

> caraway for crisis despite craft
> cherry orange zest for doomed anger
> quince for fine detail
> amber for friendship despite exhaustion
> tea for reluctant passion
> soursop for irrational attraction
> lavender for regret
>
> Not a scent that you could construct in a bottle. And not the only version of your past. But you feel the shape of it, and it's what you choose for now.

Procedural content generation—using an algorithmic process to create more outputs to a system than a human maker could practically write—has been present in games from the start. Originally this was by necessity: early computers had such limited storage and memory footprints that a game's worth of content was too big to fit in them. Random variation allowed replayability too: *Hunt the Wumpus* used pseudorandomness to distribute hazards and enemies across a fixed map, making each game different, while *Super Star Trek* generated a galaxy of sectors for each playthrough with randomly scattered Klingons and stars. The 1980 game *Rogue* [Michael Toy et al.] and its successors began a tradition of more deeply generative worlds, reaching glorious apotheosis with games like *Dwarf Fortress* and *Caves of Qud* [Freehold Games 2015]. At the core of many of these generative systems was a simple technique of nested lists, each of which might link to another list as one of its possible expansions. Games like *Nested* are pure distillations of this approach, delighting in exploring bottomless chains of permutation sprung from simple seeds.

see **1973** and **1974**

see **2006**

see **2011**

This last technique had been formalized in the 1950s by linguist Noam Chomsky as "context-free grammars," sets of rules for recursively expanding one symbol into others. Such a structure could define everything from the valid syntax of a programming language to a procedure to generate plans for new houses in the style of Frank Lloyd Wright.[6] In the domain of generative text, context-free grammars could transform high-level plans for a sentence into more and more specific subplans, bottoming out in specific pieces of text to instantiate them. A grammar for a random greeting, for instance, might look like this, with links to other asterisked symbols wrapped in brackets:

```
*Greeting: "[*Hello], [*friend]."
*Hello: "Greetings", "Hello", "Hi", "[*Extended Hello]"
*friend: "buddy", "friend", "pal"
*Extended Hello: "Such a pleasure to make your acquaintance",
"I'm delighted to meet you"
```

When expanded, `*Greeting` might then produce outputs like "Hi, buddy" or "I'm delighted to make your acquaintance, friend." As a grammar becomes more complex, with reusable symbols and deeply nested chains, it can produce enormous variety in its output, while remaining under the control of the author who creates it. Expansion grammars become even more powerful when individual random choices can influence others: one implementation might let the randomly chosen symbol `Extended Hello` set a *long-winded* flag that could influence what later content to select.

In the mid-2010s, expansion grammar–based content generators saw a surge of popularity due in large part to the debut of a new tool for easily defining them, Tracery.[4] A friendly browser-based editor and a flexible, open-source JavaScript implementation made it easy to incorporate the tool (by self-described "maker of many interesting things" Kate Compton) into ongoing projects. Soon Tracery was powering everything from Twitter bots to generative art exhibits. When Sam Ashwell set out to create *Scents & Semiosis*, he used a reimplementation of Compton's program (in a code section called "I Can't Believe It's Not Tracery") as the foundation for his text-generation system—though it would end up being only one part of a more elaborate meaning-making machine.

Ashwell had been active in the interactive fiction community since the 1990s, earning a reputation as someone who thought deeply and wrote eloquently about the medium and its potential. His games, typically unique experiments rather than orthodox epics, "always seem to be from a parallel universe where IF developed in wildly different directions," one reviewer wrote. "They don't 'fit in' with usual IF tropes."[8] *Olivia's Orphanorium* [2012], a Victorian satire by way of resource management parody game, is a typical example. In 2017 he created *Apocalypse Fuel*, a standalone generator to make locations and characters for the tabletop roleplaying game *Apocalypse World* [Meguey Baker and D. Vincent Baker, 2010]. He wrote it in Inform 7, a familiar language for making parser-based text games, though it was an odd fit for a project that had no parser and was not a game. But the language had built-in

see *Violet* **2008**

support for defining complex text variation, including the crucial ability to nest expansions:

```
To say hello: say "[one of]Greetings[or]Hello[or]Hi[or][Extended Hello]
[at random]." To say Extended Hello: say "[one of]Such a pleasure to
make your acquaintance[or]I'm delighted to meet you[at random]".
```

Ashwell created a web interface for *Apocalypse Fuel* using Vorple, an Inform 7 extension by Juhana Leinonen that let authors craft browser-based interfaces for their games to supplant or replace the traditional text-only parser, again with readable natural language syntax.

```
place a link to the command "begin" reading "Play", without showing
the command;
scroll to the end of the page;
wait for any key;
```

With Vorple and his Inform 7 Tracery port, Ashwell had both an elegant front-end and back-end for experimenting with procedural text. For a follow-up project he thought he might try making something for NaNoGenMo (National Novel Generation Month), an annual challenge since 2013 that gives procedural text enthusiasts thirty days to write code that can author a novel (via various, occasionally-strained definitions). But Ashwell's concept soon grew into something more personal: a gift for longtime friend and fellow interactive fiction author Emily Short, "according to an approach she has spoken of fondly: crafting a game for a target audience of one." As befitting a thoughtful gift, Ashwell didn't want anything too bulky or complicated, but "something that could be consumed in small sessions and with only gentle effort; I didn't want playing it to become a chore."[1] He also set it in the kind of parallel world he knew they both loved to explore: one less drab and more piquant than our own, filled with hints of evocative histories and intriguing cultures.

see *Galatea* **2000**

Short had created her own such worlds, often dabbling in procedural text herself. More recently, she had been exploring what it could do in isolation, not just as a piece of a larger game. *The Annals of the Parrigues* was a noninteractive book, a travel guide to a fictional country, that she'd written in collaboration with a handcrafted generator.[11] As Short fleshed out the book's setting, she'd come up with a thematic framework akin to something like the four elements or the suites of Tarot in our world: a system for meaning-making around which both she and her generator could structure concepts and descriptions. She eventually developed an iconography based on five symbols—Mushroom, Egg, Beeswax, Venom, and Salt—each with a set of associations and ideas that together helped sketch in an underlying consistency for a fictional culture.

But while meant to be pure worldbuilding, Short realized the framework could also describe different techniques for procedural content generation. She called them the Five Principles: "They cannot be observed simultaneously," she wrote, "or with equal attention at all times."[11] Mushroom implied unrestrained growth and fecundity—systems less concerned with the quality of individual passages than their effect on the whole, useful for generation techniques "unapologetic about repetitions" and more concerned with quantity than quality. Venom meant brightly colored, striking, deceitful, surprising—systems that varied text in places more likely to dangerously startle than go safely unnoticed. Beeswax was busy, warm, chaotic, diverse—chaneling the many voices in massive text corpora with conflicting styles, or idiosyncratic passages handwritten for particular situations. Finally, Salt signified dry, crystalline regularity—clean techniques in which the mechanism shone through—and Egg meant the elegance of living vitality and nuance, suggesting systems designed for collaboration with a flesh-and-blood author adding their unique organic spin.

Ashwell loved Short's framework. He decided his project would be very Beeswaxy: "lots of small, steady, incremental, unglamorous additions, list-sifting, running your antennae over all the parts." It would be organic and heterogeneous, filigreed and filled with unique phrases that might only appear once, or even less: "Part of what I love about parser that's often lost in hypertext IF," he wrote, "is the sense of weird discovery, of finding something amazing that you didn't *have* to find and might not have."[1] The authoring would also keep in mind the principles of Venom, allowing for surprising, interesting juxtapositions: "It's important, in procgen [procedural generation], to avoid things getting over-determined, to leave space for the fortuitous."[3] While the text would aim to seem as elegant as something handwritten, it would allow for interesting imperfections to creep in, fashioning "hopeful monsters rather than exactingly-bred show animals," as a comment in the game's source code notes.

Time for something else:

» *a smoky glass flask with a label that has been erased with black marker*
» *a black lacquer bottle*
» *an obsidian flask*

Lavender, coconut, gunpowder, three kinds of amber, sacramental soursop, raw honey and balm of Mecca. The scent brings back memories of Fillouch, who you made a promise to at Akala Annex.

» *amber is suggestive of things unexpected*
» *balm of Mecca might mean mercy in tension with effort*
» *coconut feels like deliberate honesty*
» *raw honey is suggestive of passion which causes organisation*
» *None of these feel right. Reconsider.*

Ashwell went to great lengths to ensure his system's outputs would be aesthetically pleasing more often than not, but he also recognized that in a

---

collaboration with a generative system, embracing the unexpected was not only a necessity but a boon:

> A huge problem in procgen output, generally, is the need for filtering, curation. Much of what procgen produces is rubbish and it takes human work and human taste to pick out the gems; in a lot of games, that makes run-time procgen elements a liability. The big trick of *Scents* is that it enlists the player to do that curation work, and calls it play.[3]

As Ashwell began the project, a core system emerged for generating perfumes based on the fundamentals of real scent design, which involves a combination of top, heart, and base notes. He was more concerned with evocative suggestions than strict accuracy, expecting that "people who intimately understand perfume are likely to laugh a lot at the outputs."[1] But at first the project failed to gel into a satisfying experience. It was "just a pretty text-generating toy … I wanted this to be a bit more than that, something that was *played* rather than passively absorbed."[3] The key spark came when he added a system that associated different scent notes with meanings that the player could take part in selecting. To fully explain this, we need to delve deeper into how the game's generator works.

Perfume descriptions in *Scents & Semiosis* originate with a list of "structures," templates for kinds of sentences that might describe them:

> "[pop scenttops][pop scenthearts][pop scentbases][if a random chance of 1 in 7 succeeds], [pop hintphrases][end if]"

Each top-level structure can then expand into its own set of structures for each possible component of the description:

> scenthearts is a list of texts that varies.
> scenthearts is {
> "**heart** [one of]notes [or][purely at random]of [scentpop heartnotes] **and** [scentpop heartnotes]; ",
> "[scentpop heartnotes], ",
> "[scentpop heartnotes], ",
> "[scentpop heartnotes], ",
> "[pop multiphrases], ",
> "[pop multiphrases], [scentpop heartnotes], ",
> "[scentpop heartnotes], [scentpop heartnotes], "
> }.

But as the expansions drill down toward individual words, selection becomes guided less by randomness than by mechanisms to suggest internal consistency. First, a perfume might be given one or two themes, which make it more likely that matching descriptors, connectors, or adjectives will be used when describing it:

> Woodland is a theme in startroom. The twist of woodland is {"**dank**", "**dirty**", "**feral**", "**fire**", "**forest**", "**earthy**", "**green**", "**mouldering**",

"murky", "organic", "overgrown", "prickly", "tangled", "tranquil", "vegetal", "verdant", "wild", "woody"}.

The composite of woodland is {"blooms amongst", "growing amongst", "intertwines with", "interwoven with", "tangled with", "rich with", "in a bed of"}.

The phantpre of woodland is {"arbor", "bear", "boar", "bird", "bog", "bough", "brush", "buck", "deer", "duck", "elf", "fae", "fox", "glade", "goose", "hog", "leaf", "marsh", "mire", "mist", "moss", "oak", "rain", "shade", "soil", "stink", "tangle", "tree", "willow", "wolf"}.

Themes can also have "resonances," abstract concepts to which they connect. Woodlands resonates with solitude, nature, and growth; the season of spring with beginnings and fun. Resonances in turn can affect descriptive text but also the memories and themes associated with each scent, leading to a system that tries to organically tie the elements of each perfume's description together.

> » an amber glass bottle with a pinecone stopper
>
> Melancholy lavender, rich cassia, earthy whiskey, four kinds of moss. You made this for your father on his deathbed.
>
> » *lavender is suggestive of persistent disappointment*
> » *cassia might suggest completed things*
> » *whiskey feels like dissolution*
> » *whiskey might stand for fading tragedy*
> » *None of these feel right. Reconsider.*

Here a theme for the season of fall suggested the pinecone stopper, the amber glass, and the adjective "earthy." Fall triggered associations with melancholy, loss, and endings, which in turn supplied the dying father and the associations with tragedy and dissolution. The generation is still random, but the themes and associations constrain the output into a more consistent, plausible whole.

The memories each perfume might suggest came to comprise an increasingly large portion of the system. Memories could involve gifts given or received, jobs done or favors rendered, festivals and parties attended, friends and lovers of all kinds, and more, each with their own elaborate, bespoke generator. Many of these spun off their own generators to assemble fractal nests of carefully crafted details—worldbuilding rendered in the name of an opera or the type of cloth used for a corset. Each of the nested chain of lists below, parts of the code for generating memories about good times with friends, has been truncated from its full length, often considerably:

groupmainact is a list of texts that varies. groupmainact is {
"**when** *[one of]***the two of** *[or][purely at random]***you** *[one of]***broke***[or]*

• calamity • weird • Zhegtis • rr • Monotheite • dated • resting upon • New Gardens • obscure • impasse • Monica • Helm • complicated • advancement
• torso • blue cheese • Philippe • Sīa • Egypt • o • gleaming • new beginnings • rose • kumquat • Ber • yellow • mille-feuilles • bicycle • Berdil • Thibault • ro
phrastus • skiff • Qalat Erbil • Hungary • friendship • your • ts • Wusid • paper • didn't adopt a cat • Laia • lazy • Jashuni • Kuçer • Museum • harmony • rough
vela • Johnsen • close • en • Sîbel • Qazi • ludologist • tragic • Aleppo • arcane symbols • Lima • Filip • er • Horn • summer • Weronika • Sakina • okoleha
food stores • glowing • new • Penthe • Fry • fiveleaf • jujube • Magazine • none • Maria Luisa • Sophie • mural • Amanda • damson • dignity • Paper • Angel
n • Fabre • Coricancha • Albanian • Vera • Bêdaran • Koçer • Acorns • regrettable • silver • Tamu • understood • Zofia • transformative • joyful things • Bee
box • boyfriend • intense • Opal • Gloria • Brunette • Loic • vibrant • ic • Royal • Ragusa • ā • West • brief • cornflower • snake • Defence • Monika • Tata
g • Jamalzadah • fir • butts • Orozco • Apolonia • plumeria • Dalmatian • Food and Drink • dark • sam • Ifeadigo • Jordan • grapefruit • Mammoth Cave • bac
e • Bald • Laure • Cecilia • Bold • pensive • Shajkiki • Malîn • nasty • Carr • grey • Weasel • Kristensen • Bhūī • Golden • blossom • Das • gochujang • lemor
Bayiz • cinnabar • hamantash • j • black • indulgent • Tea • Chakraborty • Corsican • Czech • p • Sanesîn • Serav • sparkling • foolish • Noel • resolute • Góm
d • complete • arrack • reseda • anxious • ridiculous • pansy • summer sausage • catalogue • annotating • the Star • reserve • Murthy • Somalian • raw • mon
bristlecone • hidden roots • theremin • Extreme Metal • with • g • Clackamas • Ar • reflexive • Çekdar • hymn • be conspiring with • Lukas • cacao • ocea
green jade • Ebubedike • END • in the past • black lacquer • Victorious • Akam • Mir • first • lilikoi • Gardens • Mahdi • it recollects • Mariusz • Ainara • devilwo
ti Monastery • spent • Japanese red • Laura • Peacemaker • breadfruit • Slug • narrativist • green • winter • entices • Marseilles • glitter • joy • Oaxacan • fori
stry with • tavern • de Koningh • Algiers • looking everywhere but at you • censor • procedural generation • a microlight aircraft • moss agate glass • lingering
ah • Camelia • astoundingly • Soho • white • prickly ash • avens • intellectual • masks • Szechuan peppercorn • bicycles • Jirīd • Palestinian • t • Dilkanî • p
ophe • Jonas • lawn bowls • enduring • irrational • for • quin • Tilde • agar • a drinks cabinet • Monk • fey • experience • ska • passionate enthusiasm • kind-h
ness • syrah • Read • Francisco • hemp • Wolf • olibanum • Yemeni • synaesthesia • still life • cherry • self-knowledge • scarlet glass • Gourmand • thick • Kelle
• gaiac wood • Spronk • weary • Rurai • moral degenerate • a • h2 • swaggers atop • taught yourself • murder • Besê • none • Cecilia • moist • homm • gre
rangpur • vexatious • none • Hare • seared • amaryllis • Archive • Peter Schoeffer's Der Gart • molasses • Serdest • m • Sandoval • food • Korean • unreliabl
stry • wood • radiant • disappointment • swamp • Parry • Bursa • Moving on • Rosa • Fruit • gold • ballad • visceral • Iron • z • Hosniya • m • unsettling • I
st • materials • Hêmen • smoky glass • buttered • fairy • the Horae • cantaloupe • Jorladj • the World • Gulavî • Deb • August • Cano • Hotel • Yannis • Mûnzi
prase • deer • orange • honey • Payedar • light • comedy • blackberry • Kesrewan • coast • birch • speakeasy • Library • i • troubled • Henrician • four kinds o
taineer • juicy • Giravi • Whale • Alba Maria • neon • ph • Khushi • paper • damask • Cornwall • s • kayaking • skeleton • Paulician • cranberries • Holm • hopel
dcore • patrician • Dey • n • titanium • Dokha • Wine • Ingle • raw • Medina • tuxedo • Laughter • Bats • Ali • rap • its niche • Teutonic Thrash Metal • swe
nspiel • was honest with you • Kaur • heady • Tamanna • sharp • white • Jager • Annex • bunk • August • vial • autumn • Genovese • warehouse • Ebionite • J
nge • Rodriguez • maps • qiviut • prairie • fucked up • Susana • impostor syndrome • Miller • modechoices • Kiçan • black glass • Sazan • Hedge • conspirac
st up a side-channel • intricate knotwork • showcase piece • synchronicity • Rabat • alpine • Kular • copper • Jadwiga • nightclub • rich with • Museum • lascivi
ma • chemist • silk • romantic • Arboretum • Hill • Liber Serapionis Aggregatus • fear • skinny • blue glass • installation • Jose Luis • Shahed • Kanta • a high-str
n line • your voice hoarse from singing • Acest • tangled • Haq • scarf • Iloegbunam • Sol • Ime • rhetoric • Parents • lachrymose • Nneka • Petit • Three • arou
liquid • white jade • Hancock • Sorzhoj • cryptid-hunter • Baboon • independent • en • Brussels • wolf • Islam • Ignacy • Raithīo • Tarot cards • community
that vaguely resembled • Siberian dwarf • wild • unasked-for • composed • Williams • half-forgotten • kabosu • Corsican • torch song • Evelina • Academy • Eu
versive • actor • Boston • de Koning • saxifrage • Hearth • Sunden • blanco • Teresa • Alexander • Biswas • obscene • Solheim • botany • Usurper • municip
• Alexandra • death • Romantic • canoe • Harun • fir • unseasonal showers • blue-green glass • Tove • horticulture • androgyne • an impossibly • hopeful • rus
aissance • al-Asadi • Rizgar • Ronga • Abbas • aspen • Baku • and • townhouse • Daly • Pakistan • craggy • green • firm • verdant • YA • thorns • Roskilde Cath
Aicha • wild • Said • Merdem • Benjamin • Isabel • precise • white-water rafting • served with every meal • composing bad poetry • arcane • couturier • ouch
lt • Waclawa • Diocletian's Palace • Herve • Arabia • Library • Diamond • you use it as an object lesson for students • trying to • Chamber • orange • a faint h
stelle • Hope • deft • finger • Naturalis Historia • peach • that was never named • a • intuitive • Chinese white • pepper • zinfandel • Ambre • Hedgehog • bi
ing • Haugland • gossiped about • transhumanist • Egill • doubt • victorious • the light of dawn • thorn • de Wit • dynamics • Turin • Testimony • Kraus • diap
rapery • in the woods • Psilanthropist • the Ellora Caves • Jamal • it was a holiday and the city hummed with celebration • Karakeçi • assiduously copied out
or you • Moldova • the unrelenting sun • Technical Death Metal • gr • classicist • in an alley near • conformity • flame • ph • badminton • fireplace nook • porcel
eloped • ander • tiger's-eye • voluptuous • Strom • Wise • Jadisri • blue glass • Park • Avsîn • ai • maintext • moon • Abedlkadr • sepia • Katia • softened wit
scarred from • asafoetida • you are reminded of • improper • amber • s • dépaysement • Sepúlveda • drummer • literary • first months of • Zina • girl • self-c
• Kubar • cut with a cameo of • kh • Bern • Antonella • Kolbrun • rich with • morning • serenity • Dîmen • with no ulterior motive • pashmina • fishing • Nichol
Alex • arctic • Lang • Baths • ts • Dijkstra • habit • winged • courtship • xylophonist • the wallpaper • spiritual • Aurelie • district • Jonna • rich • Klaudia • ne
ct • heavy-lidded • Grape • ng • a moment of distraction • a hint of • corpse • cautious • graphic • Emperor • shameful • Damascus • passant • Crowned • cr
ctured armour • Choker • raisin • archaic • Zotu • Aphrodite • beatboxer • razor-sharp • Berêz • farewell • scarf • ren • Guyan • conical • essays • Khalil • bedsi
nt • h2 • fundamental • nature • sweet black • habit of • the Pons Neronianus • Maryam • the slow burn • pink • modetxt • cabal • e • crowfoot • proto • Meriv
ehouse • Masoumeh • Banî • Fernanda • anthro • This was the • r • black glass • low • Tristan • synagogue • Darkness • matelassé • stars cold overhead • Jiqu
deviation • Dilem • promises • Barzani • flower • rye • ardent • eur • dulce de leche • panda-shadowed • the Cat • Great • Gag • Gulnav • Aas • Zîvan • wit
drawn label • and Adonis • engine oil • Damascene • Le Grant Herbier • root • from the street-vendor • forbidden • sh • stiletto • flautist • device • fencing te
• Quillfeldt closure • the Third • battle • lace • winery • Farzana • garden party • organic • ikat • smoky with • Portuguese • wide • pastries • all evening • gug
pocket • breathtakingly • the narrows • fiery • os • j • floral sidebar • dh • Carolina • Russian • wet dog • archaic • sorrel • medieval • Ugandan • Raj • ede
ng else • esoteric • vermeil • resin • aur • al-Shirazi • bolero • shepherd • wild • green glass • Duchess • esoteric • Sahota • Seafood • narrative • literary • j
boo • complementary qualities • samba • royal • Absukthi • optical • torrid • with a tacky wine-charm around the neck • Xanim • the Traitor • cafe • brutal
er • dusk • Bawer • ball • Marek • Hoffmann • mercurial • ch • copper • brushing against • houndstooth • tight with resolve • centered • y • Ezîn • vigorou
sh • bespectacled • Anglo-Indian • sorrow • Propaganda • memorial service • Loritaj • ū • finoptions • Coins • forest • worldly • it • c • Mêhvan • heavy • fondn
v • speaks to • Zeoda • Bengîn • it's a very nice dress • Atghun'id • Strategist • Hêja • was friends with everyone • disarming • Azû • editorial • ephemeral • Wit
ple • pregnant with • hygge • bookbinding • Jerusalem • Algerian • Ardan • who was a lot less awkward • rowan • winter • Kensal Green • edi • Danuta • Wit
nour • fire • green jade • Morgane • Udji • Noble • Erskine • spring • slumbers on • Zeinab • Dumont • performative • Dadyar • that causes • Sofia • Kezize

snuck*[or]***talked your way***[purely at random]* **into** *[one of][pop landmark][or][pop garden-names][purely at random][m mischief][m trouble][m fun][pop groupsting]*",
"**when you took a** *[pop boatkinds]* *[one of]***upriver***[or]***downriver***[or]***out on the water***[purely at random][pop boat-bullshit][m fun]*"
[...]
}
boat-bullshit is a list of texts that varies. boat-bullshit is {
" *[pop boatdetail][one of],[or][purely at random]* **and** *[pop boatconclusion]*",
" *[pop boatdetail]*",
" **and** *[pop boatconclusion]*",
" *[pop boatdetail]*, *[pop boatconclusion]*, **and** *[pop groupdetails]*",
" *[pop boatdetail]* **and** *[pop groupdetails]*",
"*[one of]* **and** *[pop boatconclusion]* **and** *[pop groupdetails][or]*, *[pop boatconclusion]* **and** *[pop groupdetails][purely at random]*",
[...]
}.
groupdetails is a list of texts that varies. groupdetails is {
"**talked** *[one of]***earnestly***[or]***endlessly***[or]***excitedly***[or]***intensely***[or]***shit***[purely at random]* **about** *[pop convtopics][m debate]*",
"**made** *[one of]***filthy***[m lust][or]***obscure***[m academia][or]***tasteless***[or]* **extremely domain-specific***[m academia][or]***extended***[or]***inside***[or]***allusive***[purely at random]* **jokes about** *[pop convtopics]*",
"**drank** *[one of]***wine***[or][pop oddbooze][or][pop redwines][purely at random][one of]* **that neither of you properly appreciated***[or]* **that neither of you could really afford***[or][purely at random]*",
[...]
}.
oddbooze is a list of texts that varies. oddbooze is {"**Abhainn Dearg**", "**aguardiente**", "**akvavit**", "**amaretto**", "**amari**", "**Aperol**", "**applejack**", "**anisette**", "**Ardbeg**", "**Armagnac**", "**arrack**", "**baijiu**", "**Bärenfang**", "**boukha**", *[...]*,
"**tsikoudia**", "**zivania**", "*[pop redwines]*", "*[one of][pop fruits][or]* *[pop allbasicscents][purely at random]* *[one of]***vodka***[or]***liqueur***[or]***brandy***[or]***schnapps***[purely at random]*", "*[pop fruits]* **cider**"}.

Ashwell enlisted the help of three friends from the interactive fiction community, "a few authors whose style I thought would be a good fit,"[1] to help expand the scope of his generative space: Yoon Ha Lee, who'd begun his career writing interactive fiction and was now a successful novelist; Caleb Wilson, another longtime community member; and Cat Manning, a new friend and rising game industry star who also offered to take on the role of a producer, helping keep Ashwell's hobby project on track. Each contributed new ideas—memory seeds, scent templates, evocative adjectives—which inevitably suggested new word lists and new generators. The changelog preserved in a source code comment hints at the many hand-tweaked factors that would come to define the project's unique flavor:

- NPCs can now recur across memories
- added a two-stage check that avoids (or at least greatly reduces) sexual resonances for memories about students and mentors
- tweaked probability of less-complex memories down a bit
- more tinkering with historical names, inc. monarchs
- will not fix: rosewood is the same as bois de rose, but they *feel* different
- deleted "golf" and "crusader" from the corpus, because we want to imply a better world
- hopefully fixed another a/an bug

Taken together, the massive arsenal of phrases and generators—nearly fifty thousand words of them—is capable of producing an extraordinary variety of bottles, perfumes, and memories of a world richly painted if just barely glimpsed. The code defines twenty-five varieties of lily, thirty-one kinds of citron, fifty-five plots for plays, eighty-two hints of unusual scents like kimchee or popcorn (rarely used); ninety-six kinds of animals that can decorate crests, and one hundred seventy-eight adjectives for kings, who might appear in the names of empires, as portraits embossed on bottles, or as indirect patrons. Mathematically, it is laughable understatement to say the same descriptions will never be rendered twice.

The gift was finally delivered, and Short gave Ashwell permission to share it online. There has never been anything else quite like it. Longtime interactive fiction author Victor Gijsbers said it gave him a new perspective on procgen, which he'd never before been a fan of.

> I've never really seen the *point* of procedural text generation. What's the advantage? What does it give you?… Text generated by an algorithm can surprise me, certainly, but text written by a human author can also surprise me. When I'm looking for material to read, I'm interested quality and not in quantity.
>
> … [But] the beauty and fascination of a piece like *Scents & Semiosis* is not so much in the texts it generates … rather, it is in the machinery of the generation itself. It is in the thoughtfulness and creativity exhibited by the author when he constructed the algorithm.… A windmill is a tool for turning grain into flour. But admiring the flour is not the best way of appreciating the windmill.[5]

A text-based and symbolically charged procedural perfume generator had no preexisting audience, but the game nonetheless found its way to many who appreciated it. It was nominated for a Nebula Award for Game Writing in 2021, alongside much more famous and traditional titles. It stands in sharp contrast with the Salty, Mushroomy future suggested by *AI Dungeon* and GPT—rather than infinite stories from an artificial storyteller, a handcrafted and joyfully singular experience by one human, for another. And its irregular edges and expansive additions also remind how text games, through their history, have been places sole authors can be auteurs: take risks, try mad experiments, tell gloriously personal stories with an agility that games tied to graphics can only envy.

The 1941 short story of the
same name by Jorge Luis
Borges famously dreamed
of a novel holding its own
infinite variations.

Scents & Semiosis, then, is a good note on which to end this book—but for more reasons than these. Its roots are also deeply entwined with the history of text games and interactive fiction. Written at the end of the 2010s, in an IF design language from the 2000s **2008** that evolved from a 90s project **1993** to reverse engineer Infocom's story format from the 80s **1983**, which originated in turn in the 70s with *Zork* **1977**, the technical foundations of Ashwell's game trace a rhizomatic line back through the medium's history. Though written in a language built for parser games, it has a hypertext interface like Twine **2012** or Storyspace **1995**, asking its readers to make decisions like a Choose Your Own Adventure **1979**. It reflects the growing maturity of its medium, which from a trunk made from stories of hobbits **1982** and spaceships **1991** has sprouted new shoots toward tales of loss **1998**, of love **2010**, of self-discovery **1986**, and of pain **2012**. It continues threads of algorithmic experimentation **1994 2006 2013**, but also takes care to be told with beautiful prose **1992 2009 2014**. It was completed only with help from a community, a recurring theme across this series: from the People's Computer Center where some of the earliest text game design conversations took place **1973**, through the interactive fiction newsgroups **2000**, the lifelong friendships born on MUDs **1997** and MOOs **1990**, and puzzle-solving collectives like the Cloudmakers **2001**. It is an odd little game, like so many in this series. Like them, it has been loved.

"This is not a process that you will ever complete," the ending text for *Scents & Semiosis* reminds us. The disparate elements you bring together are "not the only version of your past. But you feel the shape of it." So, I hope, can we. This journey through the first half century of a medium has been only one route through a garden of forking paths, with many side trips, tragic omissions, and lovely surprises. No one can say where the paths ahead will lead, through the next fifty years, and the next after that. But we will find new gardeners there, I'm sure, grafting and growing their own futures for interactive prose.

References

1 Ashwell, Sam Kabo. 2020a. "Scents & Semiosis." *These Heterogenous Tasks* (blog). Mar 9, 2020. heterogenoustasks.wordpress.com/2020/03/09/scents-semiosis | a Dec 7, 2021

2 Ashwell, Sam Kabo. 2020b. "@tsawac: Scents & Semiosis: A Story/Game/Toy about Perfume, Memory, and New Meanings…" Twitter thread. Mar 9, 2020. twitter.com/tsawac/status/1237097566287704064 | a Dec 7, 2021

3 Ashwell, Sam Kabo. 2020c. "The 'Semiosis' Part." *These Heterogenous Tasks* (blog). Mar 10, 2020. heterogenoustasks.wordpress.com/2020/03/10/the-semiosis-part | a Dec 7, 2021

4 Compton, Kate, Ben Kybartas, and Michael Mateas. 2015. "Tracery: An Author-Focused Generative Text Tool." In *International Conference on Interactive Digital Storytelling*, 2015. Springer.

5 Gijsbers, Victor. 2020. "Sam Kabo Ashwell, 'Scents and Semiosis' [Review]." *The Gaming Philosopher* (blog). Mar 15, 2020. gamingphilosopher.blogspot.com/2020/03/sam-kabo-ashwell-scents-and-semiosis.html | a Dec 7, 2021

6 Koning, Hank, and Julie Eizenberg. 1981. "The Language of the Prairie: Frank Lloyd Wright's Prairie Houses." *Environment and Planning B: Planning and Design* 8 (3).

7 Manning, Cat. 2021. "Scents & Semiosis Nominated for a Nebula." *The Garden of Forking Narratives* (blog). Mar 15, 2021. catacalypto.substack.com/p/scents-and-semiosis-nominated-for | a Dec 7, 2021

8 MathBrush. 2019. "A Terse, Symbolic Dark Speed IF Game." IFDB. Aug 26, 2019. ifdb.org/

viewgame?id=063nxblhu07vizfx | a Dec 7, 2021

9 Science Fiction and Fantasy Writers of America. 2021. "SFWA Announces the 56th Annual Nebula Award® Finalists." *Nebula Awards* (blog). Mar 15, 2021. nebulas.sfwa.org/sfwa-announces-the-56th-annual-nebula-award-finalists | a Dec 7, 2021

10 Short, Emily. 2014. "Procedural Text Generation in IF." *Emily Short's Interactive Storytelling* (blog). Nov 18, 2014. emshort.blog/2014/11/18/procedural-text-generation-in-if | a Dec 7, 2021

11 Short, Emily. 2015. *The Annals of the Parrigues.* Unpublished manuscript. drive.google.com/file/d/0B97d5C256qbrOHFwSUhsZE4tU0k/view?resourcekey=0-Axor8kMWbczzjkf5jbYtxA | a Dec 7, 2021

12 Short, Emily. 2016. "Five Strategies For Collaborating With A Machine." Conference talk, PROCJAM 2016, Oct 20, London. www.youtube.com/watch?v=narjui3em1k | a Dec 7, 2021

INDEX

Italicized titles are games unless otherwise noted. Authors, games, and publishers from game lists with no discussion (in decade intros and "Also by" blocks) are not indexed except when connecting to topics mentioned in body text.

ABOUT THE BOOK

Since a winter morning in 1971 when a teacher wheeled a
teletype into his classroom to debut a game about the Oregon
Trail, people have been telling interactive stories on digital
platforms. From text adventures to VR poetry, MUDS to mobile
romance sims, and chatbots to roguelikes, these games without
graphics have pioneered new techniques for interactive
storytelling, engaged imaginations with clever engines and
beautiful prose, and explored the new terrain of fiction you can
play.

50 Years of Text Games: From Oregon Trail to AI Dungeon picks
one text-based game from each year between 1971 and 2020
and studies how it works, what it's about, why it's special, and its
lasting legacy. From famous classics to overlooked gems, from
personal stories to million-word epics, and from games printed
by teletypes to games downloaded on smart watches, this is the
fascinating story of interactive fiction's first half-century.

ABOUT THE AUTHOR

Aaron A. Reed is an indie creator exploring the intersection of
writing and play. He is the author of *Blue Lacuna*, voted one of
the top ten text adventures of all time; *Subcutanean*, a novel that
changes for each new reader (Lambda Literary Awards finalist);
and the tabletop roleplaying game *Archives of the Sky*, a 2020
ENnie award winner. His previous nonfiction books are *Creating
Interactive Fiction With Inform 7* and *Adventure Games: Playing
the Outsider* (with Anastasia Salter and John Murray).